Webster's NEW WORLD™

POCKET DICTIONARY

THIRD EDITION

P9-CZV-824

WEBSTER'S NEW WORLD™

POCKET DICTIONARY

THIRD EDITION

Compiled by the Editors of
Webster's New World™ Dictionaries

MICHAEL AGNES
EDITOR IN CHIEF

MACMILLAN • USA

Webster's New World™
Pocket Dictionary, Third Edition

Copyright © 1997 by
Simon & Schuster, Inc.

This book is based on and includes material from
Webster's New World™ College Dictionary, Third Edition,
copyright © 1997, 1996, 1994, 1991, 1988 by Simon & Schuster, Inc.

Macmillan General Reference
A Simon & Schuster Macmillan Company
1633 Broadway
New York, NY 10019-6785

A Webster's New World™ Book

MACMILLAN is a registered trademark of Macmillan, Inc.

WEBSTER'S NEW WORLD DICTIONARY
is a registered trademark of Simon & Schuster, Inc.

Dictionary Editorial Offices:
New World Dictionaries
850 Euclid Avenue
Cleveland, OH 44114-3354

ISBN 0-02-861887-4

Manufactured in the United States of America

2 3 4 5 6 7   97 98 99 00 01 02

RULES FOR SPELLING

Words that end in a silent -e usually drop the *-e* when a suffix beginning with a vowel is added [*file—filing*]. However, before the suffixes *-able* and *-ous*, the *-e* is usually kept if it follows a soft *c* or *g* [*outrage—outrageous*]. The *-e* is usually kept when a suffix beginning with a consonant is added [*time—timely*].

Words that end in a single consonant preceded by a single vowel usually double that consonant when a suffix beginning with a vowel is added, if: a) the word is a monosyllable [*sin—sinning*], or b) the word has more than one syllable but is stressed on the last syllable [*refer—referring*]. If the final consonant is *not* preceded by a single vowel or, in American usage, if the last syllable is not stressed, the final consonant is usually *not* doubled [*hurl—hurling; travel—traveling*].

Words that end in a double letter usually drop one letter when a suffix beginning with the same letter is added [*free—freest*].

Words that end in -y preceded by a consonant usually change the *-y* to an *i* when a suffix that does not begin with *i* is added [*marry—married*]. If it follows a vowel, the *-y* is usually kept [*play—played*].

Words that end in -ie change the *-ie* to a *y* when the suffix *-ing* is added [*lie—lying*].

Words that end in -c usually take on a *k* when a suffix beginning with *i* or *e* is added [*picnic—picnicker*].

Words containing ie or ei: The combination *ei* is usually used following the letter *c* and is always used to represent the sound (ā). In most other native English words the combination *ie* is used.

Note that the suffix -ful, unlike the adjective full, has only one *l* [*cupful*].

Verbs ending in -cede and -ceed: Three common verbs (*exceed*, *proceed*, and *succeed*) end in *-ceed*. Most other verbs end in *-cede*.

RULES FOR FORMING PLURALS

Most nouns in English form the plural by adding *-s* or *-es*. When the singular noun ends in a sound that allows *-s* to be added and pronounced without the formation of a new syllable, *-s* is used [*book—books*]. When the singular noun ends in a sound such that *-s* cannot be joined to it and pronounced without the formation of an additional syllable, *-es* is used [*kiss—kisses; torch—torches*].

The chief exceptions to this basic rule are listed below.

Words that end in -o usually form the plural by adding *-es* [*hero—heroes*]; however, some of them do so by adding *-s* [*solo—solos*]. There is no rule that deals with the distinction.

Some words that end in -f form the plural by changing the *-f* to *v* and adding *-es* [*wolf—wolves*].

Words that end in -y preceded by a consonant usually form the plural by changing the *-y* to *i* and adding *-es* [*lady—ladies*]. If the *-y* is preceded by a vowel, they form the plural regularly, by adding *-s* [*day—days*].

Some words form the plural by a vowel change. Among the commonest examples are: *foot—feet; man—men; tooth—teeth; woman—women*.

Some words have special plurals to which none of the above general statements apply. Among them are words such as: *alumna—alumnae; child—children; phenomenon—phenomena; radius—radii; sheep—sheep*.

PRONUNCIATION KEY

	as in			*as in*
a	c*a*t		ʉ	f*ur*
ā	*a*pe		ə	*a* in *a*go
ä	c*o*t		ə	*o* in *a*tom
e	t*e*n		'	fert*i*le (furt'′l)
ē	m*e*		ch	*ch*in
i	f*i*t		ŋ	ri*ng*
ī	*i*ce		sh	*sh*e
ō	g*o*		th	*th*in
ô	f*a*ll		th	*th*en
oi	*oi*l		zh	mea*s*ure
oo	l*oo*k		n	Indicates nasal quality of preceding vowel
ōō	t*oo*l		ë	Pronounce e with mouth rounded as for ō
ou	*ou*t		′	primary stress
u	*u*p		′	secondary stress

ABBREVIATIONS USED

a.	adjective		n.	noun
abbrev.	abbreviated		Naut.	nautical
adv.	adverb		Obs.	obsolete
alt.	alternate		orig.	originally
Ar.	archaic		pl.	plural
Biol.	biology		Poet.	poetic
Br.	British		pp.	past participle
c.	century		ppr.	present participle
Chem.	chemistry		pref.	prefix
Col.	colloquial		prep.	preposition
con.	conjunction		pres.	present
Dial.	dialectal		pron.	pronoun
esp.	especially		pt.	past tense
etc.	et cetera		R.C.Ch.	Roman Catholic Church
fem.	feminine		Rom.	Roman
Fr.	French		sing.	singular
Gr.	Greek		Sl.	slang
Gram.	grammar		Sp.	Spanish
int.	interjection		sp.	spelling; spelled
L.	Latin		spec.	specifically
Math.	mathematics		suf.	suffix
Mil.	military		t.	tense
Mus.	music		Theol.	theology
myth.	mythology		v.	verb

Other abbreviations will be found on pages 329–333

EDITORIAL STAFF

Editor in Chief Michael Agnes
Project Editor Jonathan L. Goldman
Managing Editor James J. Heaney
Editor and Database Administrator Donald Stewart
Editorial Staff James E. Naso, Katherine Soltis, Andrew N. Sparks, Stephen P. Teresi, Laura Borovac Walker
Administrative, Data Processing, and Clerical Staff Alisa Murray Davis, Cynthia M. Sadonick, Betty Dziedzic Thompson
Citation Readers Batya Jundef, Joan Komic

A

a *a.*, *indefinite article* 1 one 2 each; any one

a– *pref.* not

aard´vark (ärd´-) *n.* African mammal that eats ants

ab– *pref.* away; from; down

a·back´ *adv.*, *a.* [Ar.] back —**taken aback** surprised

ab´a·cus *n.* frame with beads for doing arithmetic

ab´a·lo´ne *n.* sea mollusk

a·ban´don *v.* 1 give up entirely 2 to desert —*n.* lack of restraint

a·ban´doned *a.* 1 deserted 2 shamefully wicked 3 unrestrained

a·base´ *v.* to humble

a·bash´ *v.* embarrass

a·bate´ *v.* lessen —**a·bate´ment** *n.*

ab·at·toir´ (-ə twär´) *n.* slaughterhouse

ab·bé´ (a´bā) *n.* priest's title in France

ab´bess *n.* woman who is head of a nunnery

ab´bey *n.*, *pl.* **–beys** monastery or nunnery

ab´bot *n.* man who is head of a monastery

ab·bre´vi·ate´ *v.* shorten, as a word —**ab·bre´vi·a´tion** *n.*

ABC *n.*, *pl.* **ABC's** 1 *pl.* the alphabet 2 basics; rudiments

ab´di·cate´ *v.* give up, as a throne —**ab´di·ca´tion** *n.*

ab´do·men (*or* ab dō´-) *n.* part of the body between chest and pelvis —**ab·dom´i·nal** (-däm´-) *a.*

ab·duct´ *v.* kidnap —**ab·duc´tion** *n.* —**ab·duc´tor** *n.*

a·bed´ *adv.* in bed

ab´er·ra´tion *n.* deviation from normal, right, etc.

a·bet´ *v.* **a·bet´ted, a·bet´ting** to help, esp. in crime —**a·bet´tor, a·bet´ter** *n.*

a·bey´ance (-bā´-) *n.* temporary suspension

ab·hor´ *v.* **–horred´, –hor´ring** shun in disgust, hatred, etc. —**ab·hor´rence** *n.*

ab·hor´rent *a.* detestable

a·bide´ *v.* **a·bode´** *or* **a·bid´ed, a·bid´ing** 1 remain 2 [Ar.] reside 3 await 4 endure —**abide by** keep (a promise) or obey (rules)

a·bid´ing *a.* enduring

a·bil´i·ty *n.*, *pl.* **–ties** 1 a being able 2 talent

ab´ject´ *a.* miserable

ab·jure´ *v.* renounce on oath

a·blaze´ *adv.*, *a.* on fire

a´ble *a.* 1 having power (*to do*) 2 talented; skilled —**a´bly** *adv.*

–able *suf.* 1 that can or should be 2 tending to

a´ble-bod´ied *a.* healthy

able-bodied seaman *n.* skilled seaman: also **able seaman**

ab·lu´tion *n.* a washing of the body, esp. as a rite

ab´ne·gate´ *v.* renounce; give up —**ab´ne·ga´tion** *n.*

ab·nor´mal *a.* not normal —**ab´nor·mal´i·ty** *n.*, *pl.* **–ties** —**ab·nor´mal·ly** *adv.*

a·board´ *adv.*, *prep.* on or in (a train, ship, etc.)

a·bode´ *n.* home

a·bol´ish *v.* do away with

ab´o·li´tion *n.* an abolishing, spec. [A–] of slavery in the U.S. —**ab·o·li´tion·ist** *n.*

A´-bomb´ *n.* atomic bomb

a·bom´i·na·ble *a.* 1 disgusting 2 very bad —**a·bom´i·na·bly** *adv.*

a·bom´i·nate´ *v.* loathe —**a·bom´i·na´tion** *n.*

ab´o·rig´i·ne´ (-rij´ə nē´) *n.* first known inhabitant —**ab´o·rig´i·nal** *a.*, *n.*

a·bort´ *v.* 1 have or cause to have a miscarriage 2 cut short (a flight, etc.), as because of equipment failure

a·bor´tion *n.* miscarriage, esp. one induced —**a·bor´tive** *a.*

a·bound´ *v.* be plentiful

a·bout´ *adv.* 1 around 2 near 3 in an opposite direction 4 nearly —*a.* astir —*prep.* 1 around 2 near to 3 just starting 4 concerning

a·bout´-face´ *n.* a reversal

a·bove´ *adv.* 1 higher 2 earlier on a page —*prep.* 1 over 2 higher than —*a.* mentioned above

a·bove´board´ *a.*, *adv.* in plain view; honest(ly)

a·brade´ *v.* scrape away —**a·bra´sive** *a.*, *n.*

a·bra´sion *n.* 1 an abrading 2 abraded spot

a·breast´ *adv.*, *a.* 1 side by side 2 informed (*of*)

a·bridge´ *v.* shorten, as in wording; lessen —**a·bridg´ment, a·bridge´ment** *n.*

a·broad´ *adv.* 1 far and wide 2 outdoors 3 to or in foreign lands

ab´ro·gate´ *v.* abolish; repeal —**ab´ro·ga´tion** *n.*

a·brupt´ *a.* 1 sudden 2 brusque; curt 3 steep

abs *n.pl.* [Sl.] abdominal muscles

ab´scess´ (-ses´) *n.* inflamed, pus-filled area in body

ab·scond´ (-skänd´) *v.* flee and hide to escape the law

ab´sent (*v.:* ab sent´) *a.* 1 not present; away 2 lacking —*v.* keep (oneself) away —**ab´sence** *n.*

ab´sen·tee´ *n.* absent person —*a.* of, by, or from one who is absent —**ab´sen·tee´ism´** *n.*

absentee ballot n. ballot marked and sent to a board of elections by a voter (**absentee voter**) who cannot be present to vote in an election

ab'sent-mind'ed a. 1 not attentive 2 forgetful

absent without leave a. Mil. absent from duty without official permission

ab'sinthe, ab'sinth (-sinth) n. green, bitter liqueur

ab'so·lute' a. 1 perfect 2 complete 3 not mixed; pure 4 certain; positive 5 real —**ab'so·lute'ly** adv.

ab'so·lu'tion n. 1 forgiveness 2 remission (of sin)

ab·solve' v. to free from guilt, a duty, etc.

ab·sorb' v. 1 suck up 2 engulf wholly 3 interest greatly —**ab·sorp'tion** n. —**ab·sorp'tive** a.

ab·sorb'ent a. able to absorb moisture, etc.

ab·stain' v. do without; refrain —**ab·sten'tion** n.

ab·ste'mi·ous a. not eating or drinking too much

ab'sti·nence n. an abstaining from food, liquor, etc.

ab'stract' (a. also, n. always: ab'strakt') a. 1 apart from material objects; not concrete 2 theoretical —v. summarize —n. summary —**ab·strac'tion** n.

ab·stract'ed a. preoccupied

ab·struse' a. hard to understand

ab·surd' a. ridiculous —**ab·surd'i·ty** n., pl. **-ties**

a·bun'dance n. more than is needed —**a·bun'dant** a.

a·buse' (-by$\overline{oo}$z'; n.: -by$\overline{oo}$s') v. 1 use wrongly 2 mistreat 3 berate —n. 1 wrong use 2 mistreatment 3 vile language —**a·bu'sive** a.

a·but' v. **a·but'ted, a·but'ting** to border (on or upon)

a·but'ment n. part supporting an arch, strut, etc.

a·bys'mal (-biz'-) a. too deep to be measured

a·byss' (-bis'-) n. deep or bottomless gulf

a·ca'cia (-kā'shə) n. tree with yellow or white flowers

ac'a·dem'ic a. 1 of schools or colleges 2 of liberal arts 3 theoretical —**ac'a·dem'i·cal·ly** adv.

a·cad'e·my n., pl. **-mies** 1 private high school 2 school for special study 3 society of scholars, etc.

a·can'thus n. plant with large, graceful leaves

a cap·pel·la (ä kə pel'ə) a., adv. with no instruments accompanying: said of choral singing

ac·cede' (ak sēd') v. 1 agree (to) 2 enter upon the duties (of an office)

ac·cel'er·ate' v. 1 increase in speed 2 make happen sooner —**ac·cel'er·a'tion** n. —**ac·cel'er·a'tor** n.

ac'cent n. 1 stress on a syllable in speaking 2 mark showing this 3 distinctive way of pronouncing 4 rhythmic stress —v. emphasize

ac·cen'tu·ate' (-chōō-) v. to accent; emphasize; stress

ac·cept' v. 1 receive willingly 2 approve 3 agree to 4 believe in —**ac·cept'ance** n.

ac·cept'a·ble a. satisfactory —**ac·cept'a·bly** adv.

ac·cept'ed a. generally regarded as true, proper, etc.; conventional; approved

ac'cess' n. 1 right to enter, use, etc. 2 means of approach

ac·ces'si·ble a. 1 easy to enter, etc. 2 obtainable

ac·ces'sion n. 1 an attaining (the throne, etc.) 2 an addition or increase

ac·ces'so·ry n., pl. **-ries** 1 thing added for decoration 2 helper in a crime

ac'ci·dent n. 1 unexpected happening 2 mishap 3 chance —**ac'ci·den'tal** a.

ac'ci·dent-prone' a. likely or tending to be in or have accidents

ac·claim' v. greet with applause —n. great approval

ac'cla·ma'tion n. 1 strong approval or loud applause 2 spoken vote of "yes" by many

ac·cli'mate (ak'lə māt') v. get used to a new climate or situation: also **ac·cli'ma·tize'**

ac'co·lade' n. high praise

ac·com'mo·date' v. 1 adjust 2 do a favor for 3 have room for; lodge —**ac·com'mo·da'tion** n.

ac·com'mo·dat·ing a. obliging

ac·com'pa·ny v. **-nied, -ny·ing** 1 add to 2 go with 3 play music supporting a soloist —**ac·com'pa·ni·ment** n. —**ac·com'pa·nist** n.

ac·com'plice (-plis) n. partner in crime

ac·com'plish v. do; complete —**ac·com'plish·ment** n.

ac·com'plished a. skilled

ac·cord' v. 1 agree 2 grant —n. agreement —**according to** 1 consistent with 2 as stated by —**of one's own accord** voluntarily —**ac·cord'ance** n.

ac·cord'ing·ly adv. 1 in a fitting 2 therefore

ac·cor'di·on n. musical instrument with a bellows

ac·cost' v. approach and speak to

ac·count' v. 1 give reasons (for) 2 judge to

be —n. 1 pl. business records 2 worth 3 explanation 4 report —on account as part payment —on account of because of —on no account never —take into account consider

ac·count′a·ble a. 1 responsible 2 explainable

ac·count′ing n. the keeping of business records —**ac·count′ant** n.

ac·cou′ter (-kōō′-) v. equip

ac·cou′ter·ments (or -kōō′trə-) n.pl. personal outfit; clothes

ac·cred′it v. 1 authorize; certify 2 believe in

ac·cre′tion n. 1 growth in size 2 accumulated matter

ac·crue′ v. be added, as interest on money

ac·cu′mu·late′ v. pile up; collect —**ac·cu′mu·la′tion** n.

ac′cu·rate (-yər ət) a. exactly correct —**ac′cu·ra·cy** n. —**ac′cu·rate·ly** adv.

ac·curs′ed a. damnable

ac·cuse′ (-kyōōz′-) v. 1 to blame 2 charge with doing wrong —**ac′cu·sa′tion** n.

ac·cus′tom v. make familiar by habit or use

ac·cus′tomed a. 1 usual; customary 2 used (to)

ace n. 1 playing card with one spot 2 expert —a. [Col.] first-rate

ace in the hole n. [Sl.] any advantage held in reserve

ac′er·bate (as′-) v. 1 make sour or bitter 2 irritate

a·cer′bi·ty (-sur′-) n. sourness; sharpness —**a·cer′bic** a.

ac·e·ta·min·o·phen (ə sēt′ə min′ə fən) n. drug used to lessen fever or pain

ac·et·an·i·lide (as′ə tan′ə līd′) n. drug used to lessen pain and fever

ac′e·tate′ (as′-) n. 1 salt or ester of an acid (**a·ce′tic acid**) found in vinegar 2 fabric made of an acetate of cellulose

ac′e·tone′ n. liquid solvent for certain oils, etc.

a·cet·y·lene (ə set′'l ēn′) n. gas used in a blowtorch

ache (āk) n. dull, steady pain —v. have such pain

a·chieve′ v. 1 do; accomplish 2 get by effort —**a·chieve′ment** n.

ac′id (as′-) n. 1 sour substance 2 chemical that reacts with a base to form a salt —a. 1 sour; sharp 2 of an acid —**a·cid′ic** a. —**a·cid′i·ty** n.

acid test n. crucial, final test

a·cid′u·lous (-sij′ōō-) a. somewhat acid or sour

ac·knowl′edge v. 1 admit or recognize 2 to respond to (a greeting, etc.) 3 express

thanks for —**ac·knowl′edg·ment**, **ac·knowl′edge·ment** n.

ac′me (-mē) n. highest point

ac′ne (-nē) n. pimply skin

ac′o·lyte′ n. altar boy

ac′o·nite′ n. poisonous plant with hoodlike flowers

a′corn′ n. nut of the oak

acorn squash n. winter squash, acorn-shaped with green skin

a·cous′tics (-kōōs′-) n.pl. qualities of a room that affect sound —n. science of sound —**a·cous′tic, a·cous′ti·cal** a. —**a·cous′ti·cal·ly** adv.

ac·quaint′ v. 1 make familiar (with) 2 inform

ac·quaint′ance n. 1 personal knowledge 2 person one knows slightly

ac·qui·esce (ak′ wē es′) v. consent without protest —**ac′qui·es′cence** n. —**ac′qui·es′cent** a.

ac·quire′ v. get as one's own —**ac·quire′ment** n.

ac·qui·si·tion (ak′ wə zish′ən) n. 1 an acquiring 2 something or someone acquired —**ac·quis′i·tive** (-kwiz′-) a.

ac·quit′ v. —**quit′ted, -quit′ting** 1 declare not guilty 2 conduct (oneself) —**ac·quit′tal** n.

a·cre (ā′kər) n. measure of land, 43,560 sq. ft. —**a′cre·age** n.

ac′rid a. sharp or bitter

ac′ri·mo′ny n. bitterness, as of manner or speech —**ac′ri·mo′ni·ous** a.

ac′ro·bat′ n. performer on the trapeze, tightrope, etc. —**ac′ro·bat′ic** a.

ac′ro·bat′ics n.pl. acrobat's tricks

ac′ro·nym′ (-nim′) n. a word formed from the first letters of several words

ac′ro·pho′bi·a n. fear of being in high places

a·cross′ adv. from one side to the other —prep. 1 from one side to the other of 2 on the other side of 3 into contact with

a·cryl′ic (-kril′-) a. of certain synthetic fibers or resins used to make fibers, paints, etc.

act n. 1 thing done 2 a doing 3 a law 4 division of a play or opera —v. 1 perform in a play, etc. 2 behave 3 function 4 have an effect (on)

act′ing a. substitute

ac·tin′ic a. designating rays causing chemical change

ac′tion n. 1 a doing of something 2 thing done 3 pl. behavior 4 way of working 5 lawsuit 6 combat

ac′ti·vate′ v. make active —**ac′ti·va′tion** n.

ac′tive a. 1 acting; working 2 busy; lively; agile —**ac·tiv′i·ty** n., pl. **-ties**

ac′tor n. one who acts in plays —**ac′tress** n.fem.

ac′tu·al (-choo-) a. existing; real —**ac′tu·al′i·ty** n.

ac′tu·al·ize′ v. 1 make actual or real 2 make realistic

ac′tu·al·ly adv. really

ac′tu·ar′y n., pl. **-ies** insurance statistician —**ac′tu·ar′i·al** a.

ac′tu·ate′ v. 1 put into action 2 impel to action

a·cu′i·ty (-kyoo′-) n. keenness of thought or vision

a·cu′men (ə kyoo′-, ak′yə-) n. keenness of mind

ac′u·punc′ture (ak′yoo-) n. the practice of piercing the body with needles to treat disease or pain

a·cute′ a. 1 sharp-pointed 2 shrewd 3 keen 4 severe 5 critical 6 less than 90°: said of angles

ad n. [Col.] advertisement

A.D. of the Christian era

ad′age (-ij) n. proverb

a·da′gio (-dä′jō) a., adv. Mus. slow(ly)

ad′a·mant a. unyielding

Ad′am's apple n. bulge in the front of a man's throat

a·dapt′ v. fit or adjust as needed —**a·dapt′a·ble** a. —**ad′ap·ta′tion** n. —**a·dapt′er, a·dap′tor** n.

add v. 1 join (to) so as to increase 2 increase 3 find the sum of 4 say further —**add up** seem reasonable —**add up to** signify

ad·den′dum n., pl. **-da** thing added, as an appendix

ad′der n. small snake, sometimes poisonous

ad·dict′ (ə dikt′; n.: ad′ikt) v. give (oneself) up (to a habit) —n. one addicted, as to a drug —**ad·dic′tion** n. —**ad·dic′tive** a.

ad·di′tion n. 1 an adding 2 part added —**ad·di′tion·al** a.

ad′di·tive n. something added

ad′dle v. make or become confused —**ad′dled** a.

ad·dress′ (ə dres′; n.: also a′dres′) v. 1 speak or write to 2 write the destination on (mail, etc.) 3 apply (oneself to) —n. 1 a speech 2 place where one lives —**ad′dress·ee′** n.

ad·duce′ v. give as proof

-ade suf. 1 the act of 2 participants in 3 drink made from

ad′e·noids′ n.pl. growths in the throat behind the nose

a·dept′ (n.: a′dept′) a. highly skilled —n. an expert

ad′e·quate (-kwət) a. enough or good enough —**ad′e·qua·cy** n.

ad·here′ v. 1 stick fast 2 give support (to) —**ad·her′ence** n. —**ad·her′ent** n.

ad·he′sive a. sticking —n. sticky substance, as glue —**ad·he′sion** n.

ad hoc′ a., adv. for a specific purpose

a·dieu′ (ə dyoo′) int. goodbye

ad in′fi·ni′tum (-nīt′əm) n. [L.] endlessly

a·di·os′ (ä′dē ōs′) int. goodbye

ad′i·pose′ (-pōs′) a. fatty

ad·ja′cent (ə jā′sənt) a. near or next

ad·jec′tive (aj′ik tiv) n. word that qualifies a noun —**ad′jec·ti′val** (-tī′-) a.

ad·join′ v. be next to

ad·journ′ (-jurn′) v. suspend (a meeting, etc.) for a time —**ad·journ′ment** n.

ad·judge′ v. judge, declare, or award

ad·ju′di·cate′ v. act as judge (in or on)

ad′junct′ n. a nonessential addition

ad·jure′ v. 1 order solemnly 2 ask earnestly

ad·just′ v. 1 alter to make fit 2 regulate 3 settle rightly —**ad·just′a·ble** a. —**ad·just′ment** n.

ad·ju·tant (aj′ə tənt) n. assistant, esp. to a commanding officer

ad′-lib′ [Col.] v. **-libbed′, -lib′bing** improvise (words, etc.) —n. ad-libbed remark: also **ad lib**

ad′man n., pl. **-men** man whose work is advertising

ad·min′is·ter v. 1 manage; direct: also **ad·min′is·trate′** 2 give; attend (to) —**ad·min′is·tra′tor** n.

ad·min′is·tra′tion n. 1 an administering 2 executive officials; management —**ad·min′is·tra′tive** a.

ad′mi·ra·ble a. worth admiring —**ad′mi·ra·bly** adv.

ad′mi·ral n. high-ranking naval officer

ad′mi·ral·ty n. department of naval affairs

ad·mire′ v. have high regard for —**ad′mi·ra′tion** n.

ad·mis′si·ble a. acceptable

ad·mis′sion n. 1 an admitting 2 entrance fee 3 confession or concession

ad·mit′ v. **-mit′ted, -mit′ting** 1 let enter 2 concede or confess —**ad·mit′tance** n. —**ad·mit′ted·ly** adv.

ad·mix′ture n. mixture

ad·mon′ish v. 1 warn or advise 2 reprove mildly —**ad′mo·ni′tion** v. —**ad·mon′i·to′ry** a.

ad nau′se·am (-nô′zē-) adv. to the point of disgust

a·do′ n. fuss; trouble

a·do′be (-dō′bē) n. unburnt, sun-dried brick

ad′o·les′cence n. time between childhood and adulthood; youth —**ad′o·les′cent** a., n.

a·dopt' v. 1 take legally as one's child 2 take as one's own —**a·dop'tion** n. —**a·dop'tive** a.

a·dore' v. 1 worship 2 love greatly —**a·dor'a·ble** a. —**ad·o·ra'tion** n.

a·dorn' v. decorate; ornament —**a·dorn'ment** n.

a·dre'nal glands (ə drē'-) n.pl. two ductless glands on the kidneys

A·dren'a·lin' (ə dren'-) trademark synthetic hormone —n. [a–] this hormone when secreted by the adrenal glands, which increases strength, etc.

a·drift' adv., a. floating aimlessly

a·droit' a. skillful and clever —**a·droit'ly** adv.

ad'u·late' (aj'ə-) v. flatter servilely —**ad'u·la'tion** n. too high praise

a·dult' a. grown-up; mature —n. mature person, animal, or plant —**a·dult'hood** n.

a·dul'ter·ate' v. make impure by adding things —**a·dul'ter·ant** n., a. —**a·dul'ter·a'tion** n.

a·dul'ter·y n. sexual unfaithfulness in marriage —**a·dul'ter·er** n. —**a·dul'ter·ess** n.fem. —**a·dul'ter·ous** a.

ad·vance' v. 1 bring or go forward 2 pay before due 3 rise or raise in rank —n. 1 a move forward 2 pl. approaches to get favor —in advance ahead of time —**ad·vance'ment** n.

ad·vanced' a. 1 in front 2 old 3 ahead or higher in progress, price, etc.

ad·van'tage n. 1 superiority 2 gain; benefit —take advantage of use for one's own benefit —**ad·van·ta'geous** a.

ad'ven·ti'tious (-tish'əs) a. not inherent; accidental

ad·ven'ture n. 1 dangerous undertaking 2 exciting experience —**ad·ven'tur·er** n. —**ad·ven'ture·some** a. —**ad·ven'tur·ous** a.

ad'verb' n. word that modifies a verb, adjective, or other adverb —**ad·ver'bi·al** a.

ad'ver·sar'y n., pl. —**ies** foe; opponent

ad·verse' (or ad'vurs) a. 1 opposed 2 harmful

ad·ver'si·ty n., pl. —**ties** misfortune

ad·vert' v. refer (to)

ad'ver·tise' v. tell about publicly to promote sales, etc. —**ad'ver·tis'ing** n.

ad'ver·tise'ment (or -vur'tiz-) n. public notice, usually paid for

ad·vice' n. opinion on what to do

ad·vis'a·ble (-vīz'-) a. being good advice; wise —**ad·vis'a·bil'i·ty** n.

ad·vise' v. 1 give advice (to) 2 offer as advice 3 inform —**ad·vis'or, ad·vis'er** n. —**ad·vi'so·ry** a.

ad·vis'ed·ly adv. with due consideration

ad·vise'ment n. careful consideration

ad·vi'so·ry a. advising or empowered to advise —n., pl. —**ries** a report, esp. about weather conditions

ad'vo·cate' (-kāt'; n.: -kət) v. support or urge —n. one who supports another or a cause —**ad'vo·ca·cy** n.

adz, adze n. axlike tool

ae·gis (ē'jis) n. sponsorship

ae·on (ē'ən) n. eon

aer'ate' (er'-) v. expose to air —**aer·a'tion** n.

aer'i·al a. 1 of or like air 2 of flying —n. radio or TV antenna

aero- pref. 1 air; of air 2 of aircraft

aer·o'bic a. of exercise that conditions heart and lungs —n.pl. [sing. or pl. v.] aerobic exercises

aer'o·dy·nam'ics n. 1 science dealing with force of air in motion 2 pl. vehicle body qualities affecting movement through air

aer'o·nau'tics n. aviation —**aer'o·nau'ti·cal** a.

aer'o·sol (-sôl', -säl') a. using gas under pressure to dispense liquid or foam

aer'o·space' n. earth's atmosphere and outer space

aes·thet'ic (es thet'-) a. 1 of beauty or aesthetics 2 sensitive to art and beauty —**aes'thete'** (-thēt') n.

aes·thet'ics n. study or philosophy of beauty

a·far' adv. far away

af'fa·ble a. pleasant; sociable —**af'fa·bil'i·ty** n.

af·fair' n. 1 matter; event 2 pl. business matters 3 amorous relationship of two people not married to each other

af·fect' v. 1 act on; influence 2 stir emotionally 3 like to wear, use, etc. 4 pretend to be or feel

af'fec·ta'tion n. 1 pretense 2 artificial behavior

af·fect'ed a. 1 artificial 2 diseased 3 influenced 4 emotionally moved

af·fect'ing a. emotionally moving

af·fec'tion n. 1 fond feeling 2 disease

af·fec'tion·ate a. tender and loving

af·fi'ance v. betroth

af'fi·da'vit n. sworn statement in writing

af·fil'i·ate' (-āt'; n.: -ət) v. join as a member; associate —n. affiliated member —**af·fil'i·a'tion** n.

af·fin'i·ty n., pl. —**ties** 1 close relationship or kinship 2 attraction

af·firm' v. assert or confirm —**af'fir·ma'tion** n.

af·firm'a·tive a. affirming; positive —n. assent

af·fix' (ə fiks'; n.: af'iks) v. attach —n. thing affixed, as a prefix

af·flict′ v. cause pain to; distress —**af·flic′tion** n.

af·flu·ence n. 1 plenty 2 riches —**af′flu·ent** a.

af·ford′ v. 1 have money enough for 2 provide

af·for·est′ v. turn (land) into forest —**af·for′est·a′tion** n.

af·front′ v., n. insult

af·ghan′ (-gan′) n. crocheted or knitted wool blanket

a·field′ adv. away; astray

a·fire′ adv., a. on fire

a·flame′ adv., a. in flames

a·float′ a. 1 floating 2 at sea 3 current

a·flut′ter adv., a. in a flutter

a·foot′ adv., a. 1 on foot 2 in motion; astir

a·fore·men′tioned a. mentioned before

a·fore′said′ a. said before

a·fore′thought a. thought out beforehand; premeditated

a·foul′ adv., a. in a tangle

a·fraid′ a. 1 frightened 2 regretful

a·fresh′ adv. again; anew

Af′ri·can a. of Africa —n. native of Africa

Af′ri·can-A·mer′i·can a., n. (of) a black American of African ancestry

aft adv. near the stern

af′ter adv. 1 behind 2 later —prep. 1 behind 2 in search of 3 later than 4 because of 5 in spite of 6 in imitation of 7 for —con. later than —a. later

af′ter·birth′ n. placenta, etc. expelled after childbirth

af′ter·ef·fect′ n. an effect coming later, or as a secondary result

af′ter·life′ n. life after death

af′ter·math′ n. (bad) result

af′ter·noon′ n. time from noon to evening

af′ter·thought′ n. thought coming later or too late

af′ter·ward adv. later: also **af′ter·wards**

a·gain′ adv. 1 once more 2 besides

a·gainst′ prep. 1 opposed to 2 so as to hit 3 next to 4 in preparation for

a·gape′ adv., a. with mouth wide open

ag′ate (-ət) n. hard semiprecious stone, often striped

a·ga′ve (-gä′vē) n. desert plant with thick leaves

age n. 1 length of time of existence 2 time of getting full legal rights 3 stage of life 4 old age 5 historical period —v. grow old or make old

–age suf. act or state of; amount of; place of or for

a·ged (ā′jəd; 2: ājd) a. 1 old 2 of the age of

age′less a. 1 seemingly not older 2 eternal

a′gen·cy n., pl. –cies 1 action or means 2 firm acting for another

a·gen′da n. list of things to be dealt with

a′gent n. 1 force, or cause of an effect 2 one that acts for another

age′-old′ a. ancient

ag·gran′dize′ (ə gran′-) v. to increase in power, riches, etc. —**ag·gran′dize·ment** n.

ag′gra·vate′ v. 1 make worse 2 [Col.] vex; annoy —**ag′gra·va′tion** n.

ag′gre·gate (-gət; v.: -gāt′) a., n., v. total; mass —**ag′gre·ga′tion** n.

ag·gres′sion n. unprovoked attack —**ag·gres′sor** n.

ag·gres′sive a. 1 quarrelsome 2 bold and active —**ag·gres′sive·ly** adv.

ag·grieve′ v. offend

a·ghast′ (-gast′) a. horrified

ag·ile (aj′əl) a. quick; nimble —**a·gil′i·ty** (-jil′-) n.

ag′i·tate′ (aj′-) v. 1 stir up 2 disturb 3 talk to arouse support (for) —**ag′i·ta′tion** n. —**ag′i·ta′tor** n.

a·glow′ adv., a. in a glow

ag·nos′tic (-näs′-) n. one who doubts the existence of God —**ag·nos′ti·cism** n.

a·go′ adv., a. (in the) past

a·gog′ a. eager; excited

ag′o·nize′ v. cause agony

ag′o·ny n. great suffering

a·grar′i·an (-grer′-) a. of land and farming

a·gree′ v. 1 to consent 2 be in harmony or accord —**a·gree′ment** n.

a·gree′a·ble a. 1 pleasing 2 willing to consent

ag′ri·cul′ture n. farming —**ag′ri·cul′tur·al** a.

a·gron′o·my n. science, etc. of crop production —**a·gron′o·mist** n.

a·ground′ adv., a. on or onto the shore, a reef, etc.

a·gue (ā′gyōō) n. fever with chills

ah int. cry of pain, delight, etc.

a·ha′ int. cry of satisfaction, triumph, etc.

a·head′ adv., a. in front; forward; in advance

a·hoy′ int. Naut. hailing call

aid v., n. help

aide n. 1 assistant 2 military officer assisting a superior: also **aide′-de-camp′**, pl. **aides′**-

AIDS n. viral condition resulting in infections, cancer, etc.: usually fatal

ail v. 1 to pain 2 be ill

ai·le·ron (ā′lə rän′) n. hinged flap of an airplane wing

ail′ment n. chronic illness

aim v. 1 direct (a gun, blow, etc.) 2 intend —n. 1 an aiming 2 direction of aiming 3 intention; goal —**aim′less** a.

ain't 1 [Col.] am not **2** [Dial.] is not; are not; has not; have not

air n. **1** mixture of gases around the earth **2** appearance **3** pl. haughty manners **4** tune —v. **1** let air into **2** publicize —a. of aviation —**on the air** broadcasting on TV or radio

air base n. base for military aircraft

air'borne' a. **1** carried in the air **2** aloft

air conditioning n. controlling of humidity and temperature of air in a room, etc. —**air'-con·di'tion** v. —**air conditioner** n.

air'craft' n., pl. —**craft** machine or machines for flying

Aire'dale' (er'-) n. large terrier with a wiry coat

air'field' n. field where aircraft can take off and land

air force n. aviation branch of a country's armed forces

air'head' n. [Sl.] silly, ignorant person

air lane n. route for air travel

air'lift' n. the transporting of troops, supplies, etc. by aircraft —v. transport by airlift

air'line' n. air transport system or company: also **air line**

air'lin'er n. large, passenger aircraft of an airline

air'mail' n. mail transported by aircraft

air'man n., pl. —**men 1** aviator **2** enlisted person in U.S. Air Force

air'plane' n. motor-driven or jet-propelled aircraft

air'port' n. airfield with facilities for repair, etc.

air pressure n. pressure of the atmosphere or of compressed air

air raid n. attack by aircraft

air'ship' n. steerable aircraft that is lighter than air

air'sick' a. nauseated because of air travel

air'tight' a. too tight for air to enter or escape

air'way' n. air lane

air'y a. —**i·er**, —**i·est 1** open to the air **2** flimsy as air **3** light; graceful **4** lighthearted —**air'i·ly** adv.

aisle (īl) n. passageway between rows of seats

a·jar' adv., a. slightly open

a·kim'bo adv., a. with hands on hips

a·kin' a. similar; alike

—al suf. **1** of; like; fit for **2** act or process of

al'a·bas'ter n. whitish, translucent gypsum

a' la carte' adv., a. with a separate price for each dish

a·lac'ri·ty n. quick willingness; readiness

a' la mode' adv., a. **1** in fashion **2** served with ice cream

a·larm' n. **1** signal or device to warn or waken **2** fear —v. to frighten

alarm clock n. clock with device to sound at set time

a·larm'ist n. one who expresses needless alarm

a·las' int. cry of sorrow, etc.

alb n. priest's white robe

al'ba·core' n. kind of tuna

al'ba·tross' n. large, web-footed seabird

al·be'it (ôl-) con. although

al·bi'no (-bī'-) n., pl. —**nos** individual lacking normal coloration

al'bum n. blank book for photographs, stamps, etc.

al·bu'men (-byōo'-) n. white of an egg

al·bu'min n. protein in egg, milk, muscle, etc.

al'che·my (-kə-) n. chemistry of the Middle Ages —**al'che·mist** n.

al'co·hol' n. colorless, intoxicating liquid obtained from fermented grain, fruit, etc.

al'co·hol'ic a. of alcohol —n. one addicted to alcohol

al'co·hol·ism' n. addiction to alcohol

al'cove' n. recess; nook

al'der (ôl'-) n. small tree of the birch family

al'der·man n., pl. —**men** member of a city council

ale n. kind of beer

a·lert' a. watchful; ready —n. an alarm —v. warn to be ready —**a·lert'ness** n.

al·fal'fa n. plant used for fodder, pasture, etc.

al'gae' (-jē') n.pl. primitive water plants

al'ge·bra n. mathematics using letters and numbers in equations —**al'ge·bra'ic** a.

a·li·as (ā'lē əs) n. assumed name —adv. otherwise named

al'i·bi' (-bī') n., pl. —**bis' 1** plea that the accused was not at the scene of the crime **2** [Col.] any excuse —v. give an excuse

al·ien (āl'yən, ā'lē ən) a. foreign —n. foreigner

al'ien·ate' v. make unfriendly —**al'ien·a'tion** n.

a·light' v. **1** dismount **2** land after flight —a. lighted up

a·lign' (-līn') v. **1** line up **2** make agree —**a·lign'ment** n.

a·like' a. similar —adv. **1** similarly **2** equally

al'i·men'ta·ry canal n. the passage in the body that food goes through

al'i·mo'ny n. money paid to support one's former wife

a·live' a. **1** living; in existence **2** lively —**alive with** teeming with

al′ka·li′ (-lī′) n., pl. **-lies′** or **-lis′** substance that neutralizes acids —**al′ka·line′** a. —**al′ka·lize′** v.

al′ka·loid′ n. alkaline drug from plants, as cocaine

al′kyd′ (-kid′) n. synthetic resin used in paints, etc.

all a. 1 the whole of 2 every one of 3 complete —pron. 1 [pl. v.] everyone 2 everything 3 every bit —n. a whole —adv. entirely —**after all** nevertheless —**at all** in any way

all- pref. 1 entirely 2 for every 3 of everything

Al·lah (ä′lə) God: Muslim name

all′-A·mer′i·can a. chosen as the best in the U.S. —n. all-American team player

all′-a·round′ a. having many abilities, uses, etc.

al·lay′ v. to calm; quiet

all′-clear′ n. siren or signal that an air raid is over

al·lege′ v. declare, esp. without proof —**al′le·ga′tion** n. —**al·leg′ed·ly** adv.

al·le′giance (-lē′jəns) n. loyalty, as to one's country

al′le·go′ry n., pl. **-ries** story in which things, actions, etc. are symbolic

al·le·gret′to a., adv. Mus. moderately fast

al·le′gro′ (-le′-) a., adv. Mus. fast

al′ler·gen n. allergy-causing substance —**al′ler·gen′ic** a.

al′ler·gy n., pl. **-gies** sensitive reaction to certain foods, pollen, etc. —**al·ler′gic** a.

al·le′vi·ate′ v. relieve; ease —**al·le′vi·a′tion** n.

al′ley n., pl. **-leys** 1 narrow street 2 bowling lane

al·li′ance (-lī′-) n. 1 an allying 2 association; league

al·lied′ a. 1 united by treaty, etc. 2 related

al′li·ga′tor n. large lizard like a crocodile

alligator pear n. avocado

all′-im·por′tant a. necessary

all′-in·clu′sive a. comprehensive

al·lit′er·a′tion n. use of the same initial sound in a series of words

al′lo·cate′ v. allot —**al′lo·ca′tion** n.

al·lot′ v. **-lot′ted**, **-lot′ting** 1 distribute in shares 2 assign —**al·lot′ment** n.

all′-out′ a. thorough

all′o′ver a. over the whole surface

al·low′ v. 1 to permit 2 let have 3 grant —**allow for** leave room, time, etc. for —**al·low′a·ble** a.

al·low′ance n. 1 thing allowed 2 amount given regularly

al′loy (v.: ə loi′) n. metal mixture —v. mix (metals)

all′-pur′pose a. useful in many ways

all right a. 1 satisfactory 2 unhurt 3 correct —adv. yes

all′spice′ n. pungent spice from a berry

all′-star′ a. made up of star performers —n. member of an all-star team

all′-time′ a. unsurpassed up to the present time

al·lude′ v. refer; mention

al·lure′ v. tempt; attract —**al·lur′ing** a.

al·lu′sion n. indirect or casual mention —**al·lu′sive** a.

al·ly′ (ə lī′; n.: al′ī) v. **-lied′**, **-ly′ing** unite; join —n., pl. **-lies** country or person joined with another

al′ma ma′ter (mät′ər) n. college or school that one attended

al′ma·nac′ n. calendar with miscellaneous data

al·might′y a. all-powerful —**the Almighty** God

al′mond (ä′mənd, ôl′-) n. edible, nutlike, oval seed of a tree of the peach family

al′most′ adv. very nearly

alms (ämz) n. money, food, etc. given to the poor

al′oe′ (-ō′) n. African plant whose juice is used in ointments, etc.

a·loft′ adv. high up

a·lo·ha (ä lō′hä) n., int. love: Hawaiian "hello" or "goodbye"

a·lone′ a., adv. with no other —**let alone** not to mention

a·long′ prep. on or beside the length of —adv. 1 onward 2 together (with) 3 with one —**all along** from the beginning —**get along** manage

a·long′shore′ adv. near or beside the shore

a·long′side′ adv. at the side —prep. beside

a·loof′ (-lōōf′) adv. apart —a. cool and reserved

a·loud′ adv. loudly

al·pac′a n. 1 kind of llama 2 cloth from its long, silky wool

al′pha n. first letter of the Greek alphabet

al′pha·bet′ n. letters of a language, in the regular order —**al′pha·bet′i·cal** a.

al′pha·bet·ize′ v. arrange in alphabetical order

alpha particle n. a positively charged particle given off by a radioactive substance

alpha ray n. stream of alpha particles

al·read′y adv. by or before the given time; previously

al′so adv. in addition; too

al′so-ran′ n. [Col.] defeated contestant in a race, etc.

al′tar (-tər) n. table, etc. for sacred rites, as in a church

altar boy n. boy or man who helps a priest at religious services, esp. at Mass

al´ter *n.* change; modify —**al´ter·a´tion** *n.*

al´ter·ca´tion *n.* a quarrel

alter ego *n.* 1 one's other self 2 constant companion

al´ter·nate (-nət; *v.:* -nāt´) *a.* 1 succeeding each other 2 every other —*n.* a substitute —*v.* do, use, act, etc. by turns —**al´ter·na´tion** *n.*

alternating current *n.* electric current that reverses its direction

al·ter´na·tive *n.* choice between two or more —*a.* giving such a choice

al´ter·na´tor *n.* generator producing alternating current

al·though´ *con.* in spite of the fact that

al·tim´e·ter (al-) *n.* instrument for measuring altitude

al´ti·tude *n.* height, esp. above sea level

al´to *n., pl.* -**tos** lowest female voice

al´to·geth´er *adv.* wholly

al´tru·ism´ (al´-) *n.* unselfish concern for others —**al´tru·ist** *n.* —**al´tru·is´tic** *a.*

al´um *n.* astringent salt

a·lu´mi·num *n.* silvery, lightweight metal, a chemical element: also [Br.]**al´u·min´i·um**

a·lum´nus *n., pl.* -**ni´** (-nī´) former student of a certain school or college —**a·lum´na** *n.fem., pl.* -**nae** (-nē)

al´ways *adv.* 1 at all times 2 continually

Alz·hei·mer's disease (älts´hī´mərz) *n.* disease causing degeneration of brain cells

AM amplitude modulation

am *v.* pres. t. of BE: used with I

AM 1 before noon: also **a.m., A.M.** 2 amplitude modulation

a·mal´gam (-gəm) *n.* alloy of mercury and another metal

a·mal´ga·mate´ *v.* unite —**a·mal´ga·ma´tion** *n.*

a·man·u·en´sis (-yoo wen´-) *n., pl.* -**ses** (-sēz) a secretary: now used jokingly

am´a·ranth´ *n.* plant with showy flowers

am´a·ryl´lis (-ril´-) *n.* bulb plant with lilylike flowers

a·mass´ *v.* pile up; collect

am´a·teur (-chər) *n.* 1 one who does something for pleasure, not pay 2 unskillful person —**am´a·teur´ish** *a.*

am´a·to´ry *a.* of love

a·maze´ *v.* astonish; surprise —**a·maze´ment** *n.*

am´a·zon´ *n.* strong woman

am·bas´sa·dor *n.* top-ranking diplomatic official —**am·bas´sa·dor·ship´** *n.*

am´ber *n.* 1 yellowish fossil resin 2 its color

am´ber·gris´ (-grēs´) *n.* waxy secretion of certain whales, used in perfumes

am·bi·dex´trous *a.* using both hands with equal ease

am´bi·ence *n.* milieu; environment: also **am´bi·ance**

am´bi·ent *a.* surrounding

am·big´u·ous *a.* having two or more meanings; vague —**am·bi·gu´i·ty** *n., pl.* -**ties**

am·bi´tion *n.* 1 desire to succeed 2 success desired —**am·bi´tious** *a.*

am·biv´a·lence *n.* simultaneous conflicting feelings —**am·biv´a·lent** *a.*

am´ble *v.* move in an easy gait —*n.* easy gait

am·bro´si·a (-zhə) *n. Gr. & Rom. myth.* food of the gods

am´bu·lance (-byōo-) *n.* car to carry sick or wounded

am´bu·late´ *v.* walk

am´bu·la·to´ry *a.* 1 of walking 2 able to walk

am´bus·cade´ *n., v.* ambush

am´bush´ *n.* 1 a hiding for a surprise attack 2 the hiding place or group —*v.* to attack from hiding

a·me´ba *n.* amoeba

a·me´lio·rate´ (-mēl´yə-) *v.* improve —**a·mel´io·ra´tion** *n.*

a´men´ *int.* may it be so!

a·me´na·ble (-men´ə-, -mē´nə-) *a.* willing to obey or heed advice; responsive —**a·me´na·bly** *adv.*

a·mend´ *v.* 1 to correct 2 improve 3 revise, as a law —**a·mend´ment** *n.*

a·mends´ *n.pl.* a making up for injury, loss, etc.

a·men´i·ty *n., pl.* -**ties** 1 pleasantness 2 *pl.* courtesies 3 convenience: *often used in pl.*

a·ment´ *n.* spike of small flowers, as on a willow

A·mer´i·can *a.* 1 of America 2 of the U.S. —*n.* 1 native of America 2 U.S. citizen

A·mer´i·can·ism´ *n.* 1 U.S. custom 2 word or idiom originating in American English 3 devotion to the U.S.

A·mer´i·can·ize´ *v.* make or become American

am´e·thyst (-thist) *n.* purple quartz for jewelry

a´mi·a·ble *a.* good-natured; friendly

am´i·ca·ble *a.* friendly; peaceable —**am´i·ca·bly** *adv.*

a·mid´, a·midst´ *prep.* among

a·mid´ships *adv.* in or toward the middle of a ship

a·mi´go *n., pl.* -**gos** friend

a·mi´no acid (-mē-) *n.* any of several basic building blocks of protein

a·miss´ *adv., a.* wrong

am´i·ty *n.* friendship

am´me´ter *n.* instrument for measuring amperes

am´mo *n.* [Sl.] ammunition

am·mo'ni·a n. 1 acrid gas 2 water solution of it

am'mu·ni'tion n. bullets, gunpowder, bombs, etc.

am·ne'si·a (-zhə) n. loss of memory

am'nes·ty n. general pardon for political offenses

am·ni·o'·cen·te'sis n. extracting fluid (**am'·ni·ot'ic fluid**) from a pregnant woman

a·moe'ba (-mē-) n., pl. **–bas** or **–bae** (-bē) one-celled animal —**a·moe'bic** a.

a·mok' (-muk') a., adv. used chiefly in **run amok**, lose control and behave violently

a·mong', a·mongst' prep. 1 surrounded by 2 in the group of 3 to or for each of

a·mon·til·la'do (-män'tə lä'-) n. pale, rather dry sherry

a·mor'al (ā-) a. with no moral sense or standards

am'o·rous a. 1 fond of making love 2 full of love

a·mor'phous a. 1 shapeless 2 of no definite type

am'or·tize' v. provide for gradual payment of —**am'or·ti·za'tion** n.

a·mount' v. 1 add up (to) 2 be equal (to) —n. 1 sum 2 quantity

a·mour' (-mo͞or') n. love affair

am·per·age n. strength of an electric current in amperes

am'pere' (-pir') n. unit of electric current

am'per·sand' n. sign (&) meaning and

am·phet'a·mine' (-mēn') n. drug used as a stimulant and to lessen appetite

am·phib'i·an n. 1 land-and-water animal, as the frog 2 land-and-water vehicle —a. amphibious

am·phib'i·ous a. adapted to both land and water

am'phi·the·a'ter, am'phi·the·a'tre n. open theater with central space circled by tiers of seats

am'ple a. 1 large 2 adequate; plenty —**am'ply** adv.

am'pli·fy' v. **–fied', –fy'ing** make stronger, louder, or fuller —**am'pli·fi·ca'tion** n. —**am'pli·fi'er** n.

am'pli·tude' n. 1 extent or breadth 2 abundance

amplitude modulation n. changing of the amplitude of the radio wave according to the signal being broadcast

am'pul' n. small container for a dose of medicine to be injected: also **am'pule'**

am'pu·tate' (-pyo͞o-) v. to cut off, esp. by surgery —**am'pu·ta'tion** n.

am·pu·tee' n. one who has had a limb amputated

a·muck' n. amok

am'u·let (-yo͞o-) n. charm worn against evil

a·muse' v. 1 entertain 2 make laugh —**a·mus'ing** a. —**a·muse'ment** n.

amusement park n. entertainment area with rides, food, etc.

am'yl·ase' (-ə lās') n. enzyme that helps change starch into sugar, found in saliva

an a., indefinite article 1 one 2 each; any one

–an suf. 1 of 2 born in; living in 3 believing in

a·nach'ro·nism' (-nak'-) n. thing out of proper historical time —**a·nach'ro·nis'tic** a.

an'a·con'da n. large South American boa snake

a·nae'mi·a (-nē'-) n. anemia

an'aer·o'bic (-er-) a. able to live without air or free oxygen, as some bacteria

an'a·gram' n. word made by rearranging the letters of another word

a'nal a. of the anus

an'al·ge'sic (-jē'zik) n., a. (drug) that eases pain

an'a·log' a. 1 of electronic equipment, recordings, etc. in which the signal corresponds to physical change 2 using hands, dials, etc. to show number amounts

analog computer n. computer working by electrical analogy with a mathematical problem to be solved

an'a·logue' n. something analogous

a·nal'o·gy (-jē) n., pl. **–gies** similarity in some ways —**a·nal'o·gous** (-gəs) a.

a·nal'y·sis (-ə sis) n., pl. **–ses'** (-sēz') 1 separation of a whole into its parts to find out their nature, etc. 2 psychoanalysis —**an'a·lyst** (-list) n. —**an'a·lyt'ic, an'a·lyt'i·cal** a. —**an'a·lyze'** (-līz') v.

an'ar·chism' (-ər kiz'əm) n. opposition to all government —**an'ar·chist'** n.

an'ar·chy n. 1 absence of government and law 2 great disorder —**an·ar'chic** a.

a·nath'e·ma n. 1 person or thing accursed or detested 2 ritual curse —**a·nath'e·ma·tize'** v.

a·nat'o·mize' v. 1 dissect, as animals 2 analyze

a·nat'o·my n. 1 science of plant or animal structure 2 structure of an organism —**an'a·tom'i·cal** a.

–ance suf. 1 action or state of 2 a thing that (is)

an'ces'tor n. person from whom one is descended

an'ces'try n. 1 family descent 2 all one's ancestors —**an·ces'tral** a.

an'chor (-kər) n. 1 metal weight lowered from a ship to prevent drifting 2 one who anchors a newscast: also **an'chor·man'**, pl. **–men'**, or **an'chor·wom'an**, pl.

—wom'en, or an'chor·per'son —v. 1 hold secure 2 coordinate and report (a newscast) —at anchor anchored —an'chor·age n.

an'cho·rite' (-kə-) n. hermit

an'cho'vy (-chō'-) n., pl. –vies tiny herring

an·cient (ān'chənt, -shənt) a. 1 of times long past 2 very old —the ancients people of ancient times

an'cil·lar'y a. auxiliary

and con. 1 also 2 plus 3 as a result

an·dan·te (än dän'tā) a., adv. Mus. moderately slow

and'i'ron n. either of a pair of metal stands for logs in a fireplace

an'dro·gen n. male sex hormone

an'droid' n. fictional, human-looking robot

an'ec·dote' n. brief story

a·ne'mi·a n. deficiency of red blood cells —a·ne'mic a.

an'e·mom'e·ter n. gauge measuring wind velocity

a·nem'o·ne' (-nē') n. plant with cup-shaped flowers

a·nent' prep. [Now Rare] concerning

an'es·the'si·a (-zhə) n. loss of the sense of pain, touch, etc.

an'es·the'si·ol'o·gist n. doctor specializing in giving anesthetics

an'es·thet'ic n., a. (drug, gas, etc.) that produces anesthesia —an·es'the·tist n. —an·es'the·tize' v.

an'eu·rysm', an'eu·rism' (-yōō riz'əm) n. sac formed by swelling in an artery wall

a·new' adv. 1 once more 2 in a new way

an·gel (ān'jəl) n. messenger of God, pictured with wings and halo —an·gel'ic (an-) a.

an'gel·fish' n. spiny-finned, bright-colored tropical fish

angel food cake n. light, spongy, white cake: also angel cake

an'ger n. hostile feeling; wrath —v. make angry

an·gi·na pec'to·ris (-jī'-) n. heart disease with chest pains

an'gle n. 1 space formed by two lines or surfaces that meet 2 point of view —v. 1 bend at an angle 2 fish with hook and line 3 use tricks to get something —an'gler n.

angle iron n. piece of iron bent at a right angle, for joining two beams, etc.

an'gle·worm' n. earthworm

An'gli·cize' (-sīz') v. make English in form, sound, etc.

Anglo– pref. English (and)

An'glo-Sax'on n. 1 native of England before 12th c. 2 person of English descent 3 Old English

An·go·ra n. wool from longhaired goat or rabbit

an'gry a. –gri·er, –gri·est 1 feeling anger; enraged 2 stormy —an'gri·ly adv.

ang·strom (aŋ'strəm) n. unit for measuring length of light waves: also angstrom unit

an'guish n. great pain, worry, or grief

an'gu·lar (-gyōō-) a. having angles —an'gu·lar'i·ty n.

an'i·line (-lin) n. oily liquid made from benzene, used in dyes, etc.

an'i·mad·ver'sion n. criticism

an'i·mad·vert' v. criticize

an'i·mal n. 1 living organism able to move about 2 any four-footed creature —a. 1 of an animal 2 bestial

an'i·mate' (-māt', -mət) v. 1 give life to 2 make lively —a. 1 living 2 lively —an'i·mat'ed a. —an'i·ma'tion n. —an'i·ma'tor n.

animated cartoon n. movie made by filming series of cartoons

an'i·mism' n. belief that all things in nature have souls —an'i·mis'tic a.

an'i·mos'i·ty n. strong hatred; ill will

an'i·mus n. ill will

an'ise (-is) n. plant whose seed is used as flavoring

an'i·sette' n. a sweet, anise-flavored liqueur

ankh (aŋk) n. cross with a loop at the top, ancient Egyptian symbol of life

an'kle n. joint connecting foot and leg

an'klet n. short sock

an'nals n.pl. historical records, year by year

an·neal' v. toughen (glass or metal) by heating and then cooling slowly

an'ne·lid' n. any worm with a body of joined segments or rings, as the earthworm

an·nex' (ə neks'; n.: an'eks) v. attach or join to a larger unit —n. something annexed —an'nex·a'tion n.

an·ni'hi·late' (-nī'ə-) v. destroy —an·ni'hi·la'tion n.

an'ni·ver'sa·ry n., pl. –ries yearly return of the date of some event

an'no·tate' v. provide explanatory notes for —an'no·ta'tion n.

an·nounce' v. make known; tell about —an·nounc'er n. —an·nounce'ment n.

an·noy' v. to bother or anger —an·noy'ance n.

an'nu·al a. yearly —n. 1 plant living one year 2 yearbook —an'nu·al·ly adv.

an·nu'i·ty n., pl. –ties investment yielding fixed annual payments

an·nul' v. –nulled', –nul'ling make null and void —an·nul'ment n.

an·nun′ci·a′tion *n.* 1 an announcing 2 [A-] announcement to Mary, mother of Jesus, that she would bear Jesus

an′ode′ *n.* positive electrode

an′o·dize′ *v.* put a protective oxide film on (a metal) by an electrolytic process

an′o·dyne′ (-dīn′) *n.* anything that relieves pain

a·noint′ *v.* put oil on, as in consecrating

a·nom′a·ly *n., pl.* **-lies** unusual or irregular thing —**a·nom′a·lous** *a.*

a·non′ *adv.* 1 soon 2 at another time

a·non′y·mous (-ə məs) *a.* with name unknown or withheld; unidentified —**an′o·nym′i·ty** (-nim′-) *n.*

a·noph′e·les′ (-näf′ə lēz′) *n.* mosquito that can transmit malaria

an·oth′er *a., pron.* 1 one more 2 a different (one)

an′swer (-sər) *n.* 1 thing said or done in return; reply 2 solution to a problem —*v.* 1 reply (to) 2 serve or suit 3 be responsible —**an′swer·a·ble** *a.*

ant *n.* small insect living in colonies

-ant *suf.* 1 that has, shows, or does 2 one that

ant·ac′id *n., a.* (substance) counteracting acids

an·tag′o·nism′ *n.* hostility —**an·tag′o·nis′tic** *a.*

an·tag′o·nist *n.* opponent

an·tag′o·nize′ *v.* incur the dislike of

ant·arc′tic *a.* of or near the South Pole —*n.* antarctic region

an′te (-tē) *n.* player's stake in poker —*v.* **-ted** or **-teed, -te·ing** put in one's stake

ante- *pref.* before

ant′eat′er *n.* long-snouted mammal that feeds on ants

an′te·ced′ent (-sēd′-) *a.* prior —*n.* 1 thing prior to another 2 word or phrase to which a pronoun refers

an′te·cham′ber *n.* room leading to larger room

an′te·date′ *v.* occur before

an′te·di·lu′vi·an *a.* 1 before the Biblical Flood 2 outmoded

an′te·lope′ *n.* horned animal like the deer

an·ten′na *n., pl.* **-nae** (-ē) or **-nas** 1 feeler on the head of an insect, etc. 2 *pl.* **-nas** wire(s) for sending and receiving radio waves

an·te′ri·or *a.* 1 toward the front 2 earlier

an′te·room′ *n.* room leading to another room

an′them *n.* religious or patriotic choral song

an′ther *n.* pollen-bearing part of a stamen

an·thol′o·gize′ *v.* include in an anthology

an·thol′o·gy *n., pl.* **-gies** collection of poems, stories, etc. —**an·thol′o·gist** *n.*

an′thra·cite′ *n.* hard coal

an′thrax′ *n.* disease of cattle

an′thro·poid′ *a.* manlike —*n.* an anthropoid ape

an′thro·pol′o·gy *n.* study of the races, customs, etc. of mankind —**an′thro·pol′o·gist** *n.*

an′thro·po·mor′phism′ *n.* an attributing of human qualities to animals or things —**an′thro·po·mor′phic** *a.*

an′ti *n., pl.* **-tis** [Col.] a person opposed to something —*a.* [Col.] opposed

anti- *pref.* 1 against 2 that acts against

an′ti·air′craft′ *a.* used against hostile aircraft

an′ti·bal·lis′tic missile *n.* ballistic missile for stopping enemy ballistic missile

an′ti·bi·ot′ic (-bī-) *n.* substance produced by some microorganisms, able to kill or weaken bacteria

an′ti·bod′y *n., pl.* **-ies** substance produced in body to act against toxins, etc.

an′tic *n.* silly act; prank

an·tic′i·pate′ (-tis′-) *v.* 1 expect 2 act on before —**an·tic′i·pa′tion** *n.*

an′ti·cli′max′ *n.* sudden drop from the important to the trivial —**an′ti·cli·mac′tic** *a.*

an′ti·co·ag′u·lant *n.* drug that delays or prevents the clotting of blood

an′ti·de·pres′sant *n.* drug that lessens medical depression

an′ti·dote′ *n.* remedy to counteract a poison or evil

an′ti·freeze′ *n.* substance used to prevent freezing

an′ti·gen *n.* substance to which the body reacts by producing antibodies

an′ti·his′ta·mine (-mēn) *n.* drug used to treat allergies

an′ti·knock′ *n.* substance added to fuel of internal-combustion engines to do away with noise of too rapid combustion

an′ti·mat′ter *n.* matter in which the electrical charge of each particle is the reverse of that in the usual matter

an′ti·mo′ny *n.* silvery metal in alloys, a chemical element

an′ti·par′ti·cle *n.* any particle of antimatter

an′ti·pas′to (-päs′-) *n.* appetizer of spicy meat, fish, etc.

an·tip′a·thy *n., pl.* **-thies** strong dislike

an′ti·per′son·nel′ *a.* meant to destroy people rather than buildings or objects

an′ti·per′spi·rant (-pur′spə-) *n.* skin lotion, cream, etc. for reducing perspiration

an′ti·phon′ (-fän′) *n.* hymn, psalm, etc. sung in responsive, alternating parts —**an·tiph′o·nal** *a.*

an·tip′o·des′ (-dēz′) *n.pl.* opposite places on the globe

an′ti·quar′i·an (-kwer′-) *a.* of antiques or antiquaries —*n.* antiquary

an′ti·quar′y *n., pl.* **-ies** collector or student of antiquities

an′ti·quate′ *v.* make obsolete —**an′ti·quat′ed** *a.*

an·tique′ (-tēk′) *a.* 1 of a former period 2 out-of-date —*n.* piece of furniture, etc. from earlier times

an·tiq′ui·ty (-tik′wə-) *n., pl.* **-ties** 1 ancient times 2 great age 3 ancient relic, etc.

an′ti·sem′i·tism′ *n.* prejudice against Jews —**an′ti·sem′ite′** *n.* —**an′ti·se·mit′ic** *a.*

an′ti·sep′tic *a.* preventing infection by killing germs —*n.* antiseptic substance

an′ti·slav′er·y *a.* against slavery

an′ti·so′cial *a.* 1 not sociable 2 harmful to society

an′ti·tank′ *a.* for use against tanks in war

an·tith′e·sis *n., pl.* **-ses** (-sēz′) exact opposite —**an′ti·thet′i·cal** *a.*

an′ti·tox′in *n.* serum that counteracts a disease

an′ti·trust′ *a.* regulating business trusts

an′ti·viv′i·sec′tion·ist *n.* one opposing vivisection

ant′ler *n.* branched horn of a deer, elk, etc.

an′to·nym′ (-nim′) *n.* word opposite in meaning

a′nus (ā′-) *n.* opening at rear end of the alimentary canal

an′vil *n.* block on which to hammer metal objects

anx·i′e·ty (aŋ zī′-) *n., pl.* **-ties** worry about what may happen

anx′ious (aŋk′shəs) *a.* 1 worried 2 eagerly wishing —**anx′ious·ly** *adv.*

an′y *a.* 1 one of more than two 2 some 3 every —*pron.* [*sing.* or *pl. v.*] any person(s) or amount —*adv.* at all

an′y·bod′y *pron.* anyone

an′y·how′ *adv.* 1 in any way 2 in any case

an′y·one′ *pron.* any person

an′y·thing′ *pron.* any thing —**anything but** not at all

an′y·way′ *adv.* anyhow

an′y·where′ *adv.* in, at, or to any place

A-OK *a.* [Col.] excellent, fine, etc.: also **A′-O·kay′**

A one *a.* [Col.] superior; first-class: also **A1, A number 1**

a·or′ta (ā-) *n.* main artery leading from the heart

a·pace′ *adv.* swiftly

a·part′ *adv.* 1 aside 2 away from (one) another 3 into pieces —*a.* separated

a·part′heid′ (-pär′tāt′, -tīd′) *n.* strict ra-

cial segregation as formerly practiced in South Africa

a·part′ment *n.* room or set of rooms to live in

ap′a·thy *n.* lack of feeling or interest —**ap′a·thet′ic** *a.*

ape *n.* large, tailless monkey —*v.* imitate

a·pe·ri·tif′ (a per′ə tēf′) *n.* alcoholic drink before meals

ap′er·ture (-chər) *n.* opening

a′pex′ *n.* highest point

a·pha′si·a (-zhə) *n.* loss of power to use or understand words

a·phid (ā′fid, af′id) *n.* insect that sucks the juices of plants

aph′o·rism′ *n.* wise saying

aph′ro·dis′i·ac′ (-diz′-) *n., a.* (drug, etc.) arousing sexual desire

a′pi·ar′y *n., pl.* **-ies** collection of beehives

a·piece′ *adv.* to or for each

a·plen′ty *a., adv.* [Col.] in abundance

a·plomb (ə pläm′) *n.* poise

a·poc′a·lypse′ (-lips′) *n.* total devastation, as doomsday —**a·poc′a·lyp′tic** *a.*

a·poc′ry·phal (-rə fəl) *a.* of doubtful authenticity

ap′o·gee′ *n.* point farthest from earth in a satellite's orbit

a·po·lit′i·cal (ā′-) *a.* not concerned with political matters —**a′po·lit′i·cal·ly** *adv.*

a·pol′o·gist *n.* defender of a doctrine, action, etc.

a·pol′o·gy *n., pl.* **-gies** 1 expression of regret for a fault, etc. 2 defense of an idea, etc. —**a·pol′o·get′ic** *a.* —**a·pol′o·gize′** *v.*

ap′o·plex′y *n.* paralysis caused by a broken blood vessel in the brain —**ap′o·plec′tic** *a.*

a·pos′tate *n.* one who abandons faith, principles, etc. —**a·pos′ta·sy** *n.*

A·pos′tle (-päs′əl) *n.* 1 any of the disciples of Jesus 2 [a-] leader of a new movement —**ap′os·tol′ic** *a.*

a·pos′tro·phe (-fē) *n.* sign (′) indicating: 1) omission of letter(s) from a word 2) possessive case

a·poth′e·car′y *n., pl.* **-ies** druggist

a·poth′e·o′sis *n.* 1 deifying of a person 2 glorification of a person or thing 3 glorified ideal

ap·pall′, ap·pal′ *v.* to dismay —**ap·pall′ing** *a.*

ap′pa·ra′tus (-rat′əs, -rāt′-) *n.* tools, etc. for a specific use 2 complex device

ap·par′el *n.* clothes —*v.* clothe; dress

ap·par′ent *a.* 1 obvious; plain 2 seeming —**ap·par′ent·ly** *adv.*

ap′pa·ri′tion *n.* ghost

ap·peal′ *n.* 1 request for help 2 attraction 3 request for rehearing by a higher court —*v.* 1 make an appeal 2 be attractive

ap·pear′ (-pir′) *v.* 1 come into sight 2 seem

3 come before the public —**ap·pear′ance** n.

ap·pease′ (-pēz′) v. to quiet by satisfying —**ap·pease′ment** n.

ap·pel′lant n. one who appeals to a higher court

ap·pel′late court (-pel′ət) n. court handling appeals

ap′pel·la′tion n. a name

ap·pend′ v. add or attach

ap·pend′age (-pen′dij) n. an attached part, as a tail

ap′pen·dec′to·my n., pl. **–mies** surgical removal of the appendix

ap·pen′di·ci′tis (-sī′-) n. inflammation of the appendix

ap·pen′dix n., pl. **–dix·es** or **–di·ces′** (-də sēz′) **1** extra material at the end of a book **2** small, closed tube attached to large intestine

ap′per·tain′ v. pertain

ap′pe·ten·cy n., pl. **–cies 1** appetite **2** propensity **3** natural attraction

ap′pe·tite n. desire, esp. for food

ap′pe·tiz′ing a. stimulating the appetite; savory —**ap′pe·tiz′er** n.

ap·plaud′ v. show approval, esp. by clapping the hands; praise

ap·plause′ n. approval, esp. by clapping

ap′ple n. round, fleshy fruit —**ap′ple·sauce′** n.

apple butter n. jam made of stewed apples

ap′ple·jack n. brandy distilled from apple cider

ap·pli′ance n. device or machine, esp. for home use

ap′pli·ca·ble a. appropriate —**ap′pli·ca·bil′i·ty** n.

ap′pli·cant n. one who applies, as for a job

ap′pli·ca′tion n. **1** an applying **2** thing applied **3** formal request

ap′pli·ca′tor n. device for applying medicine, etc.

ap′pli·qué′ (-kā′) n. decoration of one fabric on another

ap·ply′ v. **–plied′, –ply′ing 1** to put on **2** put into use **3** devote (oneself) diligently **4** ask formally **5** be relevant —**ap′pli·ca·ble** a.

ap·point′ v. **1** set (a time, etc.) **2** name to an office **3** furnish —**ap·point′ee′** n. —**ap·point′ive** a. —**ap·point′ment** n.

ap·por′tion v. portion out —**ap·por′tion·ment** n.

ap′po·site (-zit) a. fitting

ap′po·si′tion n. placing of a word or phrase beside another in explanation —**ap·pos′i·tive** a., n.

ap·praise′ v. estimate the value of —**ap·prais′al** n. —**ap·prais′er** n.

ap·pre′ci·a·ble (-sha bəl) a. enough to be noticed —**ap·pre′ci·a·bly** adv.

ap·pre′ci·ate′ (-shē-) v. **1** value; enjoy **2** recognize rightly or gratefully —**ap·pre′ci·a′tion** n. —**ap·pre′ci·a·tive** a.

ap′pre·hend′ v. **1** arrest **2** understand —**ap′pre·hen′sion** n.

ap′pre·hen′sive a. anxious

ap·pren′tice n. helper who is being taught a trade —v. to place as apprentice —**ap·pren′tice·ship′** n.

ap·prise′, ap·prize′ (-prīz′) v. inform; notify

ap·proach′ v. **1** come nearer (to) **2** speak to —n. **1** a coming near **2** way of beginning **3** access

ap′pro·ba′tion n. approval

ap·pro′pri·ate′ (-āt′; a.: -ət) v. **1** take for one's own use **2** set (money) aside for some use —a. suitable —**ap·pro′pri·ate·ly** adv. —**ap·pro′pri·a′tion** n.

ap·prove′ v. **1** consent to **2** have a favorable opinion (of) —**ap·prov′al** n.

ap·prox′i·mate (-māt′; a.: -mət) v. be about the same as —a. nearly exact or correct —**ap·prox′i·ma′tion** n.

ap·pur′te·nance (-pur′-) n. **1** adjunct **2** additional right

ap·pur′te·nant a. pertaining

ap′ri·cot′ (ap′rə-, ā′prə-) a. small peachlike fruit

A′pril n. fourth month

a′pron n. to protect the front of one's clothing

ap′ro·pos′ (-pō′) a. appropriate —**apropos** of regarding

apse (aps) n. domed or vaulted projection of a church

apt a. **1** fitting; suitable **2** likely (to) **3** quick to learn

ap′ti·tude′ n. **1** ability **2** quickness to learn

aq′ua·cul′ture n. cultivation of water plants and animals for human use

Aq′ua-Lung′ trademark apparatus for breathing under water —n. [usually a-l-] such apparatus

aq′ua·ma·rine′ (ak′wə-, äk′-) n., a. bluish green: also **aq′ua**

aq′ua·naut′ (-nôt′) n. one who does undersea experiments in a watertight chamber

a·quar′i·um (-kwer′-) n. tank, etc. for keeping fish or other water animals

A·quar′i·us 11th sign of the zodiac; Water Bearer

a·quat′ic (-kwät′-, -kwat′-) a. **1** living in water **2** taking place in water

aq′ue·duct′ (ak′wə-) n. large pipe or channel bringing water from a distance

a′que·ous (ā′kwē-) a. of or like water

aqueous humor n. watery fluid between the cornea and the lens of the eye

aq·ui·line (ak′wə lĭn′) a. curved like an eagle's beak

Ar′ab n., a. **1** (native) of Arabia **2** (one) of a people now scattered through lands around Arabia

A·ra′bi·an a. of Arabia or the Arabs —n. ARAB (n. 1)

Ar′a·bic a. of the people or language of Arabia, etc. —n. this language

Arabic numerals n. figures 1, 2, 3, 4, 5, 6, 7, 8, 9, and 0

ar′a·ble a. fit for plowing

a·rach′nid (-rak′-) n. small, eight-legged animal, as the spider or mite

ar′bi·ter n. judge; umpire

ar′bi·trar′y a. using only one's own wishes or whim —ar′bi·trar′i·ly adv.

ar′bi·trate v. settle (a dispute) by using or being an arbiter —ar′bi·tra′tion n. —ar′bi·tra′tor n.

ar′bor n. place shaded by trees, shrubs, or vines

ar·bo′re·al (-bôr′ē-) a. of, like, or living in trees

ar′bo·re′tum n., pl. **-tums** or **-ta** place where many kinds of trees are grown

ar′bor·vi′tae (-vī′tē) n. evergreen tree or shrub

ar·bu′tus (-byōō′-) n. evergreen trailing plant

arc n. **1** curved line, as part of a circle **2** band of light made by electricity leaping a gap

ar·cade′ n. **1** covered passage, esp. one lined with shops **2** row of arches on columns

ar·cane′ a. secret or esoteric

arch n. curved support over an opening —v. form (as) an arch —a. **1** chief **2** mischievous; coy

arch– pref. chief; main

ar′chae·ol′o·gy (-kē-) n. study of ancient peoples, as by excavation of ruins: also sp. **ar′che·ol′o·gy** —ar′chae·o·log′i·cal a.

a·cha′ic (-kā′-) a. **1** out-of-date **2** now seldom used

arch·an′gel (ärk′-) n. angel of the highest rank

arch′bish′op (ärch′-) n. bishop of the highest rank

arch′dea′con n. church official ranking just below a bishop

arch′di′o·cese n. diocese headed by an archbishop

arch′duke′ n. ruling prince

arch′en′e·my n. chief enemy

arch′er·y n. practice or sport of shooting with bow and arrow —arch′er n.

ar′che·type′ (-kə-) n. original model —ar′che·typ′al, ar′che·typ′i·cal a.

ar′chi·pel′a·go (-kə-) n., pl. **-goes′** or **-gos′** chain of islands in a sea

ar′chi·tect′ n. one who designs buildings

ar′chi·tec′ture n. science of designing and constructing buildings —ar′chi·tec′tur·al a.

ar′chives′ (-kīvz′-) n.pl. public records or place to store them —ar′chi·vist n.

arch′way′ n. passage under an arch

arc lamp n. lamp in which light is made by an arc between electrodes

arc′tic a. of or near the North Pole —n. arctic region

ar′dent a. passionate; eager —ar′dent·ly adv.

ar′dor n. passion; zeal

ar′du·ous (-jōō-) a. laborious or strenuous

are v. pres. t. of BE: used with you, we, or they

ar′e·a (er′ē-) n. **1** region **2** total surface, measured in square units **3** scope

area code n. telephone code number for any of the areas into which U.S. and Canada are divided

a·re′na n. **1** center of amphitheater, for contests, etc. **2** area of struggle

arena theater n. theater with a central stage surrounded by seats

aren′t are not

ar′gon′ n. chemical element, gas used in light bulbs, etc.

ar′go·sy n. [Poet.] large merchant ship or fleet

ar′got (-gō, -gət) n. special vocabulary, as of thieves

ar′gu·a·ble a. supportable by argument —ar′gu·a·bly adv.

ar′gue v. **1** give reasons (for or against) **2** dispute; debate —ar′gu·ment n. —ar′gu·men·ta′tion n. —ar′gu·men′ta·tive a.

ar′gyle′ (-gīl′) a. knitted or woven in a diamond-shaped pattern, as socks

a′ri·a (ä′rē-) n. solo in an opera, etc.

–arian suf. one of specified age, belief, work, etc.

ar′id (er′-) a. **1** dry **2** dull —a·rid′i·ty n.

Ar·i·es (er′ēz′) first sign of the zodiac; Ram

a·right′ adv. correctly

a·rise′ v. a·rose′, a·ris′en, a·ris′ing **1** get up; rise **2** come into being

ar′is·toc′ra·cy n. **1** government by an upper class minority **2** upper class —a·ris′to·crat′ n. —a·ris′to·crat′ic a.

a·rith′me·tic (n.: er′ith met′ik) n. science of computing by numbers —a. of arithmetic: also ar′ith·met′i·cal a.

ark Bible boat in which Noah, etc. survived the Flood

arm n. **1** one of two upper limbs of the human body **2** anything like this **3** weapon

4 military branch **5** pl. coat of arms —v. provide with weapons —**arm in arm** with arms interlocked —**up in arms** indignant —**with open arms** cordially

ar·ma'da (-mä'-) n. fleet of warships

ar·ma·dil'lo n., pl. **-los** tropical mammal covered with bony plates

ar'ma·ments n.pl. military forces and equipment

ar'ma·ture n. revolving coil in an electric motor or dynamo

arm'chair' n. chair with supports for one's arms

armed forces n.pl. all the military, naval, and air forces of a country

arm'ful n., pl. **-fuls** as much as the arms can hold

arm'hole' n. opening for the arm in a garment

ar'mi·stice n. truce

arm'let n. ornamental band worn on the upper arm

ar'mor n. protective covering —**ar'mored** a.

armored car n. vehicle with armor plate, as a truck carrying money to or from a bank

ar·mor'i·al a. heraldic

armor plate n. protective covering of steel plates

ar'mor·y n., pl. **-ies** 1 arsenal 2 military drill hall

arm'pit' n. the hollow under the arm at the shoulder

arm'rest' n. support for the arm as on inside of car door

ar'my n., pl. **-mies** 1 large body of soldiers 2 any very large group

a·ro'ma n. pleasant odor —**ar'o·mat'ic** a.

a·rose' v. pt. of ARISE

a·round' adv., prep. 1 in a circle (about) 2 on all sides (of) 3 to the opposite direction 4 [Col.] nearby

a·rouse' v. wake; stir up

ar·peg'gi·o (-pej'ō) n., pl. **-os** chord with notes played in quick succession

ar·raign' (-rān') v. 1 bring to court for trial 2 accuse —**ar·raign'ment** n.

ar·range' v. 1 put in a certain order 2 plan 3 adjust; adapt —**ar·range'ment** n.

ar'rant (er'-) a. out-and-out

ar'ras n. 1 elaborate tapestry 2 wall hanging

ar·ray' v. 1 place in order 2 dress finely —n. 1 an orderly grouping 2 impressive display 3 finery

ar·rears' n.pl. overdue debts —**in arrears** behind in payment

ar·rest' v. 1 stop or check 2 seize 3 seize and hold by law —n. an arresting

ar·rest'ing n. interesting

ar·rive' v. 1 reach one's destination 2 come —**ar·riv'al** n.

ar'ro·gant a. haughty; overbearing —**ar'ro·gance** n.

ar'ro·gate' v. seize arrogantly

ar'row n. 1 pointed shaft shot from a bow 2 sign (←) to show direction

ar'row·head' n. pointed tip of an arrow

ar'row·root' n. starch from a tropical plant root

ar·roy'o n., pl. **-os** 1 dry gully 2 stream

ar'se·nal n. place for making or storing weapons

ar'se·nic n. silvery-white, poisonous chemical element

ar'son n. crime of purposely setting fire to property —**ar'son·ist** n.

art n. 1 skill; craft 2 aesthetic work, as painting, sculpture, music, etc. 3 pl. academic studies 4 cunning; wile —v. [Ar.] form of ARE: used with thou

art dec'o n. decorative style of the 1920's and 1930's

ar·te·ri·o·scle·ro'sis (-tir'ē-) n. hardening of the arteries

ar'ter·y n., pl. **-ies** 1 tube carrying blood from the heart 2 a main road —**ar·te'ri·al** (-tir'ē-) a.

ar·te'sian well (-tē'zhən) n. deep well with water forced up by underground water pressure

art'ful a. 1 skillful; clever 2 crafty; cunning

ar·thri'tis n. inflammation of joints —**ar·thrit'ic** a.

ar'thro·pod' n. invertebrate animal with jointed legs and segmented body

ar'thro·scope' n. surgical device for use inside a joint —**ar'thro·scop'ic** a.

ar'ti·choke' n. 1 thistlelike plant 2 its flower head, cooked as a vegetable

ar'ti·cle n. 1 single item 2 separate piece of writing, as in a magazine 3 section of a document 4 any of the words a, an, or the

ar·tic'u·late' (-lāt'; a.: -lət) v. 1 speak clearly 2 join —a. 1 clear in speech 2 jointed: usually **ar·tic'u·lat'ed** —**ar·tic'u·la'tion** n.

ar'ti·fact' n. any object made by human work

ar'ti·fice (-fis) n. 1 trick or trickery 2 clever skill

ar'ti·fi'cial a. 1 made by man; not natural 2 not genuine; affected —**ar'ti·fi'ci·al'i·ty** n.

artificial respiration n. artificial maintenance of breathing, as by forcing breath into the mouth

ar·til'ler·y n. 1 mounted guns, as cannon 2 military branch using these

ar'ti·san (-zən) n. skilled craftsman

art'ist n. person with skill, esp. in any of the fine arts

ar·tis'tic a. 1 of art or artists 2 skillful —**art'ist·ry** n.

art'less a. 1 unskillful 2 simple; natural

art'y a. **-i·er, -i·est** [Col.] affectedly artistic: also **art'sy, -si·er, -si·est**

ar'um (er'-) n. plant with flowers inside hooded leaf

as adv. 1 equally 2 for instance —con. 1 in the way that 2 while 3 because 4 though —pron. that —prep. in the role of —**as for** (or **to**) concerning —**as is** [Col.] just as it is, as damaged merchandise —**as of** on or up to (a certain time)

as·bes'tos n. fibrous mineral used in fireproofing

as·cend' (-send') v. go up; climb —**as·cen'-sion** n.

as·cend'an·cy, as·cend'en·cy n. domination —**as·cend'ant, as·cend'ent** a.

as·cent' n. 1 an ascending 2 upward slope

as'cer·tain' v. find out with certainty

as·cet'ic (-set'-) a. self-denying —n. one who denies pleasures to himself or herself —**as·cet'i·cism'** n.

a·scor'bic acid n. vitamin C

as'cot n. scarflike necktie

as·cribe' v. assign or attribute —**as·crip'-tion** n.

a·sep'tic (ā-) a. free from disease germs

a·sex'u·al (ā-) a. sexless

ash n. 1 often pl. grayish powder left from something burned 2 shade tree —**ash'en** a. —**ash'y** a.

a·shamed' a. feeling shame

a·shore' adv., a. to or on shore

ash'tray' n. container for smokers' tobacco ashes: also **ash tray**

A'sian (-zhən) n., a. (native) of the continent of Asia: also, now less preferred, **A'si·at'ic** (-zhē ət'-)

a·side' adv. 1 on or to one side 2 away 3 apart —n. an actor's words spoken aside —**aside from** except for

as'i·nine' (-nīn') n. stupid; silly —**as'i·nin'i·ty** (-nin'-) n.

ask v. 1 call for an answer to 2 inquire of or about 3 request 4 invite

a·skance' adv. 1 sideways 2 with suspicion

a·skew' (-skyōō'-) adv., a. awry

ask'ing price n. price asked by a seller, to begin bargaining

a·slant' adv., a. on a slant ≈prep. slantingly across

a·sleep' a. 1 sleeping 2 numb —adv. into sleep

a·so'cial (ā-) a. not social; avoiding others

asp n. poisonous snake

as·par'a·gus n. plant with edible green shoots

as'par·tame' n. an artificial, low-calorie sweetener

as'pect' n. 1 look or appearance 2 side or facet

as'pen n. poplar tree with fluttering leaves

as·per'i·ty n., pl. **-ties** harshness; sharpness

as·per'sion n. a slur; slander

as'phalt' n. tarlike substance used for paving, etc.

as'pho·del' n. plant like a lily, with white or yellow flowers

as·phyx'i·ate' (-fik'sē-) v. overcome by cutting down oxygen in the blood —**as·phyx'i·a'tion** n.

as'pic' n. jelly of meat juice, tomato juice, etc.

as'pi·rate' v. 1 begin (a syllable, etc.) with sound of English h 2 suck in or suck up

as'pi·ra'tion n. ambition

as'pi·ra·tor n. apparatus using suction to remove air, fluids, etc.

as·pire' v. be ambitious (to) —**as'pi·rant** n. —**as·pir'ing** a.

as'pi·rin' n. drug that relieves pain or fever

ass n. 1 donkey 2 fool

as·sail' v. attack

as·sail'ant n. attacker

as·sas'sin n. murderer

as·sas'si·nate' v. murder, esp. for political reasons —**as·sas'si·na'tion** n.

as·sault' (-sôlt') n., v. attack

assault and battery n. Law the carrying out of threatened physical harm

as'say n., v. test; attempt

as·sem'ble v. 1 gather in a group 2 put together —**as·sem'blage'** (-blij') n.

as·sem'bly n., pl. **-blies** 1 an assembling 2 group 3 [A—] legislative body

assembly line n. line of workers in a factory who assemble a product as it passes along

as·sem'bly·man n., pl. **-men** member of a legislative assembly

as·sent' v., n. consent

as·sert' v. 1 declare 2 defend, as rights —**as·ser'tion** n. —**as·ser'tive** a.

as·sess' v. 1 set a value on for taxes 2 impose a fine, tax, etc. —**as·sess'ment** n. —**as·ses'sor** n.

as'set' n. 1 valuable thing 2 pl. property, cash, etc.

as·sev'er·ate' v. declare

as·sid'u·ous (-sij'ōō-) a. diligent

as·sign' v. 1 designate 2 appoint 3 allot; give —**as·sign'ment** n.

as'sig·na'tion n. lovers' secret meeting

as·sim'i·late' v. merge; absorb —**as·sim'i·la'tion** n.

as·sist' v., n. help; aid —**as·sist'ance** n. —**as·sist'ant** a., n.

as·so'ci·ate' (-āt'; n., a.: -ət) v. 1 join 2 connect in the mind 3 join (with) as a partner, etc. —n. partner, colleague, etc. —a. associated —**as·so'ci·a'tion** n.

association football n. soccer

as'so·nance n. likeness of sound

as·sort'ed a. 1 miscellaneous 2 sorted

as·sort'ment n. variety

as·suage' (-swāj') v. ease (pain, hunger, etc.)

as·sume' v. 1 take on (a role, look, etc.) 2 undertake 3 take for granted 4 pretend to have —**as·sump'tion** n.

as·sure' v. 1 make sure; convince 2 give confidence to 3 promise 4 guarantee —**as·sur'ance** n. —**as·sured'** a.

as'ter n. daisylike flower

as'ter·isk n. sign (*) used to mark footnotes, etc.

a·stern' adv. at or toward the rear of a ship

as'ter·oid' n. any of the small planets between Mars and Jupiter

asth'ma (az'-) n. chronic disorder characterized by coughing, hard breathing, etc. —**asth·mat'ic** a.

a·stig'ma·tism' n. eye defect that keeps light rays from focusing to one point

a·stir' adv., a. in motion

as·ton'ish v. fill with sudden surprise —**as·ton'ish·ing** a. —**as·ton'ish·ment** n.

as·tound' v. astonish greatly —**as·tound'ing** a.

a·strad'dle adv. in a straddling position

as'tra·khan (-kən) n. curled fur from young lamb pelts

as'tral a. of, from, or like the stars

a·stray' adv., a. off the right path

a·stride' adv., prep. with a leg on either side (of)

as·trin'gent n., a. (substance) contracting body tissue and blood vessels

as·trol'o·gy n. pseudo science of effect of stars, etc. on human affairs —**as·trol'o·ger** n. —**as'tro·log'i·cal** a.

as'tro·naut' n. traveler in outer space

as'tro·nau'tics n. science of spacecraft and space travel —**as'tro·nau'ti·cal** a.

as'tro·nom'i·cal a. 1 of or in astronomy 2 huge, as numbers Also **as'tro·nom'ic**

as·tron'o·my n. science of the stars, planets, etc. —**as·tron'o·mer** n.

as·tute' a. shrewd; keen

a·sun'der adv. 1 into parts or pieces 2 apart or separate

a·sy'lum n. 1 place of safety 2 institution for the mentally ill, aged, etc.

a·sym'me·try (ā sim'-) n. lack of symmetry —**a'sym·met'ri·cal** a.

at prep. 1 on; in; near 2 to or toward 3 busy with 4 in the state of 5 because of

at'a·vism' n. a throwback

ate v. pt. of EAT

-ate suf. 1 make, become, or form 2 to treat with 3 of or like

at'el·ier' (-yā') n. studio

a'the·ism' n. belief that there is no God —**a'the·ist'** n. —**a'the·is'tic** a.

ath'er·o·scle·ro'sis n. formation of nodules on hardening artery walls

a·thirst' a. eager

ath'lete' n. one skilled at sports requiring strength, speed, etc. —**ath·let'ic** a. —**ath·let'ics** n.pl.

athlete's foot n. ringworm of the feet

a·thwart' prep., adv. 1 across 2 against

a·tilt' a., adv. tilted

a·tin'gle a. tingling

-ation suf. act, condition, or result of

-ative suf. of or relating to; serving to

at'las n. book of maps

ATM n. computer terminal for automatic deposit, withdrawal, etc. of bank funds

at'mos·phere' (-fir') n. 1 the air surrounding the earth 2 general feeling or spirit 3 [Col.] interesting effect produced by decoration, etc. —**at·mos·pher'ic** a.

at·oll' (a'tôl') n. coral island surrounding a lagoon

at'om n. smallest particle of a chemical element, made up of electrons, protons, etc. —**a·tom'ic** a.

atomic (or atom) bomb n. bomb whose immense power derives from nuclear fission

atomic energy n. energy released from an atom in nuclear reactions

at'om·iz'er n. device for spraying liquid in a mist

a'to·nal'i·ty (ā'-) n. Mus. organization of tones without relation to a key —**a·ton'al** a.

a·tone' v. make amends (for) —**a·tone'ment** n.

a·top' adv., prep. on the top (of)

a'tri·um n. hall or lobby rising up through several stories

a·tro'cious (-shəs) a. 1 cruel or evil 2 very bad —**a·troc'i·ty** (-träs'-) n., pl. **-ties**

at'ro·phy (-fē; v.: also -fī') v. **-phied, -phy·ing** waste away or shrink up —n. an atrophying

at'ro·pine' (-pēn') n. alkaloid used to relieve spasms

at·tach' v. 1 fasten; join 2 tie by devotion 3 seize by legal order —**at·tach'ment** n.

at'ta·ché' (-shā') n. member of a diplomatic staff

attaché case n. flat, rectangular case for carrying papers

at·tack′ v. 1 to fight or work against 2 undertake vigorously —n. 1 an attacking 2 fit of illness

at·tain′ v. 1 to gain; achieve 2 arrive at —**at·tain′a·ble** a. —**at·tain′ment** n.

at·tain′der (-dər) n. loss of civil rights and property by one sentenced to death or outlawed

at·tar′ (-ər) n. perfume made from flower petals

at·tempt′ v., n. try

at·tend′ v. 1 be present at 2 pay attention 3 go with —**attend to** take care of —**at·tend′ant** n.

at·tend′ance n. 1 at attending 2 number present

at·ten′tion n. 1 a giving heed 2 heed; notice 3 pl. kind acts —**at·ten′tive** a.

at·ten′u·ate′ v. thin out; weaken —**at·ten′u·a′tion** n.

at·test′ v. 1 declare to be true 2 be proof of

at′tic n. space just below the roof; garret

at·tire′ v. clothe; dress up —n. clothes

at′ti·tude′ n. 1 bodily posture 2 way of looking at things, or manner

at′ti·tu′di·nize′ v. to pose for effect

at·tor′ney (-tur′-) n., pl. -neys lawyer: also **attorney at law**

attorney general n. chief law officer of a government

at·tract′ v. 1 draw to itself 2 make notice or like one —**at·trac′tion** n. —**at·trac′tive** a.

at·trib·ute (ə trib′yōōt; n.: a′trə byōōt′) v. think of as belonging or owing (to) —n. characteristic —**at·trib′ut·a·ble** a. —**at′tri·bu′tion** n.

at·tri′tion (-trish′ən) n. a wearing down bit by bit

at·tune′ v. bring into harmony or agreement

ATV (ā′tē′vē′) n., pl. **ATVs** small motor vehicle for rough ground, snow, ice, and water

a·twit′ter adv., a. twittering

a·typ′i·cal (ā-) a. not typical

au′burn a., n. red-brown

auc′tion n. public sale in which items go to the highest bidder —v. sell at auction —**auc′tion·eer′** n., v.

au·da′cious (-shəs) a. 1 bold; reckless 2 insolent —**au·dac′i·ty** (-das′-) n.

au′di·ble a. loud enough to be heard —**au′di·bly** adv.

au′di·ence n. 1 group seeing or hearing a play, concert, radio or TV show, etc. 2 formal interview

au′di·o′ a. of the sound portion of a TV broadcast

au′di·o·phile′ n. devotee of hi-fi sound reproduction

au′di·o·vis′u·al a. involving both hearing and sight

au′dit v. examine and check (accounts) —n. an auditing —**au′di·tor** n.

au·di′tion n. a hearing to try out a singer, actor, etc. —v. try out in an audition

au′di·to′ri·um n. a hall for speeches, concerts, etc.

au′di·to′ry a. of hearing

au′ger (-gər) n. tool for boring holes in wood

aught (ôt) n. 1 anything 2 zero

aug·ment′ v. increase —**aug′men·ta′tion** n.

au gra·tin (ō grät′'n) a. with browned cheese crust

au′gur (-gər) v. foretell —**augur ill** (or **well**) be a bad (or good) omen —**au′gu·ry** (-gyə rē) n.

Au′gust n. eighth month

au·gust′ a. imposing

au jus (ō zhoo′) a. in its natural gravy

auk n. diving seabird

aunt (ant, änt) n. 1 sister of one's parent 2 uncle's wife

au′ra n. radiance or air about a person or thing

au′ral a. of hearing

au′re·ole′ n. halo

Au·re·o·my·cin (ôr′ē ō mī′sin) trademark antibiotic drug

au re·voir (ō′rə vwär′) n. goodbye

au′ri·cle n. outer part of the ear

au·ro′ra n. dawn

aurora bo·re·al′is (bôr′ē-) n. luminous bands in the northern night sky

aus′cul·ta′tion (-kəl-) n. a listening to chest sounds with a stethoscope

aus′pi·ces (-pə siz) n.pl. patronage

aus·pi′cious (-pish′əs) a. favorable; of good omen —**aus·pi′cious·ly** adv.

aus·tere′ (ô stir′) a. 1 strict 2 very plain; severe —**aus·ter′i·ty** (ô ster′-) n., pl. -ties

Aus·tral′i·an n., a. (native) of the continent or country of Australia

Aus′tri·an n., a. (native) of Austria

au·then′tic a. true, real, genuine, etc. —**au′then·tic′i·ty** (-tis′-) n.

au·then′ti·cate′ v. 1 make valid 2 verify 3 prove to be genuine —**au·then′ti·ca′tion** n.

au′thor n. writer or originator —**au′thor·ship′** n.

au·thor·i·tar′i·an a. enforcing or favoring strict obedience to authority

au·thor′i·ta′tive a. having or showing authority

au·thor′i·ty n., pl. -ties 1 power to command 2 pl. persons with such power 3 expert; reliable source

au′thor·ize′ v. 1 give official approval to 2 empower —**au′thor·i·za′tion** n.

au'tism' n. mental state marked by disregard of external reality —**au·tis'tic** a.

au'to n., pl. **-tos** automobile

auto– pref. self

au'to·bi·og'ra·phy n., pl. **-phies** one's own life story written by oneself —**au'to·bi'o·graph'i·cal** a.

au'to·crat' n. ruler with unlimited power —**au·toc'ra·cy** n. —**au'to·crat'ic** a.

au'to·di'dact n. person who is self-taught

au'to·graph' n. signature —v. write one's signature on

au'to·hyp·no'sis n. a hypnotizing of oneself

au'to·in·tox'i·ca'tion n. poisoning by toxic substances formed within the body

au'to·mat' n. restaurant dispensing food from coin-operated compartments

au'to·mate' v. convert to automation

au'to·mat'ic a. **1** done without conscious effort **2** operating by itself —**au'to·mat'i·cal·ly** adv.

automatic pilot n. gyroscopic instrument for piloting an aircraft, missile, etc.: also **au'to·pi'lot**

au'to·ma'tion n. automatic system of manufacture, as by electronic devices

au·tom'a·tism' n. automatic quality, action, etc.

au·tom'a·ton' n. robot

au'to·mo·bile' n. passenger vehicle propelled by an engine, for use on streets and roads —**au'to·mo'tive** a.

au'to·nom'ic a. of the nervous system regulating the heart, lungs, etc.

au·ton'o·my n. self-government —**au·ton'o·mous** a.

au'top·sy' n., pl. **-sies** examination of a corpse to find cause of death

au·tumn (ôt'əm) n. season after summer, when leaves fall —**au·tum·nal** (ô tum'nəl) a.

aux·il·i·ar·y (ôg zil'yə rē) a. **1** helping **2** subsidiary —n., pl. **-ries** auxiliary group, etc.

auxiliary verb v. verb used to help form tenses, etc., as will, shall, have, do, be, etc.

a·vail' v. be of use or help (to) —n. use or help —**avail oneself of** make use of

a·vail'a·ble a. that can be got or had —**a·vail'a·bil'i·ty** n.

av'a·lanche' n. great fall of rock, snow, etc. down a hill

a·vant-garde (ä' vänt-gärd') n. vanguard

av'a·rice (-ris) n. greed for money —**av'a·ri'cious** (-rish'əs) a.

a·vast' int. Naut. stop!

a·venge' v. get revenge for —**a·veng'er** n.

av·e·nue (-nōō') n. **1** street **2** way to something; approach

a·ver' (-vur') v. **a·verred'**, **a·ver'ring** declare to be true

av'er·age n. **1** sum divided by the number of quantities added **2** usual kind, amount, etc. —a. being the average —v. **1** figure the average of **2** do on the average —**on the average** as an average amount, rate, etc.

a·verse' a. unwilling

a·ver'sion n. dislike

a·vert' v. **1** turn away **2** prevent

a'vi·ar'y (ā'vē-) n., pl. **-ies** large cage for many birds

a'vi·a'tion n. science or work of flying airplanes —**a'vi·a'tor** n.

av'id a. eager or greedy

a'vi·on'ics n. electronics applied in aviation and astronautics

av'o·ca'do (-kä'-) n., pl. **-dos** thick-skinned tropical fruit with buttery flesh

av'o·ca'tion (-kā'-) n. hobby

a·void' v. keep away from; shun —**a·void'a·ble** a. —**a·void'ance** n.

av·oir·du·pois (av'ər də poiz') n. weight system in which 16 oz. = 1 lb.

a·vouch' v. assert; affirm

a·vow' v. declare openly; admit —**a·vow'al** n.

a·vun'cu·lar a. of an uncle

aw int. sound of protest, etc.

a·wait' v. wait for

a·wake' v. **a·woke'** or **a·waked'**, **a·waked'** or **a·wok'en**, **a·wak'ing** rouse from sleep —a. **1** not asleep **2** alert

a·wak'en v. rouse; awake —**a·wak'en·ing** n., a.

a·ward' v. give after judging —n. **1** decision, as by judges **2** prize

a·ware' a. conscious; knowing —**a·ware'ness** n.

a·wash' adv., a. **1** with water washing over the surface **2** flooded **3** afloat

a·way' adv. **1** to another place **2** aside **3** from one's keeping —a. **1** absent **2** at a distance —**do away with 1** get rid of **2** kill

awe n. reverent fear and wonder —v. inspire awe in —**awe'-struck'**, **awe'strick'en** a.

a·weigh' a. being weighed (hoisted): said of an anchor

awe'some a. causing awe

awe'-struck' a. filled with awe: also **awe'-strick'en**

aw'ful a. **1** terrifying; dreadful **2** bad —adv. [Col.] very —**aw'ful·ly** adv.

a·while' adv. for a short time

awk'ward a. **1** clumsy **2** uncomfortable **3** embarrassing —**awk'ward·ly** adv.

awl n. pointed tool for making holes in wood, etc.

awn n. bristly fibers on a head of barley, oats, etc.

awn′ing n. overhanging shade of canvas, metal, etc.

AWOL, awol (ā′wôl′) a. absent without leave

a·wry (ə rī′) adv., a. **1** with a twist to a side **2** amiss

ax, axe n., pl. **ax′es** tool for chopping wood, etc.

ax′i·om n. an evident truth —**ax′i·o·mat′ic** a.

ax′is n., pl. **ax′es′** (-ēz′) straight line around which a thing rotates —**ax′i·al** a.

ax′le n. rod on which a wheel revolves

ax′le·tree′ n. axle of a wagon, carriage, etc.

ax·o·lotl (ak′sə lät′'l) n. dark salamander of Mexico and western U.S.

aye (ā) adv. [Ar.] always

aye, ay (ī) adv., n. yes

a·za′lea (-zāl′yə) n. shrub with brightly colored flowers

az′ure (azh′-) a., n. sky blue

B

baa (bä) v., n. bleat

bab′ble v. **1** talk in a foolish or jumbled way **2** murmur —n. babbling talk or sound —**bab′bler** n.

babe n. baby

ba′bel n. tumult

ba·boon′ n. ape with doglike snout

ba·bush′ka n. scarf worn on the head

ba′by n., pl. **-bies** very young child; infant —a. **1** of, for, or like a baby **2** small or young —v. **-bied, -by·ing** pamper —**ba′by·hood′** n. —**ba′by·ish** a.

baby beef n. meat from a heifer or steer one to two years old

baby carriage n. light carriage for wheeling a baby about: also **baby buggy**

baby grand n. small grand piano

baby's breath n. plant with small white or pink flowers

ba′by·sit′ v. **-sat′, -sit′ting** take care of children when parents are away —**baby sitter** n.

bac′ca·lau′re·ate (-lôr′ē ət) n. **1** bachelor's degree **2** a talk to graduating class

bac·cha·nal (bak′ə nal′) n. drunken orgy —**bac′cha·na′li·an** (-nā′-) a.

bach′e·lor n. unmarried man —**bach′e·lor·hood′** n.

Bachelor of Arts (or **Science,** etc.) n. four-year college degree

bachelor's button n. plant with showy white, pink, or blue flowers

ba·cil′lus (-sil′-) n., pl. **-li** (-ī) kind of bacteria

back n. **1** rear or hind part **2** backbone **3** the reverse **4** football player behind the line —a. **1** at the rear **2** of the past **3** backward —adv. **1** at or to the rear **2** to a former time, place, etc. **3** in return —v. **1** move backward **2** support **3** provide a back for —**back down** retract an opinion, etc. —**back′er** n. —**back′ing** n.

back′ache′ n. an ache in the back

back′bite′ v. to slander

back′board′ n. Basketball board behind the basket

back′bone′ n. **1** spinal column **2** courage; firmness

back′break′ing a. very tiring

back′drop′ n. curtain at the back of a stage

back′field′ n. Football players behind the line

back′fire′ n. faulty ignition in an engine —v. **1** have a backfire **2** go awry, as plans

back′gam′mon n. game played on a special board

back′ground′ n. **1** the part behind, more distant, etc. **2** past events, causes, etc.

back′hand′ n. a backhanded stroke, as in tennis

back′hand′ed a. **1** with the back of the hand forward **2** insincere

back′lash′ n. sharp reaction

back′log′ n. piling up, as of work to be done

back order n. order not yet filled

back′pack′ n. knapsack —v. hike wearing a backpack

back′rest′ n. support for the back

back′side′ n. **1** back part **2** rump

back′slap′per n. [Col.] effusively friendly person

back′slide′ v. to fall back in morals, religious faith, etc.

back′stage′ adv. in theater dressing rooms, etc.

back′stretch′ n. part of a race track opposite the homestretch

back′stroke′ n. swimming stroke made while lying face upward

back talk n. [Col.] insolence

back′track′ v. to retreat

back′ward adv. **1** toward the back **2** with the back foremost **3** into the past Also **back′wards** —a. **1** turned to the rear or away **2** shy **3** retarded —**back′ward·ness** n.

back′woods′ n.pl. remote, wooded areas —**back′woods′man** n., pl. **-men**

ba′con n. cured meat from hog's back or sides

bac·te′ri·a n.pl., sing. **-ri·um** microorganisms causing diseases, fermentation, etc. —**bac·te′ri·al** a.

bac·te′ri·cide′ n. agent that destroys bacteria

bac·te′ri·ol′o·gy n. study of bacteria

bad a. **worse, worst** 1 not good 2 spoiled 3 incorrect 4 wicked 5 severe —adv. [Col.] badly —n. anything bad —**bad′ly** adv. —**bad′ness** n.

bade (bad) v. pt. of BID (v. 1 & 2)

badge n. pin or emblem worn to show rank, membership, etc.

badg′er n. burrowing animal —v. to nag; pester

bad′man′ n., pl. **-men′** desperado of the old West

bad′min′ton n. game using rackets and a feathered cork

bad′-mouth′ v. [Sl.] find fault (with)

bad′-tem′pered a. irritable

baf′fle v. puzzle; bewilder —n. deflecting screen —**baf′fling** a.

bag n. 1 container made of fabric, paper, etc. 2 suitcase 3 purse —v. **bagged, bag′ging** 1 hang loosely 2 kill or capture 3 put into a bag —**in the bag** [Sl.] certain —**bag′gy** a.

bag′a·telle′ n. a trifle

ba′gel (-gəl) n. hard bread roll like a small doughnut

bag′gage n. luggage

bag′pipe′ n. musical instrument with a bag from which air is forced into pipes: also **bag′pipes′** n.pl.

bah (bä) int. shout of scorn

bail n. money left as security to free a prisoner until trial —v. 1 get freed by giving bail 2 dip out (water) from (a boat) —**bail out** to parachute

bail′iff n. 1 court officer guarding prisoners and jurors 2 sheriff's assistant

bail′i·wick′ (bāl′ē-) n. one's field of interest or authority

bait v. 1 torment, as by insults 2 put food on (a hook, etc.) as a lure —n. anything used as a lure

baize (bāz) n. coarse, feltlike cloth

bake v. 1 cook by dry heat in an oven 2 harden by heat —**bak′er** n.

bak′er·y n., pl. **-ies** place where bread, etc. is baked

baking powder n. leavening powder

baking soda n. sodium bicarbonate, powder used as leavening and as an antacid

bal′a·lai′ka (-lī′-) n. Russian instrument like a guitar

bal′ance n. 1 instrument for weighing, with two pans 2 equilibrium 3 harmonious proportion 4 equality of or difference between credits and debits 5 remainder —v. 1 compare 2 offset; counteract 3 put, keep, or be in equilibrium 4 be equal 5 sum up or equalize the debits and credits of (an account) —**in the balance** not yet settled

balance sheet n. statement of financial status of a business

bal′co·ny n., pl. **-nies** 1 platform projecting from an upper story 2 tier of theater seats above main floor

bald a. 1 lacking hair on the head 2 plain and frank —**bald′ness** n.

bald eagle n. large eagle of North America, with white-feathered head

bal′der·dash′ (bôl′-) n. nonsense

bald′faced′ a. shameless

bald′ing a. becoming bald

bal′dric (bôl′-) n. belt over the shoulder to support a sword

bale n. large bundle, as of raw cotton —v. make into bales

ba·leen′ n. whalebone

bale′ful a. harmful; evil

balk v. 1 stop and refuse to move 2 obstruct —n. 1 hindrance; obstruction 2 Baseball illegal motion by pitcher —**balk′y** a., **-i·er, -i·est**

ball n. 1 round object; sphere 2 round or oval object used in games 3 formal social dance 4 Baseball pitched baseball that is not a strike 5 [Sl.] good time —v. form into a ball —**be on the ball** [Sl.] be alert

bal′lad n. 1 popular love song 2 folk song or poem telling a story

ball′-and-sock′et joint n. joint, as the hip, like a ball in a socket

bal′last (-əst) n. heavy matter put in a ship, etc. to keep it steady —v. to furnish with ballast

ball bearing n. 1 bearing in which the parts turn on rolling metal balls 2 one of these balls

bal′le·ri′na n. woman ballet dancer

bal·let (ba lā′) n. intricate, formalized group dance

bal·lis′tic missile n. long-range guided missile that falls free as it nears its target

bal·lis′tics n. science of the motion of projectiles

bal·loon′ n. bag that rises when filled with light gas —v. swell; expand

bal′lot n. 1 paper marked in voting 2 voting —v. to vote

ball′park′ n. baseball stadium

ball′play′er n. baseball player

ball′point′ (pen) n. pen with ink cartridge and small ball bearing for a point

ball′room′ n. large room for social dances

bal′ly·hoo′ n. exaggerated or sensational advertising or propaganda

balm (bäm) n. fragrant healing ointment or oil

balm′y a. **–i·er, –i·est** soothing, mild, etc.

ba·lo′ney n. **1** bologna **2** [Sl.] nonsense

bal′sa (bôl′-) n. lightweight wood of a tropical tree

bal′sam (bôl′-) n. **1** aromatic resin **2** tree yielding it

bal′us·ter (bal′-) n. railing post

bal′us·trade′ n. row of balusters supporting a rail

bam·boo′ n. tropical grass with hollow, treelike stems

bam·boo′zle v. **1** trick **2** confuse

ban v. **banned, ban′ning** forbid —n. formal forbidding by authorities

ba·nal (bā′nal, bə nal′) a. trite —**ba·nal′i·ty** n., pl. **–ties**

ba·nan′a n. long tropical fruit with creamy flesh

band n. **1** strip of cloth, etc. as for binding **2** stripe **3** range of radio wave lengths **4** group of people **5** group of performing musicians —v. **1** mark or tie with a band **2** join

band′age n. cloth strip to bind an injury —v. bind with a bandage

Band′-Aid′ trademark small bandage of gauze and adhesive tape —n. [**b- a-**] such a bandage: also **band′aid′**

ban·dan′na, ban·dan′a n. large, colored handkerchief

band′box′ n. light pasteboard box for hats, etc.

ban′dit n. robber; brigand —**ban′dit·ry** n.

ban′do·leer′, ban′do·lier′ (-lir′) n. broad belt holding bullets, worn over one shoulder and across the chest

band saw n. power saw that is an endless, toothed steel belt

band′stand′ n. (outdoor) platform for an orchestra

band′wag′on n. winning or popular side

ban′dy v. **–died, –dy·ing** toss or pass back and forth —a. curved outward —**ban′dy·leg′ged** a.

bane n. cause of harm or ruin —**bane′ful** a.

bang v., n. (make, or hit with) a loud noise

ban′gle n. bracelet

bangs n.pl. short hair worn across the forehead

ban′ish v. **1** to exile **2** dismiss —**ban′ish·ment** n.

ban′is·ter n. a handrail, held up by balusters, along a staircase

ban′jo n., pl. **–jos** or **–joes** stringed instrument with a circular body

bank n. **1** mound; heap **2** steep slope, as beside a river **3** row; tier **4** business handling savings, loans, etc. —v. **1** form a bank **2** put (money) in a bank **3** cover (a fire) to make last —**bank on** [Col.] rely on

—**bank′er** n.

bank account n. money deposited in a bank and credited to the depositor

bank′book′ n. book recording a bank depositor's deposits

bank card n. encoded plastic card for use at a bank ATM

bank′ing n. business of a bank

bank note n. promissory note issued by a bank

bank′roll′ n. supply of money —v. [Col.] supply with money

bank′rupt′ a. **1** legally declared unable to pay one's debts **2** lacking —n. bankrupt person —v. make bankrupt —**bank′rupt′cy** n.

ban′ner n. **1** flag **2** long strip of cloth with writing, etc. —a. foremost; leading

banns n.pl. church notice of an upcoming marriage

ban′quet n. formal dinner

ban·quette′ (-ket′) n. **1** gunner's platform in a trench **2** upholstered bench

ban′shee n. Folklore wailing female spirit

ban′tam (-təm) n. breed of small chickens —a. small

ban′ter v. tease playfully —n. genial teasing

ban′yan (-yən) n. Asian fig tree with many trunks

bap′tism′ n. rite of admission into a Christian church by dipping in or sprinkling with water —**bap·tis′mal** (-tiz′məl) a. —**bap′tize** v.

bap′tis·ter·y (or -tis trē) n., pl. **–ies** place in a church used for baptizing: also **bap′tis·try**, pl. **–tries**

bar n. **1** long, narrow piece of wood, metal, etc. **2** oblong piece, as of soap **3** obstruction **4** band or strip **5** law court **6** legal profession **7** counter or place for serving liquor **8** Mus. a measure or vertical line marking it off —v. **barred, bar′ring 1** obstruct; close **2** oppose **3** exclude —prep. excluding

barb n. sharp, back-curving point —**barbed** a.

bar·bar′i·an (-ber′-) n. uncivilized person; savage —a. uncivilized —**bar·bar′ic** a.

bar′ba·rize′ v. make or become barbarous

bar·ba·rous a. **1** uncivilized **2** crude; coarse **3** brutal —**bar′ba·rism′** n.

bar′be·cue′ n. **1** animal roasted whole over open fire **2** picnic at which such meat is served —v. **1** roast whole **2** broil in spicy sauce (**barbecue sauce**)

barbed wire n. twisted strands of wire with barbs at close intervals: also **barb′wire′** n.

bar′bel (-bəl) n. threadlike growth from lip or jaw of a fish

bar′bell′ *n.* metal bar with weights at each end, used in weight lifting

bar′ber *n.* one who cuts hair, shaves beards, etc.

bar′ber·ry (or -bə rē) *n., pl.* **-ries 1** spiny shrub with red berries **2** the berry

bar·bi′tu·rate (-bich′ōō ət) *n.* drug used as a sedative

bar′ca·role′, bar′ca·rolle′ (-rōl′) *n.* Venetian gondolier song, or such music

bard *n.* poet

bare *a.* **1** naked **2** exposed **3** empty **4** mere —*v.* uncover —**bare′foot′, bare′foot′ed** *a., adv.* —**bare′head′ed** *a., adv.*

bare′back′ *adv.* **1, 2** on a horse with no saddle

bare′-bones′ *a.* simple; basic

bare′faced′ *a.* shameless

bare′ly *adv.* only just

bar′gain (-gən) *n.* **1** agreement or contract **2** item bought at a favorable price —*v.* haggle —**bargain for** (or **on**) expect — **into** (or **in**) **the bargain** besides

bargain counter store counter with goods on sale at reduced prices

barge *n.* flat-bottomed freight boar —*v.* enter abruptly (*into*)

bar′i·tone′ (ber′ə-) *n.* male voice, or instrument, between tenor and bass

bar′i·um (ber′ē-) *n.* silver-white metallic chemical element

bark *n.* **1** outside covering of trees **2** sharp cry of a dog **3** sailing vessel —*v.* **1** utter a bark **2** scrape off the skin of

bar′keep′er *n.* **1** owner of a barroom **2** bartender

bark′er *n.* announcer at a carnival sideshow

bar′ley *n.* cereal grain

bar′maid′ *n.* waitress in a bar

bar mitz′vah (-və) *n.* religious ceremony for a Jewish boy when he becomes thirteen years old

barn *n.* farm building for livestock, storage, etc. —**barn′yard′** *n.*

bar′na·cle *n.* shellfish that clings to ships, etc.

barn′storm′ *v.* tour small towns, acting plays, etc.

ba·rom′e·ter *n.* instrument to measure atmospheric pressure —**bar′o·met′ric** *a.*

bar′on *n.* nobleman of lowest rank —**bar′on·ess** *n.fem.* —**ba·ro′ni·al** (-rō′-) *a.*

bar′on·et′ *n.* Br. man with hereditary rank of honor

ba·roque′ (-rōk′) *a.* having elaborate decoration

bar′racks *n.pl.* building(s) for housing soldiers

bar′ra·cu·da (-kōō-) *n., pl.* **-da** or **-das** fierce tropical fish

bar·rage′ (bə räzh′) *n.* curtain of artillery fire

barred *a.* **1** having bars or stripes **2** closed off with bars **3** not allowed

bar′rel *n.* **1** round, wooden container with bulging sides **2** tube of a gun

barrel organ musical instrument played by turning crank

bar′ren *a.* **1** sterile **2** unproductive

bar·rette′ (bə ret′) *n.* clasp for a girl's hair

bar′ri·cade′ *n.* barrier for defense —*v.* block with a barricade

bar′ri·er *n.* fence, wall, or other obstruction

bar′ring *prep.* excepting

bar′ris·ter *n.* in England, courtroom lawyer

bar′room′ *n.* room with a BAR (*n.* 7)

bar′row *n.* traylike frame for carrying loads

bar′tend′er *n.* person serving drinks at a BAR (*n.* 7)

bar′ter *v.* exchange (goods) —*n.* a bartering

ba·sal (bā′səl) *a.* basic

basal metabolism *n.* quantity of energy used by any organism at rest

ba·salt (bə sôlt′) *n.* dark volcanic rock

base *n.* **1** part that a thing rests on **2** basis **3** goal in some games **4** headquarters or a source of supply **5** substance reacting with an acid to form a salt —*v.* put on a base —*a.* **1** morally low **2** inferior —**base′ly** *adv.*

base′ball′ *n.* **1** team game played with a bat and ball **2** the ball used

base′board′ *n.* molding along the bottom of a wall

base hit *Baseball* play by a batter who hits and gets on base safely

base′less *a.* unfounded

base line 1 *Baseball* lane from one base to the next **2** back line on a tennis court

base′man *n., pl.* **-men** *Baseball* infielder at first, second, or third base

base′ment *n.* story just below the main floor

base on balls *Baseball* walk

base pay *n.* basic rate of pay, not counting overtime pay

base runner *n. Baseball* player at or trying to reach a base

bash *v.* [Col.] hit or attack hard

bash′ful *a.* socially timid; shy —**bash′ful·ly** *adv.*

ba′sic *a.* of or at the base; fundamental —**bas′i·cal·ly** *adv.*

bas′il (baz′-, bas′-) *n.* an herb

ba·sil′i·ca *n.* ancient kind of church building

bas′i·lisk′ (bas′-) *n.* mythical, lizardlike monster whose glance could kill

ba′sin n. 1 wide, shallow container for liquid 2 a sink 3 bay, cove, etc. 4 area drained by a river

ba′sis n., pl. **-ses** (-sēz′) 1 base or foundation 2 main constituent

bask v. warm oneself

bas′ket n. 1 container made of interwoven strips 2 goal in basketball

bas′ket·ball′ n. 1 team game with raised open nets through which a large ball must be tossed 2 this ball

bas′-re·lief′ (bä′-, bas′-) n. sculpture with figures projecting a little from the background

bass (bās) n. 1 lowest male singing voice 2 singer or instrument with low range

bass (bas) n. perchlike fish

bas′set n. short-legged hound

bas′si·net′ n. baby's bed like a large basket

bas·so (bas′ō, bäs′ō) n., pl. **-sos** bass voice or singer

bas·soon′ n. double-reed, bass woodwind instrument

bass vi·ol (vī′əl) n. double bass

bast n. plant fiber used for ropes, mats, etc.

bas′tard n. illegitimate child —a. 1 illegitimate 2 sham, not standard, etc. —**bas′tard·ize′** v.

baste v. 1 sew with loose, temporary stitches 2 moisten (a roast) with drippings, etc. —**bast′ing** n.

bas′tion (-chən) n. 1 part of a fort that juts out 2 any strong defense

bat n. 1 a club to hit a ball, as in baseball 2 nocturnal, mouselike, flying mammal —v. **bat′ted, bat′ting** 1 hit as with a bat 2 [Col.] blink

batch n. quantity taken, made, etc. in one lot

bat′ed a. held in, as the breath in fear

bath n. 1 a washing of the body 2 water, etc. for bathing or soaking something 3 bathtub 4 bathroom

bathe (bāth) v. 1 give a bath to, or take a bath 2 put into a liquid 3 cover as with liquid —**bath′er** n.

bath′ing suit n. swimsuit

bath′mat′ n. mat used in or next to a bathtub

ba·thos′ (bā′-) n. a shift from noble to trivial

bath′robe′ n. loose robe worn to and from the bath

bath′room′ n. room with a bathtub, toilet, etc.

bath′tub′ n. tub to bathe in

bath′y·scaph′ (-ə skaf′) n. deepsea diving apparatus not using a cable

ba·tik (-tēk′) n. cloth with design dyed only on parts not coated with wax

ba·tiste′ (-tēst′) n. fine, thin cotton fabric

bat mitz′vah (bät-) n. religious ceremony for a Jewish girl similar to bar mitzvah: also **bas mitz′vah** (bäs-)

ba·ton′ n. 1 stick used in leading an orchestra, etc. 2 staff serving as a symbol of office

bat·tal′ion n. subdivision of a regiment

bat′ten n. strip of wood —v. 1 fasten with battens 2 fatten; thrive

bat′ter v. 1 strike repeatedly 2 injure by hard use —n. 1 player at bat in baseball 2 mixture of flour, milk, etc. for making cakes

bat′ter·ing ram n. heavy beam, etc. to batter down gates, etc.

bat′ter·y n., pl. **-ies** 1 cell or cells providing electric current 2 set of artillery guns 3 pitcher and catcher in baseball 4 illegal beating of a person

bat′ting n. wadded fiber

bat′tle n., v. fight, esp. between armies —**bat′tler** n.

bat′tle-ax′, bat′tle-axe′ n. heavy ax formerly used as a weapon

bat′tle·dore′ n. racket for a game like badminton

bat′tle·field′ n. place of battle: also **bat′tle·ground′**

bat′tle·ment n. low wall on a tower with open spaces for shooting

battle royal n., pl. **battles royal** 1 a brawl 2 heated dispute

bat′tle·ship′ n. large warship with big guns

bat′ty a. **-ti·er, -ti·est** [Sl.] crazy, odd, queer, etc.

bau′ble n. trinket

baud (bôd) n. the number of bits per second transmitted in a computer system

baux·ite (bôk′sīt′) n. claylike aluminum ore

bawd n. a prostitute

bawd′ry n. obscene language

bawd′y a. **-i·er, -i·est** obscene —**bawd′i·ness** n.

bawl v. 1 to shout 2 to weep noisily —**bawl out** [Col.] scold angrily

bay n. 1 wide inlet of a sea or lake 2 alcove 3 recess in a wall, as for a window (**bay window**) 4 laurel tree 5 1) reddish brown 2) horse of this color —v. bark or howl in long, deep tones —**at bay** 1 with escape cut off 2 held off —**bring to bay** cut off escape of

bay′ber′ry n., pl. **-ries** 1 wax myrtle 2 its berry

bay leaf n. laurel leaf, dried and used as spice in cooking

bay′o·net′ n. blade attached to a rifle barrel —v. to stab with a bayonet

bay·ou (bī′ōō′) n. marshy inlet or outlet, as a lake

ba·zaar (-zär′) n. **1** Oriental market place **2** benefit sale for a club, etc.

ba·zoo′ka n. portable tubelike weapon for firing rockets

BB (shot) n. tiny metal shot for an air rifle (**BB gun**)

B.C. before Christ

be v. was or were, been, be′ing **1** exist; live **2** occur **3** remain; continue *Be* is also an important auxiliary verb

be- pref. **1** around **2** completely **3** away **4** about

beach n. stretch of sandy shore —v. ground (a boat)

beach′comb′er n. hobo living on a beach

beach′head′ n. shore area taken by invading troops

bea′con n. guiding light

bead n. **1** small ball of glass, etc., pierced for stinging **2** pl. string of beads **3** drop or bubble —**draw a bead on** take careful aim at —**bead′ed** a. —**bead′y** a.

bea′dle n. minor officer who keeps order in church

bea′gle n. small, short-legged hound

beak n. **1** bird's bill **2** any beaklike mouth part

beak′er n. broad glass container

beam n. **1** long, thick piece of timber, etc. **2** ship's greatest breadth **3** shaft of light **4** radiant look or smile **5** guiding radio signal —v. **1** radiate in a beam **2** smile warmly

bean n. **1** edible seed of some plants **2** pod of these

bear n. **1** large, heavy mammal with shaggy fur **2** rough, rude person —v. **bore, borne** or **born, bear′ing 1** carry **2** have or show **3** give birth to **4** produce **5** permit of **6** endure —**bear down** exert pressure —**bear on** relate to —**bear out** confirm —**bear up** endure —**bear with** tolerate —**bear′a·ble** a. —**bear′er** n.

beard n. **1** hair on a man's face **2** awn —**beard′ed** a.

bear′ing n. **1** way one carries oneself **2** relative position or direction **3** relation **4** ball, roller, etc. on which something turns or slides

bear′ish a. **1** bearlike **2** causing a drop in stock exchange prices

bear′skin′ n. **1** furry hide of a bear **2** rug, coat, etc. made from this

beast n. **1** any large four-footed animal **2** brutal, gross person —**beast′ly** a.

beast of burden n. any animal used for carrying things

beast of prey n. any animal that hunts and kills other animals for food

beat v. **beat, beat′en, beat′ing 1** strike repeatedly **2** punish by striking **3** mix by stirring **4** defeat **5** throb **6** flap (wings) **7** make (a path) by tramping —n. **1** a throbbing beat **2** habitual route **3** unit of musical rhythm —a. [Col.] tired —**beat back (or off)** drive back —**beat it!** [Sl.] go away! —**beat up (on)** [Sl.] thrash —**beat′er** n.

be·a·tif′ic a. blissful

be·at′i·fy′ v. **-fied′, -fy′ing** R.C.Ch. declare one who has died to be among the blessed in heaven

be·at′i·tude′ n. bliss

beat′-up′ a. [Sl.] worn-out, battered, dilapidated, etc.

beau (bō) n., pl. **beaus** or **beaux** (bōz) woman's lover

beau·ti·cian (-tish′ən) n. one who works styling hair, etc.

beau′ti·ful (byōō′-) a. having beauty: also **beau′te·ous** —**beau′ti·ful·ly** adv.

beau′ti·fy′ v. **-fied′, -fy′ing** make beautiful

beau′ty n., pl. **-ties 1** pleasing quality as in looks, sound, etc. **2** person or thing of beauty

beauty salon (or **shop** or **parlor**) n. place where women go for hair styling, etc.

bea′ver n. **1** amphibious animal with webbed hind feet **2** its brown fur

be·calm′ v. **1** make calm **2** make (a ship) motionless from lack of wind

be·cause′ con. for the reason that —**because of** on account of

beck n. beckoning gesture

beck′on v. call by gesture

be·cloud′ v. to obscure

be·come′ v. **-came′, -come′, -com′ing 1** come to be **2** suit —**become of** happen to

be·com′ing a. right or suitable; attractive

bed n. **1** piece of furniture to sleep on **2** plot of soil for plants **3** flat bottom or foundation **4** layer —v. **bed′ded, bed′ding** put or go to bed

be·daz′zle v. dazzle thoroughly

bed′bug′ n. small, wingless, biting insect

bed′clothes′ n.pl. bedsheets, blankets, etc.

bed′cov′er n. bedspread

bed′ding n. mattresses and bedclothes

be·deck′ v. adorn

be·dev′il v. to torment or worry —**be·dev′il·ment** n.

bed′fast′ a. bedridden

bed′fel′low n. **1** person who shares one's bed **2** any associate

be·dim′ v. **-dimmed′, -dim′ming** make (the vision) dim

bed jacket n. woman's jacket worn in bed over a nightgown

bed·lam (-ləm) n. noisy confusion

bed of roses n. [Col.] situation of ease and luxury

Bed′ou·in′ (-ōō-) n. Arab nomad

bed′pan′ n. shallow pan used as a toilet by one bedridden

be·drag′gled a. wet and dirty; messy

bed′rid·den a. confined to bed, as by long illness

bed′rock′ n. 1 solid rock under soil 2 base or bottom

bed′roll′ n. portable roll of bedding, used by campers

bed′room′ n. sleeping room

bed′sore′ n. sore on a bedridden person

bed′spread′ n. ornamental cover for a bed

bed′spring′ n. framework of springs under a mattress

bed′stead′ n. frame of a bed

bed′time′ n. one's usual time for going to bed

bee n. 1 winged insect that makes honey 2 meeting of group, as to work together

beech n. tree with gray bark and beech-nuts

beech′nut′ n. small, edible, three-cornered nut of the beech

beef n., pl. **beeves** or **beefs** 1 cow, bull, or steer 2 its meat —v. [Sl.] complain

beef′eat′er n. 1 one who eats beef 2 guard at the Tower of London

beef′steak′ n. thick cut of beef for broiling or frying

beef′y a. **-i·er, -i·est** brawny

bee′hive′ n. hive for bees

bee′keep′er n. one who keeps bees to make honey —**bee′keep′ing** n.

bee′line′ n. straight course

been v. pp. of BE

beep n. brief, shrill sound of a horn or electronic signal —v. make this sound

beep′er n. portable electronic device for contacting people

beer n. mildly alcoholic drink brewed from malt, hops, etc.

bees′wax′ n. wax from bees, used in their honeycombs

beet n. plant with edible red or white root

bee′tle n. insect with hard front wings —v. jut out

bee′tle-browed′ a. 1 having bushy eyebrows 2 frowning

be·fall′ v. **-fell′, -fall′en, -fall′ing** happen (to)

be·fit′ v. **-fit′ted, -fit′ting** be fitting for

be·fog′ v. **-fogged′, -fog′ging** make foggy 2 to confuse

be·fore′ adv. 1 in front 2 till now 3 earlier —prep. 1 ahead of 2 in sight of 3 earlier than 4 rather than —con. earlier or sooner than

be·fore′hand′ adv., a. ahead of time

be·foul′ v. 1 make filthy 2 cast aspersions on

be·friend′ v. be a friend to

be·fud′dle v. confuse

beg v. **begged, beg′ging** 1 ask for (alms) 2 entreat —**go begging** be unwanted

be·gat′ v. [Ar.] pt. of BEGET

be·get′ v. **-got′, -got′ten** or **-got′, -get′ting** 1 to father 2 to cause

beg′gar n. 1 one who lives by begging 2 very poor person —v. 1 make a beggar of 2 make seem inadequate

beg′gar·ly a. poor; mean

be·gin′ v. **-gan′, -gun′, -gin′ning** 1 start 2 originate —**be·gin′ner** n.

be·gin′ning n. 1 start 2 origin 3 first part

be·gone′ int., v. go away

be·go′nia (-gōn′yə) n. plant with showy flowers

be·grudge′ v. 1 envy the possession of 2 give reluctantly —**be·grudg′ing·ly** adv.

be·guile′ (-gīl′) v. 1 deceive or trick 2 charm 3 pass (time) pleasantly

be·half′ n. support, side, etc. —**in** (or on) **behalf of** in the interest of

be·have′ v. 1 conduct (oneself), properly 2 act

be·hav′ior n. conduct —**be·hav′ior·al** a.

be·head′ v. cut off the head of

be·he′moth (bē hē′-) n. huge animal

be·hest′ n. a command

be·hind′ adv. 1 in the rear 2 slow; late 3 to the back —prep. 1 in back of 2 later or slower than 3 supporting —a. 1 that follows 2 in arrears

be·hind′hand′ adv., a. late in payment, time, or progress

be·hold′ v. **-held′, -hold′ing** see; look at —int. look! see!

be·hold′en a. indebted

be·hoove′ v. be necessary or fitting (for)

beige (bāzh) n. grayish tan

be′ing n. 1 existence; life 2 one that lives

be·la′bor v. spend too much time on

be·lat′ed a. too late

be·lay′ v. **-layed′, -lay′ing** 1 secure (a rope) around a cleat 2 [Col.] Naut. to stop

bel can′to (kän′-) n. brilliant singing style with purity of tone

belch v. 1 expel stomach gas orally 2 eject with force —n. a belching

be·lea′guer (-lē′gər) v. 1 besiege 2 beset

bel′fry (-frē) n., pl. **-fries** bell tower

Bel′gian n., a. (native) of Belgium

be·lie′ v. **-lied′, -ly′ing** 1 misrepresent 2 prove false

be·lief′ n. 1 conviction; faith 2 trust 3 opinion

be·lieve′ v. 1 take as true 2 have faith (in)

3 suppose; guess —**be·liev'a·ble** a. —**be·liev'er** n.

be·lit'tle v. make seem little or unimportant

bell n. 1 hollow metal object that rings when struck 2 sound of a bell

bel'la·don'na n. 1 poisonous plant yielding a drug that relieves spasms 2 the drug

bell'-bot'tom a. flared at the bottom, as trousers

belle (bel) n. pretty girl

belles-let·tres (bel let're) n.pl. fiction, poetry, drama, etc.; literature

bell'hop' n. one who does errands at a hotel: also **bell'boy'**

bel'li·cose' a. quarrelsome —**bel'li·cos'i·ty** (-käs'-) n.

bel·lig'er·ent (bə lij'-) a. warlike —n. nation or person at war —**bel·lig'er·ence** n.

bell jar n. glass, bell-shaped container, used to keep air, moisture, etc. in or out: also **bell glass**

bel'low v., n. roar or shout

bel'lows' n., pl. **-lows'** collapsible device for producing a stream of air

bell pepper n. large, sweet red pepper

bells n.pl. [Col.] bell-bottom trousers

bell'weth'er n. 1 male sheep that leads a flock 2 indicator of a trend, style, etc.

bel'ly n., pl. **-lies** 1 abdomen 2 stomach —v. **-lied**, **-ly·ing** to bulge

bel'ly·ache' n. pain in the belly —v. [Sl.] complain

bel'ly·but'ton n. [Col.] the navel: also **belly button**

bel'ly·ful n. 1 more than enough to eat 2 [Sl.] all that one can bear

belly laugh n. [Col.] hearty laugh

be·long' v. have a proper place —**belong to** 1 be a part of 2 be owned by 3 be a member of

be·long'ings n.pl. possessions

be·lov'ed (-luv'əd, -luvd') a., n. dearly loved (person)

be·low' adv., a. in or to a lower place; beneath —prep. lower than; beneath

belt n. 1 encircling band, as around the waist 2 distinct area —v. strike as with a belt —**below the belt** unfair(ly)

be·mire' v. 1 make dirty with mire 2 bog down in mire

be·moan' v. lament

be·mused' a. preoccupied

bench n. 1 long seat 2 worktable 3 seat for judges 4 status of a judge —v. remove (a player) from a game

bench mark n. standard or model: also **bench'mark'**

bench warrant n. order by judge or law court for an arrest

bend v. **bent**, **bend'ing** 1 to curve, as by pressure 2 (make) yield 3 stoop —n. 1 a bending 2 bent part

be·neath' adv., a. below; underneath —prep. 1 below; under 2 unworthy of

ben'e·dic'tion n. blessing

ben'e·fac'tor n. one who has given money or aid —**ben'e·fac'tion** n. —**ben'e·fac'tress** n.fem.

ben'e·fice (-fis) n. endowed church position

be·nef'i·cence n. 1 kindness 2 kindly act or gift —**be·nef'i·cent** a.

ben'e·fi'cial (-fish'əl) a. producing benefits

ben'e·fi'ci·ar'y (-fish'ər ē) n., pl. **-ies** one receiving benefits, as from insurance

ben'e·fit n. 1 help or advantage 2 a show, etc. to raise money for a cause —v. 1 to help 2 profit

be·nev'o·lence n. the wish to do good; kindness; generosity —**be·nev'o·lent** a.

be·night'ed a. ignorant

be·nign' (-nīn') a. 1 kindly 2 favorable 3 not malignant

be·nig'nant a. benign

ben'i·son n. blessing

ben'ny n., pl. **-nies** [Sl.] amphetamine pill

bent a. 1 curved 2 determined (on) —n. inclination

bent'grass' n. low-growing grass that puts out runners, used for lawns

bent'wood' a. made of pieces of wood permanently bent

be·numb' v. make numb

Ben·ze·drine (ben'zə drēn') trademark amphetamine —n. [**b-**] this drug

ben'zene n. coal-tar derivative used as a solvent

ben'zine (-zēn) n. petroleum derivative used as a motor fuel, in dry cleaning, etc.

ben'zo·ate' n. chemical used to preserve food

be·queath' (-kwēth', -kwēth') v. 1 leave (property) to another by one's will 2 hand down —**be·quest'** n.

be·rate' v. scold severely

be·reave' v. **-reaved'** or **-reft'**, **-reav'ing** 1 deprive 2 leave forlorn, as by death —**be·reave'ment** n. —**be·reft'** a.

be·ret' (-rā') n. flat, round, soft cap

berg n. iceberg

ber'i·ber'i n. disease caused by lack of vitamin B₁

berm n. ledge along the edge of a paved road

ber'ry n., pl. **-ries** small, fleshy fruit with seeds

ber·serk' (-surk', -zurk) a., adv. in(to) a violent rage

berth (burth) n. 1 ship's place of anchorage 2 built-in bed 3 position or job

ber'yl (-əl) n. hard, bright mineral, as the emerald

be·ryl'li·um (-ril'-) *n.* rare, metallic chemical element used in alloys

be·seech' *v.* **-sought'** or **-seeched'**, **-seech'ing** ask (for) earnestly; entreat —**be·seech'ing·ly** *adv.*

be·set' *v.* **-set'**, **-set'ting** 1 attack from all sides 2 surround

be·set'ting *a.* always harassing

be·side' *prep.* 1. at the side of; near 2 as compared with 3 besides 4 aside from —*adv.* besides —**beside oneself** wild, as with fear or anger

be·sides' *adv.* 1 in addition 2 else 3 moreover —*prep.* in addition to

be·siege' *v.* 1 lay siege to; hem in 2 overwhelm, harass, etc. 3 close in on

be·smirch' *v.* to soil; sully

be·som (bē'zəm) *n.* broom made of twigs tied to a handle

be·sot'ted *a.* stupefied, as with liquor

be·speak' *v.* 1. speak for; reserve 2 indicate

best *a.* 1 most excellent 2 most suitable —*adv.* 1 in the best way 2 most —*n.* 1 best person, thing, etc. 2 the utmost —*v.* outdo; beat —**all for the best** turning out to be good —**at best** under the most favorable conditions —**get** (or **have**) **the best of** defeat or outwit —**had best** should —**make the best of** adjust to

bes'tial (-chəl) *a.* like a beast; brutal

be·stir' *v.* stir up; busy

best man *n.* main attendant of a bridegroom

be·stow' *v.* present as a gift (*on* or *upon*)

be·stride' *v.* **-strode'**, **-strid'den**, **-strid'ing** sit, mount, or stand astride

bet *n.* 1 agreement that the one proved wrong will pay something 2 thing so staked —*v.* **bet** or **bet'ted**, **bet'ting** 1 make a bet 2 stake in a bet —**bet'tor**, **bet'ter** *n.*

be·ta (bā'tə) *n.* second letter of the Greek alphabet

be·take' *v.* take (oneself); go

beta particle *n.* electron or positron ejected from an atomic nucleus during radioactive disintegration

beta ray *n.* stream of beta particles

be·tel nut (bēt'l) *n.* fruit of a tree (**betel palm**), chewed with leaves of a plant (**betel pepper**) by some Asian peoples

be·think' *v.* think of; remind (oneself)

be·tide' *v.* happen (to)

be·to'ken *v.* be a sign of

be·tray' *v.* 1 be disloyal to 2 deceive 3 seduce 4 reveal —**be·tray'al** *n.*

be·troth' (-trōth', -trôth') *v.* promise in marriage —**be·troth'al** (-trōth'-) *n.* —**betrothed'** (-trōthd') *a.*, *n.*

bet'ter *a.* 1 more excellent 2 more suitable 3 improved —*adv.* 1 in a better way 2 more —*n.* 1 a superior 2 a better thing,

etc. —*v.* to surpass or improve —**better off** in better circumstances —**get** (or **have**) **the better of** defeat or outwit —**had better** should

bet'ter·ment *n.* improvement

be·tween' *prep.* 1 in the space or time separating 2 involving 3 joining 4 in the common possession of 5 one of —*adv.* in the middle

be·twixt' *prep.*, *adv.* [Ar.] between

bev'el *n.* 1 angled part or surface 2 tool for marking angles —*v.* cut or slope at an angle

bev'er·age *n.* drink

bev'y *n.*, *pl.* **-ies** 1 group, as of girls or women 2 flock of quail

be·wail' *v.* wail over

be·ware' *v.* guard against

be·wil'der *v.* confuse —**be·wil'der·ment** *n.*

be·witch' *v.* to enchant —**be·witch'ing** *a.*

bey (bā) *n.* Turkish title of respect

be·yond' *prep.* 1 farther or later than; past 2 more than —*adv.* farther away —**the (great) beyond** whatever follows death

bez'el *n.* slanting faces of a cut jewel

bhang (baŋ) *n.* 1 hemp plant 2 its dried leaves and flowers, used as a narcotic

bi- *pref.* two or twice

bi·an'nu·al *a.* twice a year

bi·as (bī'əs) *n.* 1 diagonal or slanting line 2 prejudice —*v.* to prejudice —**on the bias** diagonally

bib *n.* cloth tied under a child's chin at meals

bibb lettuce *n.* lettuce with loose, dark-green leaves

Bi'ble sacred book of Christians or of Jews —**Bib'li·cal**, **bib'li·cal** *a.*

bib'li·og'ra·phy *n.*, *pl.* **-phies** list of writings on one subject or by one author

bib'li·o·phile' (-fil') *n.* one who loves and collects books

bib'u·lous *a.* addicted to or fond of alcoholic liquor

bi·cam'er·al *a.* having two legislative branches

bi·car'bon·ate of soda (-ət) *n.* baking soda

bi·cen·ten'ni·al *n.* 200th anniversary

bi'ceps' *n.*, *pl.* **-ceps'** large front muscle of the upper arm

bick'er *v.*, *n.* quarrel

bi·cus'pid *n.* tooth with two-pointed crown

bi'cy·cle (-si kəl) *n.* two-wheeled vehicle —*v.* ride a bicycle —**bi'cy'clist** *n.*

bid *v.* **bade** (bad) or **bid**, **bid'den** or **bid**, **bid'ding** 1 command or ask 2 tell 3 bid, **bid'ding** offer as a price —*n.* 1 amount bid 2 attempt —**bid'der** *n.*

bide *v.* **bode** or **bid'ed**, **bid'ed**, **bid'ing** 1 stay 2 dwell 3 wait —**bide one's time** wait patiently for a chance

bi·det' (-dā') *n.* bathroom fixture, for bathing crotch

bi·en'ni·al *a.* 1 every two years 2 lasting two years —*n.* plant living two years

bier (bir) *n.* frame on which a coffin is put

bi'fo'cals *n.pl.* eyeglasses with lenses having two parts, for close and far focus

big *a.* **big'ger, big'gest** 1 of great size 2 loud 3 important 4 noble —*adv.* [Col.] 1 boastfully 2 impressively —**big'ness** *n.*

big'a·my *n.* crime of marrying again while still married —**big'a·mist** *n.* —**big'a·mous** *a.*

big game *n.* large wild animals hunted for sport, as lions

big'heart'ed *a.* generous

big'horn' *n.* horned, wild sheep of Rocky Mountains

bight (bīt) *n.* 1 loop in a rope 2 curve in a coastline 3 a bay formed by such a curve

big'ot *n.* narrow-minded, intolerant person —**big'ot·ed** *a.* —**big'ot·ry** *n.*

big shot *n.* [Sl.] important person

bike *n., v.* [Col.] 1 bicycle 2 motorcycle

bi·ki'ni *n., pl.* **–nis** 1 women's very brief, two-piece swimsuit 2 very brief underpants or trunks

bi·lat'er·al *a.* on, by, or having two sides

bile *n.* 1 bitter liver secretion 2 bad temper

bilge (bilj) *n.* 1 lower part of a ship's hold 2 stale water that gathers there 3 [Sl.] nonsense

bi·lin'gual *a.* of, in, or speaking two languages

bil'ious (-yəs) *a.* 1 having a disorder of the bile or liver 2 bad-tempered

bilk *v.* to swindle

bill *n.* 1 statement of charges, as for goods 2 list of things offered 3 proposed law 4 piece of paper money 5 bird's beak —*v.* present a bill of charges to

bill'board' *n.* signboard

bil'let *n.* lodging, as for soldiers —*v.* assign to lodging

bill'fold' *n.* wallet

bil'liards (-yərdz) *n.* game played with cue and three balls on a table with raised edges

bil'lion *n.* thousand millions —**bil'lionth** *a., n.*

bil'lion·aire' *n.* one having at least a billion dollars

bill of fare *n.* menu

Bill of Rights first ten amendments to U.S. Constitution

bill of sale *n.* paper transferring ownership by sale

bil'low *n.* 1 large wave 2 swelling mass, as of smoke —*v.* surge or swell

—**bil'low·y** *a.*, **-i·er, -i·est**

bil'ly *n., pl.* **-lies** club, esp. a policeman's stick

billy goat *n.* [Col.] male goat

bi·month'ly *a., adv.* once every two months

bin *n.* box or enclosed space for storage

bi·na·ry (bī'nə rē) *a.* 1 twofold 2 of a number system with only two digits

bin·au'ral (bĭn-) *a.* of stereophonic sound reproduction

bind *v.* **bound, bind'ing** 1 tie together 2 to hold; restrain 3 encircle with (a belt, etc.) 4 bandage 5 put together (a book) with a cover 6 to obligate —**bind'er** *n.*

bind'er·y *n., pl.* **-ies** place where books are bound

bind'ing *n.* 1 anything that binds 2 covers and backing of a book

binge (binj) *n.* [Col.] spree

bin'go *n.* game played on cards with numbered squares

bin'na·cle *n.* case enclosing a ship's compass

bin·oc'u·lars (bī näk'-, bin äk'-) *n.pl.* field glasses

bi'o·chem'is·try *n.* chemistry of living organisms

bi'o·cide' *n.* poisonous chemical substance

bi'o·de·grad'a·ble (-grād'-) *a.* readily decomposed by bacteria

bi'o·feed'back *n.* technique for controlling emotions

bi·og'ra·phy *n., pl.* **-phies** one's life story written by another —**bi·og'ra·pher** *n.* —**bi'o·graph'i·cal** *a.*

biological warfare *n.* use of microorganisms, toxins, etc. to spread disease in war

bi·ol'o·gy *n.* science of plants and animals —**bi'o·log'i·cal** *a.* —**bi·ol'o·gist** *n.*

bi·on'ics *n.* science of modeling instruments or systems after living organisms

bi'op'sy *n., pl.* **-sies** removal of living body tissue for diagnosis

bi·par'ti·san (-zən) *a.* representing two parties

bi'ped' *n.* two-footed animal

birch *n.* 1 tree with smooth bark 2 its hard wood

bird *n.* warmblooded vertebrate with feathers and wings

bird'ie *n.* Golf score of one under par for a hole

bird's'-eye' *view a.* 1 view from above or at a distance 2 general view

birth *n.* 1 a being born 2 descent or origin 3 beginning —**give birth to** to bring into being —**birth'place'** *n.*

birth'day' *n.* day of birth or its anniversary

birth'mark' *n.* skin blemish present at birth

birth′rate′ n. number of births per year in an area

birth′right′ n. rights a person has by birth

bis′cuit (-kit) n. 1 small bread roll 2 [Br.] cracker

bi·sect′ v. divide into two equal parts —**bi·sec′tor** n.

bi·sex′u·al a. sexually attracted to both sexes —n. bisexual person

bish′op n. 1 clergyman heading a diocese 2 chessman moving diagonally

bish′op·ric n. diocese, rank, etc. of a bishop

bis′muth (biz′-) n. metallic chemical element whose salts are used in medicine

bi′son n., pl. **bi′son** shaggy, oxlike animal of North America

bisque n. 1 thick, creamy soup made from shellfish, etc. or strained vegetables

bis′tro (bēs′-) n., pl. **-tros** small cafe

bit n. 1 mouthpiece on a bridle, for control 2 cutting part of a drill 3 small piece or amount 4 single digit in a binary number system 5 [Col.] short time —**bit by bit** gradually —**do one's bit** do one's share

bitch n. female dog, fox, etc. —v. [Sl.] complain

bite v. **bit, bit′ten** or **bit, bit′ing** 1 seize or cut as with the teeth 2 sting, as a bee 3 cause to smart 4 swallow a bait —n. 1 a biting 2 biting quality; sting 3 wound from biting 4 mouthful 5 [Col.] light meal

bit′ing a. 1 cutting; sharp 2 sarcastic

bit′ter a. 1 sharp to the taste 2 sorrowful, painful, resentful, etc. 3 harsh —**bit′ter·ly** adv.

bit′tern n. heronlike bird

bit′ters n.pl. liquor having bitter herbs, etc.

bit′ter·sweet′ a. both bitter and sweet

bi·tu′men n. natural asphalt or similar substance made from coal, etc.

bi·tu′mi·nous coal n. soft coal, easy to burn but smoky

bi′valve′ n. mollusk with two shells, as a clam

biv·ou·ac′ (-wak′, -ōō ak′) n. temporary camp (of soldiers) —v. **-ou·acked′, -ou·ack′ing** make such a camp

bi·week′ly a., adv. once every two weeks

bi·zarre (bi zär′) a. odd; fantastic

blab v. **blabbed, blab′bing** to tattle, gossip, etc.

black a. 1 of the color of coal; opposite to white 2 having dark skin 3 without light; dark 4 dirty 5 evil 6 sad —n. 1 black pigment 2 member of a dark-skinned people, or person having African ancestry —v. to blacken —**black out** lose consciousness —**black′ness** n.

black′-and-blue′ a. discolored by a bruise

black′ball′ n., v. (a) vote against

black belt n. black belt awarded to an expert of the highest skill in judo or karate

black′ber′ry v., pl. **-ries** 1 small, edible, dark fruit 2 bramble it grows on

black′bird′ n. bird the male of which is all black

black′board′ n. smooth surface for writing with chalk

black′en v. 1 make or become black 2 slander

black eye n. discoloration of skin around the eye, as from a blow

black′guard (blag′ard) n. scoundrel; villain

black′head′ n. plug of dirt in a pore of the skin

black′jack′ n. 1 small bludgeon 2 a card game

black light n. ultraviolet or infrared radiation

black′list′ n. list of those to be punished, refused jobs, etc.

black lung (disease) n. lung disease from continual inhaling of coal dust

black′mail′ n. money extorted on threat of disclosing something disgracing —v. (try to) get blackmail from —**black′mail′er** n.

black market n. system for selling goods illegally during rationing, etc.

black′out′ n. 1 concealing of light, facts, etc. 2 a faint 3 loss of electricity in an area

black sheep n. disgraceful member of a family, etc.

black′smith′ n. one who forges iron and shoes horses

black′thorn′ n. thorny shrub with black, plumlike fruit

black′top′ n. asphalt mixture used to surface roads, etc.

black widow n. small, poisonous spider

blad′der n. sac that collects urine from the kidneys

blade n. 1 leaf of grass 2 cutting part of a knife, tool, etc. 3 flat surface, as of an oar

blame v. 1 accuse of being at fault 2 put the responsibility of (on) —n. 1 a blaming 2 responsibility for a fault —**be to blame** deserve blame —**blame′less** a. —**blame′wor′thy** a.

blanch v. 1 bleach 2 make or turn pale

bland a. mild; soothing

blan′dish v. flatter; coax —**blan′dish·ment** n.

blank a. 1 not written on 2 empty 3 utter —n. 1 (printed form with) space to be filled in 2 cartridge without a bullet —**draw a blank** [Col.] be unable to remember something

blan′ket n. 1 wool spread used as bed cover, etc. 2 a covering, as of snow —a. all-inclusive —v. to cover

blare v. sound loudly —n. loud, trumpetlike sound

blar'ney (blär'-) n. flattery

bla·sé (blä zā') a. bored

blas'phe·my' (-fə mē) n., pl. **—mies** profane abuse of God **—blas·pheme'** (-fēm') v. **—blas'phe·mous** a.

blast n. 1 strong rush of air 2 loud sound of horn, etc. 3 explosion —v. 1 explode 2 to blight; wither

blast furnace n. furnace for smelting iron ore

blast'off', **blast'-off'** n. launching of a rocket, etc.

bla'tant a. loud and vulgar **—bla'tan·cy** n.

blaze n. 1 burst of flame 2 bright light 3 vivid display 4 outburst 5 white spot on an animal's face —v. 1 burn or shine brightly 2 mark (a trail)

blaz'er n. lightweight sports jacket in a solid color

bla'zon (-zən) n. coat of arms —v. proclaim

bleach v. whiten —n. chemical that bleaches

bleach'ers n.pl. roofless stand where spectators sit

bleak a. 1 unsheltered; bare 2 cheerless; gloomy

blear (blir) v. to dim or blur, as with tears **—blear'y** a.

bleat n. cry of a sheep or goat —v. make this cry

bleed v. **bled**, **bleed'ing** 1 lose blood 2 draw blood, air, etc. from 3 [Col.] extort from

bleep n., v. beep

blem'ish v. mar; injure —n. defect; fault

blend v. 1 mix 2 shade into each other —n. 1 a blending 2 mixture

blend'er n. kitchen appliance for chopping, mixing, etc.

bless v. **blessed** or **blest**, **bless'ing** 1 make holy 2 ask divine favor for 3 make happy **—bless·ed** (bles'əd, blest) a. **—bless'ing** n.

blew v. pt. of BLOW

blight (blīt) n. 1 insect, disease, etc. that destroys plants 2 anything that destroys —v. destroy; ruin

blimp n. small airship like a dirigible

blind a. 1 without sight 2 lacking insight 3 having no outlet 4 not controlled by reason —n. 1 window shade 2 a decoy —v. make sightless **—blind'ly** adv. **—blind'ness** n.

blind date n. [Col.] date with a stranger, arranged by a third person

blind'fold' v. cover the eyes of —n. cloth used for this

blind'side' v. hit someone who is unprepared or looking away

blink v. 1 wink rapidly 2 flash on and off

—n. 1 a blinking 2 glimmer **—blink at** ignore **—on the blink** [Sl.] out of order

blink'er n. flashing light

blip n. image on radar

bliss n. great happiness **—bliss'ful** a.

blis'ter n. fluid-filled skin swelling caused by a burn, etc. —v. form blisters

blithe (blīth, blīth) a. carefree; cheerful

blitz n. sudden, overwhelming attack

bliz'zard n. severe snowstorm with high wind

bloat v. swell up

blob n. small drop or mass

bloc n. group united for a common purpose

block n. 1 solid piece 2 auction platform 3 obstruction 4 city square or street section 5 pulley in a frame 6 part taken as a unit —v. 1 obstruct 2 shape **—block out** sketch roughly **—on the block** for sale

block·ade' n. shutting off of a place by warships, etc. —v. subject to a blockade

block'bust'er n. an expensive movie, etc. intended to have wide appeal

block'bust'ing n. [Col.] frightening owners into selling homes because minority group will become neighbors

block'head' n. stupid person

block'house' n. wooden fort

blond a. 1 having light-colored hair and skin 2 light-colored Also **blonde** —n. blond man or boy **—blonde** n.fem.

blood n. 1 red fluid in the arteries and veins 2 lineage 3 kinship **—bad blood** hatred **—in cold blood** deliberately **—blood'less** a.

blood bank n. supply of blood stored for transfusions

blood'cur'dling (-kurd'liŋ) a. very frightening; terrifying

blood'hound' n. large, keen-scented tracking dog

blood'mo·bile' (-mō bēl') n. mobile unit for collecting blood for blood banks

blood'shed' n. killing

blood'shot' a. tinged with blood: said of the eyes

blood'thirst'y a. murderous

blood vessel n. artery, vein, or capillary

blood'y a. **-i·er**, **-i·est** 1 of or covered with blood 2 involving bloodshed 3 bloodthirsty —v. **-ied**, **-y·ing** stain with blood

bloom n. 1 a flower 2 time of flowering 3 healthy glow —v. be in bloom

bloom'ers n.pl. women's baggy underpants

bloop'er n. [Sl.] stupid mistake

blos'som n., v. flower

blot n. spot or stain —v. **blot'ted**, **blot'ting** 1 spot, as with ink 2 erase or cancel (out) 3 to dry with soft paper, etc. **—blot'ter** n.

blotch n. discolored spot —v. mark with blotches —**blotch′y** a., -**i·er**, -**i·est**

blouse (blous) n. shirtlike garment for girls

blow v. **blew**, **blown**, **blow′ing** 1 move, as (by) wind 2 force air out, as with the mouth 3 sound by blowing —n. 1 a blowing 2 gale 3 a hit 4 shock —**blow out** 1 extinguish 2 burst —**blow up** 1 inflate 2 explode —**blow′er** n.

blow′gun′ n. tubular weapon through which darts, etc. are blown

blow′out′ n. bursting of a tire

blow′torch′ n. small, hot-flamed torch for welding

blow′up′ n. 1 an explosion 2 enlarged photograph

blowz·y (blou′zē) a. -**i·er**, -**i·est** slovenly: also **blows′y**

blub′ber n. whale fat —v. weep loudly

bludg·eon (bluj′ən) n. short, heavy club —v. to club

blue a. 1 of the color of the clear sky 2 gloomy —n. color of the clear sky —v. use bluing on —**the blues** 1 [Col.] depressed feeling 2 slow, sad jazz song

blue baby n. baby born with bluish skin, esp. because of a heart defect

blue′bell′ n. plant with blue, bell-shaped flowers

blue′ber′ry n., pl. -**ries** small, edible, bluish berry

blue′bird′ n. small bird with blue back and wings

blue blood n. aristocrat: also **blue′blood′**

blue′-col′lar a. of industrial workers

blue′fish′ n. silvery-blue Atlantic food fish

blue′grass′ n. type of grass with bluish-green stems

blue′jay′ n. crested bird with a blue back

blue′jeans′ n.pl. jeans of blue denim

blue law n. puritanical law, esp. one prohibiting certain activities on Sunday

blue′pen′cil v. edit

blue′print′ n. 1 photographic copy, white on blue, of architectural plans, etc. 2 any detailed plan —v. make a blueprint of

bluff v. mislead by a fake, bold front —a. rough and frank —n. 1 a buffing 2 one who bluffs 3 steep bank

blu′ing n. blue rinse for white fabrics

blu′ish a. somewhat blue: also sp. **blue′ish**

blun′der n. foolish mistake —v. 1 make a blunder 2 move clumsily

blun′der·buss′ n. obsolete gun with a broad muzzle

blunt a. 1 dull-edged 2 plain-spoken —v. make dull

blur v. **blurred**, **blur′ring** 1 to smudge 2 make or become indistinct —n. indistinct thing —**blur′ry** a., -**ri·er**, -**ri·est**

blurb n. [Col.] exaggerated advertisement

blurt v. say impulsively

blush v. redden, as from shame —n. a blushing

blus′ter v. 1 blow stormily 2 speak noisily or boastfully —n. swaggering talk —**blus′ter·y** a.

bo·a (bō′ə) n. 1 large snake that crushes its prey in its coils 2 scarf of feathers

boar n. wild hog

board n. 1 broad, flat piece of wood, etc. 2 meals provided regularly for pay 3 council —v. 1 cover (up) with boards 2 get on (a ship, train, etc.) 3 get meals regularly for pay —**on board** on a ship, etc. —**board′er** n.

board′ing·house′ n. house where one can pay for a room and meals

board′walk′ n. wooden walk along a beach

boast v. 1 talk with too much pride 2 take pride in —n. thing boasted of —**boast′er** n. —**boast′ful** a.

boat n. water craft, esp. a small one —**rock the boat** [Col.] disturb the status quo —**boat′man** n., pl. -**men**

boat′ing n. rowing, sailing, etc.

boat·swain (bō′sən) n. petty officer directing deck work

bob n. 1 small hanging weight 2 float on a fishing line —v. **bobbed**, **bob′bing** 1 move jerkily 2 cut short, as hair

bob′bin n. spool for thread

bobby pin n. tight hairpin

bobby socks (or **sox**) n. [Col.] girls' short socks

bob′cat′ n. American lynx

bob′o·link′ n. songbird with a call like its name

bob′sled′ n. racing sled

bob′white′ n. small quail

bock (beer) n. a dark beer

bode v. 1 be an omen of 2 pt. of BIDE

bod·ice (bäd′is) n. snug upper part of a dress

bod′y n., pl. -**ies** 1 whole physical structure 2 trunk of a man or animal 3 main part 4 distinct mass or group 5 [Col.] person —**bod′i·ly** a., adv.

bod′y·guard′ n. guard to protect a person

body language n. unconscious bodily movements that communicate something

body stocking n. one-piece, tight-fitting garment

bod′y·suit′ n. one-piece, tight-fitting garment for torso: also **body shirt**

bog n. a small swamp —v. **bogged**, **bog′ging** sink (down) as in a bog —**bog′gy** a.

bog′gle v. 1 be startled or hesitate (at) 2 confuse

bo′gus a. not genuine

bo·gy (bō′gē) *n.*, *pl.* **–gies** imaginary evil spirit; goblin: also sp. **bo′gey** or **bo′gie**

Bo·he′mi·an *n.* one who lives unconventionally

boil *v.* 1 bubble up into vapor by heating 2 be agitated 3 cook by boiling —*n.* 1 boiling state 2 pus-filled pimple —**boil down** condense

boil′er *n.* tank for making steam or storing hot water

bois′ter·ous *a.* rough, noisy, lively, etc.

bold *a.* 1 daring; fearless 2 impudent 3 sharp and clear —**bold′ly** *adv.*

bo·le′ro (-ler′ō) *n.*, *pl.* **–ros** 1 Spanish dance 2 short, open vest

boll (bōl) *n.* pod of cotton or flax

boll weevil *n.* beetle that harms cotton pods (**bolls**)

bo·lo′gna (-lō′nē) *n.* type of smoked sausage

bol′ster (bōl′-) *n.* long pillow —*v.* prop (*up*)

bolt *n.* 1 flash of lightning 2 sliding bar that locks 3 threaded metal rod used with a nut 4 roll of cloth —*v.* 1 gulp (food) 2 rush out 3 fasten with a bolt 4 sift —**bolt upright** straight upright

bo′lus (bō′-) *n.* 1 small lump 2 large pill

bomb (bäm) *n.* 1 explosive device or missile 2 [Col.] complete failure —*v.* 1 attack with bombs 2 [Col.] be a failure

bom·bard′ *v.* attack as with artillery or bombs —**bom′bar·dier′** (-bər dir′) *n.* —**bom·bard′ment** *n.*

bom′bast′ *n.* pompous speech —**bom·bas′tic** *a.*

bomb′er *n.* airplane designed for dropping bombs

bomb′shell′ *n.* 1 bomb 2 shocking surprise

bo·na fi·de (bō′nə fīd′, bä′-) *n.* in good faith; sincere

bo·nan′za *n.* 1 rich vein of ore 2 any rich source

bon′bon′ *n.* piece of candy

bond *n.* 1 thing that binds or unites 2 binding agreement 3 interest-bearing certificate 4 surety against theft, etc. —*v.* 1 bind 2 furnish a BOND (*n.* 4)

bond′age *n.* slavery —**bond′man** *n.*, *pl.* **–men** —**bond′wom′an** *n.fem.*, *pl.* **–wom′en**

bonds′man *n.*, *pl.* **–men** one furnishing BOND (*n.* 4)

bone *n.* material of the skeleton or piece of this —*v.* 1 remove the bones from 2 [Sl.] study hard: with *up* —**make no bones about** admit freely —**bone′less** *a.*

bone′-dry′ *a.* very dry

bone meal *n.* crushed bones used as feed or fertilizer

bon′er (bōn′-) *n.* [Sl.] a blunder

bon′fire′ *n.* outdoor fire

bong *n.* deep ringing sound —*v.* make this sound

bon′go *n.*, *pl.* **–gos** either of a pair of small drums struck with the hands

bo·ni′to (-nē′tō) *n.*, *pl.* **–tos** or **–toes** kind of tuna

bon·jour (bōn zhoor′) *int.*, *n.* [Fr.] good day; hello

bon′net *n.* hat

bon′ny *a.*, *pl.* **–ni·er** or **–ni·est** handsome; pretty

bon·sai (-sī) *n.*, *pl.* **–sai** dwarfed tree or shrub

bo′nus *n.* payment over the usual or required amount

bon voy·age (voi äzh′) *int.*, *n.* pleasant journey

bon′y *a.* **–i·er**, **–i·est** 1 (full) of bones 2 lean; thin —**bon′i·ness** *n.*

boo *int.*, *n.*, *pl.* **boos** sound made to show disapproval or to startle —*v.* shout "boo" at

boo′-boo′, **boo′boo** *n.*, *pl.* **–boos** [Sl.] stupid mistake

boo′by *n.*, *pl.* **–bies** a fool

book *n.* 1 a bound, printed work 2 a division of a long literary work 3 ledger —*v.* 1 to list in a book 2 to reserve, as rooms

book′case′ *n.* set of shelves for holding books

book′end′ *n.* end piece to hold a row of books upright

book′ie *n.* [Sl.] bookmaker

book′ish *a.* 1 inclined to read or study 2 pedantic

book′keep′ing *n.* work of recording business transactions —**book′keep′er** *n.*

book′let *n.* small book

book′mak′er *n.* one who takes bets, esp. on horses

book′mark′ *n.* slip, etc. for marking a place in a book

book′worm′ *n.* one who reads or studies much

boom *v.* 1 make a deep, hollow sound 2 grow rapidly 3 promote —*n.* 1 deep sound 2 long beam on a derrick 3 spar at the foot of a sail 4 period of prosperity

boom′er·ang′ *n.* 1 Australian curved stick that returns to the thrower 2 scheme that backfires

boon *n.* benefit

boon′docks′ *n.pl.* [Col.] remote rural region

boon′dog′gle *n.* pointless work financed with public funds

boor *n.* rude person

boost *v.*, *n.* [Col.] 1 to push upward; raise 2 to support —**boost′er** *n.*

booster shot n. later injection of vaccine, to keep immunity

boot n. outer covering for the foot and leg —v. 1 to kick 2 [Col.] dismiss

boot'ee, boot'ie n. baby's knitted or cloth shoe

booth n. small stall or enclosure

boot'leg' n. **-legged', -leg'ging** sell (liquor) illegally —a. sold illegally —**boot' leg'ger** n.

boot'less a. useless

boo'ty n. plunder; spoils

booze n. [Col.] liquor

bo·rax (bôr'aks') n. a white salt used in glass, soaps, etc.

bor'der n. 1 edge; margin 2 boundary —v. put or be a border on —a. near a border —**border on** (or **upon**) be next to —**bor' der·land** n.

bor'der·line' n. boundary —a. 1 on a boundary 2 indefinite

bore v. 1 drill a hole (in) 2 weary by being dull —n. 1 inside or diameter of a tube 2 dull person or thing —**bore'dom** n.

bore v. pt. of BEAR

bo·ric acid (bôr'ik) n. powder used in solution as an antiseptic

born v. pp. of BEAR (v. 3) —a. 1 brought into life 2 by nature

borne v. pp. of BEAR (v. 1)

bo'ron' n. nonmetallic chemical element

bor·ough (bur'ō) n. 1 in some States, self-governing town 2 division of New York City

bor'row v. 1 take on loan 2 adopt (an idea)

borsch (bôrsh) n. beet soup, often served with sour cream: also **borsht** (bôrsht)

bor'zoi' n. large dog with narrow head and long legs

bosh n., int. [Col.] nonsense

bos'om (booz'-) n. breast —a. intimate, as a friend

boss n. 1 employer or supervisor 2 head politician —v. 1 supervise 2 [Col.] order about —**boss'y** a., **-i·er, -i·est**

bo'sun n. boatswain

bot'a·ny n. science of plants —**bo·tan'i·cal** a. —**bot'a·nist** n.

botch v. spoil; bungle —n. bungled work

both a., pron. the two —con., adv. equally

both'er (bäth'-) v. 1 annoy; worry 2 trouble (oneself) —n. trouble —**both'er·some** a.

bot'tle n. glass container for liquids —v. put into a bottle —**bottle up** hold in or suppress

bot'tle·neck' n. 1 narrow passage 2 any hindrance

bot'tom n. 1 lowest part; base; underside 2 basis or cause

bot'u·lism' (bäch'ə-) n. poisoning caused by bacteria in foods improperly preserved

bou·doir (bōō dwär') n. woman's private room

bouf·fant (bōō fänt') a. puffed out; full

bough (bou) n. tree branch

bought (bôt) v. pt. & pp. of BUY

bouil·lon (bōōl'yän) n. clear broth

boul'der (bōl'-) n. large rock

bou'le·vard' (bōōl'-) n. broad, tree-lined street

bounce (bouns) v. 1 spring back on impact 2 make bounce 3 leap —n. a bouncing —**bounc'y** a., **-i·er, -i·est**

bounc'ing a. healthy

bound v. 1 pt. & pp. of BIND 2 leap or bounce 3 be a limit or boundary to —a. 1 tied 2 certain (to) 3 obliged 4 with a binding 5 headed (for) 6 [Col.] determined —n. 1 a leap or bounce 2 boundary —**out of bounds** prohibited —**bound'less** a.

bound'a·ry n., pl. **-ries** anything marking a limit

boun'te·ous a. 1 generous 2 abundant

boun'ti·ful a. bounteous

boun'ty n., pl. **-ties** 1 generosity 2 gift or reward

bou·quet (bō kā', bōō'-) n. 1 bunch of flowers 2 aroma

bour·bon (bur'bən) n. corn whiskey

bour·geoi·sie (bōōr'zhwä zē') n. social middle class —**bour·geois'** (-zhwä') a., n.

bout (bout) n. 1 struggle; contest 2 spell or term

bou·tique (bōō tēk', bō-) n. small shop selling costly articles

bou·ton·niere, bou·ton·nière (bōō' tə nir') n. flower worn in a buttonhole

bo'vine' (-vīn) a. cowlike

bow (bou) v. 1 bend down in respect 2 to submit 3 weigh (down) —n. 1 bending of the head or body 2 front part of a ship —**take a bow** acknowledge applause

bow (bō) n. 1 curved stick strung with cord for shooting arrows 2 stick strung with horsehairs, for playing a violin, etc. 3 knot with broad loops —a. curved —v. play (a violin) with a bow

bow'els (bou'-) n.pl. 1 intestines 2 depths

bow'er (bou'-) n. arbor

bow·ie knife (bōō'ē, bō'-) n. long, single-edged hunting knife

bow'knot' (bō'-) n. knot usually with two loops and two ends

bowl (bōl) n. 1 hollow, rounded dish or part 2 amphitheater 3 ball for bowling —v. 1 roll (a ball) in bowling 2 move fast —**bowl over** knock over

bow'leg'ged (bō'-) a. with the legs curved out

bowl'ing n. game in which a ball is rolled along a wooden lane (**bowling alley**) at ten wooden pins

bowls n. bowling game played on a smooth lawn (**bowling green**)

bow'man (bō'-) n., pl. **-men** archer

bow'sprit (bou'-, bō'-) n. tapered spar at bow of a ship

bow tie (bō) n. necktie tied in a bow

box n. 1 container made of wood, cardboard, etc. 2 an enclosed group of seats 3 blow with the hand 4 evergreen shrub: also **box'wood'** —v. 1 put (in) or shut (up) as in a box 2 fight with the fists —**box'er** n. —**box'ing** n.

box'car' n. enclosed railroad freight car

box office n. place in a theater to buy tickets

boy n. male child —**boy'hood'** n. —**boy'ish** n.

boy'cott' v. refuse to deal with —n. a boycotting

boy'friend' n. [Col.] 1 sweetheart of a girl or woman 2 boy who is one's friend

boy scout n. member of the **Boy Scouts,** boys' club stressing outdoor life

boy'sen·ber'ry n., pl. **-ries** berry crossed from raspberry, loganberry, and blackberry

bra n. brassiere

brace v. 1 strengthen with supports 2 prepare for a shock 3 stimulate —n. 1 pair 2 clamp 3 supporting device 4 handle of a drilling tool (**brace and bit**) 5 either of the signs [ ], for connecting lines, etc.

brace'let n. decorative band for the arm

brack'et n. 1 projecting support 2 either of the signs [ ], for enclosing words 3 classification —v. 1 support with brackets 2 enclose in brackets 3 classify together

brack'ish a. salty or rank

bract n. leaf at the base of a flower or on its stalk

brad n. thin wire nail

brae (brā) n. [Scot.] hillside

brag n., v. **bragged, brag'ging** boast

brag'gart (-ərt) n. boaster

braid v. 1 interweave strands of 2 trim with braid —n. braided strip

Braille, braille (brāl) n. system of printing for the blind, using raised dots

brain n. 1 mass of nerve tissue in the head 2 pl. intelligence —v. smash the brains of —[Col.] **brain'y** a., **-i·er, -i·est**

brain'less a. foolish or stupid

brain'storm' n. [Col.] sudden idea

brain'wash' v. [Col.] indoctrinate thoroughly

brain wave n. rhythmic electric impulses in the brain

braise (brāz) v. brown (meat), then simmer it

brake n. 1 thicket 2 device to stop or slow a machine, etc. —v. stop or slow as with a brake

brake'man n., pl. **-men** train conductor's assistant

bram'ble n. prickly shrub

bran n. husks separated from grains of wheat, rice.

branch n. 1 limb of a tree 2 off shoot or division 3 tributary stream 4 local unit of an organization —v. put forth branches —**branch off** diverge —**branch out** broaden one's interest —**branch'like'** a.

brand n. 1 burning stick 2 owner's mark burned on cattle 3 iron used to brand 4 stigma 5 trademark 6 make or kind —v. mark with a brand

bran'dish v. wave about

brand'-new' a. fully new

bran'dy n., pl. **-dies** liquor distilled from wine or fruit juice

brash a. rash or insolent

brass n. 1 alloy of copper and zinc 2 [often with pl. v.] coiled musical instruments, as the trumpet, tuba, etc. 3 [Col.] rude boldness 4 [Sl.] military officer —**brass'y** a., **-i·er, -i·est**

bras·siere (brə zir') n. woman's undergarment for supporting the breasts

brass tacks n. [Col.] basic facts

brass winds n. coiled musical instruments made of metal, as the trumpet, tuba, etc. —**brass'wind'** a.

brat n. unruly child

brat·wurst (brät'wurst') n. sausage of veal and pork

braun·schwei'ger (broun'shwī'-) n. smoked liver sausage

bra·va'do (-vä'-) n. pretended courage

brave a. full of courage —n. a North American Indian warrior —v. 1 defy 2 meet with courage —**brav'er·y** n.

bra'vo (brä'-) int., n., pl. **-vos** shout of approval

brawl v. quarrel or fight noisily —n. noisy fight

brawn n. muscular strength —**brawn'y** a., **-i·er, -i·est**

bray n. sound a donkey makes —v. make this sound

bra'zen (brā'-) a. 1 of or like brass 2 shameless —**brazen it out** act unashamed of

bra·zier (brā'zhər) n. pan for holding burning coals

Bra·zil' nut n. edible, three-sided, tropical nut

breach n. 1 break in something; gap 2 violation of a promise, friendship, etc. —v. make a breach in

bread v. broke, bro'ken, break'ing 1 baked food of flour dough 2 livelihood —v. cover with bread crumbs

breadth n. width or scope

bread'win'ner n. one who supports dependents by earning money

break v. broke, bro'ken, break'ing 1 split apart; smash 2 make or become unusable 3 tame by force 4 make penniless 5 surpass (a record) 6 violate (a law) 7 interrupt 8 stop 9 make or become known —n. 1 a breaking 2 broken place 3 interruption 4 beginning (of day) 5 sudden change 6 a chance —**break in** 1 enter forcibly 2 interrupt 3 train —**break off** stop abruptly —**break out** develop pimples —**break up** 1 to separate 2 to stop 3 [Col.](make) laugh —**break'a·ble** a.

break'age n. 1 a breaking 2 loss due to breaking

break'down' n. 1 mechanical failure 2 physical or mental collapse 3 analysis

break'er n. breaking wave

break'fast (brek'fast) n. first meal of the day —v. eat breakfast

break'-in' n. forcible entering of a building, to rob it

break'neck' a. very dangerous

break'through' n. 1 act, place, etc. of breaking through resistance 2 important discovery

break'up' n. a going apart

break'wa'ter n. barrier to break the impact of waves

breast (brest) n. 1 milk-secreting gland on a woman's body 2 upper front of the body 3 the emotions —v. to face bravely —**make a clean breast of** confess

breast'bone' n. sternum

breast stroke n. swimming stroke in which arms are extended sideways from the chest

breast'work' n. low barrier to protect gunners

breath (breth) n. 1 air taken into and let out of the lungs 2 easy breathing 3 life 4 slight breeze

breathe (brēth) v. 1 inhale and exhale 2 live 3 whisper 4 rest

breath·er (brē'thər) n. [Col.] pause for rest

breath'less a. panting

breath'tak'ing a. exciting

breech n. 1 back part 2 gun part behind the barrel

breech'es (brich'-) n.pl. knickers or trousers

breed v. bred, breed'ing 1 bring forth (offspring) 2 produce 3 raise (animals) —n. 1 race; stock 2 type

breeze n. gentle wind —v. [Col.] move briskly —breez'y a., -i·er, -i·est

breeze'way' n. covered passageway, as from house to garage

breth'ren n.pl. [Ar.] brothers

bre'vi·ar'y (brē'-) n. R.C.Ch. book of daily prayers

brev'i·ty n. briefness

brew v. 1 make (beer, etc.) 2 steep (tea, etc.) 3 form —n. beverage brewed —brew'er n.

brew'er·y n., pl. -ies place where beer is brewed

bri·ar (brī'ar) n. tobacco pipe

bribe n. thing given or promised as an inducement, esp. to wrongdoing —v. offer or give a bribe to —brib'er·y n.

bric'-a-brac' n. figurines, curios, etc.

brick n. 1 building block of baked clay 2 any oblong piece —a. built of brick —v. to cover with bricks

brick'lay'ing n. work of building with bricks

bride n. woman just married or about to be married —brid'al a.

bride'groom' n. man just married or being married

brides'maid' n. any of the bride's wedding attendants

bridge n. 1 structure for crossing a river, etc. 2 thing like a bridge in shape, etc. 3 mounting for false teeth 4 card game for two pairs of players —v. build or be a bridge over

bridge'work' n. dental bridge(s)

bri·dle n. 1 head harness for a horse 2 thing that restrains —v. 1 put a bridle on 2 curb

bridle path n. path for horseback riding

brief a. short; concise —n. summary, as of a law case —v. summarize the facts for

brief'case' n. small case for carrying papers, books, etc.

bri·er (brī'-) n. 1 thorny bush 2 its root, used for making tobacco pipes

brig n. 1 two-masted ship with square sails 2 ship's prison

bri·gade' n. 1 military unit of several regiments 2 group organized for a task

bri·ga·dier' general (-dir') n. officer just above a colonel

brig'and n. roving bandit

bright a. 1 shining; full of light 2 vivid 3 cheerful 4 mentally quick —bright'en v. —bright'ly adv. —bright'ness n.

bril'liant (-yant) a. 1 shining brightly 2 splendid 3 keenly intelligent —bril'liance n. —bril'liant·ly adv.

brim n. 1 top edge of a cup, etc. 2 projecting

rim of a hat —v. **brimmed, brim′ming** fill or be full to the brim —**brim′ful** a.

brim′stone′ n. sulfur

brin′dled a. having dark streaks, as a cow: also sp. **brin′dle**

brine n. 1 water full of salt 2 ocean —**brin′y** a., **-i-er, -i-est**

bring v. **brought, bring′ing** cause to come or happen; fetch, get, lead to, etc. —**bring about** to cause —**bring forth** give birth to; produce —**bring off** accomplish —**bring out** reveal —**bring to** revive —**bring up** 1 rear (children) 2 mention

brink n. edge, as of a cliff

bri-quette′, bri-quet′ (-ket′) n. small block of charcoal

brisk a. 1 quick; energetic 2 invigorating

bris′ket n. breast meat

bris′ling n. sprat canned as a sardine

bris-tle (bris′əl) n. short, stiff hair —v. 1 stiffen like bristles 2 stiffen with anger —**bris′tly** a.

britch′es n.pl. [Col.] breeches

Brit′ish a. of Great Britain or its people

British thermal unit n. unit of heat, equal to about 252 calories

brit′tle a. hard but easily broken —**brit′tle-ness** n.

broach n. tapered bit for reaming out holes —v. 1 make a hole in 2 start a discussion of

broad a. 1 wide 2 obvious 3 tolerant 4 extensive; general —**broad′en** v.

broad′cast′ v. **-cast′** or **-cast′ed, -cast′ing** 1 spread widely 2 send by radio, TV, etc. —n. radio, TV, etc. program —adv. far and wide —**broad′cast′er** n.

broad′cloth′ n. a fine cloth

broad′en v. widen

broad jump n. long jump

broad′loom′ a. woven on a wide loom, as a carpet

broad′-mind′ed a. liberal

broad′side′ n. 1 firing of all guns on a ship's side 2 large sheet with advertising —adv. with the side facing

bro-cade′ n. cloth of a richly patterned weave —v. weave a raised design in

broc′co-li n. green-headed cauliflower

bro-chette (brō shet′) n. a skewer for broiling chunks of meat

bro-chure′ (-shoor′) n. pamphlet

bro′gan n. heavy work shoe, fitting high on the ankle

brogue (brōg) n. Irish accent

broil v. cook by direct heat

broil′er n. 1 pan or stove section for broiling 2 chicken fit for broiling

broke v. pt. of BREAK —a. [Sl.] without money

bro′ken v. pp. of BREAK —a. 1 fractured 2 not in working order 3 violated, as a vow 4 ruined 5 interrupted 6 imperfectly spoken 7 tamed

bro′ken-down′ a. 1 sick or worn out 2 out of order

bro′ken-heart′ed a. crushed by grief

bro′ker n. agent hired to buy and sell —**bro′ker-age** n.

bro′mide′ (-mīd) n. 1 sedative 2 trite saying

bro′mine′ (-mēn′) n. fuming liquid, a chemical element

bron′chi′ (-kī′) n.pl. the two main branches of the windpipe

bron′chi-al (-kē-) a. of the branches of the windpipe

bron-chi′tis (-kī′-) n. inflammation of the bronchial tubes

bron′co n., pl. **-cos** small, wild horse of the West

bron′to-saur′ (-sôr′) n. large plant-eating dinosaur: also **bron′to-saur′us**

bronze n. 1 alloy of copper and tin 2 reddish brown —v. make bronze in color

brooch (brōch, brōōch) n. large ornamental pin with a clasp

brood n. 1 birds hatched at one time 2 offspring —v. dwell on moodily

brook n. a small stream —v. endure or tolerate

brook trout n. mottled stream trout of NE North America

broom n. 1 long-handled brush for sweeping 2 kind of shrub

broom′stick′ n. broom handle

broth n. clear soup

broth′el n. house of prostitution

broth′er n. 1 male related to one by having the same parents 2 fellow member —**broth′er-hood′** n. —**broth′er-ly** a.

broth′er-in-law′ n., pl. **broth′ers-** 1 brother of one's spouse 2 sister's husband

brought v. pt. & pp. of BRING

brou-ha-ha′ (brōō′-) n. uproar

brow n. 1 eyebrow 2 forehead 3 edge of a cliff

brow′beat′ v. **-beat, -beat-en, -beat-ing** to bully

brown a. 1 chocolate-colored 2 tanned; dark-skinned —n. brown color —v. to make or become brown

brown′-bag′ v. carry (one's lunch) to work, etc.

brown′ie n. square of flat chocolate cake

brown′out′ n. dimming of lights during a power shortage

brown rice n. unpolished rice

brown′stone′ n. reddish-brown sandstone, used for building

brown sugar n. sugar with crystals coated with brown syrup

browse v. 1 feed on grass, etc. 2 to glance through books —**brows′er** n.

bru′in n. a bear

bruise (brooz) v. injure and discolor (the skin) without breaking it —n. discolored injury of the skin

bruis′er n. pugnacious man

bruit (broot) v. rumor

brunch n. [Col.] combined breakfast and lunch

bru·net′ a. having dark hair and complexion —n. brunet person

bru·nette′ (-net′) a. brunet —n. brunette woman or girl

brunt n. main impact

brush n. 1 device with bristles, wires, etc. for cleaning, painting, etc. 2 a brushing 3 skirmish 4 underbrush 5 sparsely settled land —v. 1 use a brush on 2 touch lightly 3 remove as with a brush —**brush off** dismiss —**brush up** refresh one's memory

brush′off′ n. [Sl.] rude dismissal

brusque (brusk) a. abrupt in manner —**brusque′ly** adv.

Brus′sels sprouts n. plant bearing small cabbage-like heads —n.pl. its edible heads

bru′tal a. savage, cruel, etc. —**bru·tal′i·ty** n., pl. —**ties** —**bru′tal·ly** adv.

bru′tal·ize′ v. 1 make brutal 2 treat brutally

brute a. of or like an animal; cruel, stupid, etc. —n. 1 animal 2 brutal person —**brut′ish** a.

bub′ble n. globule of air or gas in a liquid —v. 1 rise in bubbles 2 gurgle —**bub′bly** a.

bubble gum n. chewing gum for blowing into large bubbles

bub′bler n. drinking fountain that spurts water up from a nozzle

bub′ble-top′ n. bulletproof, transparent dome, as over a car

bu·bon′ic plague (byoo bän′ik) n. deadly contagious disease

buc′ca·neer′ n. pirate

buck n. 1 male deer, goat, etc. 2 a bucking 3 [Sl.] dollar —v. 1 rear up, as to throw off (a rider) 2 [Col.] resist —**pass the buck** [Col.] shift the blame

buck′et n. container with a handle, for water, etc.; pail —**buck′et·ful′** n.

bucket seat n. single contoured seat, as in sports cars

buck′eye′ n. 1 horse chestnut with shiny, brown seeds 2 the seed

buck′le n. clasp for fastening a belt, etc. —v. 1 fasten with a buckle 2 bend or

crumple —**buckle down** apply oneself

buck′ler n. round shield

buck′-pass′er n. [Col.] one who puts the blame on someone else —**buck′-pass′ing** n.

buck′ram (-rəm) n. stiff cloth

buck′shot′ n. large lead shot for a gun

buck′skin′ n. leather from skins of deer or sheep

buck′tooth′ n., pl. —**teeth′** projecting tooth —**buck′toothed′** a.

buck′wheat′ n. plant with seeds ground into dark flour

bu·col′ic (byoo käl′ik) a. rustic

bud n. small swelling on a plant, start of a leaf, shoot, or flower —v. **bud′ded, bud′ding** 1 put forth buds 2 begin to develop

Bud·dhism (bood′iz′əm, bood′-) n. a religion of Asia —**Bud′dhist** n., a.

bud′dy n., pl. —**dies** [Col.] comrade

budge v. move slightly

budg′er·i·gar′ n. Australian parakeet: also [Col.] **budg′ie**

budg′et n. 1 plan adjusting expenses to income 2 estimated cost of operating, etc. —v. 1 put on a budget 2 schedule

buff v. polish, as with soft leather —**buff′er** n.

buf′fa·lo′ n., pl. —**loes** or —**los** 1 wild ox 2 American bison —v. [Sl.] to bluff

buff′er n. anything that lessens shock

buf·fet′ (-ət) n., v. blow; slap

buf·fet′ (-fā′) n. 1 cabinet for dishes, silver, etc. 2 food which guests serve themselves as from a buffet

buf·foon′ (-foon′) n. a clown —**buf·foon′er·y** n.

bug n. 1 crawling insect, esp. when a pest 2 [Col.] germ 3 [Sl.] defect 4 [Sl.] tiny microphone

bug′bear′ n. imaginary terror: also **bug′a·boo′**, pl. —**boos′**

bug′gy n., pl. —**gies** 1 light, one-horse carriage 2 baby carriage

bu·gle (byoo′-) n. small, valveless trumpet —**bu′gler** n.

build v. **built**, **build′ing** 1 make by putting together parts 2 create, develop, etc. —n. form or structure —**build up** to make more attractive —**build′er** n.

build′ing n. structure

build′up′, build′-up′ n. [Col.] 1 praise 2 gradual increase

built′-in′ a. 1 made as part of the structure 2 inherent

built′-up′ a. 1 made higher, etc. with added parts 2 with many buildings on it

bulb n. 1 underground bud, as the onion 2 bulblike electric lamp —**bul′bous** a.

bulge *n.* outward swelling —*v.* swell out —**bulg′y** *a.*

bu·lim′i·a (byōo lē′-) *n.* an eating disorder —**bu·lim′ic** *a.*

bulk *n.* 1 size or mass, esp. if great 2 main part —*v.* have, or gain in, size or importance —*a.* not packaged —**bulk′y** *a.*, **-i·er, -i·est**

bulk′head′ *n.* vertical partition, as in a ship

bull *n.* 1 male bovine animal, or male seal, elephant, etc. 2 edict of the Pope —*a.* male

bull′dog′ *n.* heavily built dog with a stubborn grip

bull′doze′ *v.* 1 [Col.] to bully 2 move or level with a bulldozer

bull′doz′er *n.* tractor with a large shovellike blade

bul′let *n.* shaped metal piece to be shot from a gun

bul′le·tin *n.* 1 brief news item 2 regular publication of a group

bulletin board *n.* board for posting bulletins or notices

bul′let·proof′ *a.* that bullets cannot pierce

bull′fight′ *n.* spectacle in which a bull is goaded to fury, then killed —**bull′fight′er** *n.*

bull′finch′ *n.* small European songbird

bull′frog′ *n.* large frog

bull′head′ed *a.* stubborn

bull′horn′ *n.* portable electronic voice amplifier

bul·lion (bool′yən) *n.* gold or silver ingots

bull′ish *a.* 1 like a bull 2 causing a rise in stock exchange prices

bull′ock *n.* castrated bull

bull's′-eye′ *n.* target center

bul′ly *n., pl.* **-lies** one who hurts or threatens weaker people —*v.* **-lied, -ly·ing** act the bully (toward)

bul′rush′ *n.* tall grasslike plant, in marshes, etc.

bul′wark *n.* rampart; defense

bum *n.* [Col.] a vagrant —*v.* **bummed, bum′ming** [Sl.] 1 beg 2 [Col.] loaf —*a.* [Sl.] 1 poor in quality 2 false 3 lame

bum′ble *v.* blunder or stumble —**bum′bler** *n.*

bum′ble·bee′ *n.* large bee

bum′mer *n.* [Sl.] unpleasant experience

bump *v.* collide (with) —*n.* 1 light collision 2 swelling —**bump′y** *a.*, **-i·er, -i·est**

bump′er *n.* device, as on a car, for easing collisions —*a.* unusually abundant

bumper sticker *n.* sticker with slogan, etc., for a car bumper

bump′kin *n.* awkward or simple person from the country

bun *n.* small bread roll

bunch *n.* cluster of similar things —*v.* gather; group

bun′dle *n.* 1 number of things bound together 2 package —*v.* 1 make into a bundle 2 hustle (*off*) —**bundle up** dress warmly

bun′ga·low′ *n.* small house

bun′gee cord *n.* elastic cord

bun′gle *v.* do clumsily; spoil —**bun′gler** *n.*

bun′ion *n.* swelling at the base of the big toe

bunk *n.* 1 built-in bed 2 [Col.] any narrow bed 3 [Sl.] empty talk —*v.* sleep in a bunk

bunk′er *n.* 1 large bin 2 obstacle on a golf course

bunk′house′ *n.* barracks for ranch hands, etc.

bun′ny *n., pl.* **-nies** [Col.] rabbit

bunt *Baseball v.* to bat (a pitch) so it does not go beyond the infield —*n.* a bunted ball

bun′ting *n.* 1 thin cloth for flags, etc. 2 baby's hooded blanket 3 small finch

buoy (boi, bōō′ē) *n.* floating marker —*v.* 1 keep afloat 2 lift up in spirits

buoy′an·cy (boi′-) *n.* 1 ability to float 2 cheerfulness —**buoy′ant** *a.*

bur *n.* prickly seedcase

bur′den *n.* 1 load carried 2 thing hard to bear —*v.* weigh down —**bur′den·some** *a.*

bur′dock′ *n.* plant with prickly burs

bu·reau (byoor′ō) *n., pl.* **-reaus** or **-reaux** (-rōz′) 1 chest of drawers 2 government department 3 office

bu·reauc·ra·cy (byōō rä′krə sē) *n., pl.* **-cies** (government by) officials following rigid rules —**bu′reau·crat′** (byoor′ə-) *n.* —**bu′·reau·crat′ic** *a.*

burg *n.* [Col.] city or town

bur′geon (-jən) *v.* sprout

bur′ger *n.* [Col.] hamburger or cheeseburger

-burger *suf.* 1 sandwich of ground meat, etc. 2 hamburger and

bur′glar *n.* one who breaks into a building to steal —**bur′gla·ry** *n., pl.* **-ries**

bur′glar·ize′ *v.* commit burglary in

bur′gle *v.* [Col.] burglarize

Bur′gun·dy *n.* 1 kind of wine 2 purplish red

bur′i·al (ber′-) *n.* burying of a dead body

burl *n.* knot on some tree trunks 2 veneer from wood with knots —**burled** *a.*

bur′lap′ *n.* coarse cloth of hemp, etc., used for bags

bur·lesque′ (-lesk′) *n.* 1 broadly comic satire 2 type of vaudeville —*v.* imitate comically

bur′ly *a.* **-li·er, -li·est** big and strong

burn *v.* **burned** or **burnt**, **burn′ing** 1 be or set on fire 2 destroy or be destroyed by fire 3 hurt or be hurt by acid, friction, etc. 4 feel or make feel hot 5 be excited 6 [Sl.] cheat or trick —n. injury from fire, acid, etc.

burn′er n. part of a stove, etc. producing the flame

bur′nish v., n. polish

bur·noose′ n. hooded cloak worn by Arabs

burn′out′ n. state of emotional exhaustion from stress, etc.

burp v., n. [Sl.] belch

burr n. 1 rough edge left on metal 2 trilling of r 3 bur

bur′ro n., pl. **-ros** donkey

bur′row n. hole dug by an animal —v. make a burrow

bur′sa n., pl. **-sae** (-sē) or **-sas** body sac with fluid, as between tendon and bone

bur′sar (-sər) n. college treasurer

bur·si′tis n. inflammation of a sac between bone joints

burst v. **burst, burst′ing** 1 come apart suddenly; explode 2 appear, enter, etc. suddenly 3 be too full —n. a bursting

bur·y (ber′ē) v. **-ied, -y·ing** 1 put in a grave, tomb, etc. 2 cover; hide

bus n., pl. **bus′es** or **bus′ses** large motor coach

bus′boy′ n. assistant to waiter or waitress

bus·by (buz′bē) n., pl. **-bies** tall fur hat, part of some full-dress uniforms

bush n. 1 low, woody plant 2 uncleared land —**bush′y** a., **-i·er, -i·est**

bushed a. [Col.] exhausted

bush′el n. a dry measure equal to 4 pecks

bush′ing n. removable metal lining to reduce friction

bush′whack′ v. ambush

busi·ness (biz′nəs) n. 1 commerce 2 commercial or industrial establishment; store, factory, etc. 3 occupation 4 rightful concern 5 matter; affair —**busi′ness·man′** n., pl. **-men′**

busi′ness·like′ a. efficient

bus′ing, bus′sing n. a taking children by bus to a school out of their neighborhood so as to achieve racial balance

bust n. 1 sculpture of head and shoulders 2 woman's bosom —v. [Sl.] break

bus·tle (bus′əl) v. hurry busily —n. 1 a bustling 2 padding for the back of a skirt

bus·y (biz′-) a. **-i·er, -i·est** 1 active; at work 2 full of activity —v. **-ied, -y·ing** make busy —**bus′i·ly** adv. —**bus′y·ness** n.

bus′y·bod′y n., pl. **-ies** meddler

but prep. except —con. 1 yet 2 on the contrary 3 unless —adv. 1 only 2 merely —**all but** almost —**but for** if it were not for

bu′tane (byōō′-) n. organic compound used as fuel

butch a. [Col.] designating a man's close-cropped haircut

butch′er n. 1 one who kills and dresses animals for meat 2 one who sells meat 3 killer —v. 1 slaughter 2 botch —**butch′er·y** n.

but′ler n. head manservant

butt n. 1 thick end 2 stub 3 object of ridicule 4 large cask —v. 1 join end to end 2 ram with the head —**butt in(to)** [Sl.] meddle (in)

butte (byōōt) n. small mesa

but′ter n. yellow fat churned from cream —v. spread with butter —**but′ter·y** a.

butter bean n. 1 lima bean 2 wax bean

but′ter·cup′ n. a small, bright-yellow flower

but′ter·fat′ n. fatty part of milk

but′ter·fly′ n., pl. **-flies** insect with four broad, colorful wings

but′ter·milk′ n. sour milk left after churning butter

but′ter·nut′ n. white walnut tree or its edible nut

but′ter·scotch′ n. hard candy made with butter

but′tocks n.pl. fleshy, rounded parts of the hips

but′ton n. 1 small disk for fastening a garment, etc. 2 buttonlike part —v. to fasten with buttons —**on the button** [Sl.] precisely

but′ton·hole′ n. slit for a button —v. detain in talk

but′tress n. 1 outer structure supporting a wall 2 a prop —v. prop up

bux′om a. shapely, with a full bosom

buy v. **bought, buy′ing** 1 get by paying money, etc. 2 to bribe —n. [Col.] something worth its price —**buy′er** n.

buy′out′ n. the purchase of a business by employees, etc.

buzz v. hum like a bee —n. buzzing sound

buz′zard n. 1 kind of large hawk 2 kind of vulture

buzz′er n. electrical device signaling with a buzz

buzz saw n. circular saw rotated by machinery

buzz′word′ n. jargon word having little meaning, but sounding impressive

by prep. 1 near; beside 2 during 3 not later than 4 through 5 past 6 for 7 according to —adv. 1 near 2 past —**by and by** after a while —**by and large** in most respects —**by the by** incidentally

bye n. advancement to next round of tournament without having to compete

bye′-bye′ n., int. goodbye

by′gone′ a. past —n. anything past

by′law′ *n.* local law or rule

by′line′ *n.* writer's name heading a newspaper article

by′pass′ *n.* **1** road, pipe, etc. that gets around the main way **2** surgery or passage to route blood around a diseased part —*v.* **1** to detour around **2** ignore

by′path′ *n.* side path

by′prod′uct, by′-prod′uct *n.* secondary product or result

by′stand′er *n.* one standing near but not taking part

byte (bīt) *n.* string of bits: basic unit in computing

by′way′ *n.* side road

by′word′ *n.* **1** proverb **2** thing well-known for some quality

C

cab *n.* **1** taxicab **2** place in a truck, etc. where the operator sits

ca·bal (kə bal′) *n.* **1** group of conspirators **2** plot

ca·bal·le·ro (kab′ə ler′ō) *n., pl.* **–ros** [Southwest] **1** horseman **2** lady's escort

ca·ban′a *n.* **1** cabin **2** small shelter for swimmers, etc. to change clothes

cab′a·ret′ (-rā′) *n.* cafe with entertainment

cab′bage *n.* vegetable with round head of thick leaves

cab′by, cab′bie *n., pl.* **–bies** [Col.] one who drives a taxi

ca′ber·net′ (-nā′) *n.* dry red wine

cab′in *n.* **1** hut **2** a room on a ship, etc.

cab′i·net *n.* **1** case with drawers or shelves **2** [C–] body of official advisers

cab′i·net·mak′er *n.* maker of fine furniture —**cab′i·net·work′** *n.*

ca′ble *n.* **1** thick rope, often of wire **2** cablegram **3** cable TV —*v.* send a cablegram (to)

cable car *n.* car drawn up an incline by a moving cable

ca′ble·gram′ *n.* telegram sent overseas by wire

cable TV *n.* TV system transmitting via cables to subscribers

ca·bo·chon (ka′bə shän′) *n.* precious stone cut in convex shape

ca·boo′dle *n.* [Col.] lot; group

ca·boose′ *n.* crew's car on a freight train

ca·ca·o (**bean**) (kə kā′ō) *n.* seed of tropical American tree: source of chocolate

cache (kash) *n.* **1** place for hiding food, supplies, etc. **2** anything so hidden —*v.* to place in a cache

cache-pot (kash′pät′, -pō′) *n.* jar to hold a potted plant

ca·chet′ (-shā′) *n.* sign of official approval or of quality

cack′le *v., n.* (make) the shrill sound of a hen

ca·coph′o·ny (kə käf′-) *n., pl.* **–nies** harsh, jarring sound(s) —**ca·coph′o·nous** *a.*

cac′tus *n., pl.* **–tus·es** or **–ti′** (-tī′) spiny desert plant

cad *n.* ungentlemanly man

ca·dav′er (kə dav′-) *n.* corpse —**ca·dav′er·ous** *a.*

cad′die, cad′dy *n., pl.* **–ies** attendant to a golfer —*v.* **–died, –dy·ing** be a caddy

cad′dy *n., pl.* **–dies** small container, as for tea

ca′dence *n.* **1** fall of the voice in speaking **2** rhythm; measured movement

ca·den′za *n.* elaborate passage for solo instrument in a concerto

ca·det′ *n.* student at a military or naval school

cadge *v.* beg —**cadg′er** *n.*

cad′mi·um *n.* metallic chemical element used in alloys, etc.

ca·dre (ka′drē, kä′drä′) *n.* nucleus for a larger organization

Cae·sar′e·an (**section**) *n.* surgery to deliver a baby

ca·fe (ka fā′) *n.* **1** restaurant **2** barroom

caf′e·te′ri·a (-tir′ē ə) *n.* self-service restaurant

caf·fe·ine, caf·fe·in (kaf′ēn′) *n.* stimulant in coffee, tea, etc.

caf′tan′ *n.* long-sleeved robe, worn in eastern Mediterranean lands

cage *n.* openwork structure, esp. for confining animals —*v.* put in a cage

cag′er *n.* [Sl.] basketball player

ca′gey, ca′gy *a.* **–gi·er, –gi·est** [Col.] sly; cunning —**ca′gi·ly** *adv.*

ca·hoots′ *n.* [Sl.] scheming partnership

cais′son (kā′-) *n.* **1** ammunition wagon **2** watertight box for underwater construction work

cai′tiff (kā′-) *n.* mean or cowardly person —*a.* mean or cowardly

ca·jole′ *v.* coax or wheedle —**ca·jol′er·y** *n.*

Ca′jun, Ca′jan *n.* Canadian French native of Louisiana

cake *n.* **1** baked dough or batter of flour, eggs, sugar, etc. **2** solid, formed, usually flat mass —*v.* form into a hard mass

cal′a·bash′ *n.* gourdlike fruit of a tropical tree

ca′la·ma′ri *n.* squid cooked as food

cal′a·mine′ *n.* zinc compound used in lotions, etc.

ca·lam′i·ty *n., pl.* **–ties** disaster —**ca·lam′i·tous** *a.*

cal′ci·fy′ (-sə fī′) *v.* **–fied′, –fy′ing** change

into stony matter —**cal′ci·fi·ca′tion** *n.*

cal′ci·mine′ *n.* thin, watery paint for covering plaster —*v.* to cover with calcimine

cal′ci·um *n.* chemical element in bone, limestone, etc.

calcium carbonate *n.* white compound found in limestone, bones, etc.

cal′cu·late′ *v.* **1** figure by arithmetic **2** estimate —**cal′cu·la·ble** *a.* —**cal′cu·la′tion** *n.* —**cal′cu·la′tor** *n.*

cal′cu·lat′ed *a.* deliberately planned or intended

cal′cu·lat′ing *a.* **1** scheming **2** shrewd; cautious

cal′cu·lus *n.* branch of higher mathematics

cal·dron (kôl′drən) *n.* large kettle or boiler

cal′en·dar *n.* **1** table showing the days, weeks, and months of a year **2** schedule

cal′en·der *n.* machine with rollers for making paper, cloth, etc. smooth or glossy

calf *n., pl.* **calves 1** young cow or bull **2** young elephant, seal, etc. **3** fleshy part of leg below the knee

calf′skin′ *n.* leather made from the skin of a calf

cal′i·ber, cal′i·bre *n.* **1** diameter of a bullet, bore of a gun, etc. **2** quality

cal′i·brate′ *v.* mark or fix the graduations of (a measuring device) —**cal′i·bra′tion** *n.* —**cal′i·bra′tor** *n.*

cal′i·co′ *n.* cotton cloth, usually printed

cal′i·pers *n.pl.* instrument for measuring diameter

ca′liph, ca′lif (kā′-) *n.* old title of Muslim rulers

cal′is·then′ics *n.pl.* simple athletic exercises

calk (kôk) *v., n.* caulk

call *v.* **1** say loudly; shout **2** summon **3** name **4** telephone **5** stop (a game) —*n.* **1** shout or cry **2** summons **3** demand **4** need **5** short visit —**call for 1** demand **2** come and get —**call off** cancel —**call on 1** visit briefly **2** ask (one) to speak —**on call** available when called —**call′er** *n.*

cal·la (lily) (kal′ə) *n.* plant with yellow flower spike inside a large, white leaf

cal·lig′ra·phy *n.* artistic handwriting —**cal·lig′ra·pher** *n.*

call′ing *n.* vocation; trade

cal·li·o·pe′ (-lī′ə pē′) *n.* organlike musical instrument with steam whistles

cal′lous *a.* **1** hardened **2** unfeeling —**cal′lous·ly** *adv.*

cal′low *a.* inexperienced

cal′lus *n.* hard, thickened place on the skin

calm *n.* stillness —*a.* still; tranquil —*v.* make or become calm —**calm′ly** *adv.* —**calm′ness** *n.*

ca·lor′ic *a.* of heat

cal′o·rie, cal′o·ry (-rē) *n., pl.* **–ries** unit of heat or of the energy gotten from food

cal′o·rif′ic *a.* producing heat

cal′u·met′ (-yə-) *n.* pipe with long stem smoked by North American Indians in peace ceremony

ca·lum′ni·ate′ (kə lum′-) *v.* to slander —**ca·lum′ni·a′tion** *n.*

cal·um′ny *n., pl.* **–nies** slander

calve (kav) *v.* give birth to (a calf)

ca·lyp′so (-lip′-) *n., pl.* **–sos** improvised ballad sung in the West Indies

ca·lyx (kā′liks′) *n., pl.* **–lyx′es** or **–ly·ces** (-lə sēz′) sepals of a flower

cam *n.* projection on a wheel to give irregular motion, as to a shaft

ca·ma·ra·de·rie (kä′mə räd′ər ē) *n.* comradeship

cam′ber *n.* slight convexity

cam′bi·um *n.* cell layer under bark of plants from which new wood and bark grow

cam′bric (kām′-) *n.* fine linen or cotton cloth

cam′cord′er *n.* portable videotape recorder and TV camera

came *v.* pt. of COME

cam′el *n.* beast of burden with a humped back

ca·mel′li·a (-mēl′yə) *n.* large, roselike flower

Cam·em·bert′ (cheese) (-ber′) *n.* soft, creamy, rich cheese

cam′e·o′ *n., pl.* **–os′ 1** gem, etc. with figure carved on it **2** small role for notable actor

cam′er·a *n.* **1** device for taking photographs **2** TV device that first receives the images for transmission

cam′er·a·man′ *n., pl.* **–men′** operator of a movie or TV camera

cam′i·sole′ *n.* short negligee

cam′o·mile′ *n.* chamomile

cam′ou·flage′ (-ə fläzh′) *n.* a disguising of potential targets in wartime —*v.* conceal by disguising

camp *n.* **1** place with tents, huts, etc., as for vacationers or soldiers **2** supporters of a cause —*v.* set up a camp —**camp′er** *n.*

cam·paign′ (-pān′) *n.* series of planned actions, as in war, an election, etc. —*v.* wage a campaign

cam′pa·ni′le (-nē′lē) *n.* bell tower

camp′fire′ *n.* **1** outdoor fire at a camp **2** social gathering around such a fire

cam′phor (-fər) *n.* strong-smelling crystalline substance used in mothballs, medicine, etc.

camp′site′ *n.* place for camping

cam'pus n. school or college grounds —a. of students

camp'y a. [Sl.] so artificial or trite as to amuse

can v. pt. **could** auxiliary verb showing: 1 ability 2 likelihood 3 [Col.] permission

can n. metal container, as for foods —v. **canned, can'ning** preserve (food) in cans or jars —**can'ner** n.

Ca-na'di-an n., a. (native) of Canada

ca-nal' n. 1 artificial waterway 2 body duct

ca'na-pé' (-pā') n. appetizer on a cracker, etc.

ca-nard' n. false rumor

ca-nar'y n., pl. **-ies** yellow songbird kept in a cage

ca-nas'ta n. double-deck card game

can'can' n. lively dance with much high kicking

can'cel v. 1 cross out 2 make invalid 3 abolish —**can'cel-la'tion** n.

can'cer n. 1 malignant tumor 2 a spreading evil —[**C**—] fourth sign of the zodiac; Crab —**can'cer-ous** a.

can'de-la'brum (-lä'-, -lā'-) n., pl. **-bra** or **-brums** large, branched candlestick: also **can'de-la'bra,** pl. **-bras**

can'did a. frank; honest

can'di-date' n. one seeking office, etc. —**can'di-da-cy** n.

can'died (-dēd) a. sugary

can'dle n. wax taper with a wick, burned for light

can'dle-pow'er n. unit for measuring light

can'dle-stick' n. holder for a candle or candles

can'dor n. frankness

can'dy n., pl. **-dies** confection of sugar or syrup —v. **-died, -dy·ing** cook or preserve in sugar

cane n. 1 hollow, jointed stem, as of bamboo 2 walking stick 3 split rattan —v. to beat with a cane

cane'brake' n. dense growth of cane plants

ca·nine' a. of or like a dog —n. dog

canine tooth n. any of the four sharp-pointed teeth

can'is-ter n. box or can for coffee, tea, etc.

can'ker n. a sore, esp. in the mouth —**can'ker-ous** a.

can'na-bis n. 1 hemp 2 marijuana, etc. from the flowering tops of hemp

canned a. 1 preserved, as in cans 2 [Sl.] recorded for reproduction, as on TV

can'nel (coal) n. tough bituminous coal

can'ner·y n., pl. **-ies** factory for canning foods

can'ni·bal n. person who eats human flesh —**can'ni·bal·ism'** n. —**can'ni·bal·is'tic** a.

can'ni·bal·ize' v. strip (old equipment) for usable parts

can'non n., pl. **-nons** or **-non** large mounted gun

can'non·ade' n. continuous firing of artillery

can'not can not

can'ny a. **-ni·er, -ni·est** 1 cautious 2 shrewd —**can'ni·ly** adv.

ca·noe' (-nōō') n. narrow, light boat moved with paddles —v. paddle or go in a canoe

ca·no'la (oil) n. cooking oil, from the seed of the rape plant

can'on n. 1 body of church laws 2 any law 3 official list 4 clergyman serving in a cathedral 5 musical round —**can·non'i·cal, ca·non'ic** a.

can'on·ize' v. name as a saint —**can'on·i·za'tion** n.

can'o·py n., pl. **-pies** covering hung over a bed, throne, etc. —**can'o·pied** a.

cant n. 1 special vocabulary of a class; jargon 2 hypocritical talk —v. use cant

cant n., v. tilt; slant

can't cannot

can'ta·loupe', can'ta·loup' (-ə lōp') n. sweet, juicy melon

can·tan'ker·ous a. bad-tempered; quarrelsome

can·ta'ta (kən tät'ə) n. dramatic choral composition

can·teen' n. 1 general store at an army post 2 soldier's water flask

can'ter n. easy gallop —v. go at this pace

can'ti·cle n. hymn

can'ti·le'ver n. structure that is anchored at only one end

can'to n., pl. **-tos** division of a long poem

can'ton n. a state in the Swiss Republic

can·ton'ment (-tän'-, -tōn'-) n. temporary quarters for troops

can'tor n. liturgical singer in a synagogue

can'vas n. coarse cloth used for tents, sails, oil paintings, etc.

can'vas·back' n. wild duck with a grayish back

can'vass (-vəs) v. seek votes, opinions, etc. from —n. a canvassing —**can'vass·er** n.

can'yon n. a narrow valley between high cliffs

cap n. 1 brimless hat, often with a visor 2 caplike cover —v. **capped, cap'ping** 1 put a cap on 2 surpass

ca'pa·ble a. able; skilled —**capable of** able or likely to —**ca'pa·bil'i·ty** n., pl. **-ties** —**ca'pa·bly** adv.

ca·pa'cious a. roomy; wide

ca·pac'i·tor n. device for storing an electrical charge

ca·pac'i·ty n. 1 ability to contain or hold 2 volume 3 ability 4 position

cape n. 1 sleeveless coat fastened about the neck 2 land jutting into water

ca'per v. skip about playfully —n. 1 wild, foolish act 2 [Sl.] criminal act, esp. a robbery

ca'pers n.pl. tiny pickled buds used as seasoning

cap'il·lar'y a. having a tiny bore, as a tube —n., pl. **–ies** tiny blood vessel

cap'i·tal a. 1 bringing or punishable by death 2 chief; main 3 excellent —n. 1 capital letter 2 city from which a state is governed 3 money or property owned or used in business 4 capitalists collectively 5 top of a column

capital gain n. profit made from sale of stocks, etc.

cap'i·tal·ism' n. economic system in which the means of production and distribution are privately owned

cap'i·tal·ist n. owner of wealth used in business —**cap'i·tal·is'tic** a.

cap'i·tal·ize' v. 1 convert into capital 2 use to advantage: with on 3 supply capital for 4 write with a capital letter —**cap'i·tal·i·za'tion** n.

capital letter n. large letter used to begin a sentence, name, etc.

cap'i·tal·ly adv. very well

capital punishment n. penalty of death for a crime

Cap'i·tol n. building where a legislature meets

ca·pit'u·late' (-pich'ə-) v. surrender —**ca·pit'u·la'tion** n.

cap'let n. medicinal tablet with a protective coating

ca'pon' n. castrated rooster

cap·puc·ci·no (kä'pə chē'nō, kap'ə-) n. steamed coffee mixed with steamed milk

ca·price' (-prēs'-) n. whim

ca·pri'cious (-prish'əs, -prē'shəs) a. unpredictable

Cap'ri·corn' tenth sign of the zodiac; Goat

cap'size' v. upset; overturn

cap'stan n. device around which cables are wound

cap'sule n. small case, as for a dose of medicine

cap'tain n. 1 leader 2 army officer above lieutenant 3 navy officer above commander 4 master of a ship —v. to head —**cap'tain·cy** n.

cap'tion n. 1 title, as under a newspaper picture 2 TV or film subtitle

cap'tious (-shəs) a. 1 made for the sake of argument 2 quick to find fault

cap'ti·vate' v. fascinate

cap'tive a., n. (held) prisoner —**cap·tiv'i·ty** n.

cap'tor n. one who captures

cap'ture v. take by force, by surprise, etc. —n. a capturing or the thing captured

car n. 1 wheeled vehicle; esp., an automobile 2 elevator

ca·rafe' (-raf') n. bottle for water, coffee, etc.

car'a·mel (or kär'məl) n. 1 burnt sugar used to flavor 2 chewy candy

car'at n. 1 unit of weight for jewels 2 karat

car'a·van' n. group traveling together, as through a desert

car'a·van'sa·ry n., pl. **–ries** in the Orient, inn for caravans

car'a·way' n. spicy seeds used as flavoring

car'bide' n. compound of a metal with carbon

car·bine' (-bīn', -bēn') n. light, short-barreled rifle

carbo- pref. carbon

car'bo·hy'drate n. compound of carbon, hydrogen, and oxygen, as sugar or starch

car·bol'ic acid n. an acid used as an antiseptic, etc.

car'bon n. nonmetallic chemical element in all organic compounds: diamond and graphite are pure carbon

car'bon·ate' v. charge with carbon dioxide —**car'bon·a'tion** n.

carbon copy n. copy made with carbon paper

carbon dioxide n. odorless gas given off in breathing

car'bon·if'er·ous a. containing carbon or coal

carbon monoxide n. colorless, odorless, poisonous gas

carbon paper n. paper coated with a carbon preparation, used to make copies (**carbon copies**) of letters, etc.

carbon tet'ra·chlo'ride (-klôr'īd) n. cleaning fluid

Car'bo·run'dum trademark hard abrasive, esp. of carbon and silicon —n. [c-] such a substance

car'boy' n. large bottle to hold corrosive liquids

car'bun·cle n. painful inflammation below the skin

car'bu·ret'or (-bə rāt'ər) n. device in an engine for mixing air with gasoline

car'cass (-kəs) n. dead body of an animal

car·cin'o·gen n. substance causing cancer —**car'ci·no·gen'ic** a.

car·ci·no'ma n. cancer of certain tissues, esp. the epidermis

car coat n. short overcoat

card n. 1 flat piece of stiff paper 2 postcard 3 playing card 4 pl. game played with cards 5 metal comb for wool, etc. —v.

comb with a card

card′board′ *n.* stiff paper

car′di·ac′ *a.* of the heart

car′di·gan *n.* knitted jacketlike sweater

car′di·nal *a.* 1 chief; main 2 bright-red —*n.* 1 high R.C. Church official 2 red American songbird

cardinal number *n.* number used in counting, as 7, 42, etc.

cardio– *pref.* of the heart

car′di·o·gram′ *n.* electrocardiogram

car′di·o·graph′ *n.* an electrocardiograph

car′di·ol′o·gy *n.* branch of medicine dealing with the heart —**car′di·ol′o·gist** *n.*

car′di·o·vas′cu·lar *a.* of the heart and blood vessels

card′sharp′ *n.* [Col.] professional cheater at cards: also **card shark**

care *n.* 1 worry 2 watchfulness 3 charge; keeping —*v.* 1 be concerned 2 wish (to do) —**care for** 1 love or like 2 look after —**(in) care of** at the address of —**take care of** 1 look after 2 protect —**care′free′** *a.* —**care′ful** *a.* —**care′less** *a.*

ca·reen′ *v.* tilt; lurch

ca·reer′ *n.* 1 full speed 2 progress through life 3 profession or occupation

care′free′ *a.* without care

care′ful *a.* 1 cautious; wary 2 thoroughly done —**care′ful·ly** *adv.*

care′less *a.* 1 carefree 2 not paying enough attention or heed —**care′less·ness** *n.*

ca·ress′ *v.* touch lovingly —*n.* affectionate touch

car′et *n.* mark (^) to show where addition is to be made in a printed line

care′tak′er *n.* one who takes care of a building, etc.

care′worn′ *a.* weary with care

car′fare′ *n.* price of a ride on a bus, etc.

car′go *n.*, *pl.* –**goes** or –**gos** load carried by a ship, etc.

car′i·bou′ (-bōō′) *n.* North American reindeer

car·i·ca·ture (kar′i kə chər) *n.* distorted imitation or picture for satire —*v.* do a caricature of

car·i·es (ker′ēz′) *n.* decay of teeth, bones, etc.

car′il·lon′ (kar′-) *n.* set of tuned bells

car′mine (-min, -mīn′) *n.* red or purplish red

car′nage *n.* slaughter

car′nal *a.* bodily; sensual

car·na′tion *n.* 1 variety of the pink 2 its flower

car′ni·val *n.* 1 festivity 2 kind of fair, with rides, etc.

car·niv′o·rous *a.* flesh-eating —**car′ni·vore′** *n.*

car′ob *n.* tree with sweet pods used in candy, etc.

car′ol *n.* (Christmas) song of joy —*v.* sing —**car′ol·er, car′ol·ler** *n.*

car′om *n.*, *v.* hit and rebound

ca·rot′id *n.* either of two main arteries in the neck

ca·rouse′ (-rouz′) *v.*, *n.* (join in) a drinking party

car′ou·sel′, car′rou·sel′ *n.* merry-go-round

carp *n.* freshwater fish —*v.* find fault pettily

car′pel *n.* modified leaf forming a pistil

car′pen·ter *n.* construction worker who makes wooden parts —**car′pen·try** *n.*

carpenter ant *n.* large, black ant that gnaws at wood

car′pet *n.* heavy fabric for covering a floor —*v.* to cover as with a carpet

car′pet·bag′ *n.* old-fashioned traveling bag of carpeting

car′pet·ing *n.* carpets or carpet fabric

car pool *n.* group plan to rotate cars, going to and from work

car′port′ *n.* roofed shelter for an automobile

car′rel, car′rell *n.* small enclosure for study in a library

car′riage *n.* 1 horsedrawn vehicle 2 posture 3 moving part that holds and shifts something

car′ri·er *n.* one that carries

car′ri·on *n.* decaying flesh of a dead body

car′rot *n.* plant with an edible, orange-red root

car′ry *v.* –**ried**, –**ry·ing** 1 take to another place 2 lead, transmit, etc. 3 win (an election, etc.) 4 hold; support 5 bear (oneself) 6 keep in stock 7 cover a range —**be (or get) carried away** to become very emotional or enthusiastic —**carry on** 1 do or continue 2 [Col.] behave wildly —**carry out (or through)** to accomplish

car′ry·out′ *a.* of prepared food sold to be eaten elsewhere

car′sick′ *a.* nauseated from riding in a car, etc.

cart *n.* small wagon or vehicle with wheels, pushed or pulled by hand —*v.* carry in a vehicle

cart′age *n.* a carting 2 charge for this

carte′ blanche′ (blänsh′) *n.* full authority

car·tel′ *n.* national or international monopoly

car′ti·lage′ *n.* tough, elastic skeletal tissue

car·tog′ra·phy *n.* map-making —**car·tog′ra·pher** *n.*

car′ton *n.* cardboard box

car·toon′ *n.* 1 drawing that is a caricature 2 comic strip 3 film of drawn figures that seem to move —**car·toon′ist** *n.*

car'tridge *n.* 1 cylinder holding the charge and bullet or shot for a firearm 2 small container for film, etc.

cart'wheel' *n.* a sideways turning, heels over head, with the legs extended

carve *v.* 1 make or shape by cutting 2 slice —**carv'er** *n.* —**carv'ing** *n.*

car'wash' *n.* business at which cars are washed

ca·sa'ba *n.* melon with a yellow rind

cas·cade' *n.* 1 waterfall 2 a shower —*v.* fall in a cascade

case *n.* 1 example or instance 2 situation 3 lawsuit 4 form of a noun, etc. showing its relation to neighboring words 5 container 6 protective cover —*v.* 1 put in a case 2 [Sl.] examine carefully —**in case** if —**in case of** in the event of

ca'se·in (-sē-) *n.* protein constituent of milk

case'load' *n.* number of cases being handled by a court, caseworker, etc.

case'ment *n.* hinged window that opens outward

case'work' *n.* social work dealing with cases of personal and family maladjustment —**case'work'er** *n.*

cash *n.* money on hand —*v.* give or get cash for

cash'ew *n.* kidney-shaped, edible nut

cash·ier' *n.* one in charge of cash transactions —*v.* dismiss in disgrace

cash'mere' (kash'-, kazh'-) *n.* soft, fine goat's wool, or a cloth of this

cash register *n.* device for showing the amount of a sale

cas'ing *n.* 1 outer covering 2 door frame

ca·si'no *n., pl.* **-nos** hall for dancing, gambling, etc.

cask *n.* barrel for liquid

cas'ket *n.* coffin

cas·sa'va (-sä'-) *n.* tropical plant with starchy roots

cas'se·role' *n.* covered dish for baking and serving

cas·sette' *n.* case with film or tape for a camera, tape recorder, VCR, etc.

cas'sia (kash'ə) *n.* 1 bark of an Asian tree, from which cinnamon comes 2 tropical plant whose leaves yield senna

cas·si'no (-sē'-) *n.* card game

cas'sock *n.* long vestment worn by clergymen

cast *v.* **cast, cast'ing** 1 throw 2 deposit (a vote) 3 mold 4 select (an actor) —*n.* 1 a throw 2 plaster form for broken limb 3 the actors in a play 4 type or quality 5 tinge —**cast about** search —**cast aside** (or **away** or **off**) discard

cas'ta·nets' *n.pl.* two hollow pieces clicked together in one hand in rhythm

cast'a·way' *n.* shipwrecked person

caste (kast) *n.* class distinction based on birth, etc.

cast'er *n.* small swiveled wheel as on a table leg

cas'ti·gate' *v.* criticize severely —**cas'ti·ga'tion** *n.* —**cas'ti·ga'tor** *n.*

cast'ing *n.* metal cast in a mold

cast iron *n.* hard, brittle pig iron —**cast'-i'ron** *a.*

cas·tle (kas'əl) *n.* 1 large, fortified dwelling 2 ROOK (*n.* 2)

cast'off' *a.* discarded —*n.* person or thing abandoned

cas'tor oil *n.* oil used as a laxative

cas'trate' *v.* remove the testicles of —**cas·tra'tion** *n.*

cas'u·al (kazh'ōō-) *a.* 1 by chance 2 careless 3 nonchalant 4 informal

cas'u·al·ty *n., pl.* **-ties** one hurt or killed in an accident or in war

cas'u·ist·ry *n.* subtle but false reasoning

cat *n.* 1 small, soft-furred animal kept as a pet 2 any related mammal, as the lion

cat'a·clysm' (-kliz'əm) *n.* sudden, violent change —**cat'a·clys'mic** *a.*

cat'a·comb' (-kōm') *n.* tunnel-like burial place

cat'a·falque' (-falk', -fôlk') *n.* wooden framework for holding a coffin

cat'a·lep'sy *n.* loss of consciousness, with body rigidity —**cat'a·lep'tic** *a., n.*

cat'a·log', cat'a·logue' *n.* complete list, as of library books —*v.* to list

ca·tal'pa (-tal'-) *n.* tree with heart-shaped leaves

cat'a·lyst' (-list') *a.* substance that affects a chemical reaction but itself remains unchanged —**cat'a·lyt'ic** *a.*

cat'a·mount' *n.* 1 cougar 2 lynx

cat'a·pult' *n.* device for throwing or launching —*v.* shoot as from a catapult

cat'a·ract' *n.* 1 large waterfall 2 opaque condition of eye lens

ca·tarrh' (kə tär') *n.* inflammation of the respiratory passages

ca·tas'tro·phe (-trə fē) *n.* sudden great disaster —**cat'a·stroph'ic** *a.*

cat'a·ton'ic *a.* being in a stupor in which the muscles are rigid

cat'bird' *n.* songbird with a call like a cat's

cat'call' *n.* derisive call

catch *v.* **caught, catch'ing** 1 capture 2 deceive 3 surprise 4 get 5 grab 6 understand 7 take or keep hold —*n.* 1 a catching 2 thing that catches or is caught —**catch on** 1 understand 2 become popular —**catch up** to overtake —**catch'er** *n.*

catch'all' *n.* container for holding all sorts of things

catch′ing a. 1 contagious 2 attractive

catch′up n. ketchup

catch′y a. **-i·er, -i·est** 1 easily remembered 2 tricky

cat′e·chism (-kiz′əm) n. list of questions and answers to teach religious beliefs

cat′e·chize v. to question searchingly: also sp. **cat′e·chise**

cat′e·gor′i·cal a. 1 of or in a category 2 positive

cat′e·go·ry n., pl. **-ries** any of a system of classes —**cat′e·go·rize′** v.

ca′ter v. provide food, etc. for a party —**ca′ter·er** n.

cat′er·cor′nered (kat′ə-) a. diagonal —adv. diagonally Also **cat′er·cor′ner**

cat′er·pil′lar n. larva of a butterfly, moth, etc.

cat′er·waul (-wôl′) v., n. wail

cat′fish′ n. fish with long feelers about the mouth

cat′gut′ n. tough thread made from animal intestines

ca·thar′sis n. a relieving of the emotions

ca·thar′tic a. purging —n. a laxative

ca·the′dral n. large church

cath′e·ter n. tube put in the bladder to remove urine

cath′ode′ n. 1 a negatively charged electrode 2 positive terminal of a battery

cath′ode′-ray′ tube n. vacuum tube for producing X-rays when striking solids

cath′o·lic a. 1 universal 2 liberal 3 [C-] Roman Catholic —n. [C-] member of the R.C. Church —**Ca·thol′i·cism′** n. —**cath′o·lic′i·ty** n.

cat′kin n. spike of clustered small flowers

cat′nap′ n. short sleep; doze —v. take a catnap

cat′nip′ n. plant like mint

cat′-o′-nine′-tails′ n., pl. **-tails′** whip of nine knotted cords attached to a handle

CAT (kat) n. computerized photographic technique using X-rays

cat′s cradle n. game played by looping string over the fingers to make designs

cat′s′-paw′ n. a dupe

cat′sup (or kech′əp) n. ketchup

cat′tail′ n. marsh plant with long, brown spikes

cat′tle n. 1 livestock 2 cows, bulls, steers, or oxen —**cat′tle·man** n., pl. **-men**

cat′ty a. **-ti·er, -ti·est** spiteful or mean

cat′ty-cor′nered a., adv. cater-cornered: also **cat′ty-cor′ner**

cat′walk′ n. high, narrow walk

Cau·ca·soid (kô′kə soid′) n., a. (member) of one of the major groups of human beings, loosely called the *white race*: also **Cau·ca·sian** (kô kā′zhən)

cau′cus n. political meeting to choose party candidates, etc. —v. hold a caucus

cau′dal a. of the tail

caught v. pt. & pp. of CATCH

caul n. membrane enclosing the head of a fetus at birth

caul′dron n. caldron

cau′li·flow′er n. hard, white head of a cabbagelike plant

caulk (kôk) v. make watertight or airtight by filling cracks with a puttylike sealant —n. this sealant

caus′al a. of a cause or causes —**cau·sal′i·ty** n.

cau·sa′tion n. 1 a causing 2 anything making an effect

cause n. 1 thing bringing a result 2 motive 3 group movement with an aim 4 lawsuit —v. bring about

cause′way′ n. raised road, as across a marsh

caus′tic a. 1 corrosive 2 sarcastic —n. caustic substance

cau′ter·ize′ v. burn dead tissue off, as with a hot iron

cau′tion n. 1 warning 2 prudence —v. warn —**cau′tious** a.

cav′al·cade′ n. procession

cav′a·lier′ (-lir′) n. 1 knight 2 gallant gentleman —a. 1 casual 2 arrogant —**cav′a·lier′ly** adv.

cav′al·ry n., pl. **-ries** army troops on horses or in motorized vehicles —**cav′al·ry·man** n., pl. **-men**

cave n. hollow place in the earth —v. collapse (in)

cave′-in′ n. 1 a caving in 2 place where ground, etc. has caved in

cave man n. prehistoric human being who lived in caves

cav′ern n. large cave —**cav′ern·ous** a.

cav′i·ar′, cav′i·are′ (-är′) n. fish eggs eaten as a relish

cav′il v. quibble

cav′i·ty n., pl. **-ties** hole or hollow place

ca·vort′ v. prance; caper

caw n. crow's harsh cry —v. make this sound

cay·enne′ (kī-, kā-) n. ground hot red pepper

cay·use′ (kī′ōōs′) n., pl. **-us′es** small Western horse

CB a. of radio frequencies for local use by private persons —n. CB radio

CD n. compact disc

cease (sēs) v. to end; stop

cease′-fire′ n. truce

cease′less a. unceasing

ce′cum (-kəm) n., pl. **-ca** pouch at the beginning of the large intestine ce'dar n. evergreen tree with fragrant wood

cede (sēd) v. give up; transfer

ceil'ing n. 1 inner roof of a room 2 upper limit

cel'an·dine' (-dīn', -dēn') n. 1 poppy 2 buttercup

cel'e·brate' v. 1 to perform (a ritual) 2 commemorate with festivity 3 honor; praise —cel'e·bra'tion n.

cel'e·brat'ed a. famous

ce·leb'ri·ty n. 1 fame 2 pl. —ties famous person

ce·ler'i·ty n. speed

cel'er·y n. plant with edible crisp stalks

ce·les'tial (-chəl) a. 1 of the heavens 2 divine

cel'i·ba·cy n. unmarried state —cel'i·bate (-bət) a., n.

cell n. 1 small room as in a prison 2 small unit of protoplasm 3 device for generating electricity chemically 4 unit of an organization —cel'lu·lar a.

cel'lar n. room(s) below ground under a building

cel·lo (chel'ō) n., pl. —los instrument like a large violin, held between the knees in playing —cel'list n.

cel'lo·phane' (sel'ə-) n. thin transparent cellulose material, used as a wrapping

cel'lu·lite' n. fatty deposits on the hips and thighs

cel'lu·loid' n. flammable plastic substance of cellulose

cel'lu·lose' (-yōō lōs') n. substance in plant cell walls, used in making paper, etc.

Cel'si·us a. of a thermometer on which 0° is the freezing point and 100° the boiling point of water

ce·ment' n. 1 mixture of lime, clay, and water, used for paving, in mortar, etc. 2 any adhesive —v. join as with cement

cem'e·ter'y n., pl. —ies place for burying the dead

cen'ser n. container in which incense is burned

cen'sor n. one who examines books, mail, etc. to remove things considered unsuitable —v. act as a censor of —cen'sor·ship' n.

cen·so'ri·ous (-sôr'ē-) a. critical

cen'sure n., v. blame

cen'sus n. official count of population

cent n. 100th part of a dollar; penny

cen'taur' (-tôr') n. Gr. myth. monster with a man's head and trunk and a horse's body

cen·ta'vo (-tä'-) n., pl. —vos 100th part of a peso

cen·ten'ni·al n. 100th anniversary —a. of a centennial Also cen'te·nar'y (or sen ten'ər ē)

cen'ter n. 1 middle point, esp. of a circle or sphere 2 any central place, thing, or person —v. 1 put or be at the center 2 gather

cen'ter·fold' n. center facing pages of a magazine

cen'ter·piece' n. ornament for the center of a table

centi– pref. 1 hundred 2 100th part of

cen'ti·grade' a. Celsius

cen'ti·gram' n. 1/100 gram

cen·time (sän'tēm') n. 100th part of a franc

cen'ti·me'ter n. 1/100 meter

cen'ti·pede' n. wormlike animal with many pairs of legs

cen'tral a. 1 in or near the center 2 main; chief —cen'tral·ly adv.

cen'tral·ize' v. 1 bring to a center 2 organize under one control —cen'tral·i·za'tion n.

cen'tre n., v. chiefly Br. sp. of CENTER

cen·trif'u·gal force n. force that makes rotating bodies move away from the center

cen'tri·fuge' (-fyōōj') n. machine using centrifugal force to separate particles

cen·trip'e·tal force n. force that makes rotating bodies move toward the center

cen'trist n. person with moderate political opinions

cen·tu'ri·on n. military commander in ancient Rome

cen'tu·ry (-chə-) n., pl. —ries period of 100 years

ce·phal'ic (-fal'-) a. of, in, or on the head or skull

ce·ram'ics n. the making of pottery, porcelain, etc. —n.pl. pottery, etc. —ce·ram'ic a.

ce're·al (sir'ē-) n. 1 grain used for food, as wheat, oats, etc. 2 food made from grain

cer'e·bel'lum (ser'ə-) n. lower rear part of the brain

cer'e·bral (or sə rē'-) a. of the brain

cerebral palsy n. paralysis due to a lesion of the brain

cer'e·brum (or sə rē'-) n. upper, main part of the brain

cer'e·ment n. shroud

cer'e·mo'ni·al a. ritual; formal —n. system of rites

cer'e·mo'ny n., pl. —nies 1 set of formal acts; rite 2 rigid etiquette; formality —cer'e·mo'ni·ous a.

ce·rise' (-rēz', rēs') a. clear red

cer'tain a. 1 fixed; settled 2 sure; positive 3 specific, but unnamed 4 some —for certain surely —cer'tain·ly adv. —cer'tain·ty n.

cer·tif'i·cate (-kət) n. written statement

testifying to a fact, promise, etc.

cer'ti·fy' v. **-fied', -fy'ing 1** formally declare to be true, etc. **2** guarantee —**cer'ti·fi·ca'tion** n.

cer'ti·tude' n. assurance

ce·ru'le·an a. sky-blue

cer'vix' n. neckline part —**cer'vi·cal** a.

ces·sa'tion n. stop; pause

ces'sion n. a ceding

cess'pool' n. deep hole in the ground for sewage, etc.

Cha·blis' (sha blē') n. dry white wine

chafe v. **1** make warm or sore by rubbing **2** be angry

chaff n. **1** threshed husks of grain **2** worthless stuff —v. to tease; banter

chaf'ing dish (chāf'-) n. pan for cooking food at the table

cha·grin' (sha-) n. disappointment, humiliation, etc. —v. to make feel chagrin

chain n. **1** flexible series of joined links **2** pl. fetters **3** connected series —v. restrain as with chains

chain reaction n. a series of (nuclear) reactions whose products cause new reactions

chain saw n. portable power saw with an endless chain of cutting teeth

chain store n. any of a group of retail stores owned by one company

chair n. **1** seat with a back **2** office of authority

chair'lift' n. seats on a cable for carrying skiers uphill

chair'man n., pl. **-men** one who presides at a meeting —**chair'man·ship'** n. —**chair'per'son** n. —**chair'wom'an** n.fem., pl. **-wom'en**

chaise longue (shāz' lôn') n., pl. **chaise longues** couchlike chair with a long seat

chal·ced'o·ny (kal sed'-) n. colored waxlike quartz

cha·let' (sha lā') n. cottage with overhanging eaves

chal'ice (chal'is) n. cup

chalk (chôk) n. soft limestone for writing on a blackboard —**chalk up** to record —**chalk'y a., -i·er, -i·est**

chalk'board' n. blackboard

chal'lenge n. **1** demand for identification **2** a calling into question **3** call to a contest, etc. **4** anything calling for special effort —v. put a challenge to —**chal'leng·er** n.

chal'lenged a. disabled or handicapped

cham'ber (chām'-) n. **1** room **2** pl. judge's office **3** assembly or council **4** part of a gun for the cartridge

cham'ber·maid' n. maid who keeps bedrooms neat

chamber music n. music for performance by a small group

cham'bray' (sham'-) n. smooth cotton fabric

cha·me'le·on (kə mē'-) n. lizard able to change its color

cham·ois (sham'ē) n., pl. **cham'ois 1** small antelope **2** soft kind of leather

cham'o·mile' (kam'-) n. flower used in medicinal tea

champ v. chew or bite noisily —n. [Sl.] champion

cham·pagne (sham pān') n. effervescent white wine

cham·paign (sham pān') n. flat, open country

cham'pi·on n. **1** one who fights for a cause **2** winner of first place —a. best —v. defend; support —**cham'pi·on·ship'** n.

chance n. **1** luck; fortune **2** risk **3** opportunity **4** possibility —a. accidental —v. **1** happen **2** risk

chan'cel n. place around an altar for clergy and choir

chan'cel·lor n. **1** high state or church official **2** university head —**chan'cel·ler·y** n., pl. **-ies**

chan·cre (shaŋ'kər) n. sore or ulcer of syphilis

chanc'y a. -i·er, -i·est risky

chan·de·lier (shan'də lir') n. hanging lighting fixture

chan'dler n. **1** candle maker **2** retailer of supplies, as for ships

change v. **1** to substitute **2** exchange **3** alter; vary —n. **1** alteration or variation **2** variety **3** money returned as overpayment **4** small coins —**change'a·ble** a. —**change'less** a.

change of life n. menopause

change'o'ver n. a complete change

chan'nel n. **1** bed of a river, etc. **2** wide strait joining two seas **3** any passage **4** official course of action **5** assigned frequency band, esp. in TV —v. make, or send through, a channel

chant n. song with several words to each tone —v. to utter in a chant

chan'tey (shan'tē, chan'-) n. sailors' work song

chan'ti·cleer' n. rooster

Cha·nu·kah (khä'noo kä') n. Hanuka

cha·os (kā'äs') n. complete disorder —**cha·ot'ic** a.

chap n. [Col.] a fellow —v. **chapped, chap'ping** become rough and red as from the cold

cha·peau (sha pō') n., pl. **-peaus'** or **-peaux'** (-pōz') hat

chap'el n. small church

chap·er·on, chap·er·one (shap'ə rōn') n. older person in charge of unmarried people at social affairs —v. be a chaperon to

chap′lain (-lən) n. clergyman in the armed forces

chap′let n. garland

chaps n.pl. leather trousers worn by cowboys

chap′ter n. 1 main division of a book 2 branch of an organization

char v. charred, char′ring scorch

char′ac·ter (ker′-) n. 1 letter or symbol 2 trait 3 kind or sort 4 personality 5 moral strength 6 person in a play, novel, etc. 7 [Col.] eccentric person

char′ac·ter·is′tic a. typical; distinctive —n. distinguishing quality

char′ac·ter·ize′ v. 1 describe 2 be a quality of —char′ac·ter·i·za′tion n.

cha·rade′ (shə-) n. word game in pantomime

char′broil′, char′-broil′ v. broil over a charcoal fire

char′coal′ n. pieces of incompletely burned wood

chard n. beet with edible leaves and stalks

char′don·nay′ (shär′-) n. dry white wine

charge v. 1 fill (with) 2 add electricity to 3 command 4 accuse 5 ask as a price 6 ask payment (for) 7 put as a debt 8 attack —n. 1 load 2 responsibility or care (of) 3 chemical energy in a battery 4 someone in one's care 5 command 6 accusation 7 a cost 8 debt or charge 9 attack —in charge (of) in control (of)

charge account n. arrangement to pay within some future period

charg′er n. war horse

char′i·ot n. ancient, horse-drawn, two-wheeled cart —char′i·ot·eer′ n.

cha·ris′ma (kə riz′-) n. charming or inspiring quality —char′is·mat′ic a.

char′i·ty n., pl. -ties 1 leniency in judging others 2 a helping those in need 3 institution for so helping —char′i·ta·ble a.

char·la·tan (shär′lə tən) n. quack; impostor

char′ley horse n. [Col.] muscle cramp in the thigh

charm n. 1 words or thing supposed to have magic power 2 trinket on a bracelet, etc. 3 fascination; allure —v. 1 use a magical charm on 2 fascinate; delight —charm′ing a.

char′nel (house) n. place for corpses

chart n. 1 map, esp. for navigation 2 graph, table, etc. —v. make a chart of

char′ter n. official paper licensing a new company, society, chapter, etc. —v. 1 grant a charter to 2 hire

charter member n. original member of an organization

char·treuse′ (shär trōoz′) n., a. pale, yellowish green

char′wom′an n., pl. -wom′en cleaning woman

char·y (cher′ē) a. -i·er, -i·est careful; cautious —char′i·ly adv.

chase v. 1 follow in order to catch 2 drive away 3 decorate (metal) as by engraving —n. a chasing —give chase pursue

chas′er n. [Col.] water, etc. taken after liquor

chasm (kaz′əm) n. deep crack in the earth's surface

chas·sis (chas′ē, shas′-) n., pl. -sis (-ēz) 1 frame, wheels, and motor of a car 2 frame, tubes, etc. of a radio or TV

chaste a. 1 sexually virtuous 2 decent; modest 3 simple in style —chas′ti·ty n.

chas·ten (chās′ən) v. 1 punish so as to correct 2 subdue

chas·tise′ (-tīz′) v. 1 punish as by beating 2 scold sharply —chas·tise′ment n.

chat v. chat′ted, chat′ting 1 talk in a light, informal way —chat′ty a., -ti·er, -ti·est

châ·teau (sha tō′) n., pl. -teaux′ (-tōz′) mansion

chat′tel n. piece of movable property

chat′ter v. 1 talk much and foolishly 2 click together rapidly —n. a chattering

chauf·feur (shō′fər) n. man hired to drive one's car —v. act as chauffeur to

chau·vin·ism′ (shō′-) n. 1 fanatical patriotism 2 unreasoning devotion to one's race, sex, etc. —chau′vin·ist a., n.

cheap a. 1 low in price 2 of little value —adv. at a low cost —cheap′ly adv.

cheap′en v. make cheaper

cheap′skate′ n. [Sl.] stingy person

cheat n. 1 fraud 2 swindler —v. 1 deceive or defraud 2 escape

check n. 1 sudden stop 2 restraint or restrainer 3 test of accuracy, etc. 4 mark (√) used to verify 5 token to show ownership 6 bill, as at a restaurant 7 written order to a bank to pay money 8 pattern of squares 9 Chess threat to the king —int. [Col.] right! —v. 1 stop or restrain 2 test, verify, etc. 3 mark with a check 4 deposit temporarily —check in register at a hotel, etc. —check out 1 officially leave a hotel, etc. 2 collect amount owed in a supermarket, etc. —check′er n.

check′book′ n. booklet of bank checks

checked a. having a pattern of squares

check′er n. flat, round piece used in checkers

check′er·board′ n. board for checkers, with 64 squares

check′ered a. 1 having a pattern of squares 2 varied

check'ers n. game like chess, for two players

check'ing account n. bank account for writing checks

check'list' n. list to be referred to: also **check list**

check'mate' n. Chess position from which king cannot escape, ending the game —v. to put in checkmate

check'out' n. place or time for checking out

check'point' n. place where road traffic is inspected

check'room' n. room for leaving hats, coats, etc.

check'up' n. medical examination

Ched'dar (cheese) n. a hard, smooth cheese

cheek n. 1 side of face below eye 2 [Col.] impudence —**tongue in cheek** jestingly

cheep n. young bird's short, shrill sound —v. make this sound

cheer n. 1 joy; gladness 2 shout of excitement, welcome, etc. —v. 1 fill with cheer 2 urge on, praise, etc. with cheers —**cheer up** make or become glad

cheer'ful a. 1 joyful 2 bright and attractive Also **cheer'y, -i-er, -i-est** —**cheer'ful-ly** adv.

cheer'lead'er n. person who leads cheers for a team

cheer'less a. not cheerful

cheers int. [Chiefly Br.] good health!: used as a toast

cheer'y a. **-i-er, -i-est** cheerful; bright

cheese n. solid food made from milk curds

cheese'burg'er n. hamburger with melted cheese

cheese'cloth' n. cotton cloth with a loose weave

chees'y a. **-i-er, -i-est** 1 like cheese 2 [Sl.] inferior; poor

chee'tah n. animal like the leopard

chef (shef) n. head cook

chem'i-cal (kem'-) a. of, in, or by chemistry —n. substance used in or obtained by chemistry —**chem'i-cal-ly** adv.

che-mise (shə mēz') n. woman's undergarment

chem'is-try n. science dealing with the composition, reactions, etc. of substances —**chem'ist** n.

che'mo-ther'a-py (kē'mō-) n. use of drugs in treating disease

che-nille (shə nēl') n. fabric woven with tufted cord

cheque (chek) n. Br. sp. of CHECK (n. 7)

cher'ish v. 1 hold or treat tenderly 2 keep in mind

cher'ry n., pl. **-ries** tree with small, red fruit

cher'ub n., pl. **-ubs** or **-u-bim'** angel, pictured as a chubby child with wings —**che-ru'bic** (-rōō'-) a.

chess n. checkerboard game for two players using various pieces (**chess'men**)

chest n. 1 box with a lid 2 piece of furniture with drawers 3 front part of the body above the abdomen

chest'nut' n. 1 edible nut of a kind of beech 2 [Col.] trite joke —a. reddish-brown

chev-i-ot (shev'ē ət) n. twilled wool fabric

chev'ron (shev'-) n. V-shaped sleeve insignia of rank

chew v. grind with the teeth —n. something for chewing —**chew'y** a., **-i-er, -i-est**

chew'ing gum n. flavored chicle, etc. for chewing

Chi-an-ti (kē än'tē) n. a dry red wine

chic (shēk) a. smartly stylish

chi-can'er-y (shi kān'-) n., pl. **-ies** 1 trickery 2 trick

Chi-ca-no (chi kä'nō) n., pl. **-nos** Mexican-American

chick n. young chicken

chick'a-dee' n. small bird of the titmouse family

chick'en n. hen or rooster, or its edible flesh

chick'en-pox' n. infectious disease with skin eruptions

chick'pea' n. pealike plant with edible seeds

chic'le n. gummy substance from a tropical tree

chic'o-ry n. plant with leaf used in salads and root used as a coffee substitute

chide v. scold; rebuke

chief n. leader —a. main; most important —**chief'ly** adv.

chief'tain (-tən) n. chief of a clan or tribe

chif-fon (shi fän') n. sheer silk cloth

chig'ger n. a mite larva that causes itching

chi-gnon (shēn'yän') n. coil of hair worn at the back of the neck by women

Chi-hua-hua (chi wä'wä) n. tiny dog with large, pointed ears

chil'blain' n. inflamed sore caused by exposure to cold

child n., pl. **chil'dren** 1 infant 2 boy or girl before puberty 3 son or daughter —**with child** pregnant —**child'hood'** n. —**child'-like'** a.

child'birth' n. a giving birth to a child

child'ish a. silly; immature

chil'i n., pl. **-ies** 1 hot, dried pod of red pepper 2 spicy dish of beef, chilies, beans, etc.

chili sauce n. spiced sauce of chopped tomatoes, sweet peppers, onions, etc.

chill n. 1 moderate coldness 2 body coldness with shivering 3 sudden fear —a. uncomfortably cool —v. make or become cold —**chill'y** a., **-li-er, -li-est**

chill factor n. combined effect of low temperatures and high winds on exposed skin

chime n. usually pl. set of tuned bells —v. to sound as a chime

chim'ney n. passage for smoke from a furnace, etc.

chim'pan·zee' n. medium-sized African ape

chin n. face below the lips —v. **chinned, chin'ning** pull (oneself) up until the chin is above a bar being grasped

chi'na n. dishes, etc. of fine porcelain

chin·chil'la n. 1 small South American rodent 2 its costly fur

Chi·nese' n., pl. **–nese';** a. (native or language) of China

chink n. 1 crack 2 clinking sound —v. to clink

chi'no (chē'-, shē'-) n., pl. **–nos** 1 strong cotton cloth 2 pl. men's pants of chino

chintz n. glazed, printed cotton cloth

chintz'y a. **–i·er, –i'est** [Col.] cheap, stingy, etc.

chip v. **chipped, chip'ping** break or cut off bits from —n. 1 fragment 2 place where bit is chipped off 3 small disk used in gambling 4 thin slice of food 5 microchip —**chip in** [Col.] contribute

chip'munk' n. small, striped squirrel

chipped beef n. dried or smoked beef sliced into shavings

chip'per a. [Col.] lively

chi·rop'o·dist (kī răp'-) n. podiatrist

chi·rop'o·dy (kī răp'-) n. podiatry

chi'ro·prac'tic (kī'rə-) n. treatment by manipulation of body joints, etc. —**chi'ro·prac'tor** n.

chirp v. make short, shrill sounds —n. such a sound

chir'rup v., n.

chis'el (chiz'-) n. tool for chipping wood, stone, etc. —v. 1 chip with a chisel 2 [Col.] swindle —**chis'el·er, chis'el·ler** n.

chit'chat' n. small talk

chi'tin (kī'-) n. horny covering of insects, etc.

chit·ter·lings (chit'linz) n.pl. pig intestines, used for food: also **chit'lins** or **chit'lings**

chiv'al·ry (shiv'-) n. 1 medieval system of knighthood 2 courtesy, fairness, etc. —**chiv'al·rous** a.

chives n.pl. herb with slender leaves with mild onion odor

chlo·ride (klôr'īd') n. compound of chlorine

chlo'ri·nate' v. purify (water) with chlorine

chlo·rine (klôr'ēn') n. greenish gas, a chemical element

chlo'ro·form' n. colorless liquid anesthetic —v. anesthetize or kill with this

chlo'ro·phyll', chlo'ro·phyl' (-fil'-) n. green coloring in plants

chock n., v. block; wedge —adv. completely

chock'-full' a. as full as possible

choc'o·late (-lət) n. 1 ground cacao seeds 2 drink or candy made with this 3 reddish brown

choice n. 1 selection 2 right to choose 3 the one chosen —a. excellent

choir (kwīr) n. group of singers, esp. in a church

choke v. 1 stop the breathing of; suffocate 2 obstruct; clog —n. a choking

choke collar n. dog collar that tightens when leash is taut

chok'er n. closefitting necklace

chol'er (käl'-) n. [Now Rare] anger

chol'er·a n. infectious, often fatal, intestinal disease

chol·er·ic (or kə ler'-) a. having a quick temper

cho·les'ter·ol' (-ə-) n. substance in animal fats, etc.

chomp v. to champ

choose v. **chose, cho'sen, choos'ing** 1 take; select 2 prefer; decide

choos'y, choos'ey a. **–i·er, –i·est** [Col.] fussy in choosing

chop v. **chopped, chop'ping** 1 cut by blows of sharp tool 2 cut in bits —n. 1 sharp blow 2 a slice from the rib or loin

chop'per n. 1 pl. [Sl.] teeth 2 [Col.] helicopter

chop'py a. with rough, abrupt waves or motions

chops n.pl. 1 jaws 2 flesh about the mouth

chop'sticks' n.pl. two sticks used as eating utensils in some Asian countries

chop su·ey (sōō'ē) n. American-Chinese stew served with rice

cho·ral (kôr'əl) a. of or for a choir or chorus

cho·rale, cho·ral (kə ral') n. simple hymn tune

chord (kôrd) n. 1 straight line joining two points on an arc 2 three or more tones sounded together in harmony

chore n. daily task

chor'e·og'ra·phy (kôr'-) n. the devising of ballets —**chor'e·og'ra·pher** n.

chor·is·ter (kôr'-) n. choir member

chor·tle (chôrt''l) v., n. chuckle or snort

cho·rus (kôr'əs) n. 1 group of singers or of singers and dancers 2 music for group singing 3 refrain of a song —v. sing or recite in unison

chose v. pt. of CHOOSE

cho'sen v. pp. of CHOOSE —a. selected; choice

chow n. 1 medium-sized Chinese dog 2 [Sl.] food

chow'der n. fish or clam soup with vegetables

chow mein (mān) n. American-Chinese stew served on fried noodles

Christ Jesus as the Messiah

chris·ten (kris'ən) v. 1 baptize 2 name —**chris'ten·ing** n.

Chris'ten·dom (kris'ən-) n. Christians collectively

Chris'ti·an·i·ty n. religion based on teachings of Jesus —**Chris'tian** a., n.

Christ'mas n. celebration of Jesus' birth; Dec. 25

chro·mat'ic (krō-) a. 1 of color 2 Mus. in semitones

chrome n. chromium

chro'mi·um n. hard metal in alloys, a chemical element

chro'mo·some n. any of the microscopic bodies carrying the genes of heredity

chron'ic a. long-lasting or recurring —**chron'i·cal·ly** adv.

chron'i·cle n. historical record —v. to tell the history of —**chron'i·cler** n.

chron'o·log'i·cal a. in order of occurrence —**chron'o·log'i·cal·ly** adv. —**chro·nol'o·gy** n.

chro·nom'e·ter n. very accurate clock or watch

chrys'a·lis (kris'-) n. pupa or its cocoon

chrys·an'the·mum n. plant with ball-shaped flowers

chub n. freshwater fish related to the carp

chub'by a. plump

chuck v. 1 tap playfully 2 toss —n. 1 tap 2 toss 3 shoulder cut of beef 4 clamplike device as on a lathe

chuck'-full' a. chock-full

chuck'hole' n. rough hole in pavement

chuck'le v. laugh softly —n. soft laugh

chuck wagon n. wagon with kitchen for feeding cowboys

chug n. explosive sound, as of an engine —v. **chugged**, **chug'ging** make this sound

chuk'ka boot n. man's ankle-high boot

chum [Col.] n. close friend —v. **chummed**, **chum'ming** be chums —**chum'my** a.

chump [Col.] n. fool

chunk n. thick piece

chunk'y a. **-i·er**, **-i·est** [Col.] short and thickset

church n. 1 building for public worship 2 religion or religious sect

church'go'er n. one who attends church regularly —**church'go'ing** a.

church'yard' n. yard beside a church, often a cemetery

churl n. rude, surly person

churl'ish a. rude; surly

churn n. device for making butter —v. 1 shake (cream) in a churn to make butter 2 stir about vigorously

chute (shσ̄ōt) n. inclined passage for sliding things

chut'ney (chut'-) n., pl. **-neys** relish of fruits, spices, etc.

chutz'pah, chutz'pa (hσ̄ōts'-) n. [Col.] impudence; audacity

ci·ca'da (si kā'-) n. large flying insect making a shrill sound

ci'der n. juice from apples

ci·gar' n. roll of tobacco leaves for smoking

cig'a·rette', cig'a·ret' n. tobacco cut fine and rolled in paper for smoking

cig'a·ril'lo n., pl. **-los** small, thin cigar

cil'i·a n.pl. small hairlike growths

cinch n. 1 saddle girth 2 [Sl.] thing easy to do

cin·cho'na (sin kō'-) n. tree whose bark yields quinine

cinc'ture (siηk'-) n. belt or girdle —v. gird

cin'der n. 1 tiny charred piece of wood, etc. 2 pl. ashes

cin'e·ma n. used in the cinema, films collectively; the movies —**cin'e·mat'ic** a.

cin'e·ma·tog'ra·phy n. art of photography in making movies —**cin'e·ma·tog'ra·pher** n.

cin'na·mon n. brown spice from East Indian tree bark

ci·pher (sī'fər) n. 1 zero; 0 2 code 3 key to a code

cir'ca prep. about; approximately

cir·ca'di·an a. of the body cycles associated with the earth's daily rotation

cir'cle n. 1 closed, curved line always equidistant from the center 2 cycle 3 group with interests in common 4 extent; scope —v. form or go in a circle around

cir'cuit (-kət) n. 1 boundary 2 regular, routine journey 3 theater chain 4 path for electric current

cir·cu'i·tous (-kyσ̄ō'-) a. roundabout; indirect

cir'cuit·ry n. electric circuit(s)

cir'cu·lar a. 1 round 2 roundabout —n. advertisement sent to many people

cir'cu·late' v. move or spread about —**cir'cu·la·to'ry** a.

cir'cu·la'tion n. 1 movement, as of blood through the body 2 distribution

cir'cum·cise' (-sīz') v. cut off the foreskin of —**cir'cum·ci'sion** (-sizh'ən) n.

cir·cum·fer·ence n. distance around a circle, etc.

cir'cum·flex' n. pronunciation mark (^)

cir'cum·lo·cu'tion n. roundabout way of talking

cir'cum·nav'i·gate' v. sail around (the earth, etc.)

cir´cum·scribe´ v. 1 encircle 2 limit; confine

cir´cum·spect´ a. cautious; discreet —**cir´cum·spec´tion** n.

cir´cum·stance´ n. 1 connected fact or event 2 pl. financial condition 3 ceremony —**under no circumstances** never —**cir´cum·stan´tial** (-shəl) a.

cir´cum·vent´ v. outwit or prevent by cleverness

cir´cus n. a show with acrobats, animals, clowns, etc.

ci·ré (sē rā´) a. having a smooth, glossy finish

cir·rho´sis (sə rō´-) n. disease, esp. of the liver

cir·rus (sir´əs) n. fleecy, white cloud formation

cis´tern n. large storage tank, esp. for rain water

cit´a·del´ n. fortress

cite v. 1 summon by law 2 quote 3 mention as example 4 mention in praise —**ci·ta´tion** n.

cit´i·zen n. member of a nation by birth or naturalization —**cit´i·zen·ry** a. —**cit´i·zen·ship´** n.

cit´ric acid n. weak acid in citrus fruits

cit´ron n. lemonlike fruit

cit´ron·el´la n. pungent oil that repels insects

cit´rus n. orange, lemon, etc. —a. of these trees or fruits

cit´y n., pl. **-ies** large town

civ´et n. fatty secretion of an animal (**civet cat**): used in perfume

civ´ic a. of a city or citizens

civ´ics n. study of civic affairs and duties

civ´il a. 1 of citizens 2 polite 3 not military or religious —**civ´il·ly** adv.

civil disobedience n. nonviolent refusal to obey a law on grounds of one's conscience

civil engineering n. engineering that deals with the building of bridges, roads, etc.

ci·vil´ian a., n. (of a) person not in armed forces

ci·vil´i·ty n. 1 courtesy 2 pl. **-ties** polite act

civ´i·li·za´tion n. 1 high social and cultural development 2 culture of a certain time or place

civ´i·lize´ v. bring out of savagery or barbarism

civil liberties n.pl. rights of free speech, assembly, etc.

civil rights n.pl. rights of all people to equal treatment

civil servant n. civil service employee

civil service n. government employees except soldiers, legislators, and judges

civil war n. war between factions of the same nation

civ´vies n.pl. [Col.] civilian clothes: also sp. **civ´ies**

clack v. make an abrupt sharp sound —n. this sound

clad v. alt. pt. & pp. of CLOTHE

claim v. 1 demand as rightfully one's own 2 assert —n. 1 a claiming 2 right to something 3 thing claimed —**claim´ant** n.

clair·voy´ance n. supposed ability to perceive things not in sight —**clair·voy´ant** a., n.

clam n. hard-shelled, often edible, bivalve mollusk

clam´bake´ n. picnic at which clams are served

clam´ber v. climb clumsily

clam´my a. **-mi·er, -mi·est** moist, cold, and sticky

clam´or n. 1 uproar 2 noisy demand —v. make a clamor —**clam´or·ous** a.

clamp n. device for clasping things together —v. fasten with a clamp

clan n. 1 group of related families 2 group with interests in common

clan·des´tine (-tin) a. secret

clang v. make a loud ringing sound —n. this sound

clang´or n. series of clangs

clank v. make a sharp metallic sound —n. this sound

clap v. **clapped, clap´ping** 1 make the sound of flat surfaces struck together 2 to strike together, as the hands in applauding —n. sound or act of clapping —**clap´per** n.

clap·board (klab´ərd) n. tapered board for siding

clap´trap´ n. insincere, empty talk, meant to get applause

claque (klak) n. group paid to applaud at a play, opera, etc.

clar´et (klar´-) n. dry red wine

clar´i·fy´ v. **-fied´, -fy´ing** make or become clear —**clar´i·fi·ca´tion** n.

clar´i·net´ n. single-reed, woodwind instrument —**clar´i·net´ist, clar´i·net´tist** n.

clar´i·on a. clear and shrill

clar´i·ty n. clearness

clash v. 1 collide noisily 2 disagree —n. a clashing

clasp n. 1 device to fasten things 2 an embrace 3 grip of the hand —v. 1 fasten 2 hold tightly

class n. 1 group of like people or things; sort 2 social rank 3 group of students in school 4 grade or quality 5 [Sl.] excellence —v. classify —**class´mate´** n. —**class´room´** n.

clas'sic a. 1 most excellent 2 in the style of ancient Greece or Rome —n. a book, work of art, etc. of highest excellence —**the classics** writings of ancient Greece and Rome

clas·si·cal a. 1 CLASSIC (a. 2) 2 of such music as symphonies, concertos, etc.

classified advertising n. advertising under such listings as *help wanted*

clas'si·fy' v. **-fied', -fy'ing** 1 arrange in classes 2 designate as secret —**clas'si·fi·ca'tion** n.

class'mate' n. member of the same class at a school

class'room' n. room where a class is taught at a school

class'y a. **-i·er, -i·est** [Sl.] first-class; elegant

clat'ter n. series of sharp noises —v. make a clatter

clause n. 1 part of a sentence, with a subject and verb 2 provision in a document

claus·tro·pho'bi·a n. fear of enclosed places

clav'i·chord n. early kind of piano

clav'i·cle n. bone connecting the breastbone and shoulder

cla·vier (klə vir') n. 1 keyboard, as of a piano 2 any stringed keyboard instrument

claw n. 1 sharp nail of an animal's or bird's foot 2 pincers of a lobster, crab, etc. —v. scratch as with claws

clay n. firm, plastic earth, used for pottery, etc.

clean a. 1 free from dirt 2 sinless 3 free from flaws 4 complete —adv. completely —v. make clean —**clean'er** n. —**clean'ly** (klēn'-) adv.

clean'-cut' a. trim, neat, etc.

clean'ly (klen'-) a. **-li·er, -li·est** 1 having clean habits 2 always kept clean —**clean'li·ness** n.

cleanse (klenz) v. make clean or pure —**cleans'er** n.

clear a. 1 free from clouds 2 transparent 3 distinct 4 obvious 5 free from charges, guilt, obstruction, debt, etc. —adv. 1 in a clear way 2 completely —v. 1 make or become clear 2 pass or leap over 3 make as profit 4 to empty or unload 5 rid (the throat) of phlegm —**clear away** (or **off**) remove —**in the clear** in the open —**clear'ly** adv. —**clear'ness** n.

clear'ance n. clear space between two objects

clear'ing n. plot of land cleared of trees

cleat n. piece used to give firmness or secure footing

cleav'age n. a split, crack, division, etc.

cleave v. **cleft** or **cleaved, cleav'ing** split; sever

cleave v. adhere; cling

cleav'er n. butcher's tool

clef n. musical symbol to indicate pitch

cleft a., n. split

clem'a·tis (or klə mat'is) n. vine with colorful flowers

clem'ent a. 1 lenient 2 mild —**clem'en·cy** n.

clench v. close tightly

cler'gy n., pl. **-gies** ministers, priests, etc. collectively

cler'gy·man n., pl. **-men** minister, priest, etc. —**cler'gy·wom'an** n.fem., pl. **-wom'en**

cler'ic n. member of the clergy

cler'i·cal a. 1 of the clergy 2 of office clerks

clerk n. 1 office worker who keeps records, etc. 2 salesperson in a store —v. work as a clerk

clev'er a. 1 skillful 2 intelligent —**clev'er·ness** n.

clew n. 1 ball of thread, etc. 2 clue

cli·ché (klē shā') n. trite expression or idea —**cli·chéd'** a.

click n. slight, sharp sound —v. make a click

cli'ent n. 1 person or company for whom a lawyer, etc. acts 2 customer

cli·en·tele' (-tel') n. clients

cliff n. high, steep rock

cliff'hang'er, cliff'-hang'er n. highly suspenseful story, etc.

cli'mate n. average weather conditions —**cli·mat'ic** a.

cli'max n. highest point, as of interest or excitement; culmination —v. bring to a climax —**cli·mac'tic** a.

climb v. go up; ascend —n. a climbing —**climb down** to descend —**climb'er** n.

clinch v. 1 fasten (a nail) by bending the end 2 settle (an argument, etc.) 3 *Boxing* grip with the arms —n. a clinching in boxing

cling v. **clung, cling'ing** 1 hold fast 2 stay near

clin'ic n. 1 place where medical specialists practice as a group 2 outpatient department —**cli·ni'cian** (-nish'ən) n.

clin'i·cal a. 1 of medical treatment, as in clinics 2 dispassionate

clink n. short, tinkling sound —v. make this sound

clink'er n. fused mass left in burning coal

clip v. **clipped, clip'ping** 1 cut short 2 cut the hair of 3 [Col.] hit sharply 4 fasten together —n. 1 a clipping 2 [Col.] rapid pace 3 fastening device

clip'per n. 1 clipping tool 2 fast sailing ship

clip'ping n. piece cut out, as an item from a newspaper

clique (klik, klēk) *n.* small, exclusive circle of people

clit'o·ris *n.* small, sensitive organ of the vulva

cloak *n.* 1 loose, sleeveless outer garment 2 thing that conceals —*v.* conceal; hide

clob'ber *v.* [Sl.] 1 to hit repeatedly 2 defeat decisively

clock *n.* device for measuring and showing time

clock'wise' *adv., a.* in the direction in which the hands of a clock rotate

clock'work' *n.* mechanism of a clock —**like clockwork** very regularly

clod *n.* 1 lump of earth 2 dull, stupid person

clod'hop'per *n.* 1 clumsy, stupid fellow 2 coarse, heavy shoe

clog *n.* 1 thing that hinders 2 heavy shoe —*v.* **clogged, clog'ging** 1 hinder 2 block up

clois'ter *n.* 1 monastery or convent 2 covered walk along a wall —*v.* seclude

clomp *v.* walk heavily or noisily

clone *n.* exact genetic duplicate of an organism —*v.* produce as a clone

clop *n.* sound as of a hoofbeat —*v.* **clopped, clop'ping** make such sounds

close (klōs) *a.* 1 confined 2 secretive 3 stingy 4 humid; stuffy 5 near together 6 intimate 7 thorough 8 nearly alike; nearly equal —*adv.* in a close way or position —*n.* enclosed place —**close'ly** *adv.*

close (klōz) *v.* 1 shut or stop up 2 end 3 come close, as to attack —*n.* end —**close down (or up)** stop entirely —**close in** surround

close call (klōs) *n.* [Col.] narrow escape from danger: also **close shave**

closed circuit *n.* TV system only for receivers connected by cable to its circuit

close'fit'ting *a.* fitting tightly

close'-knit' *a.* closely united

clos'et (kläz'-) *n.* small room for clothes, etc. —*v.* shut in a room for private talk

close'-up' *n.* photograph, etc. taken at very close range

clo'sure (-zhər) *n.* a closing, finish, etc.

clot *n.* coagulated mass, as of blood —*v.* **clot'ted, clot'ting** coagulate

cloth *n.* 1 fabric of cotton, wool, synthetics, etc. 2 tablecloth, dustcloth, etc.

clothe (klōth) *v.* **clothed** or **clad, cloth'ing** 1 to put clothes on 2 provide with clothes

clothes (klōthz, klōz) *n.pl.* 1 clothing 2 bedclothes

cloth·ier (klōth'yər) *n.* dealer in clothes or cloth

cloth·ing (klō'thiŋ) *n.* wearing apparel; garments

clo'ture (-chər) *n.* end of debate by putting a bill to the vote

cloud *n.* 1 mass of vapor in the sky 2 mass of smoke, dust, etc. 3 thing that darkens, etc. —*v.* darken as with clouds, gloom, etc. —**cloud'y** *a.*, **-i·er, -i·est**

cloud'burst' *n.* sudden heavy rain

clout *n.* [Col.] 1 a hard hit 2 political power

clove *n.* 1 pungent spice 2 segment of a bulb

clo'ven *a.* split

clo'ver *n.* small forage plant with triple leaves

clo'ver·leaf' *n.* highway intersection with curving ramps to ease traffic

clown *n.* comic entertainer as in a circus —*v.* act like a clown

cloy *v.* surfeit by excess

club *n.* 1 stick used as a weapon, or in games 2 social group or its meeting place 3 playing card marked with a ♣ —*v.* **clubbed, club'bing** strike with a club

club'foot' *n., pl.* **-feet'** congenitally misshapen foot

cluck *n.* low, clicking sound made by a hen —*v.* make this sound

clue *n.* hint or fact that helps solve a mystery

clump *n.* 1 lump 2 cluster —*v.* tramp heavily

clum'sy (-zē) *a.* **-si·er, -si·est** awkward —**clum'si·ly** *adv.*

clung *v.* pt. & pp. of CLING

clunk'er *n.* [Sl.] old, noisy car

clus'ter *n., v.* group; bunch

clutch *v.* 1 snatch (*at*) 2 hold tightly —*n.* 1 *pl.* control 2 grip 3 device for engaging and disengaging an engine

clut'ter *n., v.* disorder

co- *pref.* 1 together 2 joint 3 equally

coach *n.* 1 big, four-wheeled carriage 2 railroad passenger car 3 bus 4 trainer of athletes, singers, etc. —*v.* be a coach (for)

co·ad'ju·tor (-aj'ə tər, -ə jōō'-) *n.* assistant, esp. to a bishop

co·ag'u·late' *v.* thicken; clot —**co·ag'u·la'tion** *n.*

coal *n.* 1 black mineral used as fuel 2 ember

co'a·lesce' (-les') *v.* unite into a single body —**co'a·les'cence** *n.*

co'a·li'tion *n.* union

coal oil *n.* kerosene

coal tar *n.* black, thick liquid made from coal, used in dyes, medicines, etc.

coarse *a.* 1 made up of large particles 2 rough 3 vulgar —**coars'en** *v.*

coast *n.* seashore —*v.* 1 slide down an incline 2 continue moving on momentum —**coast'al** *a.*

coast′er n. small tray put under a glass

coast guard n. group defending a nation's coasts, aiding ships in distress, etc.

coast′line′ n. contour of a coast

coat n. **1** sleeved outer garment **2** natural covering **3** layer, as of paint —v. cover with a layer

coat′ing n. surface layer

coat of arms n. heraldic symbols, as on a family escutcheon

coat′tail′ n. either half of the lower back part of a coat

co′au′thor n. joint author

coax v. urge or get by soothing words, etc.

co-ax′i-al cable n. cable for sending telephone, telegraph, or television impulses

cob n. corncob

co′balt′ (-bôlt′) n. gray metallic chemical element

cob′ble v. mend (shoes)

cob′bler n. **1** shoemaker **2** fruit pie

cob′ble-stone′ n. rounded stone once used for paving

co′bra n. poisonous snake of Asia and Africa

cob′web′ n. spider web

co-caine′, co-cain′ n. drug used as a narcotic or anesthetic

coc·cyx (käk′siks′) n., pl. **coc·cy′ges′** (-sī′jēz′) bone at base of spine

coch·i-ne′al (käch′ə nēl′) n. red dye from tropical insect

coch·le·a (käk′lē ə) n. spiral part of the inner ear

cock n. **1** rooster **2** any male bird **3** faucet —v. **1** tilt **2** set hammer of (a gun) to fire

cock·ade′ n. badge on a hat

cock·a·too′ n. crested Australian parrot

cocked hat n. three-cornered hat

cock′er·el n. young rooster

cock′er (spaniel) n. small spaniel with drooping ears

cock′eyed′ a. **1** cross-eyed **2** [Sl.] **1)** awry **2)** absurd

cock′le n. edible shellfish —**cockles of one's heart** one's deepest feelings

cock′pit′ n. space for pilot in an airplane

cock′roach′ n. flat-bodied, dark insect, a kitchen pest

cocks′comb′ n. red, fleshy growth on a rooster's head

cock′sure′ a. self-confident

cock′tail′ n. **1** mixed alcoholic drink **2** appetizer

cock′y a. [Col.] conceited

co′co′ n., pl. **-cos′** coconut palm or coconut

co′coa′ (-kō′) n. **1** powder made from roasted cacao seeds **2** drink made of this

cocoa butter n. fat from cacao seeds

co′co-nut′, co′coa-nut′ n. hard-shelled fruit of a palm tree, with edible white meat

co-coon′ n. silky case of certain insect larvae

cod n. N Atlantic food fish: also **cod′fish′**

co′da n. Mus. end passage

cod′dle v. pamper

code n. **1** body of laws **2** set of principles **3** set of signals or symbols for messages —v. put or write in code

co′deine′ (-dēn′) n. sedative drug derived from opium

co′de-pend′ent a. psychologically needing another who is addicted to alcohol, etc.

codg′er n. [Col.] elderly man

cod′i-cil n. addition to a will

cod′i-fy′ (or kō′də-) v. **-fied′, -fy′ing** arrange (laws) in a code

co′ed′, co′-ed′ n. [Col.] young woman at a coeducational college

co′ed-u-ca′tion n. education of both sexes in the same classes —**co′ed-u-ca′tion-al** a.

co-e′qual a., n. equal

co-erce′ (-urs′) v. force; compel —**co-er′cion** n. —**co-er′cive** a.

co-e′val a., n. contemporary

co-ex-ist′ v. exist together —**co′ex-ist′ence** n.

cof′fee n. **1** drink made from roasted seeds of a tropical shrub **2** the seeds

coffee break n. brief respite from work for having coffee, etc.

cof′fee-cake′ n. cake or roll to be eaten with coffee, etc.

cof′fee-pot′ n. pot with a spout, for brewing or serving coffee

coffee table n. small, low table for serving refreshments

cof′fer n. **1** chest for money, etc. **2** pl. treasury

cof′fin n. case in which to bury a dead person

cog n. tooth on a cogwheel

co′gent (-jənt) a. convincing —**co′gen-cy** n.

cog′i-tate′ (käj′-) v. think (about) —**cog′i-ta′tion** n.

co-gnac (kōn′yak′) n. brandy

cog′nate′ a. related; kindred

cog-ni′tion n. knowledge

cog′ni-zance n. awareness; notice —**cog′ni-zant** a.

cog-no′men n. surname

cog′wheel′ n. wheel rimmed with teeth, as in a gear

co-hab′it v. live together, esp. as if legally married

co-here′ (-hir′) v. **1** to stick together **2** be connected logically

co·her′ent (-hir′-, -her′-) a. clear and intelligible —**co·her′ence** n.

co·he′sion n. a sticking together —**co·he′sive** a.

co′ho n., pl. **-ho′** or **-hos′** small salmon

co′hort′ n. 1 group, esp. of soldiers 2 an associate

coif (koif; 2: kwäf) n. 1 closefitting cap 2 hair style

coif·fure (kwä fyoor′) n. 1 headdress 2 hairstyle

coil v. to wind in a spiral —n. anything coiled

coin n. stamped metal piece, issued as money —v. 1 make into coins 2 make up (new word) —**coin′age** n.

co′in·cide′ v. 1 occur at the same time 2 agree; match

co·in′ci·dence n. 1 a coinciding 2 accidental occurrence together of events —**co·in′ci·den′tal** a. —**co·in′ci·den′tal·ly** adv.

co·i·tus (kō′it əs) n. sexual intercourse: also **co·i′tion** (-ish′ən)

coke n. 1 fuel made by removing gases from coal 2 [Sl.] cocaine

co′la n. carbonated soft drink with flavoring from the nut of an African tree

col′an·der (kul′-, käl′-) n. perforated bowl used as a strainer

cold a. 1 low in temperature 2 feeling chilled 3 without feeling 4 unfriendly 5 [Col.] unprepared 6 [Col.] perfectly memorized 7 [Col.] unconscious —n. 1 absence of heat 2 common virus infection with sneezing, coughing, etc. —**catch cold** become ill with a cold

cold′blood′ed a. 1 having a body temperature that varies with the surroundings 2 cruel; callous

cold cream n. creamy cleanser for the skin

cold cuts n. variety of sliced cold meats and cheeses

cold shoulder n. [Col.] snub

cold sore n. blisters about the mouth during a cold

cold turkey n. [Sl.] 1 abrupt withdrawal of drugs from an addict 2 without preparing

cold war n. conflict between nations without actual war

cole′slaw′ n. salad made of shredded raw cabbage

col′ic n. sharp abdominal pain from the bowels —**col′ick·y** a.

Col′i·se′um n. large stadium

co·li′tis n. inflammation of the large intestine

col·lab′o·rate′ v. 1 to work together 2 help the enemy —**col·lab′o·ra′tion** n. —**col·lab′o·ra′tor** n.

col·lage′ (-läzh′) n. bits of objects pasted onto a surface to make a work of art

col·lapse′ v. 1 fall in or shrink 2 break down; fail 3 fold together —n. a collapsing —**col·laps′i·ble** a.

col′lar n. a band, or the part of a garment, around the neck —v. 1 put a collar on 2 seize by the collar

col′lar·bone′ n. clavicle

col′lard n. kind of kale

col·late′ (käl′āt′, kō′lāt′) v. compare or sort (texts)

col·lat′er·al a. 1 of the same descent but in a different line 2 secondary —n. thing pledged as security for a loan

col·league′ (käl′ēg′) n. fellow worker; associate

col·lect′ v. 1 gather together 2 get payment for 3 regain control of (oneself) —a., adv. with the receiver paying —**col·lect′i·ble, col·lect′a·ble** a. —**col·lec′tion** n. —**col·lec′tor** n.

col·lect′ed a. 1 gathered together 2 calm

col·lec′tive a. 1 of or as a group 2 singular in form, but referring to a group —n. 1 a collective enterprise 2 collective noun

col′lege n. 1 school of higher learning or special instruction 2 group with certain powers —**col·le′gi·an** (-jən) n. —**col·le′gi·ate** (-jət) a.

col·lide′ v. 1 come into violent contact 2 to conflict; clash

col′lie n. large, long-haired sheep dog

col·li′sion (-lizh′ən) n. 1 a colliding 2 conflict

col·lo′di·on (-dē ən) n. solution that dries into tough, elastic film

col′loid′ n. substance of insoluble particles suspended in a fluid —**col·loi′dal** a.

col·lo′qui·al (-kwē-) a. used in informal talk and writing —**col·lo′qui·al·ism′** n.

col·lo′qui·um (-kwē-) n., pl. **-qui·a** or **-qui·ums** organized conference or seminar

col·lo·quy (käl′ə kwē) n., pl. **-quies** conversation

col·lu′sion n. secret agreement for a wrong purpose

co·logne′ (-lōn′) n. scented liquid like diluted perfume

co′lon n. 1 mark of punctuation (:) 2 lower part of the large intestine

colo·nel (kur′nəl) n. officer above lieutenant colonel

co·lo′ni·al·ism′ n. economic exploitation of colonies

col′on·nade′ n. row of evenly spaced columns

col′o·ny n., pl. **-nies** 1 group of settlers from a distant land 2 land ruled by a distant country 3 community with common interests —**co·lo′ni·al** a. —**col′o·nist** n. —**col′o·nize′** v.

col′or n. 1 effect on the eyes of light waves of different wavelengths 2 pigment 3 complexion 4 pl. a flag 5 outward appearance 6 picturesque quality —v. 1 paint or dye 2 alter or distort 3 blush —**of color** not Caucasoid; spec., black —**with flying colors** with great success —**col′or·a′tion** n. —**col′or·ful** a. —**col′or·ing** n. —**col′or·less** a.

col′or·a·tu′ra (-tʊoor′ə) n. soprano with high, flexible voice: in full **coloratura soprano**

col′or-blind′ a. unable to distinguish (certain) colors

col′ored a. not Caucasoid; spec., black

col′or·fast′ a. with color that will not fade or run

co·los′sal a. huge; immense

co·los′sus n. huge or important person or thing

col′our n., v. Br. sp. of COLOR

colt n. young male horse

colt′ish a. frisky

col′um·bine′ (-bīn′) n. plant with showy, spurred flowers

col′umn (-əm) n. 1 slender upright structure 2 vertical section of printed matter 3 line of troops, etc. —**col′um·nist′** n.

com– pref. with; together

co′ma n. deep unconsciousness, as from injury —**co′ma·tose′** (-tōs′) a.

comb (kōm) n. 1 flat, toothed object for grooming the hair 2 cockscomb 3 honeycomb —v. 1 groom with a comb 2 search

com′bat′ (v.: also kəm bat′) v., n. fight; struggle —**com·bat′ant** n.

com·bat′ive a. ready or eager to fight

com′bi·na′tion n. 1 a combining 2 combined things, groups, etc. 3 series of numbers dialed to open a lock

com·bine′ (n.: käm′bīn′) v. join; unite —n. 1 machine for harvesting and threshing grain 2 commercial or political alliance

com′bo′ n., pl. **-bos′** 1 [Col.] combination 2 a small jazz ensemble

com·bus′ti·ble n., a. flammable (thing)

com·bus′tion n. a burning

come v. **came, come, com′ing** 1 move from "there" to "here" 2 arrive or appear 3 happen 4 result 5 become 6 amount (to) 7 extend —**come by** get —**come to** regain consciousness —**come up** arise in discussion

come′back′ n. 1 a return, as to power 2 witty answer

co·me′di·an n. actor who plays comic parts —**co·me′di·enne′** (-en′) n.fem.

come′down′ n. loss of status

com·e′dy n., pl. **-dies** a humorous play, TV show, etc.

come′ly (kum′-) a. **-li·er, -li·est** attractive —**come′li·ness** n.

come′-on′ n. [Sl.] inducement

co·mes′ti·bles n.pl. food

com′et n. mass of dust and gas in space, with a luminous tail

come·up′pance n. [Col.] deserved punishment

com′fort v. soothe in distress; console —n. 1 relief from distress 2 one that comforts 3 ease —**com′fort·a·ble** a.

com′fort·er n. 1 one that comforts 2 a quilt

com′fy a. **-fi·er, -fi·est** [Col.] comfortable

com′ic a. 1 of comedy 2 funny: also **com′i·cal** —n. 1 comedian 2 pl. comic strips

comic book n. booklet of comic strips

comic strip n. cartoon series, as in a newspaper

com′ing a. 1 approaching; next 2 promising success —n. arrival; approach

com′i·ty (käm′-) n., pl. **-ties** courtesy

com′ma n. punctuation mark (,)

com·mand′ v. 1 to order 2 to control 3 deserve and get —n. 1 an order 2 control 3 military force, etc. under someone's control

com′man·dant′ (-dant′, -dänt′) n. commanding officer

com′man·deer′ v. seize for military or government use

com·mand′er n. 1 leader; officer 2 naval officer below a captain

commander in chief n. top commander of a nation's armed forces

com·mand′ment n. command; law

com·man′do n., pl. **-dos** or **-does** member of a small force for raiding enemy territory

command post n. field headquarters of a military unit

com·mem′o·rate′ v. honor the memory of —**com·mem′o·ra′tion** n.

com·mence′ v. begin

com·mence′ment n. 1 beginning 2 graduation ceremony of a school, etc.

com·mend′ v. 1 entrust 2 recommend 3 to praise —**com·mend′a·ble** a. —**com′men·da′tion** n.

com·mend′a·to′ry a. praising or recommending

com·men′su·ra·ble (-shə-) a. measurable by the same standard or measure

com·men′su·rate (-sə rət) a. equal or proportionate

com′ment′ n. 1 explanatory note 2 remark 3 talk —v. make comments

com′men·tar′y n., pl. **-ies** series of explanatory notes or remarks

com·men·tate´ v. perform as a commentator

com´men·ta·tor n. radio or TV news analyst

com´merce n. trade on a large scale

com·mer´cial (-shəl) a. 1 connected with commerce 2 done for profit —n. Radio & TV paid advertisement

com·mer´cial·ize´ v. put on a profit-making basis —**com·mer´cial·i·za´tion** n.

com·min´gle v. mix; blend

com·mis´er·ate´ (-miz´-) v. sympathize (with)

com´mis·sar´ n. government official in the U.S.S.R.

com·mis´sar·y (-ser´-) n. store in an army camp for the sale of food, etc.

com·mis´sion n. 1 authority to act 2 group chosen to do something 3 percentage of a sale allotted to the agent 4 military officer's certificate of rank —v. 1 give a commission to 2 authorize —**in** (or **out of**) **commission** (not) usable

com·mis´sion·er n. governmental department head

com·mit´ v. **-mit´ted, -mit´ting 1** put in custody **2** do **3** pledge; bind —**com·mit´ment** n.

com·mit´tee n. group chosen to do something

com·mode´ n. **1** a chest of drawers **2** toilet

com·mo´di·ous a. spacious

com·mod´i·ty n., pl. **-ties** anything bought and sold

com´mo·dore´ n. former naval rank

com´mon a. **1** shared by all **2** general **3** usual; ordinary **4** vulgar **5** designating a noun that refers to any of a group —n. also pl. town's public land —**in common** shared by all

com´mon·al·ty n., pl. **-ties** common people; public

common carrier n. transportation company

common denominator n. characteristic in common

com´mon·er n. person not of the nobility

common law n. unwritten law based on custom, usage, etc.

common market n. association of countries in economic union

com´mon·place´ n. **1** trite or obvious remark **2** anything ordinary —a. ordinary

common pleas n. civil and criminal court in some States

common sense n. good sense or practical judgment

com´mon·weal´ n. public welfare

com´mon·wealth´ n. **1** people of a state **2** democracy or republic

com·mo´tion n. turmoil

com·mu´nal (or kə myoo´-) a. of a community; public

com·mune´ n. small group living communally

com·mune´ v. talk intimately

com·mu´ni·cate´ v. **1** transmit **2** give or exchange (information) **3** be connected —**com·mu´ni·ca·ble** a. —**com·mu´ni·ca´tive** a. —**com·mu´ni·ca´tor** n.

com·mu´ni·ca´tion n. **1** a communicating or means of doing this **2** message, etc.

com·mun´ion n. **1** a sharing or being close **2** group of the same religious faith **3** [C–] Holy Communion

com·mu´ni·qué´ (-kā´) n. official communication

com´mu·nism´ n. theory or system of ownership of the means of production by the community —**com´mu·nist** n.

com·mu´ni·ty n., pl. **-ties** body of people living in the same place **2** a sharing in common

community college n. junior college for a certain community

com·mute´ v. **1** lessen (a punishment, etc.) **2** travel by train, etc. to and from work —**com·mut´er** n.

com·pact´ (or käm´pakt; n.: käm´pakt) a. **1** firmly packed **2** terse —n. **1** small case for face powder, etc. **2** agreement

compact disc (or **disk**) n. digital disc for recording music, etc.

com·pac´tor n. device that compresses trash

com·pan´ion n. **1** comrade; associate **2** thing that matches or goes with another —**com·pan´ion·a·ble** a. —**com·pan´ion·ship´** n.

com·pan´ion·way´ n. stairway from a ship's deck

com´pa·ny n., pl. **-nies 1** group of people associated for some purpose **2** [Col.] guest(s) **3** military unit

com·par´a·tive a. by comparison —n. the second degree of comparison of adverbs and adjectives

com·pare´ v. **1** liken (to) **2** examine for similarities or differences **3** to form the positive, comparative, and superlative degrees of (adjective or adverb) —**beyond compare** without equal —**com´pa·ra·ble** a. —**com·par´i·son** n.

com·part´ment n. section partitioned off

com·pass (kum´pəs) n. **1** instrument for drawing circles, etc. **2** range; extent **3** instrument for showing direction

com·pas´sion n. pity —**com·pas´sion·ate** (-ət) a.

com·pat´i·ble a. in agreement

com·pa´tri·ot n. fellow countryman

com´peer´ n. peer or comrade

com·pel´ v. **-pelled´, -pel´ling** to force

com·pen´di·um n., pl. **-ums** or **-a** comprehensive summary

com´pen·sate´ v. make up for; pay —**com´pen·sa´tion** n.

com·pete´ v. vie; rival ₹ take part (*in* a contest)

com´pe·tent a. **1** capable; able **2** adequate —**com´pe·tence, com´pe·ten·cy** n.

com´pe·ti´tion (-tish´ən) n. **1** a competing; rivalry **2** contest —**com·pet´i·tive** a. —**com·pet´i·tor** n.

com·pile´ v. compose by collecting from various sources —**com´pi·la´tion** n.

com·pla´cen·cy, com·pla´cence n. **1** contentment **2** smugness —**com·pla´cent** a.

com·plain´ v. **1** express pain, dissatisfaction, etc. **2** make an accusation —**com·plaint´** n.

com·plain´ant n. plaintiff

com·plai´sant (-plā´zənt, -sənt) a. obliging

com·plect´ed a. complexioned

com´ple·ment (-mənt; v.: -ment´) n. **1** that which completes **2** entirety —v. to make complete —**com´ple·men´ta·ry** a.

com·plete´ v. **1** lacking no parts **2** finished **3** thorough; perfect —v. make complete —**com·ple´tion** n.

com·plex´ (*or* käm´pleks; n.: käm´pleks´) a. **1** having two or more parts **2** complicated —n. **1** complex whole **2** mixed-up feeling about a thing —**com·plex´i·ty** n., pl. **-ties**

com·plex´ion (-plek´shən) n. **1** color or texture of the skin **2** nature; aspect

com·plex´ioned a. having a (specified) complexion

com·pli´ance n. **1** a complying **2** tendency to give in —**com·pli´ant** a.

com´pli·cate´ v. make difficult or involved —**com´pli·cat´ed** a. —**com´pli·ca´tion** n.

com·plic´i·ty (-plis´-) n. partnership in wrongdoing

com´pli·ment (-mənt; v.: -ment´) n. something said in praise **2** pl. respects —v. pay a compliment

com´pli·men´ta·ry a. **1** giving praise **2** given free

com·ply´ v., pl. **-plied´** or **-ply´ing** conform (*with* rules) —**com·pli´ance** n. —**com·pli´ant** a.

com·po´nent a., n. (being) part of a whole

com·port´ v. **1** conduct (oneself) **2** accord (*with*) —**com·port´ment** n.

com·pose´ v. **1** make by combining **2** put in proper form **3** write (a song, poem, etc.) **4** make calm —**com·posed´** a. —**com·pos´er** n. —**com´po·si´tion** (-zish´ən) n.

com·pos´ite (-päz´it) n., a. (thing) formed of distinct parts

com·pos´i·tor (-päz´-) n. one who sets type

com´post´ n. rotting vegetation used as fertilizer

com·po´sure (-zhər) n. calmness; self-possession

com·pote´ (-pōt) n. **1** stewed fruit **2** stemmed dish

com·pound (käm´pound´; v.: *also* käm pound´) v. combine —n. **1** substance with combined elements **2** enclosed place —a. with two or more parts

compound interest n. interest paid on both the principal and the accumulated unpaid interest

com´pre·hend´ v. **1** understand **2** include —**com´pre·hen´si·ble** a. —**com´pre·hen´sion** n. —**com´pre·hen´sive** a.

com·press´ (kəm pres´; n.: käm´pres´) v. press tight —n. wet pad —**com·pres´sion** n. —**com·pres´sor** n.

com·prise´ v. consist of

com´pro·mise´ n. settlement made with concessions —v. **1** settle by compromise **2** make suspect

comp·trol´ler (kən-) n. one who regulates finances

com·pul´sion n. a forcing or being forced —**com·pul´sive** a. —**com·pul´so·ry** a.

com·punc´tion n. slight regret for wrongdoing

com·pute´ v. calculate; figure —**com´pu·ta´tion** n.

com·put´er n. an electronic machine that rapidly calculates or correlates data —**com·put´er·i·za´tion** n. —**com·put´er·ize´** v.

com´rade´ (-rad´) n. **1** a close friend **2** associate —**com´rade·ship´** n.

con adv. against —v. **conned, con´ning 1** study carefully **2** [Sl.] swindle

con·cat´e·na´tion n. connected series, as of events

con·cave´ (*or* kän´kāv´) a. curved like the inside of a sphere

con·ceal´ v. hide —**con·ceal´ment** n.

con·cede´ v. **1** admit as true **2** grant as a right

con·ceit´ (-sēt´) n. **1** vanity; pride **2** fanciful notion —**con·ceit´ed** a.

con·ceive´ v. **1** become pregnant **2** think of **3** understand —**con·ceiv´a·ble** a.

con´cen·trate´ v. **1** fix one's attention, etc. (*on*) **2** increase, as in density —n. concentrated substance —**con´cen·tra´tion** n.

concentration camp n. prison camp for political foes, ethnic minorities, etc.

con·cen´tric a. having a common center, as circles

con'cept' *n.* idea; notion

con·cep'tion *n.* 1 a conceiving 2 concept

con·cep'tu·al *a.* of conception or concepts

con·cep'tu·al·ize' *v.* form a concept of

con·cern' *v.* be related to; involve —*n.* 1 business 2 regard 3 worry

con·cerned' *a.* 1 involved or interested 2 anxious

con·cern'ing *prep.* relating to

con'cert *n.* 1 agreement 2 musical performance

con·cert'ed *a.* combined

con·cer·ti'na (-tē'-) *n.* small accordion

con·cert·ize' *v.* perform as a soloist in concerts on a tour

con·cer'to (-cher'-) *n., pl.* **-tos** composition for solo instrument(s) and orchestra

con·ces'sion *n.* 1 a conceding 2 thing conceded 3 franchise, as for selling food

con·ces'sion·aire' *n.* holder of a CONCESSION (*n.* 3)

conch (käŋk, känch) *n.* large, spiral seashell

con'ci·erge' (-sē erzh') *n.* custodian, as of an apartment house

con·cil'i·a·r *a.* of or from a council

con·cil'i·ate' *v.* make friendly —**con·cil'i·a'tion** *n.* —**con·cil'i·a'tor** *n.* —**con·cil'i·a·to'ry** *a.*

con·cise' (-sīs') *a.* short and clear; terse —**con·cise'ly** *adv.*

con'clave *n.* private meeting

con·clude' *v.* 1 finish 2 decide 3 arrange —**con·clu'sion** *n.*

con·clu'sive *a.* decisive

con·coct' *v.* prepare or plan —**con·coc'tion** *n.*

con·com'i·tant *a.* accompanying —*n.* concomitant thing

con'cord' *n.* 1 agreement 2 peaceful relations

con·cord'ance *n.* 1 agreement 2 complete list of words used in a book —**con·cord'ant** *a.*

con·cor·dat' *n.* formal agreement

con'course' *n.* 1 a crowd 2 open space for crowds

con·crete' *a.* 1 real; actual 2 specific —*n.* hard material made of sand, gravel and cement —**con·crete'ly** *adv.* —**con·cre'tion** *n.*

con'cu·bine' (-kyōō-) *n.* wife of lesser status

con·cu'pis·cence (-kyōōp'ə-) *n.* lust —**con·cu'pis·cent** *a.*

con·cur' *v.* **-curred'**, **-cur'ring** 1 occur together 2 agree —**con·cur'rence** *n.* —**con·cur'rent** *a.*

con·cus'sion *n.* 1 jarring shock 2 brain injury from a blow

con·demn' (-dem') *v.* 1 disapprove of 2 declare guilty 3 to doom 4 take for public use 5 declare unfit —**con·dem·na'tion** *n.*

con·dense' *v.* 1 make or become denser 2 express concisely —**con·den·sa'tion** *n.* —**con·dens'er** *n.*

con·densed' milk *n.* thickened milk with added sugar

con'de·scend' (-send') *v.* stoop; deign —**con'de·scen'sion** *n.*

con·dign' (-dīn') *a.* deserved; suitable

con'di·ment *n.* seasoning

con·di'tion *n.* 1 prerequisite 2 state of being 3 healthy state 4 rank —*v.* 1 to make healthy 2 make accustomed (*to*) —**on condition that** provided that —**con·di'tion·er** *n.*

con·di'tion·al *a.* qualified —**con·di'tion·al·ly** *adv.*

con·di'tioned *a.* 1 in a desired condition 2 affected by conditioning 3 accustomed (*to*)

con·dole' *v.* show sympathy —**con·do'lence** *n.*

con'dom *n.* covering for the penis, generally of rubber, worn during sexual intercourse

con'do·min'i·um *n.* separately owned unit in a multiple-unit dwelling: also **con'do'**

con·done' (-dōn') *v.* forgive or overlook

con'dor (-dər, -dôr') *n.* large vulture

con·duce' *v.* tend; lead (*to*) —**con·du'cive** *a.*

con·duct' (*v.:* kən dukt') *n.* 1 management 2 behavior —*v.* 1 to lead 2 manage 3 to direct 4 behave (oneself) 5 transmit, as electricity —**con·duc'tion** *n.* —**con·duc'tive** *a.* —**con'duc·tiv'i·ty** *n.*

con·duct'ance *n.* ability to conduct electricity

con·duc'tor *n.* 1 an orchestra leader 2 one in charge of passengers, etc. 3 thing that conducts heat, etc.

con'duit (-dōō it) *n.* pipe, tube, etc. for fluids or wires

con'dyle (-dil, -dīl') *n.* rounded process at end of a bone

cone *n.* 1 pointed, tapered figure with circular base 2 woody fruit of evergreens

co'ney *n., pl.* **-neys** rabbit or its fur

con·fec'tion *n.* candy, ice cream, etc. —**con·fec'tion·er** *n.*

con·fec'tion·er'y *n., pl.* **-ies** confectioner's shop

con·fed'er·a·cy *n., pl.* **-cies** league —[**C-**] South in the Civil War

con·fed'er·ate (-ət; *v.:* -āt') *a.* united; allied —*n.* 1 an ally 2 accomplice —*v.* unite; ally —**con·fed'er·a'tion** *n.*

con·fer' *v.* **-ferred'**, **-fer'ring** 1 give 2 meet to discuss —**con'fer·ence** *n.*

con·fess' *v.* 1 admit (a crime) 2 affirm (a

faith) 3 tell (one's sins) —**con·fes′sion** n.

con·fes′sion·al n. box where a priest hears confessions

con·fes′sor n. priest who hears confessions

con·fet′ti n. bits of colored paper thrown as at carnivals

con·fi·dant (-dant′, -dänt′) n. trusted friend —**con′fi·dante′** n.fem.

con·fide′ v. 1 trust (in) 2 share as a secret

con·fi·dence n. 1 trust 2 assurance 3 self-reliance 4 a sharing of a secret —**con′fi·dent** a.

confidence game n. swindle done by one (**confidence man**) who gains the victim's trust

con·fi·den′tial (-shəl) a. 1 secret 2 entrusted with private matters

con·fig′u·ra′tion n. form

con·fine (v.: kən fīn′) n. limit: used in pl. —v. 1 restrict 2 to shut up, as in prison —**con·fine′ment** n.

con·firm′ v. 1 to strengthen 2 approve formally 3 prove to be true 4 admit to membership in a church —**con′fir·ma′tion** n.

con·firmed′ a. firmly established; habitual

con·fis·cate′ v. seize legally —**con′fis·ca′tion** n.

con·fis′ca·to′ry a. of or effecting confiscation

con′fla·gra′tion n. big, destructive fire

con·flict′ (n.: kän′flikt′) v. be in opposition —n. 1 a fight 2 sharp disagreement

conflict of interest n. conflict between public obligation and self-interest of an official

con′flu·ence n. 1 a flowing together of streams 2 crowd

con·form′ v. 1 be in accord 2 act according to rules, customs, etc. —**con·form′ist** n. —**con·form′i·ty** n.

con·for·ma′tion n. 1 symmetrical arrangement 2 shape

con·found′ v. confuse

con·found′ed a. 1 confused 2 damned

con·front′ v. 1 face boldly 2 bring face to face —**con′fron·ta′tion** n. —**con′fron·ta′tion·al** a.

con·fuse′ v. 1 mix up 2 bewilder —**con·fu′sion** n.

con·fute′ v. prove wrong

con·geal′ (-jēl′) v. 1 freeze 2 thicken; jell

con·ge′nial (-jēn′yəl) a. friendly; agreeable —**con·ge′ni·al′i·ty** n.

con·gen′i·tal (-jen′-) a. existing from birth —**con·gen′i·tal·ly** adv.

con′ger (eel) (-gər) n. large, edible saltwater eel

con·ge′ries (-jə rēz′) n., pl. **-ries** heap or pile

con·gest′ (-jest′) v. fill too full, as with blood —**con·ges′tion** n. —**con·ges′tive** a.

con·glom′er·ate (-at) n. large corporation formed by merging many companies

con·glom′er·a′tion n. mass

con·grat′u·late′ (-grach′ə-) v. rejoice with (a fortunate person) —**con·grat′u·la·to′ry** a.

con·grat′u·la′tions n.pl. expressions of pleasure over another's good luck, etc.

con′gre·gate′ v. gather into a crowd

con′gre·ga′tion n. assembly of people, esp. for worship

con′gress n. 1 assembly 2 legislature, esp. [C-] of the U.S. —**con·gres′sion·al** a. —**con′gress·man** n., pl. **-men** —**con′gress·per′son** n. —**con′gress·wom′an** n.fem., pl. **-wom′en**

con′gru·ent a. agreeing; corresponding

con′gru·ous a. suitable —**con·gru′i·ty** n.

con′i·cal (kän′-) a. of or like a cone: also **con′ic**

con′i·fer (kän′ə-, kō′nə-) n. cone-bearing tree

con·jec′ture (-chər) n., v. guess —**con·jec′tur·al** a.

con·join′ v. join together

con′ju·gal a. of marriage

con′ju·gate′ v. give the inflectional forms of (a verb) —**con′ju·ga′tion** n.

con·junc′tion n. 1 a joining together; union 2 an occurring together 3 word used to join words, clauses, etc. —**con·junc′tive** a.

con′junc·ti′va (-tī′-) n., pl. **-vas** or **-vae** (-vē) mucous membrane covering inner eyelid and the front of the eyeball

con·junc′ti·vi′tis n. inflammation of the mucous membrane covering the eye

con·junc′ture n. combination of events creating a crisis

con′jure v. 1 practice magic 2 entreat 3 cause to appear, etc. as by magic —**con′jur·er, con′ju·ror** n.

conk [Sl.] n., v. hit on the head —**conk out** 1 fail suddenly 2 fall asleep from fatigue

con man n. [Sl.] confidence man: also **con artist**

con·nect′ v. 1 join; link 2 show or think of as related —**con·nec′tive** a.

con·nec′tion n. 1 a connecting or being connected 2 thing that connects 3 relation

con·nip′tion (fit) n. [Col.] fit of anger, hysteria, etc.: also **con·nip′tions**

con·nive′ v. 1 pretend not to look (at crime, etc.) 2 cooperate secretly in wrongdoing —**con·niv′ance** n.

con·nois·seur (kän′ə sur′) n. expert, esp. in the fine arts

con·note′ v. suggest in addition to the explicit meaning —**con′no·ta′tion** n.

con·nu′bi·al *a.* of marriage

con′quer (-kər) *v.* defeat; overcome **—con′quer·or** *n.* **—con′quest′** *n.*

con·quis′ta·dor′ (-kwis′-, -kēs′-) *n.*, *pl.* **-dors′** or **-do′res′** (-dôr′ēz′) 16th-c. Spanish conqueror of Mexico, Peru, etc.

con′science (-shəns) *n.* sense of right and wrong

con′sci·en′tious (-shē-) *a.* scrupulous; honest

con′scious (-shəs) *a.* 1 aware (*of* or *that*) 2 able to feel and think; awake 3 intentional **—con′scious·ness** *n.*

con′script′ *v.* to draft (into the armed forces) **—con·scrip′tion** *n.*

con′se·crate′ *v.* 1 set apart as holy 2 devote **—con′se·cra′tion** *n.*

con·sec′u·tive *a.* following in order without a break **—con·sec′u·tive·ly** *adv.*

con·sen′sus *n.* general opinion

con·sent′ *v.* agree **—n.** agreement or approval

con′se·quence *n.* 1 a result 2 importance

con′se·quent *a.* resulting

con′se·quen′tial (-shəl) *a.* 1 consequent 2 self-important

con′se·quent′ly *adv.* as a result; therefore

con·ser′va·tive *a.* 1 opposed to change 2 cautious **—n.** conservative person

con·serv′a·to′ry *n.* school of music, art, etc.

con·serve′ *v.* keep from being damaged, lost, etc. **—con·ser·va′tion** *n.*

con·sid′er *v.* 1 think over 2 keep in mind 3 have regard for 4 believe to be **—con·sid′er·ate** (-ət) *a.* **—con·sid′er·a′tion** *n.*

con·sid′er·a·ble *a.* large or important **—con·sid′er·a·bly** *adv.*

con·sid′ered *a.* arrived at after careful thought

con·sid′er·ing *prep.* taking into account

con·sign′ *v.* 1 entrust 2 assign 3 deliver (goods) **—con·sign′ment** *n.*

con·sist′ *v.* be made up (*of*)

con·sis′ten·cy *n.*, *pl.* **-cies** 1 thickness, as of a liquid 2 agreement 3 uniformity of action **—con·sis′tent** *a.*

con·sole′ *v.* comfort; cheer up **—con′so·la′tion** *n.*

con′sole′ *n.* floor cabinet of an organ, radio, TV, etc.

con·sol′i·date′ *v.* unite **—con·sol′i·da′tion** *n.*

con′som·mé′ (-sə mā′) *n.* clear meat soup

con′so·nant *n.* letter for a breath-blocked sound, as *p*, *t*, *l*, etc. **—a.** in harmony **—con′so·nance** *n.*

con′sort′ (*v.*: kən sôrt′) *n.* spouse, esp. of a monarch **—v.** to associate

con·sor′ti·um (or -sôr′shəm) *n.*, *pl.* **-ti·a** international alliance, as of banks

con·spec′tus *n.* 1 general view 2 summary

con·spic′u·ous *a.* 1 easy to see 2 outstanding **—con·spic′u·ous·ly** *adv.*

con·spire′ *v.* join in a plot **—con·spir′a·cy** (-spir′-) *n.* **—con·spir′a·tor** *n.*

con′sta·ble *n.* policeman

con·stab′u·lar′y *n.*, *pl.* **-ies** 1 constables, collectively 2 militarized police force

con′stant *a.* 1 not changing; fixed 2 faithful 3 continual **—n.** unchanging thing **—con′stan·cy** *n.* **—con′stant·ly** *adv.*

con′stel·la′tion *n.* group of fixed stars

con′ster·na′tion *n.* great alarm or dismay

con′sti·pate′ *v.* make it difficult to move the bowels **—con′sti·pa′tion** *n.*

con·stit′u·en·cy (-stich′ōō-) *n.* voters in a district

con·stit′u·ent *a.* 1 necessary part 2 voter **—n.** needed to form a whole

con′sti·tute′ *v.* form; set up

con′sti·tu′tion *n.* 1 structure; make up 2 basic laws of a government, etc., esp. [C—] of the U.S. **—con′sti·tu′tion·al** *a.*

con·strain′ *v.* force or restrain **—con·straint′** *n.*

con·strict′ *v.* make smaller by squeezing, etc.; contract **—con·stric′tion** *n.*

con·struct′ *v.* build; devise

con·struc′tion *n.* 1 a constructing 2 structure 3 explanation 4 arrangement of words **—con·struc′tive** *a.*

con·strue′ *v.* interpret

con′sul *n.* government official in a foreign city looking after his country's business there **—con′su·lar** *a.* **—con′su·late** (-ət) *n.*

con·sult′ *v.* 1 confer 2 ask the advice of 3 consider **—con·sult′ant** *n.* **—con′sul·ta′tion** *n.*

con·sume′ *v.* 1 destroy 2 use up 3 eat or drink up **—con·sum′er** *n.*

con·sum′er·ism′ *n.* movement to protect consumers against harmful products, etc.

con′sum·mate′ (*a.*: kən sum′it) *v.* complete **—a.** complete **—con′sum·ma′tion** *n.*

con·sump′tion *n.* 1 a consuming 2 using up of goods 3 amount used up 4 tuberculosis of the lungs

con·sump′tive *n.*, *a.* (one) having tuberculosis of the lungs

con′tact *n.* 1 a touching 2 being in touch (*with*) 3 connection **—v.** 1 place in contact 2 get in touch with

contact lens *n.* tiny, thin lens worn on the eye to improve vision

con·ta′gion (-tā′jən) *n.* a spreading of disease, an idea, etc. **—con·ta′gious** (-jəs) *a.*

con·tain′ *v.* 1 have in it 2 be able to hold 3 restrain **—con·tain′er** *n.*

con·tain′er·ize′ *v.* to ship (cargo) in huge, standardized containers

con·tam'i·nate v. make impure; pollute —**con·tam'i·nant** n. —**con·tam'i·na'tion** n.

con'tem·plate' v. 1 to watch intently 2 meditate 3 intend —**con'tem·pla'tion** n. —**con·tem'pla·tive'** a.

con·tem'po·rar'y n., a., pl. **-ries** (one) living in the same period —**con·tem'po·ra'ne·ous** a.

con·tempt' n. 1 scorn 2 disgrace 3 disrespect shown for a judge, etc.

con·tempt'i·ble a. deserving contempt

con·temp'tu·ous (-chōō əs) a. scornful; disdainful

con·tend' v. 1 struggle 2 compete 3 assert

con·tent' a. satisfied: also **con·tent'ed** —n. satisfaction —**con·tent'ment** n.

con'tent' n. 1 pl. all that is contained 2 meaning 3 capacity

con·ten'tion n. argument or struggle —**con·ten'tious** a.

con·test' (n.: kän'test') v. 1 to dispute; question 2 fight for —n. 1 struggle 2 race, game, etc. —**con·test'ant** n.

con'text' n. words surrounding a word or phrase that fix its meaning

con·tig'u·ous a. in contact

con'ti·nence n. self-restraint, esp. sexually —**con'ti·nent** a.

con'ti·nent n. large landmass —**the Continent** Europe —**con'ti·nen'tal** a.

con·tin'gen·cy (-jən-) n., pl. **-cies** uncertain event

con·tin'gent a. dependent (on); conditional —n. quota, as of troops

con·tin'u·al a. 1 repeated often 2 continuous

con·tin'ue v. 1 keep on; go on 2 endure; last 3 resume 4 extend 5 postpone —**con·tin'u·ance, con·tin'u·a'tion** n.

con'ti·nu'i·ty n., pl. **-ties** 1 continuous state or thing 2 radio script, etc.

con·tin'u·ous a. without interruption; unbroken

con·tin'u·um n., pl. **-u·a** or **-u·ums** continuous whole, quantity, or series

con·tort' v. twist out of shape —**con·tor'tion** n.

con·tor'tion·ist n. one who can twist his or her body strangely

con'tour' (-tŏŏr') n. outline of a figure, land, etc. —v. shape to contour —a. made to fit the contour of something

contra- pref. against

con'tra·band' n. smuggled goods —a. prohibited

con'tra·cep'tion n. prevention of human conception —**con'tra·cep'tive** a., n.

con·tract' (v. 2, 3: kän trakt') n. legally valid agreement —v. 1 undertake by contract 2 get; incur 3 shrink —**con·trac'tor** n. —**con·trac'tu·al** (-chōō al) a.

con·trac'tile (-til) a. able to contract

con·trac'tion n. 1 a contracting 2 shortened form

con'tra·dict' v. say or be the opposite of —**con'tra·dic'tion** n. —**con'tra·dic'to·ry** a.

con'trail' n. white trail of condensed water vapor in the wake of an aircraft

con'tra·in'di·cate' v. Med. make (the indicated drug or treatment) inadvisable

con·tral'to n., pl. **-tos** lowest female voice

con·trap'tion n. contrivance; gadget

con'tra·pun'tal a. of counterpoint

con'trar'i·wise' adv. 1 on the contrary 2 in the opposite way, order, etc.

con'trar'y a. 1 opposed; different 2 perverse —n. the opposite —**on the contrary** as opposed to what has been said —**con·trar'i·ly** adv.

con·trast' (n.: kän'trast') v. 1 compare 2 show difference —n. striking difference when compared

con'tra·vene' v. go against

con·tre·temps' (kän'trə tän') n., pl. **-temps'** (-tän') awkward mishap

con·trib'ute v. 1 give, esp. to a common fund 2 furnish (an idea, article, etc.) —**contribute to** help bring about —**con'tri·bu'tion** n. —**con·trib'u·tor** n.

con·trite' a. remorseful —**con·tri'tion** (-trish'ən) n.

con·trive' v. 1 devise; invent 2 manage; bring about —**con·triv'ance** n.

con·trol' v. **-trolled', -trol'ling** 1 regulate (finances) 2 direct 3 restrain —n. 1 authority 2 means of restraint 3 pl. regulating mechanism —**con·trol'ler** n.

con'tro·ver'sy n. debate or dispute —**con'tro·ver'sial** (-shəl) a.

con'tro·vert' v. to dispute —**con'tro·vert'i·ble** a.

con·tu·ma·cy n. disobedience —**con'tu·ma'cious** (-shəs) a.

con'tu·me·ly n. haughty rudeness

con·tu'sion n. a bruise

co·nun'drum n. a puzzle

con'ur·ba'tion n. vast area of a large city and its environs

con'va·les'cence n. (period of) recovery after illness —**con'va·lesce'** v. —**con'va·les'cent** a., n.

con·vec'tion n. transmission of heat in currents

con·vene' v. assemble; meet

con·ven'ience n. 1 a being convenient 2 comfort 3 thing that saves work, etc.

con·ven'ient a. easy to do, use, or get to; handy

con'vent n. community of nuns or their living place

con·ven'tion n. 1 an assembly 2 custom; usage

con·ven'tion·al a. 1 customary 2 conforming

con·verge' v. come together —**con·ver'gence** n. —**con·ver'gent** a.

con·ver'sant a. familiar (with)

con·ver·sa'tion n. informal talk —**con·ver·sa'tion·al** a.

conversation piece n. something unusual, as in furnishing a room, that invites comment

con·verse' (n.: kän'vərs) v. to talk —a. opposite —n. 1 conversation 2 the opposite —**con·verse'ly** adv.

con·vert' (n.: kän'vʉrt') v. change in form, use, etc. or in religion —n. person who has converted —**con·ver'sion** n. —**con·vert'er, con·vert'or** n.

con·vert'i·ble a. that can be converted —n. automobile with a folding or removable top

con·vex' a. curved outward like the outside of a sphere —**con·vex'i·ty** n.

con·vey' v. 1 carry 2 transmit —**con·vey'or, con·vey'er** n.

con·vey'ance n. 1 a conveying 2 vehicle

con·vict' (n.: kän'vikt') v. prove or find guilty —n. prisoner serving a sentence

con·vic'tion n. 1 a being convicted 2 strong belief

con·vince' v. make feel sure —**con·vinc'ing** a.

con·viv'i·al a. sociable; jovial —**con·viv'i·al'i·ty** n.

con·voke' v. call together —**con'vo·ca'tion** n.

con'vo·lu'tion n. a twist or twisting —**con'vo·lut'ed** a.

con'voy' v. escort —n. ships, etc. being escorted

con·vulse' v. shake as with violent spasms —**con·vul'sion** n. —**con·vul'sive** a.

co'ny n., pl. **-nies** coney

coo v. make the soft sound of a pigeon or dove —n. this sound

cook v. boil, bake, fry, etc. —n. one who cooks —**cook'er·y** n.

cook'book' n. book of recipes

cook'ie, cook'y n., pl. **-ies** small, sweet, flat cake

cook'out' n. meal cooked and eaten outdoors

cool a. 1 moderately cold 2 not excited 3 unfriendly 4 [Sl.] very good —n. cool place, time, etc. —v. make or become cool —**cool'ly** adv. —**cool'ness** n.

cool'ant n. fluid for cooling engines, etc.

cool'er n. refrigerator

coo'lie n., pl. **-lies** Oriental laborer

coon n. raccoon

co-op n. [Col.] a cooperative

coop n. pen for poultry —v. confine as in a coop

co·op'er·ate', co·op'er·ate' v. to work together: also **co·op'er·ate'** —**co·op'er·a'tion, co·op'er·a'tion** n.

co·op'er·a·tive, co·op'er·a·tive a. cooperating —n. collective, profit-sharing enterprise Also **co·öp'er·a·tive**

co-opt' v. get (an opponent) to join one's side

co·or'di·nate, co·or'di·nate (-nət; v.: -nāt') a. equally important —v. to harmonize; adjust Also **co·ör'di·nate** —**co·or'di·na'tion, co·or'di·na'tion** n.

coot (kōōt) n. water bird

cop n. [Sl.] policeman

cope v. deal (with) successfully —n. priest's vestment

cop'i·er n. person who copies or machine that makes copies

co'pi'lot n. assistant pilot of an aircraft

cop'ing (kō'piŋ) n. top of masonry wall

co'pi·ous a. abundant

cop'per n. reddish-brown metal, a chemical element

cop'per·head' n. a poisonous snake

cop'ra (kōp'-) n. dried coconut meat

copse n. thicket

cop'ter n. [Col.] helicopter

cop'u·late' v. have sexual intercourse —**cop'u·la'tion** n.

cop'y n., pl. **-ies** 1 thing made just like another 2 one of many books, etc. all alike —v. **-ied, -y·ing** 1 make a copy of 2 imitate

cop'y·cat' n. imitator: chiefly child's term —a. imitating a recent event

cop'y·right' n. exclusive rights over a book, song, etc. —v. protect by copyright

co·quette' (-ket') n. flirt —**quet'ted, -quet'ting;** v. flirt —**co·quet'tish** a.

cor'al n. 1 hard mass of sea animal skeletons 2 yellowish red

cord n. 1 thick string 2 wood pile of 128 cu. ft. 3 insulated electric wire —**cord'less** a.

cor'dial (-jəl) a. friendly —n. syrupy alcoholic drink —**cor'di·al'i·ty** (-jē al'-) n. —**cor'dial·ly** adv.

cor'don n. a guarding group in a line

cor'do·van n. soft leather

cor'du·roy' n. ribbed cotton fabric

core n. 1 central part, as of an apple 2 most important part —v. remove the core of

co·re·spond'ent (kō'-) n. person in divorce suit charged with adultery with one's spouse

co·ri·an'der *n.* an herb used for flavoring

cork *n.* **1** light, thick bark of a certain oak **2** stopper —*v.* stop with a cork

cork'screw' *n.* spiral device for uncorking bottles

corm *n.* bulblike underground stem of certain plants

cor'mo·rant *n.* seabird

corn *n.* **1** grain **2** grain that grows on large ears with a hard core (**corn'cob'**); maize **3** [Col.] trite humor **4** horny thickening of the skin —*v.* to pickle (meat, etc.)

cor·ne·a *n.* clear, outer layer of the eyeball —**cor'ne·al** *a.*

cor'ner *n.* **1** place where lines or surfaces meet **2** a region **3** monopoly —*v.* put into a difficult position **2** get a monopoly in —**cut corners** cut down expenses, etc.

cor'ner·back' *n. Football* either of two defensive backs behind the line of scrimmage

cor'ner·stone' *n.* stone at a corner of a building

cor'net' *n.* brass instrument like a trumpet

corn'flow'er *n.* plant with showy disk flowers

cor'nice (-nis) *n.* molding along the top of a wall, etc.

corn'meal' *n.* meal made from corn (maize)

corn'starch' *n.* starchy flour used in cooking

corn syrup *n.* sweet syrup made from cornstarch

cor'nu·co'pi·a *n.* horn-shaped container overflowing with fruits, flowers, etc.

corn'y *a.* **-i·er, -i·est** [Col.] trite or sentimental

co·rol'la (-rōl'-, -räl'-) *n.* petals of a flower

cor'ol·lar'y *n., pl.* **-ies** proposition following from one already proved

co·ro'na *n.* ring of light around the sun or moon

cor'o·nar'y *a.* of the arteries supplying the heart —*n., pl.* **-ies** thrombosis in a coronary artery: in full **coronary thrombosis**

cor'o·na'tion *n.* crowning of a sovereign

cor'o·ner *n.* official who investigates unnatural deaths

cor'o·net' *n.* small crown worn by nobility

cor'po·ral *n.* lowest ranking noncommissioned officer —*a.* of the body

corporal punishment *n.* bodily punishment, as flogging

cor'po·ra'tion *n.* group given legal status of an individual —**cor'po·rate** *a.*

cor·po·re·al (-pôr'ē-) *a.* **1** of the body **2** material

corps (kôr) *n.* **1** organized group **2** large military unit

corpse *n.* dead body

cor'pu·lent *a.* fat; fleshy —**cor'pu·lence** *n.*

cor'pus *n.* body, as of laws

cor'pus'cle (-al) *n.* cell in the blood, lymph, etc.

cor·ral' *n.* pen for horses, etc. —*v.* **-ralled'**, **-ral'ling** confine in a corral

cor·rect' *v.* **1** make right **2** mark errors of **3** punish —*a.* right, true, etc. —**cor·rec'tion** *n.* —**cor·rec'tion·al** *a.* —**cor·rec'tive** *a., n.* —**cor·rect'ly** *adv.*

cor're·late' *v.* bring into mutual relation —**cor're·la'tion** *n.*

cor·rel'a·tive *n., a.* (conjunction) showing mutual relation, as *either ... or*

cor're·spond' *v.* **1** be similar or equal to **2** communicate as by letters —**cor're·spond'ence** *n.*

cor're·spond'ent *n.* **1** person exchanging letters with another **2** journalist sending in news to a home office

cor'ri·dor (-dar, -dôr') *n.* long hall

cor·rob'o·rate' *v.* confirm —**cor·rob'o·ra'tion** *n.* —**cor·rob'o·ra'tive** *a.*

cor·rode' *v.* wear away; rust —**cor·ro'sion** *n.* —**cor·ro'sive** *a., n.*

cor'ru·gate' *v.* make fold or wrinkles in

cor·rupt' *a.* **1** rotten **2** evil **3** taking bribes —*v.* to make or become corrupt —**cor·rupt'i·ble** *a.* —**cor·rup'tion** *n.*

cor·sage' (-säzh') *n.* small bouquet worn by a woman

cor'set *n.* tight undergarment to support the torso

cor·tege' (-tezh') *n.* ceremonial procession

cor'tex' *n., pl.* **-ti·ces** (-tə sēz') outer layer of the brain, kidney, etc. —**cor'ti·cal** *a.*

cor'ti·sone' (or -zōn') *n.* hormone used to treat allergies, inflammations, etc.

co·run'dum *n.* mineral used for grinding wheels, etc.

cor·us·cate' *v.* to glitter; sparkle —**cor'us·ca'tion** *n.*

co·ry'za (-rī'-) *n.* a cold in the head

co'sign' *v.* sign jointly —**co'sign'er** *n.*

cos·met'ic (käz-) *n., a.* (preparation) for enhancing beauty —**cos'me·tol'o·gist** *n.* —**cos'me·tol'o·gy** *n.*

cos'mic *a.* **1** of the cosmos; orderly **2** vast; huge

cos'mo·naut *n.* Russian astronaut

cos'mo·pol'i·tan *a.* at home all over the world; worldly —*n.* a worldly person

cos'mos (-məs, -mōs') *n.* the universe seen as an orderly system

co'spon'sor *v., n.* (be a) joint sponsor

cost *v.* **cost, cost'ing** require the payment, etc. of —*n.* **1** price **2** loss; sacrifice —**at all**

costs by any means whatever

co′star′ *n.* any of the actors or actresses who are stars in a movie or play —*v.* **-starred′, -star′ring** make or be a costar

cos·tive (käs′tiv) *a.* constipated or constipating

cost′ly *a.* **-li·er, -li·est** expensive —**cost′li·ness** *n.*

cost of living *n.* averge cost of necessities, as food, shelter, and clothes

cos′tume′ *n.* 1 the dress of a people, period, etc. 2 set of outer clothes for some purpose

co′sy (-zē) *a.* **-si·er, -si·est** cozy —**co′si·ly** *adv.*

cot *n.* folding bed

cote *n.* small shelter for birds, sheep, etc.

co·te·rie (kōt′ər ē) *n.* social set; clique

co·til′lion (-yən) *n.* formal dance

cot′tage *n.* small house

cottage cheese *n.* soft, white cheese made from sour milk

cot′ter pin *n.* pin with two stems that can be spread apart

cot′ton *n.* 1 plant with head of soft, white fibers 2 thread or cloth from this —**cot′ton·y** *a.*

cot′ton·mouth′ *n.* water moccasin

cot′ton·seed′ *n.* 1 seed of the cotton plant 2 its oil (**cottonseed oil**) used in margarine, soap, etc.

cot′ton·wood′ *n.* poplar having seeds covered with cottony fibers

cot·y·le·don (kät′ə lēd′'n) *n.* first leaf produced by a plant embryo

couch *n.* piece of furniture to lie on —*v.* put in words

cou′gar (kōō′-) *n.* large American wild cat

cough (kôf) *v.* expel lung air in a loud burst —*n.* 1 a coughing 2 condition of frequent coughing

cough drop *n.* small tablet for relief of coughs

could *v.* pt. of CAN: *could* is also used to show slightly more doubt than *can*

could′n't can not

coun′cil *n.* an advisory, administrative, or legislative body —**coun′cil·man** *n., pl.* **-men** —**coun′cil·wom′an** *n.fem., pl.* **-wom′en**

coun′ci·lor *n.* member of a council: also, Br. sp., **coun′cil·lor**

coun′sel *n.* 1 advice 2 lawyer(s) —*v.* to advise —**coun′se·lor, coun′sel·lor** *n.*

count *v.* 1 add up to get a total 2 name numbers in order 3 include or be included 4 consider 5 be important —*n.* 1 a counting 2 total number 3 each charge in an indictment 4 nobleman —**count on** rely on

count′down′ *n.* counting off of time units, in reverse order

coun′te·nance *n.* 1 a facial expression 2 face —*v.* to sanction

count′er *n.* long table for displaying goods, serving food, etc. —*adv., a.* contrary —*v.* oppose

counter– *pref.* 1 opposite 2 against 3 in return

coun′ter·act′ *v.* act against; undo

coun′ter·at·tack′ *n., v.* attack in return

coun′ter·bal′ance *v.* to offset

coun′ter·clock′wise′ *adv., a.* like the hands of a clock moving in reverse

coun′ter·feit (-fit′) *a.* made in imitation with intent to defraud —*n.* fraudulent imitation —*v.* 1 make counterfeits 2 pretend

coun′ter·mand′ *v.* cancel (a command)

coun′ter·pane′ *n.* bedspread

coun′ter·part′ *n.* matching or corresponding thing

coun′ter·point′ *n.* harmonic interweaving of melodies

coun′ter·poise′ *n., v.* counterbalance

coun′ter·pro·duc′tive *a.* producing the opposite of what is intended

coun′ter·sign′ *n.* password —*v.* confirm another's signature by signing

coun′ter·sink′ *v.* sink a bolt or screw into a hole large enough to receive its head

coun′ter·ten′or *n.* highest tenor voice

count′ess *n.* wife or widow of a count or earl

count′less *a.* too many to count

coun′try (kun′-) *n., pl.* **-tries** 1 region 2 nation 3 rural area —*a.* rural —**coun′try·man** *n., pl.* **-men** —**coun′try·side′** *n.*

country club *n.* social club with a golf course, etc.

country music *n.* rural folk music, esp. of the South

coun′ty *n., pl.* **-ties** subdivision of a State

coup (kōō) *n., pl.* **coups** 1 bold, successful stroke 2 coup d'état

coup d'é·tat (kōō′dā tä′) *n.* sudden overthrow of a ruler

cou·ple (kup′əl) *n.* 1 a pair 2 engaged, married, etc. man and woman 3 [Col.] a few —*v.* join together

cou′plet *n.* two successive rhyming lines of poetry

cou′pling *n.* device for joining things together

cou′pon (kōō′-, kyōō′-) *n.* certificate, ticket, etc. redeemable for cash or gifts

cour′age *n.* fearless or brave quality —**cou·ra′geous** *a.*

cou′ri·er (koor′ē-, kur′ē-) *n.* messenger

course *n.* 1 path or channel 2 direction taken 3 regular mode of action 4 series

5 separate part of a meal 6 a study or series of studies —v. run —**in the course of** during —**of course 1** naturally **2** certainly

court n. **1** an open space surrounded by buildings or walls: also **court′yard′ 2** playing area **3** royal palace **4** family, advisers, etc. of a sovereign **5** courtship **6** Law 1) judge(s) 2) place where trials are held (also **court′room′**) —v. woo

cour′te·san (-zən) n. nobleman's mistress

cour′te·sy (kurt′ə-) n., pl. **–sies** polite behavior or act —**cour′te·ous** a.

court′house′ n. building housing the offices and courtrooms of a county

cour′ti·er n. attendant at a royal court

court′ly a. dignified

court′-mar′tial n., pl. **courts′-mar′tial** or **court′-mar′tials** trial by a military or naval court —v. try by such a court

court′ship′ n. period or act of courting a woman

cous′in (kuz′-) n. child of one's uncle or aunt

cove n. small bay

cov′en (kuv′-) n. witches' meeting

cov′e·nant (kuv′ə-) n. agreement; compact

cov′er v. **1** place something over **2** extend over **3** conceal **4** protect **5** include; deal with —n. thing that covers —**take cover** seek shelter —**cov′er·ing** n.

cov′er·age n. amount covered by something

cov′er·alls′ n.pl. one-piece work garment with legs

covered wagon n. large wagon with an arched canvas cover

cov′er·let n. bedspread

cov·ert (kuv′ərt, kō′vərt) n. hidden

cov′er·up′ n. an attempt to keep blunders, crimes, etc. undisclosed

cov′et v. desire ardently (what belongs to another)

cov′et·ous a. greedy

cov′ey (kuv′ē) n. small flock of birds, esp. quail

cow n. mature female of the ox, or of the elephant, seal, etc. —v. make timid

cow′ard n. one lacking courage —**cow′ard·ice′** (-ər dis′) n. —**cow′ard·ly** a., adv.

cow′boy′ n. worker who herds cattle: also **cow′hand′**

cow′er v. cringe as in fear

cow′hide′ n. leather made from the hide of a cow

cowl n. monk's hood

cow′lick′ n. tuft of hair difficult to comb flat

cowl′ing n. metal covering for an airplane engine

co′-work′er n. fellow worker

cow′slip′ n. **1** swamp plant with yellow flowers **2** English primrose

cox′comb′ (-kōm′) n. fop

cox·swain (käk′sən, -swān′) n. one who steers a boat

coy a. shy or pretending to be shy —**coy′ly** adv.

coy·o·te (kī ōt′ē, kī′ōt′) n. small prairie wolf

coz′en (kuz′-) v. cheat

co′zy a. **-zi·er, -zi·est** warm and comfortable; snug

CPU n. central processing unit

crab n. **1** shellfish with eight legs and two pincers **2** complainer

crab apple n. small, sour apple

crab′by a. **-bi·er, -bi·est** peevish —**crab′bi·ness** n.

crab grass n. weedy grass that spreads rapidly

crack v. **1** make a sudden, sharp breaking noise **2** break without separation of parts **3** [Sl.] make (a joke) **4** solve —n. **1** sudden, sharp noise **2** incomplete break **3** sharp blow **4** [Col.] try **5** [Sl.] gibe **6** [Sl.] form of cocaine —a. [Col.] first-rate —**crack down (on)** become strict (with)

crack′down′ n. a resorting to strict discipline or rules

crack′er n. thin, crisp wafer

crack′le v., n. (make) a series of slight, sharp sounds

crack′pot′ n. [Col.] fanatic

crack′up′ n. **1** crash **2** [Col.] mental breakdown

cra′dle n. baby's bed on rockers —v. put as in a cradle

craft n. **1** skill; art **2** slyness **3** pl. **craft** boat or aircraft

crafts′man n., pl. **-men** skilled workman —**crafts′man·ship′** n.

craft′y a. **-i·er, -i·est** sly; cunning —**craft′i·ly** adv.

crag n. steep, projecting rock —**crag′gy** a.

cram v. **crammed, cram′ming 1** to stuff **2** study hurriedly for a test

cramp n. **1** painful contraction of a muscle **2** pl. intestinal pain —v. hamper

cramped a. **1** confined **2** irregular and crowded

cran′ber·ry n., pl. **-ries** sour, edible, red berry

crane n. **1** long-legged wading bird **2** machine for lifting heavy weights —v. stretch (the neck)

cra′ni·um n. the skull —**cra′ni·al** a.

crank n. **1** handle for turning a shaft **2** [Col.] an eccentric —v. start or work by a crank

crank'y a. -i·er, -i·est irritable; cross

cran'ny n., pl. -nies chink

crap n. [Sl.] 1 nonsense 2 junk

crape n. crepe

craps n.pl. dice game

crash v. 1 fall, break, drop, etc. with a loud noise 2 fail 3 [Col.] get into uninvited —n. 1 loud noise 2 a crashing 3 failure, as of business 4 coarse linen

crash'-land' v. bring (an airplane) down without landing gear —crash landing n.

crass a. grossly dull

crate n. wooden packing case —v. pack in a crate

cra'ter n. bowl-shaped cavity or pit, as of a volcano

cra·vat' n. necktie

crave v. ask or long for

cra'ven a. cowardly —n. coward

crav'ing n. intense desire

craw n. bird's crop

crawl v. 1 move slowly while flat on the ground 2 creep 3 swarm with crawling things —n. 1 a crawling 2 swimming stroke

cray'fish', craw'fish' n. shellfish like a small lobster

cray'on n. small stick of chalk, wax, etc. for drawing

craze v. make or become insane —n. fad

cra'zy a. -zi·er, -zi·est insane, mad, etc. —cra'zi·ly adv. —cra'zi·ness n.

crazy quilt n. quilt of odd patches in no regular design

creak v., n. squeak

cream n. 1 oily part of milk 2 creamy cosmetic 3 best part —v. beat till smooth as cream —cream of purée of —cream'y a., -i·er, -i·est

cream cheese n. soft, white cheese of cream and milk

cream'er n. cream pitcher

cream'er·y n., pl. -ies place where dairy products are made or sold

crease n. line made by folding —v. make a crease in

cre·ate' v. make; bring about —cre·a'tion n. —cre·a'tive a. —cre·a'tor n.

crea'ture n. living being, animal or human

cre'dence n. belief; trust

cre·den'tials (-shəlz) n.pl. papers showing one's right to a certain position, etc.

cre·den'za n. buffet or sideboard

credibility gap n. disparity between a statement and the truth

cred'i·ble a. believable —cred'i·bil'i·ty n.

cred'it n. 1 belief; trust 2 reputation 3 praise or source of praise 4 trust that one will pay later 5 completed unit of study —v. 1 believe; trust 2 give credit for —cred'it·a·ble a. —cred'it·a·bly adv.

credit card n. card entitling one to charge bills

cred'i·tor n. one to whom another owes a debt

cre'do' (krē'-, krā'-) n., pl. -dos' creed

cred·u·lous (krej'ə ləs) a. believing too readily —cre·du'li·ty (krə dōō'-) n.

creed n. statement of belief

creek n. small stream

creel n. basket for fish

creep v. crept, creep'ing 1 go on hands and knees 2 go slowly or stealthily 3 grow along the ground, etc. —n. [Sl.] disgusting person —the creeps [Col.] feeling of fear, disgust, etc.

creep'y a. -i·er, -i·est causing fear, disgust, etc.

cre'mate' v. burn (a dead body) —cre·ma'tion n.

cre'ma·to'ry n., pl. -ries furnace for cremating: also cre'ma·to'ri·um, pl. -ums or -a

cre'o·sote' n. oily preservative distilled from tar

crepe, crêpe (krāp, n. 2: also krep) n. 1 thin, crinkled silk, rayon, etc. 2 a thin pancake, rolled and filled

crept v. pt. & pp. of CREEP

cre·scen'do' (-shən'-) n., pl. -dos' Mus. a growing louder

cres'cent n. shape of a quarter moon

crest n. 1 tuft on an animal's head 2 heraldic device 3 top; summit

crest'fall'en a. dejected

cre'tin n. idiot

cre·tonne' (krē tän') n. printed linen or cotton cloth

cre·vasse' (-vas') n. deep crack, as in a glacier

crev'ice n. narrow crack

crew n. group of workers, as the seamen on a ship

crew v. alt. pt. of CROW

crew'el n. yarn used in embroidery —crew'el·work' n.

crib n. 1 box for fodder 2 baby's small bed 3 wood shed for grain —v. cribbed, crib'bing 1 confine 2 [Col.] plagiarize

crib'bage' n. card game

crick n. painful cramp

crick'et n. 1 leaping insect 2 ball game played with bats and wickets

cried v. pt. & pp. of CRY

cri'er n. one who cries, shouts announcements, etc.

crime n. 1 an act in violation of a law 2 sin

crim'i·nal a. of crime —n. person guilty of crime

crim′i·nal·ist n. expert in using physical evidence to investigate crimes

crim′i·nol′o·gy n. study of crime and criminals

crimp v., n. pleat or curl

crim′son (-zən, -sən) n. deep red —v. make or become crimson

cringe (krinj) v. 1 shrink back as in fear 2 to fawn

crin′kle v. to wrinkle or rustle —**crin′kly** a.

crin′o·line (-lin′) n. 1 stiff cloth 2 hoop skirt

crip′ple n. disabled person —v. disable

cri′sis n., pl. **-ses′** (-sēz′) 1 turning point 2 crucial situation

crisp a. 1 brittle 2 clear 3 fresh; bracing

criss′cross′ n. crossed lines —v. 1 mark with crisscross 2 move crosswise —adv. crosswise

cri·te·ri·on (krī tir′ē ən) n., pl. **-ri·a** or **-ri·ons** standard; rule

crit′ic n. 1 judge of books, art, etc. 2 faultfinder

crit′i·cal a. 1 finding fault 2 of critics or their work 3 being a crisis —**crit′i·cal·ly** adv.

crit′i·cize′ v. 1 judge as a critic 2 find fault (with) —**crit′i·cism′** n.

cri·tique′ (-tēk′) n. critical analysis or review

crit′ter n. [Dial.] creature

croak v., n. (to make) a deep, hoarse sound

cro·chet′ (-shā′) v. knit with one hooked needle

crock n. earthenware jar

crocked a. [Sl.] drunk

crock′er·y n. earthenware

croc′o·dile′ n. large reptile of tropical streams

cro′cus n. small plant of the iris family

crois·sant (krə sänt′) n. a crescent-shaped bread roll

crone n. old hag

cro′ny n., pl. **-nies** close friend

crook n. 1 a bend or curve 2 [Col.] swindler

crook′ed a. 1 not straight 2 dishonest

croon v. sing in a soft tone —**croon′er** n.

crop n. 1 saclike part of a bird's gullet 2 farm product, growing or harvested 3 group 4 riding whip —v. **cropped, crop′ping** cut or bite off the ends of —**crop out** (or **up**) appear suddenly —**crop′per** n.

crop′-dust′ing n. spraying of crops with pesticides from an airplane

cro·quet′ (-kā′) n. game with hoops in the ground through which balls are hit

cro·quette′ (-ket′) n. small mass of meat, fish, etc. deep-fried

cross n. 1 upright post with another across it 2 figure of this, symbolic of Christi-

anity 3 any affliction 4 mark made by intersecting lines, bars, etc. 5 hybrid —v. 1 place, go, or lie across 2 go (over) to the other side 3 intersect 4 draw a line across 5 thwart 6 interbreed —a. 1 lying or passing across 2 irritable —**cross off** (or **out**) cancel as by drawing lines across —**cross′ing** n. —**cross′ness** n.

cross′bones′ n. picture of two crossed bones under a skull, symbolizing death

cross′bow′ n. medieval bow on a wooden frame for shooting arrows

cross′breed′ n. hybrid —v. to breed as a hybrid

cross′-coun′try a. across open country, as a race

cross′cut′ a., n., v. cut across

cross′-ex·am′ine v. Law question (an opposition witness) —**cross′-ex·am′i·na′tion** n.

cross′-eyed′ a. having the eyes turned toward the nose

cross′hatch′ v. darken (a drawing) with crossing parallel lines

cross′ing n. 1 intersection 2 place for crossing

cross′-pur′pose n. contrary purpose —**at cross-purposes** misunderstanding each other's purposes

cross′-ref′er·ence n. reference from one part to another

cross′road′ n. 1 a road that crosses another 2 pl. road intersection

cross section n. 1 part cut straight across 2 broad sample

cross′walk′ n. pedestrians' lane across a street

cross′wise′ adv. across: also **cross′ways′**

crotch n. place where branches or legs fork

crotch′et n. whim

crotch′et·y a. cantankerous

crouch v., n. stoop with legs bent low

croup (krōōp) n. disease with cough and hard breathing

crou·pi·er (krōō′pē ā′) n. one controlling a gambling table

crou′ton′ (krōō′-) n. bit of toast served in soup

crow n. 1 large, black bird with a harsh call 2 rooster's cry —v. 1 make a rooster's cry 2 exult

crow′bar′ n. long, metal bar for prying, etc.

crowd v. to throng, press, cram, etc. —n. a mass of people —**crowd′ed** a.

crown n. 1 head covering of a monarch 2 power of a monarch 3 top part, position, quality, etc. —v. 1 make a monarch of 2 honor 3 be atop 4 climax

crow's′-feet′ n.pl. wrinkles at outer corners of eyes

crow's'-nest' n. lookout platform on a ship's mast

CRT n. cathode-ray tube

cru'cial (-shəl) a. 1 decisive 2 trying

cru'ci·ble n. container for melting metals

cru'ci·fix' n. representation of Jesus on the cross

cru'ci·fy' v. **-fied'**, **-fy'ing** execute by suspending from a cross —**cru'ci·fix'ion** (-fik'shən) n.

crude a. 1 raw; unprocessed 2 rough or clumsy —**cru'di·ty**, **crude'ness** n.

cru'el a. causing suffering; pitiless —**cru'el·ty** n.

cru'et n. small bottle for vinegar, oil, etc.

cruise v. travel about, as by ship —n. voyage

cruis'er n. 1 police car 2 large, fast warship

crul'ler n. twisted doughnut

crumb (krum) n. small piece, as of bread; bit —**crumb'y** a., **-bi·er**, **-bi·est**

crum'ble v. break into crumbs —**crum'bly** a., **-bli·er**, **-bli·est**

crum'my a. **-mi·er**, **-mi·est** [Sl.] shabby, inferior.

crum'ple v. to crush into wrinkles

crunch v. chew or crush with a crackling sound —**crunch'y** a., **-i·er**, **-i·est**

cru·sade' v., n. (to engage in) united action for some idea or cause —**cru·sad'er** n.

cruse (krōōs, krōōz) n. small container for water, oil, etc.

crush v. 1 press out of shape 2 pound into bits 3 subdue —n. 1 a crushing 2 crowded mass 3 [Col.] infatuation

crust n. 1 hard outer part of bread, earth, etc. 2 dry piece of bread

crus·ta'cean (-shən) n. hard-shelled invertebrate, as a shrimp, lobster, etc.

crust'y a. bad-tempered

crutch n. support held under the arm to aid in walking

crux n. essential point

cry v. **cried**, **cry'ing** 1 utter loudly 2 sob; weep —n., pl. **cries** 1 a shout 2 entreaty 3 call of a bird, etc. —**a far cry** a great difference

cry'ba·by n., pl. **-bies** childish complainer

cry'o·gen'ics n. science dealing with very low temperatures

crypt (kript) n. underground (burial) vault

cryp'tic a. secret; mysterious —**cryp'ti·cal·ly** adv.

cryp·tog'ra·phy n. secret-code writing or deciphering —**cryp·tog'ra·pher** n.

crys'tal n. 1 clear quartz 2 clear, brilliant glass 3 solidified substance with its molecules arranged symmetrically —**crys'tal·line** (-in) a.

crys'tal·lize' v. 1 form crystals 2 take on or give definite form —**crys'tal·li·za'tion** n.

cub n. young bear, lion, etc.

cub'by·hole' n. small, enclosed space

cube n. 1 a solid with six equal, square sides 2 product obtained by multiplying a number by its square —v. 1 get the CUBE (n. 2) of 2 cut into cubes —**cu'bic**, **cu'bi·cal** a.

cu'bi·cle n. small room

cu'bit n. ancient measure of length, about 18-22 inches

cuck'old n. man whose wife is unfaithful

cuck·oo (kōō'kōō') n. brown, slender bird —a. [Sl.] crazy

cu'cum·ber n. long, green-skinned, fleshy vegetable

cud n. food regurgitated by cattle and chewed again

cud'dle v. hold or lie close and snug —**cud'dle·some**, **cud'dly** a.

cudg'el (kuj'-) v., n. (beat with) a short club

cue n. 1 signal to begin 2 hint 3 rod for striking a billiard ball —v. to signal

cuff n. 1 band or fold at the wrist of a sleeve or the bottom of a trouser leg 2 a slap —v. to slap

cui·sine' (kwi zēn') n. 1 style of cooking 2 food cooked

cul'-de-sac' n. road, etc. with only one outlet

cu'li·nar'y (kyōō'-) a. of cookery

cull v. pick over; select

cul'mi·nate' v. reach its highest point —**cul'mi·na'tion** n.

cu·lottes' (-läts') n.pl. women's trousers resembling a skirt

cul'pa·ble a. deserving blame —**cul'pa·bil'i·ty** n.

cul'prit n. one accused, or found guilty, of a crime

cult n. system of worship or group of worshipers

cul'ti·vate' v. 1 prepare (land) for crops 2 grow (plants) 3 develop, as the mind —**cul'ti·va'tion** n.

cul'ture n. 1 animal or plant breeding 2 training of the mind, taste, etc. 3 civilization of a people or period —**cul'tur·al** a.

cul'vert n. drain or waterway under a road, etc.

cum (kum, kŏŏm) prep. with

cum'ber·some a. unwieldy

cum'in n. aromatic fruit used for flavoring

cum'mer·bund' n. sash worn around the waist by men

cu·mu·la·tive (kyōō'myə-) a. increasing by additions

cu'mu·lus *n.* a cloud having rounded masses piled up

cu·ne'i·form (kyōō nē'ə-) *n.* ancient wedge-shaped writing

cun'ning *a.* 1 sly; crafty 2 pretty —*n.* craft

cup *n.* small bowl with handle, for beverages —*v.* **cupped, cup'ping** shape like a cup —**cup'ful'** *n.,* pl. **-fuls'**

cup·board (kub'ərd) *n.* cabinet for dishes, food, etc.

cup'cake' *n.* small cake

cu·pid'i·ty (kyōō-) *n.* greed

cu'po·la (kyōō'-) *n.* small dome

cu'pro·nick'el (kyōō'-) *n.* alloy of copper and nickel

cur *n.* 1 mongrel dog 2 contemptible person

cu·rate (kyoor'ət) *n.* clergyman helping a vicar or rector

cu'ra·tive *a.* having the power to cure —*n.* a remedy

cu·ra'tor *n.* one in charge, as of a museum

curb *n.* 1 chain or strap on a horse's bit for checking the horse 2 thing that restrains 3 edging along a street —*v.* to restrain

curb'stone *n.* stones making up a curb: also **curb'ing**

curd *n.* coagulated part of soured milk

cur'dle *v.* form curd

cure *n.* 1 a healing 2 remedy —*v.* 1 make well; heal 2 remedy 3 preserve (meat) —**cur'a·ble** *a.*

cure'-all' *n.* something supposed to cure everything

cu·ret·tage (kyōō ret'ij) *n.* a cleaning or scraping of the walls of a body cavity

cur'few' *n.* evening deadline for being off the streets

cu'ri·o' *n.,* pl. **-os'** odd art object

cu'ri·os'i·ty *n.* 1 desire to know; inquisitiveness 2 strange

cu'ri·ous *a.* 1 eager to know; inquisitive 2 strange

curl *v.* 1 twist (hair, etc.) into ringlets 2 curve around; coil —*n.* 1 ringlet of hair 2 any curling —**curl'er** *n.* —**curl'y** *a.,* **-i·er, -i·est**

cur'lew' *n.* wading bird

curl'i·cue' *n.* fancy curve

curl'ing *n.* game played on ice by sliding a flat stone

cur·mudg'eon (-muj'ən) *n.* cantankerous person

cur'rant *n.* 1 small, seedless raisin 2 sour berry

cur'ren·cy *n.,* pl. **-cies** 1 money circulated in a country 2 general use; prevalence

cur'rent *a.* 1 of this day, week, etc. 2 commonly accepted or known —*n.* flow of air,

water, electricity, etc.

cur·ric'u·lum *n.,* pl. **-lums** or **-la** course of study

cur'ry *n.* spicy powder or sauce —*v.* **-ried, -ry·ing** brush the coat of (a horse, etc.) —**curry favor** try to win favor, as by flattery

curse *v.* **cursed** or **curst, curs'ing** 1 call on or bring evil down on 2 swear (at) —*n.* 1 a cursing 2 evil or injury —**be cursed with** suffer from —**curs'ed** *a.*

cur'sive (-siv) *a.* of writing with joined letters

cur'sor *n.* movable indicator light on a computer screen

cur'so·ry *a.* hastily done —**cur'so·ri·ly** *adv.*

curt *a.* so brief as to be rude —**curt'ness** *n.*

cur·tail' *v.* cut short —**cur·tail'ment** *n.*

cur'tain *n.* piece of cloth hung, as at a window, to decorate or conceal —*v.* furnish as with a curtain

curt'sy *n.,* pl. **-sies** graceful bow that women make by bending the knees —*v.* **-sied, -sy·ing** make a curtsy

curve *n.* line, surface, etc. having no straight part —*v.* form or move in a curve —**cur'va·ture** *n.*

cush'ion *n.* 1 pillow or pad 2 something absorbing shock —*v.* provide with a cushion

cush'y *a.* **-i·er, -i·est** [Sl.] easy; comfortable

cusp *n.* arched, pointed end

cus'pi·dor' *n.* spittoon

cus'tard *n.* pudding made with eggs, milk, and sugar

cus·to'di·an *n.* 1 one having custody 2 janitor

cus'to·dy *n.* 1 guarding; care 2 imprisonment —**cus·to'di·al** *a.*

cus'tom *n.* 1 usual or traditional practice; usage 2 pl. duties on imported goods —*a.* made to order: also **cus'tom-built'** or **cus'tom-made'**

cus'tom·ar'y *a.* usual —**cus'tom·ar'i·ly** *adv.*

cus'tom·er *n.* one who buys

cus'tom·ize' *v.* make according to personal specifications

cut *v.* **cut, cut'ting** 1 gash 2 pierce 3 sever 4 hew 5 reap 6 trim 7 pass across 8 reduce 9 [Col.] snub —*n.* 1 a cutting 2 part cut open or off 3 reduction 4 style 5 plate engraved for printing 6 insult 7 [Col.] share, as of profits —**cut and dried** dull; boring —**cut down (on)** reduce —**cut out for** suited for

cut'back' *n.* reduction or discontinuing of production, etc.

cute a. [Col.] 1 clever 2 pretty or pleasing

cut'i·cle (kyōot'-) n. hardened skin, as at the base and sides of a fingernail

cut'lass, cut'las n. short, thick, curved sword

cut'ler·y n. cutting tools, as knives, scissors, etc.

cut'let n. small slice of meat from the ribs or leg

cut'off' n. 1 short cut road, etc. 2 device for shutting off flow of a fluid, etc.

cut'-rate' a. selling or on sale at a lower price

cut'ter n. small, swift ship

cut'throat' n. murderer —a. merciless

cut'ting n. shoot cut from a plant —a. 1 sharp 2 piercing 3 sarcastic

cut'tle·fish' n. mollusk with ten arms

–cy suf. 1 quality or state of being 2 position, rank, or office of

cy'a·nide' (sī'-) n. poisonous white compound

cy'ber·net'ics n. comparative study of electronic computers and the human nervous system

cy'ber·space' n. electronic system of linked computers for information and interaction

cy'cla·mate' n. artificial sweetener

cy'cle n. 1 complete round of regular events, or period for this 2 bicycle, tricycle, etc. —v. ride a bicycle, etc. —cy'clic, cy·cli·cal a. —cy'clist n.

cy'clone' n. storm with heavy rain and whirling winds

cy'clo·pe·di·a n. encyclopedia

cy'clo·tron' n. apparatus that speeds up particles, as to split atomic nuclei

cyg'net (sig'-) n. young swan

cyl'in·der n. round figure with two flat ends that are parallel circles —cy·lin'dri·cal a.

cym'bals n.pl. pair of round brass plates struck together for a ringing sound

cyn'ic n. one inclined to question goodness, sincerity, etc. —cyn'i·cal n. —cyn'i·cism' n.

cy'no·sure' n. center of attention

cy'press n. evergreen tree

cyst (sist) n. sac containing fluid or hard matter —cyst'ic a.

cystic fibrosis n. children's disease of the pancreas

czar (zär) n. 1 Russian emperor 2 an autocrat

D

dab v. dabbed, dab'bing put on with light, quick strokes —n. soft or moist bit —dab'ber n.

dab'ble v. 1 splash in water 2 do something superficially: (with in or at) —dab'bler n.

dace n. small freshwater fish

dachs'hund (däks'ənd) n. small dog with a long body

Da·cron (dā'krän', dak'rän') trademark synthetic fabric or fiber —n. [d–] this fabric or fiber

dad n. [Col.] father: also **dad'dy**, pl. **–dies**

daddy long'legs' n., pl. **–legs'** long-legged arachnid

da'do (dā'-) n., pl. **–does** lower part of a wall decorated differently

daf'fo·dil' n. yellow flower

daf'fy a. **–fi·er, –fi·est** [Col.] crazy; silly

daft a. 1 silly 2 insane

dag'ger n. 1 a short, sharp-pointed weapon 2 printed reference mark (†)

dahl·ia (dal'yə) n. plant with large, showy flowers

dai'ly a., adv. (done or happening) every day —n. daily newspaper

daily double n. bet won by choosing winners in two races on a program

dain'ty a. **–ti·er, –ti·est** 1 delicately pretty 2 fastidious —n., pl. **–ties** a delicacy —dain'ti·ly adv. —dain'ti·ness n.

dai·qui·ri (dak'ər ē) n. cocktail with rum, lemon juice, etc.

dair'y n., pl. **–ies** place where milk, butter, etc. are made or sold —dair'y·man n., pl. **–men**

da·is (dā'is, dī'-) n. platform

dai'sy n., pl. **–sies** flower with white rays around a yellow disk

dale n. small valley

dal'ly v. **–lied, –ly·ing** 1 to toy or flirt 2 loiter

Dal·ma·tian (-shən) n. large, black-and-white dog

dam n. 1 barrier to hold back flowing water 2 female parent of a horse, cow, etc. —v. dammed, dam'ming keep back; confine

dam'age n. 1 injury; harm 2 pl. money paid for harm done —v. do damage to

dam'ask n. fabric with figured weave —a. deep-pink

dame n. 1 lady 2 [D–] woman's title of honor in Britain 3 [Sl.] any woman

damn (dam) v. **damned, damn'ing** condemn; declare bad, doomed, etc. —a., adv. [Col.] damned —dam'na·ble a. —dam·na'tion n.

damned a. 1 condemned 2 [Col.] outrageous —adv. [Col.] very

damp n. 1 moisture 2 mine gas —a. slightly wet; moist —v. 1 moisten 2 check or deaden Also **damp'en**

damp'-dry' v. **–dried', –dry'ing** dry with some moisture retained

damp'er n. 1 one that depresses 2 valve in a flue to control the draft

dam′sel (-zəl) n. [Ar.] girl

dam′son (-zən, -sən) n. small, purple plum

dance v. move in rhythm to music —n. 1 rhythmic movement to music 2 party or music for dancing —**danc′er** n.

D and C n. medical procedure in which tissue is scraped from uterus

dan·de·li′on n. common weed with yellow flowers

dan′der n. [Col.] anger

dan′dle v. dance (a child) up and down on the knee

dan′druff n. little scales of dead skin on the scalp

dan′dy n., pl. **–dies** vain man —a. **–di·er, –di·est** [Col.] very good; first-rate

dan′ger n. 1 liability to injury, loss, etc.; peril 2 thing that may cause injury, etc. —**dan′ger·ous** a.

dan′gle v. hang loosely

Dan′ish (dān′-) a. of the people or language of Denmark —n. 1 language of Denmark 2 [also d–] pastry with a filling

dank a. disagreeably damp —**dank′ness** n.

dap′per a. trim; spruce

dap′ple a. spotted; mottled: also **dap′pled** —v. mottle

dare v. 1 have the courage (to) 2 challenge —n. a challenge —**dare say** think probable —**dar′ing** a., n.

dare′dev′il n., a. (one who is) bold and reckless

dark a. 1 with little or no light 2 not light in color 3 gloomy 4 ignorant —n. a being dark —**dark′en** v. —**dark′ness** n.

dark horse n. [Col.] one who wins or may win unexpectedly

dark′room′ n. dark room for developing photographs

dar′ling n., a. beloved

darn v. mend by sewing

dart n. 1 small pointed weapon for throwing 2 sudden movement —v. to throw or move quickly

dash v. 1 smash 2 strike violently against 3 do hastily: (with off) 4 rush —n. 1 bit of something 2 short race 3 vigor 4 mark of punctuation (—)

dash′board′ n. instrument panel in an automobile

dash′ing a. lively

das′tard n. mean coward

das′tard·ly a. cowardly

da·ta (dāt′ə, dat′-) n. facts; information

da·ta·base n. large mass of organized data in a computer: also **data base**

data proc′ess·ing n. handling of data by mechanical means or computer

date n. 1 time of an event 2 day of the month 3 social engagement 4 fruit of a tall palm —v. 1 mark with a date 2 belong to a particular time —**out of date** old-fashioned —**up to date** modern

daub v. 1 smear with sticky stuff 2 paint badly

daugh′ter n. female as she is related to her parents

daugh′ter-in-law′ n., pl. **daugh′ters–** wife of one's son

daunt v. 1 frighten 2 dishearten —**daunt′less** a.

dau′phin (-fin) n. eldest son of the French king

dav′en·port′ n. large sofa

daw′dle v. waste time; loiter

dawn v. 1 begin to be day 2 begin to be understood —n. 1 daybreak 2 beginning

day n. 1 period from sunrise to sunset 2 period of 24 hours, esp. from midnight to midnight 3 a period; era —**day′light′** n. —**day′time′** n.

day′break′ n. time of the first light in the morning

day care n. daytime care for children or adults —**day′-care′** a.

day′dream′ n. pleasant, dreamy thinking or wishing —v. have daydreams

day′light′ n. 1 sunlight 2 daytime 3 understanding

daylight saving(s) time n. time one hour later than standard

day nursery n. place for daytime care of preschool children: also **day-care center**

Day of Atonement n. Yom Kippur

day′time′ n. time between dawn and sunset

day′-to-day′ a. daily; routine

daze v. 1 stun 2 dazzle —n. dazed condition

daz′zle v. overpower with light or brilliance

DDT n. powerful insecticide

de– pref. 1 away from; off 2 reverse the action of

dea·con (dē′kən) n. one who assists a minister

de·ac′ti·vate′ v. 1 make (an explosive, etc.) inactive 2 disband (troops)

dead (ded) a. 1 not living 2 dull; inactive 3 complete —n. time of most cold, darkness, etc. —adv. completely

dead′beat′ n. [Sl.] one who avoids paying for things

dead′bolt′ n. door lock with a long, square bolt worked by a key

dead′en v. to dull

dead end n. street closed at one end —**dead′-end′** a.

dead heat n. a tie in a race

dead′line′ n. time limit

dead′lock′ n. standstill with equal forces opposed

dead′ly *a.* **–li·er, –li·est 1** fatal **2** as or until death —*adv.* extremely

dead′pan′ *a., adv.* without expression

dead′wood′ *n.* useless thing

deaf (def) *a.* **1** unable to hear **2** unwilling to respond —**deaf′en** *v.*

deaf′-mute′ *n.* deaf person who has not learned speech

deal *v.* **dealt** (delt), **deal′ing 1** distribute **2** have to do (*with*) **3** do business —*n.* transaction or agreement —**a good** (or **great**) **deal 1** large amount **2** very much —**deal′er** *n.* —**deal′ing** *n.*

dean *n.* **1** church or college official **2** senior member of a group

dear *a.* **1** much loved **2** esteemed **3** costly **4** earnest —*n.* darling

dearth (durth) *n.* scarcity

death *n.* **1** a dying or being dead **2** cause of death

death′less *a.* immortal

death′ly *a.* characteristic of death —*adv.* extremely

deb *n.* [Col.] debutante

de·ba·cle (də bäk′əl) *n.* sudden disaster

de·bar′ *v.* **–barred′, –bar′ring** exclude (*from*)

de·bark′ *v.* leave a ship or aircraft —**de′bar·ka′tion** *n.*

de·base′ *v.* to lower in quality, etc. —**de·base′ment** *n.*

de·bate′ *v.* argue in a formal way —*n.* formal argument —**de·bat′a·ble** *a.* —**de·bat′er** *n.*

de·bauch′ *v.* to corrupt —*n.* orgy —**de·bauch′er·y** *n., pl.* **–ies**

de·ben′ture (-chər) *n.* bond issued by a corporation, etc.

de·bil′i·tate′ *v.* make weak —**de·bil′i·ta′tion** *n.*

de·bil′i·ty *n.* weakness

deb′it *n.* entry in an account of money owed —*v.* enter as a debt

deb′o·nair′, deb′o·naire′ (-ner′) *a.* elegant and gracious; urbane

de·brief′ *v.* receive information from about a recent mission

de·bris′ (də brē′) *n.* broken, scattered remains; rubbish

debt (det) *n.* **1** something owed **2** state of owing

debt′or *n.* one owing a debt

de·bunk′ *v.* to expose the false claims, etc. of

de·but′ (dā byōō′, dē-) *n.* **1** first public appearance, as of an actor **2** a formal introduction into society

deb′u·tante′ (-tänt′) *n.* girl making a social debut

dec′ade′ *n.* ten-year period

dec′a·dence *n.* a declining, as in morals or art —**dec′a·dent** *a., n.*

de·caf′fein·at′ed (-kaf′ə nāt′-) *a.* having its caffeine removed

de′cal′ *n.* picture for transfer from prepared paper

Dec′a·logue′, Dec′a·log′ *n.* [*sometimes* d-] Ten Commandments

de·camp′ *v.* leave secretly

de·cant′ *v.* pour off gently

de·cant′er *n.* decorative bottle for serving wine

de·cap′i·tate′ *v.* behead —**de·cap′i·ta′tion** *n.*

de·cath′lon′ *n.* contest of ten track and field events

de·cay′ *v.* **1** fall into ruin **2** rot —*n.* a decaying; rot

de·cease′ *n.* death

de·ceased′ *a.* dead —**the deceased** dead person(s)

de·ceit′ (-sēt′) *n.* **1** act of deceiving **2** deceitful quality —**de·ceit′ful** *a.*

de·ceive′ *v.* make believe what is not true; mislead

de·cel′er·ate′ (-sel′-) *v.* to slow down —**de·cel′er·a′tion** *n.*

De·cem′ber *n.* 12th month

de′cent *a.* **1** proper **2** respectable **3** adequate —**de′cen·cy** *n.*

de·cen′tral·ize′ *v.* shift power from main to local units

de·cep′tion *n.* **1** a deceiving **2** illusion or fraud —**de·cep′tive** *a.*

dec′i·bel′ (des′-) *n.* unit for measuring loudness of sound

de·cide′ *v.* **1** settle by passing judgment **2** make up one's mind

de·cid′ed *a.* definite —**de·cid′ed·ly** *adv.*

de·cid′u·ous (-sij′ōō-) *a.* shedding leaves annually

dec′i·mal *a.* based on the number ten —*n.* a fraction with a denominator of ten or a power of ten, shown by a point (**decimal point**) before the numerator

dec′i·mate′ *v.* destroy or kill a large part of

de·ci′pher (-sī′-) *v.* translate from code or illegibility

de·ci′sion (-sizh′ən) *n.* **1** a deciding **2** judgment **3** determination

de·ci′sive (-sī′siv) *a.* **1** conclusive **2** showing decision

deck *n.* **1** floor of a ship **2** pack of playing cards —*v.* adorn; trim

de·claim′ *v.* speak in a loud, rhetorical way —**dec′la·ma′tion** *n.*

de·clare′ *v.* **1** announce formally **2** say emphatically —**dec′la·ra′tion** *n.* —**de·clar′a·tive** *a.*

de·clas′si·fy *v.* make (secret documents) public and available

de·clen'sion n. grammatical inflection of nouns, etc.

de·cline' v. 1 slope downward 2 lessen, as in force 3 refuse politely 4 *Gram.* give inflected forms of —n. 1 a failing, decay, etc. 2 downward slope

de·cliv'i·ty n. downward slope

de·code' v. translate (a coded message) into plain language

dé·col·le·té (dā käl'ə tā') a. cut low so as to bare the neck and shoulders

de·com·pose' v. 1 break up into basic parts 2 rot —de·com·po·si'tion n.

de·com·press' v. free from air pressure —de·com·pres'sion n.

de·con·gest'ant n. medicinal relief for congestion, as of nasal passages

de·con·tam'i·nate v. to rid of harmful substance

dé·cor, de·cor (dā kôr') n. decorative scheme

dec·o·rate' v. 1 adorn; ornament 2 give a medal to —dec'o·ra·tive a. —dec'o·ra'tor n. —dec'o·ra'tion n.

de·co'rum n. proper behavior, speech, etc. —dec'o·rous a. —dec'o·rous·ly adv.

de·cou·page, dé·cou·page (dā' kōō pàzh') n. the cutting out of designs from paper, etc. and mounting them on wood, etc.

de'coy n. artificial bird, etc. used as a lure —v. lure

de·crease' (or dē'krēs') v. grow or make less or smaller —n. a decreasing

de·cree' n. official order; edict —v. –creed', –cree'ing order by decree

de·crep'it a. old and worn out —de·crep'i·tude' n.

de·crim'i·nal·ize' v. eliminate or reduce the penalties for

de·cry' v. –cried', –cry'ing to denounce; censure

ded'i·cate v. 1 set apart formally 2 devote 3 inscribe —ded'i·ca'tion n.

de·duce' v. conclude by reasoning; infer

de·duct' v. subtract or take away —de·duct'i·ble a.

de·duc'tion n. 1 a deducing or deducting 2 amount deducted 3 conclusion

deed n. 1 act 2 feat of courage, etc. 3 legal document transferring property —v. to transfer by deed

deem v. think; believe

de·em'pha·size' v. make less important

deep a. 1 extending far down, in, or back 2 hard to understand 3 involved (*in*) 4 of low pitch 5 intense —n. deep place or part —adv. far down, etc. —deep'en v.

deep'-dish' pie n. pie baked in a deep dish with top crust only

deep'freeze' v. freeze (food) suddenly so as to preserve

deep'-fry' v. fry in deep pan of boiling fat or oil

deep'-seat'ed a. firmly fixed: also deep'-root'ed

deep space n. outer space

deer n., pl. deer hoofed, cud-chewing animal, the male of which bears antlers

de·es'ca·late' v. reduce in scope

de·face' v. mar

de fac'to a., adv. existing but not officially approved

de·fame' v. slander —def'a·ma'tion n.

de·fault' v., n. fail(ure) to do or pay as required

de·feat' v. 1 win victory over 2 frustrate —n. a defeating or being defeated

de·feat'ist n., a. (one) too readily accepting defeat

def'e·cate' v. excrete waste matter from bowels

de·fect' (v.: dē fekt') n. imperfection; fault —v. to desert —de·fec'tion n. —de·fec'tive a., n.

de·fend' v. 1 protect 2 support by speech or act 3 *Law* act for (an accused) —de·fend'er n.

de·fend'ant n. *Law* person sued or accused

de·fense' n. 1 a defending against attack 2 something that defends 3 defendant and his counsel —de·fense'less a. —de·fen'sive a., n.

de·fer' (-fur') v. –ferred', –fer'ring 1 postpone 2 to yield in opinion, etc.

def'er·ence n. 1 a yielding in opinion, etc. 2 respect

de·fer'ment n. a deferring or postponing

de·fi'ance n. open resistance to authority —de·fi'ant a.

de·fi'cien·cy (-fish'ən-) n., pl. –cies shortage; lack —de·fi'cient a.

deficiency disease n. disease due to lack of vitamins, minerals, etc. in the diet

def'i·cit (-sit) n. amount by which a sum of money is less than expected, etc.

de·file' v. dirty; sully —n. narrow pass

de·fine' v. 1 mark the limits of 2 state the meaning of —def'i·ni'tion n.

def'i·nite (-nit) a. 1 having exact limits 2 explicit 3 certain

de·fin'i·tive (-tiv) a. 1 conclusive 2 most nearly complete

de·flate' v. 1 collapse by letting out air 2 lessen in amount, importance, etc. —de·fla'tion n.

de·flect' v. turn to one side

de·fog'ger n. device for clearing moisture from a window in a car, etc.

de·fo'li·ant n. chemical that strips plants of leaves

de·fo'li·ate' v. remove leaves from (trees, etc.)

de·for'est v. clear (land) of trees or forest —**de·for·est·a'tion** n.

de·form' v. mar the form of —**de·form'i·ty** n., pl. **–ties**

de·formed' a. misshapen

de·fraud' v. cheat

de·fray' v. pay (the cost)

de·frost' v. rid or become rid of frost or ice

deft a. quick and skillful

de·funct' a. no longer existing

de·fuse' v. 1 remove a fuse from 2 make less tense, etc.

de·fy' (-fī') v. **–fied', –fy'ing 1** resist openly 2 dare

de·gen'er·ate' (-āt'; a., n.; -ət) v. lose normal or good qualities —a. deteriorated —n. a degenerate person —**de·gen'er·a·cy** n. —**de·gen'er·a'tion** n.

de·grade' v. lower in rank, value, etc. —**deg'ra·da'tion** n.

de·gree' n. 1 successive step in a series 2 intensity, extent, etc. 3 rank given to a college graduate 4 unit of measure, as for angles, temperature, etc.

de·hu'man·ize' v. deprive of human qualities —**de·hu'man·i·za'tion** n.

de·hu'mid·i·fy' v. **–fied', –fy'ing** remove moisture from (air, etc.) —**de·hu'mid'i·fi'er** n.

de·hy'drate' v. remove water from —**de'hy·dra'tion** n.

de·ice' v. to melt ice from (something) —**de·ic'er** n.

de'i·fy' v. **–fied', –fy'ing** make a god of —**de'i·fi·ca'tion** (-fi-) n.

deign (dān) v. condescend

de'ism' n. belief in God on purely rational grounds —**de'ist** n.

de'i·ty n., pl. **–ties** god or goddess

dé·jà vu (dā'zhä vōō') n. [Fr.] feeling that one has been in a place or has had an experience before

de·ject'ed a. sad; depressed

de·jec'tion n. depression; sadness

de·lay' v. 1 put off; postpone 2 make late; detain —n. a delaying

de·lec'ta·ble a. delightful

de'lec·ta'tion n. delight

del'e·gate (-gət; v.: -gāt') n. representative —v. 1 appoint as delegate 2 entrust to another

del'e·ga'tion n. group of delegates

de·lete' (-lēt') v. take out (a word, etc.) —**de·le'tion** n.

del'e·te'ri·ous (-tir'ē-) a. harmful to health, etc.

del'i n. [Col.] delicatessen

de·lib'er·ate' (-āt'; a.: -ət) v. consider

carefully —a. 1 done on purpose 2 not rash or hasty 3 unhurried —**de·lib'er·a'tion** n.

del'i·ca·cy n. 1 delicate quality 2 pl. **–cies** a choice food; dainty

del'i·cate a. 1 fine and lovely 2 fragile or frail 3 needing care 4 sensitive 5 considerate and tactful —**del'i·cate·ly** adv.

del'i·ca·tes'sen n. shop selling meats, fish, cheeses, etc.

de·li'cious (-lish'əs) a. very pleasing, esp. to taste or smell

de·light' v. please greatly —n. great pleasure —**de·light'ful** a.

de·lim'it v. fix the limits of

de·lin'e·ate' v. 1 draw; sketch 2 describe

de·lin'quent a. 1 not obeying duty or law 2 overdue —n. one guilty of minor crimes —**de·lin'quen·cy** n.

del'i·quesce' (-kwes') v. absorb moisture from the air

de·lir'i·um n. 1 temporary mental illness 2 wild excitement —**de·lir'i·ous** a.

de·liv'er v. 1 set free; rescue 2 assist in birth 3 utter 4 hand over 5 distribute 6 strike or throw —**de·liv'er·ance** n.

de·liv'er·y n., pl. **–ies** a delivering or something delivered

dell n. small valley

del·phin'i·um n. tall plant with flower spikes

del'ta n. 1 letter of Greek alphabet 2 soil deposit at a river mouth

de·lude' v. mislead

del'uge (-yōōj') n. 1 great flood 2 heavy rainfall —v. 1 to flood 2 overwhelm

de·lu'sion n. false, esp. psychotic, belief —**de·lu'sive** a.

de·luxe' a. very good; elegant

delve v. investigate

dem·a·gogue, dem·a·gog (dem'ə gäg') n. one who appeals to prejudices, etc. to win power —**dem'a·gog'y** (-gä'jē), **dem'a·gogu'er·y** (-gäg'ər ē) n.

de·mand' v. 1 ask for boldly 2 require —n. 1 strong request 2 requirement —**on de·mand** when presented for payment

de'mar·ca'tion, de'mar·ka'tion n. boundary line

de·mean' v. degrade

de·mean'or n. behavior

de·ment'ed a. mentally ill

de·men'tia (-shə) n. loss of mental powers

de·mer'it n. 1 fault 2 mark for poor work, etc.

demi– pref. half

dem'i·god' n. minor deity

dem'i·john' n. large, wicker-covered bottle

de·mil'i·ta·rize' v. to free from military control

de·mise' (-mīz') n. death

dem'i·tasse' (-tas') n. small cup of coffee

dem'o n., pl. **-mos** recording made to demonstrate a song, performer's talent, etc.

de·mo'bi·lize' v. to disband (troops)

de·moc'ra·cy n., pl. **-cies** 1 government in which the power is vested in all the people 2 equality of rights, etc. —**dem'o·crat'** n. —**dem'o·crat'ic** a. —**dem'o·crat'i·cal·ly** adv.

de·mog'ra·phy n. statistical study of populations —**dem'o·graph'ic** a.

de·mol'ish v. destroy; ruin —**dem'o·li'tion** n.

de'mon n. devil; evil spirit

de·mo'ni·ac' (-nē-) a. fiendish; frenzied: also **de'mo·ni'a·cal** (-nī'-)

de·mon'ic a. 1 of a demon 2 fiendish; frenzied

de'mon·ize' v. make as if a devil, evil person, etc. —**de'mon·i·za'tion** n.

dem'on·strate' v. 1 prove 2 explain with examples 3 show the working of 4 show feelings publicly —**de·mon'stra·ble** a. —**dem'on·stra'tion** n. —**dem'on·stra'tor** n.

de·mon'stra·tive a. 1 showing clearly 2 giving proof (of) 3 showing feelings openly

de·mor'al·ize' v. to lower in morale —**de·mor'al·i·za'tion** n.

de·mote' v. reduce in rank —**de·mo'tion** n.

de·mul'cent a., n. soothing (ointment)

de·mur' (-mur') v. **-murred', -mur'ring** to scruple (at) —n. objection

de·mure' (-myoor') a. coy

de·mur'rage (-mur'ij) n. 1 delay in shipping 2 compensation paid for this

den n. 1 animal's lair 2 haunt of thieves, etc. 3 small, cozy room

de·na'ture v. to make (alcohol) unfit to drink

de·ni'al n. 1 a denying 2 contradiction

de·ni'er (den'yər) n. unit to measure fineness of threads, as of nylon

den'i·grate' v. belittle —**den'i·gra'tion** n.

den'im n. coarse, twilled cotton cloth

den'i·zen n. inhabitant

de·nom'i·nate' v. to name

de·nom'i·na'tion n. 1 a name 2 specific class or kind 3 religious sect —**de·nom'i·na'tion·al** a.

de·nom'i·na'tor n. term below the line in a fraction

de·note' v. 1 indicate 2 mean explicitly —**de'no·ta'tion** n.

de·noue·ment, dé·noue·ment (dā'nōō män') n. unraveling of a plot

de·nounce' v. 1 accuse publicly 2 condemn strongly

dense a. 1 packed tightly 2 thick 3 stupid —**dense'ly** adv.

den'si·ty n. 1 number per unit 2 ratio of the mass of an object to its volume

dent n. slight hollow made in a surface by a blow —v. make a dent in

den'tal a. of the teeth

dental floss n. thread for removing food from the teeth

den'ti·frice (-fris) n. substance for cleaning teeth

den'tin (-tin) n. tissue under the enamel of teeth: also **den'tine'** (-tēn', -tin)

den'tist n. one who cares for and repairs teeth —**den'tist·ry** n.

den'ture n. often pl. set of artificial teeth

de·nude' v. make bare; strip

de·nun'ci·a'tion n. a denouncing

de·ny' v. 1 declare untrue 2 refuse to give, accept, etc. 3 deny oneself do without

de·o'dor·ize' v. counteract the odor of —**de·o'dor·ant** a., n. —**de·o'dor·iz'er** n.

de·part' v. 1 leave 2 die 3 deviate (from) —**de·par'ture** n.

de·part'ment n. 1 division 2 field of activity —**de·part'men'tal** a.

department store n. large retail store with different goods in each of many departments

de·pend' v. 1 be determined by something else 2 rely, as for support —**de·pend'ence** n. —**de·pend'en·cy** n., pl. **-cies** —**de·pend'ent** a., n.

de·pend'a·ble a. reliable —**de·pend'a·bil'i·ty** n.

de·pict' v. 1 represent by drawing, etc. 2 describe

de·pil'a·to'ry n., pl. **-ries**; a. (substance or device for) removing unwanted hair

de·plane' v. leave an airplane after it lands

de·plete' v. 1 empty (wholly) 2 exhaust —**de·ple'tion** n.

de·plore' v. be sorry about —**de·plor'a·ble** a.

de·ploy' v. Mil. spread out

de·po'nent (-pōn'-) n. Law one who testifies in writing under oath

de·pop'u·late' v. to reduce the population of

de·port' v. 1 behave (oneself) 2 expel (an alien) —**de'por·ta'tion** n.

de·port'ment n. behavior

de·pose' v. 1 remove from office 2 testify —**dep·o·si'tion** n.

de·pos'it v. 1 place for safekeeping 2 give as partial payment 3 set down —n. something deposited —**de·pos'i·tor** n.

de·pos'i·to'ry n., pl. **-ries** place to put things for safekeeping

de'pot (-pō) n. 1 warehouse 2 train or bus station

de·prave' v. make morally bad —**de·praved'** a. —**de·prav'i·ty** n.

dep're·cate' v. express disapproval of

—dep're·ca'tion n. —dep're·ca·to'ry a.

de·pre'ci·ate' (-shē-) v. 1 lessen in value 2 belittle —de·pre'ci·a'tion n.

dep're·da'tion n. a looting

de·press' v. 1 press down 2 sadden 3 lower in value, etc. —de·pres'sant a., n. —de·pressed' a.

de·pres'sion n. 1 a depressing 2 hollow place 3 dejection 4 period of reduced business and prosperity

de·prive' v. take away or withhold from —dep'ri·va'tion n.

depth n. 1 distance from the top or back 2 deepness 3 profundity 4 pl. deepest part —in depth comprehensively

dep'u·ta'tion n. delegation

de·pute' v. 1 authorize as a deputy 2 appoint in one's place

dep'u·tize' v. make a deputy

dep'u·ty n., pl. -ties substitute or agent

de·rail' v. run off the rails —de·rail'ment n.

de·rail'leur (-lər) n. device to shift gears on a bicycle

de·range' v. 1 upset or disturb 2 make insane

der'by n., pl. -bies stiff felt hat with a round crown

de·reg'u·late' v. remove regulations governing —de·reg'u·la'tion n.

der'e·lict' a. 1 abandoned 2 negligent —n. thing or person abandoned as worthless —der'e·lic'tion n.

de·ride' v. to ridicule —de·ri'sion (-rizh'ən) n. —de·ri'sive (-rī'siv) a.

de·rive' v. 1 take or get (from) 2 deduce 3 originate 4 trace to a source —der'i·va'tion n. —de·riv'a·tive n.

der'ma·ti'tis n. inflammation of the skin

der'ma·tol'o·gy n. study of the skin and its diseases —der'ma·tol'o·gist n.

der'o·gate' v. detract; disparage —der'o·ga'tion n.

de·rog'a·to'ry a. detracting; disparaging

der'rick n. 1 machine for moving heavy objects 2 framework for drilling, as over an oil well

der'ri·ere' (-ē er') n. the buttocks

der'vish n. Muslim ascetic

de·sal'i·na'tion (-sal'-) n. removal of salt from sea water to make it drinkable

de·scend' (-send') v. 1 move down 2 come from earlier times 3 derive 4 to make a sudden attack (on) —de·scent' n.

de·scend'ant n. offspring of a certain ancestor

de·scribe' v. 1 picture in words; tell about 2 trace the outline of —de·scrip'tion n. —de·scrip'tive a.

de·scry' v. -scried', -scry'ing catch sight of

des'e·crate' v. violate the sacredness of;

profane —des'e·cra'tion n.

de·seg're·gate' v. end racial segregation (in) —de·seg're·ga'tion n.

de·sen'si·tize' v. make less sensitive —de·sen'si·ti·za'tion n.

de·sert' (-zurt') v. abandon —n. often pl. reward or punishment —de·ser'tion n.

des'ert n. arid, sandy region

de·serve' v. be worthy (of) —de·serv'ing a.

des'ic·cate' v. dry up

de·sid'er·a'tum (-sid'ə rä'-, -zid'-) n., pl. -ta something needed and wanted

de·sign' v. 1 to plan 2 contrive —n. 1 plan; scheme 2 purpose 3 a pattern —by design purposely —de·sign'er n. —de·sign'ing a., n.

des'ig·nate' v. 1 to point out; specify 2 appoint —des'ig·na'tion n.

de·sire' v. wish or long for; want —n. 1 a wish 2 thing wished for 3 sexual appetite —de·sir'a·ble a. —de·sir'ous a.

de·sist' v. stop; cease

desk n. writing table

des'o·late (-lət; v.: -lāt') a. 1 lonely; forlorn 2 uninhabited 3 laid waste —v. make desolate —des'o·la'tion n.

de·spair' v. lose hope —n. loss of hope

des'per·a'do (-pə rä'-) n., pl. -does or -dos reckless outlaw

des'per·ate (-ət) a. 1 reckless from despair 2 serious —des'per·a'tion n.

des·pi'ca·ble a. deserving scorn; contemptible

de·spise' v. 1 to scorn 2 loathe

de·spite' prep. in spite of

de·spoil' v. rob; plunder

de·spond'en·cy n. loss of hope; dejection: also de·spond'ence —de·spond'ent a.

des'pot n. tyrant —des·pot'ic a. —des'pot·ism' n.

des·sert' n. sweet dish ending a meal

des'ti·na'tion n. place to which one is going

des'tine (-tin) v. 1. head for, as by fate —destined for bound or intended for

des'ti·ny n., pl. -nies (one's) fate

des'ti·tute' a. needy —destitute of lacking —des'ti·tu'tion n.

de·stroy' v. 1 tear down; demolish 2 ruin 3 kill

de·stroy'er n. fast warship

de·struct' n. deliberate destruction of a rocket, etc. —v. be automatically destroyed

de·struc'tion n. ruin —de·struc'tive a.

des'ul·to'ry a. 1 not methodical 2 random

de·tach' v. unfasten and remove —de·tach'a·ble a.

de·tached' a. aloof; impartial

de·tach'ment n. 1 separation 2 troops on special task 3 impartiality or aloofness

de·tail′ (*or* dē′tāl) *v.* 1 tell minutely 2 *Mil.* choose for a special task —*n.* 1 minute account 2 small part 3 *Mil.* special task —**in detail** item by item

de·tain′ *v.* 1 keep in custody 2 delay —**de·ten′tion** *n.*

de·tect′ *v.* discover (thing hidden, etc.) —**de·tec′tion** *n.* —**de·tec′tor** *n.*

de·tec′tive *n.* one who investigates crimes, etc.

dé·tente, de·tente (dā tänt′) *n.* lessening of tension between nations

de·ten′tion *n.* a detaining

de·ter′ *v.* **-terred′, -ter′ring** keep someone from an action —**de·ter′ment** *n.* —**de·ter′rent** *a., n.*

de·ter′gent *n.* a cleansing (substance)

de·te′ri·o·rate′ (-tir′ē-) *v.* make or become worse —**de·te′ri·o·ra′tion** *n.*

de·ter′mi·nant *n.* thing that determines

de·ter′mi·na′tion *n.* 1 firm intention 2 firmness of purpose

de·ter′mine *v.* 1 set limits to 2 decide; resolve 3 to find out exactly —**de·ter′mined** *a.*

de·test′ *v.* hate —**de·test′a·ble** *a.* —**de′tes·ta′tion** *n.*

de·throne′ *v.* to depose (a monarch)

det′o·nate′ *v.* explode —**det′o·na′tor** *n.*

de′tour *v., n.* (use) an indirect or alternate road

de·tox′ [Col.] *v.* detoxify —*n.* detoxification

de·tox′i·fy′ *v.* **-fied′, -fy′ing** remove a poison or poisonous effect from —**de·tox′i·fi·ca′tion** *n.*

de·tract′ *v.* take something desirable (*from*) —**de·trac′tor** *n.*

det′ri·ment *n.* damage; harm —**det′ri·men′tal** *a.*

de·tri′tus (-trī′-) *n.* debris; spec., rock fragments

deuce (dōōs, dyōōs) *n.* 1 playing card with two spots 2 in tennis, tie score after which one side must score twice in a row to win

de·val′ue *v.* lessen the value of: also **de·val′u·ate′**

dev′as·tate′ *v.* destroy; ravage —**dev′as·ta′tion** *n.*

de·vel′op *v.* 1 grow, improve, expand, etc. 2 work out by degrees 3 treat (film) to make the picture visible —**de·vel′op·ment** *n.* —**de·vel′op·men′tal** *a.*

de′vi·ant *n., a.* (person) deviating from social norms

de′vi·ate′ *v.* turn aside; diverge —**de′vi·a′tion** *n.*

de·vice′ *n.* 1 a plan or scheme 2 mechanical contrivance 3 a design

dev′il *n.* 1 evil spirit; esp., [*often* D–] Satan 2 wicked or reckless person —*v.* 1 to sea-

son (food) highly 2 tease —**dev′il·try** *n., pl.* **-tries** —**dev′il·ish** *a.*

dev′il-may-care′ *a.* reckless; careless

dev′il·ment *n.* mischief

dev′il's-food′ cake *n.* rich chocolate cake

de′vi·ous *a.* roundabout

de·vise′ (-vīz′) *v.* 1 to plan 2 bequeath by will

de·vi′tal·ize′ *v.* weaken

de·void′ *v.* empty (*of*)

de·volve′ *v.* pass (*on*) to another, as a duty

de·vote′ *v.* 1 dedicate 2 apply to a purpose

de·vot′ed *a.* 1 dedicated 2 loyal —**de·vot′ed·ly** *adv.*

dev′o·tee′ (-tē′, -tā′) *n.* one devoted to something

de·vo′tion *n.* 1 a devoting 2 *pl.* prayers 3 loyalty

de·vour′ *v.* 1 eat up hungrily 2 take in eagerly

de·vout′ *a.* pious or sincere

dew *n.* atmospheric moisture condensing on cool surfaces at night —**dew′y** *a.*, **-i·er, -i·est**

dew′lap′ *n.* loose skin under the throat of cattle, etc.

dex′ter·ous (-tər əs, -trəs) *a.* skillful in using one's hands, mind, etc.: also **dex′trous** (-trəs) —**dex·ter′i·ty** *n.*

dex′trose (-trōs) *n.* sugar found in plants and animals

di- *pref.* twice; double

di·a·be·tes (dī′ə bēt′ēz, -bēt′is) *n.* disease marked by excess sugar in the blood and urine —**di′a·bet′ic** *a., n.*

di·a·bol′ic *a.* devilish: also **di′a·bol′i·cal**

di′a·crit′ic *n.* a mark to show pronunciation —**di′a·crit′i·cal** *a.*

di′a·dem′ *n.* a crown

di′ag·no′sis *n.* identifying of a disease —**di′ag·nose′** *v.* —**di′ag·nos′tic** *a.*

di·ag′o·nal *a.* slanting between opposite corners —*n.* a diagonal line

di′a·gram′ *n., v.* sketch, plan, etc. to help explain

di′al *n.* 1 face of a clock, meter, etc. for indicating some variable 2 rotating disk, or numbered buttons, on a telephone —*v.* 1 tune in on a radio dial 2 call by using a telephone dial

di′a·lect′ *n.* form of speech peculiar to a region, group, etc. —**di′a·lec′tal** *a.*

di′a·lec′tic *n.* *often pl.* logical examination of ideas

di′a·logue′, di′a·log′ *n.* conversation

di·al′y·sis (-al′ə-) *n.* separation of impurities in the blood by diffusion through a membrane

di·am′e·ter *n.* 1 straight line through the

center of a circle, etc. 2 its length —di′a-met′ri-cal a.

di-a-mond (dī′mənd, dī′ə-) n. 1 precious gem of great brilliance 2 figure shaped like ♦ 3 baseball field

di′a-mond-back′ n. large, poisonous rattlesnake

di-a-per (dī′pər, dī′ə-) n. cloth worn about a baby's crotch —v. to put a diaper on

di-aph′a-nous a. gauzy

di′a-phragm′ (-fram′) n. 1 wall of muscle between chest and abdomen 2 vibrating disk producing sound waves 3 vaginal contraceptive

di′ar-rhe′a (-rē′ə)n. very loose bowel movements

di′a-ry n., pl. **-ries** daily record of personal notes

di-as-to-le (dī as′tə lē′) n. usual rhythmic expansion of the heart —di-a-stol′ic a.

di′a-ther′my n. use of electric current to heat tissues below the skin

di-a-ton′ic a. of any standard musical scale of eight tones

di′a-tribe′ n. denunciation

dice n.pl., sing. **die** small, spotted cubes, used in gambling —v. cut into cubes

di-chot′o-my (-kät′-) n., pl. **-mies** division into two parts

dick n. [Sl.] detective

dick′er v. barter; haggle

dick′ey n. detachable collar or shirt front

dic′tate′ v. 1 speak (something) for another to write down 2 command —n. an order —dic·ta′tion n.

dic′ta′tor n. an absolute ruler; tyrant —dic′ta·to′ri·al a. —dic·ta′tor·ship′ n.

dic′tion n. 1 choice of words 2 enunciation

dic′tion-ar′y n., pl. **-ies** book of words alphabetically listed and defined

dic′tum n. formal opinion

did v. pt. of DO

di-dac′tic a. meant to teach

did′dle v. [Col.] 1 to cheat 2 waste time

did′n't did not

die v. **died**, **dy′ing** 1 stop living 2 to end 3 [Col.] wish very much —n. 1 sing. of DICE 2 device for molding, stamping, etc. —die away (or down) cease gradually —die off die one by one until all are gone —die out go out of existence

die′-hard′, **die′hard′** n. stubborn, resistant person

die-sel (dē′zəl, -səl) n. [often D—] internal-combustion engine that burns fuel oil

di′et n. 1 one's usual food 2 special food taken as for health —v. follow a diet, as to lose weight —di′e-tar′y a.

di′e-tet′ics n. study of food as needed for health

di′e-ti′tian (-tish′ən) n. planner of diets —di′e-tet′ic a.

dif′fer v. 1 to be different or unlike 2 disagree

dif′fer-ence n. 1 a being unlike 2 distinguishing characteristic 3 disagreement 4 amount by which two quantities differ —dif′fer-en′tial (-shəl) a., n.

dif′fer-ent a. 1 not alike 2 distinct 3 unusual

differential gear (or **gear′ing**) n. arrangement allowing one axle to turn faster than another

dif′fer-en′ti-ate′ (-shē-) v. 1 be or make different 2 distinguish between

dif′fi-cult′ a. hard to do, learn, deal with, etc. —dif′fi-cul′ty n., pl. **-ties**

dif′fi-dent a. shy —dif′fi-dence n.

dif-frac′tion n. a breaking up of light as into the colors of the spectrum

dif-fuse′ (-fyōōs′; v.: -fyōōz′) a. 1 spread out 2 wordy —v. spread widely —dif-fu′sion n.

dig v. **dug**, **dig′ging** 1 turn up (soil), as with a spade 2 make or get by digging —n. [Col.] sarcastic remark

di′gest′ (v.: di jest′) n. summary —v. 1 to change (food) in the stomach, etc. so that it can be absorbed 2 absorb mentally —di-gest′i-ble a. —di-ges′tion n. —di-ges′tive a.

dig′it (dij′-) n. 1 any number from 0 to 9 2 a finger or toe

dig′i-tal a. 1 of a digit 2 showing time, temperature, etc. in a row of digits 3 designating a recording method in which sounds or images are converted into electronic bits 4 of a computer processing data by electronic means

digital clock n. timepiece that shows the time in a row of digits

dig′i-tal′is n. 1 plant with long spikes of flowers 2 heart medicine made from its leaves

dig′ni-fied′ a. having or showing dignity

dig′ni-fy′ v. **-fied′**, **-fy′ing** give dignity to

dig′ni-tar′y n., pl. **-ies** person of high position

dig′ni-ty n. 1 worthiness 2 high repute; honor 3 calm stateliness

di-gress′ v. wander from the subject, as in talking —di-gres′sion n. —di-gres′sive a.

dike n. embankment to hold back the sea, etc.

di-lap′i-dat′ed (-dāt′-) a. falling to pieces

di′late′ (or dī lāt′) v. make or become wider —di-la′tion n.

dil′a-to′ry a. 1 causing delay 2 slow

di-lem′ma n. perplexing situation

dil′et-tante′ (-tänt′, tant′) n. dabbler in the arts

dil′i·gent a. careful and industrious —**dil′i·gence** n.

dill n. plant with aromatic seeds

dil′ly-dal′ly v. –**lied,** –**ly·ing** waste time

di·lute′ v. weaken as by mixing with water —a. diluted —**di·lu′tion** n.

dim a. **dim′mer, dim′mest** not bright or clear —v. **dimmed, dim′ming** make or grow dim

dime n. silver coin equal to ten cents

di·men′sion n. **1** any measurable extent **2** pl. measurement in length, breadth, and, often, height

di·min′ish v. lessen

di·min′u·tive a. tiny

dim′i·ty n. a thin cotton cloth

dim′mer n. device for dimming electric lights

dim′ple n. small, natural hollow, as on the cheek

dim′wit′ n. [Sl.] stupid person —**dim′wit′ted** a.

din n. confused clamor —v. **dinned, din′ning 1** make a din **2** keep repeating

din′-din′ n. [Col.] dinner

dine v. **1** eat dinner **2** give dinner to

din′er n. **1** railroad car for serving meals **2** restaurant built like this

di·nette′ (-net′) n. small dining room or alcove

ding n. sound of a bell: also **ding′-dong′**

din·ghy (diṇ′gē) n., pl. –**ghies** small boat

din′gy (-jē) a. –**gi·er,** –**gi·est** dirty; shabby

dink′y a. –**i·er,** –**i·est** [Col.] small

din′ner n. chief daily meal

din′ner·ware′ n. dishes

di′no·saur′ (-sôr′) n. huge extinct reptile

dint n. force: now chiefly in by dint of

di′o·cese (-sis, -sēz′) n. district headed by a bishop —**di·oc′e·san** (-äs′ə sən) a.

di′ode′ n. device used esp. as a rectifier

di·ox′ide n. oxide with two oxygen atoms per molecule

dip v. **dipped, dip′ping 1** plunge into liquid for a moment **2** scoop up **3** sink or slope down —n. **1** a dipping **2** sauce into which food may be dipped **3** downward slope

diph·the·ri·a (dif thir′ē ə) n. acute infectious disease of the throat

diph′thong (dif′-, dip′-) n. sound made by gliding from one vowel to another in one syllable

di·plo′ma n. certificate of graduation from a school

di·plo′ma·cy n. **1** the conducting of relations between nations **2** tact —**dip′lo·mat′** n. —**dip′lo·mat′ic** a.

dip′per n. long-handled cup, etc. for dipping

dip′so·ma′ni·a n. insatiable desire for alcoholic drink —**dip′so·ma′ni·ac′** n.

dip′stick′ n. graduated rod for measuring depth

dire a. **1** dreadful; terrible **2** urgent

di·rect′ a. **1** straight **2** frank **3** immediate **4** exact —v. **1** manage; guide **2** order **3** aim —adv. directly —**di·rect′ly** adv. —**di·rec′tor** n.

direct current n. electric current moving in one direction

di·rec′tion n. **1** management; guidance **2** pl. instructions **3** an order **4** the point one faces or moves toward —**di·rec′tion·al** a.

di·rec′tive (-tiv) n. an order

di·rec′to·ry n., pl. –**ries** book of names and addresses of a specific group

dire′ful a. dire

dirge (durj) n. song of mourning

dir·i′gi·ble (-ij′ə-) n. airship

dirk n. long dagger

dirt n. **1** dust, filth, etc. **2** earth; soil

dirt′y a. –**i·er,** –**i·est 1** soiled **2** obscene **3** mean **4** unfair **5** rough —v. –**ied,** –**y·ing** to soil —**dirt′i·ness** n.

dis v. **dissed, dis′sing** [Sl.] **1** insult **2** disapprove of

dis– pref. **1** the opposite of **2** reverse the action of

dis·a′ble v. make unable or unfit; cripple —**dis′a·bil′i·ty** n., pl. –**ties**

dis′a·buse′ v. rid of false ideas

dis′ad·van′tage n. drawback; handicap; detriment —**dis′ad·van·ta′geous** a.

dis′ad·van′taged a. poor

dis·af·fect′ v. make hostile —**dis·af·fec′tion** n.

dis′a·gree′ v. **1** differ **2** quarrel **3** give distress: with with —**dis′a·gree′ment** n.

dis′a·gree′a·ble a. **1** unpleasant **2** quarrelsome

dis·al·low′ v. reject

dis′ap·pear′ v. **1** go out of sight **2** cease being —**dis′ap·pear′ance** n.

dis′ap·point′ v. spoil the hopes of —**dis′ap·point′ment** n.

dis′ap·prove′ v. **1** have an unfavorable opinion **2** reject —**dis′ap·prov′al** n.

dis·arm′ v. **1** remove weapons from **2** make friendly —**dis·ar′ma·ment** n.

dis′ar·range′ v. disorder

dis′ar·ray′ n., v. disorder

dis′as·sem′ble v. take apart

dis′as·so′ci·ate′ v. sever association with

dis·as′ter n. sudden misfortune; calamity —**dis·as′trous** a.

dis′a·vow′ v. deny knowing or approving —**dis′a·vow′al** n.

dis·band′ v. break up

dis·bar′ v. –**barred′,** –**bar′ring** deprive of the right to practice law

dis·be·lieve' v. fail to believe (in) —**dis'be·lief'** n.

dis·burse' v. pay out

disc n. 1 disk 2 phonograph record, etc.

dis·card' (n.: dis'kärd') v. throw away —n. thing discarded

disc brake n. brake with two pads that press on a disc

dis·cern' (di surn', -zurn') v. perceive —**dis·cern'i·ble** a.

dis·cern'ing a. astute

dis·charge' (n.: dis'chärj') v. 1 dismiss 2 unload 3 shoot 4 emit 5 do (a duty) —n. a discharging or thing discharged

dis·ci'ple n. follower; pupil

dis'ci·pli·nar'i·an n. enforcer of discipline

dis'ci·pline (-plin) n. 1 orderly training or conduct 2 punishment —v. 1 train; control 2 punish —**dis'ci·pli·nar'y** a.

disc jockey n. one who plays recordings on the radio, in a nightclub, etc.

dis·claim' v. disown; deny

dis·claim'er n. denial or rejection of responsibility

dis·close' v. to reveal —**dis·clo'sure** n.

dis'co n., pl. **-cos** nightclub for dancing to recorded music

dis·col'or v. to stain; tarnish —**dis'col·or·a'tion** n.

dis·com'fit v. upset; embarrass —**dis·com'fi·ture** n.

dis·com'fort n. lack of comfort or cause of this

dis'com·mode' v. to inconvenience

dis'com·pose' v. fluster —**dis'com·po'sure** n.

dis'con·cert' v. confuse

dis'con·nect' v. to separate

dis'con·nect'ed a. 1 separated 2 incoherent

dis·con'so·late (-lat) a. very unhappy

dis'con·tent' n. dissatisfaction: also **dis'con·tent'ment** n.

dis'con·tent'ed a. not contented

dis'con·tin'ue v. to stop —**dis'con·tin'u·ous** a.

dis'cord' n. 1 disagreement 2 dissonance; harsh sound —**dis·cord'ant** a.

dis'co·thèque' (-tek') n. disco

dis'count' (v.: also dis kount') v. 1 deduct, as from a price 2 disregard in part or entirely —n. deduction

dis·coun'te·nance v. embarrass

dis·cour'age v. 1 deprive of hope or confidence 2 dissuade 3 work against —**dis·cour'age·ment** n.

dis'course' n. talk or formal lecture —v. to talk

dis·cour'te·ous a. impolite —**dis·cour'te·sy** n.

dis·cov'er v. 1 be the first to find, see, etc. 2 find out —**dis·cov'er·y** n., pl. **-ies**

dis·cred'it v. 1 disbelieve 2 cast doubt on 3 disgrace —n. 1 doubt 2 disgrace

dis·creet' a. careful; prudent —**dis·creet'ly** adv.

dis·crep'an·cy n., pl. **-cies** inconsistency

dis·crete' (di skrēt') a. separate; distinct

dis·cre'tion (di skresh'ən) n. 1 freedom to decide 2 prudence —**dis·cre'tion·ar'y** a.

dis·crim'i·nate' v. 1 distinguish 2 show partiality —**dis·crim'i·na'tion** n. —**dis·crim'i·na·to'ry** a.

dis·cur'sive (-siv) a. rambling

dis'cus n. heavy disk thrown in a contest

dis·cuss' v. talk or write about —**dis·cus'sion** n.

dis·dain' v., n. scorn —**dis·dain'ful** a.

dis·ease' n. (an) illness —**dis·eased'** a.

dis'em·bark' v. go ashore

dis'em·bod'y v. -bod'ied, -bod'y·ing to free from bodily existence

dis'en·chant' v. disillusion —**dis'en·chant'ment** n.

dis'en·gage' v. disconnect

dis'en·tan'gle v. extricate

dis·fa'vor n. 1 dislike 2 a being disliked

dis·fig'ure v. spoil the looks of; mar —**dis·fig'ure·ment** n.

dis·fran'chise' v. deprive of the right to vote: also **dis'en·fran'chise'**

dis·gorge' v. to vomit

dis·grace' n. shame; dishonor —v. to bring shame upon —**dis·grace'ful** a.

dis·grun'tle v. make sulky

dis·guise' (-gīz') v. make unrecognizable —n. thing, as clothing or makeup, used for disguising

dis·gust' n. sickening dislike; loathing —v. cause disgust in —**dis·gust'ed** a. —**dis·gust'ing** a.

dish n. 1 plate, etc. for food 2 kind of food

dis·ha·bille' (dis'ə bēl') n. state of being only partly dressed

dish'cloth' n. cloth for washing dishes

dis·heart'en v. discourage

di·shev'el v. muss up (hair, etc.); rumple

dis·hon'est a. not honest —**dis·hon'es·ty** n.

dis·hon'or n., v. shame; disgrace —**dis·hon'or·a·ble** a.

dish'wash'er n. a person or machine that washes dishes

dis'il·lu'sion v. 1 to free from illusion 2 make disappointed

dis'in·cline' v. make unwilling

dis'in·clined' a. unwilling

dis'in·fect' v. kill bacteria in —**dis'in·fect'ant** n.

dis'in·gen'u·ous (-jen'-) a. not candid

dis'in·her'it v. to deprive of an inheritance

dis·in'te·grate v. separate into parts; break up —**dis·in'te·gra'tion** n.

dis·in·ter·est·ed a. 1 impartial 2 indifferent

dis·joint' v. 1 put out of joint 2 dismember

dis·joint'ed a. without unity or coherence

disk n. 1 thin, flat, circular thing 2 thin plate for storing computer data 3 disc

disk·ette (di sket') n. floppy disk

disk jockey n. disc jockey

dis·like' v., n. (have) a feeling of not liking

dis·lo·cate' v. 1 put out of joint 2 disarrange —**dis'lo·ca'tion** n.

dis·lodge' v. force from its place

dis·loy'al a. not loyal —**dis·loy'al·ty** n.

dis'mal (diz'-) a. dreary

dis·man'tle v. take apart

dis·may' v. make afraid; daunt —n. loss of courage

dis·mem'ber v. tear apart —**dis·mem'ber·ment** n.

dis·miss' v. 1 request or allow to leave 2 discharge 3 set aside —**dis·miss'al** n.

dis·mount' v. 1 get off 2 take from its mounting

dis'o·bey' v. refuse or fail to obey —**dis'o·be'di·ence** n. —**dis'o·be'di·ent** a.

dis·or'der n. 1 confusion 2 commotion 3 ailment —v. to cause disorder in —**dis·or'der·ly** a.

dis·or'gan·ize' v. throw into confusion —**dis·or'gan·i·za'tion** n.

dis·o'ri·ent' v. confuse mentally

dis·own' v. refuse to acknowledge as one's own

dis·par'age v. belittle —**dis·par'age·ment** n.

dis·pa·rate (-rət) a. not alike

dis·par'i·ty n., pl. **–ties** difference; unlikeness

dis·pas'sion·ate a. free from emotion or bias

dis·patch' (n. 2, 3: also dis'pach') v. 1 send 2 finish quickly 3 kill —n. 1 speed 2 message 3 news story —**dis·patch'er** n.

dis·pel' v. **-pelled'**, **-pel'ling** drive away

dis·pen'sa·ble a. not important

dis·pen'sa·ry n., pl. **–ries** place in a school, etc. for getting medicines or first aid

dis·pense' v. 1 deal out 2 prepare and give out —**dispense with** do without —**dis·pen·sa'tion** n. —**dis·pens'er** n.

dis·perse' v. scatter —**dis·per'sal** n. —**dis·per'sion** n.

dis·pir'it·ed a. dejected

dis·place' v. 1 move from its usual place 2 replace —**dis·place'ment** n.

dis·placed' person n. one forced from his or her country, esp. by war

dis·play' v. to show; exhibit —n. exhibition

dis·please' v. annoy; offend —**dis·pleas'ure** n.

dis·port' v. 1 to play 2 amuse (oneself)

dis·pose' v. 1 arrange 2 incline mentally —**dispose of** 1 settle 2 get rid of —**dis·pos'a·ble** a. —**dis·pos'al** n. —**dis·po·si'tion** n.

dis·pos'er n. 1 one that disposes 2 kitchen device for grinding up garbage

dis'·pos·sess' v. to force to give up property; oust

dis'pro·por'tion n. lack of proportion —**dis'pro·por'tion·ate** a.

dis·prove' v. prove false

dis·pu·ta'tious a. fond of arguing

dis·pute' v., n. 1 debate 2 quarrel —**in dispute** not settled —**dis·put'a·ble** a. —**dis'pu·ta'tion** n.

dis·qual'i·fy' v. **-fied'**, **-fy'ing** make ineligible —**dis·qual'i·fi·ca'tion** n.

dis·qui'et v. make uneasy

dis'qui·si'tion n. treatise

dis're·gard' v. ignore —n. lack of attention

dis're·pair' n. worn state

dis're·pute' n. bad reputation —**dis·rep'u·ta·ble** a.

dis're·spect' n. lack of respect —**dis're·spect'ful** a.

dis·robe' v. undress

dis·rupt' v. break up; disorder —**dis·rup'tion** n. —**dis·rup'tive** a.

dis·sat·is·fy' v. **-fied'**, **-fy'ing** make discontented —**dis'sat·is·fac'tion** n.

dis·sect' (or dī'sekt') v. 1 cut apart so as to examine 2 analyze closely —**dis·sec'tion** n.

dis·sem'ble v. feign; pretend

dis·sem'i·nate' v. spread widely —**dis·sem'i·na'tion** n.

dis·sen'sion n. strife

dis·sent' v. disagree —n. difference of opinion

dis'ser·ta'tion n. formal essay

dis·serv'ice n. harm

dis'si·dence n. disagreement —**dis'si·dent** a., n.

dis·sim'i·lar a. not alike

dis'si·pate' v. 1 vanish or dispel 2 squander 3 indulge in wild, harmful pleasure —**dis'si·pa'tion** n.

dis·so'ci·ate' v. sever association (with)

dis'so·lute' a. dissipated and immoral

dis'so·lu'tion n. a dissolving or breaking up

dis·solve' v. 1 melt 2 pass or make pass into solution 3 break up 4 end 5 disappear or make disappear

dis'so·nance n. lack of harmony, esp. in sound; discord —**dis'so·nant** a.

dis·suade' (-swād') v. cause to turn from a purpose

dis·taff' n. staff for holding flax, wool, etc. in spinning —a. female

dis'tance n. 1 length between two points 2 aloofness 3 faraway place

dis'tant a. 1 far apart; remote 2 away 3 aloof

dis·taste' n. dislike —**dis·taste'ful** a.

dis·tem'per n. infectious disease of dogs, etc.

dis·tend' v. swell —**dis·ten'tion, dis·ten'sion** n.

dis·till' v. subject to or obtain by distillation

dis'til·la'tion n. process of purifying a mixture by heating it and condensing the vapor

dis·till'er·y n., pl. **-ies** place for distilling liquor —**dis·till'er** n.

dis·tinct' a. 1 not alike 2 separate 3 definite

dis·tinc'tion n. 1 a keeping distinct 2 quality that differentiates 3 fame; eminence

dis·tinc'tive a. making distinct

dis·tin'guish v. 1 perceive or show a difference 2 classify 3 make famous —**dis·tin'guish·a·ble** a. —**dis·tin'guished** a.

dis·tort' v. 1 twist out of shape 2 misrepresent —**dis·tor'tion** n.

dis·tract' v. 1 divert (the mind, etc.) 2 confuse 3 derange —**dis·trac'tion** n.

dis·traught' a. 1 harassed 2 crazed

dis·tress' v., n. pain, trouble, worry, etc.

dis·trib'ute v. 1 deal out 2 spread out 3 arrange —**dis'tri·bu'tion** n.

dis·trib'u·tor n. 1 one who distributes, deals in a product, etc. 2 device distributing electricity to spark plugs in a gasoline engine

dis'trict n. 1 division of a state, etc. 2 region

district attorney n. prosecuting attorney of a district

dis·trust' n. lack of trust —v. to mistrust —**dis·trust'ful** a.

dis·turb' v. 1 break up the quiet or settled order of 2 make uneasy 3 interrupt —**dis·turb'ance** n.

dis·u·nite' v. divide; separate

dis·use' n. lack of use

ditch n. channel dug out for drainage, etc. —v. [Sl.] get rid of

dith'er n. excited state

dit'to mark n. mark (") in lists showing the item above is to be repeated: also **dit'to**, pl. **-tos**

dit'ty n., pl. **-ties** short, simple song

di·u·ret'ic (-yōō-) a., n. (substance) increasing urine discharge

di·ur'nal (-ur'-) a. daily

di'va (dē'-) n. prima donna

di·van' (dī'van) n. large sofa

dive v. **dived** or **dove, dived, div'ing** 1 plunge into water 2 plunge suddenly or deeply —n. 1 sudden plunge 2 [Col.] cheap saloon

di·verge' v. 1 branch off 2 deviate

di'vers (-vərz) a. various

di·verse' (-vurs') a. 1 different 2 varied

di·ver'si·fy' v. **-fied', -fy'ing** vary

di·ver'sion n. 1 a diverting 2 pastime; amusement

di·ver'si·ty n. variety

di·vert' v. 1 turn aside (from) 2 amuse

di'ver·tic·u·li'tis (dī'-) n. inflammation of sac opening out from intestine

di·vest' v. strip or deprive (of)

di·vide' v. 1 separate into parts 2 apportion 3 Math. separate into equal parts by a divisor —n. ridge —**di·vis'i·ble** (-viz'-) a.

div'i·dend' n. 1 number to be divided 2 sum divided among stockholders, etc.

di·vine' a. 1 of God or a god 2 excellent —n. clergyman —v. 1 prophesy 2 guess

divining rod n. forked stick alleged to dip when held over underground water

di·vin'i·ty n. 1 a being divine 2 pl. **-ties** a god

di·vi'sion n. 1 a dividing 2 thing that divides 3 segment, group, etc. 4 section of an army corps

di·vi'sive a. causing disagreement

di·vi'sor n. number by which the dividend is divided

di·vorce' n. 1 legal dissolution of a marriage 2 separation —v. separate from, as by divorce

di·vor·cée' (-sā') n. divorced woman —**di·vor·cé'** (-sā') n.masc.

di'vot n. turf dislodged by a golf club

di·vulge' v. make known

diz'zy a. **-zi·er, -zi·est** 1 giddy; confused 2 causing dizziness —**diz'zi·ly** adv. —**diz'zi·ness** n.

DJ n. disc jockey

DNA n. basic material of chromosomes that transmits hereditary pattern

do v. **did, done, do'ing** 1 perform (an action) 2 finish 3 cause 4 deal with as required 5 have as one's work 6 get along 7 be adequate Do is also an important auxiliary verb —**do in** [Sl.] kill —**do's** (or **dos**) **and don'ts** [Col.] things permitted and things forbidden —**do without** get along without —**have to do with** relate to —**do'er** n.

Do'ber·man pin'scher (-shər) n. large dog with short, dark hair

doc·ile (däs'əl) a. easy to train —**do·cil'i·ty** n.

dock n. 1 landing pier; wharf 2 water between piers 3 place for the accused in a courtroom —v. 1 bring or come to a dock 2 cut short 3 deduct from

dock'et n. list of cases to be tried by a law court

dock'yard' n. shipyard

doc'tor n. 1 person with the highest degree

from a university 2 physician or surgeon —v. [Col.] 1 try to heal 2 tamper with

doc′tri·naire′ (-ner′) a. adhering strictly to a doctrine

doc′trine (-trin) n. something taught, as a religious tenet

doc′u·ment n. written record relied on as evidence —v. to support by documents

doc′u·men·ta·ry a. 1 of or supported by documents 2 recording news events dramatically —n., pl. —ries documentary film

dod′der v. shake as from old age

dodge v. 1 move quickly aside 2 avoid; evade —n. 1 a dodging 2 a trick

do′do n. 1 large extinct bird 2 [Sl.] stupid person

doe n. female deer, rabbit, etc.

does (duz) v. pres. t. of DO: used with he, she, or it

doe′skin′ n. leather from the skin of a female deer

does′n't does not

doff v. take off; remove

dog n. 1 domesticated animal of the wolf family 2 mean fellow —v. dogged, dog′ging follow like a dog

dog′ear′ n. turned-down corner of a page —dog′eared′ a.

dog′ged a. stubborn

dog′ger·el n. trivial, monotonous verse

do·gie (dō′gē) n. stray calf

dog′ma n. strict doctrine

dog·mat′ic a. 1 of a dogma 2 positive in stating opinion; arrogant —dog·mat′i·cal·ly adv. —dog′ma·tism′ n.

dog′wood′ n. tree with pink or white flowers

doi′ly n., pl. —lies small mat to protect a table, etc.

do′ings n.pl. actions

dol′drums (dōl′-) n.pl. low spirits

dole n. money paid to the unemployed by the government: with the —v. give (out) sparingly

dole′ful a. sad; sorrowful

doll n. child's toy made to resemble a person

dol′lar n. U.S. monetary unit, equal to 100 cents

dol′lop n. small quantity of something soft

dol′ly n., pl. —lies 1 [Col.] doll 2 low, wheeled frame for moving heavy objects

dol′men (dōl′-, däl′-) n. monument with stone laid across upright stones

do·lor·ous (dō′lar-, däl′ar-) a. sorrowful

dol′phin n. sea mammal with a beaklike snout

dolt n. stupid person —dolt′ish a.

-dom suf. 1 rank or domain of 2 state of being

do·main′ n. 1 territory under one ruler 2 field of activity

dome n. large, round roof

do·mes′tic a. 1 of home or family 2 of one's country 3 tame —n. a maid, cook, etc. —do·mes′ti·cal·ly adv. —do′mes·tic′i·ty n.

do·mes′ti·cate v. to tame —do·mes′ti·ca′tion n.

dom′i·cile (-sīl′) n. home

dom′i·nate v. 1 rule or control 2 to rise high above —dom′i·nance n. —dom′i·nant a. —dom′i·na′tion n.

dom′i·neer′ v. rule harshly

do·min′ion n. 1 rule; power 2 governed territory

dom′i·noes′, dom′i·nos′ n. game with tiles marked with dots

don v. donned, don′ning put on (clothes)

don n. Spanish gentleman

do′nate′ v. give; contribute —do·na′tion n.

done (dun) v. pp. of DO

don′key n., pl. —keys horse-like animal with long ears

don′ny·brook′ n. rowdy fight

do′nor n. one who donates

don't do not

doo′dle v., n. scribble

doom n. 1 a judgment 2 fate 3 ruin —v. 1 condemn 2 destine to a tragic fate

dooms′day′ n. the end of the world

door n. 1 movable panel for closing an entrance 2 entrance, with or without a door: also door′way′ n. —out of doors outdoors

door′bell′ n. bell rung by one wishing to enter

door′man′ n., pl. —men′ one whose work is opening doors, hailing taxicabs, etc.

door′step′ n. step from outer door to path, lawn, etc.

dope n. 1 [Col.] narcotic 2 [Sl.] information 3 [Col.] stupid person —v. to drug

dor′mant a. 1 sleeping 2 quiet; inactive

dor′mer n. an upright window structure in a sloping roof

dor′mi·to·ry n., pl. —ries 1 room with many beds 2 building with many bedrooms Also dorm

dor′mouse′ n., pl. —mice′ small, squirrel-like rodent

dor′sal a. of the back

do′ry n., pl. —ries small, flat-bottomed fishing boat

dose n. amount of medicine taken at one time —v. to give doses of —dos′age n.

do·sim′e·ter n. device that measures radiation absorbed

dos′si·er (-sē ā′) n. documents about a person

dost (dust) v. [Ar.] do: used with thou

dot n. tiny mark or round spot —v. **dot'ted, dot'ting** mark with dots

dot'age (dōt'-) n. feebleness of old age

dot'ard n. one in his or her dotage

dote v. be too fond

doth (duth) v. [Ar.] does

dot'-ma'trix a. of computer printing in which characters are formed of tiny dots

dou'ble a. 1 of or for two 2 twice as much or as many —adv. twofold or twice —n. 1 twice as much or as many 2 a duplicate 3 Baseball hit putting the batter on second —v. 1 make or become double 2 fold 3 duplicate 4 turn backward 5 serve two purposes, etc. —**on the double** [Col.] quickly

double bass (bās) n. largest, deepest-toned instrument of violin family

dou'ble-cross' v. [Col.] to betray —**dou'ble-cross'er** n.

double date [Col.] n. social engagement shared by two couples —**dou'ble-date'** v.

dou'ble-deck'er n. 1 vehicle, etc. with upper deck 2 [Col.] two-layer sandwich

dou'ble-head'er n. two games played in succession

dou'ble-park' v. to park next to another vehicle parked at a curb

double play n. baseball play that puts out two players

double standard n. rules applied unequally

dou'blet n. formerly, man's tight jacket

dou'bly adv. twice

doubt (dout) v. 1 be uncertain about 2 to disbelieve —n. 1 wavering of belief 2 uncertainty —**no doubt** certainly —**doubt'ful** a.

doubt'less adv. certainly

douche (dōōsh) n. liquid jet for cleaning a body part —v. use a douche (on)

dough (dō) n. 1 thick mixture of flour, liquid, etc. for baking 2 [Sl.] money

dough'nut' n. small, fried cake, usually ring-shaped

dour (door, dour) a. gloomy

douse (dous) v. 1 thrust into liquid 2 drench 3 [Col.] extinguish (a light)

dove (dōv) v. alt. pt. of DIVE

dove (duv) n. kind of pigeon

dove'tail' (duv'-) n. joint formed by fitting together wedge-shaped parts —v. join closely, as with dovetails

dow'a-ger n. wealthy widow

dow'dy a. **-di-er, -di-est** not neat or not stylish

dow'el n. peg fitted into holes to join two pieces

dow'er n. widow's inheritance

down adv. 1 to or in a lower place, state, etc. 2 to a later time 3 in cash 4 in writing —a. 1 descending 2 in a lower place 3 gone, paid, etc. down 4 discouraged —prep. down toward, into, along, etc. —v. put down —n. 1 descent 2 misfortune 3 soft feathers or hair 4 pl. high, grassy land —**down with!** overthrow!

down'cast' a. 1 directed downward 2 sad

down'er n. [Sl.] any sedative

down'fall' n. sudden fall, as from power

down'grade' n. downward slope —adv., a. downward —v. to demote

down'heart'ed a. sad

down'hill' adv., a. down a slope; downward

down'-home' a. of rural folk or rural life

down'play' v. minimize

down'pour' n. a heavy rain

down'right' adv. thoroughly —a. 1 utter 2 plain

down'scale' a. for people who are not affluent or stylish

down'spout' n. pipe for carrying rainwater from roof gutter

Down's syndrome n. congenital disease marked by mental deficiency

down'stairs' adv., a. to or on a lower floor —n. lower floor or floors

down'swing' n. 1 downward swing of golf club 2 downward trend

down'-to-earth' a. sensible

down'town' n. city's business district

down'trod'den a. oppressed

down'turn' n. downward trend

down'ward adv., a. toward a lower place, etc.: also **down'wards** adv.

down'y a. soft and fluffy

dow'ry n. property a bride brings to her husband at marriage

doze v., n. sleep; nap

doz'en n. set of twelve

drab a. **drab'ber, drab'best** dull —**drab'ness** n.

draft n. 1 drink 2 rough sketch of a writing 3 plan 4 current of air 5 written order for money 6 selection for compulsory military service 7 depth of water a ship displaces —v. 1 select to serve 2 make a plan, outline, etc. for —a. drawn from a cask —**on draft** ready to be drawn from a cask

draft'ee' n. one drafted for military service

drafts'man n., pl. **-men** one who draws plans of structures or machinery

draft'y a. **-i-er, -i-est** open to drafts of air

drag v. **dragged, drag'ging** 1 pull or be pulled with effort, esp. along the ground 2 search (a river bottom, etc.) as with a net 3 pass slowly —n. 1 hindrance 2 [Sl.] puff of a cigarette, etc.

drag'net' n. 1 net dragged along water bottom 2 a system for catching criminals

drag'on n. large, mythical reptile breathing out fire

drag'on·fly' n., pl. **–flies'** long insect with four wings

dra·goon' n. armed cavalryman —v. force to do something

drag race n. race between cars accelerating from a standstill on a short, straight course

drain v. 1 draw off (liquid, etc.) gradually 2 empty 3 exhaust, as energy 4 flow off —n. channel; pipe

drain'age n. 1 a draining or system for draining 2 that which is drained off

drain'pipe' n. large pipe carrying off water, etc.

drake n. male duck

dram n. 1 apothecaries' weight, ⅛ oz. 2 small drink of alcoholic liquor

dra'ma n. 1 a play 2 art of writing and staging plays

dra·mat'ic n. 1 of drama 2 vivid, exciting, etc.

dra·mat'ics n. performing or producing of plays

dram'a·tist n. playwright

dram'a·tize' v. 1 make into a drama 2 regard or show in a dramatic manner —**dram'a·ti·za'tion** n.

drank v. pt. of DRINK

drape v. cover or hang as with cloth in loose folds —n. curtain: usually used in pl.

drap'er·y n., pl. **–ies** curtain

dras'tic a. severe; harsh —**dras'ti·cal·ly** adv.

draught (draft) n., v., a. draft

draughts (drafts) n.pl. [Br.] game of checkers

draw v. **drew, drawn, draw'ing** 1 pull 2 attract 3 inhale 4 take out; get 5 come; move 6 write (a check) 7 deduce 8 stretch 9 make (lines, pictures, etc.) as with a pencil —n. 1 stalemate 2 thing that attracts

draw'back' n. disadvantage

draw'bridge' n. bridge that can be raised

drawer (drôr) n. 1 sliding box in a table, etc. 2 pl. underpants

draw'ing n. 1 art of sketching 2 picture sketched

drawing card n. entertainment drawing large audience

drawing room n. parlor

drawl n. slow, prolonged manner of speech —v. to speak with a drawl

drawn a. haggard

dray n. wagon for heavy loads

dread (dred) v. await with fear or distaste —n. fear —a. inspiring fear —**dread'ful** a.

dream n. 1 images, etc. seen during sleep 2 reverie 3 fond hope —v. **dreamed** or

dreamt (dremt), **dream'ing** have dreams —**dream'y** a.

drear'y a. **–i·er, –i·est** dismal —**drear'i·ness** n.

dredge n. apparatus for scooping up mud, etc. as in deepening channels —v. 1 enlarge with a dredge 2 gather (up) as with a dredge 3 sprinkle with flour

dregs n.pl. 1 particles at the bottom in a liquid 2 most worthless part

drench v. soak

dress v. 1 clothe 2 adorn 3 treat (a wound, etc.) 4 prepare (a fowl, etc.) by skinning, etc. —n. 1 clothes 2 woman's garment —**dress up** improve the look of, as by decorating —**dress'mak'er** n.

dress'er n. chest of drawers with a mirror

dress'ing n. 1 bandages, etc. 2 salad sauce 3 stuffing for roast fowl

dress'y a. **–i·er, –i·est** elegant

drew v. pt. of DRAW

drib'ble v. 1 flow in drops 2 drool —n. dribbling flow

drib'let n. small amount

dried v. pt. & pp. of DRY

dri'er n. device or substance that dries

drift v. be carried along, as by a current —n. 1 snow, etc. driven into a heap 2 trend 3 meaning —**drift'er** n.

drift'wood' n. wood that has drifted ashore

drill n. 1 tool for boring 2 systematic training 3 seeding machine 4 coarse, twilled cloth —v. 1 bore with a drill 2 train systematically —**drill'er** n.

drink v. **drank, drunk, drink'ing** swallow (liquid) —n. 1 liquid for drinking 2 alcoholic liquor

drip v. **dripped, drip'ping** fall or let fall in drops —n. a dripping

drip'-dry' a. of clothing that needs little or no ironing

drive v. **drove, driv'en** (driv'-), **driv'ing** 1 force to go, do, pierce, etc. 2 operate, or go in, a vehicle —n. 1 trip in a vehicle 2 paved road 3 energy 4 urge 5 campaign —**drive at** to mean —**driv'er** n.

drive'-in' n. place for eating, etc. in one's car

driv'el n. silly tale

drive'way' n. path for cars

driz'zle v., n. rain in fine, mistlike drops

drogue (drōg) n. device towed behind aircraft to slow it

droll a. quaintly amusing

drom'e·dar'y n., pl. **–ies** one-humped camel

drone n. 1 male honeybee 2 constant hum —v. 1 to hum 2 talk monotonously

drool v. drip saliva

droop v. 1 sink or bend down 2 lose vitality

—n. a drooping **—droop′y** *a.*, **-i·er, -i·est** **—droop′i·ly** *adv.*

drop *n.* 1 small, round mass, as of falling liquid 2 tiny amount 3 sudden fall 4 distance down **—v. dropped, drop′ping** 1 fall or let fall 2 to send 3 utter (a hint, etc.) **—drop in** visit **—drop out** stop taking part **—drop′per** *n.*

drop′cloth′ *n.* large cloth, etc. used as cover when painting

drop′-off′ *n.* a steep drop or decline

drop′out′ *n.* student who leaves school before graduating

drop′sy *n.* abnormal amount of fluid in the body

dross *n.* rubbish; refuse

drought (drout) *n.* spell of dry weather

drove *v.* pt. of DRIVE **—n.** herd of cattle, etc.

drown *v.* 1 die or kill by suffocation in water 2 muffle (sound, etc.): with *out*

drowse *v.* be sleepy; doze **—drows′y** *a.*, **-i·er, -i·est**

drub *v.* **drubbed, drub′bing** 1 thrash 2 defeat **—drub′bing** *n.*

drudge *n.* one who does hard or dull work **—v.** do such work **—drudg′er·y** *n.*

drug *n.* 1 medicinal substance 2 narcotic **—v. drugged, drug′ging** add or give a drug to

drug′gist *n.* pharmacist **—drug′store′** *n.*

dru′id *n.* member of religious order in ancient British Isles and France

drum *n.* 1 hollow cylinder covered with a membrane and used as a percussion instrument 2 container, as for oil 3 eardrum **—v. drummed, drum′ming** beat as on a drum **—drum up** solicit (business) **—drum′mer** *n.*

drum′lin *n.* long ridge or hill

drum major *n.* one who leads a marching band **—drum ma′jor·ette′** (-et′) *n.fem.*

drum′stick′ *n.* 1 stick for beating a drum 2 lower leg of a cooked fowl

drunk *v.* pp. of DRINK **—a.** overcome by alcohol **—n.** [Sl.] drunken person **—drunk′ard** *n.*

drunk′en *a.* intoxicated **—drunk′en·ness** *n.*

dry *a.* **dri′er, dri′est** 1 not wet 2 lacking rain 3 thirsty 4 not sweet 5 matter-of-fact 6 dull **—v. dried, dry′ing** to make or become dry **—dry′ly** *adv.*

dry′ad *n.* tree nymph

dry′-clean′ *v.* to clean (garments) with a solvent, as naphtha **—dry cleaner** *n.*

dry′er *n.* a drier

dry goods *n.* cloth (products)

dry ice *n.* carbon dioxide in a solid state

dry run *n.* [Col.] rehearsal

dry′wall′ *n.* plaster board used for interior walls of a house, etc.

du′al *a.* 1 of two 2 double

du·al′i·ty *n.*, *pl.* **-ties** a being two, or double

dub *v.* **dubbed, dub′bing** 1 confer a title upon 2 insert (dialogue, etc.) in film soundtrack

du′bi·ous *a.* doubtful

du′cal *a.* of a duke

duc·at (duk′ət) *n.* a former European coin

duch′ess *n.* duke's wife

duch′y *n.*, *pl.* **-ies** land ruled by a duke

duck *n.* 1 flat-billed, webfooted swimming bird 2 cloth like canvas but lighter **—v.** 1 dip under water briefly 2 bend suddenly, as to avoid a blow 3 [Col.] avoid

duck′bill′ *n.* small, egg-laying water mammal

duck′ling *n.* young duck

duck′pins′ *n.* bowling game with small pins and balls

duct *n.* tube or channel for fluid **—duct′less** *a.*

duc′tile (-təl) *a.* 1 that can be drawn thin 2 easily led

dud *n.* [Col.] 1 bomb, etc. that fails to explode 2 failure

dude *n.* 1 dandy; fop 2 [Sl.] man or boy

dudg·eon (duj′ən) *n.* anger

due *a.* 1 owed 2 suitable 3 expected to arrive **—adv.** exactly **—n.** anything due **—due to** 1 caused by 2 [Col.] because of

due bill *n.* receipt for money paid, exchangeable for goods, etc. only

du′el *n.* planned formal fight between two armed persons **—v.** fight a duel **—du′el·ist** *n.*

dues *n.pl.* 1 fee or tax 2 money paid for membership

du·et′ *n.* musical composition for two performers

duf′fel bag *n.* large canvas bag for clothes, etc.: also **duf′fle bag**

duf′fer *n.* [Col.] unskilled golfer

dug *v.* pt. & pp. of DIG

dug′out′ *n.* 1 boat hollowed out of a log 2 *Baseball* shelter for players when not in the field

DUI *n.* citation for driving under the influence of alcohol, etc.

duke *n.* nobleman next in rank to a prince **—duke′dom** *n.*

dul′cet (-sət) *a.* pleasant to hear

dul′ci·mer (-sə-) *n.* stringed musical instrument

dull *a.* 1 stupid 2 sluggish 3 boring 4 not sharp 5 not bright **—v.** make or become dull **—dul′ly** *adv.*

dull′ard *n.* stupid person

du′ly *adv.* properly

dumb a. 1 unable to talk 2 silent 3 [Col.] stupid

dumb'bell' n. short bar joining two weights, used in exercising

dumb'wait'er n. small elevator for food, etc.

dum'found', dumb'found' v. make speechless; amaze

dum'my n., pl. **-mies** 1 humanlike figure for displaying clothes 2 imitation 3 [Sl.] stupid person —a. sham

dump v. 1 unload in a heap 2 throw away —n. a place for dumping rubbish —(down) **in the dumps** dejected

dump'ling n. 1 piece of boiled dough 2 crust filled with fruit

Dump'ster trademark large, metal trash bin —n. [**d-**] such a trash bin

dump truck n. truck with tilting container for unloading

dump'y a. **-i-er, -i-est** 1 squat; stumpy 2 [Col.] ugly; run-down

dun a. dull grayish-brown —v. dunned, dun'ning to demand money owed

dunce n. stupid person

dune n. hill of drifted sand

dung n. animal excrement

dun'ga-rees' n.pl. work clothes of coarse cotton

dun'geon (-jən) n. dark underground prison

dunk v. 1 dip (food) into coffee, etc. 2 Basketball thrust (the ball) into the basket

du'o n., pl. **-os** performers of a duet

du'o-de'num n. first section of small intestine

dupe n. person easily tricked —v. deceive

du'plex' n. house with two separate family units

du'pli-cate (-kət; v.: -kāt´) a. 1 double 2 exactly alike —n. exact copy —v. 1 make a copy 2 make happen again —**du'pli-ca'tion** n. —**du'pli-ca'tor** n.

du-plic'i-ty (-plis´-) n., pl. **-ties** cunning deception

du'ra-ble a. lasting a long time —**du'ra-bil'i-ty** n.

du-ra'tion n. time that a thing continues or lasts

du-ress' n. coercion

dur'ing prep. 1 throughout 2 in the course of

du-rum (door´əm) n. hard wheat used for pasta, etc.

dusk n. evening twilight

dust n. finely powdered matter, esp. earth —v. 1 sprinkle with powder 2 wipe dust from —**dust'y** a., **-i-er, -i-est**

dust'pan' n. pan into which floor dust is swept

Dutch a., n. (of) the people or language of the Netherlands —**go Dutch** [Col.] have

each pay own expenses

du'ti-ful a. showing respect; obedient: also **du'te-ous** —**du'ti-ful-ly** adv.

du'ty n., pl. **-ies** 1 respect owed, as to parents 2 sense of obligation, justice, etc. 3 thing one must do 4 tax, as on imports

dwarf n. unusually small being or thing —v. 1 stunt in growth 2 make seem small —a. stunted

dwell v. dwelt or dwelled, dwell'ing make one's home —**dwell on** (or upon) talk or think about at length

dwelling (place) n. residence

DWI n. citation for driving while intoxicated

dwin'dle v. decrease

dyb-buk (dib´ək) n. dead person's spirit in Jewish folklore

dye n. coloring matter in solution —v. dyed, dye'ing to color with a dye —**dy'er** n.

dyed'-in-the-wool' a. not changing, as in beliefs

dy'ing v. ppr. of DIE

dy-nam'ic a. 1 of energy 2 energetic; forceful —**dy-nam'i-cal-ly** adv.

dy-nam'ics n. science of motions produced by forces

dy'na-mism' n. energetic quality

dy'na-mite' n. powerful explosive —v. blow up with dynamite

dy'na-mo' n., pl. **-mos'** 1 generator: earlier term 2 dynamic person

dy'nas-ty n., pl. **-ties** family line of rulers

dys-en'ter-y (dis´-) n. disease characterized by bloody diarrhea

dys-func'tion n. abnormal functioning —**dys-func'tion-al** a.

dys-lex'i-a n. impairment of reading ability —**dys-lec'tic, dys-lex'ic** a., n.

dys-pep'si-a n. indigestion

E

each a., pron. every one of two or more —adv. apiece

ea'ger a. keenly desiring

ea'gle n. large bird of prey with sharp vision

ea'gle-eyed' a. having keen vision

ear n. 1 organ of hearing 2 sense of hearing 3 attention 4 grain-bearing spike of a cereal plant

ear'drum' n. thin membrane inside the ear

earl n. Br. nobleman

ear'ly adv., a. **-li-er, -li-est** 1 near the beginning 2 before the expected or usual time

ear'mark' v. reserve for a special purpose

ear'muffs' n.pl. warm covering for the ears

earn v. 1 receive for one's work 2 get as deserved 3 gain as profit

ear´nest a. serious or sincere —**in earnest** 1 serious 2 with determination

earn´ings n.pl. 1 wages 2 profits, interest, etc.

ear´phone´ n. receiver as for a telephone, held to the ear

ear´ring´ n. ear ornament

ear´shot´ n. distance within which a sound can be heard

ear´split´ting a. very loud

earth n. 1 the planet we live on 2 land 3 soil

earth´en a. made of clay

earth´en·ware´ n. dishes, etc. made of baked clay

earth´ling n. human being

earth´ly a. 1 terrestrial 2 worldly 3 conceivable

earth´quake´ n. a shaking of the crust of the earth

earth´work´ n. embankment; fortification

earth´worm´ n. common worm in soil

earth´y a. **-i·er, -i·est** 1 of or like earth 2 coarse

ease n. 1 comfort 2 poise 3 facility —v. 1 to comfort 2 relieve 3 facilitate 4 shift carefully

ea·sel (ē´zal) n. a stand to hold an artist's canvas

ease´ment n. right one may have in another's land

eas´i·ly adv. 1 with ease 2 without a doubt

east n. 1 direction in which sunrise occurs 2 region in this direction —[E—] the Orient —a., adv. in, toward, or from the east —**east´er·ly** a., adv. —**east´ern** a. —**east´ern·er** n. —**east´ward** a., adv. —**east´wards** adv.

Eas´ter n. spring Christian festival

eas´y a. **-i·er, -i·est** 1 not difficult 2 without worry, pain, etc. 3 comfortable 4 not stiff 5 not strict 6 unhurried —adv. [Col.] easily —**take it easy** [Col.] 1 refrain from anger, etc. 2 relax

eas´y·go´ing a. not worried, rushed, or strict

eat v. **ate, eat´en, eat´ing** 1 chew and swallow (food) 2 wear away, corrode, etc. 3 make by eating

eats n.pl. [Col.] food

eaves n.pl. projecting edge of a roof

eaves´drop´ v. **-dropped´, -drop´ping** listen secretly

ebb n., v. 1 flow back toward the sea: said of the tide 2 decline

eb´on·y n.,pl. **-ies** hard, dark, tropical wood —a. black

e·bul´lient (e bool´yant) a. bubbling with joy —**e·bul´lience** n.

ec·cen´tric (ek sen´-) a. 1 having its axis off center 2 odd in conduct —n. eccentric person —**ec´cen·tric´i·ty** (-tris´-) n.,pl. **-ties**

ec·cle´si·as´tic n. clergyman —a. ecclesiastical

ec·cle´si·as´ti·cal a. of the church or clergy

ech´e·lon´ (esh´-) n. 1 steplike formation of troops, ships, or planes 2 level of command

ech·o (ek´ō) n.,pl. **-oes** repetition of a sound by reflection of sound waves —v. 1 resound 2 repeat

é·clair (ā kler´) n. oblong pastry filled with custard, etc.

é·clat (ā klä´) n. 1 striking effect 2 fame

ec·lec´tic a. using various sources

e·clipse´ n. the obscuring of the sun by the moon, or of the moon by the earth's shadow —v. surpass

e·clip´tic n. sun's apparent annual path

e´co·cide´ n. destruction of the environment

e·col´o·gy n. science dealing with organisms in their environment —**ec´o·log´i·cal** a. —**e·col´o·gist** n.

ec´o·nom´ic (or ē´kə-) a. 1 of the management of income, expenditures, etc. 2 of economics

ec´o·nom´i·cal a. thrifty —**ec´o·nom´i·cal·ly** adv.

ec´o·nom´ics n. science that deals with the production, distribution, and use of wealth —**e·con´o·mist** n.

e·con´o·mize´ v. be thrifty

e·con´o·my n., pl. **-mies** 1 management of finances 2 thrift 3 system of producing and consuming wealth

ec´o·sys´tem (or ē´kō-) n. community of animals, plants, etc.

ec´ru (-rōō´) a., n. light tan

ec´sta·sy n.,pl. **-sies** overpowering joy —**ec·stat´ic** a.

ec´u·men´i·cal a. of the Christian Church as a whole

ec´u·men·ism´ n. movement to unify Christian churches

ec·ze´ma (or eg´-) n. itchy, scaly skin disease

-ed suf. 1 having or being 2 pt. and pp. ending of many verbs

E´dam (cheese) n. mild yellow cheese

ed´dy n., pl. **-dies** little whirlpool or whirlwind —v. **-died, -dy·ing** to whirl

e·de´ma n. dropsy

E´den Bible garden where Adam and Eve first lived

edge n. 1 blade's cutting side 2 brink 3 border 4 [Col.] advantage —v. 1 put an edge on 2 move sideways —**on edge** tense

edg´ing n. trimming on an edge

edg'y a. **-i·er, -i·est** tense

ed'i·ble a. fit to be eaten

e'dict' n. public order

ed'i·fice (-fis) n. large, imposing building

ed'i·fy' v. **-fied', -fy'ing** instruct or improve morally **—ed'i·fi·ca'tion** n.

ed'it v. 1 revise, select, etc. (writing) for publication 2 be in charge of (a newspaper, etc.) 3 prepare (film, etc.) by cutting, etc. **—ed'i·tor** n.

e·di'tion n. 1 form in which a book is published 2 total copies of a book, etc. published at one time

ed'i·to'ri·al n. article in a newspaper, etc. stating the opinions of the editor or publisher **—a.** of an editor **—ed'i·to'ri·al·ize'** v.

ed'u·cate' v. develop the knowledge, skill, etc. of by schooling **—ed'u·ca'tion** n. **—ed'u·ca'tor** n.

-ee suf. 1 recipient of an action 2 one in a specified condition

eel n. snakelike fish

e'er (er) adv. [Poet.] ever

ee'rie, ee'ry (ir'ē) a. **-ri·er, -ri·est** weird; uncanny **—ee'ri·ly** adv.

ef·face' v. erase; wipe out

ef·fect' n. 1 a result 2 influence 3 meaning 4 pl. belongings **—v.** bring about **—in ef·fect** 1 actually 2 in operation **—take effect** begin to act

ef·fec'tive a. 1 producing a desired result 2 in operation **—ef·fec'tive·ly** adv.

ef·fec'tu·al (-chōō əl) a. EFFECTIVE (a. 1) **—ef·fec'tu·al·ly** adv.

ef·fem'i·nate (-nət) a. showing womanly traits; unmanly

ef'fer·vesce' (-ves') v. to bubble **—ef'fer·ves'cent** a.

ef·fete' (-fēt') a. spent and sterile

ef·fi·ca'cious a. effective

ef·fi'cient (-fish'ənt) a. effective with a minimum of effort, expense, etc. **—ef·fi'cien·cy** n. **—ef·fi'cient·ly** adv.

ef'fi·gy n., pl. **-gies** statue or image; esp., a crude figure as for mock hanging

ef'flu·ent n. outflow of a sewer, etc.

ef'fort n. 1 use of energy to do something 2 attempt

ef·fron'ter·y n. impudence

ef·fu'sive (-fyōo'-) a. gushing

e.g. for example

e·gal'i·tar'i·an a. advocating full equality for all

egg n. 1 oval body from which young of birds, fish, etc. are hatched 2 ovum **—v.** to urge on

egg'head' n. [Sl.] intellectual

egg'nog' n. drink made of eggs, milk, sugar, etc.

egg'plant' n. large, purple, pear-shaped vegetable

e·gis (ē'jis) n. aegis

eg·lan·tine (-tīn', -tēn') n. kind of pink rose

e'go n. 1 the self 2 conceit

e'go·cen'tric a. self-centered

e'go·ism' n. 1 selfishness 2 conceit **—e'go·ist** n. **—e'go·is'tic** a.

e'go·tism' n. 1 excessive reference to oneself 2 self-conceit **—e'go·tist** n. **—e'go·tis'tic,** or **e'go·tis'ti·cal** a.

ego trip n. [Sl.] self-fulfilling or vain experience

e·gre'gious (-jəs) a. flagrant

e'gress' n. an exit

e'gret' n. heron having long, white plumes

E·gyp'tian (ē jip'shən) n., a. (native) of Egypt

eh (ā, e) int. sound expressing surprise, doubt, etc.

ei'der (ī'-) n. large sea duck with soft, fine down (**ei'der·down'**)

eight a., n. one more than seven **—eighth** a., n.

eight'een' a., n. eight more than ten **—eight'eenth'** a., n.

eight'y a., n., pl. **-ies** eight times ten **—eight'i·eth** a., n.

ei'ther (ē'thər, ī'-) a., pron. one or the other (of two) **—con.** correlative used with or **—adv.** any more than the other

e·jac'u·late' v. 1 eject (esp. semen) 2 exclaim suddenly **—e·jac'u·la'tion** n.

e·ject' v. throw out; expel

eke (ēk) v. 1 barely manage to make (a living): with out

e·lab'o·rate' (-rāt'; a.: -rət) v. add details **—a.** in great detail

é·lan (ā län') n. spirited self-assurance; dash

e·lapse' v. pass, as time

e·las'tic a. springing back to shape **—n.** band, etc. with rubber in it **—e·las·tic'i·ty** (-tis'-) n.

e·las'ti·cize' v. make elastic

e·late' v. make proud, happy, etc. **—e·la'tion** n.

el'bow' n. joint between the upper and lower arm **—v.** shove as with the elbows

elbow grease n. [Col.] hard work

el'bow·room' n. ample space

eld'er a. older **—n.** 1 older person 2 church official 3 shrub with dark berries

el'der·ber'ry n., pl. **-ries** 1 the elder 2 its berry

eld'er·ly a. somewhat old

eld'est a. oldest

e·lect' v. select, esp. by voting **—a.** specially chosen **—e·lec'tion** n.

e·lec'tion·eer' v. canvass votes in an election

e·lec'tive a. 1 filled by election 2 optional —n. optional subject in school

e·lec'tor n. 1 qualified voter 2 member of the electoral college

e·lec'tor·al college n. assembly that formally elects the U.S. president

e·lec'tor·ate (-ət) n. the body of qualified voters

e·lec'tric, e·lec'tri·cal a. of, charged with, or worked by electricity

e·lec·tri'cian (-trish'ən) n. one who installs and repairs electrical apparatus

e·lec·tric'i·ty (-tris'-) n. 1 form of energy with magnetic, chemical, and radiant effects 2 electric current

e·lec'tri·fy' v. –fied', –fy'ing 1 equip for the use of electricity 2 thrill

e·lec'tro·car'di·o·gram' n. tracing showing electrical changes in the heart

e·lec'tro·car'di·o·graph n. an instrument for making electrocardiograms

e·lec'tro·cute' v. kill by electricity —e·lec'tro·cu'tion n.

e·lec'trode' n. terminal of an electric source

e·lec'tro·en·ceph'a·lo·gram' (-sef'-) n. tracing showing electrical activity in brain

e·lec'tro·en·ceph'a·lo·graph' n. instrument for making electroencephalograms

e·lec'trol'y·sis (-träl'ə-) n. breakdown into ions of a chemical compound in solution by electrical current

e·lec'tro·lyte' (-līt') n. substance which in solution conducts electric current —e·lec'tro·lyt'ic (-lit'-) a.

e·lec'tro·mag'net n. soft iron core made magnetic by an electric current —e·lec'tro·mag·net'ic a. —e·lec'tro·mag·net'ism' n.

electromagnetic wave n. wave generated by an oscillating electric charge

e·lec'tro·mo'tive a. producing an electric current

e·lec'tron' n. negatively charged particle in an atom —e·lec'tron'ic a.

electronic mail n. messages sent to and from computer terminals, as by telephone lines

e·lec'tron'ics n. science of electronic action

electron microscope n. instrument using electrons to enlarge the image of an object

electron tube n. electronic device used in radio, etc.

e·lec'tro·plate' v. coat with metal by electrolysis

e·lec'tro·ther'a·py n. treatment of disease using electricity, as by diathermy

el'e·gant a. tastefully luxurious —el'e·gance n.

el'e·gy (-jē) n., pl. –gies poem lamenting a dead person —el·e·gi'ac (-jī'-) a.

el'e·ment n. 1 natural environment 2 basic part or feature 3 Chem. substance that cannot be separated into different substances except by nuclear disintegration —the elements wind, rain, etc. —el'e·men'tal a.

el'e·men'ta·ry a. of fundamentals; introductory

elementary school n. school of the first six (or eight) grades

el'e·phant n. huge, thick-skinned mammal with a long trunk and ivory tusks

el'e·phan'tine' (-tīn', -tēn') a. huge, clumsy, etc.

el'e·vate' v. 1 raise 2 raise in rank 3 elate

el'e·va'tion n. 1 high place 2 height, as above sea level

el'e·va'tor n. 1 suspended cage for hoisting or lowering goods or people 2 warehouse for grain

e·lev'en a., n. one more than ten —e·lev'enth a., n.

elf n., pl. elves small fairy —elf'in a.

e·lic'it (-lis'-) v. draw forth

e·lide' v. slur over

el'i·gi·ble a. qualified —n. eligible person —el'i·gi·bil'i·ty n.

e·lim'i·nate' v. 1 remove 2 excrete —e·lim'i·na'tion n.

e·lite' (ā lēt') n. best or most powerful part of a group

e·lit'ism' n. government or control by an elite —e·lit'ist a., n.

e·lix'ir (-ər) n. drug in alcoholic solution

elk n. large deer

ell n. 1 extension at right angles to main part 2 L-shaped joint 3 former measure of length equal to 45 inches

el·lipse' n. closed curve that is a symmetrical oval —el·lip'ti·cal a.

el·lip'sis n. 1 omission of a word or words 2 mark (...) showing this

elm n. tall shade tree

el'o·cu'tion n. art of public speaking

e·lon'gate' v. lengthen —e·lon'ga'tion n.

e·lope' v. run away to marry —e·lope'ment n.

el'o·quent a. vivid or forceful in expression —el'o·quence n.

else a. 1 different; other 2 in addition —adv. 1 otherwise 2 if not

else'where' adv. in or to some other place

e·lu'ci·date' v. explain

e·lude' v. escape; evade

e·lu'sive a. hard to grasp; baffling

elves n. pl. of ELF

e·ma′ci·ate (-shē-, -sē-) v. make too thin —**e·ma′ci·a′tion** n.

e-′mail′ n. electronic mail

em′a·nate v. come or issue —**em′a·na′tion** n.

e·man′ci·pate′ v. set free —**e·man′ci·pa′tion** n. —**e·man′ci·pa′tor** n.

e·mas′cu·late v. castrate

em·balm′ (-bäm′) v. preserve (a dead body)

em·bank′ment n. bank of earth, etc. as to keep back water

em·bar′go n., pl. **–goes** legal restriction of commerce or shipping

em·bark′ v. 1 go aboard a ship 2 begin; start —**em′bar·ka′tion** n.

em·bar′rass v. cause to feel self-conscious —**em·bar′rass·ment** n.

em′bas·sy n., pl. **–sies** staff or headquarters of an ambassador

em·bat′tled a. ready for battle

em·bed′ v. **–bed′ded, –bed′ding** set firmly (in)

em·bel′lish v. 1 decorate 2 add details, often untrue —**em·bel′lish·ment** n.

em′ber n. glowing piece of coal or wood

em·bez′zle v. steal (money entrusted) —**em·bez′zle·ment** n. —**em·bez′zler** n.

em·bit′ter v. make bitter

em·bla′zon v. 1 decorate 2 display openly

em′blem n. visible symbol; sign —**em′blem·at′ic** a.

em·bod′y v. **–ied, –y·ing** 1 give form to 2 include —**em·bod′i·ment** n.

em·bold′en v. make bold

em′bo·lism′ n. obstruction of a blood vessel

em·boss′ v. decorate with raised designs

em·bou·chure (äm′boo shoor′) n. way of putting lips on mouthpiece of a wind instrument

em·brace′ v. 1 hug lovingly 2 adopt, as an idea 3 include —n. an embracing

em·broi′der v. ornament with needlework —**em·broi′der·y** n., pl. **–ies**

em·broil′ v. get involved

em′bry·o′ (-brē-) n., pl. **–os′** animal or plant in earliest stages of development —**em′bry·on′ic** a.

em·cee′ v. **–ceed′, –cee′ing;** n. [Col.] (act as) master of ceremonies

e·mend′ v. correct, as a text —**e′men·da′tion** n.

em′er·ald n. green jewel

e·merge′ v. come out; appear —**e·mer′gence** n.

e·mer′gen·cy n., pl. **–cies** sudden occurrence demanding quick action

e·mer′i·tus a. retired, but keeping one's title

em′er·y n. hard corundum used for grinding, etc.

e·met′ic n., a. (substance) causing vomiting

em′i·grate′ v. leave one country to settle in another —**em′i·grant** a., n. —**em′i·gra′tion** n.

é·mi·gré, e·mi·gré (em′i grā′) n. one forced to flee for political reasons

em′i·nent a. prominent or high —**em′i·nence** n.

eminent domain n. right of a government to take private property for public use

e·mir (i mir′) n. Muslim ruler

em′is·sar′y n., pl. **–ies** one sent on a mission

e·mit′ v. **e·mit′ted, e·mit′ting** 1 send out; discharge 2 utter —**e·mis′sion** n. —**e·mit′ter** n.

e·mol′li·ent n., a. (medicine) for soothing the skin

e·mol′u·ment (-yoo-) n. salary

e·mote′ v. [Col.] show emotion dramatically

e·mo′tion n. strong feeling, as of love, fear, anger, etc. —**e·mo′tion·al** a.

e·mo′tion·al·ize′ v. deal with in an emotional way

em·pa·thet′ic a. showing empathy

em′pa·thize′ v. have empathy (with)

em′pa·thy n. ability to share another's feelings

em′per·or n. ruler of an empire —**em′press** n.fem.

em′pha·sis n., pl. **–ses** (-sēz′) 1 stress; importance 2 stress on a syllable

em′pha·size′ v. to stress

em·phat′ic a. 1 using emphasis 2 forcible —**em·phat′i·cal·ly** adv.

em′phy·se′ma (-fə-) n. disease of the lungs

em′pire′ n. group of countries under one sovereign

em·pir′i·cal (-pir′-) a. based on experiment or experience

em·place′ment n. prepared position for a large gun

em·ploy′ v. 1 use 2 keep busy 3 hire or have as workers —n. employment

em·ploy·ee, em·ploy·e (-ē) n. person working for another for pay

em·ploy′er n. one who employs others for pay

em·ploy′ment n. 1 an employing or being employed 2 work; occupation

em·pow′er v. 1 authorize 2 enable

emp′ty a. **–ti·er, –ti·est** 1 with nothing or no one in it 2 worthless —v. **–tied, –ty·ing** 1 make or become empty 2 pour out —n., pl. **–ties** empty bottle, etc. —**emp′ti·ness** n.

em·py·re·an (-pir′ē-) n. 1 highest heaven 2 the sky

e·mu′ n. ostrichlike bird

em′u·late′ v. try to equal or surpass —**em′u·la·tion** n.

e·mul'si·fy' v. **-fied'**, **-fy'ing** form into an emulsion

e·mul'sion n. oil suspended in watery liquid

en– pref. **1** to put on **2** to make **3** in or into

–en suf. **1** make or become **2** get or give **3** made of

en·a'ble v. make able

en·act' v. **1** pass, as a law **2** act out

en·am'el n. **1** glassy coating fused to metal **2** white coating of teeth **3** hard, glossy paint —v. coat with enamel —**en·am'el·ware'** n.

en·am'or v. fill with love; charm

en bloc adv. all together

en·camp' v. set up, or put in, a camp —**en·camp'ment** n.

en·cap'su·late' v. **1** enclose in a capsule **2** condense

en·case' v. enclose

–ence suf. act, state, or result: also **–ency**

en·ceph'a·li'tis n. inflammation of the brain

en·chant' v. charm; delight

en·chi·la'da (-lä'-) n. tortilla rolled with meat inside

en·cir'cle v. surround

en·clave' n. foreign land inside another country

en·close' v. **1** surround; shut in **2** insert in an envelope —**en·clo'sure** n.

en·code' v. put (a message) into code

en·co'mi·um n. high praise

en·com'pass v. **1** surround **2** contain

en·core' (än'-) int. again! —n. song, etc. added by demand

en·coun'ter v. **1** meet unexpectedly **2** fight —n. **1** unexpected meeting **2** fight

en·cour'age v. **1** give courage or hope to **2** help —**en·cour'age·ment** n.

en·croach' v. intrude (on) —**en·croach'ment** n.

en·crust' v. incrust —**en'crus·ta'tion** n.

en·cum'ber v. **1** hinder **2** burden —**en·cum'brance** n.

en·cyc'li·cal (-sik'-) n. papal letter to bishops

en·cy'clo·pe'di·a n. book or set of books on one or all branches of knowledge —**en·cy'clo·pe'dic** a.

end n. **1** last part; finish **2** destruction **3** tip **4** purpose —v. finish; stop —a. final —**end'ing** n.

en·dan'ger v. put in danger

en·dear' v. make beloved

en·dear'ment n. affection

en·deav'or (-dev'-) v. try hard —n. earnest attempt

en·dem'ic a. prevalent in a place, as a disease

en'dive n. salad plant

end'less a. **1** eternal; infinite **2** lasting too long **3** with the ends joined to form a ring

end'most' a. farthest

en'do·crine' (**gland**) (-krin') n. any of the ductless glands that regulate bodily functions

en·dorse' v. **1** sign on the back of (a check) **2** approve —**en·dorse'ment** n.

en·dow' v. **1** provide with some quality **2** give money to —**en·dow'ment** n.

en·dur'ance n. ability to last, stand pain, etc.

en·dure' v. **1** stand (pain, etc.) **2** tolerate **3** last

end'ways' adv. **1** lengthwise **2** end to end Also **end'wise'**

en·e'ma n. therapeutic flushing of the rectum

en'e·my n., pl. **-mies** person or nation hostile to another; foe

en'er·gize' v. give energy to

en'er·gy n., pl. **-gies** **1** vigor; power **2** capacity to do work —**en·er·get'ic** a.

en·er·vate' v. weaken

en·fee'ble v. weaken

en·fold' v. **1** wrap up **2** embrace

en·force' v. **1** impose by force **2** make people obey (a law) —**en·force'ment** n. —**en·forc'er** n.

en·fran'chise' v. **1** free from slavery **2** give the right to vote

en·gage' v. **1** bind by a promise of marriage **2** involve oneself **3** hire **4** attract and hold **5** enter into conflict with **6** interlock; mesh —**en·gaged'** a. —**en·gage'ment** n.

en·gag'ing a. charming

en·gen'der v. cause

en'gine n. **1** a machine using energy to develop mechanical power **2** locomotive

en'gi·neer' n. **1** one trained in engineering **2** locomotive driver —v. manage skillfully

en'gi·neer'ing n. practical use of sciences in industry, building, etc.

Eng'lish a., n. (of) the people or language of England

en·grave' v. cut (designs) on (a metal plate, etc.), as for printing —**en·grav'er** n. —**en·grav'ing** n.

en·gross' (-grōs') v. take the full attention of

en·gulf' v. swallow up

en·hance' v. make greater

e·nig'ma n. baffling matter, person, etc. —**en'ig·mat'ic, e'nig·mat'i·cal** a.

en·join' v. **1** to command **2** prohibit by law

en·joy' v. **1** get pleasure from **2** have the use of —**enjoy oneself** have a good time —**enjoy'a·ble** a. —**en·joy'ment** n.

en·large' v. make larger —**enlarge on** (or **upon**) discuss fully —**en·large'ment** n.

en·light'en v. free from ignorance, prejudice, etc.

en·list' v. 1 enroll in an army, etc. 2 engage in a cause —**en·list'ment** n.

en·liv'en v. liven up

en masse' adv. all together

en·mesh' v. entangle

en'mi·ty n. ill will

en·no'ble v. dignify

en·nui' (än'wē') n. boredom

e·nor'mi·ty n., pl. **–ties** 1 great wickedness 2 outrageous act

e·nor'mous a. huge; vast

e·nough' a., adv. as much as is needed —n. amount needed —int. no more!

en·plane' v. board an airplane

en·quire' v. inquire —**en·quir'y** n., pl. **–ies**

en·rage' v. put into a rage

en·rap'ture v. fill with delight

en·rich' v. make rich(er) —**en·rich'ment** n.

en·roll' v. put or be put in a list, as a member, etc. —**en·roll'ment** n.

en route (en rōōt', än-) adv., a. [Fr.] on the way

en·sconce' v. place snugly

en·sem'ble (än säm'-) n. 1 total effect 2 costume of matching parts 3 group of musicians playing together

en·shrine' v. hold as sacred

en·shroud' v. hide

en'sign' (-sīn', n. 2: -sən) n. 1 flag 2 lowest-ranking navy officer

en'si·lage (-sə lij') n. green fodder in silo

en·slave' v. make a slave of

en·snare' v. catch as in a snare

en·sue' v. follow; result

en·tail' v. make necessary

en·tan'gle v. trap; confuse

en·tente (än tänt') n. agreement between nations

en'ter v. 1 come or go in 2 put in a list, etc. 3 join 4 begin —**enter into** 1 take part in 2 form a part of — **enter on (or upon)** begin

en'ter·i'tis n. inflammation of the intestine

en'ter·prise' n. 1 important undertaking 2 energy and boldness

en'ter·pris'ing a. full of energy and boldness

en'ter·tain' v. 1 amuse 2 act as host to 3 consider, as an idea —**en'ter·tain'er** n. —**en'ter·tain'ment** n.

en·thrall' v. fascinate

en·throne' v. place on throne

en·thuse' (-thōōz') v. [Col.] act or make enthusiastic

en·thu'si·asm' n. eager interest —**en·thu'si·ast'** n. —**en·thu'si·as'tic** a.

en·tice' v. tempt

en·tire' a. complete; whole —**en·tire'ly** adv. —**en·tire'ty** n.

en·ti'tle v. 1 give a title to 2 give a right to

en'ti·ty n., pl. **–ties** thing having real existence

en·tomb' v. put in a tomb; bury

en'to·mol'o·gy n. study of insects

en·tou·rage (än'tōō räzh') n. retinue; attendants

en'trails n.pl. inner organs; spec., intestines

en'trance (v.: en trans') n. 1 act of entering 2 door, gate, etc. 3 permission to enter —v. to delight

en'trant n. one who enters a contest

en·trap' v. catch in a trap

en·treat' v. ask earnestly

en·treat'y n., pl. **–ies** earnest request; prayer

en·tree, en·trée (än'trā') n. main dish

en·trench' v. set securely —**en·trench'ment** n.

en·tre·pre·neur (än'trə prə noor') n. one who organizes and operates a business

en'tro·py n. tendency of energy system to run down

en·trust' v. assign the care of (to)

en'try n., pl. **–tries** 1 entrance 2 item in a list, etc. 3 contestant

en·twine' v. twist together or around

e·nu'mer·ate' v. name one by one —**e·nu'mer·a'tion** n.

e·nun'ci·ate' v. 1 to state 2 pronounce (words) clearly —**e·nun'ci·a'tion** n.

en'u·re'sis n. inability to control urination

en·vel'op v. 1 wrap up 2 surround —**en·vel'op·ment** n.

en've·lope' n. covering, esp. for a letter

en·ven'om v. 1 put venom into 2 fill with hate

en·vi'ron·ment n. surroundings —**en·vi'ron·men'tal** a.

en·vi'ron·men'tal·ist n. person working to solve environmental problems

en·vi'rons n.pl. suburbs

en·vis'age (-viz'-) v. imagine

en·vi'sion v. imagine

en'voy' (än'-, en'-) n. 1 messenger 2 diplomatic official

en'vy n. 1 discontent and ill will over another's advantages, etc. 2 object of such feeling —v. feel envy toward —**en'vi·a·ble** a. —**en'vi·ous** a.

en'zyme' (-zīm') n. a catalyst formed in body cells

e'on n. very long time

ep'au·let' (ep'ə-) n. shoulder ornament on a uniform

e·pee, é·pée (ā pā') n. rigid sword for fencing

e·pergne (ē purn′) n. a footed dish for candy, flowers, etc.

e·phem′er·al a. short-lived

ep′ic n. long poem about a hero's deeds —a. heroic

ep′i·cen′ter n. focal point, as of an earthquake

ep′i·cure′ n. one with a fine taste for foods and liquors —**ep′i·cu·re′an** a.

ep′i·dem′ic n., a. (disease) that spreads rapidly

ep′i·der′mis n. outermost layer of the skin

ep′i·glot′tis n. thin lid of cartilage covering windpipe during swallowing

ep′i·gram′ n. witty saying

ep′i·lep′sy n. disease marked by convulsive fits, etc. —**ep′i·lep′tic** a., n.

ep′i·logue′, ep′i·log′ (-lôg′) n. part added at the end of a novel, play, etc.

e·pis′co·pal a. of or governed by bishops

ep′i·sode′ n. incident —**ep′i·sod′ic** a.

e·pis′tle (-pis′əl) n. 1 letter 2 [E–] Bible letter of an Apostle

ep′i·taph′ n. inscription on a tomb

ep′i·thet′ n. word or phrase characterizing a person, etc.

e·pit′o·me′ (-mē′) n. 1 typical part or thing 2 summary —**e·pit′o·mize′** v.

ep′och (-ək) n. period marked by certain events —**ep′och·al** a.

ep·ox′y n. resin used in strong glues, enamels, etc.

Ep′som salts (or **salt**) n. salt used as a cathartic

eq′ua·ble (ek′wə-) a. even; calm —**eq′ua·bly** adv.

e′qual a. of the same quantity, value, rank, etc. —n. person or thing that is equal —v. be, or do something, equal to —**equal to**, capable of —**e·qual′i·ty** n. —**e′qual·ize′** v. —**e′qual·ly** adv.

equal mark (or **sign**) n. sign (=) indicating equality

e′qua·nim′i·ty (ek′wə-, ē′kwə-) n. composure

e·quate′ v. treat, regard, or express as equal

e·qua′tion n. 1 an equating 2 equality of two quantities as shown by the equal mark

e·qua′tor n. imaginary circle around the earth, equidistant from the North and South Poles —**e′qua·to′ri·al** a.

e·ques′tri·an a. of horses or horsemanship —n. a rider or acrobat on horseback

equi– pref. equal, equally

e′qui·dis′tant a. equally distant

e′qui·lat′er·al a. having all sides equal

e′qui·lib′ri·um n. state of balance

e′quine′ a. of a horse

e′qui·nox′ n. time when the sun crosses the equator, making night and day of equal length everywhere

e·quip′ v. -**quipped′**, -**quip′ping** fit out, as for an undertaking —**e·quip′ment** n.

eq′ui·page′ (-pij) n. horse and carriage with servants

eq′ui·poise′ n. equilibrium

eq′ui·ta·ble a. fair; just

eq′ui·ta′tion n. horsemanship

eq′ui·ty n. 1 fairness 2 value of property beyond amount owed on it

e·quiv′a·lent a. equal in quantity, meaning, etc. —n. equivalent thing

e·quiv′o·cal a. 1 purposely ambiguous 2 doubtful —**e·quiv′o·cate′** v.

–**er** suf. one that

e′ra n. period of time

e·rad′i·cate′ v. wipe out —**e·rad′i·ca′tion** n.

e·rase′ v. rub out, as writing —**e·ras′er** n. —**e·ras′a·ble** a.

e·ra′sure (-shər) n. place where something was erased

ere (er) con., prep. [Ar. or Poet.] before

e·rect′ a. upright —v. 1 construct; build 2 set upright —**e·rec′tion** n.

e·rec′tile (-təl, -tīl′) a. that becomes rigid when filled with blood

erg n. unit of work

er·mine (ur′min) n. weasel with white fur in winter

e·rode′ v. wear away —**e·ro′sion** n.

e·rog′e·nous (-räj′-) a. sensitive to sexual stimulation

e·rot′ic a. causing sexual feelings or desires

e·rot′i·ca n.pl. [sing. or pl. v.] erotic books, etc.

err (ur, er) v. 1 be wrong 2 violate a moral code

er′rand n. short trip to do a thing

er′rant a. wandering

er·ra′ta (-rät′ə) n.pl., sing. **-tum** printing errors

er·rat′ic a. irregular; odd

er·ro′ne·ous a. wrong

er′ror n. 1 mistake; blunder 2 mistaken belief

er′satz′ (-zäts′) a. being an inferior substitute

erst′while′ a. former

e·ruct′ v. to belch —**e·ruc′ta′tion** n.

er′u·dite′ a. learned; scholarly —**er′u·di′tion** n.

e·rupt′ v. 1 burst forth 2 break out in a rash —**e·rup′tion** n.

–**er·y** suf. 1 a place to or for 2 act or product of 3 condition of

er·y·sip′e·las (er′i-) n. acute skin disease

e·ryth·ro·cyte (e rith′rō sīt′) n. mature red blood cell

es′ca·late′ v. rise, expand, or increase

—es·ca·la'tion n.

es·ca'la·tor n. moving stairway on an endless belt

es·cal·lop, es·cal·op (e skäl'əp, -skal'-) n., v. scallop

es'ca·pade' n. reckless adventure or prank

es·cape' v. 1 get free 2 slip away from —n. act or means of escape

es·cap·ee' n. one who has escaped

es·cape'ment n. notched wheel regulating movement in a clock

es·cap'ism' n. tendency to escape reality by fantasy

es'ca·role' n. plant with leaves used in salads

es·carp'ment n. cliff

es·chew' v. shun

es'cort' (v.: es kôrt')n. person(s) accompanying another to protect, honor, etc. —v. go with as an escort

es'crow' n. state of a deed held by a third party until conditions are fulfilled

es·cutch'eon (-ən) n. shield bearing a coat of arms

Es'ki·mo' n., a. (member) of a people living in Greenland, arctic N. America, etc.

Eskimo dog n. strong dog used by Eskimos to pull sleds

e·soph'a·gus n., pl. -gi' (-jī') passage between the pharynx and stomach

es'o·ter'ic a. known by few

ESP n. extrasensory perception

es'pa·drille' n. flat canvas shoe with rope sole

es·pal'ier (-yər) n. tree growing flat on lattice

es·pe'cial a. special; chief —es·pe'cial·ly adv.

Es'pe·ran'to (-rän'-) n. artificial international language

es'pi·o·nage' (-näzh') n. a spying

es'pla·nade' (or -näd') n. a public walk

es·pouse' (e spouz') v. 1 marry 2 support (an idea or cause) —es·pous'al n.

es·pres'so n. coffee made by forcing steam through ground coffee beans

es·py' (e spī') v. -pied', -py'ing catch sight of; see

Es'quire' n. title of courtesy put after a man's surname, or, in U.S., after a lawyer's name: abbrev. Esq.

es·say' (n.: es'ā)v. to try —n. 1 a try 2 short personal writing on one subject —es'say·ist n.

es'sence n. 1 basic nature 2 substance in concentrated form 3 perfume

es·sen'tial (-shəl) n., a. (something) necessary

es·tab'lish v. 1 set up; fix 2 to found 3 prove —es·tab'lish·ment n.

es·tate' n. 1 one's possessions 2 piece of land with a residence

es·teem' v. value highly —n. high regard

es'ter n. organic salt

es·thete' n. aesthete —es·thet'ic a.

es'ti·ma·ble a. worthy of esteem

es'ti·mate' (-mat'; n.: -mət) v. figure roughly, as size or cost —n. 1 rough calculation 2 opinion —es'ti·ma'tion n.

es·trange' v. make unfriendly

es'tro·gen n. female sex hormone

es'tu·ar'y (-tyōō-, -chōō-) n., pl. -ies wide mouth of a river

et cet'er·a and so forth: abbrev. etc.

etch v. put a design on metal plates or glass with acid, often for making prints —etch'ing n.

e·ter'nal a. 1 everlasting 2 forever the same

e·ter'ni·ty n. 1 a being eternal 2 endless time

eth'ane' n. gaseous hydrocarbon used as fuel

e'ther n. an anesthetic

e·the're·al (-thir'ē-) a. 1 light; delicate 2 heavenly

eth'ic n. 1 ethics 2 particular moral standard or value

eth'i·cal a. 1 of ethics 2 proper; right

eth'ics n.pl. moral standards; system of morals

eth'nic a. of any of the many peoples of mankind —n. member of a nationality group in a larger community

eth·nic'i·ty (-nis'-) n. ethnic affiliation

eth·nol'o·gy n. study of the world's peoples and cultures —eth'no·log'i·cal a.

e'thos' (-thäs') n. characteristic attitudes, beliefs, etc.

eth'yl (-al) n. carbon-hydrogen radical of common alcohol, etc.

eth'yl·ene' n. flammable, smelly gaseous hydrocarbon

e'ti·ol'o·gy (ēt'ē-) n., pl. -gies cause of a disease, etc.

et'i·quette (-kət) n. social forms; good manners

é'tude' (ā'-) n. Mus. instrumental piece stressing a technique

et'y·mol'o·gy n., pl. -gies 1 origin of a word 2 study of word origins

EU European Union

eu'ca·lyp'tus (yōō'kə lip'-) n. a subtropical evergreen

Eu'cha·rist (-kə-) n. Holy Communion

eu'chre (-kər) n. card game played with 32 cards

eu·gen'ics n. science of improving the human race by heredity control —eu·gen'ic a.

eu′lo·gy n., pl. **–gies** praise —**eu′lo·gize′** v.

eu′nuch (-nək) n. castrated man

eu′phe·mism′ n. mild word replacing an offensive one —**eu′phe·mis′tic** a.

eu·pho′ni·ous a. pleasant sounding —**eu′pho·ny** n.

eu·pho′ri·a n. feeling of well-being —**eu·phor′ic** a.

eu·re′ka int. cry of triumph

Eu′ro·pe′an n., a. (native) of Europe

eu·ryth′mics n.pl. rhythmical body movements to music

eu·sta′chi·an tube (-stā′kē ən, -stā′shən) n. tube between middle ear and pharynx

eu′tha·na′si·a (-nā′zhə) n. painless death to end suffering

e·vac′u·ate′ v. 1 make empty 2 to discharge (excrement) 3 remove 4 withdraw (from) —**e·vac′u·a′tion** n.

e·vac′u·ee′ n. person evacuated from area of danger

e·vade′ v. avoid by deceit, indirect answer, etc. —**e·va′sion** n. —**e·va′sive** a.

e·val′u·ate′ v. find the value of —**e·val′u·a′tion** n.

ev′a·nes′cent a. fleeting

e·van·gel′i·cal a. of the Gospels or New Testament

e·van′ge·list n. 1 [E—] Gospel writer 2 revivalist preacher —**e·van′ge·lism′** n. —**e·van′ge·lize′** v.

e·vap′o·rate′ v. 1 change into vapor 2 condense by heating 3 vanish —**e·vap′o·ra′tion** n.

eve n. 1 [Poet.] evening 2 evening before a holiday 3 time just before

e′ven a. 1 flat; level 2 constant; uniform 3 calm 4 equal 5 divisible by two 6 exact —adv. 1 indeed 2 exactly 3 still —v. make or become even —**even if though** —**e′ven·ly** adv.

e′ven·hand′ed a. fair; just

eve′ning n. end of day and beginning of night

e·vent′ n. 1 an occurrence 2 sports contest in a series —**in any event** no matter what happens —**in the event of** in case of

e′ven-tem′pered a. not quickly angered or excited

e·vent′ful a. full of events; important

e·ven′tu·al (-chōō-) a. final —**e·ven′tu·al·ly** adv.

e·ven′tu·al′i·ty n., pl. **–ties** possible outcome

ev′er adv. 1 always 2 at any time 3 at all

ev′er·glade′ n. swampy land

ev′er·green′ n., a. (tree or plant) having green leaves all year

ev′er·last′ing a. eternal

ev′er·more′ adv. forever; constantly

ev′er·y a. 1 each of a group 2 all possible —**every now and then** occasionally —**every other** each alternate —**ev′er·y·bod′y**, **ev′er·y·one′** pron. —**ev′er·y·thing′** pron. —**ev′er·y·where′** adv.

ev′er·y·day′ a. 1 daily 2 usual; common

e·vict′ v. put (a tenant) out by law —**e·vic′tion** n.

ev′i·dence n. 1 sign; indication 2 proof —v. make evident

ev′i·dent a. easy to see; clear —**ev′i·dent′ly** adv.

e′vil a. 1 morally bad 2 harmful —n. wickedness —**e′vil·do′er** n. —**e′vil·ly** adv.

e·vince′ v. show plainly (a quality, feeling, etc.)

e·vis′cer·ate′ (-vis′ər-) v. remove the entrails from

e·voke′ v. call forth; produce —**ev′o·ca′tion** n.

ev′o·lu′tion n. 1 an evolving 2 theory that all species developed from earlier forms —**ev′o·lu′tion·ar′y** a.

e·volve′ v. develop gradually; unfold

ewe (yōō) n. female sheep

ew′er n. large, wide-mouthed water pitcher

ex– pref. former

ex·ac′er·bate′ (eg zas′-) v. aggravate —**ex·ac′er·ba′tion** n.

ex·act′ a. strictly correct; precise —v. demand and get —**ex·ac′ti·tude** n. —**ex·act′ly** adv.

ex·act′ing a. strict; hard

ex·ag′ger·ate′ v. make seem greater than it really is; overstate —**ex·ag′ger·a′tion** n.

ex·alt′ v. 1 raise in dignity 2 praise 3 fill with joy —**ex′al·ta′tion** n.

ex·am′ n. examination

ex·am′ine v. 1 inspect 2 test by questioning —**ex·am′i·na′tion** n.

ex·am′ple n. 1 sample 2 a warning 3 illustration 4 model

ex·as′per·ate′ v. annoy; vex —**ex·as′per·a′tion** n.

ex′ca·vate′ v. 1 make a hole in 2 unearth 3 dig out —**ex′ca·va′tion** n. —**ex′ca·va′tor** n.

ex·ceed′ v. 1 go beyond (a limit) 2 surpass

ex·ceed′ing a. extreme —**ex·ceed′ing·ly** adv.

ex·cel′ v. **–celled′**, **–cel′ling** be better than

Ex·cel′len·cy n., pl. **–cies** title of honor

ex·cel′lent a. unusually good —**ex′cel·lence** n.

ex·cel′si·or′ n. wood shavings used for packing

ex·cept′ prep. leaving out; but —v. exclude —**except for** if it were not for

ex·cept′ing prep. except

ex·cep′tion n. 1 person or thing excluded

2 case to which a rule does not apply 3 objection —**take exception to** object

ex·cep′tion·al *a.* 1 unusual 2 gifted or handicapped

ex′cerpt′ (*v.*: ek surpt′) *n.* passage selected from a book, etc. —*v.* select; extract

ex·cess′ (*a.*: ek′ses′) *n.* 1 more than is needed 2 surplus —*a.* extra —**ex·ces′sive** *a.*

ex·change′ *v.* 1 to trade; barter 2 to interchange —*n.* 1 an exchanging 2 thing exchanged 3 place for exchanging —**ex·change′a·ble** *a.*

ex·cheq′uer (-chek′ər) *n.* 1 treasury 2 funds

ex·cise′ (*v.*: ek sīz′) *n.* tax on certain goods within a country: also **excise tax** —*v.* cut out —**ex·ci′sion** (-sizh′ən) *n.*

ex·cite′ *v.* 1 make active 2 arouse; stir the feelings of —**ex·cit′a·ble** *a.* —**ex·cite′ment** *n.*

ex·claim′ *v.* utter sharply —**ex′cla·ma′tion** *n.*

exclamation point (or mark) *n.* mark of punctuation (!)

ex·clude′ *v.* keep out or shut out —**ex·clu′sion** *n.*

ex·clu′sive *a.* 1 not shared 2 snobbish —**exclusive of** not including —**ex·clu′sive·ly** *adv.*

ex′com·mu′ni·cate′ *v.* expel from communion with a church —**ex′com·mu′ni·ca′tion** *n.*

ex·co′ri·ate (-kôr′ē-) *v.* denounce

ex′cre·ment *n.* waste material from the bowels

ex·cres′cence *n.* outgrowth, esp. an abnormal one

ex·crete′ *v.* eliminate (waste) from the body —**ex·cre′tion** *n.* —**ex′cre·to′ry** *a.*

ex·cru′ci·at′ing (-shē āt′-) *a.* very painful; agonizing

ex′cul·pate′ *v.* exonerate —**ex′cul·pa′tion** *n.*

ex·cur′sion *n.* short trip, esp. for pleasure

ex·cuse′ (ek skyōōz′; *n.*: ek skyōōs′) *v.* 1 apologize for 2 overlook (an offense or fault) 3 release from a duty, etc. 4 let leave 5 justify —*n.* 1 apology 2 something that excuses 3 pretext —**ex·cus′a·ble** *a.*

ex′e·cra·ble *a.* detestable

ex′e·crate′ *v.* 1 denounce 2 loathe; abhor —**ex′e·cra′tion** *n.*

ex′e·cute′ *v.* 1 carry out; do 2 put to death legally 3 make valid (a will, etc.) —**ex′e·cu′tion** *n.*

ex′e·cu′tion·er *n.* official who puts to death legally

ex·ec′u·tive *a.* 1 having to do with man-

aging 2 administering laws, etc. —*n.* one who administers affairs

ex·ec′u·tor *n.* one who carries out the provisions of a legal will

ex·em′plar (-plər, -plär′) *n.* model; pattern

ex·em′pli·fy′ *v.* -**fied′**, -**fy′ing** show by example

ex·empt′ *v., a.* free(d) from a rule or obligation —**ex·emp′tion** *n.*

ex′er·cise′ *n.* 1 active use 2 activity to develop the body, a skill, etc. 3 *pl.* program, as at a graduation ceremony —*v.* 1 use 2 do or give exercises 3 exert

ex·ert′ *v.* put into action

ex·er′tion *n.* 1 act of exerting 2 effort

ex·hale′ *v.* breathe forth —**ex′ha·la′tion** *n.*

ex·haust′ *v.* 1 use up 2 drain 3 tire out —*n.* discharge from an engine —**ex·haust′i·ble** *a.* —**ex·haus′tion** *n.*

ex·haus′tive *a.* thorough

ex·hib′it (eg zib′-) *v., n.* show; display —**ex·hib′i·tor** *n.*

ex′hi·bi′tion (ek′sə-) *n.* 1 a (public) showing 2 that which is shown

ex′hi·bi′tion·ist *n.* one who likes to show off —**ex′hi·bi′tion·ism′** *n.*

ex·hil′a·rate′ (eg zil′-) *v.* stimulate —**ex·hil′a·ra′tion** *n.*

ex·hort′ (eg zôrt′) *v.* urge earnestly —**ex′hor·ta′tion** *n.*

ex·hume′ *v.* dig out of the earth

ex′i·gen·cy *n., pl.* -**cies** urgency

ex·ig′u·ous *a.* scanty

ex′ile′ *n.* 1 a prolonged, often enforced, living away from one's country 2 person in exile —*v.* send into exile

ex·ist′ *v.* 1 be 2 occur 3 live —**ex·ist′ence** *n.*

ex·is·ten′tial *a.* of existence

ex′it *n.* a (way of) leaving

ex′o·dus *n.* departure

ex of·fi·ci·o (ə fish′ē ō′) *adv.* by virtue of one's position

ex·on′er·ate′ *v.* to free from blame

ex·or′bi·tant *a.* excessive —**ex·or′bi·tance** *n.*

ex′or·cise′, ex′or·cize′ *v.* drive out (an evil spirit), as by magic —**ex′or·cism′** *n.*

ex·ot′ic *a.* 1 foreign 2 strangely beautiful, etc.

ex·pand′ *v.* 1 spread out 2 enlarge —**ex·pan′sion** *n.*

ex·panse′ *n.* wide extent

ex·pan′sive *a.* 1 broad 2 warm and open in talk, etc.

ex·pa′ti·ate′ (-pā′shē-) *v.* speak or write at length

ex·pa′tri·ate′ (-āt′; *n., a.*: -ət) *v., n., a.* exile(d)

ex·pect' v. 1 look for as likely or due 2 [Col.] suppose —**be expecting** [Col.] be pregnant —**ex·pect'an·cy** n. —**ex·pect'ant** a. —**ex'pec·ta'tion** n.

ex·pec'to·rant n. medicine to bring up phlegm

ex·pec'to·rate' v. to spit

ex·pe'di·ent a. 1 useful for the purpose 2 based on self-interest —n. a means to an end —**ex·pe'di·en·cy** n.

ex'pe·dite' v. speed up; facilitate —**ex'pe·dit'er** n.

ex'pe·di'tion n. 1 a journey, as for exploration 2 those on such a journey

ex'pe·di'tious (-dish'əs) a. prompt

ex·pel' v. **-pelled', -pel'ling** 1 force out 2 dismiss by authority

ex·pend' v. spend; use up —**ex·pend'a·ble** a.

ex·pend'i·ture n. 1 spending of money, time, etc. 2 amount spent

ex·pense' n. 1 cost 2 pl. the charges met with in one's work, etc.

ex·pen'sive a. high-priced

ex·pe'ri·ence n. 1 a living through an event 2 thing one has done or lived through 3 skill gotten by training, work, etc. —v. have experience of

ex·per'i·ment n., v. test to discover or prove something —**ex·per'i·men'tal** a. —**ex·per'i·men·ta'tion** n.

ex'pert a. very skillful —n. one with great skill or knowledge in a field

ex'per·tise' (-tēz', -tēs') n. skill or knowledge of an expert

ex'pi·ate' v. atone for —**ex'pi·a'tion** n.

ex·pire' v. 1 die 2 end 3 exhale —**ex'pi·ra'tion** n.

ex·plain' v. 1 make plain or understandable 2 account for —**ex'pla·na'tion** n. —**ex·plan'a·to·ry** a.

ex'ple·tive n. oath or exclamation

ex'pli·ca·ble a. that can be explained

ex'pli·cate' v. explain fully

ex·plic'it a. clearly stated; definite

ex·plode' v. 1 burst noisily 2 discredit —**ex·plo'sion** n.

ex'ploit' (v.: ek sploit') n. bold deed —v. use to advantage —**ex'ploi·ta'tion** n.

ex·plore' v. 1 investigate 2 travel in (a region) for discovery —**ex'plo·ra'tion** n. —**ex·plor'a·to·ry** a.

ex·plo'sive a. of or like an explosion —n. substance that can explode

ex·po'nent n. 1 interpreter 2 example or symbol 3 Math. symbol at upper right showing times as a factor

ex·port' (n.: eks'pôrt') v. send (goods) to another country for sale —n. something exported —**ex'por·ta'tion** n.

ex·pose' v. 1 lay open, as to danger 2 reveal 3 to subject photographic film to light —**ex·po'sure** n.

ex'po·sé' (-zā') n. disclosure of a scandal

ex'po·si'tion n. 1 explanation 2 public exhibition

ex·pos'i·to·ry a. explaining

ex·pos'tu·late' (-päs'chə-) v. reason with a person in protest

ex·pound' v. explain fully

ex·press' v. 1 put into words 2 reveal; show 3 symbolize —a. 1 explicit 2 exact 3 fast and direct —adv. by express —n. an express train, bus, delivery service, etc.

ex·pres'sion n. 1 an expressing or way of expressing 2 certain word or phrase 3 look, etc. that shows how one feels —**ex·pres'sion·less** a. —**ex·pres'sive** a.

ex·pres'sion·ism' n. art, writing, etc. expressing inner experience

ex·press'way' n. divided highway for high-speed traffic

ex·pro'pri·ate' v. take (land, etc.) for public use —**ex·pro'pri·a'tion** n.

ex·pul'sion n. an expelling or being expelled

ex·punge' v. erase

ex'pur·gate' v. delete (from) as a censor

ex'qui·site a. 1 beautiful, delicate, etc. 2 very keen

ex'tant a. still existing

ex·tem'po·re (-rē) adv., a. without preparation: also **ex·tem'po·ra'ne·ous** a.

ex·tem'po·rize' v. speak, do, etc. extempore

ex·tend' v. 1 prolong 2 expand 3 stretch forth 4 offer

ex·ten'sion n. 1 an extending 2 an addition

ex·ten'sive a. vast; far-reaching

ex·tent' n. 1 size 2 scope 3 vast area

ex·ten'u·ate' v. lessen the seriousness of (an offense)

ex·te'ri·or a. on or from the outside —n. the outside

ex·ter'mi·nate' v. to destroy entirely —**ex·ter'mi·na'tion** n. —**ex·ter'mi·na'tor** n.

ex·ter'nal a. 1 on or from the outside 2 superficial

ex·tinct' a. no longer existing or active

ex·tinc'tion n. a dying out; annihilation

ex·tin'guish v. 1 put out (a fire) 2 destroy

ex'tir·pate' v. root out

ex·tol', ex·toll' v. **-tolled', -tol'ling** praise highly

ex·tort' v. get (money) by threats, etc. —**ex·tor'tion** n.

ex'tra a. more than expected; additional —n. extra person or thing —adv. especially

extra– pref. outside, besides

ex·tract' (n.: eks'trakt') v. **1** pull out **2** get by pressing, distilling, etc. **3** select —n. something extracted —**ex·trac'tion** n.

ex'tra·cur·ric'u·lar a. not part of required curriculum

ex'tra·dite' v. return (a fugitive) —**ex'tra·di'tion** n.

ex'tra·ne'ous a. **1** from outside **2** not pertinent

ex·tra·or'di·nar'y (ek strôr'-) a. very unusual

ex·trap'o·late' v. to estimate on basis of known facts —**ex·trap'o·la'tion** n.

ex'tra·sen'so·ry a. apart from normal sense perception

ex·trav'a·gant a. **1** excessive **2** wasteful —**ex·trav'a·gance** n.

ex·trav'a·gan'za n. spectacular show

ex·treme' a. **1** utmost **2** final **3** excessive or drastic **4** radical —n. extreme degree, state, etc. —**ex·treme'ly** adv.

ex·trem'i·ty (ek strem'-) n., pl. **-ties 1** end **2** extreme need, danger, etc. **3** pl. hands and feet

ex'tri·cate' v. set free

ex·trin'sic (-sik, -zik) a. **1** not essential **2** external

ex'tro·vert' n. one not given to introspection —**ex'tro·ver'sion** n. —**ex'tro·vert'ed** a.

ex·trude' v. force through a small opening **2** project —**ex·tru'sion** n.

ex·u'ber·ant a. **1** very healthy and lively **2** luxuriant —**ex·u'ber·ance** n.

ex·ude' v. **1** discharge **2** radiate

ex·ult' v. rejoice greatly —**ex·ult'ant** a. —**ex'ul·ta'tion** n.

ex·ur'bi·a n. communities beyond the suburbs —**ex·ur'ban·ite'** n., a.

eye n. **1** organ of sight **2** vision **3** a look **4** attention —v. eyed, **eye'ing** or **ey'ing** look at

eye'ball' n. ball-shaped part of the eye

eye'brow' n. bony arch over the eye, or the hair on this

eye'ful' n. [Sl.] striking person or thing

eye'glass'es n.pl. pair of lenses to help faulty vision

eye'lash' n. hair on the edge of the eyelid

eye'let n. small hole, as for a hook, cord, etc.

eye'lid' n. either of two folds of flesh that cover and uncover the eyeball

eye'-o'pen·er n. surprising news, sudden realization, etc.

eye'sight' n. power of seeing

eye'sore' n. ugly sight

eye'tooth' n.,pl. **-teeth'** upper canine tooth

eye'wit'ness n. one who has seen something happen

F

fa'ble n. **1** brief tale having a moral **2** untrue story

fab'ric n. cloth

fab'ri·cate' v. **1** make **2** make up (a reason, etc.)

fab'u·lous a. **1** fictitious **2** incredible **3** [Col.] wonderful

fa·çade, fa·cade (fə säd') n. main face of a building

face n. **1** front of the head **2** (main) surface **3** appearance **4** dignity —v. **1** turn, or have the face turned, toward **2** confront —**make a face** to grimace —**on the face of it** apparently —**fa'cial** (-shəl) a.

face'less a. anonymous

face lifting n. **1** plastic surgery to remove wrinkles from the face **2** altering an exterior Also **face lift**

face'-sav'ing a. preserving one's self-respect

fac'et (fas'-) n. **1** a surface of a cut gem **2** aspect

fa·ce'tious (fə sē'shəs) a. joking, esp. at the wrong time

face value n. **1** value on a bill, bond, etc. **2** seeming value

fa'cial (-shəl) a. of or for the face —n. treatment of the skin of the face with massage, creams, etc.

facial tissue n. soft tissue paper used as a handkerchief, etc.

fac'ile (fas'əl) a. **1** easy **2** superficial

fa·cil'i·tate' v. make easier

fa·cil'i·ty n., pl. **-ties 1** ease or skill **2** pl. things that help do something **3** building, etc. for some activity

fac·sim'i·le (-lē) n. exact copy

fact n. **1** actual happening **2** truth —**in fact** really

fac'tion n. **1** clique **2** dissension —**fac'tion·al** a. —**fac'tious** a.

fac·ti'tious a. forced or artificial

fac'toid' n. trivial or useless fact

fac'tor n. **1** causal element **2** Math. any of the quantities multiplied together

fac'to·ry n., pl. **-ries** building in which things are manufactured

fac·to'tum n. handyman

fac'tu·al (-chōō-) a. of facts; real

fac'ul·ty n., pl. **-ties 1** natural power or aptitude **2** staff of teachers

fad n. passing fashion —**fad'dish** a.

fade v. **1** (make) lose color or strength **2** die out

fag v. fagged, **fag'ging** make tired

fag'ot, fag'got n. bundle of sticks or twigs

Fahr·en·heit (fer′ən hīt′) *a.* of a thermometer on which the boiling point of water is 212°, the freezing point 32°

fail *v.* 1 fall short 2 weaken 3 become bankrupt 4 not succeed 5 neglect 6 not pass a test or course

fail′ing *n.* 1 failure 2 fault —*prep.* lacking

faille (fīl) *n.* soft, ribbed fabric of silk or rayon

fail′-safe′ *a.* of a system for preventing accidental operation, as of nuclear weapons

fail′ure *n.* 1 act of failing 2 one that fails

faint *a.* 1 weak, dim, etc. 2 weak and dizzy —*n.* state of temporary unconsciousness —*v.* fall into a faint —**faint′ness** *n.*

fair *a.* 1 beautiful 2 blond 3 clear and sunny 4 just 5 according to the rules 6 average —*adv.* in a fair way —*n.* exposition with exhibits, amusements, etc. —**fair′ly** *adv.* —**fair′ness** *n.*

fair′y *n., pl.* **–ies** tiny imaginary being in human form, with magic powers

faith *n.* 1 unquestioning belief, esp. in religion 2 particular religion 3 loyalty

faith′ful *a.* 1 loyal 2 exact —**faith′ful·ly** *adv.*

faith′less *a.* disloyal

fake *v., n., a.* sham

fa·kir (fə kir′) *n.* Muslim or Hindu religious mendicant

fa·la·fel (-lä′-) *n.* deep-fried patty of ground chickpeas

fal′con (fal′-, fôl′-) *n.* hawk trained to hunt —**fal′con·ry** *n.*

fall *v.* **fell, fall′en, fall′ing** 1 to drop or descend 2 tumble 3 occur —*n.* 1 a falling 2 autumn 3 overthrow or ruin 4 amount of what has fallen 5 *pl.* a waterfall —**fall back** retreat —**fall off** lessen or worsen —**fall on** (or **upon**) to attack —**fall out** quarrel —**fall through** fail —**fall to** begin

fal′la·cy *n., pl.* **–cies** 1 false idea; error 2 false reasoning —**fal·la′cious** *a.*

fal′li·ble *a.* liable to error —**fal·li·bil′i·ty** *n.*

fal·lo′pi·an tube *n.* [also **F- t-**] either of two tubes carrying ova to the uterus

fall′out′ *n.* 1 descent of radioactive particles after a nuclear explosion 2 these particles

fal·low (fal′ō) *a.* 1 plowed but unplanted 2 inactive

false *a.* 1 not true 2 lying 3 unfaithful 4 not real —**fal′si·fy′** *v.*, **–fied′, –fy′ing** —**fal′si·ty** *n.*

false′hood′ *n.* a lie or lying

fal·set′to *n.* artificial, high-pitched singing

fal′ter *v.* 1 stumble 2 stammer 3 waver

fame *n.* great reputation

fa·mil′i·al (-yəl) *a.* of or common to a family

fa·mil′iar *a.* 1 friendly; intimate 2 too intimate; presumptuous 3 closely acquainted (with) 4 well-known —**fa·mil′i·ar′i·ty** *n.* —**fa·mil′i·ar·ize′** *v.*

fam′i·ly *n., pl.* **–lies** 1 parents and their children 2 relatives 3 lineage 4 group of related things

fam′ine (-in) *n.* 1 widespread food shortage 2 starvation

fam′ish *v.* be hungry; starve

fam′ished *a.* very hungry

fa′mous *a.* having fame

fan *n.* 1 device to move air for cooling, etc. 2 [Col.] enthusiastic supporter —*v.* **fanned, fan′ning** 1 blow air toward 2 stir up 3 spread (out)

fa·nat′ic *a.* too enthusiastic or zealous: also **fa·nat′i·cal** —*n.* fanatic person —**fa·nat′i·cism′** *n.*

fan′ci·er *n.* person with a special interest, esp. plant or animal breeding

fan′cy *n., pl.* **–cies** 1 playful imagination 2 notion, whim, etc. 3 a liking —*a.* **–ci·er, –ci·est** 1 extravagant 2 elaborate 3 of superior quality —*v.* **–cied, –cy·ing** 1 imagine 2 be fond of 3 suppose —**fan′ci·ful** *a.* —**fan′ci·ness** *n.*

fan′cy-free′ *a.* carefree

fan′fare′ *n.* 1 blast of trumpets 2 showy display

fang *n.* long, pointed tooth

fan′ta·size′ *v.* have fantasies (about)

fan·tas′tic *a.* 1 strange 2 grotesque 3 extravagant —**fan·tas′ti·cal·ly** *adv.*

fan′ta·sy *n., pl.* **–sies** 1 fancy 2 illusion; reverie 3 fantastic poem, play, etc.

far *a.* **far′ther, far′thest** distant —*adv.* 1 very distant 2 very much —**by far** very much — (**in**) **so far as** to the extent that

far′a·way′ *a.* distant

farce *n.* 1 exaggerated comedy 2 absurd thing —**far′ci·cal** *a.*

fare *v.* get along —*n.* 1 transportation charge 2 paying passenger 3 food

fare·well′ (*a.:* fer′wel′) *int.* goodbye —*a., n.* parting (wishes)

far′-fetched′ *a.* not reasonable; strained

far′-flung′ *a.* extensive

fa·ri′na *n.* flour or meal eaten as cooked cereal

farm *n.* land used to raise crops or animals —*v.* cultivate (land) 2 let out (work or workers) on contract —**farm′er** *n.* —**farm′house′** *n.* —**farm′ing** *n.*

farm′hand′ *n.* hired farm worker

farm′yard′ *n.* yard around or enclosed by farm buildings

far′-off′ *a.* distant

far′-out′ *a.* [Col.] nonconformist; avant-garde

far′-reach′ing *a.* having wide range, influence, etc.

far'sight'ed *a.* 1 planning ahead 2 seeing far objects best

far'ther *a.* 1 more distant 2 additional —*adv.* 1 at or to a greater distance or extent 2 in addition

far'thest *a.* most distant —*adv.* at or to the greatest distance

fas'ci-nate' *v.* hold spellbound; captivate —**fas'ci-na'tion** *n.*

fas-cism (fash'iz'əm) *n.* militaristic dictatorship —**fas'cist** *n., a.*

fash'ion *n.* 1 kind; sort 2 manner 3 current style —*v.* make; form

fash'ion-a-ble *a.* stylish

fast *a.* 1 firm 2 loyal 3 unfading 4 rapid; quick 5 of loose morals —*adv.* 1 firmly 2 rapidly —*v.* abstain from food —*n.* period of fasting

fas'ten *v.* 1 attach 2 make secure; fix —**fas'ten-er** *n.*

fas'ten-ing *n.* thing used to fasten

fast'-food' *a.* of a business serving quickly prepared food

fas-tid'i-ous *a.* not easy to please; particular

fast'-talk' *v.* [Col.] persuade with fast, smooth talk

fast time [Col.] daylight-saving time

fat *a.* **fat'ter, fat'test** plump —*n.* oily animal substance —**fat'ty** *a.,* **-ti-er, -ti-est**

fa'tal *a.* causing death

fa'tal-ism' *n.* belief that all events are destined by fate —**fa'tal-ist** *n.* —**fa'tal-is'tic** *a.*

fa-tal'i-ty *n., pl.* **-ties** death caused by disaster

fate *n.* 1 power supposedly making events inevitable 2 one's lot in life 3 outcome 4 death; ruin —**fate'ful** *a.*

fat'ed *a.* destined

fa'ther *n.* 1 male parent 2 founder; creator 3 Christian priest —*v.* beget, found, etc. —[F-] God —**fa'ther-hood'** *n.* —**fa'ther-ly** *a.*

fa'ther-in-law' *n., pl.* **fa'thers-in-law'** father of one's wife or husband

fa'ther-land' *n.* one's native land

fath-om (fath'əm) *n. Naut.* six feet —*v.* understand

fa-tigue' (-tēg') *n.* weariness —*v.* to weary

fat'ten *v.* make or get fat

fat'u-ous (fach'-) *a.* foolish

fau'cet *n.* device with valve to draw liquid from a pipe

fault *n.* 1 flaw 2 error 3 blame —**find fault (with)** criticize —**fault'less** *a.*

fault'y *a.,* **-i-er, -i-est** defective

faun *n.* Roman deity, half man and half goat

fau'na *n.* the animals of a certain region

faux pas (fō pä') *n., pl.* **faux pas'** (-päz') social blunder

fa'vor *n.* 1 approval 2 partiality 3 kind act

4 small gift —*v.* 1 show favor toward 2 resemble Also, Br. sp., **fa'vour** —**in favor of** approving —**fa'vor-a-ble** *a.*

fa'vor-ite *a., n.* preferred (one) —**fa'vor-it-ism'** *n.*

fawn *v.* 1 show affection as by licking 2 flatter servilely —*n.* baby deer

fax *n.* 1 electronic sending of pictures, print, etc., as over telephone lines 2 device for such sending —*v.* send by fax

faze *v.* [Col.] disturb

fear *n.* 1 anxious anticipation of danger, pain, etc. 2 awe —*v.* 1 be afraid (of) 2 be in awe (of) —**fear'ful** *a.* —**fear'less** *a.*

fear'some *a.* 1 dreadful 2 frightened

fea'si-ble (fē'zə-) *a.* 1 possible 2 probable 3 suitable —**fea'si-bil'i-ty** *n.*

feast *n.* 1 religious festival 2 banquet —*v.* 1 have a feast (for) 2 delight

feat *n.* bold and daring deed

feath'er *n.* 1 one of the outgrowths covering a bird 2 kind —**feath'er-y** *a.*

feath'er-bed'ding *n.* use of extra workers to make more jobs, as by union contract

fea'ture *n.* 1 *pl.* form of the face or its parts 2 special part, article, etc. 3 main attraction —*v.* make a feature of

Feb'ru-ar'y (-roo-, -yoo-) *n.* second month

fe'ces' (-sēz') *n.pl.* excrement —**fe'cal** (-kəl) *a.*

feck'less *a.* 1 ineffective 2 careless

fe'cund *a.* fertile

fed'er-al *a.* 1 of a union of states under a central government 2 of the central government, esp. [F-] of the U.S.

fed'er-al-ize' *v.* 1 unite in a federal union 2 put under federal authority

fed'er-ate' *v.* unite in a federation

fed'er-a'tion *n.* union of states or groups; league

fe-do'ra *n.* man's felt hat

fee *n.* charge for some service or right

fee'ble *a.* weak; not strong —**fee'bly** *adv.*

feed *v.* **fed, feed'ing** 1 give food to 2 supply as fuel, material, etc. 3 gratify 4 eat —*n.* fodder

feed'back' *n.* 1 transfer of part of the output back to the input, as of electricity or information 2 a response

feel *v.* **felt, feel'ing** 1 touch 2 have a feeling (of) 3 be aware of 4 believe 5 be or seem to be 6 grope —*n.* 1 sense of touch 2 way a thing feels —**feel like** [Col.] have a desire for

feel'er *n.* 1 antenna or other organ of touch 2 remark or offer made to elicit opinions

feel'ing *n.* 1 sense of touch 2 sensation 3 an emotion 4 *pl.* sensitiveness 5 sympathy 6 opinion

feet *n.* pl. of FOOT

feign (fān) v. 1 make up (an excuse) 2 pretend

feint (fānt) n. pretended attack, as in boxing —v. make a feint

feist·y (fīs'tē) a. **-i·er, -i·est** [Col.] 1 lively 2 quarrelsome, belligerent, etc.

feld'spar' n. hard, crystalline mineral

fe·lic'i·tate' (-lis'-) v. congratulate —**fe·lic'i·ta'tion** n.

fe·lic'i·tous a. appropriate

fe·lic'i·ty n. 1 happiness 2 pl. **-ties** apt and pleasant expression

fe'line a. of or like a cat —n. a cat

fell v. 1 pt. of FALL 2 knock down 3 cut down

fel'low n. 1 an associate 2 an equal 3 a mate 4 man or boy —a. associated —**fel'low·ship'** n.

fel'on n. criminal

fel'o·ny n. major crime —**fe·lo'ni·ous** a.

felt n. fabric made of fibers pressed together

fe'male' a. 1 designating of or the sex that bears offspring 2 feminine —n. female person or animal

fem'i·nine (-nin) a. of or like women or girls; female —**fem'i·nin'i·ty** n.

fem'i·nism n. movement to win equal rights for women —**fem'i·nist** n., a.

fe'mur n. thighbone

fen n. swamp; bog

fence n. 1 barrier of posts, wire, etc. 2 dealer in stolen goods —v. 1 enclose with a fence 2 engage in fencing —**fenc'er** n.

fenc'ing n. sport of fighting with foils or swords

fend v. ward (off) —**fend for oneself** manage by oneself

fend'er n. a guard over an automobile wheel

fen'nel n. an herb used to flavor

fer'ment' (v.: fər ment') n. 1 thing causing fermentation 2 agitation —v. undergo or cause fermentation (in)

fer'men·ta'tion n. chemical change caused by yeast, bacteria, etc.

fern n. nonflowering plant with fronds

fe·ro'cious (-shəs) a. savage; fierce —**fe·roc'i·ty** n.

fer'ret n. kind of weasel —v. search (out)

fer'ric, fer'rous a. of iron

Fer'ris wheel n. large, revolving wheel with hanging seats, as in amusement parks

fer'rule (-əl) n. metal ring or cap around the end of a cane, etc. to strengthen it

fer'ry v. **-ried, -ry·ing** take across a river, etc. in a boat —n., pl. **-ries** boat used for ferrying: also **fer'ry·boat'**

fer'tile (furt''l) a. 1 producing abundantly 2 able to produce young, fruit, etc. —**fer·til'i·ty** n.

fer·til·ize' v. 1 make fertile 2 spread fer-

tilizer on 3 make fruitful by introducing a male germ cell —**fer'til·i·za'tion** n.

fer·til'iz·er n. manure, chemicals, etc. to enrich the soil

fer'ule (-əl) n. flat stick or ruler used to punish a child

fer'vent a. intense; ardent

fer'vid a. fervent

fer'vor n. ardor; zeal

fes'tal a. joyous; merry

fes'ter v. 1 form pus 2 rankle

fes'ti·val n. time or day of celebration

fes'tive a. joyous; merry

fes·tiv'i·ty n., pl. **-ties** 1 gaiety 2 pl. things done in celebration

fes·toon' n. garland, etc. hanging in loops —v. adorn with festoons

fet'a (cheese) n. soft, white cheese

fetch v. 1 go after and bring back; get 2 sell for

fetch'ing a. attractive

fete, fête (fāt, fet) n. festival; outdoor party —v. honor with a fete; entertain

fet'id a. stinking

fet'ish n. 1 object thought to have magic power 2 object of irrational devotion

fet'lock' n. leg joint above a horse's hoof

fet'ter n. ankle shackle —v. restrain as with fetters

fet'tle n. used chiefly in **in fine fettle**, in good condition

fe'tus n. unborn young —**fe'tal** a.

feud (fyōōd) n. deadly quarrel, as between families —v. engage in a feud

feu'dal·ism' n. medieval system with lords, vassals, and serfs —**feu'dal** a.

fe'ver n. abnormally high body temperature —**fe'ver·ish'** a.

few a. not many —pron., n. a small number

fez n. conical Turkish hat

fi·an·cé (fē'än sā') n. man to whom one is betrothed —**fi'an·cée'** (-sā') n.fem.

fi·as'co (fē-) n., pl. **-coes** or **-cos** utter failure

fi'at' (fī'-, fē'-) n. a decree

fib n. petty lie —v. **fibbed, fib'bing** tell a fib

fi'ber, fi'bre n. 1 threadlike part(s) forming organic tissue 2 threadlike part(s) used for weaving, etc. —**fi'brous** a.

Fi'ber·glas' trademark material made of fine filaments of glass —n. [f-] this material: also **fi'ber·glass'**

fi'ber·op'tic a. of synthetic fibers for transmitting light

fi'bril·la'tion (fib'ri-) n. rapid series of heart contractions, causing weak heartbeats

fi'broid' a. like or made of fibrous tissue

fi·bro'sis n. abnormal growth of fibrous tissue

fib'u·la (-yōō-) n., pl. **-lae** (-lē') or **-las**

thinner bone of lower leg

fick'le a. tending to change one's mind

fic'tion n. literary work(s) with imaginary characters and events —**fic'tion·al** a.

fic·ti'tious (-tish'əs) a. imaginary

fic'tive a. 1 of fiction 2 imaginary

fi'cus n., pl. **–cus** tropical plant with leathery leaves

fid'dle n. [Col.] violin —v. 1 [Col.] play a violin 2 fidget (with) —**fid'dler** n.

fi·del'i·ty n. faithfulness

fidg'et (fij'-) v. make nervous movements —**fidg'et·y** a.

fie (fī) int. shame!

field n. 1 piece of open land, esp. one for crops, grazing, etc. 2 expanse 3 area for athletic event 4 sphere of knowledge or activity 5 all contestants

field glasses n.pl. portable, telescopic eyeglasses

field goal n. 1 Basketball basket toss from play, scoring two points 2 Football goal kicked from the field, scoring three points

field hand n. hired farm worker

fiend (fēnd) n. 1 devil 2 [Col.] addict —**fiend'ish** a.

fierce a. 1 savage; wild 2 violent —**fierce'ly** adv.

fi'er·y a. **–i·er, –i·est** flaming, hot, etc. 2 ardent

fi·es'ta (fē-) n. festival

fife n. small, shrill flute

fif'teen' a., n. five more than ten —**fif'teenth'** a., n.

fifth a. preceded by four others —n. 1 one after the fourth 2 one of five equal parts 3 fifth of a gallon

fif'ty a., n., pl. **–ties** five times ten —**fif'ti·eth** a., n.

fig n. sweet, chewy fruit with seed-filled pulp

fight n., v. **fought, fight'ing** struggle; battle; contest —**fight'er** n.

fig'ment n. thing imagined

fig'ur·a·tive a. using metaphors, similes, etc.

fig'ure n. 1 outline; shape 2 person 3 likeness of a person or thing 4 illustration 5 design 6 a number 7 sum of money —v. 1 compute 2 be conspicuous 3 [Col.] predict —**figure out** solve

fig'ure·head' n. leader with no real power

figure of speech n. a vivid expression, use a metaphor or simile

fig'u·rine' (-rēn') n. small statue

fil'a·ment n. threadlike part

fil'bert n. hazelnut

filch v. steal (something trivial)

file n. 1 container for keeping papers in order 2 orderly arrangement of papers, etc.

3 line of persons or things 4 ridged tool for scraping, etc. —v. 1 put papers, etc. in order 2 move in a file 3 smooth or grind with a file

fi·let (fi lā') n., v. fillet

filet mi·gnon (min yōn') n. thick cut of beef tenderloin

fil'i·al a. of or suitable to a son or a daughter

fil'i·bus'ter n. obstruction of a bill in a legislature, as by a long speech —v. obstruct a bill in this way

fil'i·gree' n. lacelike work of fine wire

fil'ings n.pl. small pieces scraped off with a file

fill v. 1 make or become full 2 put into or hold (a job or office) 3 supply things ordered —n. anything that fills —**fill in** 1 make complete 2 substitute —**fill out** 1 make or become larger, etc. 2 complete (a blank form)

fil·let (fi lā') n. boneless piece of fish or meat —v. to bone (fish, etc.)

fill'ing n. thing used to fill something else

filling station n. service station

fil'lip n. stimulus; tonic

fil'ly n., pl. **–lies** young mare

film n. 1 thin coating 2 flexible cellulose material used in photography 3 1) series of pictures flashed on a screen in rapid succession so that things in them seem to move 2) story in this form —v. make a FILM (n. 3)

film'strip' n. strip of film with stills of pictures, charts, etc. on some subject

film'y a. **–i·er, –i·est** blurred

fil'ter n. thing used for straining out particles, etc. from a fluid, etc. —v. 1 pass through a filter 2 remove with a filter 3 pass slowly —**fil·tra'tion** n.

filter tip n. cigarette with a tip of cellulose, etc. to filter the smoke

filth n. 1 foul dirt 2 obscenity —**filth'i·ness** n. —**filth'y** a., **–i·er, –i·est**

fin n. winglike, membranous organ on a fish

fi·na'gle v. use, or get by, trickery —**fi·na'gler** n.

fi'nal a. 1 last 2 conclusive —n. pl. last of a series of contests —**fi·nal'i·ty** n. —**fi'nal·ly** adv. —**fi'nal·ist** n. —**fi'nal·ize'** v.

fi·na'le (-nal'ē) n. last part of a musical work

fi·nance' (or fi'nans') n. 1 pl. funds 2 science of managing money matters —v. supply money for —**fi·nan'cial** (-shəl) a. —**fin'an·cier'** (-sir') n.

finch n. small songbird

find v. **found, find'ing** 1 come upon; discover 2 learn 3 recover (a thing lost) 4 decide —n. something found

fine a. 1 excellent 2 not heavy or coarse 3

sharp 4 discriminating 5 very well —n. money paid as a penalty —v. cause to pay a fine

fine arts n.pl. painting, sculpture, music, etc.

fin'er·y n. showy clothes

fi·nesse' n. skill in handling delicate situations

fin'ger n. any of the parts (five with the thumb) at the end of the hand —v. to handle —**fin'ger·nail'** n. —**fin'ger·tip'** n.

fin'ger·board' n. part of a stringed instrument to which the strings are pressed

fin'ger·print' n. impression of the lines of a fingertip

fin'ick·y a. too particular; fussy

fi·nis (fin'is) n.; pl. **–nis·es** the end; finish

fin'ish v. 1 to end 2 complete 3 use up 4 perfect; polish —n. 1 last part; end 2 polish or perfection 3 way a surface is finished

fi'nite' a. having limits

Finn n. Finnish person

Finn'ish a., n. (of) the people or language of Finland

fiord (fyôrd) n. sea inlet bordered by steep cliffs

fir n. evergreen tree

fire n. 1 flame 2 thing burning 3 ardor 4 discharge of guns —v. 1 make burn 2 shoot (a gun, etc.) 3 discharge from a job —**on fire** burning —**under fire** under attack —**fire'proof'** v., a.

fire'arm' n. rifle, pistol, etc.

fire'bomb' n. incendiary bomb —v. attack, etc. with a firebomb

fire'crack'er n. noisy explosive rolled in paper

fire engine n. truck equipped for firefighting

fire escape n. outside stairway to escape a burning building

fire'fight'er n. one who fights fires —**fire'fight'ing** n.

fire'fly' n. winged beetle with a glowing abdomen

fire'man n., pl. **–men** 1 firefighter 2 stoker

fire'place' n. place built in a wall for a fire

fire'plug' n. street hydrant

fire'proof' v., a. (make) not easily destroyed by fire

fire'trap' n. building unsafe in the case of fire

fire'wood' n. wood used as fuel

fire'works' n.pl. firecrackers, rockets, etc. for noisy or brilliant displays

firm a. 1 solid 2 fixed; stable 3 strong and steady —v. make firm —n. business company —**firm'ness** n.

fir'ma·ment n. [Poet.] sky

first a., adv. before any others —n. 1 first

one 2 beginning

first aid n. emergency care for injuries —**first'-aid'** a.

first'-class' a. of the highest quality —adv. with the best accommodations

first'hand' a., adv. from the source; direct(ly)

first lady n. [often **F- L-**] wife of the U.S. president

first lieutenant n. military officer ranking just above second lieutenant

first'ly adv. in the first place

first'-rate' a. excellent

firth n. narrow inlet of the sea

fis'cal a. financial

fish n., pl. **fish**; for different kinds, **fish'es** coldblooded animal with gills and fins, living in water —v. 1 to catch fish 2 angle (for) —**fish'er·man** n., pl. **–men** —**fish'er·y** n., pl. **–ies**

fish'hook' n. hook for catching fish

fish'y a. **–i·er, –i·est** 1 like a fish 2 [Col.] questionable

fis·sion (fish'ən) n. a splitting apart

fis·sure (fish'ər) n. a cleft or crack

fist n. clenched hand

fist'ful n. handful

fist'i·cuffs' n.pl. boxing

fit v. **fit'ted** or **fit, fit'ting** 1 be suitable to 2 be the proper size, etc. (for) 3 adjust to fit 4 equip —a. **fit'ter, fit'test** 1 suited 2 proper 3 healthy —n. 1 way of fitting 2 seizure as of coughing 3 outburst —**fit'ness** n.

fit'ful a. not regular; spasmodic

fit'ting a. proper —n. 1 adjustment 2 pl. fixtures

five a., n. one more than four

fix v. 1 fasten or set firmly 2 determine 3 adjust or repair 4 prepare (food, etc.) 5 [Col.] influence by bribery, etc. —n. 1 [Col.] predicament 2 [Sl.] clear understanding —**fix up** [Col.] set in order —**fixed** a.

fix·a'tion n. obsession

fix'ings' n.pl. [Col.] accessories or trimmings

fix'ture n. any of the attached furnishings of a house

fizz v., n. (make) a hissing, bubbling sound

fiz'zle v. 1 to fizz 2 [Col.] fail

fjord (fyôrd) n. fiord

flab n. [Col.] sagging flesh

flab'ber·gast' v. amaze

flab'by a. **–bi·er, –bi·est** 1 limp and soft 2 weak

flac·cid (flak'sid, flas'id) a. flabby

flag n. 1 cloth with colors or designs, used as a national symbol, etc. 2 iris (flower) —v. **flagged, flag'ging** 1 to signal with flags 2 grow weak —**flag'pole', flag'staff'** n.

flag'el·late' (flaj'-) v. to whip —**flag'el·la'-tion** n.

flag'on (flag'-) n. container for liquids

flag'pole' n. pole for flying a flag: also **flag'staff'**

fla'grant a. glaringly bad —**fla'gran·cy** n.

flag'ship' n. 1 commander's ship 2 chief member of a network

flag'stone' n. flat paving stone

flail n. implement used to thresh grain by hand —v. 1 use a flail 2 beat

flair n. aptitude; knack

flak n. 1 fire of antiaircraft guns 2 [Col.] criticism

flake n. 1 soft, thin mass 2 chip or peeling —v. form into flakes —**flak'y** a., **-i·er, -i·est**

flam·bé' (fläm bā') a. served with flaming rum, etc.

flam·boy'ant a. showy —**flam·boy'ance** n.

flame n. tongue(s) of fire; blaze —v. burst into flame

fla·men'co n. Spanish gypsy music or dancing

flame'out' n. failure of combustion in jet engine in flight

fla·min'go n. pink, long-legged wading bird

flam'ma·ble a. easily set on fire

flange (flanj) n. projecting rim on a wheel, etc.

flank n. 1 side of an animal between the ribs and the hip 2 side of anything —v. be at, or go around, the side of

flan'nel n. soft, napped cloth of wool, etc.

flan'nel·ette', flan'nel·et' (-et') n. soft, fleecy, cotton cloth

flap n. 1 flat, loose piece 2 motion or sound of a swinging flap —v. flutter

flare v. 1 blaze up 2 spread outward —n. 1 bright, unsteady blaze 2 brief, dazzling signal light 3 sudden outburst 4 a spreading outward

flare'-up' n. sudden outburst

flash v. 1 send out a sudden, brief light 2 sparkle 3 move suddenly 4 [Col.] show briefly —n. 1 sudden, brief light 2 an instant 3 bit of late news

flash'back' n. interruption in a story by a return to some earlier episode

flash'bulb n. bulb giving brief, bright light, for taking photographs

flash'card' n. one of a set of cards used as an aid to memorizing

flash'cube' n. rotating cube with flash-bulbs in four sides

flash'ing n. metal roofing for joints, etc.

flash'light' n. portable electric light

flash'y a. **-i·er, -i·est** gaudy; showy

flask n. kind of bottle

flat a. **flat'ter, flat'test** 1 smooth and level

2 broad and thin 3 lying spread out 4 absolute 5 without taste or sparkle 6 dull; lifeless 7 emptied of air 8 Mus. below true pitch —adv. in a flat way —n. 1 flat surface or part 2 deflated tire 3 Mus. note ½ step below another: symbol (♭) 4 apartment —**flat'ten** n.

flat'bed' n. trailer, etc. having no sides

flat'car' n. railroad car without sides

flat'fish' n. fish with a very broad, flat body

flat'foot' n. foot with the sole's arch flattened

flat'-out' a. [Col.] 1 at full, speed, effort, etc. 2 absolute

flat'ter v. 1 praise insincerely 2 gratify the vanity of —**flat'ter·y** n.

flat'u·lent (flach'ə-) a. having or making gas in the stomach

flat'ware' n. flat tableware

flaunt (flônt) v. show off

fla'vor n. taste of a substance —v. give flavor to

fla'vor·ing n. added essence, etc. that flavors food

flaw n. defect —**flawed** a. —**flaw'less** a.

flax n. plant with fibers that are spun into linen thread

flax'en a. pale yellow

flay v. strip the skin from

flea n. small jumping insect that is parasitic

fleck n., v. spot

fledg'ling (flej'-) n. young bird just able to fly

flee v. **fled, flee'ing** escape swiftly, as from danger

fleece n. wool covering a sheep —v. to swindle —**fleec'y** a., **-i·er, -i·est**

fleet n. 1 group of warships under one command 2 any similar group, as of trucks, planes, etc. —a. swift

fleet'ing a. passing swiftly

flesh n. 1 tissue between the skin and the bones 2 pulp of fruits and vegetables 3 the body —**flesh'y** a., **-i·er, -i·est**

flew v. pt. of FLY

flex v. 1 bend, as an arm 2 contract, as a muscle

flex'i·ble a. 1 easily bent; pliable 2 adaptable

flick n. light, quick stroke —v. strike, throw, etc. with such a stroke

flick'er v. move, burn, or shine unsteadily —n. dart of flame or light

fli'er n. 1 aviator 2 handbill or leaflet

flight n. 1 act or power of flying 2 distance flown 3 group of things flying together 4 trip by airplane 5 set of stairs 6 a fleeing —**flight'less** a.

flight'y a. **-i·er, -i·est** unsettled; frivolous

flim'sy *a.* **-si·er, -si·est 1** easily broken **2** trivial

flinch *v.* draw back, as from a blow

fling *v.* throw with force —*n.* **1** a flinging **2** [Col.] a try **3** [Col.] brief love affair

flint *n.* a hard quartz

flip *v.* **flipped, flip'ping** toss with a quick jerk —*a.* [Col.] flippant

flip'pant *a.* frivolous and disrespectful —**flip'pan·cy** *n.*

flip'per *n.* flat limb adapted for swimming, as in seals

flip side *n.* [Col.] reverse side (of a phonograph record)

flirt *v.* **1** play at love **2** trifle —*n.* one who plays at love —**flir·ta'tion** *n.* —**flir·ta'tious** *a.*

flit *v.* **flit'ted, flit'ting** move lightly and rapidly

float *n.* **1** thing that stays on the surface of a liquid **2** flat, decorated vehicle in a parade —*v.* **1** stay on the surface of a liquid **2** drift gently in air, etc. **3** put into circulation, as a bond issue

flock *n.* group, esp. of animals —*v.* gather in a flock

flock'ing *n.* tiny fibers put on wallpaper, etc. as a velvetlike surface: also **flock**

floe *n.* large sheet of floating ice

flog *v.* **flogged, flog'ging** beat, thrash, or whip

flood *n.* **1** overflowing of water on land **2** great outpouring —*v.* to overflow

flood'light' *n.* lamp casting a very bright, broad light

floor *n.* **1** bottom surface of a room, etc. **2** story in a building **3** permission to speak —*v.* **1** furnish with a floor **2** knock down

floor'ing *n.* material for making a floor

floor show *n.* show with singers, dancers, etc., as in a nightclub

flop *v.* **flopped, flop'ping 1** move, drop, or flap about clumsily **2** [Col.] fail —*n.* a flopping —**flop'py** *a.*

floppy (disk) *n.* small, flexible computer disk

flo'ra *n.* the plants of a region

flo'ral *a.* of or like flowers

flor'id *a.* **1** ruddy **2** gaudy

flo'rist *n.* one who grows or sells flowers

floss *n.* **1** soft, silky fibers **2** dental floss —*v.* clean (the teeth) with dental floss

flo·til'la *n.* small fleet

flot'sam *n.* floating debris or cargo of a shipwreck

flounce *v.* move with quick, flinging motions —*n.* a ruffle

floun'der *v.* struggle or speak clumsily —*n.* kind of edible flatfish

flour *n.* a powdery substance ground from grain

flour'ish *v.* **1** thrive **2** be in one's prime **3** brandish —*n.* **1** sweeping motion or stroke **2** fanfare

flout *v.* mock or scorn

flow *v.* **1** move as water does **2** move smoothly **3** proceed **4** hang loose —*n.* a flowing or thing that flows

flow'chart' *n.* diagram showing steps in a process

flow'er *n.* **1** petals and pistil of a plant **2** a plant grown for its blossoms **3** best part —*v.* **1** to produce blossoms **2** become its best

flow'er·pot' *n.* container with earth for a plant to grow in

flow'er·y *a.* **-i·er, -i·est** showy in expression

flown *v.* pp. of FLY

flu *n.* influenza

flub [Col.] *v.* **flubbed, flub'bing** bungle —*n.* blunder

fluc'tu·ate' (-chōō-) *v.* keep changing, as prices

flue *n.* shaft in a chimney

flu'ent *a.* speaking or writing easily —**flu'en·cy** *n.*

fluff *n.* loose, soft mass —*v.* **1** make fluffy **2** bungle

fluff'y *a.* **-i·er, -i·est** soft and light

flu'id *a.* **1** able to flow **2** not fixed —*n.* liquid or gas —**flu·id'i·ty** *n.*

fluke *n.* **1** anchor blade **2** [Col.] stroke of luck

flung *v.* pt. & pp. of FLING

flunk *v.* [Col.] to fail

flunk'y *n., pl.* **-ies** low, servile person

fluo·res'cent (flôr es'ənt) *a.* giving off cool light —**fluo·res'cence** *n.*

fluo'ri·date' (flôr'ə-) *v.* add fluorides to (water) —**fluo'ri·da'tion** *n.*

fluo·ride (flôr'īd') *n.* fluorine salt

fluo·rine (flôr'ēn') *n.* yellowish gas, a chemical element

fluo'ro·scope' (flôr'ə-) *n.* kind of X-ray machine

flur'ry *n., pl.* **-ries 1** gust of wind, rain, or snow **2** sudden commotion

flush *v.* **1** to redden in the face **2** start up from cover, as a bird **3** wash out —*n.* a blush; glow —*a.* **1** well-supplied **2** level (*with*) **3** direct

flus'ter *v.* make confused

flute *n.* tubelike wind instrument —**flut'ist** *n.*

flut'ed *a.* grooved

flut'ter *v.* wave, move, or beat rapidly or irregularly —*n.* **1** a fluttering **2** confusion —**flut'ter·y** *a.*

flux *n.* **1** a flowing **2** constant change **3** substance used to help metals fuse

fly *v.* **flew** or (*v.* 5) **flied, flown** or (*v.* 5) **flied,**

fly'ing 1 move through the air by using wings **2** wave or float in the air **3** move swiftly **4** flee **5** hit a fly in baseball **6** travel in or pilot (aircraft) —n., pl. **flies 1** flap concealing buttons, etc. in a garment **2** baseball batted high **3** winged insect

fly'catch'er n. small bird that catches flying insects

fly'er n. flier

flying colors n. notable success

flying fish n. fish with winglike fins that glides in the air

flying saucer n. unidentified flying object

fly'leaf' n. blank leaf at the front or back of a book

fly'pa'per n. sticky paper set out to catch flies

fly'wheel' n. wheel that regulates a machine's speed

FM frequency modulation

foal n. young horse

foam n. **1** bubbly mass on liquids **2** spongy mass of rubber, plastic, etc. —v. form foam —**foam'y** a., **-i·er, -i·est**

foam rubber n. rubber foam

fob n. pocket-watch chain or ornament on it

fo'cus n., pl. **-cus·es** or **-ci** (-sī') **1** point where rays of light meet **2** adjustment of lens distance for clear image **3** center of activity —v. **1** bring into focus **2** concentrate —**fo'cal** a.

fod'der n. coarse food for cattle, horses, etc.

foe n. enemy

fog n. **1** thick mist **2** mental confusion —v. **fogged, fog'ging** make or become foggy —**fog'gy** a., **-gi·er, -gi·est** —**fog'gi·ness** n.

fog'horn' n. horn blown to warn ships in a fog

fo·gy (fō'gē) n., pl. **-gies** old-fashioned person

foi'ble n. small weakness in character

foil v. thwart —n. **1** thin fencing sword **2** thin sheet of metal **3** one that enhances another by contrast

foist v. impose by fraud

fold v. **1** double (material) over **2** intertwine **3** wrap up —n. **1** folded layer **2** pen for sheep

-fold suf. times as many

fold'a·way' a. that can be folded together and stored

fold'er n. **1** folded sheet of cardboard to hold papers **2** booklet of folded sheets

fo'li·age n. plant leaves

fo'li·o' n., pl. **-os'** largest regular size of book

folk n., pl. **folk** or **folks** people —a. of the common people

folk'lore' n. beliefs, legends, etc. of a people

folk song n. song made and handed down

among the common people —**folk singer** n.

folk'sy a. **-si·er, -si·est** [Col.] friendly or sociable

fol'li·cle n. small sac or gland, as in the skin

fol'low v. **1** come or go after **2** go along **3** take up (a trade) **4** result (from) **5** obey **6** pay attention to **7** understand —**follow out** (or **up**) carry out fully —**fol'low·er** n.

fol'low·ing a. next after —n. group of followers

fol'ly n., pl. **-lies** foolish state, action, belief, etc.

fo·ment' v. incite

fond a. loving; tender —**fond of** liking —**fond'ly** adv.

fon'dle v. to caress

fon·due', fon·du' n. oil, melted cheese, etc. for dipping cubes of meat, bread, etc.

font n. basin for holy water

food n. substance taken in by an animal or plant to enable it to live and grow

food poi'son·ing n. any sickness caused by eating food contaminated by bacteria, chemicals, etc.

fool n. **1** silly person **2** dupe —v. **1** be silly or playful **2** trick

fool'har'dy a. **-di·er, -di·est** foolishly daring; rash

fool'ish a. silly; unwise

fool'proof' a. simple, safe, etc.

foot n., pl. **feet 1** end part of the leg, on which one stands **2** bottom; base **3** measure of length, 12 inches —v. [Col.] pay (a bill) —**on foot** walking —**under foot** in the way

foot'ball' n. **1** team game played on a field with an inflated leather ball **2** this ball

foot'hill' n. low hill at the foot of a mountain

foot'hold' n. place for the feet, as in climbing

foot'ing n. **1** secure placing of the feet **2** basis for relationship

foot'lights' n.pl. lights at the front of a stage floor

foot'loose' a. free to go or do as one likes

foot'man n., pl. **-men** male servant assisting a butler

foot'note' n. note at the bottom of a page

foot'print' n. mark left by a foot

foot'rest' n. support for foot or feet

foot'step' n. **1** sound of a step **2** footprint

foot'stool' n. stool for a seated person's feet

fop n. vain man fussy about his clothes, etc. —**fop'pish** a.

for prep. **1** in place of **2** in the interest

of 3 in favor of **4** with the purpose of 5 in search of **6** meant to be received, used, etc. by **7** with respect to **8** because of **9** to the extent or duration of —con. because

for′age n. fodder —v. to search for food

for′ay n., v. raid

for·bear′ v. –bore′, –borne′, –bear′ing 1 refrain (from) 2 control oneself —**for·bear′ance** n.

for·bid′ v. –bade′ (-bad′) or –bad′, –bid′den, –bid′ding not permit; prohibit

for·bid′ding a. frightening

force n. 1 strength; power 2 coercion 3 effectiveness **4** organized group, as an army —v. 1 make do something; compel 2 break open 3 impose, produce, etc. by force —**force′ful** a.

forced a. 1 compulsory 2 not natural

for′ceps n., pl. –ceps small tongs or pincers

for′ci·ble a. with force —**for′ci·bly** adv.

ford n. shallow place in a river —v. cross at a ford

fore adv., a., n. (in or toward) the front part —int. Golf warning shout

fore– pref. before; in front

fore′arm′ n. arm between the elbow and wrist

fore′bear′ n. ancestor

fore·bode′ v. foretell

fore′cast′ v. –cast′ or –cast′ed, –cast′ing predict —n. prediction —**fore′cast′er** n.

fore·cas·tle (fōk′səl, fôr′kas′əl) n. forward deck or front part of a ship

fore·close′ v. take away the right to redeem (a mortgage) —**fore·clo′sure** a.

fore′fa′ther n. ancestor

fore′fin′ger n. finger nearest the thumb

fore′front′ n. extreme front

fore′go′ing a. preceding

fore·gone′ a. previous

fore′ground′ n. part of a scene nearest the viewer

fore′hand′ n. racket stroke with palm of hand turned forward

fore′head′ n. part of the face above the eyebrows

for′eign (-in) a. 1 of or from another country 2 not characteristic —**for′eign-born′** a. —**for′eign·er** n.

foreign minister n. cabinet member in charge of foreign affairs

fore′knowl′edge n. knowledge of something beforehand

fore′leg′ n. front leg of animal

fore′man n., pl. –men 1 man in charge of workers 2 chairman of a jury

fore′most′ a., adv. first

fore′noon′ n. time before noon

fo·ren′sic a. 1 of or suitable for public debate 2 of scientific techniques of crime investigation

fore′or·dain′ v. predestine

fore′play′ n. touching, etc. before sexual intercourse

fore′run′ner n. person or thing foretelling another

fore·see′ v. –saw′, –seen′, –see′ing see or know beforehand

fore·shad′ow v. presage

fore·short′en v. shorten some lines in drawing to make some parts seem farther away

fore′sight′ n. 1 power to foresee 2 prudence

fore′skin′ n. fold of skin over the end of the penis

for′est n. tract of land covered with trees

fore·stall′ v. prevent by acting beforehand

for′es·ta′tion n. planting or care of forests

for′est·ry n. science of the care of forests —**for′est·er** n.

fore·tell′ v. –told′, –tell′ing predict

fore′thought′ n. foresight

for·ev′er adv. 1 for all time 2 at all times

fore·warn′ v. warn beforehand

fore′wom′an n.pl. –wom′en woman serving as a foreman

fore′word′ n. preface

for′feit (-fit) n. penalty —v. lose as a penalty —**for′fei·ture** (-fə chər) n.

for·gath′er v. assemble; meet

forge n. 1 furnace for heating metal to be wrought 2 smith's shop —v. 1 shape by heating and hammering 2 counterfeit (a signature) 3 advance slowly

for′ger·y n., pl. –ies 1 crime of forging documents, signatures, etc. 2 anything forged

for·get′ v. –got′, –got′ten or –got′, –get′ting 1 be unable to remember 2 neglect —**for·get′ful** a.

for·get′-me-not′ n. plant with small, blue flowers

for·give′ v. –gave′, –giv′en, –giv′ing give up wanting to punish; pardon —**for·give′ness** n. —**for·giv′ing** a.

for·go′ v. –went′, –gone′, –go′ing do without

fork n. 1 pronged instrument for lifting 2 place of branching —v. to branch

fork′lift′ n. mobile lifting device in warehouses, etc.

for·lorn′ a. 1 abandoned 2 wretched; miserable

form n. 1 shape; figure 2 mold 3 style; customary behavior **4** document to be filled in —v. 1 to shape 2 develop (habits) 3 constitute —**form′less** a.

for′mal a. 1 according to custom, rule, etc. 2 stiff; prim 3 for use at ceremonies —**for′mal·ize′** v. —**for′mal·ly** adv.

form·al'de·hyde' n. disinfectant and preservative

for·mal'i·ty n. 1 an observing of customs, rules, etc. 2 pl. **–ties** formal act

for'mat' n. general arrangement, as of a book

for·ma'tion n. 1 a forming 2 thing formed; structure —**form'a·tive** a.

for'mer a. 1 of the past 2 being the first mentioned —**for'mer·ly** adv.

for'mi·da·ble a. 1 causing fear 2 hard to handle

for'mu·la n., pl. **–las** or **–lae'** (-lē') 1 fixed expression or rule 2 set of symbols expressing a mathematical rule, chemical compound, etc. —**for'mu·late'** v. —**for'mu·la'tion** n.

for'ni·ca'tion n. sexual intercourse between unmarried people —**for'ni·cate'** v.

for·sake' v. **–sook'**, **–sak'en**, **–sak'ing** abandon; desert

for·swear' v. 1 swear to give up 2 commit perjury

for·syth'i·a (-sith'-) n. shrub with yellow flowers

fort n. fortified place for military defense

for·te (fôr'tā'; n.: fôrt) a., adv. Mus. loud —n. what one does well

forth adv. 1 forward 2 out; into view

forth'com'ing a. 1 about to appear 2 ready at hand

forth'right' a. frank

forth·with' adv. at once

for'ti·fi·ca'tion n. 1 a fortifying 2 a fort

for'ti·fy' v. **–fied'**, **–fy'ing** to strengthen, enrich, etc.

for·tis'si·mo' a., adv. Mus. very loud

for'ti·tude' n. calm courage

fort'night' n. two weeks

for'tress n. fortified place

for·tu'i·tous a. 1 accidental 2 lucky

for'tu·nate (-chə nət) a. lucky —**for'tu·nate·ly** adv.

for'tune n. 1 luck; fate 2 good luck 3 wealth

for'tune-tell'er n. one claiming to foretell others' future —**for'tune-tell'ing** n.

for'ty a., n., pl. **–ties** four times ten —**for'ti·eth** a., n.

fo'rum n. meeting for public discussion

for'ward a. 1 at, to, or of the front 2 advanced 3 bold —adv. ahead: also **for'wards** —v. 1 promote 2 send on

fos'sil n. hardened plant or animal remains, as in rock —a. 1 of a fossil 2 taken from the earth —**fos'sil·ize'** v.

fos'ter v. 1 bring up 2 promote —a. in a family but not by birth or adoption

fought v. pt. & pp. of FIGHT

foul a. 1 filthy 2 stormy 3 outside the rules or limits 4 very bad —n. foul hit, blow, etc. —v. 1 make filthy 2 entangle 3 make a foul

foul'-up' n. [Col.] mix-up; mess

found v. 1 pt. & pp. of FIND 2 establish —**found'er** n.

foun·da'tion n. 1 establishment or basis 2 base of a wall, house, etc. 3 philanthropic fund or institution

foun'der v. 1 fall or go lame 2 fill and sink, as a ship

found'ling n. deserted child

found'ry n., pl. **–ries** place where metal is cast

fount n. source

foun'tain n. 1 spring of water 2 jet of water or basin for it 3 source

foun'tain·head' n. source

fountain pen n. pen getting ink from its own reservoir

four a., n. one more than three —**fourth** a., n.

four'score' a., n. eighty

four'some n. group of four people

four'square' a. 1 firm 2 frank —adv. frankly

four'teen' a., n. four more than ten —**four'teenth'** a., n.

fowl n. 1 any bird 2 domestic bird, as the chicken

fox n. small, wild, doglike animal —v. to trick —**fox'y** a., **–i·er**, **–i·est**

fox'glove' n. plant with long spikes of flowers

fox'hole' n. hole dug as protection against gunfire

fox terrier n. small terrier with smooth or wiry coat

fox trot n. ballroom dance

foy'er n. entrance hall

fra'cas (frā'-) n. brawl

frac'tion n. 1 part of a whole, as ¾, ½, etc. 2 small part

frac'tious a. unruly

frac'ture n. a break, esp. in a bone —v. to break; crack

frag'ile (fraj'əl) a. easily broken —**fra·gil'i·ty** n.

frag'ment n. 1 part broken away 2 incomplete part —**frag'men·tar'y** a.

fra'grant a. sweet-smelling —**fra'grance** n.

frail a. 1 fragile 2 delicate or weak —**frail'ty** n., pl. **–ties**

frame v. 1 make, form, build, etc. 2 enclose in a border 3 [Sl.] make seem guilty by a plot —n. 1 framework 2 framing border or case 3 mood

frame'-up' n. [Col.] falsifying of evidence to make seem guilty

frame'work' n. supporting or basic structure

franc n. Fr. monetary unit

fran′chise (-chīz′) n. **1** special right **2** right to vote **3** business with right to provide product or service

fran′gi·ble a. breakable

frank a. outspoken; candid —v. send (mail) free —**frank′ly** adv. —**frank′ness** n.

frank′furt·er n. smoked link sausage; wiener

frank′in·cense n. gum resin burned as incense

fran′tic a. wild with anger, worry, etc. —**fran′ti·cal·ly** adv.

frap·pé (fra pā′) n. dessert of partly frozen fruit juices

fra·ter′nal a. **1** brotherly **2** of a fellowship society

fra·ter′ni·ty n., pl. **–ties 1** brotherliness **2** college social club for men **3** group with like interests

frat′er·nize v. be friendly

fraud n. **1** a cheating or tricking; dishonesty **2** hypocrite; cheat

fraud′u·lent (frô′jə-) a. **1** using fraud **2** done by fraud

fraught a. filled (with)

fray n. quarrel or fight —v. make or become ragged

fraz′zle [Col.] v. wear out —n. frazzled state

freak n. abnormal animal or plant —a. abnormal

freck′le n. small brown spot on the skin —v. to spot with freckles

free a. **fre′er, fre′est 1** not under another's control **2** loose, clear, unrestricted, etc. **3** without cost —adv. **1** without cost **2** in a free way —v. **freed, free′ing** make free —**free from** (or of) without

free′boot′er n. a pirate

free′dom n. **1** independence **2** liberty **3** ease of movement **4** a right

free fall n. unchecked fall through the air, esp. part of parachutist's jump before parachute opens

free′-for-all′ n. a brawl

free′lance′, free′-lance′ a. selling services to individual buyers

free′load′er n. [Col.] one imposing on others for free food, etc.

free′think′er n. religious skeptic

free′way′ n. multiple-lane highway with interchanges

freeze v. **froze, fro′zen, freez′ing 1** change into, or become covered with, ice **2** make or become very cold **3** kill or damage by cold **4** fix (prices, etc.) at a set level —n. a freezing

freeze′-dry′ v. **–dried′, –dry′ing** preserve (food) by freezing quickly and drying

freez′er n. refrigerator for freezing and storing foods

freight (frāt) n. **1** goods transported **2** transportation of goods or its cost **3** train for freight

freight′er n. ship for freight

French a., n. **(of)** the people or language of France —**French′man** n., pl. **–men**

French dressing n. orange-colored salad dressing

French fried a. fried in deep fat

French fries n.pl. potatoes cut in strips and fried in deep fat

French horn n. brass musical instrument with a coiled tube

fre·net′ic a. frantic

fren′zy n., pl. **–zies** wild excitement —**fren′zied** a.

fre′quen·cy n., pl. **–cies 1** frequent occurrence **2** number of times anything recurs in a given period

frequency modulation n. changing of the frequency of the radio wave according to the signal being broadcast

fre′quent a. **1** occurring often **2** constant —v. go to habitually

fres′co n., pl. **–coes** or **–cos** painting done on wet plaster

fresh a. **1** not spoiled, stale, worn out, etc. **2** new **3** refreshing **4** not salt: said of water —**fresh′en** v.

fresh′et n. flooded stream

fresh′man n., pl. **–men** first-year student in high school or college

fresh′wa′ter a. living in water that is not salty

fret v. **fret′ted, fret′ting**; n. to worry —n. **1** worry **2** ridge on fingerboard of banjo, guitar, etc. —**fret′ful** a.

fret′work′ n. ornate openwork

fri′a·ble (frī′-) a. easily crumbled

fri′ar n. R.C.Ch. member of a religious order

fric′as·see′ n. stewed pieces of meat

fric′tion n. **1** rubbing of one object against another **2** conflict —**fric′tion·al** a.

Fri′day n. sixth day of the week

fried v. pt. & pp. of **FRY**

friend n. **1** person one knows well and likes **2** ally —**friend′ship′** n.

friend′ly a. **–li·er, –li·est** kindly; helpful

frieze (frēz) n. decorative band around a wall, etc.

frig·ate (frig′ət) n. fast sailing warship

fright n. sudden fear

fright′en v. **1** make afraid **2** drive (away) with fear

fright′ful a. **1** causing fright **2** disgusting

frig·id (frij′id) a. very cold —**fri·gid′i·ty** n.

frill n. 1 ruffle 2 [Col.] fancy ornament —**frill′y** a.

fringe n. border, as of loose threads —v. to edge, as with a fringe

fringe benefit n. payment other than wages, as in pension, insurance, etc.

frip′per·y n.,pl. **–ies** showy display, clothes, etc.

frisk v. to frolic

frisk′y a. **-i·er, -i·est** lively —**frisk′i·ness** n.

frit′ter v. waste (money, etc.) bit by bit —n. small fried cake

friv′o·lous a. 1 trivial 2 silly —**fri·vol′i·ty** n.,pl. **–ties**

frizz, friz′zle v. to form tight curls —**friz′zy** a.

fro adv. back: used only in **to and fro**, back and forth

frock n. 1 dress 2 robe

frog n. 1 leaping web-footed animal 2 braided loop —**frog in the throat** hoarseness

frol′ic n. merry time; fun —v. **-icked, -ick·ing** have fun —**frol′ic·some** a.

from prep. 1 beginning at 2 out of 3 originating with 4 out of the possibility, reach, etc. of 5 as not being like 6 because of

frond n. fern or palm leaf

front n. 1 forward part 2 first part 3 land along a street, ocean, etc. 4 outward behavior —a. of or at the front —v. to face —**front′age** n. —**fron′tal** a.

fron·tier′ n. 1 border of a country 2 new or unexplored field —**fron·tiers′man** n.,pl. **–men**

fron′tis·piece′ n. picture facing the title page

front′-run′ner n. leading candidate, runner, etc.

frost n. 1 temperature causing freezing 2 frozen dew or vapor —v. cover with frost or frosting —**frost′y** a., **-i·er, -i·est**

frost′bite′ n. injury from intense cold —**frost′bit′ten** a.

frost′ing n. 1 icing 2 dull finish on glass

froth n., v. foam —**froth′y** a., **-i·er, -i·est**

fro′ward a. stubborn

frown v. 1 contract the brows 2 look with disapproval (on) —n. a frowning

frow′zy a. slovenly

froze v. pt. of FREEZE

fro′zen v. pp. of FREEZE

fruc′tose′ n. sugar in honey, sweet fruit, etc.

fru′gal a. thrifty or sparing —**fru·gal′i·ty** n.

fruit n. 1 pulpy, edible product of a plant or tree 2 result; product —**fruit′ful** a. —**fruit′less** a.

fruit′cake′ n. rich cake with fruit, nuts, etc.

fru·i′tion (-ish′ən) n. 1 the bearing of fruit 2 fulfillment

frump n. dowdy woman —**frump′y** a.

frus′trate′ v. thwart; block —**frus·tra′tion** n.

fry v. **fried, fry′ing** cook in hot fat or oil —n. young fish

fry′er n. 1 utensil for deep-frying foods 2 tender chicken for frying

fuch′sia (fyo̅o̅′shə) n. plant with purplish-red flowers —a. purplish-red

fudge n. soft candy made of butter, sugar, etc.

fu′el n. thing burned for heat or power —v. supply with or get fuel

fu′gi·tive a. 1 fleeing 2 fleeting —n. one who has fled from the law, etc.

fugue (fyo̅o̅g) n. musical work with theme in counterpoint

–ful suf. 1 full of 2 having the qualities of 3 apt to 4 quantity that will fill

ful′crum n. support on which a lever turns

ful·fill′, ful·fil′ v. **-filled′, -fill′ing** carry out or complete, as a promise or duty —**ful·fill′ment, ful·fil′ment** n.

full a. 1 containing all there is space for 2 having much in it 3 complete 4 ample —n. greatest amount, etc. —adv. 1 completely 2 exactly —**full′ness** n. —**full′y** adv.

full′-blown′ a. matured

full dress n. formal dress

full′-fledged′ a. fully developed; of full status

full′-grown′ a. fully grown

full house n. poker hand with three of a kind and a pair

full′-scale′ a. 1 to the utmost degree 2 of full size

full′-time′ a. of work, etc. using all one's regular working hours

ful′mi·nate′ (ful′-) v. 1 explode 2 denounce strongly

ful′some (fo̅o̅l′-) a. sickeningly insincere

fum′ble v. grope or handle clumsily —n. a fumbling

fume n. offensive smoke or vapor —v. 1 give off fumes 2 show anger

fu′mi·gate′ v. fill with fumes so as to kill vermin, germs, etc.

fun n. 1 lively play; merry time 2 source of gaiety —**make fun of** ridicule

func′tion n. 1 special or typical action, use, duty, etc. 2 formal ceremony or social affair —v. do its work —**func′tion·al** a.

func·tion·ar′y n.,pl. **-ies** an official

fund n. 1 supply; store 2 money set aside for a purpose 3 pl. ready money

fun′da·men′tal a., n. basic (thing)

fun′da·men′tal·ism′ n. religious beliefs based literally on the Bible —**fun′da·men′tal·ist** n., a.

fu′ner·al n. ceremonies for burial or cremation

funeral director n. manager of place (**funeral home** or **parlor**) for funerals

fu·ne′re·al (-nir′ē-) a. sad; gloomy

fun′gus n., pl. **-gi′** (-jī′, -gī′) or **-gus·es** any of the mildews, molds, mushrooms, etc. —**fun′gous** a.

funk n. [Col.] depressed mood

fun′nel n. 1 slim tube with a cone-shaped mouth 2 ship's smokestack —v. to pour as through a funnel

fun′ny a. **-ni·er**, **-ni·est** 1 amusing 2 [Col.] odd

fur n. soft, thick hair on an animal —**fur′ry** a., **-ri·er**, **-ri·est**

fur·be·low′ (-bə lō′) n. fancy trimming

fu′ri·ous a. full of fury

furl v. roll up tightly, as a flag

fur′long′ n. ⅛ of a mile

fur′lough (-lō) n. a military leave of absence —v. grant a furlough to

fur′nace (-nəs) n. structure in which heat is produced

fur′nish v. 1 put furniture into 2 supply

fur′nish·ings n.pl. 1 furniture and fixtures, as for a house 2 things to wear

fur′ni·ture n. chairs, beds, etc. in a room, etc.

fu·ror (fyoor′ôr′) n. 1 widespread enthusiasm 2 fury

fur′ri·er n. one who processes, or deals in, furs

fur′ring n. thin wood strips put on a wall, floor, etc. before boards or plaster

fur′row n. 1 groove made in the ground by a plow 2 deep wrinkle —v. make furrows in

fur′ther a. 1 additional 2 more distant —adv. 1 to a greater extent 2 in addition 3 at or to a greater distance —v. to promote —**fur′ther·ance** n.

fur′ther·more′ adv. besides

fur′thest a. most distant —adv. at or to the greatest distance or extent

fur′tive (-tiv) a. done or acting in a stealthy way

fu′ry n. 1 wild rage 2 violence

fuse v. melt (together) —n. 1 wick that is lighted to set off an explosive 2 safety device that breaks an electric circuit when the current is too strong —**fu′sion** n.

fu′se·lage (-läzh′) n. body of an airplane

fu′sil·lade′ (-läd′, -lād′) n. simultaneous discharge of many guns

fu′sion n. 1 a melting together 2 blending 3 nuclear fusion

fuss n. nervous, excited state —v. bustle about or worry over trifles —**fuss′y** a., **-i·er**, **-i·est**

fus′ty a. **-ti·er**, **-ti·est** 1 musty 2 old-fashioned

fu·tile (fyoōt′'l) a. useless —**fu·til′i·ty** n.

fu′ton′ (foō′-) n. thin floor mattress

fu′ture a. that is to be or come —n. 1 time that is to come 2 what is going to be; prospects —**fu′tur·is′tic** a.

fu·tu′ri·ty (-toor′ə-) n. quality of being future

fuzz n. loose, light particles; fine hairs —**fuzz′y** a., **-i·er**, **-i·est**

G

G trademark film rating indicating content suitable for persons of all ages

gab n., v. **gabbed**, **gab′bing** [Col.] chatter —**gab′by** a., **-bi·er**, **-bi·est**

gab·ar·dine′ (-ər dēn′) n. cloth with a diagonal weave

gab′ble v., n. jabber

ga′ble n. triangular wall enclosed by the sloping ends of a roof —**ga′bled** a.

gad v. **gad′ded**, **gad′ding** roam about restlessly —**gad′a·bout′** n.

gad′fly′ n. 1 large, stinging fly 2 one who annoys in exciting or stirring others

gadg′et (gaj′-) n. small mechanical device

gaff n. large hook on a pole for landing fish

gaffe n. a blunder

gag v. **gagged**, **gag′ging** 1 retch or cause to retch 2 keep from speaking, as with a gag —n. 1 something put into the mouth to prevent speech 2 joke

gage n. 1 pledge 2 challenge 3 gauge —v. gauge

gag′gle n. 1 flock of geese 2 any group or cluster

gai′e·ty (gā′-) n. 1 cheerfulness 2 merriment

gai′ly adv. 1 merrily 2 brightly

gain n. 1 increase 2 profit —v. 1 earn 2 win 3 get as an addition or advantage 4 reach 5 make progress —**gain on** draw nearer to, as in a race

gain′ful a. profitable

gain·say′ v. **-said′**, **-say′ing** deny or contradict

gait n. manner of walking or running

gal n. [Col.] girl

ga′la a. festive —n. festival

gal·ax·y n., pl. **-ies** very large group of stars —**ga·lac′tic** a.

gale n. 1 strong wind 2 outburst, as of laughter

gall (gôl) n. 1 bile 2 tumor on plant tissue 3 [Col.] impudence —v. annoy

gal′lant a. 1 brave and noble 2 polite to women —**gal′lant·ry** n., pl. **-ries**

gall´blad´der n. sac attached to the liver, in which excess bile is stored

gal´le·on n. large Spanish ship of 15th-16th centuries

gal·le·ri´a n. large arcade or court with a glass roof

gal´ler·y n., pl. **–ies** 1 covered walk 2 outside balcony 3 theater balcony 4 place for art exhibits

gal´ley n., pl. **–leys** 1 ancient sailing ship with oars 2 ship's kitchen

gal´li·vant´ v. gad about for pleasure

gal´lon n. four quarts

gal´lop n. fastest gait of a horse —v. go or make go at a gallop

gal´lows n., pl. **–lows·es** or **–lows** structure for hanging condemned persons

gall´stone´ n. abnormal stony mass in the gallbladder

ga·lore´ adv. in great plenty

ga·losh´es n.pl. high overshoes

gal·van´ic a. of electric current, esp. from a battery

gal´va·nize´ v. 1 startle 2 plate (metal) with zinc

gam´bit n. opening move in chess

gam´ble v. 1 play games of chance for money 2 take a risk 3 bet —n. risk; chance —**gam´bler** n.

gam´bol v., n. frolic

game n. 1 amusement or sport with competing players 2 wild animals hunted for sport —v. gamble —a. 1 plucky 2 ready (for) 3 [Col.] lame —**the game is up** failure is certain

game plan n. long-range strategy

gam·ete (gam´ēt) n. reproductive cell

gam´ma ray n. electromagnetic radiation with short wavelength

gam´ut n. the entire range, esp. of a musical scale

gam´y (gām´-) a. **-i·er**, **-i·est** 1 strongly flavored 2 slightly tainted

gan´der n. male goose

gang n. group working or acting together —**gang up on** [Col.] attack as a group

gan´gling a. thin and tall

gan´gli·on n. mass of nerve cells

gang´plank´ n. movable ramp from a ship to the dock

gan´grene´ n. decay of body tissue from lack of blood supply —**gan´gre·nous** a.

gang´ster n. member of a gang of criminals

gang´way´ n. 1 passageway 2 gangplank —int. clear the way!

gant´let (gônt´-, gant´-) n. punishment of being beaten as one runs between two rows of men

gan´try n., pl. **–tries** wheeled framework with a crane, etc.

gaol (jāl) n. Br. sp. of JAIL

gap n. 1 opening or break 2 blank space

gape v. 1 open wide 2 stare with the mouth open

gar n. long fish with a long snout: also **gar´fish´**

ga·rage´ (-räzh´, -räj´) n. shelter or repair shop for automobiles, etc.

garb n. clothing; style of dress —v. clothe

gar´bage (-bij) n. waste parts of food

gar´ble v. distort (a story, etc.)

gar´den n. 1 plot for flowers, vegetables, etc. 2 fertile area 3 public park —v. make, or work in, a garden —**gar´den·er** n.

gar·de´ni·a (-dēn´yə) n. waxy white flower

Gar·gan´tu·an, gar·gan´tu·an (-chōō-) a. huge

gar´gle v. rinse the throat —n. liquid for gargling

gar´goyle´ n. gutter spout in the form of a sculptured grotesque creature

gar´ish (gar´-) a. gaudy

gar´land n. wreath of flowers, leaves, etc.

gar´lic n. strong-smelling plant bulb, used to season

gar´ment n. piece of clothing

gar´ner v. gather and store

gar´net n. deep-red gem

gar´nish v. decorate (food) —n. decoration for food

gar´nish·ee´ v. attach (a debtor's wages, etc.) to pay the debt

gar´ret (gar´-) n. attic

gar´ri·son n. fort or the troops in it —v. provide with troops

gar·rote´ (-rōt´, -rät´) v. strangle —n. device for strangling

gar´ru·lous (gar´-) a. talking much —**gar·ru´li·ty** n.

gar´ter n. elastic band to hold up a stocking

gas n. 1 fluid substance that can expand; vapor: some gases are used as fuel 2 gasoline —v. gassed, gas´sing attack with gas —**gas´e·ous** a.

gash v. cut deep into —n. deep cut

gas´ket n. rubber or metal ring sealing a joint, etc.

gas´o·hol´ n. fuel mixture of gasoline and alcohol

gas´o·line´ (-lēn´) n. liquid fuel from petroleum

gasp v. catch the breath with effort —n. a gasping

gas station n. service station

gas´sy a. **-si·er**, **-si·est** flatulent

gas´tric a. of the stomach

gas·tri´tis (-trīt´is) n. inflammation of the stomach

gas·tron´o·my n. art of good eating —**gas´tro·nom´i·cal** a.

gas′tro·pod′ n. kind of mollusk, as a snail or slug

gate n. 1 hinged door in a fence or wall 2 number of paid admissions

gate′-crash′er n. [Col.] one who attends without invitation or payment

gate′way′ n. entrance with a gate

gath′er v. 1 bring or come together; collect 2 infer 3 draw into pleats —n. a pleat —**gath′er·ing** n.

gauche (gōsh) a. tactless

gau′cho (-), pl. –**chos** South American cowboy

gaud′y a. –**i·er**, –**i·est** showy but tasteless —**gaud′i·ly** adv.

gauge (gāj) n. 1 standard measure 2 device for measuring —v. 1 to measure 2 to estimate

gaunt a. haggard; thin

gaunt′let n. 1 long glove with a flaring cuff 2 gantlet —**throw down the gauntlet** challenge

gauze n. loosely woven material —**gauz′y** a.

ga·vage′ (-väzh′) n. forced feeding through a stomach tube

gave v. pt. of GIVE

gav′el n. chairman's small mallet

ga·votte′ (-vät′) n. 17th-c. dance like the minuet

gawk v. stare stupidly

gawk′y a. –**i·er**, –**i·est** clumsy; ungainly

gay a. 1 joyous and lively 2 bright 3 homosexual

gaze v. look steadily; stare —n. steady look

ga·ze′bo (-zē′-, -zā′-) n., pl. –**bos** or –**boes** small, open, roofed building in garden or park

ga·zelle′ n. swift antelope

ga·zette′ n. newspaper

gaz′et·teer′ n. dictionary of geographical names

gaz·pa′cho (gäz pä′-) n. cold, Spanish vegetable soup

gear n. 1 equipment 2 system of toothed wheels that mesh 3 such a wheel —v. 1 connect by gears 2 adjust

gear′shift′ n. device for changing transmission gears

geck′o n., pl. –**os** or –**oes** tropical lizard

gee (jē) int. [Sl.] exclamation of surprise, etc.

geese n. pl. of GOOSE

gee′zer (gē′-) n. [Sl.] eccentric old man

Gei′ger counter (gī′gər) n. instrument for measuring radioactivity

gei′sha (gā′-) n., pl. –**sha** or –**shas** Japanese woman entertainer

gel (jel) n. jellylike substance

gel′a·tin n. jellied substance extracted from bones, hoofs, vegetables, etc. —**ge·lat′i·nous** a.

geld (geld) v. castrate (a horse, etc.) —**geld′ing** n.

gel′id (jel′-) a. frozen

gem n. precious stone

Gem′i·ni′ (-nī′, -nē′) third sign of the zodiac; Twins

gen·darme′ (zhän-) n. armed French police officer

gen′der n. classification of words as masculine, feminine, or neuter

gene n. unit of heredity in chromosomes

ge′ne·al′o·gy (jē′nē äl′-) n. history of ancestry —**ge′ne·a·log′i·cal** a.

gen·er·a (jen′ər ə) n. pl. of GENUS

gen′er·al a. 1 of or for all 2 widespread 3 usual 4 not specific —n. high-ranking army officer —**in general** usually —**gen′er·al·ly** adv.

gen′er·al′i·ty n., pl. –**ties** nonspecific idea or statement —**gen′er·al·ize′** v.

gen′er·ate′ v. cause to be; produce —**gen′er·a·tive** a.

gen′er·a′tion n. 1 production 2 all persons born about the same time 3 average time (30 years) between generations —**gen′er·a′tion·al** a.

gen′er·a′tor n. machine for changing mechanical into electrical energy

ge·ner′ic a. 1 inclusive; general 2 of a genus —**ge·ner′i·cal·ly** adv.

gen′er·ous a. 1 giving readily; unselfish 2 ample —**gen′er·os′i·ty** n.

gen′e·sis n. origin —[**G–**] first book of the Bible

genetic code n. arrangement of chemical substances in DNA molecules transmitting genetic information

ge·net′ics n. study of heredity —**ge·net′ic** a. —**ge·net′i·cist** n.

ge′ni·al (jēn′-) a. kindly; amiable —**ge′ni·al′i·ty** n.

ge·nie (jē′nē) n. 1 magic spirit that can be summoned 2 jinni

gen′i·tals n.pl. external sex organs —**gen′i·tal** a.

gen′i·tive (-tiv) a., n. Gram. (in) the case showing possession or origin

gen′ius (jēn′yəs) n. 1 great mental or creative ability 2 person having this

gen′o·cide′ n. systematic killing of a whole people

gen·re (zhän′rə) n. kind or type

gen·teel′ a. (overly) polite, refined, etc.

gen′tian (-shən) n. plant with blue, fringed flowers

gen′tile′ (-tīl′) a., n. [also G–] non-Jewish (person)

gen·til′i·ty n. politeness

gen'tle a. 1 mild; moderate 2 kindly; patient —**gen'tly** adv.

gen'tle-folk' n.pl. well-bred people: also **gen'tle-folks'**

gen'tle-man n., pl. -**men** 1 well-bred, courteous man 2 any man: polite term

gen'tri-fy' v. -**fied'**, -**fy'ing** raise to a higher status or condition —**gen'tri-fi-ca'tion** n.

gen'try n. people just below the nobility

gen'u-flect' v. bend the knee, as in worship —**gen'u-flec'tion** n.

gen'u-ine (-in) a. 1 real; true 2 sincere

ge'nus (jē'-) n., pl. **gen'er-a** or sometimes **ge'nus-es** class; kind, esp. in biology

ge'o-cen'tric a. with the earth as a center

ge'o-des'ic a. of a dome with a gridlike framework

ge'o-det'ic a. of the measurement of the earth

ge-og'ra-phy n. science of the earth's surface, climates, plants, animals, etc. —**ge-og'ra-pher** n. —**ge'o-graph'i-cal**, **ge'o-graph'ic** a.

ge-ol'o-gy n. science of the earth's crust and of rocks and fossils —**ge'o-log'i-cal** (-läj'-) a. —**ge-ol'o-gist** n.

ge'o-mag-net'ic a. of the earth's magnetic properties —**ge'o-mag'ne-tism** n.

ge-om'e-try n. branch of mathematics dealing with plane and solid figures —**ge'o-met'ric**, **ge'o-met'ri-cal** a.

ge'o-phys'ics n. science of the effects of weather, tides, etc. on the earth —**ge'o-phys'i-cal** a.

geor-gette (jôr jet') n. thin, crinkled fabric, for dresses, etc.

ge'o-sta'tion-ar'y a. of an orbiting satellite staying above same point over earth's surface: also **ge'o-syn'chro-nous**

ge'o-ther'mic a. of heat inside the earth: also **ge'o-ther'mal**

ge-ra'ni-um n. plant with showy flowers

ger'bil n. small rodent

ger'i-at'rics (jer'-) n. branch of medicine dealing with diseases of old age

germ n. 1 microscopic, disease-causing organism 2 seed, bud, etc. 3 origin

Ger'man n., a. (native or language) of Germany

ger-mane' a. relevant

ger-ma'ni-um n. a chemical element used in transistors, semiconductors, etc.

ger'mi-cide' n. anything used to destroy germs

ger'mi-nal a. in earliest stage of growth

ger'mi-nate' v. sprout, as from a seed —**ger'mi-na'tion** n.

ger'on-tol'o-gy (jer'-) n. study of aging —**ger'on-tol'o-gist** n.

ger'ry-man'der (jer'-) v. divide (voting area) unfairly to benefit one party

ger'und (jer'-) n. verbal noun ending in -**ing**

ges-ta'tion (jes-) n. pregnancy

ges-tic'u-late' v. to gesture

ges'ture n. movement of part of the body, to express ideas, feelings, etc. —v. make gestures

get v. **got**, **got** or **got'ten**, **get'ting** 1 come to have; obtain 2 come, go, or arrive 3 bring 4 make or become 5 [Col.] 1) be obliged 2) possess 3) baffle 4) understand —**get along** manage —**get around** circumvent —**get away** escape —**get by** [Col.] survive; manage —**get over** recover from —**get through** 1 finish 2 survive —**get together** 1 assemble 2 [Col.] reach an agreement —**get up** rise (from sleep, etc.)

get'a-way' n. 1 a starting, as in a race 2 an escape

get'-go' n. [Col.] beginning

get'-to-geth'er n. informal gathering

gew-gaw (gyōō'gô') n. trinket

gey'ser (gī'zər) n. gushing hot spring

ghast'ly (gast'-) a. -**li-er**, -**li-est** 1 horrible 2 pale as a ghost

gher'kin (gur'-) n. small pickle

ghet-to (get'ō) n., pl. -**tos** or -**toes** section of a city lived in by members of a minority group

ghost n. supposed disembodied spirit of a dead person —**ghost'ly** a.

ghost'writ'er n. a writer of speeches, etc. for another pretending to be the author

ghoul (gōōl) n. supposed evil spirit that feeds on the dead —**ghoul'ish** a.

GI n., pl. **GI's** or **GIs** [Col.] enlisted soldier

gi'ant n. person or thing of great size, strength, etc. —a. like a giant

gib'ber (jib'-) v. speak incoherently

gib'ber-ish n. confused talk

gib'bet (jib'-) n. a gallows

gib'bon (gib'-) n. small, slender, long-armed ape

gibe (jīb) v., n. taunt

gib'let (jib'-) n. edible internal part of a fowl

gid'dy a. -**di-er**, -**di-est** 1 dizzy 2 frivolous —**gid'di-ness** n.

gift n. 1 a present 2 a giving 3 natural ability

gift'ed a. talented

gig n. [Sl.] job, esp. playing jazz

gi-gan'tic a. huge

gig'gle v. laugh in a nervous, silly way —n. such a laugh

gig'o-lo' (jig'-) n., pl. -**los'** man supported by his female lover

Gi-la monster (hē'lə) n. stout, poisonous lizard

gild v. **gild'ed** or **gilt**, **gild'ing** 1 to cover with a layer of gold **2** make better than it is

gill (gil; *n.* 2: jil) *n.* **1** breathing organ of a fish **2** ¼ pint

gilt *n.* surface layer of gold

gilt′-edged′ *a.* of highest value, quality, etc., as securities

gim′bals (gim′-) *n.pl.* pair of free-swinging balls that keep ship's compass level

gim′crack (jim′-) *n.* object that is showy but useless

gim′let (gim′-) *n.* small tool for making holes

gim′mick *n.* [Col.] tricky or deceptive device

gin *n.* **1** an alcoholic liquor **2** machine for separating cotton from the seeds

gin′ger *n.* spice from the root of a tropical herb

ginger ale *n.* nonalcoholic drink flavored with ginger

gin′ger·bread′ *n.* cake flavored with ginger

gin′ger·ly *a., adv.* careful(ly) or timid(ly)

gin′ger·snap′ *n.* crisp ginger cookie

ging·ham (giŋ′əm) *n.* cotton cloth in stripes or checks

gin·gi·vi·tis (jin′jə vīt′is) *n.* inflammation of gums

gink·go (giŋ′kō) *n., pl.* **-goes** tree with fan-shaped leaves

Gip′sy *n., pl.* **-sies** Gypsy

gi·raffe′ *n.* large African animal with a very long neck

gird *v.* **girded** or **girt**, **gird′ing 1** encircle **2** prepare for action

gird′er *n.* large beam for supporting a floor, etc.

gir′dle *n.* **1** a belt **2** light, flexible corset

girl *n.* female child or young woman —**girl′ish** *a.*

girl′friend′ *n.* **1** sweetheart of a boy or man **2** girl who is one's friend **3** woman friend of a woman

girl scout *n.* member of the **Girl Scouts**, girls' club stressing healthful activities

girth *n.* **1** horse's belly band **2** circumference

gist (jist) *n.* main point

give *v.* **gave, giv′en, giv′ing 1** hand over; deliver **2** cause to have **3** produce **4** utter **5** perform **6** bend, etc. from pressure —*n.* a bending, etc. under pressure —**give away** [Col.] expose —**give forth** (or **off**) emit —**give in** yield —**give out 1** make public **2** distribute **3** become worn out —**give up 1** relinquish **2** stop

give′a·way *n.* thing given away or sold cheap

giv′en *a.* **1** bestowed **2** accustomed **3** stated

giz′mo, gis′mo *n., pl.* **-mos** [Sl.] gadget or gimmick

giz′zard *n.* muscular second stomach of

a bird

gla·cé (gla sā′) *a.* candied, as fruit

gla′cier (-shər) *n.* large mass of ice moving slowly down a slope —**gla′cial** (-shəl) *a.*

glad *a.* **glad′der, glad′dest 1** happy **2** causing joy **3** pleased —**glad′ly** *adv.* —**glad′ness** *n.*

glad′den *v.* make glad

glade *n.* clearing in a forest

glad′i·a′tor *n.* **1** in ancient Rome, a fighter in public shows **2** any fighter

glad′i·o′lus *n.* plant with tall spikes of funnel-shaped flowers: also **glad′i·o′la**

glam′or·ize′ *v.* make glamorous

glam′our, glam′or *n.* bewitching charm —**glam′or·ous, glam′our·ous** *a.*

glance *v.* **1** strike and go off at an angle **2** look briefly —*n.* a glimpse

gland *n.* body organ that secretes a substance —**glan′du·lar** (-jə lər) *a.*

glare *v.* **1** shine with a dazzling light **2** stare fiercely —*n.* **1** dazzling light **2** fierce stare **3** glassy surface, as of ice

glar′ing *a.* flagrant

glass *n.* **1** hard, brittle substance, usually transparent **2** drinking vessel, mirror, etc. made of this *pl.* eyeglasses or binoculars

glass′ware′ *n.* glass articles

glass′y *a.* **-i·er, -i·est 1** like glass **2** expressionless

glau·co′ma *n.* eye disease

glaze *v.* **1** furnish with glass **2** give a glossy finish **3** cover with a sugar coating —*n.* glassy coating

gla′zi·er (-zhər) *n.* one who fits glass in windows

gleam *n.* **1** faint glow of light **2** brief show, as of hope —*v.* send out a gleam

glean *v.* collect slowly, as grain left by reapers

glee *n.* joy —**glee′ful** *a.*

glee club *n.* singing group

glen *n.* secluded valley

glib *a.* **glib′ber, glib′best** fluent, esp. in a shallow way

glide *v.* to move or descend smoothly and easily —*n.* a smooth, easy flow or descent

glid′er *n.* engineless airplane carried by air currents

glim′mer *v., n.* (give) a faint, flickering light

glimpse *n.* brief, quick view —*v.* catch a glimpse of

glint *v., n.* gleam

glis·ten (glis′ən) *v., n.* sparkle

glitch *n.* [Sl.] mishap, error, etc.

glit′ter *v., n.* sparkle

glitz *n.* [Col.] gaudy showiness —**glitz′y** *a.*, **-i·er, -i·est**

gloam′ing *n.* twilight

gloat v. feel or show malicious pleasure

glob n. rounded lump

glob'al·ism' n. world-wide outlook

globe n. 1 ball-shaped thing 2 the earth, or a model of it —**glob'al** a.

globe'-trot'ter n. world traveler

glob'u·lar a. 1 spherical 2 of globules

glob'ule' n. small drop

glock-en-spiel (gläk'ən spēl') n. instrument with tuned metal bars played with hammers

gloom n. 1 darkness 2 dark place 3 sadness —**gloom'y** a., -i·er, -i·est

glo'ri·fy' v. -fied', -fy'ing 1 give glory to; honor 2 make seem greater —**glo'ri·fi·ca'tion** n.

glo'ri·ous a. full of glory 2 splendid

glo'ry n., pl. -ries 1 great praise or fame 2 splendor 3 heavenly bliss —v. -ried, -ry·ing exult (*in*)

gloss (glôs) n. 1 surface polish 2 explanation; footnote —v. to smooth (*over*), as an error —**gloss'y** a., -i·er, -i·est

glos'sa·ry n., pl. -ries list of difficult terms with definitions, as for a book

glos'so·la'li·a n. speaking of unintelligible sounds in religious ecstasy

glot'tis n. opening between the vocal cords —**glot'tal** a.

glove (gluv) n. 1 covering for the hand with sheaths for the fingers 2 padded mitt for boxing —**gloved** a.

glow v. 1 give off bright or steady light 2 be elated 3 be bright with color —n. 1 bright or steady light 2 brightness, warmth, etc.

glow'er (glou') v., n. stare with sullen anger

glow'worm' n. phosphorescent insect or larva

glu'cose' n. the sugar in fruits and honey

glue n. thick, adhesive liquid —v. stick together as with glue —**glu'ey** a.

glum a. **glum'mer, glum'mest** gloomy

glut v. **glut'ted, glut'ting** feed, fill, or supply to excess —n. excess

glu'ten n. sticky protein substance in wheat flour

glu'ti·nous a. sticky

glut'ton n. one who eats too much —**glut'ton·ous** a.

glut'ton·y n. overeating

glyc'er·in (glis'-) n. glycerol: also sp. **glyc'er·ine**

glyc'er·ol' n. colorless, syrupy liquid used in lotions, etc.

gly'co·gen (glī'ka-) n. substance in animal tissues that is changed into glucose

gnarl (närl) n. knot on a tree —v. to twist

gnash (nash) v. grind (the teeth) together

gnat (nat) n. small insect

gnaw (nô) v. 1 wear away by biting 2 torment —**gnaw'ing** a.

gneiss (nīs) n. rock like granite formed in layers

gnome (nōm) n. dwarf

gnu (nōō, nyōō) n. African antelope

go v. **went, gone, go'ing** 1 move along; pass or proceed 2 depart 3 work, as a clock 4 be or become 5 fit or suit 6 belong in a place —n. 1 a success 2 [Col.] energy 3 [Col.] a try —**go back on** [Col.] break, as a promise —**go in for** [Col.] engage or indulge in —**go off** explode —**go out** 1 be extinguished 2 go to social affairs, parties, etc. —**go over** 1 examine 2 do again —**go through** 1 endure 2 search —**go under** fail —**let go** release one's hold

goad n. 1 pointed stick 2 spur —v. urge on

goal n. 1 place where a race, trip, etc. ends 2 end striven for 3 place to put the ball or puck to score

goal'keep'er n. player guarding a goal: also **goal'ie** or **goal'tend'er**

goat n. cud-chewing horned animal —**get someone's goat** [Col.] annoy someone

goat·ee' n. pointed beard on a man's chin

goat'herd' n. herder of goats

goat'skin' n. (leather made from) skin of goat

gob n. 1 lump or mass 2 [Sl.] U.S. sailor

gob'ble n. cry of a male turkey —v. 1 make this cry 2 eat greedily —**gob'bler** n.

gob·ble·dy·gook' n. [Sl.] pompous, wordy talk or writing with little meaning

go'-be·tween' n. one acting between two persons

gob'let n. stemmed glass

gob'lin n. evil spirit

God monotheistic creator and ruler of the universe —n. [g-] any divine being —**god'dess** n.fem. —**god'like'** a.

god'child' n. the person (**god'daugh'ter** or **god'son'**) that a godparent sponsors

god'hood' n. state of being a god

god'less a. irreligious 2 wicked

god'ly a. -li·er, -li·est devoted to God; devout

god'par'ent n. spiritual sponsor (**god'fa'ther** or **god'moth'er**) of an infant, esp. at baptism

god'send' n. something unexpected but much needed

go'fer, go'-fer n. [Sl.] employee who does minor tasks

gog'gle v. stare with bulging eyes —n. pl. large spectacles to protect the eyes against dust, etc.

go'ing n. 1 departure 2 degree of ease in traveling —a. 1 working 2 current

goi'ter, goi'tre n. enlargement of the thyroid gland

gold n. 1 yellow, precious metal, a chemical element 2 money; wealth 3 bright yellow —a. of gold —**gold'en** a.

golden ager n. [Col.] retired person 65 or older

gold'en·rod' n. plant with long, yellow flower clusters

gold'-filled' a. of cheap metal overlaid with gold

gold'finch' n. small, yellow American song-bird

gold'fish' n. small yellowish fish, kept in ponds, etc.

gold'smith' n. skilled maker of gold articles

golf n. outdoor game in which a small ball is driven, with special clubs, into holes —**golf'er** n.

go'nad n. ovary or testicle

gon'do·la (or gän dō'lə) n. boat used on the canals of Venice —**gon'do·lier'** (-lir'-) n.

gone v. pp. of GO

gon'er n. person sure to die, be ruined, etc.

gong n. metal disk that resounds loudly when struck

gon'or·rhe'a (-rē'ə) n. venereal disease

goo n. 1 anything sticky 2 sentimentality **goo'ber** n. peanut

good a. **bet'ter, best** 1 having proper qualities 2 beneficial 3 of moral excellence 4 enjoyable, happy, etc. 5 considerable —n. 1 worth or virtue 2 benefit —**good'ness** n.

good'bye', good'-bye' int., n. farewell: also written **good'by'** or **good'-by'**

Good Friday n. Friday before Easter

good'-heart'ed a. kind

good'-look'ing a. handsome

good'ly a. rather large

good'-na'tured a. pleasant

goods n.pl. 1 personal property 2 wares 3 fabric

good'y n., pl. **-ies** [Col.] thing good to eat

goof [Sl.] n. 1 a blunder 2 stupid or silly person —v. 1 to blunder 2 waste time: with off —**goof'y** a., **-i·er, -i·est**

gook n. [Sl.] sticky or slimy substance

goon n. [Sl.] 1 hired thug 2 stupid person

goop n. [Sl.] sticky, semiliquid substance

goose n., pl. **geese** 1 long-necked water bird like a large duck 2 silly person —**cook one's goose** [Col.] spoil one's chances

goose'ber'ry n., pl. **-ries** sour berry used for jam, etc.

goose flesh n. rough skin caused by cold, fear, etc.: also **goose bumps**

goose'liv'er n. smoked liver sausage

go'pher n. burrowing rodent

gore n. 1 clotted blood 2 tapered cloth inserted to add width —v. 1 pierce as with a tusk 2 insert gores in —**gor'y** a., **-i·er, -i·est**

Gore'-Tex' trademark synthetic material used to make clothing repel water

gorge n. deep, narrow pass —v. eat or stuff greedily

gor'geous (-jəs) a. magnificent

go·ril'la n. largest of the apes, native to Africa

gor'mand·ize' v. eat like a glutton

gosh int. call of surprise

gos'ling (gäz'-) n. young goose

gos'pel n. 1 [often G—] teachings of Jesus and the Apostles 2 belief proclaimed as true

gos'sa·mer n. filmy cobweb or cloth —a. filmy

gos'sip n. 1 one who chatters about others 2 such idle talk —v. indulge in gossip —**gos'sip·y** a.

got v. pt. & pp. GET

got'ten v. alt. pp. of GET

Gou'da (cheese) (gou'-, gōō'-) n. mild cheese

gouge (gouj) n. 1 chisel for cutting grooves 2 such a groove —v. 1 scoop out as with a gouge 2 [Col.] overcharge —**goug'er** n.

gou·lash (gōō'läsh') n. stew seasoned with paprika

gou·ra·mi (goor'ə mē) n. brightly colored fish, often kept in aquariums

gourd (gôrd, goord) n. 1 bulb-shaped fruit of a trailing plant 2 its dried shell hollowed out for use

gour·mand (goor mänd', gôr-) n. one who likes to eat

gour·met (goor mā', gôr-) n. judge of fine foods and drinks

gout n. disease with painful swelling of the joints

gov'ern v. 1 control 2 influence; determine

gov'ern·ess n. woman hired to teach children at home

gov'ern·ment n. 1 control; rule 2 system of ruling 3 those who rule —**gov'ern·men'tal** a.

gov'er·nor n. 1 one who governs; esp., head of a State 2 device to control engine speed automatically

gown n. 1 woman's dress 2 long robe, as for a judge

grab v. **grabbed, grab'bing** snatch suddenly —n. a grabbing

grab'by a. **-bi·er, -bi·est** avaricious

grace n. 1 beauty of form, movement, etc. 2 favor; good will 3 delay granted for payment due 4 prayer of thanks at a meal 5 God's love for man —v. **graced, grac'ing** dignify or adorn —**in the good graces of** in favor with —**grace'ful** a. —**grace'ful·ly** adv.

grace'less a. 1 ignorant of propriety 2 clumsy

gra'cious (-shəs) a. kind, polite, charming, pleasing, etc.

grack'le n. small blackbird

gra·da'tion n. 1 arrangement in steps 2 stage in a series

grade n. 1 degree in a scale of rank or quality 2 slope 3 any of the school years through the 12th 4 mark or rating, as on a test —v. 1 classify; sort 2 give a GRADE (n. 4) to 3 make (ground) sloped or level

grade crossing n. place where a road crosses a railroad

grade school n. elementary school

gra'di·ent n. slope, or degree of slope

grad'u·al (graj'-) a. little by little —**grad'u·al·ly** adv.

grad'u·al·ism' n. principle of gradual social change

grad'u·ate (-ət; v.: -āt') n. one who completed a course of study at a school or college —v. 1 give a diploma to (a graduate) 2 become a graduate 3 mark with degrees for measuring —**grad'u·a'tion** n.

graf·fi'ti (-fēt'ē) n.pl., sing. **-to** crude drawings or writing on a public wall, etc.

graft n. 1 shoot, etc. of one plant inserted in another to grow 2 transplanting of skin, etc. 3 dishonest gain of money by public officers —v. insert (a graft)

gra·ham (grā'əm) a. made of unsifted, whole-wheat flour

Grail n. in legend, cup used by Jesus

grain n. 1 seed of wheat, corn, etc. 2 cereal plants 3 particle, as of salt or sand 4 smallest unit of weight 5 natural markings on wood, leather, etc.

grain'y a. **-i·er, -i·est** 1 of wood that shows grain 2 granular —**grain'i·ness** n.

gram n. metric unit of weight (¹⁄₂₈ of an ounce)

-gram suf. a writing or drawing

gram'mar n. system of speaking and writing a language —**gram·mar'i·an** (-mer'-) n. —**gram·mat'i·cal** a.

gran'a·ry (grān'-, gran'-) n., pl. **-ries** building for storing grain

grand a. great in size, beauty, importance, etc.; imposing, splendid, etc. —n. [Sl.] a thousand dollars

grand'child' n. child (**grand'daugh'ter** or **grand'son'**) of one's son or daughter

gran'deur (-jər, -dyoor) n. great size, beauty, etc.; splendor

grandfather clock n. clock in tall, upright case

gran·dil'o·quent a. bombastic

gran'di·ose' (-ōs') a. 1 very grand 2 too grand

grand jury n. jury with power to indict persons for trial

grand'par'ent n. parent (**grand'fa'ther** or **grand'moth'er**) of one's father or mother

grand piano n. large piano with a horizontal case

grand slam n. home run hit with a runner on each base

grand'stand' n. structure for spectators of outdoor sports —v. [Col.] show off to get attention or applause

grange (grānj) n. 1 farm 2 [G—] association of farmers

gran'ite (-it) n. very hard crystalline rock

gran'ny n., pl. **-nies** [Col.] grandmother

gra·no'la n. breakfast cereal of oats, honey, nuts, etc.

grant v. 1 consent to or give 2 concede —n. something granted —**take for granted** consider as a fact

grant'in-aid' n., pl. **grants-** grant of funds by a foundation, etc. to an artist, scientist, etc.

gran'u·lar a. of or like grains or granules

gran'u·late' v. form into granules —**gran'u·la'tion** n.

gran'ule n. small grain

grape n. small, round fruit growing in clusters

grape'fruit' n. large citrus fruit with a yellow rind

grape hyacinth n. small plant with blue, bell-shaped flowers

grape'vine' n. 1 woody vine with grapes 2 rumor

graph n. a diagram that shows changes in value

-graph suf. 1 that writes 2 thing written

graph'ic a. 1 vivid; in lifelike detail 2 of the arts of drawing, printing, etc. —**graph'i·cal·ly** adv.

graph'ics n. 1 graphic arts 2 design in graphic arts

graph'ite' n. soft, black carbon in pencils, etc.

graph·ol'o·gy n. study of handwriting —**graph·ol'o·gist** n.

grap'nel n. device with hooks or claws for grasping

grap'ple n. 1 grapnel 2 grip in wrestling —v. 1 grip and hold 2 struggle

grasp v. 1 grip; seize 2 comprehend —n. 1 a grip 2 control 3 power to grasp

grasp'ing a. greedy

grass n. 1 green plant grown for lawns 2 cereal plant 3 pasture —**grass'y** a.

grass'hop'per n. leaping insect with long hind legs

grass'land' n. open land with grass; prairie

grass'-roots' a. of common people having basic political opinions

grate v. 1 form into particles by scraping 2 rub with a harsh sound 3 irritate —n. 1 frame of bars to hold fuel 2 framework of bars over an opening

grate'ful a. thankful

grat'i·fy' v. -fied', -fy'ing 1 please 2 indulge —grat'i·fi·ca'tion n.

grat'ing n. GRATE (n. 2)

gra·tis (grāt'is, grat-) adv., a. free

grat'i·tude' n. thankful appreciation

gra·tu'i·tous a. 1 free of charge 2 uncalled-for

gra·tu'i·ty n., pl. -ties gift of money for a service

grave a. 1 serious 2 solemn —n. burial place, esp. a hole in the ground

grav'el n. bits of rock —v. cover with gravel

grav'el·ly a. hoarse or rasping

grav'en (grāv'-) a. carved

grav'en image (grāv'-) n. idol of stone or wood

grave'stone' n. tombstone

grave'yard' n. cemetery

grav'id (grav'-) a. pregnant

grav'i·tate' v. be attracted

grav'i·ta'tion n. Physics force of mutual attraction between masses

grav'i·ty n. 1 seriousness 2 weight 3 Physics gravitation; esp., the pull on bodies toward earth's center

gra'vy n., pl. -vies juice from cooking meat

gray n. mixture of black and white —a. 1 of this color 2 dreary —gray'ish a.

gray'beard' n. old man

gray matter n. 1 grayish brain tissue 2 [Col.] intelligence

graze v. 1 feed on growing grass, etc. 2 rub lightly in passing —n. a grazing

grease n. 1 melted animal fat 2 thick oily lubricant —v. put grease on —greas'y a., -i·er, -i·est

grease'paint' n. greasy stage makeup

great a. 1 much larger, more, or better than average 2 being one generation removed —great'ly adv.

Great Dane n. large, strong dog with short hair

Gre'cian (-shən) a. Greek

greed n. excessive desire, as for wealth —greed'y a., -i·er, -i·est —greed'i·ly adv.

Greek n., a. (native or language) of Greece

green n. 1 color of grass 2 pl. leafy vegetables 3 smooth turf —a. 1 of the color green 2 unripe 3 inexperienced —green'ness n.

green'belt' n. area around a city, reserved for parks or farms

green'er·y n. green foliage

green'-eyed' a. very jealous

green'horn' n. beginner

green'house' n. heated glass building for growing plants

green thumb n. knack for growing plants

greet v. address, meet, or receive in a certain way

greet'ing n. act or words of one who greets

gre·gar'i·ous (-ger'-) a. sociable

gre·nade' n. small bomb usually thrown by hand

gren'a·dier' (-dir') n. Br. soldier of a special regiment

gren'a·dine' (-dēn') n. syrup made from pomegranates

grew v. pt. of GROW

grey n., a. Br. sp. of GRAY

grey'hound' n. swift dog

grid n. 1 GRATE (n. 2) 2 network of crossed lines, as on a map

grid'dle n. flat pan for cooking pancakes, etc.

grid'i'ron n. 1 framework of bars on which to broil 2 football field

grid'lock' n. traffic jam allowing no movement at all

grief n. deep sorrow —come to grief fail

griev'ance n. complaint or a basis for it

grieve v. be or make sad

griev'ous a. 1 causing grief 2 deplorable —griev'ous·ly adv.

grif'fin n. mythical beast, part eagle and part lion

grill n. 1 gridiron 2 restaurant serving grilled foods —v. 1 broil 2 question relentlessly

grille n. open grating forming a screen

grim a. grim'mer, grim'mest 1 fierce 2 hideous; ghastly —grim'ly adv.

gri·mace' (or grim'is) n. twisting of the facial features —v. make grimaces

grime n. sooty dirt —grim'y a., -i·er, -i·est

grin v. grinned, grin'ning smile broadly —n. such a smile

grind v. ground, grind'ing 1 crush into bits 2 sharpen, smooth, etc. by friction 3 rub harshly 4 work by cranking —n. hard task

grind'stone' n. revolving stone for sharpening, etc.

grip n. 1 firm hold 2 handclasp 3 a handle 4 a valise —v. gripped, grip'ping hold firmly

gripe v. 1 cause pain in the bowels of 2 [Sl.] complain —n. [Sl.] complaint

grippe (grip) n. influenza

gris'ly (griz'-) a. -li·er, -li·est ghastly

grist n. grain to be ground

gris'tle (-əl) n. cartilage

grit n. 1 rough bits of sand, etc. 2 obstinate courage —v. grit'ted, grit'ting grind (the teeth) —grit'ty a., -ti·er, -ti·est

grits *n.pl.* coarsely ground grain

griz′zled, griz′zly *a.* gray

grizzly bear *n.* large, ferocious North American bear

groan *v., n.* (utter) a deep sound of pain, etc.

gro′cer *n.* storekeeper who sells food, etc.

gro′cer·y *n., pl. -ies* 1 store of a grocer 2 *pl.* goods sold by a grocer

grog *n.* rum and water

grog′gy *a.* **-gi·er, -gi·est** dazed or sluggish

groin *n.* fold where the abdomen joins either thigh

groom *n.* 1 man who tends horses 2 bridegroom —*v.* 1 make neat 2 train

groove *n.* 1 narrow furrow 2 channel 3 routine —*v.* make a groove in

grope *v.* feel or search about blindly

gross (grōs) *a.* 1 flagrant 2 coarse 3 total —*n.* 1 overall total 2 *pl.* **gross** twelve dozen —*v.* earn before deductions —**gross out** 1 disgust, offend, etc.

gross national product *n.* value of a nation's output of goods and services

gro·tesque′ (-tesk′) *a.* 1 distorted 2 absurd

grot′to *n., pl.* **-toes** or **-tos** 1 cave 2 cavelike shrine, place, etc.

grouch *n.* [Col.] 1 one who grumbles 2 sulky mood —**grouch′y** *a.*, **-i·er, -i·est**

ground *v.* 1 pt. & pp. of GRIND 2 set or keep on the ground 3 base 4 instruct (*in*) —*n.* 1 land; earth 2 *pl.* tract of land 3 distance 4 *often pl.* cause or basis 5 background 6 *pl.* dregs —*a.* of or on the ground

ground crew *n.* group of workers who maintain aircraft

ground′er *n.* batted ball that rolls or bounces along the ground

ground hog *n.* woodchuck: also **ground′hog′**

ground′less *a.* without reason

ground rule *n.* any basic rule

ground swell *n.* violent rolling of the ocean

ground′work′ *n.* foundation

group *n.* persons or things gathered or classed together —*v.* form a group

group′ie *n.* [Col.] fan of rock groups

grouse *n.* game bird

grout *n.* thin mortar

grove *n.* small group of trees

grov′el (gruv′-, gräv′-) *v.* 1 crawl abjectly 2 behave humbly

grow *v.* **grew, grown, grow′ing** 1 develop 2 increase 3 become 4 raise (crops) —**grow up** to mature

growl *n.* rumbling sound, as of an angry dog —*v.* make this sound

grown′-up′ (*n.*: -up′) *a., n.* adult

growth *n.* 1 a growing 2 something that grows

grub *v.* **grubbed, grub′bing** 1 dig or dig up 2 work hard —*n.* 1 wormlike larva, esp.

of a beetle 2 [Sl.] food

grub′by *a.* **-bi·er, -bi·est** dirty; untidy

grub′stake′ *n.* [Col.] money advanced for an enterprise

grudge *v.* begrudge —*n.* resentment or a reason for this

gru′el *n.* thin cereal broth

gru′el·ing, gru′el·ling *a.* very tiring; exhausting

grue′some *a.* causing loathing and horror

gruff *a.* 1 rough and surly 2 hoarse —**gruff′ly** *adv.*

grum′ble *v.* mutter in discontent —**grum′bler** *n.*

grump′y *a.* **-i·er, -i·est** peevish; surly

grun′gy *a.* **-gi·er, -gi·est** [Sl.] dirty, messy, etc.

grunt *v., n.* (utter with) the deep sound of a hog

gua·no (gwä′nō) *n.* manure of bats or seabirds

guar·an·tee′ (gar′-) *n.* 1 pledge to replace something sold if faulty 2 assurance 3 pledge or security for another's debt or obligation —*v.* 1 give a guarantee for 2 assure Also **guar′an·ty** —**guar′an·tor′** *n.*

guard *v.* 1 protect; defend 2 keep from escape 3 take precautions (*against*) —*n.* 1 a person or thing that guards 2 careful watch

guard′ed *a.* 1 kept safe 2 cautious

guard′house′ *n. Mil.* jail

guard′i·an *n.* 1 one legally in charge of a minor, etc. 2 custodian

guard′rail′ *n.* protective railing

gua′va (gwä′-) *n.* yellow tropical fruit

gu′ber·na·to′ri·al *a.* of a governor or governor's office

guer·ril·la, gue·ril′la (gə-) *n.* fighter who makes raids behind enemy lines

guess *v.* 1 estimate; judge 2 suppose —*n.* surmise

guess′work′ *n.* 1 a guessing 2 view based on this

guest *n.* 1 one entertained at another's home, etc. 2 paying customer, as at a hotel —*a.* 1 for guests 2 performing by invitation

guf·faw′ *n., v.* laugh in a loud, coarse burst

guide *v.* 1 show the way to 2 control —*n.* person or thing that guides —**guid′ance** *n.*

guide′book′ *n.* book for tourists

guided missile *n.* war missile guided by radio or radar

guide′line′ *n.* principle for directing policies, etc.

guild (gild) *n.* association to promote mutual interests

guile (gīl) *n.* deceit

guil·lo·tine (gil′ə tēn′) *n.* instrument for beheading

guilt *n.* **1** fact of having committed an offense **2** painful feeling that one has done a wrong

guilt′y *a.* **-i·er, -i·est** having or showing guilt —**guilt′i·ly** *adv.*

guin·ea (gin′ē) *n.* former English coin, equal to 21 shillings

guinea fowl (or **hen**) *n.* speckled domestic fowl

guinea pig *n.* small rodent used in experiments

guise (gīz) *n.* assumed or false appearance

gui·tar′ *n.* musical instrument usually with six strings plucked or strummed —**gui·tar′ist** *n.*

gulch *n.* deep narrow valley

gulf *n.* **1** ocean area partly enclosed by land **2** wide chasm **3** vast separation

gull *n.* **1** gray and white seabird **2** dupe —*v.* cheat

gul′let *n.* esophagus

gul′li·ble *a.* easily tricked —**gul′li·bil′i·ty** *n.*

gul′ly *n., pl.* **-lies** narrow ravine

gulp *v.* swallow greedily or hastily —*n.* a gulping

gum *n.* **1** sticky substance from some plants **2** an adhesive **3** flesh around the teeth —*v.* **gummed, gum′ming** make sticky —**gum′my** *a.* **-mi·er, -mi·est**

gum′bo *n., pl.* **-bos** soup made with okra pods

gum′drop′ *n.* chewy candy

gump′tion *n.* [Col.] initiative

gun *n.* weapon for shooting projectiles —*v.* **gunned, gun′ning** **1** to shoot or hunt with a gun **2** to increase the speed of (an engine)

gun′fire′ *n.* firing of guns

gung′-ho′ *a.* [Col.] enthusiastic

gunk *n.* [Sl.] thick, messy substance

gun′man *n., pl.* **-men** armed gangster

gun′ner·y *n.* the making or firing of large guns —**gun′ner** *n.*

gun′ny *n., pl.* **-nies** sack made of coarse fabric

gun′play′ *n.* exchange of gunshots

gun′pow′der *n.* explosive powder used in guns, etc.

gun′ship′ *n.* armed helicopter

gun′shot′ *n.* shot fired from a gun

gun′smith′ *n.* one who makes or repairs small guns

gun·wale (gun′əl) *n.* upper edge of a boat's side

gup′py *n., pl.* **-pies** tiny tropical fish

gur′gle *n.* bubbling sound —*v.* make this sound

gur′ney *n.* wheeled stretcher or cot used in hospitals

gu·ru′ *n.* Hindu spiritual advisor or teacher

gush *v.* **1** flow copiously **2** talk too emotionally —*n.* a gushing —**gush′er** *n.*

gus′set *n.* a triangular piece inserted in a garment

gust *n.* **1** sudden rush of air **2** sudden outburst

gus′ta·to′ry *a.* of the sense of taste

gus′to *n.* zest; relish

gut *n.* **1** intestine **2** cord made of intestines **3** *pl.* [Col.] courage —*v.* **gut′ted, gut′ting** destroy the interior of

gut′less *a.* [Col.] lacking courage

guts′y *a.* **-i·er, -i·est** [Col.] courageous, forceful, etc.

gut′ta-per′cha *n.* rubberlike substance from some trees

gut′ter *n.* channel to carry off rain water, etc.

gut′tur·al (-ər əl) *a.* sounded in the throat; rasping

guy *n.* **1** guiding rope **2** [Sl.] boy or man

guz′zle *v.* drink greedily

gym (jim) *n.* [Col.] gymnasium

gym·na′si·um *n.* place for physical training and sports

gym·nas′tics *n.pl.* **1** exercises for the muscles **2** sport employing acrobatics, etc. —**gym′nast′** *n.* —**gym·nas′tic** *a.*

gy′ne·col′o·gy (gī′nə-) *n.* medical science of women's diseases —**gy′ne·col′o·gist** *n.*

gyp (jip) *n., v.* **gypped, gyp′ping** [Col.] swindle

gyp′sum *n.* calcium sulfate, a white chalky mineral

Gyp′sy *n., pl.* **-sies** [*also* g–] one of a wandering people

gy′rate′ (jī′-) *v.* to whirl —**gy·ra′tion** *n.*

gy′ro·scope′ *n.* wheel mounted in a ring and spinning rapidly, used as a stabilizer —**gy′ro·scop′ic** *a.*

H

ha *int.* exclamation of surprise, triumph, etc.

ha′be·as cor′pus *n.* writ requiring a court to decide the legality of a prisoner's detention

hab′er·dash′er *n.* dealer in men's hats, shirts, etc. —**hab′er·dash′er·y** *n., pl.* **-ies**

ha·bil′i·ments *n.pl.* attire

hab′it *n.* **1** costume **2** custom **3** fixed practice

hab′it·a·ble *a.* fit to live in

hab′i·tat′ *n.* natural living place

hab′i·ta′tion *n.* dwelling

hab′it-form′ing *a.* resulting in addiction

ha·bit′u·al (-bich′⁄oo-) *a.* **1** done by habit **2** constant **3** usual —**ha·bit′u·al·ly** *adv.*

ha·bit′u·ate′ *v.* accustom

ha·bit′u·é′ (-ā′) *n.* constant frequenter of a place

hack *v.* **1** chop roughly **2** cough harshly —*n.* **1** gash **2** harsh cough **3** vehicle for hire **4** old, worn-out horse **5** a literary drudge

hack′er *n.* **1** unskilled golfer **2** talented amateur computer user

hack′les *n.pl.* hairs on a dog's back that bristle

hack′neyed (-nēd′) *a.* trite; stale

hack′saw′ *n.* saw for cutting metal: also **hack saw** *n.*

had *v.* pt. & pp. of HAVE

had′dock *n.* small ocean fish used as food

Ha·des (hā′dēz′) *n.* hell

had′n't had not

haft *n.* handle, as of an ax

hag *n.* ugly old woman

hag′gard *a.* having a wasted, worn look; gaunt

hag′gle *v.* argue about terms, price, etc.

hah (hä) *int.* ha

hai′ku′ (hī′-) *n.* three-line Japanese poem

hail *n.* **1** greeting **2** frozen raindrops **3** shower of or like hail —*int.* shout of greeting, etc. —*v.* **1** cheer **2** shout to **3** pour down (like) hail

hail′stone′ *n.* piece of hail

hair *n.* **1** threadlike outgrowth from the skin **2** growth of these, as on the head —**split hairs** quibble —**hair′y** *a.*, **-i′er**, **-i′est**

hair′breadth′ *n.* very short distance —*a.* very narrow

hair′cut′ *n.* act or style of cutting the hair

hair′do′ (-dōō′) *n.*, *pl.* **-dos′** hair style

hair′dress′er *n.* person whose work is arranging hair

hair′line′ *n.* **1** thin line **2** outline of hair above the forehead

hair′piece′ *n.* wig

hair′pin′ *n.* wire for keeping hair in place —*a.* U-shaped

hair′-rais′ing *a.* [Col.] horrifying

hair′style′ *n.* special style of hair: also **hair′do′**, *pl.* **-dos′**

hal′cy·on (-sē ən) *a.* tranquil

hale *a.* healthy; robust —*v.* force to go

half *n.*, *pl.* **halves** either of the two equal parts of a thing —*a.* **1** being a half **2** partial —*adv.* **1** to the extent of a half **2** partially

half′-breed′ *n.* one with parents of different races: offensive term

half brother (or sister) *n.* brother (or sister) by one parent only

half′heart′ed *a.* with little enthusiasm or interest

half′tone′ *n.* semitone

half′track′ *n.* army vehicle with a continuous tread instead of rear wheels

half′way′ *a.* **1** midway between points **2** partial —*adv.* to the halfway point

half′-wit′ted *a.* feebleminded —**half′-wit′** *n.*

hal′i·but *n.* large flounder

hal′i·to′sis *n.* bad-smelling breath

hall *n.* **1** public building with offices **2** large room for meetings, shows, etc. **3** vestibule **4** passageway

hal·le·lu′jah, hal·le·lu′iah (-yə) *int.*, *n.* praise (to) God

hall′mark′ *n.* mark of quality

hal′low *v.* make or regard as holy —**hal′lowed** *a.*

Hal′low·een′, Hal′low·e′en′ *n.* evening of Oct. 31

hal·lu′ci·na′tion *n.* apparent perception of sights, etc. not really present —**hal·lu′ci·nate′** *v.* —**hal·lu′ci·na·to′ry** *a.*

hal·lu′ci·no·gen *n.* drug that produces hallucinations

hall′way′ *n.* corridor

ha′lo *n.* ring of light

halt *v.* **1** to stop **2** to limp **3** hesitate —*n.* a stop —**halt′ing·ly** *adv.*

hal′ter *n.* **1** rope for tying an animal **2** woman's backless upper garment

halve (hav) *v.* **1** divide into halves **2** reduce to half

halves *n.* pl. of HALF

hal′yard (-yərd) *n.* rope for raising a flag, etc.

ham *n.* **1** upper part of a hog's hind leg **2** [Col.] amateur radio operator

ham′burg·er *n.* **1** ground beef **2** cooked patty of such meat, often in a bun Also **ham′burg**

ham′let *n.* small village

ham′mer *n.* tool with a metal head for pounding —*v.* pound, drive, shape, etc. as with a hammer

ham′mock *n.* bed of canvas, etc. swung from ropes

ham′per *v.* hinder; impede —*n.* large basket

ham′ster *n.* small rodent kept as a pet

ham′string′ *n.* tendon back of the knee

hand *n.* **1** end of the arm beyond the wrist **2** side or direction **3** active part **4** handwriting **5** applause **6** help **7** hired worker **8** pointer on a clock **9** cards held by a player in a card game —**a.** of, for, or by the hand —*v.* give as with the hand —**at hand** near —**hand down** bequeath —**hand in hand** together —**hands down** easily —**on hand** available —**hand′ful′** *n.*

hand′bag′ *n.* woman's purse

hand′ball′ *n.* game in which players hit a ball against a wall with the hand

hand′bill′ *n.* printed notice passed out by hand

hand′book′ *n.* compact book of instructions or facts

hand′clasp′ *n.* handshake

hand′cuff′ *n.* one of a pair of shackles for the wrists —*v.* put handcuffs on

hand′gun′ *n.* firearm held with one hand, as a pistol

hand′i·cap′ *n.* **1** difficulty or advantage given to some contestants to equalize their chances **2** hindrance **3** physical disability —*v.*, **-capped′**, **-cap′ping** hinder

hand′i·craft′ *n.* work calling for skill with the hands

hand′i·work′ *n.* result of one's actions

hand·ker·chief (haŋ′kər chif′) *n.* small cloth for wiping the nose, etc.

han′dle *n.* part of tool, etc. by which it is held —*v.* **1** touch, lift, etc. with the hand **2** manage **3** deal with **4** deal in; sell

han′dle·bar′ *n. often pl.* curved bar for steering a bicycle, etc.

hand′made′ *adv.* made by hand, not by machine

hand′out′ *n.* **1** gift to a beggar, etc. **2** leaflet, etc. handed out

hand′pick′ *v.* choose with care

hand′rail′ *n.* rail along a staircase, etc.

hand′shake′ *n.* clasping of hands in greeting

hand′some *adv.* **1** good-looking in a manly or impressive way **2** sizable **3** gracious

hand′spring′ *n.* a turning over in midair with the hands touching the ground

hand′-to-hand′ *a.* at close quarters

hand′-to-mouth′ *a.* with just enough to live on

hand′writ′ing *n.* writing done by hand —**hand′writ′ten** *a.*

hand′y *a.*, **-i·er**, **-i·est 1** nearby **2** easily used **3** clever with the hands —**hand′i·ly** *adv.*

hand′y·man′ *n., pl.* **-men′** man who does odd jobs

hang *v.* **hung** *or* (*v.* 3) **hanged**, **hang′ing 1** to attach or be attached from above **2** attach so as to swing freely **3** kill by suspending from a rope about the neck **4** attach to walls **5** droop —*n.* **1** way a thing hangs **2** way a thing is done —**hang around** [Col.] loiter —**hang back** hesitate, as from shyness —**hang on 1** keep hold **2** persevere —**hang up 1** end a telephone call **2** delay

hang′ar *n.* aircraft shelter

hang′dog′ *a.* abject; cowed

hang′er *n.* that on which something is hung

hang′man *n., pl.* **-men** man who hangs convicted criminals

hang′nail′ *n.* bit of torn skin next to a fingernail

hang′o′ver *n.* sickness resulting from being drunk

hang′-up′ *n.* [Sl.] personal problem one finds hard to cope with

hank *n.* skein of yarn

han′ker *v.* long (*for*)

Ha·nu·ka (hä′noo kä′) *n.* Jewish festival

hap′haz′ard *a.* not planned; random —*adv.* by chance

hap′less *a.* unlucky

hap′pen *v.* **1** take place **2** occur by chance **3** have the luck or occasion

hap′pen·ing *n.* event

hap′py *a.*, **-pi·er**, **-pi·est 1** showing pleasure or joy **2** lucky **3** apt —**hap′pi·ly** *adv.* —**hap′pi·ness** *n.*

hap′py-go-luck′y *a.* easygoing

har·a-ki·ri (här′ə kir′ē) *n.* Japanese ritual suicide

ha·rangue (-raŋ′) *v., n.* (to address in) a noisy or scolding speech

har·ass (hə ras′, har′əs) *v.* trouble or attack constantly —**har·ass′ment** *n.*

har·bin·ger (här′bin jər) *n.* forerunner

har′bor *n.* protected inlet for ships —*v.* **1** to shelter **2** hold in the mind

hard *a.* **1** firm or solid **2** powerful **3** difficult to do, understand, etc. **4** harsh —*adv.* **1** with energy **2** with strength **3** firmly —**hard and fast** strict —**hard′en** *v.*

hard′-bit′ten *a.* tough; stubborn

hard′-boiled′ *a.* **1** boiled until solid **2** [Col.] tough; unfeeling

hard′-core′ *adv.* absolute

hard hat *n.* **1** protective helmet **2** [Sl.] worker wearing a hard hat

hard′head′ed *a.* **1** shrewd **2** stubborn

hard′heart′ed *a.* cruel

har′di·hood′ *n.* boldness, vigor, etc.

hard′-line′ *a.* politically unyielding

hard′ly *adv.* **1** barely **2** not likely

hard′-nosed′ *a.* [Col.] tough and stubborn

hard sell *n.* high-pressure salesmanship

hard′ship′ *n.* thing hard to bear, as poverty, pain, etc.

hard′tack′ *n.* unleavened bread in hard wafers

hard′ware′ *n.* **1** metal articles, as tools, nails, etc. **2** electronic equipment

hard′wood′ *n.* tough timber with a compact texture

har′dy *a.*, **-di·er**, **-di·est 1** bold and resolute **2** robust —**har′di·ness** *n.*

hare *n.* rabbit, esp. one of the larger kind

hare′brained′ *a.* senseless

hare′lip′ *n.* congenital cleft of the upper lip

ha·rem (her′əm) *n.* **1** quarters for the

women in a Muslim's house 2 these women

hark v. [Poet.] listen

hark·en v. hearken

har′le·quin n. masked clown

har′lot n. prostitute

harm n., v. hurt; damage —**harm′ful** a. —**harm′less** a.

har·mon′i·ca n. small wind instrument held to the mouth

har′mo·nize′ v. 1 be, sing, etc. in harmony 2 bring into harmony

har′mo·ny n. 1 pleasing agreement of parts 2 agreement in ideas, action, etc. 3 pleasing combination of musical tones —**har·mon′ic** a. —**har·mon′i·cal·ly** adv. —**har·mo′ni·ous** a.

har′ness n. straps, etc. for hitching a horse to a wagon, etc. —v. 1 put harness on 2 control for use

harp n. stringed musical instrument played by plucking —v. keep talking or writing (on) —**harp′ist** n.

har·poon′ n. barbed shaft for spearing whales —v. to strike or catch with a harpoon

harp′si·chord′ n. early keyboard instrument

har′ri·dan (har′-) n. shrewish old woman

har′row (har′-) n. frame with spikes or disks for breaking up plowed land —v. 1 draw a harrow over 2 distress

har′ry (har′-) v. -ried, -ry·ing harass; torment

harsh a. 1 rough to the ear, eye, taste, etc. 2 cruel or severe —**harsh′ly** adv. —**harsh′ness** n.

hart n. male deer; stag

har′vest n. 1 a season's crop or the gathering of it 2 season for this —v. reap

has v. pres. t. of HAVE: used with he, she, or it

has′-been′ n. [Col.] one whose popularity is past

hash n. a cooked mixture of chopped meat, potatoes, etc.

hash′ish′ (-ēsh′) n. narcotic made from Indian hemp

has′n't has not

hasp n. clasplike fastening for a door, lid, etc.

has′sle n. [Col.] annoying or troubling situation —v. [Sl.] annoy; harass

has′sock n. firm cushion used as a footstool, etc.

hast v. [Ar.] have: with thou

haste n. hurry or rush

has·ten (hās′ən) v. to hurry

hast′y a. -i·er, -i·est done with haste —**hast′i·ly** adv.

hat n. head covering, often with a brim

hatch v. 1 bring or come forth from (an egg) 2 contrive (a plot) —n. hatchway or its lid

hatch′back′ n. automobile with rear lid over wide storage area

hatch′er·y n., pl. -ies place for hatching eggs

hatch′et n. short ax

hatch′way′ n. opening in a ship's deck, or in a floor

hate v. dislike strongly —n. strong dislike: also **ha′tred**

hate′ful a. deserving hate

hath v. [Ar.] has

haugh·ty (hôt′ē) a. -ti·er, -ti·est scornfully proud —**haugh′ti·ly** adv. —**haugh′ti·ness** n.

haul v. 1 pull; drag 2 transport by truck, etc. —n. 1 amount caught 2 load or distance transported

haunch n. hip, rump, and upper thigh

haunt v. 1 visit often 2 recur often to —n. place often visited

haunt′ed a. supposedly frequented by ghosts

haunt′ing a. not easily forgotten

hau·teur (hō tur′) n. scornful pride

have v. had, hav′ing 1 hold; possess 2 experience 3 hold mentally 4 get; take 5 beget 6 engage in 7 cause to do, be, etc. 8 permit 9 be forced Have is also an important auxiliary verb —n. rich person or nation —**have on** be wearing —**have to do with** deal with

ha′ven n. shelter; refuge

have′-not′ n. poor person or nation

have′n't have not

hav′er·sack′ n. bag for provisions, worn on the back

hav′oc n. great destruction —**play havoc with** ruin

hawk n. bird of prey —v. 1 peddle (goods) in the streets 2 clear the throat

hawk′er n. peddler

haw′ser (-zər) n. cable for anchoring or towing a ship

haw′thorn′ n. small tree with red berries

hay n. grass, clover, etc. cut and dried —**hay′stack′** n.

hay fever n. allergy to pollen that affects one like a cold

hay′mow′ (-mou′) n. pile of hay in a barn

hay′stack′ n. pile of hay outdoors

hay′wire′ a. [Col.] wrong or crazy

haz′ard n. 1 chance 2 risk; danger 3 obstacle on a golf course —v. to risk —**haz′ard·ous** a.

haze n. 1 mist of fog, smoke, etc. 2 vagueness —**ha′zy** a., -zi·er, -zi·est

ha′zel n. 1 tree bearing small nut (**ha′zel·nut′**) 2 reddish brown

H′-bomb′ n. hydrogen bomb

he pron. 1 the male mentioned 2 anyone

head n. 1 part of the body above or in front of the neck 2 mind 3 top or front part 4 leader 5 crisis 6 poise —a. 1 chief 2 at the head —v. 1 to lead 2 set out; go —**head off** intercept —**head over heels** completely —**lose one's head** lose self-control —**not make head or tail of** not understand —**over one's head** beyond one's understanding —**turn one's head** make one vain

head'ache' n. pain in the head

head'dress' n. decorative head covering

head'first' adv. headlong

head'ing n. title; caption

head'light' n. light at the front of a vehicle

head'line' n. title of newspaper article —v. feature

head'long a., adv. 1 with the head first 2 rash(ly)

head'-on' a., adv. 1 with the head or front foremost 2 directly

head'phone' n. often pl. device with tiny speakers worn over the ears

head'quar'ters n.pl. center of operations; main office

head'room' n. space overhead

head'start n. early start or other competitive advantage

head'stone' n. grave marker

head'strong' a. obstinate

head'wa'ters n.pl. sources of a river

head'way' n. progress

head'y a. -i-er, -i-est 1 intoxicating 2 rash

heal v. cure or mend

health n. 1 soundness of body and mind 2 physical condition —**health'ful** a. —**health'y** a., -i-er, -i-est

heap n., v. pile; mass

hear v. heard, hear'ing 1 receive (sounds) through the ear 2 listen to 3 be told —**not hear of** not permit

hear'ing n. 1 ability to hear 2 chance to be heard

heark•en (här'kən) v. listen

hear'say' n. gossip; rumor

hearse (hurs) n. vehicle to carry a body to the grave

heart n. 1 organ that circulates the blood 2 vital part 3 love, sympathy, courage, etc. 4 figure shaped like ♥ —**by heart** from memory —**take to heart** take (too) seriously

heart'ache' n. sorrow

heart'break' n. great sorrow

heart'bro'ken a. overwhelmed with sorrow —**heart'break'ing** a.

heart'burn' n. burning sensation in the stomach

heart'en v. encourage

heart'felt' a. sincere

hearth (härth) n. 1 floor of a fireplace 2 home

heart'less a. unkind

heart'-rend'ing a. agonizing

heart'sick' a. very sad

heart'strings' n.pl. deepest feelings

heart'-to-heart' a. intimate

heart'y a. -i-er, -i-est 1 cordial 2 vigorous 3 strong and healthy 4 nourishing —**heart'i-ly** adv.

heat n. 1 hotness, or the perception of it 2 strong feeling 3 single race, etc. in a series 4 sexual excitement in animals —v. to make or become hot —**heat'ed-ly** adv. —**heat'er** n.

heath n. tract of open wasteland

hea•then (hē'thən) a., n. (of) one not a Jew, Christian, or Muslim

heath'er (heth'-) n. low plant with purple flowers

heave v. heaved or hove, heav'ing 1 lift, or lift and throw, with effort 2 make (a sigh) with effort 3 rise and fall in rhythm 4 retch or vomit —n. act of heaving

heav'en Theol. the place where God and his angels are —n. 1 pl. sky 2 state of bliss —**heav'en-ly** a.

heav'y a. -i-er, -i-est 1 weighing much 2 very great, intense, etc. 3 sorrowful —n., pl. -ies stage villain —**heav'i-ly** adv. —**heav'i-ness** n.

heav'y-du'ty a. made to withstand hard use

heav'y-hand'ed a. awkward

heav'y-heart'ed a. sad

heav'y-set' a. stout; stocky

He'brew n. language of ancient and modern Israel —a. of the Jews

heck'le v. annoy with questions, taunts, etc. —**heck'ler** n.

hec'tare' n. measure of land, 10,000 sq. meters

hec'tic a. rushed, frenzied, etc. —**hec'ti-cal-ly** adv.

he'd 1 he had 2 he would

hedge n. dense row of shrubs —v. 1 put a hedge around 2 avoid direct answers

hedge'hog' n. porcupine

he'don-ist n. pleasure-seeker —**he'don-ism'** n. —**he'do-nis'tic** a.

heed n. careful attention —v. pay heed (to) —**heed'ful** a. —**heed'less** a.

heel n. 1 back part of the foot 2 part of shoe, etc. at the heel —v. 1 furnish with heels 2 follow closely 3 lean to one side, as a ship

heft [Col.] n. heaviness —v. to lift —**heft'y** a., -i-er, -i-est

he-gem'o-ny (hi jem'-) n. dominance of one nation over others

heif'er (hef'-) n. young cow

height n. 1 highest point or degree 2 dis-

height'en v. make or become higher, greater, etc.

Heim·lich maneuver (hīm'lik) n. emergency technique for dislodging an object in the windpipe

hei'nous (hā'-) a. outrageous

heir (er) n. one who inherits another's property, etc. —**heir'ess** n.fem.

heir'loom' n. a possession handed down in a family

heist (hīst) [Sl.] n. a robbery —v. rob or steal

held v. pt. & pp. of HOLD

hel'i·cop'ter n. aircraft with a horizontal propeller above the fuselage

he'li·o·cen'tric a. having the sun as center

he'li·o·trope' n. plant with clusters of purple flowers

hel'i·port' n. flat area for helicopters to land and take off

he'li·um n. very light, nonflammable gas, a chemical element

he'lix n., pl. **–lix·es** or **–li·ces** (hel'ə sēz') spiral —**hel'i·cal** a.

he'll 1 he will 2 he shall

hell Theol. place of torment for sinners after death —n. state of evil or great suffering —**hell'ish** a.

Hel·len'ic a. Greek

hell'gram·mite' (-grəm-) n. fly larva used as fish bait

hel'lion (-yən) n. [Col.] person fond of mischief; rascal

hel·lo' int. exclamation of greeting

helm n. 1 tiller or wheel to steer a ship 2 control

hel'met n. protective head covering of metal, etc.

helms'man n., pl. **–men** man who steers a ship

help v. 1 give assistance (to); aid 2 to remedy 3 avoid 4 serve —n. 1 aid; assistance 2 remedy 3 one that helps 4 hired helper(s) —**help'er** n. —**help'ful** a.

help'ing n. portion of food served to one person

help'less n. 1 unable to help oneself 2 unprotected

help'mate' n. wife or husband: also **help·meet**

hel'ter-skel'ter adv., a. in or showing haste or confusion

hem v. **hemmed, hem'ming** 1 fold the edge of and sew down 2 surround or confine 3 clear the throat audibly —n. hemmed edge —**hem and haw** hesitate in speaking

hem'a·tite' n. kind of iron ore

he'ma·tol'o·gy n. study of blood and its diseases —**he'ma·tol'o·gist** n.

hem'i·sphere' n. 1 half a sphere 2 any of the halves (N or S, E or W) of the earth

hem'lock' n. 1 evergreen tree 2 poisonous weed

hemo– pref. blood

he'mo·glo'bin n. coloring matter of red blood cells

he'mo·phil'i·a n. inherited condition in which the blood fails to clot —**he' mo·phil' i·ac'** n.

hem'or·rhage' (-ər ij') n. heavy bleeding —v. bleed heavily

hem'or·rhoids' (-ər oidz') n.pl. swollen veins near the anus —**hem' or·rhoi'dal** a.

hemp n. tall plant with fibers used to make rope, etc.

hem'stitch' n. ornamental stitch, used esp. at a hem

hen n. female of the chicken or certain other birds

hence adv. 1 from this place or time 2 therefore

hence·forth' adv. from now on

hench'man n., pl. **–men** helper or follower, esp. of a criminal

hen'na n. reddish-brown dye from a tropical shrub

hen'peck' v. to domineer over (one's husband)

hen'pecked' a. nagged or dominated by one's wife

he·pat'ic a. of the liver

hep'a·ti'tis n. inflammation of the liver

her pron. objective case of SHE —a. of her

her'ald n. 1 messenger 2 forerunner —v. foretell

her'ald·ry n. 1 study of coats of arms, etc. 2 pomp —**he·ral'dic** a.

herb (urb, hurb) n. nonwoody plant, now esp. one used as seasoning or in medicine —**herb'al** (hur'bəl, ur'-) a.

herb'age n. pasturage; grass

herb'al·ist n. one who grows or sells herbs

her'bi·cide' (hur'-, ur'-) n. chemical used to kill plants, esp. weeds

her·biv'o·rous (hər-) a. plant-eating

her'cu·le'an a. having or involving great strength, courage, etc.

herd n. cattle, etc. feeding or living together —v. form into a herd or group

herds'man n., pl. **–men** one who tends a herd

here adv. 1 in, at, or to this place 2 at this point; now —n. this place

here'a·bout' adv. near here: also **here'a·bouts'**

here·af'ter adv. from now on —n. state after death

here·by' adv. by this means

he·red'i·tar'y adv. of, or passed down by, heredity or inheritance

he·red´i·ty n. passing on of characteristics to offspring or descendants

here·in´ adv. in this place, matter, writing, etc.

her´e·sy (her´-) n., pl. **–sies** unorthodox opinion or religious belief **—her´e·tic** n. **—he·ret´i·cal** a.

here´to·fore´ adv. until now

her´it·a·ble a. that can be inherited

her´it·age´ n. tradition, etc. handed down from the past

her·maph´ro·dite´ n. one with both male and female parts **—her·maph´ro·dit´ic** a.

her·met´ic a. airtight: also **her·met´i·cal** **—her·met´i·cal·ly** adv.

her´mit n. one who lives alone in a secluded place

her´ni·a n. rupture, as of the abdominal wall

her´ni·ate´ v. form a hernia

he·ro (hir´ō) n., pl. **–roes** 1 brave, noble person, esp. a man 2 central male character in a story **—he·ro´ic·a.** **—her·o·ine** (her´ō in) n.fem. **—her´o·ism´** n.

her´o·in n. narcotic

her´on n. wading bird

hero sandwich n. meat, cheese, etc. in long, sliced roll

her´pes´ (-pēz´) n. viral disease causing blisters

her´ring n. food fish of the Atlantic

her´ring·bone´ n. pattern of parallel, slanting lines

hers pron. that or those belonging to her

her·self´ pron. intensive or reflexive form of SHE

hertz n., pl. **hertz** international unit of frequency, as of waves

he's 1 he is 2 he has

hes´i·tate´ (hez´-) v. 1 feel unsure; waver 2 pause **—hes´i·tan·cy** n. **—hes´i·tant** a. **—hes´i·ta´tion** n.

het´er·o·dox´ a. unorthodox, as in religious beliefs **—het´er·o·dox´y** n.

het´er·o·ge´ne·ous a. 1 dissimilar 2 varied

het´er·o·sex´u·al a. of or having sexual desire for those of the opposite sex **—n.** heterosexual person

heu·ris´tic (hyōō-) a. helping to learn, as by self-teaching

hew v. **hewed, hewed** or **hewn, hew´ing** chop, as with an ax

hex n. spell bringing bad luck; jinx

hex´a·gon´ n. figure with 6 angles and 6 sides **—hex·ag´o·nal** a.

hey (hā) int. exclamation to get attention, etc.

hey´day´ n. peak period

hi int. [Col.] word of greeting

hi·a´tus n. gap or interruption

hi·ba·chi (hi bä´chē) n. charcoal-burning cooking grill

hi´ber·nate´ v. spend the winter in a sleeplike state **—hi´ber·na´tion** n. **—hi´ber·na´tor** n.

hi·bis´cus n. plant with large, colorful flowers

hic´cup´ n. muscle spasm that stops the breath **—v.** have a hiccup Also **hic´cough´**

hick n. [Col.] unsophisticated country person: contemptuous term

hick´o·ry n., pl. **–ries** 1 hardwood tree 2 its nut

hide v. **hid, hid´den** or **hid, hid´ing** 1 put, or be, out of sight 2 keep secret **—n.** animal skin or pelt

hide´a·way´ n. [Col.] secluded place

hide´bound´ n. narrow-minded

hid´e·ous a. very ugly

hide´-out´ n. [Col.] hiding place, as for gangsters

hie v. **hied, hie´ing** or **hy´ing** hasten

hi´er·ar´chy (-är´kē) n., pl. **–chies** (rule by) officials or clergy in graded ranks **—hi´er·ar´chi·cal** a.

hi´er·o·glyph´ics (hī´er ə glif´-, hī´rə glif´-) n.pl. picture writing, as of the ancient Egyptians **—hi´er·o·glyph´ic** a., n.

hi´-fi´ a. of high fidelity

high a. 1 tall 2 to, at, or from a height 3 above others in rank, size, cost, etc. 4 raised in pitch; shrill 5 elated 6 [Sl.] drunk or influenced by drugs **—adv.** in or to a high level, etc. **—n.** 1 high level, degree, etc. 2 the gear arrangement giving greatest speed **—high´ly** adv.

high´ball´ n. liquor mixed with soda water, etc.

high´brow´ n., a. [Col.] intellectual

high´fa·lu´tin a. [Col.] pompous: also **high´-fa·lu´ting**

high fidelity n. accurate reproduction of sound

high´-flown´ a. too showy

high frequency n. radio frequency between 3 and 30 megahertz

high´hand´ed a. arrogant

high´land n. mountainous region

high´light´ n. brightest or most interesting part, scene, etc.

high´-mind´ed a. having high ideals or principles

high´ness n. 1 height 2 [H—] title of royalty

high´-pres´sure a. using persuasive methods

high´-rise´ n. tall building

high school n. school from grades 8 (or 9) through 12

high seas n.pl. ocean waters not belonging to any nation

high′-spir′it·ed a. lively

high′-strung′ a. excitable

high′-tech′ a. of complex technology

high′-ten′sion a. carrying a high voltage

high′way′ n. main road

high′way·man n., pl. **-men** highway robber

hi′jack′ v. [Col.] steal (goods in transit) by force

hike v., n. **1** (take) a long walk **2** [Col.] increase

hi·lar′i·ous a. very funny or merry —**hi·lar′i·ty** n.

hill n. mound of land —**hill′y** a., **-i·er, -i·est**

hill′bil′ly n., pl. **-lies** [Col.] native of mountains or backwoods of southern U.S.: sometimes a contemptuous term

hill′ock n. small hill

hilt n. handle of a sword, dagger, etc.

him pron. objective case of HE

him·self′ pron. intensive or reflexive form of HE

hind a. back; rear —n. female of the red deer

hin′der v. keep back; stop or thwart —**hin′drance** n.

hind′most′ a. farthest back

hind′sight′ n. recognition, after the event, of what one should have done

Hin′du′ n. native or language of India —a. **1** of Hindus **2** of Hinduism

Hin′du·ism′ n. main religion of India

hinge n. joint on which a door, etc. swings —v. **1** attach by a hinge **2** depend

hint n. slight indication —v. give a hint

hin′ter·land′ n. remote area

hip n. part between the upper thigh and the waist

hip′pie n. [Sl.] young person, esp. of 1960's, alienated from conventional society

hip′po·drome′ n. arena

hip′po·pot′a·mus n., pl. **-mus·es** or **-mi′** (-mī′) large, thick-skinned animal of Africa

hire v. pay for the services or use of —n. amount paid in hiring

hire′ling n. one who will do almost anything for pay

hir′sute′ (hur′-) a. hairy

his pron. that or those belonging to him —a. of him

His·pan′ic n. Spanish-speaking Latin American living in U.S.

hiss n. prolonged s sound —v. **1** make this sound **2** disapprove of by hissing

his′to·ry n., pl. **-ries** study or record of past events —**his·to′ri·an** n. —**his·tor′i·cal, his·tor′ic** a.

his′tri·on′ics (-trē-) n.pl. dramatics —**his′tri·on′ic** a.

hit v. **hit, hit′ting 1** come against with force; bump **2** give a blow (to); strike **3** affect strongly **4** come (on or upon) —n. **1** a blow **2** collision **3** successful song, play, etc. —**hit′ter** n.

hit′-and-run′ a. of a car driver who leaves after hitting a victim: also **hit′-skip′**

hitch v. **1** move with jerks **2** fasten with a hook, knot, etc. —n. **1** a tug; jerk **2** hindrance **3** kind of knot

hitch′hike′ v. travel by asking for rides from motorists —**hitch′hik′er** n.

hith′er adv. to this place

hith′er·to′ adv. until now

hive n. **1** colony of bees or its shelter **2** pl. skin allergy with raised, itching patches

hoa·gy, hoa·gie (hō′gē) n., pl. **-gies** hero sandwich

hoard n. hidden supply —v. accumulate and store away (money, etc.) —**hoard′er** n.

hoar′frost′ a. frozen dew

hoarse a. sounding rough and husky

hoar′y a. **-i·er, -i·est 1** white **2** white-haired and old **3** very old

hoax n. a trick; practical joke —v. to fool

hob′ble v. **1** to limp **2** hamper by tying the legs —n. a limp

hob′by n., pl. **-bies** pastime activity —**hob′by·ist** n.

hob′by·horse′ n. stick with horse's head: child's toy

hob′gob′lin n. **1** elf **2** bugbear

hob′nail′ n. broad-headed nail for shoe soles

hob′nob′ v. **-nobbed′, -nob′bing** be friendly (with)

ho′bo′ n., pl. **-bos′** or **-boes′** a vagrant; tramp

hock n. hind-leg joint that bends backward —v. [Sl.] to pawn

hock′ey n. team game played on ice skates

ho′cus-po′cus n. **1** magic tricks **2** trickery

hod n. **1** trough for carrying bricks, etc. **2** coal scuttle

hodge′podge′ n. a jumble

hoe n. garden tool with a thin blade on a long handle —v. **hoed, hoe′ing** cultivate with a hoe

hoe′down′ n. lively dance

hog n. **1** pig **2** [Col.] greedy person —v. **hogged, hog′ging** [Sl.] take all of

hogs′head′ n. large barrel

hog′tie′ v. [Col.] hinder from action

hog′wash′ n. insincere words

hoi pol·loi′ (-pə loi′) n. the common people

hoist v. raise, esp. with a crane, etc. —n. apparatus for lifting

hoke v. [Sl.] treat in a sentimental or contrived way

hok′ey (hōk′-) n. [Sl.] overly sentimental

ho′kum n. [Sl.] nonsense

hold v. **held, hold′ing 1** keep in the hands **2**

keep in a certain position 3 keep back 4 occupy 5 have (a meeting, etc.) 6 contain 7 regard 8 remain unyielding —n. 1 grip 2 a strong influence 3 ship's interior below deck —**get hold of** acquire —**hold up** 1 delay 2 rob

hold′ings n.pl. property, esp. stocks or bonds, owned

hold′out′ n. one who refuses to perform, join in, etc.

hold′o′ver n. [Col.] one staying on from former time

hold′up′ n. 1 a delay 2 robbery

hole n. 1 hollow place 2 burrow 3 an opening, tear, etc. —**hole up** hibernate, as in a hole

hol′i·day (häl′ə-) n. 1 religious festival 2 work-free day, usually set aside by law

ho′li·ness n. a being holy

hol′lan·daise′ sauce (-dāz′) n. creamy sauce of butter, egg yolks, etc.

hol′ler v., n. [Col.] shout

hol′low a. 1 having a cavity within it 2 concave; sunken 3 insincere 4 deep-toned and dull —n. 1 cavity 2 small valley —v. make or become hollow

hol′ly n. evergreen shrub with red berries

hol′ly·hock′ n. tall plant with large, showy flowers

hol·o·caust (häl′ə kôst′) n. great destruction, esp. of people or animals by fire

hol′o·graph′ n. document handwritten by author

hol′ster n. leather pistol case

ho′ly a. **-li·er, -li·est** 1 sacred 2 sinless 3 deserving reverence or worship

Holy Communion n. church rite in which bread and wine are received as (symbols of) the body and blood of Jesus

Holy Ghost (or **Spirit**) third person of the Trinity

hom′age (häm′-, äm′-) n. anything done to show honor or respect

home n. 1 place where one lives 2 household or life around it —a. 1 domestic 2 central —adv. 1 at or to home 2 to the target —**home′less** a. —**home′made′** a.

home′land′ n. native land

home′ly a. **-li·er, -li·est** 1 simple 2 plain; ugly

home plate n. Baseball last base touched in scoring a run

home run n. Baseball hit by which the batter scores a run

home′sick′ a. longing for home —**home′sick′ness** n.

home′spun′ n. cloth made of yarn spun at home —a. plain or simple

home′stead′ (-sted′) n. 1 a home and its grounds 2 public land granted as a farm

home′stretch′ n. final part of racetrack, project, etc.

home′ward adv., a. toward home: also **home′wards** adv.

home′work′ n. schoolwork done outside the classroom

hom′i·cide′ n. 1 a killing of one person by another 2 one who kills another —**hom′i·ci′dal** a.

hom′i·let′ics n. art of writing or preaching sermons

hom′i·ly n., pl. **-lies** sermon

hom′i·ny n. coarsely ground dry corn

homo- pref. same; equal

ho′mo·ge′ne·ous a. 1 similar 2 made up of similar parts

ho·mog′e·nize′ (-mäj′-) v. make uniform throughout —**ho·mog′e·nous** a.

hom′o·graph′ n. word with same spelling as another but having a different meaning

hom′o·nym′ (-nim′) n. word pronounced like another but having a different meaning and, usually, spelling

Ho·mo sa·pi·ens (hō′mō sā′pē enz′) n. man; human being

ho′mo·sex′u·al a. of having homosexual desire for those of the same sex —n. homosexual person

hon′cho n., pl. **-chos′** [Sl.] person in charge; chief

hone n. fine whetstone —v. sharpen on a hone

hon′est (än′-) a. 1 not cheating, stealing, or lying; upright 2 sincere or genuine 3 frank and open —**hon′es·ty** n.

hon′ey n. sweet, syrupy substance made by bees (**hon′ey·bees′**)

hon′ey·comb′ n. structure of wax cells made by bees to hold their honey, etc. —v. fill with holes

hon′ey·dew′ melon n. muskmelon with a whitish rind

hon′ey·moon′ n. vacation for a newly married couple —v. have a honeymoon

hon′ey·suck′le n. a vine with small, fragrant flowers

honk n. 1 call of a wild goose 2 sound of an auto horn —v. make this sound

hon′ky-tonk′ n. [Sl.] cheap, noisy nightclub

hon′or (än′-) n. 1 high regard 2 good reputation 3 adherence to right principles 4 glory or credit 5 [H—] title of certain officials 6 something showing respect 7 source of respect of fame —v. 1 treat with respect or high regard 2 confer an honor on 3 accept as valid

hon′or·a·ble a. deserving honor —**hon′or·a·bly** adv.

hon′o·ra′ri·um (-rer′ē-) *n.* fee paid for professional services

hon′or·ar′y *a.* done, given, or held as an honor

hon′or·if′ic *a.* signifying honor, as a title

hon′our *n.* Br. sp. of HONOR

hood *n.* 1 covering for the head and neck 2 cover over an automobile engine 3 [Sl.] hoodlum —**hood′ed** *a.*

-hood *suf.* 1 state or quality 2 whole group of

hood′lum *n.* ruffian

hoo′doo *n., pl.* **-doos** [Col.] bad luck or its cause

hood′wink′ *v.* deceive

hoof *n., pl.* **hoofs** or **hooves** horny covering on the feet of cattle, horses, etc.

hook *n.* 1 bent piece of metal used to catch or hold something, spec., one for catching fish 2 sharp curve or curving motion —*v.* catch, fasten, hit, etc. with a hook —**hook up** connect, as a radio

hook·ah, hook·a (hŏŏ′kə) *n.* tobacco pipe for drawing smoke through water

hook′er *n.* [Sl.] a prostitute

hook′up′ *n.* connection of parts, as in radio

hook′worm′ *n.* a small intestinal roundworm

hook′y *n.* used only in **play hooky**, be a truant

hoo′li·gan *n.* ruffian

hoop *n.* large, circular band

hoop′la *n.* [Col.] excitement

hoop skirt *n.* woman's skirt worn over hoop framework

hoo·ray′ *int., n.* hurrah

hoose′gow′ (-gou) *n.* [Sl.] jail

hoot *n.* 1 cry an owl makes 2 shout of scorn —*v.* utter a hoot or hoots

hop *v.* **hopped, hop′ping** leap on one foot, or with all feet at once —*n.* 1 a hopping 2 [Col.] a dance 3 *pl.* dried cones of a vine, used to flavor beer, etc.

hope *n.* 1 trust that what is wanted will happen 2 object of this —*v.* want and expect —**hope′ful** *a.* —**hope′less** *a.*

hop′per *n.* trough from which material is conveyed

hop′sack′ing *n.* coarse cloth

hop′scotch′ *n.* children's hopping game

horde *n.* a crowd; pack

hore′hound′ *n.* medicine or candy made from a bitter plant

ho·ri′zon *n.* line where sky and earth seem to meet

hor′i·zon′tal *a.* 1 parallel to the horizon 2 level

hor′mone *n.* substance that is formed by a gland and stimulates an organ

horn *n.* 1 bonelike growth on the head of a cow, etc. 2 brass musical instrument —**horned** *a.*

hor′net *n.* large wasp

horn′pipe′ *n.* sailor's dance

horn′y *a.* **-i·er, -i·est** 1 hard; callous 2 [Sl.] easily aroused sexually

hor′o·scope′ *n.* chart of the zodiac used by astrologers

hor·ren′dous *a.* horrible

hor′ri·ble *a.* 1 causing horror 2 [Col.] very bad, ugly, etc. —**hor′ri·bly** *adv.*

hor′rid *a.* horrible

hor′ri·fy′ *v.* **-fied′, -fy′ing** 1 make feel horror 2 [Col.] shock greatly

hor′ror *n.* 1 strong fear or dislike 2 cause of this

hors d'oeuvre (ôr′ durv′) *n., pl.* **hors′ d'oeuvres′** appetizer

horse *n.* 1 large animal domesticated for pulling loads, carrying a rider, etc. 2 supporting frame on legs —**horse around** [Sl.] 1 engage in horseplay 2 waste time —**hors′y** *a.*

horse′back′ *adv., n.* (on) the back of a horse

horse chestnut *n.* 1 tree with large brown seeds 2 its seed

horse′hair′ *n.* stiff fabric made from hair of horse's mane or tail

horse′man *n., pl.* **-men** skilled rider of horses —**horse′man·ship′** *n.* —**horse′wom′an** *n., pl.* **-wom′en**

horse′play′ *n.* rough play

horse′pow′er *n.* unit of power output, as of engines

horse′rad′ish *n.* plant with a pungent edible root

horse′shoe′ *n.* flat, U-shaped, metal plate nailed to a horse's hoof

hor′ta·to′ry *a.* exhorting

hor′ti·cul′ture *n.* art of growing flowers, fruits, etc. —**hor′ti·cul′tur·al** *a.*

ho·san′na (-zan′-) *int., n.* shout of praise to God

hose *n.* 1 *pl.* **hose** stocking 2 flexible tube to convey liquids

ho′sier·y (-zhər-) *n.* stockings

hos′pice (-pis) *n.* shelter for travelers, sick, poor, etc.

hos′pi·ta·ble (-pit ə-) *a.* friendly to guests —**hos′pi·tal′i·ty** *n.*

hos′pi·tal *n.* place of medical care for sick and injured —**hos′pi·tal·ize′** *v.*

host *n.* 1 man who entertains guests 2 great number

hos′tage *n.* person held as a pledge

hos′tel *n.* lodging place

host′ess *n.* 1 woman who acts as a host 2 woman in charge of seating in a restaurant

hos´tile (-təl) a. 1 of or like an enemy 2 unfriendly

hos·til´i·ty n., pl. **–ties** 1 enmity 2 pl. warfare

hos´tler (-lər) n. one caring for horses in stable or inn

hot a. **hot´ter, hot´test** 1 high in temperature; very warm 2 spicy; peppery 3 angry, violent, eager, etc. 4 close behind 5 [Col.] fresh or new —**hot´ly** adv.

hot´bed´ n. glass-covered bed of earth, for forcing plants

hot´-blood´ed a. excitable

hot cake n. pancake

hot dog n. [Col.] wiener

ho·tel´ n. place with rooms, food, etc. for travelers

hot´head´ed a. easily angered —**hot´head´** n.

hot´house´ n. greenhouse

hot line n. phone or telegraph line for emergencies

hot plate n. small, portable stove

hot rod n. [Sl.] car rebuilt for speed —**hot rod´der** n.

hot´shot´ n. [Sl.] one thought of as skillful, important, etc.

hound n. breed of hunting dog —v. keep pursuing

hour n. 1 ¹⁄₂₄ of a day; 60 minutes 2 a particular time —**hour´ly** a., adv.

hour´glass´ n. instrument for measuring time by the flow of sand in it

hou·ri (hoo´rē) n. nymph in Muslim paradise

house (v.: houz) n. 1 building to live in 2 family 3 building for specified use 4 business firm 5 legislative assembly —v. cover, shelter, lodge, etc. —**keep house** take care of a home

house´break´ing n. breaking into another's house to steal

house´bro´ken a. trained to live in a house, as a dog

house´hold´ n. 1 all those living in one house 2 home and its affairs

house´hold´er n. 1 owner of a house 2 head of a household

house´keep´er n. a woman who manages a home

house´warm´ing n. party after moving into a new home

house´wife´ n., pl. **–wives** woman running a home

house´work´ n. work of cleaning, cooking, etc. in a house

hous´ing (houz´-) n. 1 shelter or lodging; houses 2 enclosing frame, box, etc.

hov´el (huv´-) n. small, miserable dwelling

hov´er (huv´-) v. 1 flutter in the air near one place 2 linger close by

how adv. 1 in what way 2 in what condition 3 why 4 to what extent

how´dah (-də) n. seat on the back of an elephant or camel

how·ev´er adv. 1 by whatever means 2 to whatever degree —con. nevertheless

how´itz·er n. short cannon

howl n. 1 long, wailing cry of a wolf, dog, etc. 2 similar cry, as of pain —v. 1 utter a howl 2 laugh in scorn, mirth, etc.

howl´er n. [Col.] funny blunder

how´so·ev´er adv. however

hoy´den n. tomboy

hua·ra·ches (wə rä´chěz, hə-) n.pl. flat sandals

hub n. 1 center of a wheel 2 center of activity, etc.

hub´bub´ n. tumult

hu´bris (hyoo´-) arrogance

huck´le·ber´ry n., pl. **–ries** edible dark-blue berry

huck´ster n. peddler

hud´dle v. 1 to crowd close together 2 draw (oneself) up tightly —n. confused crowed or heap

hue n. color; tint —**hue and cry** loud outcry

huff v. to blow; puff —n. burst of anger —**huff´y** a., **-ier, -iest**

hug v. **hugged, hug´ging** 1 embrace 2 keep close to —n. embrace

huge a. very large; immense

hu´la n. native Hawaiian dance

hulk n. 1 body of an old, dismantled ship 2 big, clumsy person or thing —**hulk´ing** a.

hull n. 1 outer covering of a seed or fruit 2 main body of a ship —v. remove the hulls from

hul´la·ba·loo´ n. clamor

hum v. **hummed, hum´ming** 1 sing with closed lips 2 make a low, steady murmur —n. this sound

hu´man a. of or like a person or people —n. a person: also **human being** —**hu´man·ly** adv.

hu·mane´ a. kind, merciful, etc. —**hu·mane´ly** adv.

hu´man·ism´ n. system of thought based on interests and ideals of humankind —**hu´man·ist** n.

hu·man´i·tar´i·an n. one devoted to promoting the welfare of humanity —a. helping humanity

hu·man´i·ty n. 1 a being human or humane 2 the human race

hu´man·ize´ v. make human or humane

hu´man·kind´ n. people

hu´man·oid´ a., n. nearly human (creature)

hum´ble a. 1 not proud; modest 2 lowly;

unpretentious —v. to make humble —**hum′bly** adv.

hum′bug′ n. fraud; sham

hum′drum′ adv. monotonous

hu′mer·us n. bone of upper arm

hu′mid a. damp; moist

hu·mid′i·fy′ v. **-fied′, -fy′ing** make humid —**hu·mid′i·fi′er** n.

hu·mid′i·ty n. 1 dampness 2 amount of moisture in the air

hu′mi·dor′ n. jar, etc. for keeping tobacco moist

hu·mil′i·ate′ v. lower the pride or dignity of; mortify —**hu·mil′i·a′tion** n.

hu·mil′i·ty n. humbleness

hum′ming·bird′ n. tiny bird able to hover

hum′mock (-ək) n. low, rounded hill

hu·mon′gous (-mäŋ′-, -muŋ′-) a. [Sl.] huge

hu′mor n. 1 comical quality, talk, etc. 2 ability to see or express what is funny 3 mood 4 whim —v. indulge Also, Br. sp., **hu′mour** —**hu′mor·ist** n. —**hu′mor·ous** a.

hump n. rounded bulge —v. to arch; hunch

hump′back′ n. (person having) a back with a hump

hu′mus n. dark soil made up of decayed leaves, etc.

hunch v. arch into a hump —n. 1 a hump 2 feeling not based on facts

hunch′back′ n. humpback

hun′dred a., n. ten times ten —**hun′dredth** a., n.

hun′dred·weight′ n. unit of weight, 100 pounds

hung v. pt. & pp. of HANG

Hun·gar′i·an (-ger′-) a., n. (of) the people or language of Hungary

hun′ger n. 1 need or craving for food 2 strong desire —v. feel hunger (for) —**hun′gry** a., **-gri·er, -gri·est** —**hun′gri·ly** adv.

hunk n. [Col.] large piece

hun′ker v. squat

hunt v. 1 search out (game) to catch or kill 2 search; seek 3 chase —n. a chase or search —**hunt′er** n.

hur′dle n. 1 frame for jumping over in a race 2 obstacle —v. 1 jump over 2 overcome (an obstacle)

hur′dy-gur′dy n., pl. **-dies** barrel organ

hurl v. throw with force or violence —**hurl′er** n.

hurl′y-burl′y n. turmoil

hur·rah′ int., n. shout of joy, approval, etc.

hur·ray′ int., n. hurrah

hur′ri·cane′ n. violent storm from the tropics

hur′ry v. **-ried, -ry·ing** move, act, etc. with haste; rush —n. rush; haste —**hur′ried·ly** adv.

hurt v. **hurt, hurt′ing** 1 cause pain or injury to 2 damage 3 offend 4 have pain —n. pain, injury, or harm —**hurt′ful** a.

hur′tle v. move or throw swiftly or with violence

hus′band n. married man —v. manage thriftily

hus′band·ry n. 1 thrifty management 2 farming

hush v. make or become silent —n. silence; quiet

hush puppy n. cornmeal fritter

husk n. dry covering of some fruits and seeds —v. remove the husk from

husk′y a. **-i·er, -i·est** 1 hoarse 2 big and strong —n. [also H–] arctic dog used for pulling sleds

hus′sy n., pl. **-sies** bold or shameless woman

hus′tings n. (place for) political campaigning

hus′tle (-əl) v. 1 shove roughly 2 move, work, etc. quickly or energetically —n. a hustling

hus′tler (-lər) n. [Sl.] 1 one who gets money dishonestly 2 a prostitute

hut n. shedlike cabin

hutch n. 1 chest or cupboard 2 pen or coop for small animals

hy′a·cinth′ n. plant with spikes of flowers

hy′brid n. offspring of two animals or plants of different species, etc.

hy′brid·ize′ v. produce hybrids; crossbreed —**hy′brid·i·za′tion** n.

hy′dra n. tiny freshwater polyp

hy·dran′ge·a (-drān′jə) n. shrub with large clusters of flowers

hy′drant n. large pipe with a valve for drawing water from a water main

hy·drau′lic (-drô′-) a. 1 worked by force of a moving liquid 2 of hydraulics

hy·drau′lics n. study and use of the mechanical properties of liquids

hydro- pref. 1 water 2 hydrogen

hy′dro·car′bon n. compound of hydrogen and carbon

hy′dro·chlo′ric acid (-klôr′ik) n. acid formed from hydrogen and chlorine

hy′dro·e·lec′tric a. of the production of electricity by water power

hy′dro·foil′ n. (winglike structure on) high-speed watercraft that skims just above water

hy′dro·gen n. colorless gas, the lightest chemical element

hy·drog′e·nat′ed (-drāj′-) a. treated with hydrogen

hydrogen bomb n. very destructive atomic bomb

hydrogen peroxide n. liquid bleach and disinfectant

hy·drol′y·sis n. chemical reaction of a compound with water that produces a weak acid or base or both

hy′dro·pho′bi·a n. rabies

hy′dro·plane′ n. **1** small, highspeed motorboat with hydrofoils **2** seaplane

hy′dro·pon′ics n. science of growing plants in liquid mineral solutions

hy′dro·ther′a·py n. treatment of disease by external use of water

hy·drox′ide′ n. substance containing the radical OH

hy·e′na n. wolflike animal of Africa and Asia

hy′giene′ (-jēn′) n. set of principles for health

hy′gi·en′ic (-jē en′-, -jen′-) a. **1** of hygiene or health **2** sanitary

hy·grom′e·ter n. device for measuring humidity

hy′men n. membrane covering part of the opening of the vagina

hymn (him) n. song of praise, esp. a religious one

hym′nal n. book of hymns: also **hymn′book′**

hype (hīp) [Sl.] n. sensational publicity —v. promote in a sensational way —**hype up** stimulate

hyper- pref. over; excessive

hy·per′bo·le (-ba lē) n. exaggeration for effect —**hy′per·bol′ic** a.

hy′per·crit′i·cal a. too critical

hy′per·sen′si·tive a. too sensitive

hy′per·ten′sion n. abnormally high blood pressure

hy′per·thy′roid a. of or having excessive activity of the thyroid gland

hy′per·ven′ti·la′tion n. extreme rapid breathing, often causing dizziness, etc.

hy′phen n. mark (-) used between parts or syllables of a word

hy′phen·ate′ v. join or write with a hyphen —**hy′phen·a′tion** n.

hyp·no′sis (hip-) n. sleeplike state in which one responds to the hypnotist's suggestions —**hyp·not′ic** a.

hyp′no·tize′ v. induce hypnosis in —**hyp′no·tism′** n. —**hyp′no·tist** n.

hypo- pref. **1** under **2** less than; deficient in

hy′po·chon′dri·ac′ (-kän′-) n. one who suffers from abnormal anxiety over his or her health

hy·poc′ri·sy (hi-) n., pl. **-sies** condition of being, or action of, a hypocrite

hyp′o·crite′ (-krit′) n. one who pretends to have a virtue, feeling, etc. he or she does not have —**hyp′o·crit′i·cal** a.

hy′po·der′mic a. injected under the skin —n. syringe and needle for giving hypodermic injections

hy·pot′e·nuse′ (-n<u>oo</u>s′) n. side of right-angled triangle opposite the right angle

hy·poth′e·sis n. tentative explanation

hy′po·thet′i·cal a. based on a hypothesis; supposed

hy′po·thy′roid a. of or having deficient activity of the thyroid gland

hys·sop (his′sap) n. fragrant plant of mint family

hys′ter·ec′to·my (his′-) n. surgical removal of the uterus

hys·te′ri·a n. outbreak of wild emotion —**hys·ter′i·cal** a.

hys·ter′ics n.pl. hysteria

I

I pron. person speaking or writing

i′bex′ n. wild goat

i′bis n. large wading bird

-ible suf. that can or should be **2** tending to

i′bu·pro′fen (ī′byoo-) n. drug that relieves pain or fever

-ic, -ical suf. **1** of or having to do with **2** like **3** produced by **4** containing

ICBM intercontinental ballistic missile

ice n. **1** water frozen solid by cold **2** frozen dessert of fruit juice, sugar, etc. —v. **1** change into ice **2** cool with ice **3** cover with icing —**iced** a.

ice′berg′ n. great mass of ice afloat in the sea

ice′box′ n. refrigerator, esp. in which ice is used

ice′break′er n. sturdy boat for breaking through ice

ice cream n. frozen cream dessert

ice milk n. frozen dessert less rich than ice cream

ice skate n. shoe with a metal runner for gliding on ice —**ice′-skate′** v.

ich′thy·ol′o·gy (ik′thē-) n. study of fishes —**ich′thy·ol′o·gist** n.

i′ci·cle n. hanging stick of ice

ic′ing n. sweet, soft coating for cakes; frosting

i′con′ n. sacred image or picture

i·con′o·clast′ n. one who attacks venerated institutions or ideas

-ics suf. art or science

i′cy a. **i′ci·er, i′ci·est 1** full of or covered with ice **2** very cold —**i′ci·ly** adv. —**i′ci·ness** n.

id n. part of mind thought to be source of psychic energy

I'd 1 I had **2** I would

i·de′a n. **1** mental conception; a thought or belief **2** a plan or scheme

i·de·al n. 1 conception of something in its perfect form 2 perfect model —a. thought of as, or being, an ideal —i·de′al·ly adv.

i·de·al·ism′ n. conception of, or striving for, an ideal —i·de′al·ist n. —i·de·al·is′tic a.

i·de·al·ize′ v. regard or show as perfect —i·de′al·i·za′tion n.

i·den′ti·cal a. the same —i·den′ti·cal·ly adv.

i·den′ti·fy′ v. -fied′, -fy′ing 1 show to be a certain one 2 associate closely (with) —i·den′ti·fi·ca′tion n.

i·den′ti·ty n., pl. -ties 1 state or fact of being the same 2 individuality

i′de·ol′o·gy (ī′dē-, id′ē-) n., pl. -gies system of beliefs, as of a group —i′de·o·log′i·cal a.

id′i·om n. 1 set phrase with a special meaning 2 usual way of expression in words —id′i·o·mat′ic a.

id′i·o·path′ic a. of a disease with unknown cause

id′i·o·syn′cra·sy (-sin′-) n., pl. -sies personal oddity

id′i·ot n. foolish or stupid person —id′i·o·cy n. —id′i·ot′ic a.

i′dle a. 1 useless 2 baseless 3 not busy or working 4 lazy —v. 1 loaf 2 be or make idle —i′dler n. —i′dly adv.

i′dol n. image or object worshiped or adored

i·dol′a·try n. worship of idols —i·dol′a·ter n. —i·dol′a·trous a.

i′dol·ize′ v. adore as an idol

i′dyll, i′dyl (-dəl) n. short poem about pleasant rural life —i·dyl′lic (-dil′-) a.

i.e. that is to say

if con. 1 in case that 2 although 3 whether —as if as it would be if

if′fy a. [Col.] not definite

ig′loo n., pl. -loos′ Eskimo hut made of snow blocks

ig′ne·ous a. 1 of fire 2 produced by great heat

ig·nite′ v. 1 set fire to 2 catch fire

ig·ni′tion n. 1 an igniting 2 electrical system for igniting the gases in an engine

ig·no′ble a. not noble; base

ig′no·min′y n. shame; disgrace —ig′no·min′i·ous a.

ig′no·ra′mus (-rā′məs, -ram′əs) n., pl. -mus·es ignorant person

ig′no·rant a. 1 showing lack of knowledge 2 unaware —ig′no·rance n.

ig·nore′ v. pay no attention to

i·gua′na (i gwä′-) n. large tropical lizard

ilk n. kind; sort

I′ll 1 I shall 2 I will

ill a. worse, worst 1 bad 2 sick —n. an evil or disease —adv. worse, worst 1 badly 2 scarcely —ill at ease uncomfortable

ill′-ad·vised′ a. unwise

ill′-bred′ a. rude; impolite

il·le′gal a. against the law —il·le′gal·ly adv.

il·leg′i·ble a. hard or impossible to read —il·leg′i·bil′i·ty n. —il·leg′i·bly adv.

il·le·git′i·mate (-mət) a. 1 born of unwed parents 2 contrary to law, rules, etc. —il·le·git′i·ma·cy n.

ill′-fat′ed a. unlucky

ill′-got′ten a. obtained unlawfully or dishonestly

il·lib′er·al a. 1 without culture 2 narrowminded

il·lic′it (-lis′-) a. improper or unlawful

il·lim′it·a·ble a. without limit; immeasurable

il·lit′er·ate (-ət) a. unable to read —n. illiterate person —il·lit′er·a·cy n.

ill′-man′nered a. impolite; rude

ill′ness n. sickness; disease

il·log′i·cal a. not logical

ill′-suit′ed a. not appropriate

ill′-tem′pered a. irritable

ill′-timed′ a. inappropriate

ill′-treat′ v. to treat unkindly, unfairly, etc. —ill′-treat′ment n.

il·lu′mi·nate′ v. 1 light up 2 explain 3 decorate —il·lu′mi·na′tion n.

il·lu′mine v. light up

ill′-use′ v. abuse —n. cruel treatment: also **ill′-us′age**

il·lu′sion n. 1 false idea 2 misleading appearance —il·lu′sive, il·lu′so·ry a.

il·lus′trate′ v. 1 explain, as by examples 2 furnish (books, etc.) with pictures —il′lus·tra′tion n. —il·lus′tra·tive a. —il′lus·tra′tor n.

il·lus′tri·ous a. famous

ill will n. hate; dislike

I′m I am

im- pref. in-: used before b, m, or p

im′age n. 1 a representation, as a statue 2 reflection in a mirror, etc. 3 mental picture; idea 4 copy —v. reflect

im′age·ry n. 1 images 2 descriptions

i·mag′i·nar′y a. existing only in the imagination

i·mag′i·na′tion n. 1 power to form mental pictures or ideas 2 thing imagined —i·mag′i·na·tive a.

i·mag′ine v. 1 conceive in the mind 2 suppose —i·mag′i·na·ble a.

im·bal′ance n. lack of balance in proportion, force, etc.

im′be·cile (-səl) a. stupid —n. person who is mentally deficient —im′be·cil′ic a. —im′be·cil′i·ty n.

im·bed′ v. embed

im·bibe′ v. 1 drink (in) 2 absorb into the mind

im·bro′glio (-brōl′yō) n., pl. -glios involved misunderstanding or disagreement

im·bue' (-byōō') v. 1 saturate 2 dye 3 fill, as the mind

im'i·tate' v. 1 copy or mimic 2 resemble —**im'i·ta'tion** n., a. —**im'i·ta'tor** n.

im·mac'u·late (-yōō lat) a. 1 perfectly clean 2 without a flaw 3 pure; sinless

im'ma·nent a. present everywhere: said of God

im'ma·te'ri·al a. 1 unimportant 2 spiritual

im'ma·ture' a. not fully grown or developed —**im'ma·tu'ri·ty** n.

im·meas'ur·a·ble a. boundless; vast —**im·meas'ur·a·bly** adv.

im·me'di·a·cy n. direct relation to present time, place, etc.

im·me'di·ate (-at) a. 1 closest 2 instant 3 direct —**im·me'di·ate·ly** adv.

im'me·mo'ri·al a. very old

im·mense' a. vast; huge —**im·men'si·ty** n.

im·merse' v. 1 plunge into a liquid 2 engross —**im·mer'sion** n.

im'mi·grant n. one who immigrates —a. immigrating

im'mi·grate' v. enter a country, etc. in order to settle there —**im'mi·gra'tion** n.

im'mi·nent a. likely to happen without delay —**im'mi·nence** n.

im·mo'bile (-bal) a. not moving or movable —**im·mo·bil'i·ty** n. —**im·mo'bi·lize'** v.

im·mod'er·ate (-at) a. without restraint; excessive

im·mod'est a. indecent —**im·mod'es·ty** n.

im·mor'al a. not moral; esp., unchaste —**im·mo·ral'i·ty** n.

im·mor'tal a. 1 living forever 2 having lasting fame —n. immortal being —**im·mor·tal'i·ty** n.

im·mov'a·ble a. 1 firmly fixed 2 unyielding

im·mune' a. 1 exempt from or protected against something bad, as a disease, etc. —**im·mu'ni·ty** n. —**im'mu·ni·za'tion** n. —**im'mu·nize'** v.

immune system n. system protecting body from disease by producing antibodies

im'mu·nol'o·gy n. study of immunity to disease

im·mure' (im myoor') v. to shut up within walls

im·mu'ta·ble a. unchangeable —**im·mu'ta·bly** adv.

imp n. 1 young demon 2 mischievous child

im·pact' n. (force of) a collision

im·pact'ed a. describing a tooth lodged tight in jaw

im·pair' v. make worse, less, etc. —**im·pair'ment** n.

im·pa'la (-pä'lə, -pal'e) n. reddish African antelope

im·pale' v. pierce through with something pointed

im·pal'pa·ble a. that cannot be felt or easily perceived

im·pan'el v. Law choose (a jury) from a jury list

im·part' v. 1 give 2 tell

im·par'tial a. fair; just —**im·par'ti·al'i·ty** n.

im·pass'a·ble a. that cannot be traveled over

im'passe (-pas') n. deadlock

im·pas'sioned a. passionate; fiery

im·pas'sive a. calm

im·pas'to (-päs'-) n. painting with paint laid thickly on the canvas

im·pa'tient a. annoyed because of delay, etc. —**im·pa'tience** n.

im·peach' v. try (an official) on a charge of wrongdoing —**im·peach'ment** n.

im·pec'ca·ble a. flawless

im'pe·cu'ni·ous a. having no money; poor

im·ped'ance (-pēd'-) n. total resistance in a circuit to the flow of an electric current

im·pede' v. hinder

im·ped'i·ment n. thing that impedes; spec., a speech defect

im·ped'i·men'ta n.pl. encumbrances

im·pel' v. –**pelled'**, –**pel'ling** 1 drive forward 2 force

im·pend' v. be imminent —**im·pend'ing** a.

im·pen'e·tra·ble a. that cannot be penetrated

im·pen'i·tent a. not ashamed

im·per'a·tive a. 1 necessary; urgent 2 of the mood of a verb expressing a command

im'per·cep'ti·ble a. not easily perceived; subtle

im·per'fect a. 1 not complete 2 not perfect

im'per·fec'tion n. 1 a being imperfect 2 fault

im·pe'ri·al (-pir'ē-) a. of an empire, emperor, or empress

imperial gallon n. Br. gallon, equal to 1⅕ U.S. gallons

im·pe'ri·al·ism' n. policy of forming and maintaining an empire, as by subjugating territories, etc. —**im·pe'ri·al·ist** a., n.

im·per'il v. endanger

im·pe'ri·ous a. domineering

im·per'ish·a·ble a. indestructible

im·per'ma·nent a. not permanent

im·per'son·al a. 1 without reference to any one person 2 not existing as a person

im·per'son·ate' v. 1 assume the role of 2 mimic —**im·per'son·a'tion** n.

im·per'ti·nent a. 1 not relevant 2 insolent —**im·per'ti·nence** n.

im·per·turb'a·ble a. calm; impassive

im·per'vi·ous a. 1 incapable of being penetrated 2 not affected by: with to

im·pe·ti'go (-tī'-) n. skin disease with pustules

im·pet'u·ous (-pech'-) *a.* impulsive; rash —**im·pet'u·os'i·ty** *n.*

im'pe·tus *n.* 1 force of a moving body 2 stimulus

im·pinge' *v.* 1 strike, hit, etc. (*on*) 2 encroach (*on*)

im'pi·ous (-pē-) *a.* not pious —**im·pi'e·ty** (-pī'-) *n.*

im·pla'ca·ble (-plak'ə-, -plā'kə-) *a.* not to be appeased

im·plant' *v.* 1 plant firmly 2 insert surgically —*n.* implanted organ, etc.

im·plau'si·ble *a.* not plausible

im'ple·ment *n.* tool or instrument —*v.* put into effect

im'pli·cate' *v.* show to be a party to a crime, etc.

im'pli·ca'tion *n.* 1 an implying or implicating 2 something implied

im·plic'it (-plis-) *a.* 1 implied 2 absolute

im·plode' *v.* burst inward —**im·plo'sion** *n.*

im·plore' *v.* beseech

im·ply' *v.* **-plied', -ply'ing** hint; suggest

im·po·lite' *a.* discourteous

im·pol'i·tic *a.* unwise

im·pon'der·a·ble *a.* not measurable or explainable —*n.* anything imponderable

im·port' (*n.*: im'pôrt') *v.* 1 bring (goods) into a country 2 signify —*n.* 1 thing imported 2 meaning 3 importance —**im'por·ta'tion** *n.*

im·por'tant *a.* 1 having much significance 2 having power or authority —**im·por'tance** *n.*

im·por'tune' *v.* urge repeatedly —**im·por'tu·nate** (-chə nət) *a.*

im·pose' *v.* put on (a burden, tax, etc.) —**impose on** 1 take advantage of 2 cheat —**im'po·si'tion** *n.*

im·pos'ing *a.* impressive

im·pos'si·ble *a.* that cannot be done, exist, etc. —**im·pos'si·bil'i·ty** *n.*, *pl.* **-ties**

im·pos'tor *n.* cheat pretending to be what he is not

im'po·tent (-pə-) *a.* lacking power; helpless —**im'po·tence** *n.*

im·pound' *v.* seize by law

im·pov'er·ish *v.* make poor

im·prac'ti·ca·ble *a.* that cannot be put into practice

im·prac'ti·cal *a.* not practical

im'pre·cate' *v.* to curse —**im'pre·ca'tion** *n.*

im'pre·cise' *a.* not precise; not clear, etc.

im·preg'na·ble *a.* that cannot be overcome by force

im·preg'nate' *v.* 1 make pregnant 2 saturate —**im'preg·na'tion** *n.*

im'pre·sa·ri·o' (-sä'-) *n.*, *pl.* **-os'** manager, as of concerts

im·press' (*n.*: im'pres') *v.* 1 to stamp 2 af-

fect the mind or emotions of 3 to fix in the memory —*n.* an imprint —**im·pres'sive** *a.*

im·pres'sion *n.* 1 a mark 2 effect produced on the mind 3 vague notion

im·pres'sion·a·ble *a.* sensitive; easily influenced

im·pres'sion·ism' *n.* style of art, music, etc. reproducing a brief, immediate impression —**im·pres'sion·ist** *n.* —**im·pres'sion·is'tic** *a.*

im'pri·ma·tur (-mät'ər) *n.* permission, esp. to publish

im·print' (*n.*: im'print') *v.* mark or fix as by pressing —*n.* 1 a mark; print 2 characteristic effect

im·pris'on *v.* put in prison

im·prob'a·ble *a.* unlikely

im·promp'tu' *a.*, *adv.* without preparation; offhand

im·prop'er *a.* not proper

im'pro·pri'e·ty (-prī'-) *n.*, *pl.* **-ties** improper act

im·prove' *v.* make or become better or more valuable —**im·prove'ment** *n.*

im·prov'i·dent *a.* unthrifty

im'pro·vise' *v.* 1 compose and perform without preparation 2 make or do with whatever is at hand —**im·prov'i·sa'tion** *n.*

im·pru'dent *a.* rash; indiscreet —**im·pru'dence** *n.*

im'pu·dent (-pyōō-) *a.* insolent —**im'pu·dence** *n.*

im·pugn' (-pyōōn') *v.* to challenge as false

im'pulse' *n.* 1 driving force; impetus 2 sudden inclination to act —**im·pul'sive** *a.*

im·pu'ni·ty *n.* freedom from punishment or harm

im·pure' *a.* 1 dirty 2 immoral 3 adulterated —**im·pu'ri·ty** *n.*, *pl.* **-ties**

im·pute' *v.* attribute

in *prep.* 1 contained by 2 wearing 3 during 4 at the end of 5 with regard to 6 because of 7 into —*adv.* to or at the inside —*n.* 1 *pl.* those in power 2 [Col.] special access —**in that** because —**in with** associated with

in– *pref.* 1 in, into, or toward 2 no, not, or lacking: add *not* or *lack of* to meaning of base word in list below

in'a·bil'i·ty

in'ac·ces'si·ble

in·ac'cu·ra·cy

in·ac'cu·rate

in·ac'tive

in·ad'e·qua·cy

in·ad'e·quate

in'ad·mis'si·ble

in'ad·vis'a·ble

in·an'i·mate

in·ap'pli·ca·ble

in'ap·pro'pri·ate

in·apt'
in·ar·tic'u·late
in'at·ten'tion
in·au'di·ble
in'aus·pi'cious
in·ca'pa·ble
in'ca·pac'i·ty
in'ci·vil'i·ty
in'co·her'ence
in'co·her'ent
in'com·bus'ti·ble
in'com·pat'i·ble
in'com'pre·hen'si·ble
in'con·ceiv'a·ble
in'con·clu'sive
in·con'gru·ous
in·con'sid·er·a·ble
in·con'sid·er·ate
in'con·sis'ten·cy
in'con·sis'tent
in·con'stant
in·con'ti·nence
in'con·tro·vert'i·ble
in'cor·rect'
in'cor·rupt'i·ble
in·cur'a·ble
in·de'cent
in'de·ci'sion
in'de·ci'sive
in·dec'o·rous
in·def'i·nite
in'di·gest'i·ble
in'di·rect'
in'dis·cern'i·ble
in'dis·creet'
in'dis·cre'tion
in'dis·pu'ta·ble
in'dis·tinct'
in'dis·tin·guish·a·ble
in'di·vis'i·ble
in·ed'i·ble
in'ef·fec'tive
in'ef·fec'tu·al
in·ef'fi·ca·cy
in'ef·fi'cient
in·e·las'tic
in'el'e·gant
in·el'i·gi·ble
in'e·qual'i·ty
in·eq'ui·ta·ble
in·eq'ui·ty
in'ex·act'
in'ex·cus'a·ble
in'ex·haust'i·ble
in'ex·pe'di·ent
in'ex·pen'sive
in'ex·tin'guish·a·ble
in·fer'tile
in·fre'quent
in·glo'ri·ous

in·grat'i·tude'
in'har·mo'ni·ous
in·hos'pi·ta·ble
in'hu·mane'
in'ju·di'cious
in·of·fen'sive
in·op'er·a·tive
in·op'por·tune'
in·sep'a·ra·ble
in'sig·nif'i·cance
in'sig·nif'i·cant
in·sol'u·ble
in·solv'a·ble
in'sta·bil'i·ty
in'suf·fi'cient
in'sur·mount'a·ble
in·tan'gi·ble
in·tol'er·a·ble
in·tol'er·ance
in·tol'er·ant
in·var'i·a·ble
in·vul'ner·a·ble

in ab·sen'ti·a (-sen'shə) *adv.* although not present

in·ac'ti·vate' *v.* make no longer active

in'ad·vert'ent *a.* not on purpose; accidental —**in'ad·vert'ence** *n.*

in·al'ien·a·ble (-āl'yən-) *a.* that cannot be taken away

in·ane' *a.* lacking sense; silly —**in·an'i·ty** *n.*

in'as·much' as' *adv.* because

in·au'gu·rate' (-ô'gyə-) *v.* **1** formally induct into office **2** begin; open —**in·au'gu·ral** *a.* —**in·au'gu·ra'tion** *n.*

in'board' *a.* inside the hull of a boat

in'born' *a.* present at birth; natural

in'bound' *a.* going inward

in'breed' *v.* breed by continually mating from the same stock

in·cal'cu·la·ble *a.* too great to be calculated

in'can·des'cent *a.* **1** glowing with heat **2** shining

in'can·ta'tion *n.* words chanted in magic spells

in·ca·pac'i·tate' (-pas'-) *v.* make unable or unfit

in·car'cer·ate' *v.* imprison —**in·car'cer·a'tion** *n.*

in·car'nate (-nət) *a.* in human form; personified —**in·car·na'tion** *n.*

in·cen'di·ar'y (-sen'-) *a.* **1** causing fires **2** stirring up strife —*n.* one who willfully sets fire to property

in'cense' (*v.:* in sens') *n.* **1** substance burned to produce a pleasant odor **2** this odor —*v.* enrage

in·cen'tive *n.* motive or stimulus

in·cep'tion *n.* a beginning

in·ces'sant *a.* constant

in'cest' *n.* sexual intercourse between close

relatives —**in·ces'tu·ous** (-chōō əs) *a.*

inch *n.* measure of length, 1/12 foot —*v.* to move very slowly, by degrees —**every inch** in all respects

in·cho·ate' (-kō'ət) *a.* just begun

in'ci·dence *n.* range of occurrence or effect

in'ci·dent *n.* event

in'ci·den'tal *a.* 1 happening along with something more important 2 minor —*n.* 1 something incidental 2 *pl.* miscellaneous items —**in'ci·den'tal·ly** *adv.*

in·cin'er·ate' *v.* burn to ashes

in·cin'er·a'tor *n.* furnace for burning trash

in·cip'i·ent *a.* just beginning to exist or appear

in·cise' (-sīz') *v.* cut into; engrave

in·ci'sion (-sizh'ən) *n.* 1 a cutting into 2 a cut; gash

in·ci'sive (-sī'siv) *a.* piercing; acute

in·ci'sor (-zər) *n.* any of the front cutting teeth

in·cite' *v.* urge to action —**in·cite'ment** *n.*

in·clem'ent *a.* stormy

in·cline' (*n.:* in'klīn') *v.* 1 lean; bend; slope 2 tend 3 have a preference 4 influence —*n.* a slope —**in'cli·na'tion** *n.*

in·close' *v.* enclose

in·clude' *v.* have or take in as part of a whole; contain —**in·clu'sion** *n.*

in·clu'sive *a.* 1 including everything 2 including the items mentioned

in·cog'ni'to (-tē'-) *adv., a.* disguised under a false name

in'come *n.* money one gets as wages, salary, rent, etc.

in'com'ing *a.* coming in

in'com·mu'ni·ca'do (-kä'dō) *adv., a.* unable or not allowed to communicate

in·com'pa·ra·ble *a.* beyond comparison; matchless

in'com·pe'tent *a.* (one) without adequate skill or knowledge —**in·com'pe·tence** *n.*

in'com·plete' *a.* lacking a part or parts; unfinished

in'con·se·quen'tial *a.* unimportant

in'con·sol'a·ble *a.* that cannot be comforted or cheered

in'con·spic'u·ous *a.* attracting little attention

in'con·test'a·ble *a.* certain

in·con'ti·nent *a.* unable to control one's natural functions —**in·con'ti·nence** *n.*

in'con·ven'ience *n.* 1 lack of comfort, etc. 2 inconvenient thing —*v.* cause bother, etc. to —**in'con·ven'ient** *a.*

in·cor'po·rate' *v.* 1 combine; include 2 merge 3 form (into) a corporation —**in·cor'po·ra'tion** *n.*

in·cor'ri·gi·ble *a.* too bad to be reformed

in·crease' (*or* in'krēs') *v.* make or become

greater, larger, etc. —*n.* 1 an increasing 2 amount of this

in·creas'ing·ly *adv.* more and more

in·cred'i·ble *a.* too unusual to be believed

in·cred'u·lous (-krej'-) *a.* showing doubt —**in·cre·du'li·ty** *n.*

in'cre·ment *n.* 1 an increasing 2 amount of this

in·crim'i·nate' *v.* involve in, or make appear guilty of, a crime —**in·crim'i·na'tion** *n.*

in·crust' *v.* cover with, or form into, a crust

in'cu·bate' *v.* sit on and hatch (eggs) —**in'cu·ba'tion** *n.*

in'cu·ba'tor *n.* 1 heated container for hatching eggs 2 similar device in which premature babies are kept

in·cul'cate' *v.* fix in the mind, as by insistent urging

in·cum'bent *a.* resting (*on* or *upon* one) as a duty —*n.* holder of an office, etc.

in·cur' *v.* **-curred'**, **-cur'ring** bring upon oneself

in·cur'sion *n.* raid

in·debt'ed *a.* 1 in debt 2 owing gratitude

in·debt'ed·ness *n.* 1 a being indebted 2 amount owed

in'de·ci'pher·a·ble (-sī'fər-) *a.* illegible

in·deed' *adv.* certainly —*int.* exclamation of surprise, doubt, sarcasm, etc.

in'de·fat'i·ga·ble *a.* not tiring; tireless

in'de·fen'si·ble *a.* that cannot be defended or justified

in·del'i·ble *a.* that cannot be erased, washed out, etc. —**in·del'i·bly** *adv.*

in·del'i·cate (-kət) *a.* lacking propriety; coarse

in·dem'ni·fy' *v.* repay for or insure against loss —**in·dem'ni·ty** *n.*

in·dent' *v.* 1 to notch 2 space in from the regular margin —**in'den·ta'tion** *n.*

in·den'ture *v.* bind by a contract to work for another

in'de·pend'ent *a.* not ruled, controlled, supported, etc. by others —**in'de·pend'ence** *n.*

in'-depth' *a.* thorough

in'de·scrib'a·ble *a.* beyond the power of description

in'de·struct'i·ble *a.* that cannot be destroyed

in'de·ter'mi·nate (-nət) *a.* not definite; vague

in'dex *n., pl.* **-dex'es** or **-di·ces'** (-di sēz') 1 the forefinger: also **index finger** 2 indication 3 alphabetical list of names, etc. in a book showing pages where they can be found —*v.* make an index of or for

In'di·an *n., a.* 1 (native) of India 2 (member) of any of the aboriginal peoples of the Western Hemisphere: also **American Indian**

in·di·cate′ v. 1 point out; show 2 be a sign of —**in′di·ca′tion** n. —**in·dic′a·tive** a. —**in′di·ca′tor** n.

in·dict′ (-dīt′) v. charge with a crime —**in·dict′ment** n.

in·dif·fer·ent a. 1 neutral 2 unconcerned 3 of no importance 4 fair, average, etc. —**in·dif′fer·ence** n.

in·dig′e·nous (-dij′-) a. native

in′di·gent a. poor; needy —**in′di·gence** n.

in·di·ges′tion n. difficulty in digesting food

in·dig′nant a. angry at unjust or mean action —**in′dig·na′tion** n.

in·dig′ni·ty n., pl. —**ties** an insult to one's pride

in′di·go′ n. 1 blue dye 2 deep violet-blue

in·dis·crim′i·nate (-nət) a. making no distinctions

in′dis·pen′sa·ble a. absolutely necessary

in′dis·posed′ a. 1 slightly ill 2 unwilling

in′dis·sol′u·ble a. that cannot be dissolved or destroyed

in′di·vid′u·al (-vij′-) n. single person, thing, or being —a. 1 single 2 of, for, or typical of an individual —**in′di·vid′u·al·ly** adv.

in′di·vid′u·al·ism′ n. the leading of one's life in one's own way —**in′di·vid′u·al·ist** n.

in′di·vid′u·al′i·ty n. distinct characteristics

in·doc′tri·nate′ v. teach a doctrine or belief to —**in·doc′tri·na′tion** n.

in′do·lent (-də-) a. idle; lazy —**in′do·lence** n.

in·dom′i·ta·ble a. unyielding; unconquerable

in′door′ a. being, belonging, done, etc. in a building

in′doors′ adv. in or into a building

in′du·bi·ta·ble a. that cannot be doubted

in·duce′ v. 1 persuade 2 bring on; cause —**in·duce′ment** n.

in·duct′ v. 1 install in an office, a society, etc. 2 bring into the armed forces —**in·duct·ee′** n.

in·duc′tion n. 1 an inducting 2 a coming to a general conclusion from particular facts

in·dulge′ v. 1 satisfy a desire 2 gratify the wishes of —**in·dul′gence** n. —**in·dul′gent** a.

in·dus′tri·al a. having to do with industries or people working in industry

in·dus′tri·al·ist n. owner or manager of a large industry

in·dus′tri·al·ize′ v. build up industries in

industrial park n. area zoned for industry and business

in·dus′tri·ous a. working hard and steadily

in′dus·try n., pl. —**tries** 1 steady effort 2 any branch of manufacture or trade

—**ine** suf. of or like

in·e′bri·ate (-āt′; n.: -ət) v. make drunk —n. drunkard —**in·e′bri·a′tion** n.

in·ef′fa·ble a. too sacred to be spoken

in′e·luc′ta·ble a. not to be avoided or escaped

in·ept′ a. 1 unfit 2 foolishly wrong 3 awkward —**in·ep′ti·tude′**, **in·ept′ness** n.

in·ert′ a. 1 unable to move or act 2 dull; slow 3 without active properties

in·er′ti·a (-sha) n. tendency of matter to remain at rest, or to continue moving in a fixed direction

in′es·cap′a·ble a. that cannot be escaped

in·es′ti·ma·ble a. too great to be estimated

in·ev′i·ta·ble a. certain to happen —**in·ev′i·ta·bil′i·ty** n.

in·ex′o·ra·ble a. unrelenting —**in·ex′o·ra·bly** adv.

in′ex·pe′ri·enced a. lacking experience or skill

in·ex′pert a. not skillful

in′ex·pli·ca·ble a. that cannot be explained

in′ex·press′i·ble a. that cannot be expressed

in′ex·tri·ca·ble a. 1 that one cannot get free from 2 that cannot be disentangled

in·fal′li·ble a. never wrong

in′fa·my (-fə mē) n. 1 disgrace 2 great wickedness —**in′fa·mous** a.

in′fant n. baby —a. 1 of infants 2 in an early stage —**in′fan·cy** n. —**in′fan·tile** a.

in′fan·try n. soldiers trained to fight on foot —**in′fan·try·man** n., pl. —**men**

in·farct′ n. area of dying tissue: also **in·farc′tion**

in·fat′u·ate (-fach′ oo̅-) v. inspire with unreasoning passion —**in·fat′u·a′tion** n.

in·fect′ v. make diseased —**in·fec′tion** n.

in·fec′tious a. 1 caused by microorganisms in the body 2 tending to spread to others

in·fer′ v. —**ferred′**, —**fer′ring** conclude by reasoning —**in′fer·ence** n.

in·fe′ri·or (-fir′ē-) a. 1 lower in space, order, status, etc. 2 poor in quality —**in·fe′ri·or′i·ty** n.

in·fer′nal a. of hell; hellish

in·fer′no′ n., pl. —**nos′** hell

in·fest′ v. overrun in large numbers

in′fi·del′ (-fə-) n. one who rejects (a) religion

in′fi·del′i·ty n. unfaithfulness

in′field′ n. Baseball area enclosed by base lines —**in′field′er** n.

in′fight·ing n. personal conflict within a group

in·fil′trate′ v. 1 filter 2 pass through —**in′fil·tra′tion** n.

in·fi·nite (-nit) *a.* 1 lacking limits; endless 2 vast

in·fin·i·tes·i·mal *a.* too small to be measured

in·fin·i·tive *n.* form of a verb without reference to person, tense, etc.

in·fin·i·ty *n.* unlimited space, time, or quantity

in·firm′ *a.* weak; feeble —**in·fir′mi·ty** *n., pl.* **-ties**

in·fir′ma·ry *n.* hospital

in·flame′ *v.* 1 excite 2 make red, sore, and swollen —**in·flam·ma·tion** *n.* —**in·flam′ma·to′ry** *a.*

in·flam′ma·ble *a.* flammable

in·flate′ *v.* make swell out, as with gas

in·fla′tion *n.* 1 an inflating 2 increase in the currency in circulation resulting in a fall in its value and a rise in prices —**in·fla′tion·ar·y** *a.*

in·flect′ *v.* 1 vary the tone of (the voice) 2 change the form of (a word) to show tense, etc. —**in·flec′tion** *n.*

in·flex′i·ble *a.* stiff, fixed, unyielding, etc.

in·flict′ *v.* cause to suffer (a wound, punishment, etc.) —**in·flic′tion** *n.*

in′-flight′ *a.* done while an aircraft is in flight

in·flo·res′cence (-res′əns) *n.* 1 producing of blossoms 2 flowers

in′flu·ence *n.* 1 power to affect others 2 one with such power —*v.* have an effect on —**in′flu·en′tial** *a.*

in′flu·en′za *n.* acute, contagious viral disease

in′flux′ *n.* a flowing in

in·form′ *v.* give information (to) —**in·form′er** *n.*

in·for′mal *a.* 1 not following fixed rules 2 casual; relaxed —**in′for·mal′i·ty** *n., pl.* **-ties**

in·form′ant *n.* person who gives information

in′for·ma′tion *n.* news or knowledge imparted —**in′form′a·tive** *a.*

infra– *pref.* below

in·frac′tion *n.* violation of a law, etc.

in·fran′gi·ble (-jə-) *a.* unbreakable

in′fra·red′ *a.* of those invisible rays having a penetrating, heating effect

in′fra·struc′ture *n.* basic installations and facilities, as roads

in·fringe′ *v.* break (a law, etc.) —**infringe on** encroach on (others′ rights) —**in·fringe′ment** *n.*

in·fu′ri·ate′ *v.* enrage

in·fuse′ *v.* 1 instill 2 inspire 3 to steep —**in·fu′sion** *n.*

–ing *suf.* used to form the present participle

in·gen′ious (-jēn′-) *a.* clever; resourceful —**in·ge·nu′i·ty** *n.*

in·gé·nue (an′zhə nōō′, än′-) *n.* role of an inexperienced young woman in a play, etc.

in·gen′u·ous (-jen′-) *a.* 1 frank 2 naive

in·gest′ *v.* take (food, drugs, etc.) into the body

in·got (iŋ′gət) *n.* mass of metal cast as a bar, etc.

in·grained′ *a.* firmly fixed

in′grate′ *n.* ungrateful person

in·gra′ti·ate′ (-grā′shē-) *v.* get (oneself) into another′s favor

in·gre′di·ent *n.* component part of a mixture

in′gress′ *n.* entrance

in′grown′ *a.* grown inward, esp. into the flesh

in·hab′it *v.* live in

in·hab′it·ant *n.* person or animal inhabiting a place

in·hal′ant *n.* medicine, etc. to be inhaled

in′ha·la′tor *n.* 1 apparatus for inhaling medicine 2 respirator

in·hale′ *v.* breathe in —**in′ha·la′tion** *n.*

in·hal′er *n.* 1 respirator 2 INHALATOR (*n.* 1)

in·her′ent (-hir′-, -her′-) *a.* inborn; natural; basic

in·her′it *v.* 1 receive as an heir 2 have by heredity —**in·her′it·ance** *n.*

in·hib′it *v.* restrain; check —**in′hi·bi′tion** *n.*

in·hu′man *a.* cruel, brutal, etc. —**in′hu·man′i·ty** *n.*

i·nim′i·cal *a.* 1 hostile 2 harmful; adverse

in·im′i·ta·ble *a.* that cannot be imitated

in·iq·ui·ty (i nik′wə tē) *n., pl.* **-ties** sin or wicked act —**in·iq′ui·tous** *a.*

in·i′tial (i nish′əl) *a.* first —*n.* first letter of a name —*v.* mark with one′s initials —**in·i′tial·ly** *adv.*

in·i′ti·ate′ *v.* 1 begin to use 2 teach the fundamentals to 3 admit as a new member —**in·i′ti·a′tion** *n.*

in·i′ti·a·tive *n.* 1 first step 2 ability to get things started

in·ject′ *v.* 1 force (a fluid) into tissue, etc. with a syringe, etc. 2 throw in; insert —**in·jec′tion** *n.*

in·junc′tion *n.* order or command, esp. of a court

in′jure *v.* do harm to; hurt —**in·ju′ri·ous** *a.*

in′ju·ry *n., pl.* **-ries** harm or wrong

in·jus′tice *n.* 1 a being unjust 2 unjust act

ink *n.* colored liquid for writing, printing, etc. —*v.* mark or color with ink —**ink′y** *a.*, **-i·er, -i·est**

ink'blot' n. pattern of blots of ink used in a psychological test

ink'ling n. hint or notion

in'land a., adv. in or toward a country's interior

in'-law n. [Col.] a relative by marriage

in'lay' v. **-laid', -lay'ing** decorate a surface with pieces of wood, etc. set in —n., pl. **-lays'** 1 inlaid decoration 2 filling in a tooth

in'let' n. narrow strip of water going into land

in'mate' n. one kept in a prison, hospital, etc.

in'most' a. innermost

inn n. hotel or restaurant

in'nate' a. inborn; natural

in'ner a. 1 farther in 2 more secret

inner city n. crowded or blighted central section of a city

in'ner·most' a. 1 farthest in 2 most secret

in'ning n. Baseball round of play in which both teams have a turn at bat

in'no·cent a. 1 without sin 2 not guilty 3 harmless 4 artless —n. innocent person —**in'no·cence** n.

in·noc'u·ous a. harmless

in'no·va'tion n. new method, device, etc. —**in'no·va'tor** n.

in·nu·en'do (in'yoō-) n., pl. **-does** or **-dos** a hint or sly remark

in·nu'mer·a·ble a. too numerous to be counted

in·oc'u·late' v. inject a vaccine so as to immunize —**in·oc'u·la'tion** n.

in·or'di·nate (-nat) a. excessive

in·or·gan'ic a. not living; not animal or vegetable

in'put' n. 1 what is put in, as power into a machine or data into a computer 2 opinion or advice —v. feed (data) into a computer —**in'put'ter** n.

in'quest' n. judicial inquiry, as by a coroner

in·quire' v. 1 ask; question 2 investigate (into) —**in·quir'y** (in'kwə rē, in kwīr'ē) n., pl. **-ies**

in'qui·si'tion n. 1 investigation 2 strict suppression, as of heretics by a tribunal —**in·quis'i·tor** n.

in·quis'i·tive (-kwiz'-) a. asking many questions; prying

in'roads' n.pl. an advance, esp. an encroachment

in·sane' a. 1 mentally ill; crazy 2 of or for insane people —**in·san'i·ty** n.

in·sa'ti·a·ble (-sā'shə bəl) a. that cannot be satisfied

in·scribe' v. mark or engrave (words, etc.) on —**in·scrip'tion** n.

in·scru'ta·ble a. that cannot be understood

in'sect' n. small animal with six legs, as a fly

in·sec'ti·cide' n. substance used to kill insects

in·se·cure' a. 1 not safe 2 anxious 3 not firm —**in'se·cu'ri·ty** n.

in·sem'i·nate' v. sow or impregnate —**in·sem'i·na'tion** n.

in·sen'sate' a. not feeling

in·sen'si·ble a. 1 unconscious 2 unaware

in·sen'si·tive a. not sensitive or responsive —**in·sen'si·tiv'i·ty** n.

in·sert' (n.: in'surt') v. put into something else —n. a thing inserted —**in·ser'tion** n.

in·set' v. set in —n. something inserted

in'shore' adv., a. near or in toward the shore

in'side' n. inner side or part —a. 1 internal 2 secret —adv. 1 within 2 indoors —prep. in

in·sid'er n. one having confidential information

in·sid'i·ous a. sly, treacherous, tricky, etc.

in'sight' n. understanding of a thing's true nature

in·sig'ni·a n.pl. badges, emblems, etc., as of rank or membership

in·sin·cere' a. deceptive or hypocritical —**in·sin·cer'i·ty** n.

in·sin'u·ate' v. 1 hint; imply 2 to get in artfully —**in·sin'u·a'tion** n.

in·sip'id a. tasteless; dull

in·sist' v. demand strongly 2 maintain a stand —**in·sist'ence** n. —**in·sist'ent** a.

in'so·far' adv. to the degree that: with as

in'sole' n. (removable) inside sole of a shoe

in'so·lent (-sə-) a. showing disrespect —**in'so·lence** n.

in·sol'vent a. bankrupt

in·som'ni·a n. abnormal inability to sleep —**in·som'ni·ac'** n.

in'so·much' as adv. inasmuch as

in·sou'ci·ant (-sōō'sē-) a. calm; carefree

in·spect' v. 1 look at carefully 2 examine officially —**in·spec'tion** n. —**in·spec'tor** n.

in·spire' v. 1 stimulate, as to a creative effort 2 arouse (a feeling) 3 inhale —**in'spi·ra'tion** n.

in·stall' v. 1 put formally in office 2 establish in a place 3 fix in place for use —**in'stal·la'tion** n.

in·stall'ment, in·stal'ment n. any of the several parts of a payment, magazine serial, etc.

installment plan n. system by which debts, as for purchases, are paid in installments

in'stance n. 1 example 2 occasion 3 instigation

in'stant a. 1 immediate 2 quick to prepare —n. moment —**in'stant·ly** adv.

in·stan·ta·ne·ous a. done or happening in an instant

in·stead' adv. in place of the other

in'step' n. upper surface of the arch of the foot

in'sti·gate' v. urge on to an action; incite —**in'sti·ga'tion** n. —**in'sti·ga'tor** n.

in·still', in·stil' v. put in gradually; implant

in'stinct' n. 1 inborn tendency to do a certain thing 2 knack —**in·stinc'tive** a.

in'sti·tute' v. establish —n. organization for promoting art, science, etc.

in'sti·tu'tion n. 1 establishment 2 established law, custom, etc. 3 institute —**in'sti·tu'tion·al** a. —**in'sti·tu'tion·al·ize'** v.

in·struct' v. 1 teach 2 direct —**in·struc'tion** n. —**in·struc'tive** a. —**in·struc'tor** n.

in'stru·ment n. 1 means; agent 2 tool or device for doing exact work 3 device producing musical sound

in'stru·men'tal a. 1 serving as a means 2 of, for, or by musical instruments

in'stru·men·tal'i·ty n., pl. **-ties** means; agency

in'sub·or'di·nate (-nət) a. disobedient

in'sub·stan'tial (-shəl) a. 1 unreal 2 weak or flimsy

in·suf'fer·a·ble a. intolerable

in'su·lar (-sə-, -syoo-) a. 1 of an island 2 narrow in outlook

in'su·late' v. 1 protect with a material to prevent the loss of electricity, heat, etc. 2 set apart —**in'su·la'tion** n. —**in'su·la'tor** n.

in'su·lin n. pancreatic hormone used to treat diabetes

in·sult' n. act or remark meant to hurt the feelings —v. subject to an insult

in·su'per·a·ble a. that cannot be overcome

in·sur'ance (-shoor'-) n. 1 an insuring contract whereby a company guarantees payment for loss, death, etc. 3 amount for which a thing is insured

in·sure' v. 1 make sure 2 protect 3 get or give insurance on

in·sured' n. person insured against loss

in·sur'er n. company that insures others against loss

in·sur'gent a. rising up in revolt; rebelling —n. a rebel —**in·sur'gence** n.

in'sur·rec'tion n. rebellion

in·tact' a. kept whole

in·ta'glio' (-tal'yō') n., pl. **-ios'** design carved below the surface

in'take' n. 1 amount taken in 2 place in a pipe, etc. where fluid is taken in

in'te·ger n. whole number

in'te·gral (or in teg'rəl) a. 1 essential to completeness 2 entire

in'te·grate' v. 1 form into a whole; unify 2 desegregate —**in'te·gra'tion** n.

in'te·grat'ed circuit n. electronic circuit on a chip of semiconductor material

in·teg'ri·ty n. 1 honesty, sincerity, etc. 2 wholeness

in·teg'u·ment n. skin, rind, shell, etc.

in'tel·lect' n. 1 ability to reason 2 high intelligence

in'tel·lec'tu·al a. 1 of the intellect 2 needing or showing high intelligence —n. one with intellectual interests

in'tel·lec'tu·al·ize' v. examine rationally, not emotionally

in·tel'li·gence n. 1 ability to learn, or solve problems 2 news; information —**in·tel'li·gent** a.

in·tel'li·gi·ble a. that can be understood; clear

in·tem'per·ate (-ət) a. not moderate; excessive

in·tend' v. 1 to plan; purpose 2 to mean

in·tend'ed n. [Col.] one's prospective wife or husband

in·tense' a. 1 very strong, great, deep, etc. 2 very emotional —**in·ten'si·fy'** v., **-fied'**, **-fy'ing** —**in·ten'si·fi·ca'tion** n. —**in·ten'si·ty** n.

in·ten'sive a. 1 thorough 2 Gram. emphasizing

in·tent' a. firmly fixed in attention or purpose —n. purpose; intention

in·ten'tion n. thing intended or planned; purpose —**in·ten'tion·al** a.

in·ter' (-tur') v. **-terred'**, **-ter'ring** bury

inter– pref. 1 between; among 2 with each other

in'ter·act' v. to act on one another —**in'ter·ac'tion** n. —**in'ter·ac'tive** a.

in'ter·breed' v. **-bred'**, **-breed'ing** to cross varieties of in breeding

in'ter·cede' (-sēd') v. 1 plead for another 2 mediate —**in'ter·ces'sion** (-sesh'ən) n.

in'ter·cept' v. seize or interrupt on the way —**in'ter·cep'tion** n.

in'ter·change' (n.: in'tər chānj') v. 1 exchange 2 alternate —n. 1 an interchanging 2 traffic entrance or exit on a freeway —**in'ter·change'a·ble** a.

in'ter·col·le'giate (-jət) a. between or among colleges

in'ter·com' n. communication system, as between rooms

in'ter·con·nect' v. connect with one another

in'ter·con'ti·nen'tal a. able to travel between continents

in'ter·course' n. 1 dealings between people, countries, etc. 2 sexual union

in'ter·de·nom'i·na'tion·al a. between or among religious denominations

in'ter·de·pend'ence n. mutual dependence
—in'ter·de·pend'ent a.

in'ter·dict' (n.: in'tər dikt') v. 1 prohibit 2
restrain —n. prohibition —in'ter·dic'tion
n.

in·ter·est (in'trist) n. 1 feeling of curiosity
or concern 2 thing causing this feeling 3
share in something 4 welfare; benefit 5
group with a common concern 6 (rate of)
payment for the use of money —v. have
the interest or attention of

in'ter·est·ed a. 1 influenced by personal
interest 2 feeling or showing interest

in'ter·est·ing a. exciting curiosity or attention

in'ter·face' n. point or means of interaction
—v. interact with

in'ter·fere' (-fir') v. 1 come between; in-
tervene 2 meddle —interfere with hinder
—in'ter·fer'ence n.

in'ter·im n. time between; meantime —a.
temporary

in·te'ri·or (-tir'ē-) a. 1 inner 2 inland 3
private —n. 1 interior part 2 domestic
affairs of a country

in'ter·ject' v. throw in between; insert

in'ter·jec'tion n. 1 an interjecting 2 thing
interjected 3 Gram. exclamation

in'ter·lace' v. join as by weaving together

in'ter·lard' v. intersperse

in'ter·line' v. write between the lines of

in'ter·lock' v. lock together

in'ter·loc'u·to·ry a. Law not final, as a
decree

in'ter·lop'er n. intruder

in'ter·lude' n. thing that fills time, as music
between acts of a play

in'ter·mar'ry v. –ried, –ry·ing marry, as persons of different races, religions, etc.
—in'ter·mar'riage n.

in'ter·me'di·ar·y a. intermediate —n., pl.
–ies go-between

in'ter·me'di·ate (-ət) a. in the middle; in
between

in·ter'ment n. burial

in'ter·mez'zo' (-met'sō') n., pl. –zos' or
–zi' (-sē') short musical piece

in·ter·mi·na·ble a. lasting, or seeming to
last, forever

in'ter·min'gle v. mix together

in'ter·mis'sion n. interval, as between acts
of a play

in'ter·mit'tent a. periodic; recurring at intervals

in·tern' (v.: in turn') n. doctor in training
at a hospital —v. confine within an area

in·ter'nal a. 1 inner 2 within a country —in·
ter'nal·ize' v.

internal medicine n. diagnosis and nonsur-
gical treatment of disease

in'ter·na'tion·al a. 1 among nations 2 for
all nations —in'ter·na'tion·al·ize' v.

in'ter·ne'cine (-nē'sin) a. destructive to
both sides

In'ter·net' n. extensive computer network
of thousands of smaller networks

in·tern'ist n. doctor specializing in internal
medicine

in'ter·of'fice a. between offices of an organization

in'ter·per'son·al a. between persons

in'ter·plan'e·tar'y a. between planets

in'ter·play' n. action or influence on each
other

in·ter'po·late' v. to insert (extra words, etc.)

in'ter·pose' v. place or come between; interrupt

in·ter'pret v. explain or translate —in·
ter'pre·ta'tion n. —in·ter'pret·er n.

in'ter·ra'cial a. among or for persons of
different races

in'ter·re·lat'ed a. closely connected with
one another

in·ter'ro·gate' (-ter'-) v. question formally
—in·ter'ro·ga'tion n.

in'ter·rog'a·tive n., a. (word) asking a question

in'ter·rupt' v. 1 break in on (talk, etc.) 2
obstruct —in'ter·rup'tion n.

in'ter·scho·las'tic a. between or among
schools

in'ter·sect' v. 1 divide by passing across 2
cross each other —in'ter·sec'tion n.

in'ter·sperse' v. scatter among other things

in'ter·state' a. between or among states of
a country

in·ter·stice (-stis) n. crevice

in'ter·twine' v. twist together

in'ter·ur'ban a. going between towns or
cities

in'ter·val n. 1 space between things 2 time
between events 3 difference in musical
pitch —at intervals now and then

in'ter·vene' v. 1 come or be between 2 come
in so as to help settle something —in'ter·
ven'tion n.

in'ter·view' n. meeting of people, as to confer, ask questions, etc. —v. have an interview with

in·tes'tate' a. not having made a will

in·tes'tine (-tin) n. usually pl. alimentary
canal from the stomach to the anus —in·
tes'tin·al a.

in'ti·mate' (-māt'; a., n.: -mət) v. hint —a.
1 most personal 2 very familiar —n. an
intimate friend —in'ti·ma·cy n., pl. –cies
—in'ti·ma'tion n.

in·tim'i·date' v. make afraid as with threats
—in·tim'i·da'tion n.

in'to prep. 1 toward and within 2 to the

form, state, etc. 3 [Col.] involved in or concerned with

in′to·na′tion n. manner of utterance with regard to rise and fall in pitch

in·tone′ v. utter in a chant

in to′to adv. as a whole

in·tox′i·cate′ v. 1 make drunk 2 excite greatly —**in·tox′i·cant** n. —**in·tox′i·ca′tion** n.

intra- pref. within; inside

in·trac′ta·ble a. unruly

in′tra·mu′ral a. among members of a school or college

in·tran′si·gent a. refusing to compromise —**in·tran′si·gence** n.

in·tran′si·tive (-tiv) a. not taking a direct object, as some verbs

in′tra·ve′nous a. into or within a vein

in·trep′id a. fearless

in′tri·cate (-kət) a. hard to follow because complicated —**in′tri·ca·cy** n., pl. —**cies**

in·trigue′ (-trēg′) v. 1 to plot secretly 2 excite the curiosity of —n. 1 secret plot 2 secret love affair

in·trin′sic (sik, -zik) a. real; essential —**in·trin′si·cal·ly** adv.

in′tro·duce′ v. 1 insert 2 bring into use 3 make acquainted with 4 give experience of 5 begin —**in′tro·duc′tion** n. —**in′tro·duc′to·ry** a.

in′tro·spec′tion n. a looking into one's own thoughts, feelings, etc.

in′tro·vert′ n. one more interested in his inner feelings than in external events —**in′tro·ver′sion** n. —**in′tro·vert′ed** a.

in·trude′ v. force oneself upon others without welcome —**in·trud′er** n. —**in·tru′sion** n. —**in·tru′sive** a.

in·tu·i′tion (-ish′ən) n. immediate knowledge of something without conscious reasoning —**in·tu′i·tive** a.

in′un·date′ v. flood —**in′un·da′tion** n.

in·ure′ (-yoor′) v. accustom to pain, trouble, etc.

in·vade′ v. enter forcibly, as to conquer —**in·vad′er** n. —**in·va′sion** n.

in′va·lid n. one who is ill or disabled

in·val′id a. not valid, sound, etc. —**in·val′i·date′** v.

in·val′u·a·ble a. priceless

in·vec′tive n. strong critical or abusive language

in·veigh′ (-vā′) v. talk or write bitterly (against)

in·vei′gle (-vē′-, -vā′-) v. trick or lure into an action

in·vent′ v. 1 produce (a new device) 2 think up —**in·ven′tor** n.

in·ven′tion n. 1 an inventing 2 power of inventing 3 something invented

—**in·ven′tive** a.

in′ven·to′ry n., pl. —**ries** complete list or stock of goods

in·verse′ (or in′vurs′) a. inverted; directly opposite —n. inverse thing

in·vert′ v. 1 turn upside down 2 reverse —**in·ver′sion** n.

in·ver′te·brate (-brət) n., a. (animal) having no backbone

in·vest′ v. 1 install in office 2 furnish with authority 3 put (money) into business, etc. for profit —**in·vest′ment** n. —**in·ves′tor** n.

in·ves′ti·gate′ v. search (into); examine —**in·ves′ti·ga′tion** n. —**in·ves′ti·ga′tor** n.

in·ves′ti·ture n. formal investing, as with an office

in·vet′er·ate (-ət) a. firmly fixed; habitual

in·vid′i·ous a. offensive, as an unfair comparison

in·vig′or·ate′ v. enliven

in·vin′ci·ble a. unconquerable —**in·vin′ci·bil′i·ty** n.

in·vi′o·la·ble a. not to be profaned or injured

in·vi′o·late a. kept sacred or unbroken

in·vis′i·ble a. not visible or not evident —**in·vis′i·bil′i·ty** n. —**in·vis′i·bly** adv.

in′vi·ta′tion n. 1 an inviting 2 message or note used in inviting

in′vi·ta′tion·al a. only for those invited to take part

in·vite′ v. 1 ask to come somewhere or to do something 2 request 3 give occasion for

in·vit′ing a. alluring

in vi′tro′ (-vē′-) a. kept alive apart from the organism, as in a test tube

in′vo·ca′tion n. prayer for blessing, help, etc.

in′voice′ n. itemized list of goods or services provided; bill

in·voke′ v. call on (God, etc.) for help, etc.

in·vol′un·tar′y a. 1 not done by choice; unintentional 2 not consciously controlled

in′vo·lu′tion n. 1 entanglement 2 intricacy

in·volve′ v. 1 complicate 2 draw into difficulty, etc. 3 include 4 require 5 occupy the attention of —**in·volve′ment** n.

in′ward a. 1 internal 2 directed toward the inside —adv. 1 toward the inside 2 into the mind or soul Also **in′wards** adv. —**in′ward·ly** adv.

i′o·dine′ n. chemical element used in medicine, etc.

i′o·dize′ v. treat with iodine

i·on′ (ī′an, -än′) n. electrically charged atom or group of atoms

—**ion** suf. 1 act or state of 2 result of

i′on·ize′ v. separate into ions or become electrically charged —**i′on·i·za′tion** n.

i·on′o·sphere′ n. outer part of earth's atmosphere

i·o´ta *n.* a jot

IOU *n.* signed note acknowledging a debt

–ious *suf.* having; characterized by

ip·e·cac (ip´ə kak´) *n.* emetic made from a plant root

ip´so fac´to [L.] by that very fact

IQ *n.* number showing one's level of intelligence, based on a test

I·ra´ni·an (-rā´-, -rä´-) *n., a.* (native) of Iran

I·ra·qi (i rä´kē, -rak´ē) *n., a.* (native) of Iraq

i·ras´ci·ble (-ras´ə-) *a.* easily angered

i·rate´ *a.* very angry

ire *n.* anger; wrath

ir´i·des´cent *a.* showing a play of rainbowlike colors —**ir´i·des´cence** *n.*

i´ris *n.* 1 colored part of the eye, around the pupil 2 plant with sword-shaped leaves and showy flowers

I´rish *a., n.* (of) the people or language of Ireland —**I´rish·man** *n., pl.* **-men**

irk *v.* annoy; tire out

irk´some *a.* annoying; tiresome

i·ron (ī´ərn) *n.* 1 strong metal that is a chemical element 2 device used for smoothing wrinkles from cloth 3 *pl.* iron shackles 4 golf club with metal head —*a.* 1 of iron 2 strong —*v.* press with a hot iron —**iron out** smooth away

i´ron·clad´ *a.* 1 covered with iron 2 difficult to change or break

iron lung *n.* large respirator enclosing the body

i·ro·ny (ī´rə nē) *n., pl.* **-nies** 1 expression in which what is meant is the opposite of what is said 2 event that is the opposite of what is expected —**i·ron´ic, i·ron´i·cal** *a.*

ir·ra´di·ate´ *v.* 1 expose to X-rays, ultraviolet rays, etc. 2 shine; radiate

ir·ra´tion·al *a.* lacking reason or good sense

ir·rec´on·cil´a·ble *a.* that cannot be reconciled or made to agree

ir´re·deem´a·ble *a.* that cannot be brought back, changed, etc.

ir·ref´u·ta·ble (*or* ir´i fyoot´-) *a.* that cannot be disproved —**ir·ref´u·ta·bly** *adv.*

ir·reg´u·lar *a.* 1 not conforming to rule, standard, etc. 2 not straight or uniform —**ir·reg´u·lar´i·ty** *n.*

ir·rel´e·vant *a.* not to the point —**ir·rel´e·vance** *n.*

ir·re·li´gious *a.* not religious

ir·re·me´di·a·ble *a.* that cannot be remedied or corrected

ir·rep´a·ra·ble *a.* that cannot be repaired or remedied

ir´re·press´i·ble *a.* that cannot be held back

ir´re·proach´a·ble *a.* blameless; faultless

ir´re·sist´i·ble *a.* that cannot be resisted

ir·res´o·lute´ *a.* not resolute; wavering

ir´re·spec´tive *a.* regardless (*of*)

ir´re·spon´si·ble *a.* lacking a sense of responsibility

ir´re·triev´a·ble *a.* that cannot be recovered

ir·rev´er·ent *a.* showing disrespect —**ir·rev´er·ence** *n.*

ir·re·vers´i·ble *a.* that cannot be reversed, annulled, etc.

ir·rev´o·ca·ble *a.* that cannot be undone or changed —**ir·rev´o·ca·bly** *adv.*

ir´ri·gate´ *v.* 1 supply with water by means of ditches, etc. 2 wash out (a body cavity) —**ir´ri·ga´tion** *n.*

ir´ri·ta·ble *a.* easily irritated or angered —**ir´ri·ta·bil´i·ty** *n.*

ir´ri·tate´ *v.* 1 to anger; annoy 2 make sore —**ir´ri·tant** *a., n.* —**ir´ri·ta´tion** *n.*

ir·rupt´ *v.* 1 burst (into) 2 increase abruptly in population

is *v.* pres. t. of BE: used with *he, she,* or *it*

–ise *suf.* chiefly Br. sp. of –IZE

–ish *suf.* 1 like; like that of 2 somewhat

i´sin·glass´ (ī´zin-) *n.* 1 gelatin made from fish bladders 2 mica

Is·lam (is´läm´, iz´-) *n.* Muslim religion —**Is·lam´ic** *a.*

is´land *n.* land mass surrounded by water —**is´land·er** *n.*

isle (īl) *n.* island

is·let (ī´lət) *n.* very small island

ism *n.* doctrine, theory, system, etc. whose name ends in *-ism*

–ism *suf.* 1 theory or doctrine of 2 act or result of 3 condition or qualities of 4 an instance of

is´n't is not

i´so·bar´ *n.* line on a map connecting points of equal barometric pressure

i´so·late´ *v.* place alone —**i´so·la´tion** *n.*

i´so·la´tion·ist *n.* one who believes his or her country should not get involved with other countries

i´so·mer *n.* chemical compound whose molecules have same atoms as another, but differently arranged

i´so·met´ric *a.* 1 of equal measure 2 of exercises in which muscles tense against each other

i·sos·ce·les (ī säs´ə lēz´) *a.* designating a triangle with two equal sides

i´so·tope´ *n.* any of two or more forms of an element with different atomic weights

Is·rae·li (iz rā´lē) *n., a.* (native) of Israel

Is·ra·el·ite (iz´rē ə līt´) *n.* one of the people of ancient Israel

is´sue *n.* 1 result 2 offspring 3 point under dispute 4 an issuing or amount issued —*v.* 1 emerge 2 result 3 put out; give out 4 publish —**at issue** disputed —**take issue** disagree —**is´su·ance** *n.*

–ist *suf.* 1 one who practices or 2 adherent of

isth·mus (is'məs) *n.* strip of land connecting two larger bodies of land

it *pron.* the animal or thing mentioned *It* is also used as an indefinite subject or object

I·tal·ian *n., a.* (native or language) of Italy

i·tal·ic *a., n.* (of) type in which the letters slant upward to the right —**i·tal'i·cize'** *v.*

itch *n.* 1 tingling of the skin, with the desire to scratch 2 restless desire —*v.* have an itch —**itch'y** *a.*, **-i·er, -i·est**

-ite *suf.* 1 inhabitant of 2 adherent of

i'tem *n.* 1 article; unit 2 bit of news

i'tem·ize' *v.* list the items of

it'er·ate' *v.* repeat —**it'er·a'tion** *n.*

i·tin'er·ant *a.* traveling —*n.* traveler

i·tin'er·ar'y *n., pl.* **-ies** 1 route 2 plan of a journey

-itis *suf.* inflammation of

its *a.* of it

it's 1 it is 2 it has

it·self' *pron.* intensive or reflexive form of IT

-ity *suf.* state or quality

I've 1 have

-ive *suf.* 1 of, or having the nature of 2 tending to

i'vo·ry *n., pl.* **-ries** 1 hard, white substance in elephants' tusks, etc. 2 tusk of elephant, etc. 3 creamy white

i'vy *n., pl.* **i'vies** climbing evergreen vine

-ize *suf.* 1 make or become 2 unite with 3 engage in

J

jab *v., n.* **jabbed, jab'bing** punch or poke

jab'ber *v.* talk quickly or foolishly —*n.* chatter

jack *n.* 1 device to lift something 2 playing card with picture of male royal attendant 3 *Naut.* small flag 4 electric plug-in receptacle —*v.* used in **jack up**, *1*) lift with a jack *2*) [Col.] raise (prices, etc.)

jack'al *n.* wild dog of Asia or Africa

jack'ass' *n.* 1 male donkey 2 fool

jack'daw' *n.* European crow

jack'et *n.* 1 short coat 2 outer covering

jack'-in-the-box' *n.* toy consisting of a box with a figure springing out

jack'-in-the-pul'pit *n.* plant with a hooded flower spike

jack'knife' *n.* large pocketknife —*v.* bend at the middle

jack'-o'-lan'tern *n.* hollow pumpkin cut to look like a face and used as a lantern

jack'pot' *n.* cumulative stakes, as in a poker game

jack rabbit *n.* large hare of W North America

Jac·quard' (jə kärd') *n.* fabric with a figured weave

jade *n.* 1 hard, green stone 2 worn-out horse 3 loose woman —*v.* tire or satiate —**jad'ed** *a.*

jade'ite' *n.* variety of jade

jade plant *n.* house plant with thick leaves

jag'ged *a.* having sharp points; notched or ragged

jag'uar' (-wär') *n.* animal like a large leopard

jail *n.* prison for short-term confinement —*v.* to put or keep in a jail —**jail'er, jail'or** *n.*

ja·la·pe·ño (hä'lə pän'yō) *n.* Mexican hot pepper

ja·lop'y *n., pl.* **-pies** [Sl.] old, worn-out automobile

jal'ou·sie' (-ə sē') *n.* window or door made of slats fixed as in a Venetian blind

jam *v.* **jammed, jam'ming** 1 cram; stuff 2 crush or crowd 3 wedge tight —*n.* 1 a jamming 2 [Col.] a difficult situation 3 spread made by boiling fruit and sugar

jamb (jam) *n.* side post of a doorway

jam'bo·ree' *n.* noisy revel

jan'gle *v., n.* (make or cause to make) a harsh, inharmonious sound

jan'i·tor *n.* one who takes care of a building —**jan'i·to'ri·al** *a.*

Jan'u·ar'y *n.* first month

Jap'a·nese' *n., pl.* **-ese'**; *a.* (native or language) of Japan

jar *v.* **jarred, jar'ring** 1 make a harsh sound 2 jolt —*n.* 1 jolt 2 wide-mouthed container

jar·di·niere' (-nir') *n.* large flower pot

jar'gon *n.* special vocabulary of some work, class, etc.

jas·mine, jas·min (jaz'min) *n.* shrub with fragrant flowers

jas'per *n.* colored quartz

jaun·dice (jôn'dis) *n.* disease that turns the skin, eyeballs, etc. yellow —*v.* make bitter with envy

jaunt *n.* short pleasure trip

jaun'ty *a.* **-ti·er, -ti·est** easy and carefree

jav'e·lin *n.* light spear thrown in contests

jaw *n.* either of the two bony parts that hold the teeth —*v.* [Sl.] to talk

jaw'bone' *n.* lower bone of jaw —*v.* try to persuade by using one's high position

jaw'break'er *n.* piece of hard candy

jay *n.* 1 bird of the crow family 2 blue-jay

jay'walk' *v.* cross a street heedlessly —**jay'walk'er** *n.*

jazz *n.* popular American music with strong rhythms —*v.* [Sl.] make exciting or elaborate: with *up*

jazz'y *a.* **-i·er, -i·est** [Sl.] lively, flashy, etc.

jeal'ous (jel'-) *a.* 1 resentfully suspicious

or envious **2** watchful in guarding **—jeal'ous·ly** n., pl. **-ies**

jeans n.pl. trousers or overalls of twilled cotton cloth

jeep n. small, rugged, orig. military automobile

jeer v. ridicule —n. derisive comment

Je·ho'vah God

je·june' a. childish

je·ju'num n. middle part of the small intestine

jell v. **1** become, or make into, jelly **2** [Col.] become definite

jel'ly n., pl. **-lies 1** soft, gelatinous food made from cooked fruit syrup **2** gelatinous substance

jel'ly·bean' n. small, bean-shaped candy

jel'ly·fish' n. jellylike sea animal with tentacles

jel'ly·roll' n. thin cake spread with jelly and rolled up

jeop'ard·ize' (jep'-) v. to risk; endanger

jeop'ard·y n. danger; peril

jerk n. **1** sharp pull **2** muscular twitch **3** [Sl.] disagreeable person —v. **1** move with a jerk **2** twitch **—jerk'y** a., **-i·er, -i·est**

jer'kin n. snug, usually sleeveless jacket

jerk'wa'ter a. [Col.] small, unimportant, etc.

jer'ky n. dried strips of meat

jer'ry·built' a. poorly built

jer'sey n. **1** soft, knitted cloth **2** pl. **-seys** upper garment of this

jest v., n. **1** joke **2** ridicule **—jest'er** n.

Je'sus founder of the Christian religion

jet v. **jet'ted, jet'ting 1** shoot out in a stream **2** travel by jet airplane —n. **1** liquid or gas in such a stream **2** spout that shoots a jet **3** jet-propelled airplane **4** black mineral —a. **1** jet-propelled **2** black

jet lag n. fatigue, etc. from adjusting to jet travel over great distances

jet'lin'er n. commercial jet passenger plane

jet propulsion n. propulsion by means of gases from a rear vent **—jet'-pro·pelled'** a.

jet'sam n. cargo thrown overboard to lighten a ship

jet'ti·son v. **1** throw (goods) overboard to lighten a ship **2** discard

jet'ty n., pl. **-ties 1** wall built into the water **2** landing pier

Jew n. **1** descendant of people of ancient Israel **2** believer in Judaism **—Jew'ish** a.

jew'el n. **1** gem **2** small gem used as a watch bearing

jew'el·er, jew'el·ler n. one who deals in jewelry

jew'el·ry n. jewels, or ornaments with jewels

jib n. triangular sail ahead of all other sails

jibe v. **1** shift a sail, or the course, of a ship **2** [Col.] be in accord **3** to gibe —n. a gibe

jif'fy n. [Col.] an instant

jig n. **1** lively dance **2** device to guide a tool —v. **jigged, jig'ging** dance (a jig)

jig'ger n. glass of 1½ oz. for measuring liquor

jig'gle v. move in slight jerks —n. a jiggling **—jig'gly** a.

jig'saw' n. saw with a narrow blade set in a frame: also **jig saw**

jigsaw puzzle n. picture cut into pieces that are to be fitted together again

jilt v. reject (a lover)

jim'my n., pl. **-mies** short crowbar used by burglars —v. **-mied, -my·ing** pry open

jim'son weed n. poisonous weed with trumpet-shaped flowers

jin'gle v. make light, ringing sounds —n. **1** jingling sound **2** light verse

jin'go·ism' n. warlike chauvinism **—jin'go·ist** n.

jin·ni' n., pl. **jinn** supernatural being in Muslim folklore

jin·rik'i·sha' (-rik'shô') n. two-wheeled Asian carriage pulled by one or two men

jinx [Col.] n. person or thing supposed to cause bad luck —v. bring bad luck to

jit'ter·y [Col.] a. nervous or restless **—the jitters** nervous feeling

jive n. [Sl.] foolish or insincere talk —v. [Col.] be in accord; jibe

job n. **1** a piece of work **2** employment; work —a. done by the job —v. handle (goods) as a middleman

job'ber n. one who buys goods in quantity and sells them to dealers

job lot n. goods, often of various sorts, for sale as one quantity

jock n. [Sl.] **1** disc jockey **2** male athlete

jock'ey n. race-horse rider —v. maneuver for advantage

jo·cose' a. joking; playful

joc'u·lar a. joking; full of fun **—joc'u·lar'i·ty** n.

joc'und a. genial; gay

jodh·purs (jäd'pərz) n.pl. riding breeches

jog v. **jogged, jog'ging 1** nudge; shake **2** move at a slow, steady, jolting pace —n. **1** nudge **2** jogging pace **3** part that changes direction sharply

jog'ging n. steady trotting as exercise **—jog'ger** n.

jog'gle v., n. jolt; jounce

join v. **1** to connect; unite **2** become a part or member of

join'er n. **1** carpenter of interior woodwork **2** [Col.] one who joins many clubs

joint n. **1** place where two things are joined

2 one of the parts of a jointed whole **3** [Sl.] any building, esp. a cheap bar —*a.* **1** common to two or more **2** sharing with another —*v.* connect by a joint —**out of joint 1** dislocated **2** disordered —**joint'ly** *adv.*

joist *n.* any of the parallel timbers holding up planks of a floor, etc.

joke *n.* **1** anything said or done to arouse laughter **2** thing not to be taken seriously —*v.* make jokes

jok'er *n.* **1** one who jokes **2** deceptive clause, as in a contract **3** extra playing card used in some games

jol'ly *a.* -**li-er**, -**li-est** merry —**jol'li-ness** *n.* —**jol'li-ty** *n.*

jolt *v.*, *n.* **1** jar; jerk **2** shock or surprise

jon'quil *n.* narcissus with yellow or white flower

josh *v.* [Col.] tease, fool, etc.

jos'tle (-al) *v.* shove roughly

jot *n.* very small amount —*v.* **jot'ted**, **jot'ting** write (*down*) briefly

jounce *v.* jolt or bounce

jour'nal (jur'-) *n.* **1** diary **2** record of proceedings **3** a newspaper or magazine **4** book for business records **5** part of an axle, etc. that turns in a bearing

jour'nal-ism' *n.* newspaper writing and editing —**jour'nal-ist** *n.* —**jour'nal-is'tic** *a.*

jour'ney *n.* a trip —*v.* to travel

jour'ney-man *n.*, *pl.* -**men** worker skilled at a trade

joust (joust, just) *n.*, *v.* fight with lances on horseback

jo'vi-al *a.* merry; jolly

jowl *n.* **1** cheek **2** *pl.* fleshy, hanging part under the jaw

joy *n.* gladness; delight —**joy'ful** *a.* —**joy' ous** *a.*

joy ride *n.* [Col.] reckless, speedy ride in a car, just for fun

joy'stick' *n.* **1** [Sl.] control stick of airplane **2** manual control device for video games, etc.

ju'bi-lant *a.* rejoicing —**ju'bi-la'tion** *n.*

ju'bi-lee' *n.* **1** a 50th or 25th anniversary **2** time of rejoicing

Ju'da-ism' *n.* Jewish religion

judge *v.* **1** hear and decide cases in a law court **2** determine the winner **3** appraise or criticize **4** think; suppose —*n.* one who judges

judg'ment *n.* **1** a deciding **2** legal decision **3** opinion **4** ability to make wise decisions Also sp. **judge'ment**

judg·men'tal *a.* making judgments, esp. harsh judgments; critical

Judgment Day *n.* time of divine judgment of all people

ju-di'cial (-dish'əl) *a.* **1** of judges, courts, etc. **2** careful in thought

ju-di'ci-ar'y (-dish'ē er'ē, -dish'ar ē) *a.* of judges or courts —*n.*, *pl.* -**ries 1** part of government that administers justice **2** judges collectively

ju-di'cious (-dish'əs) *a.* showing good judgment —**ju-di'cious-ly** *adv.*

ju'do *n.* kind of jujitsu used for self-defense

jug *n.* container for liquids, with a small opening and a handle

jug'ger-naut' *n.* relentless irresistible force

jug'gle *v.* **1** do tricks with (balls, etc.) **2** handle in a tricky way —**jug'gler** *n.*

jug'u-lar (vein) *n.* either of two large veins in the neck

juice *n.* liquid from fruit or cooked meat —**juic'y** *a.*, -**i-er**, -**i-est**

ju-jit'su' *n.* Japanese wrestling using leverage

ju'jube' (-jōōb', -jōō bē') *n.* gelatinous, fruit-flavored candy

juke'box' *n.* coin-operated phonograph: also **juke box**

ju-li-enne' *a.* cut into strips: said of vegetables, etc.

Ju-ly' *n.* 7th month

jum'ble *v.*, *n.* (mix into) a confused heap

jum'bo *a.* very large

jump *v.* **1** spring from the ground, etc. **2** leap or make leap over **3** move or change suddenly **4** rise or raise suddenly, as prices —*n.* **1** a jumping **2** distance jumped **3** sudden move or change —**jump at** accept eagerly —**jump'er** *n.*

jump'er *n.* sleeveless dress worn over a blouse, etc.

jump'suit' *n.* coveralls, worn for work or leisure

jump'y *a.* -**i-er**, -**i-est 1** moving jerkily **2** nervous

jun'co *n.*, *pl.* -**cos** small bird with gray or black head

junc'tion *n.* **1** a joining **2** place where things join

junc'ture *n.* **1** junction **2** point of time

June *n.* 6th month

jun'gle *n.* dense forest in the tropics

jun-ior (jōōn'yər) *a.* **1** the younger: written *Jr.* **2** of lower rank, etc. —*n.* **1** high school or college student in the next-to-last year

junior college *n.* school with courses two years beyond high school

ju'ni-per *n.* small evergreen with berry-like cones

junk *n.* **1** old metal, paper, etc. **2** Chinese ship with flat bottom **3** [Col.] worthless thing(s); rubbish —*v.* [Col.] to discard; scrap —**junk'y** *a.*, -**i-er**, -**i-est**

junk'er *n.* [Sl.] old, worn-out car, etc.

jun′ket n. 1 pleasure trip 2 milk thickened as curd

junk′ie, junk′y n., pl. **–ies** [Sl.] narcotics addict

jun′ta (hoon′-, jun′-) n. military group seizing political power

ju′ris·dic′tion n. (range of) authority, as of a court

ju′ris·pru′dence n. 1 science or philosophy of law 2 a system of laws

ju′rist n. an expert in law

ju′ror n. member of a jury

ju′ry n., pl. **–ries** group of people chosen to give a decision, esp. in a law case

just a. 1 right or fair 2 righteous 3 well-founded 4 correct; exact —adv. 1 exactly 2 only 3 barely 4 a very short time ago 5 [Col.] quite; really —**just now** a moment ago —**just′ly** adv.

jus′tice (-tis) n. 1 a being just 2 reward or penalty as deserved 3 the upholding of what is just 4 a judge

justice of the peace n. local magistrate in minor cases

jus′ti·fy′ v. **–fied′, –fy′ing** 1 show to be just, right, etc. 2 free from blame —**jus′ti·fi′a·ble** a. —**jus′ti·fi′a·bly** adv. —**jus′ti·fi·ca′tion** n.

jut v. **jut′ted, jut′ting** stick out

jute n. strong fiber used to make burlap, rope, etc.

ju′ve·nile (-və nīl′, -nəl) a. 1 young; immature 2 of or for juveniles —n. child or young person

jux′ta·pose′ v. put side by side —**jux′ta·po·si′tion** n.

K

kad′dish (käd′-) n. Jewish mourner's prayer

Kai·ser (kī′zər) n. title of former Austrian and German rulers

kale n. a cabbage with spreading, curled leaves

ka·lei′do·scope′ (-lī′-) n. small tube containing bits of colored glass that change patterns as the tube is turned —**ka·lei′do·scop′ic** (-skäp′-) a.

kan′ga·roo′ n. leaping marsupial of Australia

ka′o·lin n. white clay, used to make porcelain, etc.

ka′pok′ n. silky fibers from tropical trees, used for stuffing pillows, etc.

ka·put′ (-poot′) a. [Sl.] ruined, destroyed, etc.

kar·a·kul (kar′ə kul′) n. curly black fur from the fleece of Asian lambs

kar′at n. one 24th part (of pure gold)

ka·ra′te (-rät′ē) n. self-defense by blows with side of open hand

kar′ma n. fate

ka′ty·did′ n. insect resembling the grasshopper

kay′ak (kī′-) n. Eskimo canoe

ka·zoo′ n. toy musical instrument into which one hums

ke·bab (kə bäb′) n. small pieces of meat broiled on a skewer

keel n. center piece along the bottom of a ship —**keel over** turn or fall over

keen a. 1 sharp 2 piercing 3 perceptive; acute 4 eager 5 intense —**keen′ly** adv.

keep v. **kept, keep′ing** 1 fulfill; observe 2 protect; take care of 3 preserve 4 retain 5 continue 6 hold and not let go 7 refrain —n. food and shelter —**keep to oneself** 1 avoid others 2 to refrain from telling —**keep′er** n.

keep′ing n. 1 care or protection 2 conformity

keep′sake′ n. souvenir

keg n. small barrel

kelp n. brown seaweed

ken n. range of knowledge

ken′nel n. 1 doghouse 2 often pl. place where dogs are bred or kept

kerb n. Brit. sp. of CURB

ker′chief (-chif) n. 1 cloth worn around the head or neck 2 handkerchief

ker′nel n. 1 grain or seed 2 soft, inner part of a nut or fruit pit

ker′o·sene′, ker′o·sine′ (-sēn′) n. oil distilled from petroleum

kes′trel n. European falcon

ketch n. sailing vessel

ketch′up n. thick sauce of tomatoes, spices, etc.

ket′tle n. 1 pot used in cooking 2 teakettle

ket′tle·drum′ n. hemispheric copper drum with an adjustable parchment top

key n. 1 device for working a lock 2 lever pressed in operating a piano, typewriter, etc. 3 thing that explains, as a code 4 controlling factor 5 mood or style 6 low island 7 Mus. scale based on a certain keynote —a. controlling —v. bring into harmony —**key up** excite —**key in** input (data) with a keyboard —**key′hole′** n.

key′board′ n. row(s) of keys of a piano, computer terminal, etc.

key′note′ n. 1 Mus. lowest, basic note of a scale 2 basic idea

key′stone′ n. central, topmost stone of an arch

kha·ki (kak′ē) a., n. yellowish-brown (uniform)

kib·butz' (-boots') *n.*, *pl.* **-but·zim'** (-boo tsēm') Israeli collective farm

kib'itz *v.* [Col.] act as meddlesome onlooker —**kib'itz·er** *n.*

ki'bosh *n.* [Sl.] end —**put the kibosh on** check, squelch, etc.

kick *v.* **1** strike (out) with the foot **2** recoil, as a gun **3** [Col.] complain —*n.* **1** a kicking **2** [often *pl.*] [Col.] thrill

kick'back' *n.* [Sl.] forced or secret rebate

kick'off' *n.* kick in football that begins a play

kick'stand' *n.* metal bar on a bicycle to hold it upright

kid *n.* **1** young goat **2** leather from its skin: also **kid'skin'** **3** [Col.] child —*v.* **kid'ded**, **kid'ding** [Col.] tease, fool, etc. —**kid'der** *n.*

kid'dy, **kid'die** *n.*, *pl.* **-dies** [Col.] child

kid'nap' *v.* **-napped'**, **-nap'ping** seize and hold a person, esp. for ransom —**kid'nap'per** *n.*

kid'ney *n.*, *pl.* **-neys** the urine-forming gland

kidney bean *n.* seed of common garden bean

kiel·ba·sa (kēl bä'sə) *n.*, *pl.* **-si** (-sē) or **-sas** smoked Polish sausage

kill *v.* **1** make die; slay **2** destroy **3** spend (time) idly —*n.* **1** a killing **2** animal(s) killed —**kill'er** *n.*

kill'ing *n.* murder **2** [Col.] sudden great profit

kill'-joy' *n.* spoiler of pleasure for others

kiln (kil, kiln) *n.* oven for baking bricks, etc.

ki·lo (kē'lō, kil'ō) *n.*, *pl.* **-los** kilogram

kilo- *pref.* one thousand

kil'o·byte' *n.* 1, 024 bytes

kil'o·cy'cle *n.* kilohertz

kil'o·gram' *n.* 1,000 grams

kil'o·hertz' *n.* 1,000 hertz

kil'o·me'ter (or ki läm'ət ər) *n.* 1,000 meters

kil'o·watt' *n.* 1,000 watts

kilt *n.* skirt worn by men of Northern Scotland

kil'ter *n.* [Col.] used chiefly in **out of kilter**, not in working order

ki·mo'no *n.*, *pl.* **-nos** Japanese robe

kin *n.* relatives; family

kind *a.* sort; variety —*a.* gentle, generous, etc. —**in kind** in the same way —**kind of** [Col.] somewhat —**kind'ly** *a.*, *adv.* —**kind'ness** *n.*

kin'der·gar'ten *n.* class or school for children about four to six years old —**kin'der·gart'ner**, **kin'der·gar'ten·er** (-gärt'nər) *n.*

kind'heart'ed *a.* kind

kin'dle *v.* **1** set on fire **2** start burning **3** excite

kin'dling *n.* bits of wood, etc. for starting a fire

kin'dred *n.* relatives; kin —*a.* related or similar

kine *n.* [Ar.] cows; cattle

ki·net'ic *a.* of motion

kin'folk' *n.pl.* family; relatives: also **kin'folks'**

king *n.* **1** male ruler of a state **2** playing card with a king's picture **3** chess piece that has to be captured

king'dom *n.* country ruled by a king or queen

king'fish'er *n.* fish-eating diving bird

king'-size' *a.* [Col.] larger than usual size

kink *n.*, *v.* curl or twist —**kink'y** *a.*, **-i·er**, **-i·est**

kin'ship' *n.* **1** family relationship **2** close connection

kins'man *n.*, *pl.* **-men** male relative —**kins'wom·an** *n.fem.*, *pl.* **-wom'en**

ki·osk (kē'äsk') *n.* small, open structure used as a newsstand, etc.

kip'per *n.* salted and dried or smoked herring

kirk *n.* [Scot.] church

kis'met (kiz'-) *n.* fate

kiss *v.* caress with the lips in affection or greeting —*n.* **1** act of kissing **2** kind of candy

kit *n.* **1** set of tools, etc. **2** box or bag for it

kitch'en *n.* place for preparing and cooking food

kitch'en·ette', **kitch'en·et'** *n.* small kitchen

kitch'en·ware' *n.* kitchen utensils

kite *n.* **1** kind of hawk **2** light frame covered with paper, tied to a string, and flown in the wind

kith and kin *n.* friends and relatives

kitsch (kich) *n.* pretentious but shallow popular art, etc.

kit'ten *n.* young cat: also **kit'ty**, *pl.* **-ties**

kit'ten·ish *a.* coy

kit'ty-cor'nered *a.*, *adv.* cater-cornered

ki·wi (kē'wē) *n.*, *pl.* **-wis** flightless bird of New Zealand

Klee'nex *trademark* soft tissue paper used as a handkerchief, etc. —*n.* [**k-**] a piece of such paper

klep'to·ma'ni·a *n.* persistent impulse to steal —**klep'to·ma'ni·ac'** *n.*

knack *n.* special ability

knack·wurst (näk'wurst') *n.* thick, spicy sausage

knap'sack' *n.* bag to carry supplies on the back

knave *n.* dishonest person; rogue —**knav'ish** *a.*

knav'er·y *n.* dishonesty

knead *v.* press and squeeze

knee *n.* joint between thigh and lower leg

knee′cap′ *n.* movable bone at the front of the knee

knee′-deep′ *a.* very much involved

knee′-jerk′ *a.* [Col.] automatic and predictable

kneel *v.* **knelt** or **kneeled, kneel′ing** rest on the bent knee or knees

knell *n.* slow tolling of a bell, as at a funeral

knew *v.* pt. of KNOW

knick′ers *n.pl.* breeches gathered below the knees: also **knick′er·bock′ers**

knick′knack′ *n.* small, showy article

knife *n., pl.* **knives** sharp cutting blade set in a handle —*v.* stab with a knife

knight *n.* **1** medieval chivalrous soldier **2** British man holding honorary rank **3** chessman like a horse's head —**knight′hood′** *n.*

knit *v.* **knit′ted** or **knit, knit′ting 1** make by looping yarn with needles **2** draw or grow together

knit′wear′ *n.* knitted clothing

knob *n.* round handle, etc. —**knob′by** *a.*, **–bier, –bi·est**

knock *v.* **1** hit; strike; rap **2** make a pounding noise **3** [Col.] find fault with —*n.* **1** hit; blow **2** a pounding noise —**knock down** take apart —**knock off** [Col.] **1** stop working **2** deduct —**knock out** make unconscious —**knock′er** *n.* —**knock′out′** *n.*

knock′-kneed′ *a.* having legs that bend inward at the knees

knock′out′ *n.* **1** [Sl.] very attractive person or thing **2** boxing victory when an opponent can no longer fight

knock′wurst *n.* knackwurst

knoll (nōl) *n.* little hill; mound

knot *n.* **1** lump in tangled thread, etc. **2** a tying together of string, rope, etc. **3** small group **4** hard lump in wood where a branch has grown **5** one nautical mile per hour —*v.* **knot′ted, knot′ting** form a knot (in)

knot′ty *a.* **–ti·er, –ti·est 1** full of knots **2** puzzling

know *v.* **knew, known, know′ing 1** be informed (about) **2** be aware (of) **3** be acquainted with

know′-how′ *n.* [Col.] technical skill

know′ing *a.* **1** having knowledge **2** shrewd; cunning

knowl·edge (näl′ij) *n.* things known or learned —**knowl′edge·a·ble** *a.*

knuck′le *n.* joint of a finger —**knuckle down** work hard —**knuckle under** surrender

ko·a′la (-ä′-) *n.* tree-dwelling marsupial of Australia

kohl·ra·bi (kōl′rä′bē) *n., pl.* **–bies** kind of cabbage

kook (kōōk) *n.* [Sl.] silly, eccentric person —**kook′y, kook′ie** *a.*

Ko·ran (kə ran′, kôr′an′) the sacred book of Muslims

Ko·re′an *n., a.* (native or language) of Korea

ko′sher *a.* fit to eat according to Jewish dietary laws

kow·tow (kou′tou′) *v.* show great deference (to)

ku·chen (kōō′kən) *n.* breadlike cake, with raisins, etc.

ku′dos′ (-däs′, -dōs′) *n.* credit for achievement

kud·zu (kood′zōō′) *n.* fast-growing vine with large leaves

kum′quat′ (-kwät′) *n.* small, oval, orangelike fruit

kung′ fu′ *n.* system of self-defense like karate

L

lab *n.* [Col.] laboratory

la′bel *n.* card, etc. marked and attached to an object to show its contents, etc. —*v.* **1** attach a label to **2** classify as

la′bi·a *n.pl., sing.* **–bi·um** liplike folds of the vulva

la′bi·al *a.* of the lips

la′bor *n.* **1** work **2** task **3** all workers **4** process of childbirth —*v.* **1** work hard **2** move with effort

lab′o·ra·to′ry (lab′rə–) *n., pl.* **–ries** place for scientific work or research

la′bored *a.* with effort

la′bor·er *n.* a worker; esp., an unskilled worker

la·bo′ri·ous *a.* difficult

labor union *n.* association of workers to further their interests

la′bour *n., v.* Br. sp. of LABOR

la·bur′num *n.* shrub with drooping yellow flowers

lab′y·rinth′ (-ə-) *n.* maze

lac (lak) *n.* resinous source of shellac

lace *n.* **1** string used to fasten together parts of a shoe, etc. **2** openwork fabric woven in fancy designs —*v.* **1** fasten with a lace **2** intertwine **3** whip

lac′er·ate′ (las′–) *v.* tear jaggedly —**lac′er·a′tion** *n.*

lace′work′ *n.* lace, or any openwork like it

lach′ry·mose′ (lak′ri-) *a.* tearful; sad

lack *n.* state of not having enough or any —*v.* have little or nothing of

lack′a·dai′si·cal (-dā′zi–) *a.* showing lack of interest

lack'ey n., pl. **-eys 1** menial male servant **2** toady

lack'lus'ter a. dull

la·con'ic a. concise; brief

lac·quer (lak'ər) n. a varnish, often like enamel —v. coat with lacquer

la·crosse' n. ball game using long-handled sticks

lac'te·al a. of or like milk

lac'tic a. **1** of milk **2** of an acid in sour milk

lac'tose' n. sugar found in milk

la·cu'na (-kyōō'-) n. gap; space

lac'y a. **-i·er, -i·est** of or like lace —**lac'i·ness** n.

lad n. boy; youth

lad'der n. series of rungs framed by two s¹depieces for climbing up or down

lade v. **lad'ed, lad'ed** or **lad'en, lad'ing** to load

lad'en a. **1** loaded **2** burdened

lad'ing n. a load; cargo

la'dle n. long-handled, cuplike spoon for dipping —v. dip out with a ladle

la'dy n., pl. **-dies 1** well-bred, polite woman **2** any woman —a. female —**la'dy-like'** a.

la'dy-bug' n. small beetle with a spotted back

la'dy-fin'ger n. small finger-shaped spongecake

la'dy-like' a. refined; well-bred

la'dy-love' n. sweetheart

la'dy-slip'per n. orchid with flowers like slippers

lag v. **lagged, lag'ging** fall behind —n. **1** falling behind **2** amount of this

la'ger (beer) (lä'-) n. a beer aged for several months

lag'gard a. backward; slow —n. one who falls behind

la·gniappe, la·gnappe (lan yap') n. gratuity

la·goon' n. **1** shallow lake joined to a larger body of water **2** water inside an atoll

laid v. pt. & pp. of LAY

laid'-back' a. [Sl.] easygoing

lain v. pp. of LIE (recline)

lair n. animal's den

lais·sez faire (les'ā fer') n. noninterference

la'i·ty n. all laymen, as a group

lake n. large inland body of water

lam n. [Sl.] headlong flight —v. **lammed, lam'ming** [Sl.] flee

la'ma (lä'-) n. Buddhist priest or monk in Tibet

la'ma·ser'y n., pl. **-ies** monastery of lamas

La·maze' (lə mäz') n. training program in natural childbirth

lamb (lam) n. **1** young sheep **2** its flesh as food

lam·baste' (-bāst') v. [Col.] beat or scold soundly

lam'bent a. **1** flickering **2** glowing softly **3** light and graceful

lame a. **1** crippled **2** stiff and painful **3** poor; ineffectual —v. make lame

la·mé (la mā') n. cloth interwoven with metal threads

lame duck n. elected official whose term goes beyond a reelection defeat

la·mel'la n., pl. **-lae** (-ē) or **-las** thin plate, layer, etc.

la·ment' v. feel or show deep sorrow for —n. **1** a lamenting **2** elegy; dirge —**lam'en·ta·ble** a. —**lam'en·ta'tion** n.

lam'i·na n., pl. **-nae** (-nē) or **-nas** thin scale or layer

lam'i·nate' v. form of or into thin layers —**lam'i·nat'ed** a. —**lam'i·na'tion** n.

lamp n. **1** device for producing light **2** such a device set in a stand

lamp'black' n. fine soot used as a black pigment

lam·poon' n. written satirical attack —v. to attack in a lampoon

lamp'post' n. post supporting a street lamp

lam'prey (-prē) n., pl. **-preys** eellike water animal

la·nai (lə nä'ē, -nī') n. veranda

lance n. **1** long spear **2** lancet —v. cut open with a lancet

lan'cer n. cavalry soldier armed with a lance

lan'cet n. surgical knife

land n. **1** solid part of earth's surface **2** country or region **3** ground; soil **4** real estate —v. **1** put or go on shore or land **2** catch **3** [Col.] get or secure

land'ed a. **1** owning land **2** consisting of land

land'fall' n. sighting of land

land'fill' n. place for burying garbage

land'hold'er n. land owner

land'ing n. **1** a coming to shore **2** pier; dock **3** platform at the end of stairs **4** an alighting

land'locked' a. **1** surrounded by land **2** confined to fresh water

land'lord' n. man who leases land, houses, rooms, etc. to others —**land'la'dy** n.fem.

land'lub'ber n. one with little experience at sea

land'mark' n. **1** identifying feature of a locality **2** important event

land'mass' n. large area of land

land'-of'fice business n. [Col.] booming business

land'scape' n. (picture of) natural scenery —v. plant lawns, bushes, etc. on

land'slide' n. **1** sliding of rocks or earth down a slope **2** overwhelming victory

lane n. narrow path, road, etc.

lan′guage (-gwij) n. 1 speech or writing 2 any means of communicating

lan′guid a. 1 weak 2 listless; sluggish

lan′guish v. 1 become weak 2 long; pine —**lan′guish·ing** a.

lan′guor (-gər) n. lack of vigor —**lan′guor·ous** a.

lank a. tall and lean

lank′y a. **-i·er, -i·est** awkwardly tall and lean

lan′o·lin′ n. fatty substance obtained from wool

lan′tern n. transparent case holding a light

lan′tern-jawed′ a. having long, thin jaws and sunken cheeks

lan′yard (-yərd) n. Naut. short rope

lap n. 1 front part from the waist to the knees of a sitting person 2 place in which one is cared for 3 one circuit of a race track 4 overlapping part —v. **lapped, lap′ping** 1 fold or wrap 2 lay or extend partly over 3 dip up with the tongue 4 splash lightly

la·pel′ n. fold-back part at the upper front of a coat

lap′i·dar′y (-der′-) n., pl. **-ies** one who cuts and polishes gems

lap′is laz′u·li′ (-yōō lī′) n. azure, opaque semiprecious stone

lap robe n. heavy blanket, etc. laid over the lap

lapse n. 1 small error 2 a falling into a lower condition 3 passing, as of time —v. 1 fall into a certain state 2 deviate from virtue 3 become void

lap′top′ n. portable microcomputer including a screen, keyboard, battery, etc.

lar′board (-bərd) n., a. left; port

lar′ce·ny n., pl. **-nies** theft —**lar′ce·nous** a.

larch n. kind of pine tree

lard n. melted fat of hogs —v. cover with lard

lard′er n. (place for keeping) food supplies

large a. of great size or amount —adv. in a large way —**at large** 1 free; not jailed 2 in general —**large′ness** n.

large′ly adv. mainly

large′-scale′ a. extensive

lar·gess′, lar·gesse′ n. generous giving

lar′go a., adv. Mus. slow and stately

lar′i·at n. a rope; esp., a lasso

lark n. 1 any of various songbirds 2 merry time —v. to play or frolic

lark′spur′ n. delphinium

lar′va n., pl. **-vae′** (-vē′) insect in the earliest stage after hatching —**lar′val** a.

lar·yn·gi·tis (lar′in jīt′is) n. inflammation of the larynx

lar′ynx (-iŋks) n. upper end of the trachea

la·sa′gna (-zän′yə) n. wide noodles baked with layers of cheese, ground meat, tomato sauce, etc.

las·civ′i·ous (lə siv′-) a. showing or exciting lust

la′ser (-zər) n. device that concentrates light rays in an intense beam

lash n. 1 striking part of a whip 2 a stroke as with a whip 3 eyelash —v. 1 strike or drive as with a lash 2 swing sharply 3 tie with a rope, etc. —**lash out** speak angrily

lass n. young woman

las′si·tude′ n. weariness

las′so′ n., pl. **-sos′** or **-soes′** rope with a sliding noose, for catching cattle, etc. —v. catch with a lasso

last a. 1 after all others 2 only remaining 3 most recent —adv. 1 after all others 2 most recently —n. 1 last one 2 footlike form for making shoes —v. stay in use, etc. —**at last** finally

last hurrah n. final attempt or appearance

last′ly adv. in conclusion

last straw n. final trouble causing defeat, anger, etc.

latch n. fastening for a door, window, etc., esp. a bar that fits into a notch —v. fasten with a latch

late a. 1 after the expected time 2 near the end of a period 3 recent 4 recently dead —adv. 1 after the expected time 2 near the end of a period 3 recently —**of late** recently

late′ly adv. recently

la′tent a. undeveloped

lat′er adv. after some time

lat′er·al a. sideways

la′tex′ n. milky fluid in certain plants and trees

lath (lath) n. framework for plaster, as thin strips of wood

lathe (lāth) n. machine for shaping wood, metal, etc. with a cutting tool

lath′er n. 1 foam formed by soap and water 2 foamy sweat —v. cover with or form lather

Lat′in n. 1 language of ancient Rome 2 speaker of a Latin language —a. of or derived from Latin

lat′i·tude′ n. 1 freedom of opinion, action, etc. 2 distance in degrees from the equator

la·trine′ (-trēn′) n. toilet for the use of many people

lat·te (lä′tä) n. espresso coffee mixed with steamed milk

lat′ter a. 1 nearer the end 2 last mentioned of two

lat′tice (-is) n. a structure of crossed strips of wood, etc.

lat′tice-work′ n. 1 lattice 2 lattices collectively

laud (lôd) v., n. praise —**laud′a·to′ry** a.

laud′a·ble a. praiseworthy

laud′a·num n. solution of opium in alcohol

laugh (laf) v. make vocal sounds showing mirth, scorn, etc. —n. act of laughing: also **laugh′ter** —**laugh′a·ble** a.

laugh′ing-stock′ n. object of ridicule

launch v. 1 send into space 2 set afloat 3 begin —n. a large motorboat

launch pad n. platform for launching a rocket, etc.

laun′der v. wash or wash and iron (clothes, linens, etc.) —**laun′dress** n.fem.

laun′dro·mat′ n. self-service laundry

laun′dry n., pl. **-dries** 1 place for laundering 2 things (to be) laundered

lau′rel n. 1 evergreen with large, glossy leaves 2 pl. fame; victory

la·va (lä′və, lav′ə) n. rock from a volcano

lav′a·to′ry n., pl. **-ries** 1 washbowl 2 room with toilet and washbowl

lav′en·der n. pale purple

lav′ish n. very generous —v. give or spend freely

law n. 1 any of the rules of conduct made by a government 2 obedience to these 3 profession of lawyers 4 fundamental rule 5 series of natural events always happening in the same way —**law′break′er** n. —**law′mak′er** n.

law′-a·bid′ing a. obeying the law

law′ful a. LEGAL (a. 1)

law′less a. disobeying law

law′mak′er n. one who makes laws

lawn n. grass cut short

lawn mower n. machine to cut lawn grass

law′suit′ n. case before a court for decision

law′yer n. person licensed to practice law

lax a. 1 not tight 2 not strict —**lax′i·ty** n.

lax′a·tive n., a. (medicine) making the bowels move

lay v. **laid, lay′ing** 1 put down on something 2 set in place 3 put or place 4 produce (an egg) 5 settle; allay 6 to bet 7 devise 8 to present or assert —n. 1 position; arrangement 2 short poem —a. of or for laymen —**lay aside** (or **away** or **by**) save for future use

lay v. pt. of LIE (recline)

lay′a·way′ n. method of buying by making a deposit to hold item until full payment

lay′er n. single thickness

lay·ette′ n. complete outfit for a newborn baby

lay′man n., pl. **-men** one not belonging to the clergy or to a given profession

lay′off′ n. temporary unemployment

lay′out′ n. arrangement

lay′o′ver n. stop in a journey

laze v. idle or loaf

la·zy a. **-zi·er, -zi·est** 1 not willing to work 2 sluggish —**la′zi·ly** adv. —**la′zi·ness** n.

Lazy Su′san n. revolving food tray

leach v. extract or lose (a soluble substance)

lead (lēd) v. **led, lead′ing** 1 direct or guide as by going before 2 be at the head of 3 go or pass 4 bring as a result 5 move first in a game, etc. —n. 1 guidance 2 first place 3 distance ahead 4 clue 5 leading role —**lead off** begin —**lead on** lure —**lead up to** prepare the way for —**lead′er** n. —**lead′er·ship′** n.

lead (led) n. 1 heavy, soft metal, a chemical element 2 graphite used in pencils

lead′en (led′-) a. 1 of lead 2 heavy 3 gloomy

lead′ing (lēd′-) a. chief

leaf n., pl. **leaves** 1 flat, thin, usually green part growing from a plant stem 2 sheet of paper, etc. —v. turn the pages of

leaf′let n. 1 small leaf 2 folded printed sheet

leaf′y a. **-i·er, -i·est** having many leaves

league (lēg) n. 1 association of nations, groups, etc. 2 unit of distance, about 3 miles —v. join in a league

leak v. 1 pass or let pass out or in accidentally 2 become known gradually —n. accidental crack that allows leaking —**leak′y** a., **-i·er, -i·est**

leak′age n. 1 a leaking 2 amount that leaks

lean v. 1 bend or slant 2 rely (on) 3 tend 4 to rest against something —a. 1 with little or no fat 2 meager —**lean′ness** n.

lean′ing n. tendency

lean′-to′ n., pl. **-tos′** structure whose sloping roof abuts a wall, etc.

leap v. **leapt** or **lept** or **leaped, leap′ing** jump (over) —n. a jump

leap′frog′ n. game in which players leap over the backs of others —v. **-frogged′, -frog′ging** leap or skip (over)

leap year n. every fourth year, having 29 days in February

learn v. 1 get knowledge or skill by study 2 hear (of) 3 memorize —**learn′ing** n.

learn′ed a. having or showing much learning

lease n. contract by which property is rented —v. give or get by a lease

leash n. strap or chain for holding a dog, etc. in check

least a. smallest —adv. in the smallest

degree —n. smallest in degree, etc. —at least at any rate

leath'er n. animal skin that has been tanned —**leath'er·y** a.

leave v. **left, leav'ing 1** let remain **2** to have remaining behind or after one **3** bequeath **4** go away (from) —n. **1** permission **2** permitted absence from duty —**leave out** omit —**take one's leave** depart

leav'en (lev'-) n. **1** yeast, etc. used to make dough rise: also **leav'en·ing 2** permeating influence —v. affect with leaven

leaves n. pl. of LEAF

leav'ings n.pl. remnants

lech'er n. lewd man —**lech'er·ous** a.

lec'i·thin (les'ə-) n. fatty compound in living cells

lec'tern n. reading stand

lec'ture n. **1** informative talk **2** a scolding —v. give a lecture (to) —**lec'tur·er** n.

led v. pt. & pp. of LEAD (guide)

ledge n. **1** shelf **2** projecting ridge of rocks

ledg'er n. book of final entry for transactions

lee a., n. (on) the side away from the wind —**lee'ward** n., a., adv.

leech n. bloodsucking worm

leek n. onionlike vegetable

leer n. malicious or suggestive grin —v. look with a leer

leer'y a. wary

lees n.pl. dregs; sediment

lee'ward (also Naut. lōō'ərd) a. away from the wind —n. lee side —adv. toward the lee

lee'way' n. [Col.] margin of time, money, etc.

left a. of that side toward the west when one faces north —n. **1** left side **2** liberal or radical party, etc. —adv. toward the left

left v. pt. & pp. of LEAVE

left'-hand'ed a. **1** using the left hand more easily **2** for the left hand **3** insincere —adv. with the left hand

left'ist n., a. liberal or radical

left'o'ver n., a. (something) remaining

leg n. **1** limb used for standing and walking **2** thing like a leg in shape or use

leg'a·cy n., pl. **-cies** something handed down to one, esp. by a will

le'gal a. **1** of, based upon, or permitted by law **2** of lawyers —**le·gal'i·ty** n. —**le'gal·ize'** v. —**le'gal·ly** adv.

le'gal·ese' (-ēz') n. legal jargon, often thought of as incomprehensible

legal tender n. money legally acceptable for payment

leg'ate (-ət) n. papal envoy

le·ga'tion n. envoy with staff and headquarters

le·ga'to (li gät'ō) a., adv. Mus. in a smooth, even style

leg'end n. **1** traditional tale **2** inscription, title, etc. —**leg'end·ar'y** a.

leg'er·de·main' n. sleight of hand

leg'gings n.pl. coverings for protecting the legs

leg'horn' n. [often L-] a kind of small chicken

leg'i·ble a. that can be read —**leg'i·bly** adv.

le'gion (-jən) n. **1** large body of soldiers **2** great number

le'gion·naire' n. member of a legion

leg'is·late' v. **1** make laws **2** bring (about) by laws —**leg'is·la'tion** n. —**leg'is·la'tive** a. —**leg'is·la'tor** n.

leg'is·la'ture n. group of persons who make laws

le·git'i·mate (-mət) a. **1** born of a married couple **2** lawful **3** reasonable

le·git'i·mize' v. legalize, authorize, justify, etc.

leg'man' n., pl. **-men'** assistant who does routine work outside the office

leg·ume (leg'yōōm') n. plant with pods, as the pea and bean —**le·gu'mi·nous** a.

lei (lā) n., pl. **leis** garland or wreath with flowers

lei·sure (lē'zhər, lezh'ər) a., n. free (time) for rest, play, etc.

lei'sure·ly a. slow —adv. in an unhurried manner

lem'ming n. small arctic rodent

lem'on n. small, sour, yellow citrus fruit

lem'on·ade' n. drink of lemon juice, sugar, and water

le'mur (lē'-) n. small mammal related to the monkey

lend v. **lent, lend'ing 1** let another use (a thing) temporarily **2** let out (money) at interest **3** impart —**lend'er** n.

length n. **1** distance from end to end **2** extent in space or time **3** long stretch —**at length** finally —**length'wise'** a., adv.

length'en v. make or become longer

length'y a. **-i·er, -i·est** long; esp., too long

le'ni·ent a. merciful; gentle —**le'ni·en·cy, le'ni·ence** n.

lens n. **1** curved piece of glass, plastic, etc. for adjusting light rays passing through it: used in cameras, telescopes, etc. **2** similar part of the eye

Lent n. period of 40 weekdays before Easter

lent v. pt. & pp. of LEND

len'til n. small edible seed of a pealike plant

Le'o n. fifth sign of the zodiac; Lion

le'o·nine' a. like a lion

leop'ard (lep'-) n. large, black-spotted wildcat of Asia and Africa

le′o·tard *n.* a dancer's tight-fitting, one-piece garment

lep′er *n.* one having leprosy

lep′re·chaun′ (-kôn′) *n.* Irish fairy in the form of a little man who can reveal hidden treasure

lep′ro·sy *n.* disease with skin ulcers, scaling, etc.

les′bi·an (lez′-) *a., n.* female homosexual

le′sion (-zhən) *n.* injury of an organ or tissues

less *a.* not so much, so great, etc. —*adv.* to a smaller extent —*n.* a smaller amount —*prep.* minus

–less *suf.* 1 without 2 that does not 3 that cannot be

les·see′ *n.* one to whom property is leased

less′en *v.* make or become less

less′er *a.* smaller, less, etc.

les′son *n.* 1 exercise for a student to learn 2 something learned by experience

les′sor′ *n.* one giving a lease

lest *con.* for fear that

let *v.* 1 allow; permit 2 leave 3 rent 4 cause to flow, as blood —*n.* hindrance *Let* is also used as an auxiliary verb —**let down 1** lower 2 disappoint —**let up 1** relax 2 cease

let′down′ *n.* a disappointment

le′thal *a.* fatal; deadly

leth′ar·gy *n.* lack of energy —**le·thar′gic** *a.*

let′ter *n.* 1 a character of the alphabet 2 message sent by mail 3 literal meaning 4 *pl.* literature —*v.* mark with letters —**let′tered** *a.*

let′ter·head′ *n.* 1 name, etc. of a person or firm as a heading on letter paper 2 a sheet of this paper

let′ter·per′fect *a.* entirely correct

let′ter·qual′i·ty *a.* producing printed characters of similar quality to typewritten characters

let′tuce (-əs) *n.* plant with crisp, green leaves used in salads

let′up′ *n.* [Col.] 1 a slackening 2 stop or pause

leu·ke′mi·a (loo-) *n.* disease characterized by an abnormal increase in the white blood corpuscles

lev′ee *n.* river embankment to prevent flooding

lev′el *n.* 1 instrument for determining the horizontal 2 horizontal plane, line, etc. 3 height 4 position, rank, etc. —*a.* 1 flat and even 2 even in height (*with*) —*v.* 1 make or become level 2 demolish —**lev′el·er** *n.*

lev′el·head′ed *a.* sensible

lev′er (or lē′vər) *n.* bar turning on a fulcrum, used to lift or move weights

lev′er·age *n.* action or power of a lever

le·vi′a·than (-vī′-) *n.* 1 *Bible* sea monster 2 huge thing

Le·vi's (lē′vīz) *trademark* denim trousers

lev′i·tate′ *v.* (make) rise and float in the air —**lev′i·ta′tion** *n.*

lev′i·ty *n.* improper gaiety; frivolity

lev′y *v.* -ied, -y·ing 1 impose (a tax, etc.) 2 enlist (troops) 3 wage (war) —*n., pl.* -ies a levying or something levied

lewd (lood) *a.* indecent

lex′i·cog′ra·phy *n.* work of writing a dictionary —**lex′i·cog′ra·pher** *n.*

lex′i·con′ *n.* dictionary

li′a·bil′i·ty *n., pl.* -ties 1 a being liable 2 debt 3 disadvantage

li′a·ble *a.* 1 legally responsible 2 subject to 3 likely

li·ai·son (lē ā′zän′) *n.* 1 communication between military units 2 illicit love affair

li′ar *n.* one who tells lies

lib *n.* liberation

li·ba′tion *n.* 1 wine or oil poured in honor of a god 2 alcoholic drink

li′bel *n.* statement in writing that may unjustly hurt a reputation —*v.* make a libel against —**li′bel·ous, li′bel·lous** *a.*

lib′er·al *a.* 1 generous 2 not strict 3 tolerant 4 favoring reform —*n.* person who favors reform —**lib′er·al·ism′** *n.* —**lib′er·al′i·ty** *n.* —**lib′er·al·ize′** *v.*

liberal arts *n.pl.* literature, philosophy, history, etc.

lib′er·al′i·ty *n., pl.* -ties 1 generosity 2 tolerance

lib′er·ate′ *v.* set free; release —**lib′er·a′tion** *n.* —**lib′er·a′tor** *n.*

lib′er·tar′i·an *n.* advocate of full civil liberties

lib′er·tine′ (-tēn′) *n.* sexually promiscuous person

lib′er·ty *n., pl.* -ties 1 freedom from slavery, etc. 2 a particular right 3 *pl.* excessive familiarity —**at liberty 1** not confined 2 permitted (*to*)

li·bi′do (-bē′-) *n.* sexual urge —**li·bid′i·nous** *a.*

Li′bra (lē′-) seventh sign of the zodiac; Scales

li′brar′y *n., pl.* -ies collection of books or a place for it —**li·brar′i·an** *n.*

li·bret′to *n., pl.* -tos or -ti (-ē) text of an opera, etc. —**li·bret′tist** *n.*

lice *n.* pl. of LOUSE

li′cense *n.* 1 legal permit 2 freedom from rules 3 freedom that is abused —*v.* permit formally Also, Br. sp., **li′cence**

li·cen′tious (-shəs) *a.* morally unrestrained

li·chen (lī′kən) *n.* mosslike plant growing on rocks, trees, etc.

lic′it (lis′-) *a.* lawful

lick v. 1 pass the tongue over 2 [Col.] beat or conquer —n. 1 a licking 2 small quantity —**lick up** consume by licking

lic·o·rice (lik′ər ish) n. 1 black flavoring from a plant root 2 candy with this flavoring

lid n. 1 movable cover 2 eyelid —**lid′ded** a.

lie v. **lay, lain, ly′ing** 1 be horizontal or rest horizontally 2 be or exist —n. position; lay

lie v. **lied, ly′ing** make a false statement knowingly —n. thing said in lying

lie detector n. polygraph

liege (lēj) n. feudal lord or vassal

lien (lēn) n. legal claim on another's property until a debt is paid

lieu (lōō) n. used chiefly in **in lieu of**, instead of

lieu·ten′ant n. 1 low-ranking commissioned officer 2 deputy —**lieu·ten′an·cy** n., pl. —**cies**

lieutenant governor n. elected State official who may substitute for a governor

life n., pl. **lives** 1 active existence of plants and animals 2 living things 3 time of being alive 4 way of living 5 a biography 6 liveliness —**life′less** a. —**life′like′** a.

life′boat′ n. small rescue boat carried by a ship

life′guard′ n. swimmer employed to prevent drownings

life jacket (or **vest**) n. life preserver like a jacket or vest

life′long′ a. lasting for life

life pre·serv′er n. device for keeping a body afloat

life′sav′er n. [Col.] person or thing that gives help in time of need

life′-size′ a. as big as the thing represented

life′style′ n. individual's way of life: also sp. **life style**

life′time′ a., n. (lasting for) the length of one's life

lift v. 1 bring higher; raise 2 go up; rise 3 [Sl.] steal —n. 1 a lifting 2 lifting force 3 raising of one's spirits 4 help; aid 5 ride in the direction one is going 6 [Br.] elevator

lift′off′ n. vertical takeoff of a spacecraft, etc.

lig′a·ment n. connective tissue for bones or organs

lig′a·ture n. 1 a thing for tying, as surgical thread 2 letters united, as **th**

light n. 1 Radiant energy by which one sees 2 brightness 3 lamp, lantern, etc. 4 daylight 5 thing to ignite something 6 aspect 7 knowledge —a. 1 bright 2 pale; fair 3 not heavy 4 not important 5 easy to bear or do 6 happy 7 dizzy 8 moderate —adv. 1 palely 2 lightly —v. **light′ed** or **lit, light′ing** 1 ignite 2 furnish with light 3 brighten

4 be lighted 5 come to rest 6 happen (on) —**in the light of** considering

light′en v. make or become brighter, less heavy, etc.

light′er n. 1 person or thing that ignites something 2 barge for loading or unloading large ships

light′-fin′gered a. thievish

light′head′ed a. 1 dizzy 2 flighty

light′heart′ed a. free from care; cheerful

light′house′ n. tower with a light to guide ships

light′ly adv. 1 gently 2 very little 3 cheerfully 4 carelessly

light′-mind′ed a. frivolous

light′ning n. flash of light in the sky from a discharge of atmospheric electricity

lightning bug n. firefly

lightning rod n. metal rod to divert lightning

light′-year′ n. distance that light travels in a year, about 6 trillion miles

lik′a·ble, like′a·ble a. pleasant, friendly, etc.

like a. similar; equal —prep. 1 similar(ly) to 2 typical of 3 in the mood for 4 indicative of —con. [Col.] 1 as 2 as if —v. 1 be fond of; enjoy 2 wish —n. 1 an equal 2 pl. preferences —**like crazy** (or **mad**) [Col.] wildly —**lik′ing** n.

–like suf. like

like′ly a. 1 credible 2 probable; expected 3 suitable —adv. probably —**like′li·hood′** n.

like′-mind′ed a. having the same ideas, tastes, etc.

lik′en (līk′-) v. compare

like′ness n. 1 a being like 2 picture; copy

like′wise′ adv. 1 in the same way 2 also; too

li′lac′ n. shrub with tiny, pale-purple flower clusters

lilt n. light, swingy rhythm

lil′y n., pl. —**ies** plant with trumpet-shaped flowers

lil′y-liv′ered a. cowardly

lily of the valley n., pl. **lilies of the valley** plant with a spike of bell-shaped flowers

li′ma bean (lī′-) n. large, flat, edible bean in pods

limb (lim) n. 1 arm, leg, or wing 2 large tree branch

lim′ber v., a. (make or become) flexible

lim′bo′ n. place of oblivion

Lim′burg·er (**cheese**) n. white, strong-smelling cheese

lime n. 1 white substance obtained from limestone 2 a green, lemonlike fruit

lime′light′ n. prominent position before the public

lim′er·ick n. rhymed, funny poem of five lines

lime′stone′ n. rock used in building, making lime, etc.

lim′it n. 1 point where something ends 2 pl. bounds —v. set a limit to —**lim′i·ta′tion** n.

lim′it·ed a. confined

limn (lim) v. portray in pictures or words

lim′ou·sine′ (-ə zēn′) n. large, luxury automobile: also [Col.] **lim′o**, pl. **-os**

limp v., n. (walk with) lameness —a. not firm

limp′et n. shellfish that clings to rocks, etc.

lim′pid a. transparent

lin′den n. tree with heart-shaped leaves

line n. 1 cord, rope, etc. 2 wire, pipe, etc. 3 long, thin mark 4 boundary 5 outline 6 a row or series 7 conformity 8 transportation system 9 route; course 10 stock of goods 11 short letter —v. 1 mark with lines 2 form a line: with up 3 put, or serve as, a lining in

lin·e·age (lin′ē ij) n. line of descent; ancestry

lin′e·al a. 1 directly descended 2 linear

lin′e·a·ment n. distinctive facial feature

lin′e·ar a. 1 of a line or lines 2 of length

line′man n., pl. **-men** person who puts up telephone or other electric lines

lin′en n. 1 cloth of flax 2 things of linen or cotton

lin′er (lin′-) n. ship or airplane of a LINE (n. 8)

line′up′ n. a row of persons or things

lin′ger v. 1 continue to stay 2 loiter

lin·ge·rie (län′zhə rā′) n. women's underwear

lin′go n., pl. **-goes′** unfamiliar jargon

lin·gui′ne (-gwē′nē) n. flat, narrow spaghetti: also **lin·gui′ni**

lin′guist (-gwist) n. one adept in several languages

lin·guis′tics n. science of (a) language

lin′i·ment n. medicated liquid for the skin

lin′ing (līn′-) n. material covering an inner surface

link n. 1 loop in a chain 2 thing that connects —v. join; connect —**link′age** n.

links n.pl. place where golf is played

lin·o′le·um n. hard, smooth floor covering

lin′seed′ oil n. yellow oil from seed of flax

lint n. bits of thread, fluff, etc. from cloth —**lint′y** a., **-i·er**, **-i·est**

lin′tel n. horizontal piece over a door or window

li′on n. 1 large animal of the cat family, found in Africa and SW Asia 2 very strong, brave person 3 a celebrity —**li′on·ess** n.fem.

li′on·heart′ed a. very brave

li′on·ize′ v. treat as a celebrity

lip n. 1 upper or lower edge of the mouth 2 thing like a lip, as a cup's rim

lip′o·suc′tion n. surgical removal of fatty tissue by suction

lip reading n. recognition of words by watching a speaker's lips —**lip′-read′** v.

lip′stick′ n. small stick of rouge to color the lips

liq′ue·fy′ (lik′wi-) v. **-fied′**, **-fy′ing** change to a liquid

li·queur (li kur′, -koor′) n. sweet alcoholic liquor

liq′uid a. 1 readily flowing 2 readily changed into cash —n. substance that flows easily

liq′ui·date′ v. 1 settle the accounts of (a business) 2 pay (a debt) 3 change into cash —**liq′ui·da′tion** n.

liq′uor (-ər) n. alcoholic drink, as whiskey

li·ra (lir′ə) n., pl. **-re** (-ā) or **-ras** Italian monetary unit

lisle (līl) n. fabric woven of strong cotton thread

lisp v. substitute the sounds "th" and "th" for the sounds of "s" and "z" —n. act or sound of lisping

lis′some, lis′som a. lithe and graceful

list n. series of names, words, etc. set forth in order —v. put in a list

list v. tilt to one side, as a ship —n. a listing

lis′ten (-ən) v. 1 try to hear 2 pay attention

list′ing n. 1 making of a list 2 entry in a list

list′less a. indifferent because ill, sad, etc.

list price n. retail price

lists n.pl. area where knights jousted

lit′a·ny n., pl. **-nies** prayer with responses

li′ter (lē′-) n. metric unit of capacity (61.025 cubic inches)

lit′er·al a. 1 precise; exact; strict 2 prosaic 3 restricted to fact —**lit′er·al·ly** adv.

lit′er·ar′y a. having to do with literature

lit′er·ate (-ət) a. educated; esp., able to read and write —**lit′er·a·cy** n.

lit′er·a·ture′ n. 1 all the valuable writings of a specific time, nation, etc. 2 all writings on some subject

lithe (līth) a. bending easily

lith′i·um n. the lightest metal, a chemical element

lith′o·graph′ n. print made from stone or metal treated with grease and water —**li·thog′ra·phy** n.

lit′i·gant n. party to a lawsuit

lit′i·gate′ v. to contest in a lawsuit —**lit′i·ga′tion** n.

lit′mus paper n. treated paper that turns blue in bases and red in acids

li′tre n. Br. sp. of LITER

lit′ter n. 1 portable couch 2 stretcher 3

young borne at one time by a dog, cat, etc. **4** things lying about in disorder —v. make untidy

lit'ter·bug' n. one who litters public places with rubbish

lit'tle a. **1** small in size or amount **2** short; brief **3** not important —adv. **1** slightly **2** not at all —n. small amount or short time —**little by little** gradually —**not a little** very

lit'to·ral a. of or along the shore

lit'ur·gy n., pl. –gies ritual for public worship —**li·tur'gi·cal** a.

liv'a·ble a. fit or pleasant to live in

live (liv) v. **1** have life **2** stay alive; endure **3** pass one's life in a certain way **4** have a full life **5** feed (on) **6** reside

live (līv) a. **1** having life **2** energetic **3** of interest now **4** still burning **5** unexploded **6** carrying electrical current **7** broadcast while happening

live'li·hood' n. means of supporting oneself

live'long' (liv'-) a. whole

live'ly a. –li·er, –li·est **1** full of life **2** exciting **3** cheerful **4** having much bounce —**live'li·ness** n.

liv·en (līv'-) v. cheer (up)

liv'er n. organ in vertebrates that makes bile

liv'er·wurst' n. sausage made of ground liver

liv'er·y n., pl. –ies **1** uniform as of a servant **2** business of renting horses and carriages

lives v. pl. of LIFE

live'stock' n. animals kept or raised on a farm

liv'id a. **1** discolored by a bruise; black-and-blue **2** grayish-blue

liv'ing a. **1** having life **2** in active use **3** of persons alive **4** true; lifelike **5** of life **6** enough to live on —n. **1** a being alive **2** livelihood **3** way that one lives

living room n. room for lounging, entertaining, etc.

living wage n. wage high enough to live on in some comfort

liz'ard n. reptile with a long tail and four legs

lla·ma (lä'-) n. South American camellike animal

lo int. look! see!

load n. **1** amount carried **2** burden —v. **1** put (a load) in or on **2** burden **3** put ammunition into

load'star' n. lodestar

load'stone' n. lodestone

loaf n., pl. **loaves** bread, etc. baked in one piece —v. waste (time) —**loaf'er** n.

loam n. rich soil

loan n. **1** act of lending **2** something lent, esp. money at interest —v. lend

loath (lōth) a. reluctant

loathe (lōth) v. abhor —**loath'some** a.

loath'ing (lōth'-) n. intense dislike

lob v. **lobbed, lob'bing** toss or hit (a ball) in a high curve —n. a toss or hit made this way

lob'by n., pl. **–bies 1** entrance hall **2** group of lobbyists —v. **–bied, –by·ing** act as a lobbyist

lob'by·ist n. one who tries to influence legislators

lobe n. rounded projection

lob'ster n. edible sea animal with large pincers

lobster tail n. edible tail of any of various crayfish

lo'cal a. of or for a particular place or area —n. **1** bus, etc. making all stops **2** branch, as of a labor union —**lo'cal·ly** adv.

lo·cale' (-kal') n. a place or setting for events, etc.

lo·cal'i·ty n., pl. **–ties** place or district

lo'cal·ize' v. limit or trace to a certain place

lo'cate' v. **1** establish in a certain place **2** find or show the position of

lo·ca'tion n. **1** a locating **2** position; place

loch (läk) n. [Scot.] **1** lake **2** arm of the sea

lock n. **1** device for fastening a door, etc. as with a key **2** part of a canal between gates **3** curl of hair —v. **1** fasten with a lock **2** shut (in or out) **3** jam or link together

lock'er n. chest, closet, etc. that can be locked

lock'et n. little case worn on a necklace

lock'jaw' n. tetanus

lock'out' n. a locking out of employees to force agreement to employer's terms

lock'smith' n. one who makes or repairs locks and keys

lock'up' n. a jail

lo·co a. [Sl.] crazy; insane

lo'co·mo'tion n. act or power of moving about

lo'co·mo'tive n. engine for a railroad train

lo'cust n. **1** grasshopper-like insect **2** cicada **3** tree with white flowers

lo·cu'tion (-kyoo'-) n. phrase or phraseology

lode n. vein or stratum of metallic ore

lode'star' n. star by which one directs one's coarse

lode'stone' n. magnetic iron ore

lodge n. **1** a house for special use **2** chapter of a society —v. **1** to house or dwell for a time **2** put in **3** come to rest —**lodg'er** n.

lodg'ing n. **1** place to live **2** pl. rented rooms

loft n. **1** space below a roof **2** upper story of a warehouse, etc. **3** gallery —v. send (a ball) high into the air

loft'y a. **-i·er, -i·est** 1 very high 2 noble 3 haughty —**loft'i·ness** n.

log n. 1 section cut from a tree trunk 2 daily record of a ship's, etc. progress 3 logarithm —v. **logged, log'ging** 1 cut down trees and remove the logs 2 enter in a ship's log —**log on** (or **off**) enter information to begin (or end) activity on a computer terminal

lo'gan·ber'ry (-) n., pl. **-ries** purple-red berry

log'a·rithm (-rith əm) n. Math. power to which a base number must be raised to get a given number

loge (lōzh) n. theater box

log'ger·head' n. stupid fellow —**at loggerheads** in disagreement

log'ic (läj'-) n. 1 science of reasoning 2 (correct) reasoning —**lo·gi·cian** (lō jish'ən) n.

log'i·cal a. 1 using or used in logic 2 expected as a result —**log'i·cal·ly** adv.

lo·gis'tics n. military science of moving and supplying troops

log'jam' n. obstacle or deadlock

lo'go' n. distinctive symbol, etc., as a trademark

log'roll'ing n. mutual exchange of favors, esp. among lawmakers

lo'gy (-gē) a. **-gi·er, -gi·est** [Col.] dull or sluggish

-logy suf. science or study of

loin n. 1 lower back from ribs to hipbone 2 pl. hips and lower abdomen

loin'cloth' n. cloth worn about the loins, as by some tribes

loi'ter v. 1 spend time idly 2 move slowly

loll (läl) v. 1 lounge about 2 droop or let hang loosely

lol'li·pop', lol'ly·pop' n. piece of candy on a stick

lol'ly·gag' v. **-gagged', -gag'ging** [Col.] waste time aimlessly

lone a. by oneself or itself

lone'ly a. **-li·er, -li·est** 1 alone and unhappy 2 unfrequented —**lone'li·ness** n.

lon'er (lōn'-) n. [Col.] one who avoids the company of others

lone'some a. having or causing a lonely feeling

long a. 1 measuring much 2 in length 3 of great length 4 tedious 5 far-reaching 6 well supplied —adv. 1 for a long time 2 for the time of 3 at a remote time —v. to wish earnestly; yearn —**as** (or **so**) **long as** 1 while 2 since 3 provided that —**before long** soon

long'-dis'tance a. to or from distant places —adv. by long-distance telephone

long distance n. telephone service for long-distance calls

lon·gev'i·ty (-jev'-) n. 1 long life 2 length of time

long'-faced' a. glum

long'hand' n. ordinary handwriting

long'ing n. earnest desire

lon'gi·tude' n. distance, in degrees, east or west of a line through Greenwich, England

lon'gi·tu'di·nal a. 1 of length 2 of longitude

long jump n. a jump for distance

long'-lived' (-līvd', livd') a. having a long life span

long'-play'ing a. of a phonograph record playing at 33 ⅓ revolutions per minute

long'-range' a. covering a long distance or time

long'shore'man n., pl. **-men** one whose work is loading and unloading ships

long'-term' a. for a long time

long ton n. 2,240 pounds

long'ways' adv. lengthwise

long'-wind'ed (-win'dəd) a. wordy and tiresome

look v. 1 direct the eyes so as to see 2 search 3 seem —n. 1 an act of looking 2 appearance 3 [Col.] pl. personal appearance —int. 1 see! 2 pay attention! —**look after** care for —**look into** investigate —**look up to** admire

look'ing glass n. glass mirror

look'out' n. 1 careful watching 2 guard; sentry

look'-see' n. [Sl.] quick look

loom n. machine for weaving —v. come into sight suddenly

loon n. ducklike bird

loon'y a. **-i·er, -i·est** [Sl.] crazy; insane

loop n. line, figure, etc. that curves back to cross itself —v. make a loop

loop'hole' n. means of evading something

loose (lōōs) a. 1 free 2 not firm or tight 3 inexact 4 sexually immoral —v. 1 to free 2 make less tight, etc. 3 release —**on the loose** not confined; free —**loose'ly** adv. —**loos'en** v.

loot n., v. plunder —**loot'er** n.

lop v. **lopped, lop'ping** cut off

lope v., n. (move with) a long, swinging stride

lop'sid'ed a. heavier, lower, etc. on one side

lo·qua'cious (-kwā'shəs) a. very talkative

lord n. 1 master 2 Br. nobleman —[**L-**] 1 God 2 Jesus Christ

lore n. knowledge

lor·gnette (lôrn yet') n. eyeglasses on a handle

lor'ry n., pl. **-ries** [Br.] motor truck

lose (lōōz) v. **lost, los'ing** 1 become unable

to find **2** have taken from one by accident, death, etc. **3** fail to keep **4** fail to win

loss n. **1** a losing, or damage, etc. resulting from losing something **2** person, thing, etc. lost

lost a. **1** ruined **2** missing or mislaid **3** wasted

lot n. **1** deciding of a matter by chance **2** fate **3** piece of land **4** group **5** [Col.] *often pl.* great amount or number —*adv.* very much

lo'tion n. liquid for softening or healing the skin

lot'ter·y n., *pl.* **–ies** game in which numbered chances on prizes are sold

lot'to n. a game like bingo

lo'tus n. tropical waterlily

loud a. **1** strong in sound **2** noisy **3** [Col.] flashy —*adv.* in a loud way —**loud'ly** *adv.* —**loud'ness** n.

loud'mouthed' (-mouth d', -moutht') a. talking in a loud, irritating way

loud'speak'er n. device, as in a radio, for changing electric waves into sound and amplifying it

lounge v. **1** sit in a relaxed way **2** to be idle —n. **1** room furnished for lounging **2** couch

louse (lous) n., *pl.* **lice** small insect parasite —**louse up** [Sl.] botch; ruin

lous'y (lou'zē) a. **–i·er, –i·est** **1** infested with lice **2** [Sl.] inferior, contemptible, etc. **3** [Sl.] well supplied (*with*)

lout n. stupid fellow

lou'ver (loo'-) n. **1** an opening with boards slanted to let in air and keep out rain **2** such a board

love n. **1** strong affection **2** object of this **3** in tennis, a score of zero —v. feel love (for) —**in love** feeling love —**make love** woo, embrace, etc. —**lov'a·ble, love'a·ble** a. —**lov'er** n. —**lov'ing·ly** adv.

love'lorn' a. pining from love

love'ly a. **–li·er, –li·est 1** beautiful **2** [Col.] very enjoyable —**love'li·ness** n.

love seat n. small sofa for two

lov'ing a. feeling or expressing love

loving cup n. large drinking cup with two handles, often given as a prize

low a. **1** not high **2** below others in rank, size, cost, etc. **3** gloomy **4** deep in pitch **5** vulgar **6** not loud —*adv.* in or to a low level, etc. —n. **1** low level, degree, etc. **2** gear arrangement giving least speed **3** moo —v. to moo —**lay low** kill —**lie low** stay hidden

low'brow' n., a. [Col.] nonintellectual

low'-cal' a. having few calories

low'down' (a.: lō'doun') n. [Sl.] pertinent facts: with *the* —a. [Col.] mean or contemptible

low'er (lō'-) a. below in rank, etc. —v. **1** let or put down **2** make or become less in amount, value, etc.

low'er (lou'-) v. **1** to scowl **2** appear threatening

low'er·case' a., n. (of or in) small, rather than capital, letters

low frequency n. radio frequency between 30 and 300 kilohertz

low'-key' a. subdued; not intense

low'land n. land lower than land around it

low'ly a. **1** of low rank **2** humble —**low'li·ness** n.

low'-mind'ed a. having a coarse, vulgar mind

lox n. smoked salmon

loy'al a. faithful to one's friends, country, etc. —**loy'al·ly** adv. —**loy'al·ty** n., *pl.* **–ties**

loy'al·ist n. supporter of the government during a revolt

loz'enge n. cough drop, small piece of hard candy, etc.

LP n. long-playing record

LSD n. chemical compound used as a psychedelic drug

lu·au (loo'ou') n. Hawaiian feast

lube n. [Col.] a lubrication or lubricant

lu'bri·cant a. that lubricates —n. oil, grease, etc.

lu'bri·cate' v. apply oil or grease to reduce friction —**lu'bri·ca'tion** n.

lu'cid a. **1** clear **2** sane **3** shining —**lu·cid'i·ty** n. —**lu'cid·ly** adv.

luck n. **1** chance; fortune **2** good fortune —**luck'less** a.

luck'y a. **–i·er, –i·est** having, resulting in, or thought to bring good luck —**luck'i·ly** adv.

lu'cra·tive a. profitable

lu'cre (-kər) n. riches; money: chiefly humorously derogatory

lu'cu·brate' v. work or study hard, esp. late at night —**lu'cu·bra'tion** n.

lu'di·crous (-krəs) a. so incongruous as to be funny

luff v. head a ship toward the wind

lug v. **lugged, lug'ging** carry with effort —n. **1** earlike handle or support **2** bolt, used with lug nut, to mount a wheel

luge (loozh) n. racing sled

lug'gage n. suitcases, trunks, etc.

lu·gu'bri·ous (lə goo'-) a. mawkishly mournful

luke'warm' a. **1** slightly warm **2** lacking enthusiasm

lull v. **1** soothe by gentle sound or motion **2** calm —n. short period of calm

lull'a·by n., pl. **–bies** song for lulling a baby to sleep

lum·ba'go n. pain in the lower back

lum'bar (-bär', -bər) a. of or near the loins

lum'ber n. wood sawed into beams, boards, etc. —v. move heavily and clumsily —**lum'ber·ing** n.

lum'ber·jack' n. man who cuts timber for the sawmill

lum'ber·man n., pl. **–men** lumber dealer

lu'mi·nar'y n., pl. **–ies** famous person

lu'mi·nes'cence (-əns) n. giving off light without heat —**lu'mi·nes'cent** a.

lu'mi·nous a. bright; shining —**lu'mi·nos'i·ty** n.

lum'mox (-əks) n. [Col.] clumsy person

lump n. 1 a mass of something 2 a swelling —a. in a lump or lumps —v. to group together —**lump'y** a., **–i'er, –i'est**

lump sum n. total sum paid at one time

lu'nar (-nər) a. of the moon

lu·na'tic a. 1 insane 2 utterly foolish —n. an insane person —**lu'na·cy** n.

lunch n. midday meal —v. eat lunch

lunch'eon (lun'chən) n. formal lunch

lunch'eon·ette' n. small restaurant serving light lunches

luncheon meat n. meat processed in loaves, etc., ready to eat

lung n. organ in the chest for breathing

lunge n. 1 sudden thrust 2 forward plunge —v. make a lunge

lung'fish' n. fish having lungs as well as gills

lu'pine (-pin) n. plant with spikes of rose, white, or blue flowers

lu'pus n. disease with skin lesions

lurch v. sway suddenly to one side —n. 1 lurching movement 2 danger; trouble

lure (loor) n. 1 thing that attracts 2 fish bait —v. attract; entice

lu'rid (loor'id) a. 1 shocking 2 glowing strangely

lurk v. 1 to stay or be hidden, ready to attack 2 to move furtively

lus'cious (lush'əs) a. 1 delicious 2 pleasing

lush a. of or having luxuriant growth

lust n. 1 strong sexual desire 2 strong desire, as for power —v. feel an intense desire —**lust'ful** a.

lus'ter n. 1 gloss; brightness 2 brilliant fame —**lus'trous** (-trəs) a.

lust'y a., **–i·er, –i·est** vigorous; robust —**lust'i·ly** adv.

lute n. a stringed, guitarlike instrument

lut'ist n. lute player: also **lu'ta·nist**

lux·u'ri·ant (lug zhoor'-, luk shoor'-) a. 1 growing in abundance 2 richly ornamented —**lux·u'ri·ance** n.

lux·u'ri·ate' v. 1 live in luxury 2 revel (in)

lux·u'ri·ous a. 1 giving a feeling of luxury 2 fond of luxury

lux'u·ry n., pl. **–ries** costly comfort(s) or pleasure(s) —a. characterized by luxury

-ly suf. 1 like 2 in a specified way, or at a specified time or place 3 in sequence 4 every

lye (lī) n. strong alkaline substance

ly'ing v. ppr. of LIE

ly'ing-in' a. 1 n. (of or for) childbirth

lymph (limf) n. clear, yellowish body fluid —**lym·phat'ic** a.

lynch (linch) v. kill by mob action, without lawful trial, as by hanging

lynx (links) n. North American wildcat

ly·on·naise (lī'ə nāz') a. made with fried, sliced onions

lyre (līr) n. ancient instrument like a small harp

lyr'ic (lir'-) a. 1 suitable for singing 2 expressing the poet's emotions —n. 1 lyric poem 2 pl. words of a song

lyr'i·cal a. 1 lyric 2 very enthusiastic, etc. —**lyr'i·cal·ly** adv.

M

ma n. [Col.] mother

ma'am n. [Col.] madam

ma·ca'bre (-käb'rə, -käb') a. grim and horrible

mac·ad'am n. 1 small broken stones, used to make some roads 2 such a road

mac'a·ro'ni n. tubes of flour paste, cooked for food

mac'a·roon' n. cookie made with almonds or coconut

ma·caw' n. large parrot

mace n. 1 heavy, spiked club 2 official's staff 3 spice made from ground nutmeg shell —[M-] trademark combined tear gas and nerve gas

mac'er·ate' (mas'-) v. soften by soaking

ma·che'te (-shet'ē) n. large, heavy knife

Mach·i·a·vel'li·an (mak'-) a. crafty, deceitful, etc.

mach'i·na'tion (mak'-) n. wily or evil scheme

ma·chine' (-shēn') n. 1 device with moving parts, for doing work 2 group in control of a political party —a. of or done by machines —v. to shape, etc. by machinery

machine gun n. automatic gun

ma·chin'er·y n. 1 machines 2 working parts

ma·chin'ist n. one who makes or operates machines

Mach number (mäk) n. number for the ratio of airspeed to the speed of sound

ma′cho a. overly virile, domineering, etc.

mack′er·el n. edible fish of N Atlantic

mack′i·naw (coat) n. short, heavy coat, often plaid

mack′in·tosh′ n. raincoat of rubberized cloth

mac′ra·mé′ (-mä′) n. coarse yarn, etc. knotted in designs

macro- pref. large

mac′ro·cosm′ n. universe

ma′cron (-krən) n. pronunciation mark (̄)

mad a. **mad′der**, **mad′dest** 1 insane 2 frantic 3 foolish 4 angry —**mad′ly** adv. —**mad′ness** n.

mad′am n. polite title for a woman

ma·dame (mə däm′) n., pl. **mes·dames′** (mā′däm′) married woman: Fr. for *Mrs.*

mad′cap′ a. reckless; wild

mad′den v. make mad —**mad′den·ing** a.

mad′der n. 1 vine with berries 2 red dye made from its root

made v. pt. & pp. of MAKE

ma·de·moi·selle (mad′ə mə zel′) n. unmarried woman: Fr. for *Miss*

made′-to-or′der a. made to customer's specifications

made′-up′ a. 1 invented; false 2 with cosmetics applied

mad′house′ n. 1 insane asylum 2 place of turmoil

mad′man′ n., pl. **-men′** insane person

Ma·don′na n. picture or statue of the Virgin Mary

ma′dras n. fine cotton cloth, usually striped

mad′ri·gal n. part song for small group

mael′strom (māl′-) n. violent whirlpool

maes·tro (mīs′-) n. master, as in music

Ma′fi·a secret, criminal society

mag′a·zine′ (-zēn′) n. 1 periodical publication 2 storage place, as for military supplies 3 supply chamber, as in a rifle

ma·gen′ta n. purplish red

mag′got n. wormlike larva —**mag′got·y** a.

Ma·gi (mā′jī′) n.pl. wise men in the Bible

mag′ic n. 1 use of charms, spells, etc. 2 sleight of hand —a. of or as if by magic: also **mag′i·cal** —**mag′i·cal·ly** adv.

ma·gi·cian (-jish′ən) n. one who does magic

mag′is·te′ri·al (maj′-) a. authoritative

mag′is·trate′ (maj′-) n. official who administers the law —**mag′is·tra·cy** n.

mag′ma n. molten rock

mag·nan′i·mous a. generous in forgiving; noble —**mag′na·nim′i·ty** n.

mag′nate n. influential person in business

mag·ne′sia (-zhə) n. white powder (magnesium oxide) used as a laxative

mag·ne′si·um (-zē əm) n. light, silvery metal, a chemical element

mag′net n. piece of iron, steel, etc. that attracts iron or steel

magnetic tape n. thin plastic tape magnetized for recording

mag′net·ism′ n. 1 properties of magnets 2 personal charm —**mag·net′ic** a.

mag′net·ize′ v. 1 make a magnet of 2 to charm

mag·ne′to n., pl. **-tos** small electric generator

mag′ne·tom′e·ter n. device for measuring magnetic forces

mag·nif′i·cent a. 1 grand and stately; splendid 2 exalted —**mag·nif′i·cence** n.

mag′ni·fy′ v. **-fied′**, **-fy′ing** 1 increase apparent size of, as with a lens 2 exaggerate —**mag′ni·fi·ca′tion** n. —**mag′ni·fi′er** n.

mag′ni·tude′ n. greatness of size, extent, or importance

mag·no′li·a n. tree with large, fragrant flowers

mag′pie′ n. noisy bird of the crow family

Mag′yar′ n. person or language of Hungary

ma·ha·ra·jah, ma·ha·ra′ja n. in India, a prince, formerly the ruler of a native state —**ma·ha·ra′ni, ma·ha·ra′nee** n.fem.

ma·hat′ma (or -hät′-) n. in India, wise and holy person

mah′-jongg′, mah′jong′ n. Chinese game played with small tiles

ma·hog′a·ny n. reddish-brown wood of a tropical tree

ma·hout′ (-hout′) n. in India, elephant driver

maid n. 1 an unmarried, esp. young, woman 2 woman or girl servant

maid′en n. [Now Rare] young unmarried woman —a. 1 of or for a maiden 2 unmarried 3 first; earliest —**maid′en·hood′** n. —**maid′en·ly** a.

maid′en·hair′ n. delicate fern

mail n. 1 letters, etc. sent by postal service 2 postal system 3 metal mesh armor —a. of mail —v. send by mail —**mail′box′** n. —**mail′man′** n., pl. **-men′**

mail carrier n. one who carries and delivers mail

maim v. cripple; disable

main a. chief; leading; principal —n. 1 chief pipe in a system 2 [Poet.] ocean —**in the main** mostly —**with might and main** with all one's strength —**main′ly** adv.

main′frame′ n. large computer connected to several terminals

main′land′ n. main part of a continent

main′spring′ n. chief spring in a clock, etc.

main′stay′ n. main support

main′stream′ n. prevailing trend

main·tain′ v. 1 keep up; carry on 2 keep in working condition 3 declare to be true 4 support

main'te·nance n. 1 a maintaining 2 means of support

maî·tre d'hô·tel (me'trə dô'tel') n. [Fr.] chief of waiters

maize (māz) n. corn

maj'es·ty n. 1 grandeur; dignity 2 [M—] title for a sovereign —**ma·jes'tic** a. —**ma·jes'ti·cal·ly** adv.

ma·jol'i·ca n. Italian glazed pottery

ma'jor a. 1 greater in size, rank, etc. 2 Mus. semitone higher than the minor —n. 1 military officer above a captain 2 main field of study —v. specialize (in a subject)

ma'jor-do'mo n. man in charge of a great house

ma'jor-ette' n. girl who leads a marching band

major general n. officer above brigadier general

ma·jor'i·ty n. 1 more than half 2 full legal age

make v. made, mak'ing 1 bring into being; build, create, etc. 2 cause to be 3 amount to; equal 4 acquire; earn 5 cause success of 6 execute, do, etc. 7 force; compel 8 [Col.] get a place on (a team) —n. 1 act of making 2 style or build —**make away with** steal —**make believe** pretend —**make out** 1 see 2 succeed —**make over** change —**make up** 1 put together 2 invent 3 compensate 4 stop quarreling —**mak'er** n.

make'-be·lieve' n. pretense —a. pretended

make'shift' a., n. (as) a temporary substitute

make'up', make'-up' n. 1 way a thing is put together 2 cosmetics

mal- pref. bad or badly

mal'ad·just'ed a. badly adjusted, as to one's environment —**mal'ad·just'ment** n.

mal'a·droit' a. clumsy

mal'a·dy n., pl. –dies illness

ma·laise' (-lāz') n. vague feeling of illness

mal'a·mute' (-myōot') n. breed of sled dog used by Eskimos

mal'a·prop'ism' n. ridiculous misuse of words

ma·lar'i·a (-ler'-) n. disease with chills and fever, carried by mosquitoes

ma·lar'key, ma·lar'ky n. [Sl.] nonsensical talk

mal'a·thi'on (-thī'än') n. kind of organic insecticide

mal'con·tent' a., n. dissatisfied (person)

male a. 1 of the sex that fertilizes the ovum 2 of, like, or for men or boys —n. a male person, animal, or plant

mal'e·dic'tion n. a curse

mal'e·fac'tor n. evildoer —**mal'e·fac'tion** n.

ma·lev'o·lent a. wishing harm to others —**ma·lev'o·lence** n.

mal·fea'sance (-fē'zəns) n. wrongdoing in public office

mal'for·ma'tion n. faulty formation —**mal·formed'** a.

mal·func'tion v. fail to work as it should —n. failure

mal'ice (-is) n. ill will; wish to harm —**ma·li'cious** (-lish'əs) a.

ma·lign' (-līn') v. speak evil of —a. evil; harmful

ma·lig'nant a. 1 evil 2 very harmful 3 likely to cause death —**ma·lig'nan·cy** n.

ma·lin'ger v. feign illness to escape duty —**ma·lin'ger·er** n.

mall n. 1 shaded public walk 2 enclosed shopping center

mal'lard n. wild duck

mal'le·a·ble a. that can be hammered or pressed into shape —**mal'le·a·bil'i·ty** n.

mal'let n. hammer with a wooden head

mal'low n. family of plants including the hollyhock

mal·nour'ished a. improperly nourished

mal'nu·tri'tion n. faulty diet; lack of nourishment

mal'oc·clu'sion n. faulty position of teeth so that they do not meet properly

mal·o'dor·ous a. having a bad smell; stinking

mal·prac'tice n. improper practice, as by a doctor

malt n. barley, etc. soaked and dried for use in brewing and distilling

malt'ed (milk) n. drink of milk, malt, ice cream, etc.

mal·treat' v. to abuse —**mal·treat'ment** n.

ma'ma, mam'ma n. mother: child's word

mam'mal n. any vertebrate the female of which suckles its offspring

mam'ma·ry a. of milk-secreting glands

mam·mog'ra·phy n. X-ray technique to detect breast tumors

mam'mon n. riches as an object of greed

mam'moth n. huge, extinct elephant —a. huge

man n. 1 human being; person 2 adult male person 3 human race —v. manned, man'ning furnish with men for work, etc. —**to a man** with no exception

man'a·cle n., v. handcuff

man'age v. 1 to control or guide 2 have charge of 3 succeed in doing —**man'age·ment** n. —**man'ag·er** n.

man'aged care n. medical system using certain doctors and hospitals to reduce costs

man'a·ge'ri·al (-jir'ē-) a. of a manager

ma·ña·na (mä nyä'nä) adv., n. [Sp.] tomorrow

man'a·tee' n. large mammal living in tropical waters

man'da·rin n. 1 high official of former Chinese empire 2 [M—] main Chinese dialect

man'date' n. 1 an order; command 2 the will of voters as expressed in elections 3 commission given to a nation to administer a region 4 such a region —**man'da·to·ry** a.

man'di·ble n. lower jaw

man'do·lin' n. musical instrument with from 8 to 12 strings

man'drake' n. root formerly used in medicine

man'drel, man'dril (-drəl) n. spindle in a lathe to support work

man'drill (-dril) n. large African baboon

mane n. long hair on the neck of a horse, lion, etc.

man'-eat'er n. animal that eats human flesh

ma·nège' (ma nezh') n. art of riding and training horses

ma·neu'ver (-nōō'-) n. 1 a planned movement of troops, warships, etc. 2 scheme —v. 1 perform maneuvers 2 get, etc. by some scheme

man'ga·nese' n. grayish metal in alloys, a chemical element

mange (mānj) n. parasitic skin disease of animals —**man'gy** a., **-gi·er, -gi·est**

man·ger (mān'jər) n. box from which livestock feed

man'gle v. 1 mutilate by hacking, etc. 2 botch 3 press in a mangle —n. machine with rollers for ironing

man'go n., pl. **-goes** or **-gos** yellow-red tropical fruit

man'grove n. tropical tree with branches that send down roots to form trunks

han'dle'dle v. handle roughly

man'hole' n. hole for entering a sewer, etc.

man'hood' n. 1 time of being a man 2 manly qualities

man'-hour' n. one hour of work by one person

man'hunt' n. hunt for a fugitive

ma'ni·a n. 1 wild insanity 2 obsession —**man'ic** a.

ma'ni·ac' n. violently insane person —**ma·ni'a·cal** (-nī'-) a.

man·ic-de·pres'sive a. having alternating periods of mania and mental depression

man'i·cure' v., n. trim, polish, etc. (of) the fingernails —**man'i·cur'ist** n.

man'i·fest' a. obvious —v. reveal; show —n. list of a ship's cargo —**man'i·fes·ta'tion** n.

man'i·fes'to n., pl. **-toes** or **-tos** public declaration

man'i·fold' a. of many parts, sorts, etc. —n.

pipe with several outlets, as for carrying exhaust from an engine

man'i·kin n. mannequin

Ma·nil'a (paper) n. tan paper for wrapping, etc.

ma·nip'u·late' v. 1 handle skillfully 2 manage unfairly or dishonestly —**ma·nip'u·la'tion** n. —**ma·nip'u·la'tive** a.

man'ne·quin (-kin) n. model of the human body, as for displaying clothes

man'ner n. 1 way; style 2 habit 3 pl. (polite) ways of behaving 4 kind; sort

man'ner·ism' n. (affected) peculiarity of manner

man'ner·ly a. polite

man'nish a. masculine

man'-of-war' n. warship

man'or n. large estate

man'pow'er n. 1 human physical strength 2 the collective strength of a nation, etc.

man'sard (roof) (-särd) n. roof with two slopes on each side

manse n. residence of a minister or clergyman

man'sion n. large, imposing house

man'slaugh'ter n. unintentional killing of a person

man'tel n. frame around or shelf above a fireplace

man·til'la n. woman's scarf for the hair and shoulders

man'tis n. large, predatory insect

man'tle n. 1 sleeveless cloak 2 thing that covers —v. to cover

man'tra n. Hindu hymn or text chanted as a prayer

man'u·al a. made or done by hand —n. handbook

man'u·fac'ture n. making of goods by machinery —v. make, esp. by machinery —**man'u·fac'tur·er** n.

man'u·mit' v. **-mit'ted, -mit'ting** free from slavery —**man'u·mis'sion** n.

ma·nure' n. animal waste as fertilizer

man'u·script' n. written or typed book, article, etc.

man'y a. **more, most** numerous —n., pron. large number (of persons or things)

map n. drawing of the features of a region, the earth's surface, the sky, etc. —v. **mapped, map'ping** 1 to make a map of 2 plan

ma'ple n. 1 large shade tree 2 its hard wood 3 flavor of syrup or sugar made

mar v. **marred, mar'ring** damage; spoil

mar'a·bou' (-bōō') n. (plumes of) a stork of Africa or India

ma·ra'ca n. pebble-filled musical rattle

mar'a·schi'no cherry (-skē'-, -shē'-) n. cherry in a syrup

mar'a·thon n. **1** foot race of about 26 mi. **2** any endurance contest

ma·raud'er n. raider —**ma·raud'ing** a.

mar'ble n. hard limestone, white or colored —a. of or like marble

mar'ble·ize' v. make look like marble

March n. third month

march v. **1** walk with regular steps **2** advance steadily —n. **1** a marching **2** progress **3** distance marched **4** marching music

mar'chion·ess (-shən is) n. wife or widow of a marquess

Mar'di Gras' (-grä') n. last day before Lent begins

mare n. female horse, mule, donkey, etc.

mar'ga·rine (-rin) n. a spread like butter, of vegetable oil and skim milk

mar'gin n. **1** edge, as the blank border of a page **2** extra amount in reserve —**mar'gin·al** a.

ma·ri·a·chi (mär'ē ä'chē) n. **1** (member of) a strolling band in Mexico **2** its music

mar'i·gold' n. plant with yellow or orange flowers

mar'i·jua'na, mar'i·hua'na (-wä'nə) n. narcotic from the hemp plant

ma·rim'ba n. kind of xylophone

ma·ri'na (-rē'-) n. small harbor with docks

mar'i·nade' n. spiced pickling solution for meat, fish, etc.

mar'i·nate' v. soak in spiced vinegar, brine, etc.

ma·rine' a. of or in the sea, ships, etc. —n. member of the Marine Corps

mar'i·ner n. sailor

mar'i·o·nette' n. puppet

mar'i·tal a. of marriage

mar'i·time' a. **1** on or near the sea **2** of sailing

mar'jo·ram n. plant used for flavoring

mark n. **1** spot, scratch, etc. **2** sign or label **3** sign of quality **4** grade **5** impression **6** target; goal —v. **1** put a mark on **2** show by a mark **3** characterize **4** listen to **5** rate —**mark'er** n.

mark'down' n. price decrease

marked a. **1** having a mark **2** noticeable

mar'ket n. **1** place where goods are sold **2** store selling food **3** buying and selling **4** demand for (goods, etc.) —v. buy or sell —**mar'ket·a·ble** a. —**mar'ket·er** n.

mar'ket·place' n. **1** an outdoor market **2** the world of business

mark'ing n. arrangement of marks, as on fur, etc.

marks'man n., pl. **-men** one who shoots well —**marks'man·ship'** n.

mark'up' n. price increase

mar'lin n. large, slender, deep-sea fish

mar'ma·lade' n. preserve of oranges or other fruits

mar'mo·set' n. small monkey

mar'mot n. thick-bodied rodent, as the woodchuck

ma·roon' n., a. dark brownish red —v. put (a person) ashore in a lonely place

mar·quee' (-kē') n. rooflike projection over an entrance

mar'quess (-kwis) n. **1** British nobleman above an earl **2** marquis

mar'que·try (-kə-) n. fancy inlaid work in furniture, etc.

mar'quis (-kwis) n. nobleman above an earl or count —**mar·quise'** (-kēz') n.fem.

mar'qui·sette' (-ki zet') n. thin, netlike cloth

mar'riage (-ij) n. **1** married life **2** wedding —**mar'riage·a·ble** a.

mar'row n. **1** soft core inside bones **2** central part

mar'ry v. **-ried, -ry·ing 1** join as husband and wife **2** take as spouse **3** unite

marsh n. swamp —**marsh'y** a., **-i·er, -i·est**

mar'shal n. **1** highest ranking officer in some armies **2** Federal officer like a sheriff **3** head of a police or fire department —v. arrange (troops, ideas, etc.)

marsh'mal'low n. soft, white, spongy candy

mar·su'pi·al n. animal with a pouch for carrying its young

mart n. market

mar'ten n. **1** weasellike animal **2** its fur; sable

mar'tial (-shəl) a. **1** of war **2** military **3** warlike

martial art n. system of self-defense from Japan, etc.: usually used in pl.

martial law n. military rule over civilians

mar'tin n. kind of swallow

mar'ti·net' n. strict disciplinarian

mar·ti'ni n., pl. **-nis** cocktail

mar'tyr (-tər) n. one who suffers or dies for his beliefs —v. treat as a martyr —**mar'tyr·dom** n.

mar'vel n. wonderful thing —v. be amazed —**mar'vel·ous** a.

Marx'ism' n. doctrine of socialism —**Marx'ist** a., n.

mar'zi·pan' n. candy of ground almonds, egg white, etc.

mas·car'a (-kar'ə) n. cosmetic to color eyelashes

mas'con' *n.* dense material beneath the moon's surface

mas'cot' *n.* animal or thing kept for good luck

mas'cu·line (-kyoo lin) *a.* of or like men or boys; male —**mas'cu·lin'i·ty** *n.*

ma'ser (-zər) *n.* device that emits radiation in a narrow beam

mash *n.* 1 grain crushed in water for brewing, etc. 2 moist feed mixture for horses, etc. —*v.* crush into a soft mass

mask *n., v.* cover to conceal or protect the face

mas'o·chist (-ə kist) *n.* one who gets pleasure from being hurt —**mas'o·chism'** *n.* —**mas'o·chis'tic** *a.*

ma'son *n.* construction worker in brick, stone, etc.

ma'son·ry *n.* mason's work

masque (mask) *n.* 1 MASQUERADE (*n.* 1) 2 elaborate verse play

mas'quer·ade' (-kər-) *n.* 1 party with masks and costumes 2 disguise —*v.* be disguised

mass *n.* 1 quantity of matter 2 large number 3 size 4 [**M**—] *R.C.Ch.* service of the Eucharist —*v.* gather into a mass —**the masses** the common people

mas'sa·cre (-kər) *n.* indiscriminate killing —*v.* kill in large numbers

mas·sage' (mə säzh') *n.* rubbing and kneading of part of the body —*v.* give a massage

mas·seur' (mə sur') *n.* a man whose work is massaging —**mas·seuse'** (-sōōz') *n.fem.*

mas'sive *a.* big and heavy

mass media *n.pl.* newspapers, magazines, radio, and TV

mass number *n.* number of neutrons and protons in the nucleus of an atom

mass production *n.* production in large quantities

mast *n.* tall, upright pole on a ship, supporting sails

mas·tec'to·my *n., pl.* **–mies** surgical removal of a breast

mas'ter *n.* 1 man who rules others or is in control 2 expert —*a.* 1 of a master 2 chief; main —*v.* 1 control 2 become expert in

mas'ter·ful *a.* 1 domineering 2 expert; skillful: also **mas'ter·ly**

master key *n.* key that opens every one of a set of locks

mas'ter·mind' *v., n.* (be) an ingenious planner of (a project)

Master of Arts (or Science, etc.) *n.* advanced college degree

master of ceremonies *n.* person who presides at an entertainment, banquet, etc.

mas'ter·piece' *n.* thing made or done with expert skill

mas'ter·y *n.* 1 control 2 victory 3 expert skill

mast'head' *n.* part of a newspaper, etc. giving address, publisher, etc.

mas'ti·cate' *v.* chew up —**mas'ti·ca'tion** *n.*

mas'tiff *n.* big, strong dog

mas'to·don' *n.* extinct animal like the elephant

mas'toid' *a., n.* (of) a bony projection behind the ear

mas'tur·bate' *v.* practice genital self-excitation —**mas'tur·ba'tion** *n.*

mat *n.* 1 flat piece, as of woven straw, for protecting a floor, etc. 2 thick tangled mass 3 border around a picture —*v.* **mat'ted, mat'ting** 1 cover with a mat 2 weave or tangle together

mat'a·dor' *n.* bullfighter

match *n.* 1 short sliver with a tip that catches fire by friction 2 person or thing like another 3 contest 4 marriage —*v.* 1 be equal (to) 2 put in opposition 3 get an equivalent to

match'less *a.* without equal

match'mak'er *n.* arranger of marriages

mate *n.* 1 one of a pair 2 husband or wife 3 lower officer on a ship —*v.* join, as in marriage

ma·te'ri·al *n.* 1 what a thing is made of 2 fabric —*a.* 1 physical 2 essential

ma·te'ri·al·ism' *n.* 1 concern with physical things only 2 belief that everything has a physical cause —**ma·te'ri·al·is'tic** *a.*

ma·te'ri·al·ize' *v.* give or take material form

ma·te'ri·al·ly *adv.* 1 physically 2 considerably

ma·te'ri·el' *n.* military supplies

ma·ter'nal *a.* of, like, or from a mother

ma·ter'ni·ty *n.* motherhood —*a.* for pregnant women

math *n.* [Col.] mathematics

math'e·mat'ics *n.* science dealing with quantities and forms, their relationships, etc. —**math'e·mat'i·cal** *a.* —**math'e·ma·ti'cian** (-tish'ən) *n.*

mat·i·nee, mat·i·née (mat'n ā') *n.* afternoon performance of a play, etc.

mat'ins *n.pl.* morning prayer

ma'tri·arch' (-ärk') *n.* woman who rules her family or tribe —**ma'tri·ar'chal** *a.*

ma·tric'u·late' *v.* enroll, as in college —**ma·tric'u·la'tion** *n.*

mat'ri·mo'ny *n.* marriage —**mat'ri·mo'ni·al** *a.*

ma'trix' *n., pl.* **–tri·ces'** (-trə sēz') or **–trix'es** that within which a thing develops

ma'tron *n.* 1 wife or widow 2 woman manager of domestic affairs, as of a prison

matte (mat) *n.* dull surface or finish —*a.* not glossy

mat′ted a. closely tangled

mat′ter n. 1 physical substance of a thing 2 thing or affair 3 occasion 4 importance 5 trouble —v. be of importance —**as a matter of fact** really —**no matter** regardless of

mat′ter-of-fact′ a. sticking to facts; literal

mat′ting n. woven straw, etc. used as for mats

mat′tock (-ək) n. kind of pickax

mat′tress n. casing filled with cotton, springs, etc., for use on a bed

ma·ture′ (-toor′, -choor′) a. 1 fully grown, developed, etc. 2 due for payment —v. make or become mature —**ma·tu′ri·ty** n.

mat·zo (mät′sə) n., pl. **-zot**, **-zoth** (-sôt), or **-zos** (piece of) unleavened bread eaten at Passover

maud′lin a. foolishly sentimental

maul v. handle roughly

maun′der v. talk or move aimlessly

mau·so·le′um n. large, imposing tomb

mauve (mōv, môv, mäv) n. pale purple

mav′er·ick n. 1 lost, unbranded calf 2 political independent

maw n. 1 bird's crop 2 throat, gullet, jaws, etc.

mawk′ish a. sentimental in a sickening way

maxi- pref. maximum, very large, very long

max·il′la n. upper jawbone

max′im n. concise saying that is a rule of conduct

max′i·mize′ v. to increase to a maximum

max′i·mum a., n. greatest possible (quantity or degree)

May n. fifth month

may v. pt. **might** auxiliary verb showing: 1 possibility 2 permission

may′be adv. possibly

may′flow′er n. early spring flower

may′fly′ n., pl. **-flies′** delicate winged insect

may′hem n. 1 crime of maiming a person intentionally 2 deliberate destruction or violence

may′o′ n. [Col.] mayonnaise

may′on·naise′ (-nāz′) n. creamy salad dressing

may′or n. head of a city —**may′or·al·ty** n.

maze n. confusing network of paths

maz·el tov (mä′zəl tōv′) n., int. [Heb.] good luck

ma·zur′ka n. lively Polish dance

M.C. Master of Ceremonies

me pron. objective case of I

mead n. alcoholic liquor made from honey

mead·ow (med′ō) n. level field of grass

mea′ger a. 1 poor; scanty 2 thin Br. sp. **mea′gre**

meal n. 1 any of the times for eating 2 food served then 3 coarsely ground grain, etc. —**meal′y** a.

meal′y-mouthed′ a. not sincere

mean v. **meant** (ment), **mean′ing** 1 intend 2 intend to express 3 signify 4 have a certain importance —a. 1 low in quality or rank 2 poor or shabby 3 ignoble, petty, unkind, etc. 4 stingy 5 halfway between extremes —n. 1 middle point 2 pl. [sing. or pl. v.] that by which a thing is gotten or done 3 pl. wealth —**by all** (or **no**) **means** certainly (not) —**by means of** by using —**mean′ly** adv. —**mean′ness** n.

me·an′der v. 1 wind back and forth 2 wander idly

mean′ing n. what is meant, indicated, etc. —**mean′ing·ful** a. —**mean′ing·less** a.

mean′time′ adv., n. (during) the intervening time: also **mean′while′**

mea′sles (-zəlz) n. contagious disease, usually of children

mea′sly a. **-sli·er**, **-sli·est** [Col.] slight, worthless, mean

meas′ure (mezh′-) v. 1 find out the extent, dimensions, etc. of 2 mark off a certain amount 3 be a thing for measuring 4 be of specified dimensions —n. 1 dimensions, capacity, etc. 2 unit of measuring 3 system of measuring 4 instrument for measuring 5 definite quantity 6 course of action 7 a law 8 notes and rests between two bars on a musical staff —**meas′ur·a·ble** a. —**meas′ure·less** a. —**meas′ure·ment** n.

meat n. 1 flesh of animals used as food 2 edible part 3 essence —**meat′y** a., **-i·er**, **-i·est**

me·chan′ic (-kan′-) n. worker who repairs machines

me·chan′i·cal a. 1 of or run by machinery 2 machinelike —**me·chan′i·cal·ly** adv.

me·chan′ics n. 1 science of motion and the effect of forces on bodies 2 knowledge of machinery 3 technical aspect

mech′a·nism′ (mek′-) n. 1 working parts of a machine 2 system of interrelated parts

mech′a·nize′ v. 1 to make mechanical 2 to equip with machinery, trucks, etc. —**mech′a·ni·za′tion** n.

med′al n. flat, inscribed piece of metal given as an honor or reward

med′al·ist n. one who wins a medal

me·dal′lion (-yən) n. 1 large medal 2 a round, medallike design

med′dle v. interfere in another's affairs —**med′dler** n. —**med′dle·some** a.

me′di·a n. alt. pl. of MEDIUM

me′di·an n., a. (number, point, etc.) in the middle

me′di·ate′ v. (try to) settle (differences) between two parties —**me′di·a′tion** n. —**me′di·a′tor** n.

med·ic *n.* [Col.] 1 doctor 2 army medical corpsman

Med·ic·aid' [*also* m–] State and Federal program helping the poor pay medical bills

med·i·cal *a.* having to do with the practice or study of medicine —**med'i·cal·ly** *adv.*

Med·i·care' [*also* m–] Federal program helping the elderly pay medical bills

med'i·cate' *v.* treat with medicine —**med'i·ca'tion** *n.*

me·dic'i·nal (-dis'-) *a.* that is or is used as a medicine

med'i·cine (-sən) *n.* 1 science of treating and preventing disease 2 drug, etc. used in treating disease

medicine man among North American Indians, etc., a man supposed to have healing powers

me'di·e'val (mē'dē-, med'ē-) *a.* of or like the Middle Ages

me'di·o·cre (-kər) *a.* ordinary; average —**me'di·oc'ri·ty** (äk'-) *n., pl.* –**ties**

med'i·tate' *v.* 1 think deeply 2 plan —**med'i·ta'tion** *n.* —**med'i·ta·tive** *a.*

me'di·um *a.* intermediate in amount, degree, etc. —*n., pl.* –**di'ums** or –**di'a** 1 medium thing or state 2 thing through which a force acts 3 means, agency, etc. 4 surrounding substance

med'ley *n.* 1 mixture of unlike things 2 musical piece made up of several songs

meek *a.* 1 patient and mild 2 easily imposed on

meer'schaum (-shəm) *n.* (tobacco pipe made of) white, claylike mineral

meet *v.* **met, meet'ing** 1 come upon 2 be present at the arrival of 3 be introduced (to) 4 come into contact (with) 5 come together 6 satisfy 7 pay —*n.* a meeting —*a.* suitable

meet'ing *n.* 1 a coming together 2 a gathering of people 3 junction

mega- *pref.* 1 large, great 2 a million of

meg'a·byte' *n.* million bytes

meg'a·hertz' *n., pl.* –**hertz'** million hertz

meg'a·lo·ma'ni·a *n.* delusion of grandeur or power

meg'a·lop'o·lis *n.* vast urban area

meg'a·phone' *n.* funnel-shaped device to increase the volume of the voice

meg'a·ton' *n.* explosive force of a millions tons of TNT

mel'an·cho'li·a (-kō'-) *n.* extreme depression

mel'an·chol'y (-käl'ē) *n.* sadness and mental depression —*a.* sad or saddening

mé·lange' (mā lônzh') *n.* mixture or medley

mel'a·nin *n.* dark pigment of skin, etc.

mel·a·no'ma *n., pl.* –**mas** or –**ma·ta** skin tumor

Mel'ba toast *n.* very crisp, thinly sliced toast

meld *v.* to blend; merge

me·lee, mê·lée (mā'lā') *n.* brawling group fight

mel'io·rate' (mēl'yə-) *v.* make or become better

mel·lif'lu·ous *a.* smooth and sweet, as sounds: also **mel·lif'lu·ent** —**mel·lif'lu·ence** *n.*

mel'low *a.* full, rich, gentle, etc.; not harsh —*v.* make or become mellow

me·lo'di·ous *a.* 1 having melody 2 pleasing to hear

mel'o·dra'ma *n.* sensational, extravagant drama —**mel'o·dra·mat'ic** *a.*

mel'o·dra·mat'ics *n.pl.* melodramatic behavior

mel'o·dy *n., pl.* –**dies** a tune, song, etc. —**me·lod'ic** *a.*

mel'on *n.* large, juicy, many-seeded fruit

melt *v.* 1 change from solid to liquid, as by heat 2 dissolve 3 disappear or merge gradually 4 soften

melt'down' *n.* dangerous melting of fuel in a nuclear reactor

melting pot *n.* place in which various immigrants are assimilated

mem'ber *n.* 1 distinct part, as an arm 2 person in an organization

mem'ber·ship' *n.* 1 state of being a member 2 all the members

mem'brane' *n.* thin tissue lining an organ or part —**mem'bra·nous** *a.*

me·men'to *n., pl.* –**tos** or –**toes** souvenir

mem'o *n., pl.* –**os** memorandum

mem'oirs' (-wärz') *n.pl.* account of one's past life

mem'o·ra·bil'i·a *n.pl.* things worth remembering

mem'o·ra·ble *a.* worth remembering

mem'o·ran'dum *n., pl.* –**dums** or –**da** short note to remind one of something

me·mo'ri·al *n.* anything meant to help people remember a person or event

me·mo'ri·al·ize' *v.* commemorate

mem'o·rize' *v.* to commit to memory

mem'o·ry *n., pl.* –**ries** 1 power or act of remembering 2 something or everything remembered 3 commemoration 4 device in a computer, etc. that stores information

men *n.* pl. of MAN

men'ace *n.* a threat —*v.* to threaten

mé·nage (mā näzh') *n.* household: also **me·nage**

me·nag'er·ie (-naj'-, -nazh'-) *n.* collection of wild animals

mend *v.* 1 repair 2 make or become better

—n. mended place —**on the mend** improving —**mend′er** n.

men·da′cious a. lying —**men·dac′i·ty** n.

men′di·cant n. beggar

men′folk′ n.pl. [Col.] men

me′ni·al a. servile —n. servant

men·in·gi′tis (-jīt′is) n. inflammation of membranes of the brain and spinal cord

me·nis′cus n. curved upper surface of a column of liquid

men′o·pause′ n. permanent cessation of menstruation

me·no′rah n. Jewish candelabrum

men′ses′ (-sēz′) n.pl. monthly menstrual flow

men′stru·ate′ v. have a flow of blood monthly from the uterus —**men′stru·al** a. —**men′stru·a′tion** n.

men·su·ra′tion (-sha-) n. a measuring

-ment suf. 1 result of 2 a means for 3 act of 4 state of being

men′tal a. 1 of or in the mind 2 for the mentally ill —**men′tal·ly** adv.

men·tal′i·ty n. mental power, attitude, outlook, etc.

mental retardation n. congenital lowness of intelligence

men′thol′ (-thôl′) n. derivative of oil of peppermint —**men′tho·lat′ed** a.

men′tion n. brief reference —v. refer to briefly

men′tor n. wise advisor

men′u n., pl. **-us** list of choices of meals, computer functions, etc.

me·ow′, me·ou′ v., n. (make) the sound of a cat

mer·can·tile′ (-tīl′, -tēl′) a. of merchants or trade

mer′ce·nar′y a. thinking mainly of money —n., pl. **-ies** soldier paid to serve in a foreign army

mer′cer·ized′ a. treated, as cotton, to strengthen it

mer′chan·dise′ (-dīz′; n.: also -dīs′) v. buy and sell —n. things bought and sold

mer′chant n. 1 dealer in goods 2 storekeeper

mer′chant·man n., pl. **-men** ship used in commerce

merchant marine n. ships of a nation used in trade

mer·ci′ (mer sē′) int. [Fr.] thank you

mer·cu′ri·al (-kyoor′ē-) a. changeable, fickle, etc.

mer′cu·ry n. silvery liquid metal, a chemical element

mer′cy n., pl. **-cies** 1 kindness; forbearance 2 power to forgive —**at the mercy of** in the power of —**mer′ci·ful** a. —**mer′ci·less** a.

mercy killing n. euthanasia

mere a. **mer′est** no more than; only

mere′ly adv. only; simply

mer·e·tri′cious (-trish′əs) a. flashy; tawdry

mer·gan′ser n. large duck

merge v. unite or combine so as to lose identity

merg′er n. a merging, or thing formed by merging

me·rid′i·an n. 1 highest point 2 circle through the earth's poles

me·ringue′ (-raŋ′) n. egg whites and sugar beaten stiff

me·ri′no (mə rē′-) n., pl. **-nos** (silky wool of) a hardy breed of sheep

mer′it n. 1 worth; value 2 something deserving praise —v. deserve

mer′i·to′ri·ous a. deserving reward, praise, etc.

mer′maid n. imaginary creature like a woman with a fish's tail

mer′ry a. **-ri·er, -ri·est** full of fun —**make merry** have fun —**mer′ri·ly** adv. —**mer′ri·ment** n. —**mer′ry·mak′ing** n.

mer′ry-go-round′ n. revolving platform with seats, as in amusement parks

mer′ry-mak′ing n. fun; festivity —**mer′ry·mak′er** n.

me′sa (mā′-) n. high plateau with steep sides

mes′ca·line (-lin) n. psychedelic drug from a cactus plant (**mes·cal′**)

mes·dames′ (mā däm′) n. pl. of MADAM, MADAME, or MRS.

mesh n. (cord or wire of) a net or network —v. 1 to entangle 2 interlock

mes′mer·ize′ (mez′-) v. hypnotize —**mes′mer·ism′** n. —**mes′mer·ist** n.

mes·quite, mes·quit′ (-kēt′) n. spiny shrub

mess n. 1 a jumble 2 trouble 3 untidy condition 4 communal meal as in the army —v. 1 make dirty, jumbled, etc. 2 meddle —**mess′i·ness** n. —**mess′y** a., **-i·er, -i·est**

mes′sage n. 1 a communication 2 important idea

mes′sen·ger n. one who carries a message, etc.

mess hall n. room or building where soldiers, etc. regularly eat

Mes·si′ah (-sī′-) 1 Judaism expected deliverer of the Jews 2 Christianity Jesus —n. [**m-**] expected savior or liberator —**Mes′si·an′ic** a.

Messrs. (mes′ərz) pl. of MR.

mes·ti′zo (-tē′-) n., pl. **-zos** or **-zoes** one of American Indian and Spanish parentage

met v. pt. & pp. of MEET

me·tab′o·lism′ n. changing of food by organisms into energy, cells, etc. —**met′a·bol′ic** a.

met′a·car′pus n., pl. **-pi** (-pī′) part of the

hand between the wrist and the fingers

met'al n. 1 shiny, usually solid, chemical element 2 an alloy —a. of metal —**me·tal'lic** adv.

met'al·lur'gy n. science of refining metals —**met'al·lur'gi·cal** a. —**met'al·lur'gist** n.

met'a·mor'pho·sis n., pl. **-ses'** (-sēz') 1 change in form 2 any change

met'a·phor' n. word for one thing used for another —**met'a·phor'ic, met'a·phor'i·cal** a.

met'a·phys'ics n. [sing. v.] philosophy that deals with first principles —**met'a·phys'i·cal** a.

me·tas'ta·sis n., pl. **-ses'** (-sēz') spread of cancer cells through the bloodstream —**me·tas'ta·size'** vi.

met'a·tar'sal a. of the part of the foot between ankle and toes

met'a·tar'sus n., pl. **-si** (-sī') part of the foot between the ankle and the toes

mete (mēt) v. allot

me'te·or n. fiery meteoroid traveling through the earth's atmosphere —**me'te·or'ic** a.

me'te·or·ite' n. part of a meteor fallen to earth

me'te·or·oid' n. small, solid body traveling through outer space at high speed

me'te·or·ol'o·gy n. science of weather, climate, etc. —**me'te·or·o·log'i·cal** a. —**me'te·or·ol'o·gist** n.

me'ter n. 1 rhythmic pattern in verse 2 metric unit of length (39.37 in.) 3 device to measure flow of fluid —**met'ric** a. —**met'ri·cal** a.

meth'a·done' (-dōn') n. synthetic narcotic used in medicine

meth'ane n. colorless, odorless, inflammable gas

meth'a·nol' (-nôl') n. toxic liquid used as fuel, antifreeze, etc.

me·thinks' v. [Ar.] it seems to me

meth'od n. 1 way; process 2 system

me·thod'i·cal a. orderly

meth'od·ol'o·gy n., pl. **-gies** system of methods

me·tic'u·lous a. very careful about details; fussy

mé·tier (mā tyā') n. one's trade, etc.

me'tre n. Br. sp. of METER

met'ric a. 1 of the meter (unit of length) 2 of the metric system 3 metrical

met'ri·cal a. 1 of or composed in meter or verse 2 used in measurement —**met'ri·cal·ly** adv.

met'ri·ca'tion n. a changing to the metric system

metric system n. decimal system of weights and measures

met'ro·nome' n. device that beats time at a set rate

me·trop'o·lis n. main or important city —**met'ro·pol'i·tan** a.

met'tle n. spirit; courage —**on one's mettle** ready to do one's best

met'tle·some a. spirited; ardent

mew v. n. meow

mewl v. to cry weakly, like a baby

mews n.pl. [Br.] stables or carriage houses, now often made into dwellings

Mex'i·can n., adv. (native) of Mexico

mez'za·nine' (-nēn') n. 1 low story built between two main stories 2 first few rows of balcony seats

mez'zo-so·pra'no (met'sō-) n. voice or singer between soprano and contralto

mi·as'ma (mī az'-) n. vapor from swamps, once believed poisonous

mi'ca (mī'-) n. mineral that forms into thin, heat-resistant layers

mice n. pl. of MOUSE

micro- pref. small

mi'crobe' n. minute organism, esp. one causing disease

mi'cro·chip' n. electronic circuit on a tiny piece of semiconductor material

mi'cro·com·put'er n. small computer for home use, etc.

mi'cro·cosm' n. universe on a small scale

mi'cro·fiche' (-fēsh') n. film card on which greatly reduced microfilm is recorded

mi'cro·film' n. film on which documents, etc. are recorded in a reduced size

mi·crom'e·ter n. instrument for measuring very small distances, angles, etc.

mi'cron' n. one millionth of a meter

mi'cro·or·gan·ism' n. microscopic organism

mi'cro·phone' n. instrument for changing sound waves into electric impulses

mi'cro·scope' n. device for magnifying minute objects

mi'cro·scop'ic a. so small as to be invisible except through a microscope

mi'cro·wave' n. radio or infrared wave used in radar, cooking, etc. —v. a. (to cook) using microwaves

mid, 'mid prep. [Poet.] amid

mid- pref. middle of

mid'air' n. point not in contact with any surface

mid'day' n., a. noon

mid'dle a. halfway between two points, etc. —n. middle point or part

mid'dle-aged' a. in the time between youth and old age

Middle Ages a period in Europe, A.D. 476 - c. 1450

mid'dle·man' n., pl. **-men'** 1 one who buys

from a producer and sells at wholesale or retail 2 go-between

middle school n. school with, usually, grades five through eight

mid′dling a. of middle size, quality, etc.

mid′dy n., pl. **-dies** loose blouse with a sailor collar

midge n. small gnat

midg′et n. very small person —adv. miniature

mid′land a., n. (of) the middle region of a country

mid′night′ n. twelve o'clock at night

mid′riff n. part of body between abdomen and chest

mid′ship′man n., pl. **-men** naval officer trainee

midst n. the middle —prep. [Poet.] in the midst of

mid′sum′mer n. period about June 21

mid′way′ a., adv. in the middle; halfway —n. location for side shows, etc. at a fair

mid′wife′ n., pl. **-wives′** woman who helps others in childbirth —mid′wife′ry n.

mid′win′ter n. period about December 22

mien (mēn) n. one's manner

miff v. [Col.] offend

might v. pt. of MAY: might is also used to show less possibility or permission than may —n. strength; force

might′y a. **-i·er, -i·est** powerful, great, etc. —adv. [Col.] very —might′i·ly adv.

mi′graine′ n. periodic headache

mi′grate′ v. move from one place or region to another, as with the change in season —mi′grant a., n. —mi·gra′tion n. —mi′gra·to′ry a.

mi·ka′do (mi kä′-) n., pl. **-dos** emperor of Japan

mike n. [Col.] microphone

mil n. .001 of an inch

milch a. kept for milking

mild a. 1 gentle 2 weak in taste —mild′ly adv.

mil′dew′ n. whitish fungus on plants, damp cloth, etc.

mile n. unit of measure, 5,280 ft.

mile′age n. 1 total miles traveled 2 allowance per mile for traveling expenses

mil′er n. contestant in mile races

mile′stone′ n. significant event

mi·lieu (mēl yoo′) n. surroundings; environment

mil′i·tant a. ready to fight —mil′i·tan·cy n.

mil′i·ta·rism′ n. 1 warlike spirit 2 maintenance of strong armed forces —mil′i·ta·rist n. —mil′i·ta·ris′tic a.

mil′i·ta·ry a. of soldiers, war, etc. —n. the army

mil′i·tate′ v. work (for or against)

mi·li′tia (-lish′ə) n. citizens trained for emergency military service

milk n. 1 white liquid secreted by female mammals for suckling their young 2 any liquid like this —v. draw milk from (a mammal) —milk′y a., -i·er, -i·est —milk′i·ness n.

milk′man′ n., pl. **-men′** man who sells or delivers milk

milk of magnesia n. milky-white liquid used as laxative, etc.

milk′shake′ n. frothy drink of milk, flavoring, and ice cream

milk′sop′ n. sissy

milk′weed′ n. plant with a milky juice

mill n. 1 place for grinding grain into flour 2 machine for grinding 3 factory 4 ¹⁄₁₀ of a cent —v. 1 grind by or in a mill move (around or about) confusedly, as a crowd —mill′er n.

mill′age n. taxation in mills per dollar of valuation

mil·len′ni·um n., pl. **-ni·ums** or **-ni·a** 1 Theol. 1,000-year period of Christ's future reign on earth 2 period of peace and joy

mil′let n. cereal grass

milli- pref. ¹⁄₁₀₀₀ part of

mil′li·gram′ n. one thousandth of a gram

mil′li·li′ter n. one thousandth of a liter

mil′li·me′ter n. one thousandth of a meter

mil′li·ner n. one who makes or sells women's hats

mil′li·ner′y n. 1 women's hats 2 business of a milliner

mil′lion n., a. a thousand thousands —mil′lionth a., n.

mil′lion·aire′ n. one having at least a million dollars

mill′stone′ n. 1 flat, round stone used for grinding grain, etc. 2 heavy burden

mill′wright′ n. worker who installs or repairs heavy machinery

milt n. fish sperm

mime n., v. clown or mimic

mim′e·o·graph′ n. machine for making stenciled copies of typewritten matter —v. make (such copies) of

mim′ic v. **-icked, -ick·ing** 1 imitate, as to ridicule 2 to copy closely —n. one who mimics —mim′ic·ry n.

mi·mo′sa n. flowering tree or shrub of warm climates

min′a·ret′ n. mosque tower

mince v. 1 cut into small pieces 2 lessen the force of (words) 3 act with affected daintiness —minc′ing a.

mince′meat′ n. pie filling of raisins, spices, suet, etc.

mind n. 1 center of thought, feeling, etc. 2 intellect 3 sanity 4 memory 5 opinion, intention, etc. —v. 1 observe 2 obey 3 take care of 4 be careful about 5 object to —bear (or keep) in mind remember —have in mind intend —make up one's mind reach a decision —put in mind remind

mind'ful a. aware of

mind's eye n. the imagination

mine pron. that or those belonging to me —n. 1 large excavation from which to extract ores, coal, etc. 2 great source of supply 3 explosive device hidden under land or water —v. 1 dig (ores, etc.) from a mine 2 hide mines in —**min'er** n.

min'er·al n. ore, rock, etc. found naturally in the earth —a. of or containing minerals

mineral jelly n. petrolatum

min'er·al'o·gy n. science of minerals —**min'er·al'o·gist** n.

mineral oil n. oil from petroleum used as a laxative

mineral water n. water having mineral salts or gases

mi·ne·stro·ne (min'ə strō'nē) n. thick vegetable soup

min'gle v. 1 mix or become 2 join with others

mini- pref. miniature; very small; very short

min'i·a·ture n. tiny copy, model, painting, etc. —a. minute

min'i·a·tur·ize' v. make in a small, compact form

min'i·bike' n. small motorcycle

min'i·bus' n. very small bus

min'i·cam' n. portable TV camera

min'i·com·put'er n. computer between a mainframe and a microcomputer in power, etc.

min'i·mize' v. reduce to or estimate at a minimum

min'i·mum n. 1 smallest quantity possible 2 lowest degree reached —a. lowest or least possible —**min'i·mal** a.

min'ing n. work of removing ores, etc. from a mine

min'ion (-yən) n. faithful or servile follower

min'is·cule' a. minuscule: a misspelling

min'i·skirt' n. skirt ending well above the knee

min'is·ter n. 1 head of a governmental department 2 diplomatic official below an ambassador 3 one who conducts religious services —v. give help; serve —**min'is·tra'tion** n. —**min'is·te'ri·al** (-tir'ē-) a.

min'is·try n., pl. —tries 1 office of a clergyman 2 clergy 3 government department headed by a minister —a. ministering

min'i·van' n. small passenger van with windows all around and back seats

mink n. 1 weasellike mammal 2 its valuable fur

min'now (-ō) n. very small freshwater fish

mi'nor a. 1 lesser in size, rank, etc. 2 Mus. semitone lower than the major —n. 1 one under full legal age 2 secondary field of study

mi·nor'i·ty n., pl. —ties 1 smaller part or number 2 racial, religious, etc. group that differs from the larger groups 3 time of being a minor

min'strel n. 1 traveling singer of the Middle Ages 2 entertainer in an old-style U.S. variety show

mint n. 1 place where the government makes coins 2 large amount 3 aromatic plant with leaves used for flavoring —v. coin (money)

min'u·end' n. number from which another is to be subtracted

min'u·et' n. slow, stately dance of 18th c.

mi'nus prep. less —a. 1 negative 2 less than —n. sign (-) showing subtraction or negative quantity

mi·nus·cule (min'ə skyōōl') a. tiny; minute

min·ute (min'it) n. 1 sixtieth part of an hour 2 moment 3 pl. official record

mi·nute (mī nōōt', -nyōōt') a. 1 very small 2 exact —**mi·nute'ly** adv.

mi·nu·ti·ae (mi nōō'shə, -nyōō'-) n.pl. trifling details

minx n. bold or saucy girl

mir'a·cle n. 1 event that seems to contradict scientific laws 2 remarkable thing —**mi·rac'u·lous** a.

mi·rage (mi räzh') n. optical illusion caused by reflection of light

mire n. deep mud or slush —v. stick or cause to get stuck as in mire

mir'ror n. coated glass that reflects images

mirth n. gaiety with laughter —**mirth'ful** a.

mis- pref. wrong(ly); bad(ly)

mis'ad·ven'ture n. bad luck

mis·an'thrope' n. one who hates all people: also **mis·an'thro·pist** —**mis'an·throp'ic** a. —**mis·an'thro·py** n.

mis·ap·ply' v. —**plied'**, —**ply'ing** apply badly or wrongly

mis'ap·pre·hend' v. understand wrongly —**mis'ap·pre·hen'sion** n.

mis·ap·pro'pri·ate' v. use (funds, etc.) dishonestly —**mis·ap·pro'pri·a'tion** n.

mis·be·got'ten a. illegitimate

mis·be·have' v. behave badly —**mis'be·hav'ior** n.

mis·cal'cu·late' v. misjudge —**mis'cal·cu·la'tion** n.

mis·car'ry v. 1 go wrong 2 lose a fetus

before full term —**mis·car′riage** (or mis·
kar′ij) n.

mis·cast′ v. cast (an actor) in an unsuitable
role

mis·ce·ge·na′tion (mis′i jə-) n. interracial
marriage

mis′cel·la′ne·ous a. of various kinds; mixed

mis′cel·la′ny n., pl. -**nies** collection of various kinds

mis·chance′ n. bad luck

mis′chief (-chif) n. **1** harm or damage **2**
prank **3** teasing —**mis′chie·vous** (-chə-)
a.

mis·ci·ble (mis′ə-) a. that can be mixed

mis′con·ceive′ v. misunderstand —**mis′-
con·cep′tion** n.

mis·con′duct n. wrong conduct

mis′con·strue′ v. misinterpret

mis′cre·ant n. villain

mis·deal′ (n.: mis′dēl′) v.-**dealt′**,-**deal′ing**
deal (playing cards) wrongly —n. wrong
deal

mis·deed′ n. crime, sin, etc.

mis′de·mean′or n. Law minor offense

mis′di·rect′ v. direct wrongly or badly
—**mis′di·rec′tion** n.

mi′ser (-zər) n. stingy hoarder of money
—**mi′ser·ly** a.

mis·er·a·ble (miz′-) a. **1** in misery **2** causing misery **3** bad, poor, etc. —**mis′er·a·bly**
adv.

mis′er·y n., pl. -**ies** pain, poverty, distress,
etc.

mis·file′ v. file in the wrong place

mis·fire′ v. fail to go off

mis·fit′ v. fit improperly —n. **1** improper
fit **2** maladjusted person

mis·for′tune n. **1** trouble **2** mishap, calamity, etc.

mis·giv′ings n.pl. feelings of fear, doubt,
etc.

mis·gov′ern v. govern badly —**mis·gov′ern·
ment** n.

mis·guide′ v. mislead

mis·han′dle v. abuse

mish′mash′ n. a jumble

mis′in·form′ v. give wrong information to

mis′in·ter′pret v. to interpret wrongly
—**mis′in·ter′pre·ta′tion** n.

mis·judge′ v. judge wrongly

mis·la′bel v. label wrongly

mis·lay′ v. -**laid′**, -**lay′ing** put in a place
later forgotten

mis·lead′ v. **1** lead astray **2** deceive

mis·man′age v. manage badly

mis·match′ (n.: mis′mach′) v. match badly
—n. bad match

mis·name′ v. give an inappropriate name
to

mis·no′mer n. name wrongly applied

mi·sog′y·nist (-säj′ə-) n. one who hates
women —**mi·sog′y·ny** n.

mis·place′ v. put in a wrong place

mis′play′ v. play wrongly —n. wrong play

mis′print′ n. printing error

mis·pri′sion (-prizh′ən) n. misconduct by a
public official

mis′pro·nounce′ v. pronounce wrongly

mis·quote′ v. quote incorrectly

mis·read′ (-rēd′) v.-**read′** (-red′), -**read′ing**
read wrongly and so misunderstand

mis′rep·re·sent′ v. give a false idea of

mis·rule′ (or mis rool′) n. bad government

miss v. **1** fail to hit, meet, do, see, hear, etc.
2 avoid **3** note or feel the loss of —n. **1**
failure to hit, etc. **2** unmarried woman **3**
[M—] title used before her name

mis′sal (-əl) n. R.C.Ch. prayer book for Mass
for the year

mis·shap′en (-shāp′-) a. badly shaped; de-
formed

mis′sile (-əl) n. object to be thrown or shot

miss′ing a. absent; lost

mis′sion n. **1** special task or duty **2** group
or station of missionaries **3** diplomatic
delegation

mis′sion·ar′y n., pl. -**ies** person sent by a
church to make converts, esp. abroad

mis′sive n. letter or note

mis·spell′ v. spell incorrectly

mis·spend′ v. -**spent′**, -**spend′ing** spend
improperly or wastefully

mis·state′ v. state wrongly —**mis·state′ment**
n.

mis′step′ n. **1** wrong step **2** mistake in
conduct

mist n. mass of water vapor; thin fog

mis·take′ v. -**took′**, -**tak′en**, -**tak′ing** understand or perceive wrongly —n. error

mis·tak′en a. wrong or incorrect

mis′ter n. title before a man's name: usually
Mr.

mis′tle·toe′ (mis′əl-) n. evergreen plant
with white berries

mis·treat′ v. treat badly —**mis·treat′ment** n.

mis′tress n. **1** woman in charge or control **2** woman who has sexual intercourse
with and is supported by a man without
marriage

mis·tri′al n. Law trial made void by an
error, etc.

mis·trust′ n. lack of trust —v. have no trust
in; doubt

mist′y a. -**i·er**, -**i·est** **1** like or covered with
mist **2** vague or indistinct

mis′un·der·stand′ v. -**stood′**, -**stand′ing** understand incorrectly

mis′un·der·stand′ing n. **1** failure to understand **2** a quarrel

mis·use´ (-yooz´; n.: -yoos´) v. 1 use improperly 2 abuse —n. incorrect use

mite n. 1 tiny, parasitic arachnid 2 tiny amount

mi´ter n. 1 tall cap of a bishop 2 corner joint of two pieces cut at an angle

mit´i·gate´ v. make or become less severe —**mit´i·ga´tion** n.

mi·to´sis n. process of cell division

mitt n. 1 padded baseball glove 2 [Sl.] hand

mit´ten n. glove without separate finger pouches

mix v. **mixed** or **mixt, mix´ing** 1 stir or come together in a single mass 2 make by mixing ingredients 3 combine —n. mixture, or its ingredients —**mix up** 1 confuse 2 involve (in)

mixed a. 1 blended 2 of different kinds 3 of both sexes

mix´ture n. 1 a mixing 2 thing mixed

mix´-up´ n. confusion

mne·mon´ic (nē-) a. of or helping the memory

moan n. low, mournful sound —v. 1 utter (with) a moan 2 complain

moat n. deep, usually water-filled ditch around a castle

mob n. crowd, esp. a disorderly one —v. **mobbed, mob´bing** crowd around and attack

mo´bile (-bəl, -bīl´; n.: -bēl´) a. 1 readily movable or adaptable 2 easy in changing social status —n. abstract sculpture suspended to move in the air —**mo·bil´i·ty** n.

mobile home n. large trailer outfitted as a home

mo´bi·lize´ v. make or become ready, as for war —**mo´bi·li·za´tion** n.

moc´ca·sin n. heelless slipper of soft leather

mo´cha (-kə) n. kind of coffee

mock v. 1 ridicule 2 mimic and deride —a. false

mock´er·y n., pl. -**ies** 1 a mocking 2 poor imitation

mock´ing·bird´ n. small bird with imitative call

mock´-up´ n. full-scale model

mode n. 1 way of acting or doing 2 fashion

mod´el n. 1 small copy of something 2 one to be imitated 3 style 4 one who poses for an artist 5 one who displays clothes by wearing them —a. serving as a model —v. 1 plan or form 2 work as a model

mo´dem n. device converting computer data for transmission, as by telephone

mod´er·ate (-ət; v.: -āt´) a. avoiding extremes —n. moderate person —v. 1 to make or become moderate 2 preside over (a debate, etc.) —**mod´er·ate·ly** adv. —**mod´er·a´tion** n. —**mod´er·a´tor** n.

mod´ern a. of recent times; up-to-date —n. modern person —**mod´ern·is´tic** a. —**mod´ern·ize´** v.

mod´est a. 1 not conceited 2 decent 3 moderate —**mod´es·ty** n.

mod´i·cum n. small amount

mod´i·fy´ v. -**fied´**, -**fy´ing** change or limit slightly —**mod´i·fi·ca´tion** n. —**mod´i·fi´er** n.

mod´ish (mōd´-) a. fashionable

mod´u·late´ (mäj´ə-) v. adjust or vary, as the pitch of the voice —**mod´u·la´tion** n.

mod·ule (mäj´ool) n. detachable section with a special function —**mod´u·lar** a.

mo´gul n. important person

mo´hair´ n. goat-hair fabric

Mo·ham´med·an a., n. Muslim —**Mo·ham´-med·an·ism´** n.

moi´e·ty n., pl. -**ties** 1 half 2 indefinite part

moire (mwär) n. fabric with a wavy pattern: also **moi·ré** (mwä rā´)

moist a. slightly wet

mois´ten (-ən) v. make moist

mois´ture n. slight wetness

mois´tur·ize´ v. make moist —**mois´tur·iz´er** n.

mo´lar n. back tooth

mo·las´ses n. dark syrup left after sugar is refined

mold n. 1 hollow form in which a thing is shaped 2 thing shaped in it 3 furry, fungous growth —v. 1 make in a mold 2 shape 3 become moldy

mold´er v. crumble

mold´ing n. decorative strip of wood, etc.

mold´y a. -**i·er**, -**i·est** of or covered with MOLD (n. 3)

mole n. 1 small, dark, congenital spot on the skin 2 small, burrowing animal

mol´e·cule´ n. smallest particle of a substance that can exist alone —**mo·lec´u·lar** a.

mole´hill´ n. small ridge made by a burrowing mole

mole´skin´ n. strong cotton fabric with soft nap

mo·lest´ v. to trouble or harm —**mo´les·ta´tion** n.

mol´li·fy´ v. -**fied´**, -**fy´ing** soothe; make calm

mol´lusk, mol´lusc n. invertebrate with soft body in a shell

mol´ly·cod´dle v. pamper

molt v. shed hair, skin, etc. before getting a new growth

mol´ten (mōl´-) a. melted by heat

mom n. [Col.] mother

mo·ment n. brief period of, or certain point in, time

mo·men·tar´i·ly adv. 1 for a short time 2 at any moment

mo·men·tar´y a. lasting for only a moment

mo·men´tous a. very important

mo·men´tum n. impetus of a moving object

mom´my n., pl. –mies mother: child's word

mon´arch (-ərk, -ärk´) n. hereditary ruler —**mo·nar´chi·cal** (-när´ki-) a.

mon´ar·chy n., pl. –ies government by a monarch —**mon´ar·chist** n.

mon´as·ter´y n., pl. –ies residence for monks

mo·nas´tic a. of or like monks or nuns —n. monk —**mo·nas´ti·cism** n.

mon·au´ral (-ôr´əl) a. of sound reproduction using one channel

Mon´day n. second day of the week

mon´e·tar´y a. 1 of currency 2 of money

mon´ey n., pl. –eys or –ies 1 metal coins or paper notes used as the legal medium of exchange 2 wealth —**make money to** become wealthy

mon´ey·bags´ n. [Col.] rich person

mon´eyed (-ēd) a. rich

mon´ey·mak´er n. something financially profitable —**mon´ey·mak´ing** a., n.

money order n. order for payment issued at a bank, etc.

Mon´gol·oid´ n., a. (member) of the large human group including most of the Asian people

mon´goose´ n., pl. –goos´es ferretlike animal of India

mon´grel n., a. (animal or plant) of mixed breed

mon´i·tor n. 1 student who helps keep order, etc. 2 TV receiver or computer video screen —v. watch, or check on

monk n. man who is a member of an ascetic religious order

mon´key n., pl. –keys small, long-tailed primate —v. [Col.] meddle; trifle

monkey business n. [Col.] foolishness, deceit, etc.

mon´key·shines´ n.pl. [Col.] playful tricks or pranks

monkey wrench n. wrench with an adjustable jaw

monk's cloth n. heavy cloth with a weave like that of a basket

mon´o n. mononucleosis

mono- pref. one; alone

mon´o·cle n. eyeglass for one eye

mo·nog´a·my n. practice of being married to only one person at a time —**mo·nog´a·mous** a.

mon´o·gram´ n. initials of a name, made into a design

mon´o·graph´ n. book or article on a single subject

mon´o·lith´ n. pillar, statue, etc. made of a single, large stone —**mon´o·lith´ic** a.

mon´o·logue´, mon´o·log´ n. 1 long speech 2 skit for one actor only

mon´o·ma´ni·a n. excessive interest in one thing —**mon´o·ma´ni·ac´** n.

mon´o·nu´cle·o´sis n. acute viral disease with fever, tiredness, etc.

mo·nop´o·ly n., pl. –lies 1 total control of something, esp. of a product or service 2 company having this —**mo·nop´o·lis´tic** a. —**mo·nop´o·lize´** v.

mon´o·rail´ n. railway with cars on a single rail

mon´o·syl´la·ble n. word of one syllable —**mon´o·syl·lab´ic** a.

mon´o·the·ism´ n. belief that there is only one God —**mon´o·the·is´tic** a.

mon´o·tone´ n. sameness of tone, pitch, color, etc.

mo·not´o·ny n. 1 lack of variety 2 tiresome sameness —**mo·not´o·nous** a.

mon·ox´ide n. oxide with one oxygen atom per molecule

mon·sieur (mə syur´) n., pl. **mes´sieurs** (mes´ərz, mā syur´) gentleman: Fr. for Mr.

Mon·si´gnor (-sēn´yər) n. R.C.Ch. title of high rank

mon·soon´ n. wind bringing rainy season to S Asia

mon´ster n. huge or very abnormal plant or animal

mon´strous a. 1 horrible 2 huge 3 very abnormal —**mon·stros´i·ty** n., pl. –ties

mon·tage (-täzh´) n. superimposing of images, as in a movie

Mon·tes·so´ri method n. (-sôr´ē) n. method of teaching children, emphasizing training of senses

month n. any of the 12 divisions of the year

month´ly a. happening, appearing, etc. every month —n., pl. –lies monthly periodical —adv. every month

mon´u·ment n. 1 memorial statue, building, etc. 2 famous work —**mon´u·men´tal** a.

moo v., n. (make) the vocal sound of a cow

mooch [Sl.] v. get by begging, etc. —**mooch´er** n.

mood n. 1 state of mind 2 verb form to express a fact, wish, or order

mood´y adv. –i·er, –i·est 1 changing in mood 2 gloomy

moon n. body that revolves around a planet, spec. around the earth —v. look dreamy or listless —**moon´beam´** n. —**moon´light´** n.

moon′light′ing n. the holding of a second job along with a main job

moon′lit′ a. lighted by the moon

moon′scape′ n. surface of the moon

moon′shine′ n. 1 moonlight 2 [Col.] whiskey made illegally —**moon′shin′er** n.

moon′shot′ n. launching of a spacecraft to the moon

moon′stone′ n. milky-white gem

moon′struck′ a. 1 crazed 2 romantically dreamy

moon′walk′ n. a walking about on the moon's surface

Moor n. Muslim of NW Africa —**Moor′ish** a.

moor n. open wasteland —v. to secure by cables, ropes, etc.

moor′ings n.pl. cables, or place, for mooring a ship

moose n., pl. **moose** largest animal of the deer family

moot a. debatable

mop n. rags, sponge, etc. on a stick, as for washing floors —v. **mopped, mop′ping** clean up, as with a mop

mope v. be gloomy

mo′ped′ n. bicycle with a small motor

mop′pet n. [Col.] little child

mo-raine′ (-rān′) n. heap of rocks, etc. left by a glacier

mor′al a. 1 of or dealing with right and wrong 2 good; virtuous 3 giving sympathy, but no active help —n. 1 moral lesson 2 pl. moral rules or standards —**mor′al·ly** adv.

mo-rale′ (-ral′) n. degree of courage, discipline, etc.

mo-ral′i·ty n. 1 moral quality 2 virtue

mor′al·ize′ v. discuss moral questions —**mor′al·ist** n.

mo-rass′ n. bog; swamp

mor′a·to′ri·um n. authorized delay or stopping of some activity

mo′ray (eel) n. voracious eel

mor′bid a. 1 diseased 2 gloomy or unwholesome —**mor-bid′i·ty** n.

mor′dant a. sarcastic

more a., n. 1 greater (in) amount or degree 2 (something) additional —adv. 1 to a greater degree 2 in addition —**more or less** somewhat

more-o′ver adv. besides

mo-res (môr′ēz′, -āz′) n.pl. customs with the force of law

morgue (môrg) n. place where bodies of accident victims, etc. are taken, as for autopsy

mor′i·bund′ a. dying

morn n. [Poet.] morning

morn′ing n. first part of the day, till noon

morning glory n. vine with trumpet-shaped flowers

morning sickness n. nausea during pregnancy

mo-roc′co n. fine, soft leather made of goatskin

mo′ron′ n. person who is mentally somewhat deficient —**mo·ron′ic** a.

mo-rose′ (-rōs′) a. gloomy

mor′phine′ (-fēn′) n. opium drug used to relieve pain

mor-phol′o·gy n. form and structure, as in biology

mor′row n. [Poet.] 1 morning 2 the following day

Morse code n. code of dots and dashes used in telegraphy

mor′sel n. bit, as of food

mor′tal a. 1 that must die 2 causing death 3 very great; extreme —n. human being —**mor′tal·ly** adv.

mor·tal′i·ty n. 1 a being mortal 2 death rate

mor′tar n. 1 bowl for pulverizing things with a pestle 2 small cannon 3 cement mixture used between bricks, etc.

mor′tar·board′ n. 1 square board for carrying mortar 2 academic cap with square, flat top

mort′gage (môr′gij) n. deed pledging property as security for a debt —v. pledge (property) in a mortgage

mor·ti′cian (-tish′ən) n. undertaker

mor′ti·fy′ v. **-fied′, -fy′ing** 1 shame; humiliate 2 control (desires) by fasting, etc. —**mor′ti·fi·ca′tion** n.

mor·tise (môrt′is) n. hole cut for a tenon to fit in

mor′tu·ar′y (-chōō-) n., pl. **-ies** place to keep dead bodies before burial

mo-sa′ic (-zā′-) n. design made of colored stones inlaid in mortar

mo′sey (-zē) v. [Sl.] amble along

Mos′lem (mäz′-) n., a. Muslim

mosque (mäsk) n. Muslim place of worship

mos·qui·to (mə skēt′ō) n., pl. **-toes** or **-tos** small biting insect that sucks blood

moss n. tiny green plant growing in clusters on rocks, etc. —**moss′y** a.

moss′back′ n. 1 turtle's back covered with algae 2 [Col.] conservative person

most a. 1 greatest in amount or number 2 almost all —n. the greatest amount or number —adv. to the greatest degree —**make the most of** take full advantage of

most′ly adv. 1 mainly; chiefly 2 usually; generally

mote n. speck, as of dust

mo-tel′ n. roadside hotel for motorists

moth n. four-winged insect like a butterfly

moth′ball′ n. small ball of crystalline substance: its fumes repel moths

moth′er n. 1 female parent 2 woman head

of a convent: in full **mother superior** —*a.*
1 of or like a mother 2 native —*v.* be a
mother to —**moth'er·hood'** *n.* —**moth'er·**
ly *a.*

moth'er-in-law' *n., pl.* **moth'ers-** mother of
one's husband or wife

moth'er·land' *n.* one's native land

moth'er-of-pearl' *n.* hard, shiny lining of
some shells

mo·tif' (-tēf') *n.* main theme of an artistic
work

mo·tile (-til) *a.* that can move —**mo·til'i·ty**
n.

mo·tion *n.* 1 a moving; change of position
2 gesture 3 proposal made at a meeting
—*v.* make, or direct by, gestures —**mo'**
tion·less *a.*

motion picture *n.* a FILM (*n.* 3)

mo'ti·vate' *v.* provide with motive —**mo'ti·**
va'tion *n.* —**mo'ti·va'tor** *n.*

mo'tive *n.* reason for doing something
—*adv.* of motion

mot'ley *a.* of many different elements; varied

mo'to-cross' *n.* cross-country motorcycle
race

mo'tor *n.* 1 machine using electricity to
make something work 2 engine; esp., a
gasoline engine —*a.* 1 of or run by a motor 2 of or for motor vehicles 3 producing motion 4 of muscular movements —*v.*
to travel in an automobile —**mo'tor·ist**
n.

mo'tor·bike' *n.* [Col.] 1 bicycle with motor
2 light motorcycle

mo'tor·boat' *n.* boat propelled by a motor

mo'tor·cade' *n.* procession of cars

mo'tor·car' *n.* automobile

mo'tor·cy'cle *n.* two-wheeled, engine-
powered vehicle

mo'tor·ize' *v.* equip with a motor or motor vehicles

motor vehicle *n.* car, truck, bus, etc.

mot'tle *v.* to blotch

mot'to *n., pl.* **-toes** or **-tos** maxim or phrase,
as used on seals, coins, etc., that shows
one's ideals, etc.

mould (mōld) *n., v.* chiefly Br. sp. of MOLD
—**mould'y** *a.*, **-i·er, -i·est**

moult (mōlt) *v.* chiefly Br. sp. of MOLT

mound *n.* heap of earth, etc.

mount *v.* 1 climb; go up 2 get up on 3 increase in amount 4 fix on or in a mounting
—*n.* 1 act of mounting 2 horse to ride 3
mounting 4 mountain

moun'tain *n.* very high rise of land on
earth's surface

moun'tain·eer' *n.* 1 mountain dweller 2
mountain climber

mountain goat *n.* long-haired antelope of
Rocky Mountains

mountain lion *n.* cougar

moun'tain·ous *a.* 1 full of mountains 2 very
big

moun'te·bank' *n.* charlatan

mount'ed *a.* 1 with a mounting 2 on horseback

Mount'ie, Mount'y *n., pl.* **-ies** [Col.] member of the Royal Canadian Mounted Po-
lice

mount'ing *n.* a backing, support, setting,
etc.

mourn (môrn) *v.* feel or show grief or sorrow
(for) —**mourn'er** *n.* —**mourn'ful** *a.*

mourn'ing *n.* 1 grief at a death 2 mourners'
black clothes

mouse (mous) *n., pl.* **mice** 1 small rodent 2
timid person 3 hand-held device for controlling images on a computer video screen
—**mous'y, mous'ey** *a.*, **-i·er, -i·est**

mousse (mōōs) *n.* chilled dessert of egg,
gelatin, etc.

mous'tache' *n.* mustache

mouth (mouth; *v.*: mouth) *n.* 1 opening in
the face for food 2 any opening —*v.* form
(words) with the mouth soundlessly
—**mouth'ful'** *n.*

mouth organ *n.* harmonica

mouth'piece' *n.* 1 part held in or near the
mouth 2 spokesman for another

mouth'wash' *n.* liquid for rinsing the
mouth

mouth'wa'ter·ing *a.* tasty

mouth'y *a.*, **-i·er, -i·est** talkative

mou·ton (mōō'tän') *n.* lamb fur made to
resemble beaver, etc.

move *v.* 1 change the place of 2 set or keep
in motion 3 change one's residence 4 be
active or take action 5 cause 6 stir emotionally 7 propose (a resolution) —*n.* 1
movement or action 2 *Games* one's turn
—**mov'a·ble, move'a·ble** *a.*, **-er.** —**mov'er**
n.

move'ment *n.* 1 a moving or way of moving 2 action toward a goal 3 moving parts
of a clock, etc. 4 *Mus.* main division of a
composition

mov'ie *n.* a FILM (*n.* 3) —**the movies** 1 film
industry 2 a showing of a film

mow (mō) *v.* **mowed, mowed** or **mown, mow'**
ing 1 cut down (grass) 2 kill; knock down
—**mow'er** *n.*

mow (mou) *n.* heap of hay, esp. in a barn

moz'za·rel'la (mät'sə-) *n.* soft, white
cheese with mild flavor

Mr. title used before a man's name

Mrs. title used before a married woman's
name

Ms. (miz) title used instead of *Miss* or *Mrs.*

much a. **more**, **most** great in quantity, degree, etc. —adv. 1 greatly 2 nearly —n. 1 great amount 2 something great

mu·ci·lage (myōō′si lij′) n. gluey or gummy adhesive

muck n. 1 black earth 2 dirt; filth

muck′rake′ v. expose corruption in politics and business —**muck′rak′er** n.

mu′cous (myōō′-) a. 1 of or secreting mucus 2 slimy

mucous membrane n. membrane lining body cavities

mu′cus n. slimy secretion of mucous membranes

mud n. soft, wet earth

mud′dle v. 1 mix up; confuse 2 act confusedly —n. mess, confusion, etc.

mud′dle·head′ed a. confused

mud′dy a. **-di·er**, **-di·est** 1 full of or covered with mud 2 clouded or obscure —v. **-died**, **-dy·ing** make or become muddy

mud′sling′ing n. unfair verbal attack

mu·ez′zin (myōō-) n. crier calling Muslims to prayer

muff n. cylindrical covering to warm the hands —v. bungle; miss

muf′fin n. bread baked in a small cupcake mold

muf′fle v. 1 wrap up warmly 2 deaden (sound), as on an automobile

muf′fler n. 1 thick scarf 2 device to deaden noise, as on an automobile

muf′ti n. civilian clothes

mug n. 1 heavy drinking cup 2 face 3 official photograph of a criminal or suspect: in full **mug shot**

mug′gy a. **-gi·er**, **-gi·est** hot and humid

muk′luk′ n. Eskimo boot

mu·lat·to (mə lat′ō) n., pl. **-toes** or **-tos** one with a black parent and a white parent

mul′ber′ry n., pl. **-ries** tree with berrylike fruit

mulch v., n. (use) a cover of leaves, peat, etc. around plants

mulct (mulkt) v. take from by fraud

mule n. 1 offspring of a male donkey and a female horse 2 lounging slipper

mul′ish (myōō′-) a. stubborn

mull v. 1 ponder 2 heat and flavor, as wine

mul′lein (-in) n. tall plant with downy leaves

mul′let n. an edible fish

mul′li·gan stew n. meat stew

mul′li·ga·taw′ny n. meat soup flavored with curry

mul′lion (-yən) n. vertical bar between windowpanes

multi– pref. of or having many or several

mul′ti·far′i·ous a. of many kinds; varied

mul′ti·ple a. having many parts, etc. —n. product of two numbers, one specified

mul′ti·ple-choice′ a. listing several answers to choose from

multiple sclerosis n. disease of nervous system

mul′ti·plex′ a. of a system for combining signals sent over one circuit, etc.

mul′ti·pli·cand′ n. the number to be multiplied by another

mul′ti·plic′i·ty (-plis′-) n. great number

mul′ti·ply′ n. **-plied′**, **-ply′ing** 1 to increase in number, degree, etc. 2 find the product (of) by adding a certain number a certain number of times —**mul′ti·pli·ca′tion** n. —**mul′ti·pli′er** n.

mul′ti·stage′ a. operating by successive propulsion systems, as a missile or rocket

mul′ti·tude′ n. large number

mul′ti·tu′di·nous a. many

mum n. [Col.] chrysanthemum —a. silent

mum′ble v. speak or say indistinctly —n. mumbled utterance

mum′bo jum′bo n. meaningless ritual or talk

mum′mer n. actor, esp. one with a mask or disguise

mum′mer·y n., pl. **-ies** foolish ritual; false show

mum′mi·fy′ v. **-fied′**, **-fy′ing** make into or become a mummy

mum′my n., pl. **-mies** ancient embalmed body

mumps n. disease in which the salivary glands swell

munch v. chew noisily

mun′dane′ a. of the world

mu·nic′i·pal (-nis′-) a. of a city or town

mu·nic′i·pal′i·ty n., pl. **-ties** city or town having its own local government

mu·nif′i·cent a. very generous —**mu·nif′i·cence** n.

mu·ni′tions n.pl. weapons and ammunition for war

mu·ral (myoor′əl) a. of or on a wall —n. picture painted on a wall

mur′der v. kill (a person) unlawfully and with malice —n. act of murdering —**mur′der·er** n.

mur′der·ous a. 1 of or like murder 2 guilty of, or ready to, murder

murk n. darkness; gloom —**murk′y** a., **-i·er**, **-i·est**

mur′mur n. 1 low, steady sound 2 mumbled complaint —v. 1 make a murmur 2 say in a low voice

mur′rain (-in) n. a plague, esp. of cattle

mus′ca·tel′ n. wine made from kind of sweet grape (**mus′cat**)

mus′cle (-əl) n. 1 tissue forming the fleshy

parts that move the body **2** any single part of this tissue **3** strength

mus´cle-bound´ a. having some muscles enlarged and less elastic

mus´cu·lar a. **1** of or done by muscle **2** strong

muscular dys·tro·phy (dis´trə fē) n. disease in which muscles waste away

mus´cu·la·ture (-chər) n. muscular system of a body, limb, etc.

muse v. think deeply —n. spirit inspiring an artist

mu·se´um n. place for displaying artistic, historical, or scientific objects

mush n. **1** thick, soft mass **2** boiled cornmeal **3** [Col.] maudlin sentimentality —int. shout urging on sled dogs —v. travel over snow —**mush´y** a., **-i·er**, **-i·est**

mush´room´ n. fleshy, umbrella-shaped fungus, often edible —v. grow rapidly

mu´sic n. **1** songs, symphonies, etc. **2** art of composing or performing these

mu´si·cal a. of, fond of, or set to music —n. play or film with singing and dancing —**mu´si·cal·ly** adv.

mu´si·cale´ (-kal´) n. social affair with musical program

mu·si´cian (-zish´ən) n. person skilled in music

mu´si·col´o·gy n. study of history and forms of music —**mu´si·col´o·gist** n.

musk n. strong-smelling animal secretion, used in perfumes —**musk´y** a., **-i·er**, **-i·est**

mus´kel·lunge´ n. large, edible pike: also **mus´kie**

mus´ket n. long gun —**mus´ket·eer´** n.

musk´mel´on n. cantaloupe

musk´rat´ n. water rodent

Mus´lim (muz´-, mooz´-) n. follower of the religion of Mohammed —a. of Islam or Muslims

mus´lin (muz´-) n. strong cotton cloth, as for sheets

muss v. make messy —n. [Col.] mess —**muss´y** a.

mus´sel n. bivalve mollusk

must v. auxiliary verb showing: **1** obligation **2** probability **3** certainty —n. [Col.] thing that must be done

mus·tache´ (-tash´) n. hair grown out on the upper lip of men

mus´tang´ n. small, wild horse

mus´tard n. yellow, spicy powder or paste

mus´ter v. **1** to bring or come together, as troops **2** summon —n. a mustering

mus´ty a. **-ti·er**, **-ti·est** stale and moldy

mu·ta·ble a. changeable

mu´tant n. animal or plant different from parents

mu·ta´tion n. a change, esp. a sudden variation in a plant or animal —**mu´tate´** v.

mute a. **1** silent **2** not able to speak —n. **1** one unable to speak; spec., a deaf-mute **2** device to mute a musical instrument —v. soften the sound of

mu´ti·late´ v. cut off or damage part of

mu´ti·ny n., pl. **-nies**; v. **-nied**, **-ny·ing** revolt, as against one's military superiors —**mu´ti·neer´** n. —**mu´ti·nous** a.

mutt n. [Sl.] mongrel dog

mut´ter v. **1** speak or say in low, indistinct tones **2** grumble —n. muttered utterance

mut´ton n. flesh of (grown) sheep used as food

mu´tu·al (-chōō-) a. **1** of or for one another **2** in common —**mu´tu·al·ly** adv.

muu·muu (mōō´mōō´) n. long, loose Hawaiian dress

muz´zle n. **1** snout **2** device for an animal's mouth to prevent biting **3** front end of a gun barrel —v. **1** put a muzzle on **2** prevent from talking

my a. of me

my·e·li´tis (mī´ə līt´is) n. inflammation of bone marrow or spinal cord

my´na, my´nah n. Asian starling

my·o´pi·a n. nearsightedness —**my·op´ic** (-äp´-) a.

myr´i·ad (mir´-) n. great number —a. very many

myrrh (mur) n. resin used in incense, perfume, etc.

myr´tle n. **1** evergreen shrub **2** creeping evergreen plant

my·self´ pron. intensive or reflexive form of I

mys´ter·y n., pl. **-ies 1** unexplained or unknown thing **2** obscurity or secrecy —**mys·te´ri·ous** a.

mys´tic a. **1** of mysticism **2** occult or mysterious —n. believer in mysticism

mys´ti·cal a. **1** spiritually symbolic **2** mystic

mys´ti·cism´ n. belief that God can be known directly

mys´ti·fy´ v. **-fied´**, **-fy´ing** perplex or puzzle —**mys´ti·fi·ca´tion** n.

mys·tique´ (-tēk´) n. mystical or fascinating quality of a person, etc.

myth n. **1** traditional story explaining some phenomenon **2** fictitious person or thing —**myth´i·cal** a.

my·thol´o·gy n., pl. **-gies 1** study of myths **2** myths of a certain people —**myth´o·log´i·cal** a.

N

nab v. [Col.] seize or arrest

na·bob (nā′bäb′) n. very rich or important person

na·cre (nā′kər) n. mother-of-pearl

na′dir n. lowest point

nag v. **nagged, nag′ging** scold or urge constantly —n. 1 one who nags 2 inferior horse

nai·ad (nā′ad, nī′-) n. in myths, nymphs living in water

nail n. 1 horny layer at the ends of the fingers and toes 2 narrow, pointed piece of metal driven into pieces of wood to hold them —v. fasten as with nails

na·ive, na·ïve (nä ēv′) a. innocent; simple —**na·ive·té′, na·ïve·té′** (-tā′) n.

na′ked a. 1 without clothing or covering 2 plain

nam′by-pam′by a.; n., pl. **–bies** insipid, indecisive (person)

name n. 1 word or words for a person, thing, or place 2 reputation —a. well-known —v. 1 give a name to 2 mention or identify by name 3 appoint

name′less a. 1 without a name 2 obscure; vague

name′ly adv. that is to say

name′sake′ n. person named after another

nan′ny goat n. female goat

nap v. **napped, nap′ping** sleep briefly —n. 1 short sleep 2 fuzzy surface of fibers on cloth

na′palm′ (-päm′) n. jellylike gasoline used in bombs, etc.

nape n. back of the neck

naph′tha (naf′-, nap′-) n. oily liquid used as a solvent, etc.

naph′tha·lene′ n. crystalline substance made from coal tar

nap′kin n. small piece of paper or cloth to protect clothes while eating

narc n. [Sl.] police agent enforcing narcotics laws

nar′cis·sism′ (-sə-) n. self-love —**nar′cis·sist** n.

nar·cis′sus (-sis′-) n. flowering bulbous plant

nar·cot′ic n. drug that causes deep sleep and lessens pain —a. of or like a narcotic

nar′rate′ v. tell a story —**nar′ra′tor** n.

nar·ra′tion n. 1 a narrating 2 a narrative

nar′ra·tive a. in story form —n. story; account

nar′row a. 1 not wide 2 intolerant 3 limited in size, degree, etc. —v. lessen in width, extent, etc.

nar′row-mind′ed a. bigoted

nar·whal (när′wəl) n. small whale with a long tusk

nar′y a. [Dial.] used in **nary a**, not any

na′sal (-zəl) a. of or through the nose

na′sal·ize′ v. speak with nasal sound —**na′sal·i·za′tion** n.

nas′cent (or nā′sənt) a. starting to be or develop

nas·tur′tium (-shəm) n. yellowish-red flower

nas′ty a. **–ti·er, –ti·est** 1 dirty 2 obscene 3 unpleasant; mean —**nas′ti·ly** adv. —**nas′ti·ness** n.

na′tal a. of (one's) birth

na′tion n. 1 a people with history, language, etc. in common 2 people under one government

na′tion·al a. of a whole nation —n. citizen

na′tion·al·ism′ n. 1 patriotism 2 advocacy of national independence —**na′tion·al·ist** a., n. —**na′tion·al·is′tic** a.

na′tion·al′i·ty n., pl. **–ties** nation, esp. of one's birth or citizenship

na′tion·al·ize′ v. transfer control of to a government —**na′tion·al·i·za′tion** n.

na′tion·wide′ a. throughout the whole nation

na′tive a. 1 belonging to a region or country by birth, source, etc. 2 being or of the place of one's birth 3 inborn —n. native person, animal, or plant

na′tive-born′ a. born in a specified place

na·tiv′i·ty n. birth

nat′ty a. **–ti·er, –ti·est** neat and stylish

nat′u·ral (nach′-) a. 1 of or dealing with nature 2 not artificial 3 innate 4 lifelike; usual 5 to be expected 6 Mus. neither sharp nor flat —**nat′u·ral·ly** adv.

natural childbirth n. childbirth without anesthesia but with prior training

natural history n. study of nature

nat′u·ral·ism′ n. art or writing about people and things as they really are

nat′u·ral·ist n. one who studies plants and animals

nat′u·ral·ize′ v. confer citizenship upon (an alien) —**nat′u·ral·i·za′tion** n.

natural resources n.pl. coal, oil, water power, etc.

natural sciences n.pl. biology, chemistry, physics, etc.

na′ture n. 1 basic quality of a thing 2 inborn character 3 kind; sort 4 physical universe or [also N–] its forces 5 natural scenery

naught (nôt) n. 1 nothing 2 zero

naugh′ty a. **–ti·er, –ti·est** 1 mischievous 2

not nice or proper —**naugh'ti·ly** adv.
—**naugh'ti·ness** n.

nau·sea (-shə, -zhə) n. 1 feeling of wanting to vomit 2 disgust —**nau'se·ate'** (-shē-, -zē-) v. —**nau'seous** a.

nau'ti·cal a. of sailors, ships, or navigation

nautical mile n. unit of linear measure used in navigation, equal to c. 6,076 ft.

nau'ti·lus n. tropical mollusk

na'val a. of or for a navy, its ships, etc.

nave n. main, long part of some churches

na'vel n. small, abdominal scar where the umbilical cord was attached

nav'i·ga·ble a. 1 wide or deep enough for ship travel 2 that can be steered

nav'i·gate' v. 1 travel through or on (air, sea, etc.) in a ship or aircraft 2 steer (a ship, etc.) —**nav'i·ga'tion** n. —**nav'i·ga'tor** n.

na'vy n., pl. **-vies** 1 entire fleet of warships, etc. of a nation 2 very dark blue: also **navy blue**

navy bean n. small, white bean

nay n. 1 denial 2 negative vote or voter

Na·zi (nät'sē) n., a. (adherent) of the German fascist party (1933-45) —**Na'zism'** n.

NC-17 trademark film rating indicating no one under 17 may be admitted

neap tide n. lowest high tide, occurring twice a month

near adv. at a short distance —a. 1 close in distance, time, etc. 2 intimate 3 stingy —v. to draw near to —prep. close to —**near'ness** n.

near'by' a., adv. near; close at hand

near'ly adv. almost

near miss n. result that is not quite successful

near'sight'ed a. seeing only near objects distinctly

neat a. 1 tidy; clean 2 skillful 3 trim in form —**neat'ly** adv. —**neat'ness** n.

neb'u·la n., pl. **-lae** (-lē') or **-las** cloudlike patch seen in the night sky —**neb'u·lar** a.

neb'u·lous a. vague

nec'es·sar'i·ly adv. 1 because of necessity 2 as a necessary result

nec'es·sar'y a. 1 that must be had or done; essential 2 inevitable —n., pl. **-ies** necessary thing

ne·ces'si·tate' v. make (something) necessary

ne·ces'si·ty n., pl. **-ties** 1 great need 2 something necessary 3 poverty

neck n. 1 part that joins the head to the body 2 narrow part, as of a bottle —v. [Sl.] to hug, kiss, and caress passionately —**neck and neck** very close as to outcome

neck'er·chief n. kerchief worn around the neck

neck'lace (-ləs) n. chain of gold, beads, etc. worn around the neck

neck'tie' n. decorative neck band worn with a shirt

neck'wear' n. neckties, scarves, etc.

ne·crol'o·gy (ne-) n. list of people who have died

ne·cro'sis n. death or decay of tissue in some body part

nec'tar n. 1 sweet liquid in flowers 2 delicious drink

nec'tar·ine' (-tə rēn') n. smooth-skinned peach

nee, née (nā) a. born

need n. 1 lack of something required; also, the thing lacking 2 poverty or distress —v. 1 have need of 2 to be obliged Need is also used as an auxiliary verb —**if need be** if it is required

need'ful a. necessary

nee'dle n. 1 a very slender, pointed piece, as for sewing, knitting, playing phonograph records, etc. 2 anything needleshaped —v. [Col.] goad; tease

nee'dle·point' n. embroidery of woolen threads on canvas

need'less a. unnecessary

nee'dle·work' n. sewing, embroidery, crocheting, etc.

need'y a. **-i·er, -i·est** very poor; destitute

ne'er (ner) adv. [Poet.] never

ne'er'-do-well' a., n. lazy and irresponsible (person)

ne·far'i·ous (-fer'-) a. very wicked

ne·gate' v. deny or nullify —**ne·ga'tion** n.

neg'a·tive a. 1 saying "no" 2 not positive 3 of the electricity made by friction on resin 4 being less than zero —n. 1 a negative word, reply, etc. 2 battery plate of lower potential 3 photographic plate or film in which light and shadow are reversed

ne·glect' v. 1 fail to do 2 fail to care for properly —n. a neglecting —**ne·glect'ful** a.

neg'li·gee' (-zhā') n. woman's dressing gown

neg'li·gent a. habitually careless —**neg'li·gence** n.

neg'li·gi·ble a. trivial

ne·go'ti·ate' (-shē āt') v. 1 discuss so as to agree on 2 arrange for (a loan, etc.) 3 transfer or sell 4 move across —**ne·go'ti·a·ble** a. —**ne·go'ti·a'tion** n. —**ne·go'ti·a'tor** n.

Ne'gro a., n., pl. **-groes** (of) a member of dark-skinned peoples of Africa, or a person having African ancestors; black —**Ne'groid'** a.

neigh (nā) v., n. (utter) the cry of a horse

neigh′bor n. 1 one that lives or is near another 2 fellow human being —a. nearby —v. live or be near

neigh′bor·hood′ n. one part of a city or the people in it —in the neighborhood of [Col.] near or nearly

neigh′bor·ly a. friendly

nei′ther (nē′-, nī′-) a., pron. not one or the other (of two) —con. correlative used with nor

nem′e·sis n. inevitable cause of one's downfall or defeat

neo— pref. new; recent

ne′o·co·lo′ni·al·ism′ n. exploiting of a supposedly independent region by a foreign power

ne·ol′o·gism′ (-äl′ə jiz′ əm) n. new word

ne′on′ n. inert gas used in electric signs, a chemical element

ne′o·phyte′ (-fīt′) n. novice

ne′o·plasm′ (-plaz′ əm)n. abnormal growth of tissue, as a tumor

neph′ew (nef′yōō) n. 1 son of one's brother or sister 2 son of one's brother-in-law or sister-in-law

ne·phri′tis (-frīt′is) n. inflammation of the kidneys

nep′o·tism′ n. giving of jobs, etc. to relatives

nerd n. [Sl.] one regarded as dull, ineffective, etc.

nerve n. 1 cordlike fiber carrying impulses to and from the brain 2 courage 3 pl. nervousness 4 [Col.]impudence —get on someone's nerves [Col.] make someone nervous or annoyed

nerve center n. 1 group of nerve cells working together 2 headquarters

nerve gas n. poisonous liquid that paralyzes: used in warfare

nerve′-rack′ing a. very trying to one's composure or patience: also sp. **nerve′-wrack′ing**

nerv′ous a. 1 of nerves 2 easily upset; restless 3 fearful —**nerv′ous·ness** n.

nervous system n. all the nerve cells and nervous tissues of an organism

nerv′y a. **-i·er, -i·est** 1 bold 2 [Col.] impudent; brazen

-ness suf. quality; state

nest n. 1 place where a bird or other animal raises its young 2 cozy place 3 set of things in increasing sizes —v. make a nest

nest egg n. money put aside

nes′tle (-əl) v. 1 settle down or hold close for comfort 2 lie sheltered

net n. 1 openwork fabric as of string, for snaring fish, etc. 2 fine net to hold the hair 3 netlike cloth 4 net amount —a. left over after deductions, etc. —v. net′ted, net′ting 1 to snare 2 to gain

neth′er a. under

net′ting n. net fabric

net′tle n. weed with stinging hairs —v. annoy

net′work′ n. 1 arrangement of wires or threads as in a net 2 system of roads, computers, etc. 3 chain of radio or TV stations

neu′ral (noor′əl, nur′-) a. of a nerve or nerves

neu·ral′gi·a (-jə) n. pain along a nerve path

neu·ri′tis (-rīt′is) n. inflammation of nerves —**neu·rit′ic** a.

neuro— pref. of nerves

neu·rol′o·gy n. branch of medicine dealing with the nervous system —**neu·rol′o·gist** n.

neu′ron′ n. nerve cell and its processes

neu·ro′sis n., pl. **-ses′** (-sēz′) mental disorder with abnormally intense anxieties, obsessions, etc. —**neu·rot′ic** a., n.

neu′ter a. neither masculine nor feminine —v. castrate or spay (an animal)

neu′tral a. 1 supporting neither side in a war or quarrel 2 not one or the other 3 having no decided color —n. 1 neutral nation, etc. 2 position of disengaged gears —**neu·tral′i·ty** n.

neu′tral·ize′ v. counteract the effectiveness of

neu′tron′ n. uncharged particle of an atom

nev′er adv. 1 at no time 2 in no way

nev′er·the·less′ adv., con. in spite of that; however

new a. 1 appearing, thought of, made, etc. for the first time 2 unfamiliar or foreign 3 fresh 4 unused 5 modern; recent 6 more 7 beginning again —adv. 1 again 2 recently

new blood n. new people as a source of new ideas, vigor, etc.

new′born′ a. 1 just born 2 reborn

new′com′er n. recent arrival

new′fan′gled a. new and strange

new′ly adv. recently

new′ly·wed′ n. recently married person

news n. 1 new information 2 (reports of) recent events

news′boy′ n. boy who sells or delivers newspapers

news′cast′ n. radio or TV news broadcast —**news′cast′er** n.

news′let′ter n. special group's news bulletin, issued regularly

news′man′ n., pl. **-men′** male newscaster or reporter —**news′wom′an** n., pl. **-wom′en**

news′pa′per n. daily or weekly news publication

news'print' n. cheap paper used for newspapers, etc.

news'stand' n. a stand for the sale of newspapers, etc.

news'wor'thy a. timely and important or interesting

news'y a. **-i·er, -i·est** [Col.] having much news

newt n. small salamander

New Testament second part of the Christian Bible

next a. nearest; closest —adv. in the nearest time, place, etc.

next'-door' a. in or at the next house, building, etc.

nex'us n., pl. **-us·es** or **-us** connection or link

ni'a·cin n. nicotinic acid

nib n. 1 bird's beak 2 (pen) point

nib'ble v. eat with quick, small bites —n. small bite

nice a. 1 pleasant, kind, good, etc. 2 precise; accurate 3 refined —**nice'ly** adv.

ni'ce·ty n., pl. **-ties** 1 accuracy 2 refinement 3 small detail; fine point 4 something choice or dainty

niche (nich) n. 1 recess in a wall for a statue, etc. 2 especially suitable position

nick v. make a small cut, chip, etc. in or on —n. small cut, chip, etc. —**in the nick of time** exactly when needed

nick'el n. 1 rust-resistant metal, a chemical element 2 nickel and copper coin worth 5 cents

nick'name' n. 1 a substitute name, as "Slim" 2 familiar form of a proper name, as "Bob" —v. give a nickname to

nic'o·tine' (-tēn') n. poisonous liquid in tobacco leaves

nic'o·tin'ic acid (-tin'-) n. member of the vitamin B complex

niece (nēs) n. 1 daughter of one's sister or brother 2 daughter of one's sister-in-law or brother-in-law

nig'gard·ly a. stingy; miserly

nigh (nī) adv., a., prep. [Dial.] near

night n. period of darkness between sunset and sunrise —**night'time'** n.

night blindness n. poor vision in near darkness or dim light

night'cap' n. 1 cap worn in bed 2 [Col.] alcoholic drink taken just before bedtime

night clothes n.pl. clothes to be worn in bed, as pajamas

night'club' n. place for eating, drinking, dancing, etc. at night

night crawl'er n. large earthworm that comes to the surface at night

night'fall' n. close of the day

night'gown' n. sleeping gown for women and children

night'hawk' n. 1 night bird 2 night owl

night'ie n. [Col.] nightgown

night'in·gale' n. a European thrush that sings at night

night life n. pleasure-seeking activity at night, as in nightclubs

night'ly a., adv. (done or happening) every night

night'mare' n. frightening dream or experience

night owl n. one who stays up late

night'shade' n. belladonna or related plant

night'shirt' n. shirtlike nightgown, esp. for men

night'spot' n. [Col.] nightclub

night stand n. small bedside table

night stick n. long, heavy club carried by a policeman

night'time' n. night

ni·hil·ism (nī'ə liz'əm, nē'-) n. general rejection of usual beliefs in morality, religion, etc. —**ni'hil·ist** n.

nil n. nothing

nim'ble a. quick in movement or thought —**nim'bly** adv.

nim'bus n. 1 rain cloud 2 halo

nin'com·poop' n. fool

nine a., n. one more than eight —**ninth** a., n.

nine'teen' a., n. nine more than ten —**nine'teenth'** a., n.

nine'ty a., n., pl. **-ties** nine times ten —**nine'ti·eth** a., n.

nin'ja n. in former times, a trained Japanese assassin

nin'ny n., pl. **-nies** a fool

nip v. **nipped, nip'ping** 1 pinch or bite 2 pinch off 3 spoil, as by frost —n. 1 stinging cold 2 small drink of liquor —**nip and tuck** very close as to outcome

nip'per n. 1 pl. pliers, pincers, etc. 2 claw of a crab or lobster

nip'ple n. 1 protuberance on a breast or udder 2 thing shaped like this

nip'py a. **-pi·er, -pi·est** sharp; biting

nir·va'na (-vä'-) n. Buddhism perfect, passionless bliss

nit n. egg of a louse

ni'ter n. salt used in explosives, fertilizer, etc.: also, Br. sp., **ni'tre**

nit'-pick'ing n. a fussy —**nit'pick'er** n.

ni'trate' n. salt of nitric acid

ni'tric acid n. corrosive acid containing nitrogen

ni'tro·cel'lu·lose' (-yōō lōs') n. pulplike substance, used in making explosives, etc.

ni'tro·gen n. colorless, odorless gas, a chemical element —**ni·trog'e·nous** (-träj'-) a.

ni'tro·glyc'er·in, ni'tro·glyc'er·ine (-glis'-

ər in) *n.* thick, explosive oil, used in dynamite

nit·ty-grit·ty *n.* [Sl.] basic facts, issues, etc.

nit'wit' *n.* stupid person

nix *int.* [Sl.] no! stop!

no *adv.* 1 not at all 2 not so —*a.* not a —*n.*, *pl.* **noes** 1 refusal 2 negative vote

no·bil'i·ty *n.*, *pl.* **–ties** 1 noble state or rank 2 people of noble rank

no'ble *a.* 1 highly moral 2 grand; splendid 3 of high hereditary rank —*n.* person of high rank —**no'ble·man** *n.*, *pl.* **–men** —**no'bly** *adv.*

no'bod·y *pron.* no one —*n.*, *pl.* **–ies** unimportant person

noc·tur'nal *a.* 1 of the night 2 done, happening, etc. at night

noc·turne' *n.* romantic musical composition

nod *v.* **nod'ded, nod'ding** 1 bend the head quickly 2 show (assent) thus 3 let the head fall forward in dozing —*n.* a nodding

node *n.* 1 knob; swelling 2 point on a stem from which a leaf grows

nod·ule (näj'ōōl') *n.* small knot or rounded lump

No·el, No·ël (nō el') *n.* Christmas

no'-fault' *a.* of car insurance paying for damages without blame being fixed

nog'gin *n.* [Col.] the head

no'-good' *a.* [Sl.] despicable

noise *n.* sound, esp. a loud, unpleasant sound —*v.* spread (a rumor) —**noise'less** *a.*

noi'some *a.* 1 unhealthful 2 foul-smelling

nois'y *a.* **-i·er, -i·est** 1 making noise 2 full of noise —**nois'i·ly** *adv.* —**nois'i·ness** *n.*

no'mad' *n.* 1 member of a wandering tribe 2 wanderer —**no·mad'ic** *a.*

no'men·cla'ture (-klā'chər) *n.* system of names

nom'i·nal *a.* 1 in name only 2 relatively small —**nom'i·nal·ly** *adv.*

nom'i·nate' *v.* 1 appoint; name 2 name as a candidate —**nom'i·na'tion** *n.*

nom'i·na·tive *a.*, *n. Gram.* (in) the case of the subject of a verb

nom'i·nee' *n.* a person who is nominated

non– *pref.* not: see list below

non'ab·sorb'ent
non·ac'tive
non'ag·gres'sion
non'al·co·hol'ic
non'be·liev'er
non'com·bus'ti·ble
non'com·mer'cial
non'con·form'ist
non'con·ta'gious
non'es·sen'tial

non'ex·ist'ent
non·fac'tu·al
non·fa'tal
non·fic'tion
non·flow'er·ing
non·fly'ing
non·func'tion·al
non'in·ter·fer'ence
non'in·ter·ven'tion
non·ir'ri·tat·ing
non·ma·lig'nant
non·me·tal'lic
non·mil'i·tar·y
non'of·fi'cial
non·pay'ment
non·per'ish·a·ble
non·poi'son·ous
non·po·lit'i·cal
non·po'rous
non'pro·duc'tive
non'pro·fes'sion·al
non·prof'it·a·ble
non're·li'gious
non'res·i·den'tial
non·smok'er
non'sup·port'ing
non'sus·tain'ing
non·tax'a·ble
non·tech'ni·cal
non·tox'ic

non'age (-ij) *n.* state of being under legal age

non'a·ligned' *a.* not aligned with either side in a conflict

nonce *n.* the present time

non'cha·lant' (-shə länt') *a.* casually indifferent —**non'cha·lance'** *n.*

non'com' *n.* [Col.] noncommissioned officer

non'com·bat·ant *n.* 1 civilian in wartime 2 soldier not in combat

non'com·mis'sioned officer *n.* enlisted person in the armed forces

non'com·mit'tal *a.* not taking a definite stand

non'con·duc'tor *n.* thing that does not conduct electricity, heat, etc.

non'de·script' *a.* of no definite class or type

none (nun) *pron.* 1 no one 2 not any —*adv.* not at all

non·en'ti·ty *n.*, *pl.* **–ties** unimportant person

none'the·less' *adv.* nevertheless: also **none the less**

non·fer'rous *a.* of metals other than iron

non·met'al *n.* element that is not a metal, as carbon

non'pa·reil' (-pə rel') *a.* without equal; peerless

non'par·ti·san *a.* not of any single party, faction, etc.

non·plus′ v. –**plused′** or –**plussed′**, –**plus′ing** or –**plus′sing** thoroughly bewilder

non′prof′it a. not for profit

non′res′i·dent n., a. (person) not living in the locality of his work, etc.

non′sec·tar′i·an a. not connected with a specific religion

non′sense′ n. absurd or meaningless words or acts —**non·sen′si·cal** a.

non′ se′qui·tur (-sek′wi-) n. remark having no relation to something just said

non′stop′ a., adv. without a stop

non′sup·port′ n. failure to support a legal dependent

non·un′ion a. not belonging to, or done by, a labor union

non′vi′o·lent a. not using violence —**non′vi·o·lence** n.

noo′dle n. flat strip of dry dough

nook n. **1** corner **2** small secluded spot

noon n. twelve o'clock in the daytime; midday: also **noon′day′** or **noon′time′**

no one pron. no person

noose n. loop with a slipknot for tightening it

nor con. and not (either)

norm n. standard or model

nor′mal a. **1** usual; natural **2** average —n. what is normal; usual state —**nor′mal·cy**, **nor·mal′i·ty** n.

nor′mal·ly adv. **1** in a normal way **2** usually

north n. direction or region to the right of one facing the sunset —a., adv. in, toward, or from the north —**north′er·ly** a., adv. —**north′ern** a. —**north′ern·er** n. —**north′ward** a., adv. —**north′wards** adv.

north′east′ n. direction or region between north and east —a., adv. in, toward, or from the northeast —**north′east′er·ly** a., adv. —**north′east′ern** a. —**north′east′ward** a., adv. —**north′east′wards** adv.

northern lights n.pl. aurora borealis

North Pole northern end of the earth's axis

North Star bright star almost directly above the North Pole

north′west′ n. direction or region between north and west —a., adv. in, toward, or from the northwest —**north′west′er·ly** a., adv. —**north′west′ern** a. —**north′west′ward** a., adv. —**north′west′wards** adv.

Nor·we′gian (-jən) n., a. (native or language) of Norway

nose n. **1** part of the face with two openings for breathing and smelling **2** sense of smell **3** thing like a nose —v. **1** find, as by smell **2** push with the front forward **3** meddle (in) —**nose out** defeat narrowly

nose′bleed′ n. bleeding from the nose

nose cone n. foremost part of a rocket or missile

nose dive n. **1** swift downward plunge of an airplane, nose first **2** sharp drop, as of prices

nose drops n. medication put into the nose in drops

nose′gay′ n. bunch of flowers

nos·tal′gi·a (-jə) n. a longing for something past or far away —**nos·tal′gic** a.

nos′tril n. either of two outer openings of the nose

nos′trum n. quack medicine

nos′y, nos′ey (nōz′-) a. –**i·er**, –**i·est** [Col.] inquisitive

not adv. in no manner, degree, etc.

no′ta·ble a., n. remarkable or outstanding (person) —**no′ta·bly** adv.

no′ta·rize′ v. certify (a document) as a notary

no′ta·ry n., pl. –**ries** one authorized to certify documents, etc.: in full **notary public**

no·ta′tion n. **1** (use of) a system of symbols, as in music **2** a note

notch n. **1** a V-shaped cut **2** [Col.] a step; degree —v. to cut notches in

note n. **1** brief writing, comment, letter, etc. **2** notice; heed **3** written promise to pay **4** musical tone or its symbol **5** importance —v. **1** to notice **2** make a note of —**compare notes** exchange views

note′book′ n. book for keeping memorandums, etc.

not′ed a. renowned; famous

note′wor′thy a. outstanding

noth′ing n. **1** no thing **2** unimportant person or thing **3** zero —adv. not at all —**for nothing 1** free **2** in vain **3** without reason —**noth′ing·ness** n.

no′tice n. **1** announcement or warning **2** a short review **3** attention —v. observe —**take notice** observe

no′tice·a·ble a. **1** easily seen **2** significant —**no′tice·a·bly** adv.

no′ti·fy′ v. –**fied′**, –**fy′ing** give notice to; inform —**no′ti·fi·ca′tion** n.

no′tion n. **1** general idea **2** belief; opinion **3** whim **4** pl. small wares

no·to′ri·ous a. widely known, esp. unfavorably —**no′to·ri′e·ty** n.

no′-trump′ n. Bridge a bid to play with no suit being trumps

not′with·stand′ing prep., adv. in spite of (that)

nou′gat (nōō′-) n. candy of sugar paste with nuts

nought (nôt) n. **1** nothing **2** zero

noun n. word that names a person, thing, etc.

nour′ish (nur′-) a. feed to promote life and growth —**nour′ish·ment** n.

no′va n., pl. –**vas** or –**vae** (-vē) star that

brightens intensely and then gradually dims

nov′el a. new and unusual —n. long fictional narrative

nov′el·ist n. writer of novels

nov′el·ty n., pl. **-ties** 1 newness 2 novel thing 3 small, cheap toy, etc.

No·vem′ber n. 11th month

no·ve′na n. R.C.Ch. special prayers for nine days

nov′ice n. 1 one in a religious order before taking final vows 2 beginner

no·vi·ti·ate (nō vish′ē ət) n. period of being a novice: also, Br. sp., **no·vi′ci·ate**

No′vo·cain′ trademark procaine: also sp. **No′vo·caine′**

now adv. 1 at this moment; at present 2 at that time; then 3 with things as they are —con. since —n. the present time —**now and then** occasionally: also **now and again**

now′a·days′ adv. in these days; at the present time

no′where′ adv. not in, at, or to any place

no′wise′ adv. in no way

nox·ious (näk′shəs) a. harmful to health or morals

noz′zle n. small spout at the end of a hose, etc.

nu·ance′ (-äns′) n. slight change in color, meaning, etc.

nub n. 1 lump or small piece 2 [Col.] gist

nub′by a. **-bi·er**, **-bi·est** rough and knotty, as cloth

nu′bile (-bil, -bīl′) a. sexually attractive: said of a young woman

nu′cle·ar a. of, like, or forming a nucleus or nuclei

nuclear family n. family including parents and their children living in one household

nuclear fission n. splitting of nuclei of atoms, with the release of much energy, as in the atomic bomb

nuclear fusion n. fusion of nuclei of atoms, with the release of much energy, as in the hydrogen bomb

nuclear reactor n. device for creating controlled chain reaction, as for producing energy

nu′cle·us n., pl. **-cle·i′** (-klē ī′) or **-cle·us·es** central part, spec. of an atom or of a living cell

nude a., n. naked (figure) —**nu′di·ty** n.

nudge v. push gently, as with the elbow to get someone's attention —n. gentle push

nud′ism′ n. practice or cult of going nude —**nud′ist** a., n.

nug′get n. lump of gold ore

nui′sance (nōō′-) n. annoying act, person, etc.

nuke v., n. [Sl.] (attack with) nuclear weapon

null a. without legal force: also **null and void**

nul′li·fy v. **-fied′**, **-fy′ing** 1 make null 2 make useless —**nul′li·fi·ca′tion** n.

numb (num) a. not able to feel —v. make numb

num′ber n. 1 symbol or word showing how many or what place in a series 2 total 3 often pl. many 4 quantity 5 single issue of a periodical 6 one part of a program of entertainment 7 form of a word showing it to be singular or plural —v. 1 to count 2 give a number to 3 include 4 to total or contain

num′ber·less a. countless

nu′mer·al n. figure, letter, or word expressing a number

nu′mer·a′tor n. part above the line in a fraction

nu·mer′i·cal a. 1 of, in, or having to do with number(s) 2 (expressed) by numbers Also **nu·mer′ic** —**nu·mer′i·cal·ly** adv.

nu′mer·ol′o·gy n. divination by numbers

nu′mer·ous a. 1 very many 2 large in number

nu′mis·mat′ics n. study or collecting of coins —**nu·mis′ma·tist** n.

num′skull′ n. stupid person

nun n. woman living in a convent under vows

nun′ci·o′ (-shē ō′) n., pl. **-os′** papal ambassador

nun′ner·y n., pl. **-ies** [Ar.] convent

nup′tial (-shəl) a. of marriage or a wedding —n. pl. a wedding

nurse n. 1 one trained to care for the sick, help doctors, etc. 2 nursemaid —v. 1 take care of (an invalid, child) 2 try to cure; treat 3 suckle 4 protect or conserve 5 nourish

nurse′maid′ n. woman hired to care for children

nurs′er·y n., pl. **-ies** 1 room set aside for children 2 place where trees and plants are raised for sale

nursery rhyme n. poem for children

nursery school n. school for children about three to five years old

nurs′ing home n. residence providing care for the infirm, chronically ill, disabled, etc.

nur′ture n. training; care —v. 1 nourish 2 train; rear

nut n. 1 dry fruit with a kernel inside a hard shell 2 the kernel 3 small metal block for screwing onto a bolt, etc. 4 [Sl.] odd or silly person 5 [Sl.] fan; devotee

nut′crack′er n. device for cracking nutshells

nut′hatch′ n. small songbird

nut′meat′ n. kernel of a nut

nut′meg n. aromatic seed grated and used as a spice

nut′pick′ n. small device for digging out nut kernels

nu′tri·a (-trē-) n. soft, brown fur of a South American rodent

nu′tri·ent a., n. nutritious (substance)

nu′tri·ment n. food

nu·tri′tion (-trish′ən) n. 1 process of taking in and assimilating food 2 food —**nu′tri·tive** (-tiv) a.

nu·tri′tious a. nourishing

nuts a. [Sl.] crazy; silly

nut′shell′ n. shell of a nut

nut′ty a. **-ti·er, -ti·est** 1 containing nuts 2 tasting like nuts 3 [Sl.] crazy, enthusiastic, etc.

nuz′zle v. 1 to push against with the nose 2 snuggle

ny′lon′ n. 1 synthetic material made into thread, etc. 2 pl. stockings of this

nymph (nimf) n. minor Greek or Roman nature goddess

nym′pho·ma′ni·a n. uncontrollable sexual desire in a woman —**nym′pho·ma′ni·ac′** a., n.

O

O int. 1 exclamation in direct address 2 oh

oaf n. stupid, clumsy fellow —**oaf′ish** a.

oak n. hardwood tree bearing acorns —**oak′en** a.

oa′kum n. hemp fiber used to caulk seams in boats

oar n. pole with a broad blade at one end, for rowing —**oars′man** n., pl. **-men**

oar′lock′ n. device supporting an oar in rowing

o·a′sis n., pl. **-ses′** fertile place with water in the desert

oat n. usually pl. 1 a cereal grass 2 its grain —**oat′en** a.

oath n. 1 sworn declaration to tell the truth, etc. 2 word used in cursing

oat′meal′ n. ground or rolled oats, cooked as porridge

ob′bli·ga′to (-gät′ō) n., pl. **-tos** or **-ti** (-ē) elaborate musical accompaniment to a piece

ob′du·rate (-dər ət) a. 1 stubborn; unyielding; inflexible 2 not repenting —**ob′du·ra·cy** n.

o·be′di·ent a. obeying or willing to obey —**o·be′di·ence** n. —**o·be′di·ent·ly** adv.

o·bei′sance (-bā′-, -bē′-) n. 1 bow, curtsy, etc. 2 homage

ob′e·lisk n. slender, tapering, four-sided pillar

o·bese′ a. very fat —**o·be′si·ty** n.

o·bey′ v. 1 carry out orders (of) 2 be guided by

ob·fus′cate′ v. to obscure; confuse —**ob′fus·ca′tion** n.

o·bit′u·ar′y (-bich′ōō-) n., pl. **-ies** notice of death, often with a short biography: also **o′bit**

ob′ject (v.: əb jekt′) n. 1 thing that can be seen or touched 2 person or thing to which action, etc. is directed 3 purpose; goal 4 Gram. word receiving the action of the verb or governed by a preposition —v. feel or express opposition or disapproval —**ob·jec′tor** n.

ob·jec′tion n. 1 expression of disapproval 2 a reason for objecting

ob·jec′tion·a·ble a. offensive; disagreeable

ob·jec′tive a. 1 real or actual; not subjective 2 without bias 3 Gram. of the case of an object of a preposition or verb —n. goal —**ob′jec·tiv′i·ty** n. —**ob·jec′tive·ly** a.

object lesson n. practical example of some principle

ob·jet d′art (äb′zhä där′) n., pl. **ob′jets d′art′** (-zhä-) small object of artistic value

ob′jur·gate′ v. rebuke; upbraid —**ob′jur·ga′tion** n.

ob′late′ a. Geometry flattened at the poles

ob·la′tion n. sacrifice or offering to God or a god

ob′li·gate′ v. bind by a promise, sense of duty, etc. —**ob′li·ga′tion** n. —**ob·lig′a·to′ry** a.

o·blige′ (-blīj′) v. 1 compel, as by law or duty 2 make indebted; do a favor for

o·blig′ing a. helpful

ob·lique′ (ō blēk′) a. 1 slanting 2 not direct —**ob·liq′ui·ty** n.

ob·lit′er·ate′ v. 1 blot out 2 destroy —**ob·lit′er·a′tion** n.

ob·liv′i·on n. 1 state of being forgotten 2 forgetful state

ob·liv′i·ous a. not aware

ob′long′ a. rectangular and longer than broad —n. oblong figure

ob′lo·quy (-kwē) n. widespread censure or disgrace

ob·nox′ious (-näk′shəs) a. offensive

o′boe n. double-reed woodwind instrument

ob·scene′ (-sēn′) a. offensive to decency —**ob·scen′i·ty** (-sen′-) n., pl. **-ties**

ob·scure′ a. 1 dim 2 not clear or distinct 3 not well-known —v. make obscure —**ob·scu′ri·ty** n.

ob′se·quies′ (-kwēz′) n.pl. funeral rites

ob·se′qui·ous (-kwē-) a. servile

ob·serv′ance (-zurv′-) n. 1 the observing of a law, etc. 2 customary act, rite, etc.

ob·serv'ant a. 1 attentive 2 perceptive; alert

ob·serv'a·to'ry n., pl. **–ries** building for astronomical research

ob·serve' v. 1 adhere to (a law, etc.) 2 celebrate (a holiday, etc.) 3 notice; watch 4 to remark —**ob·serv'a·ble** a. —**ob'ser·va'tion** n. —**ob·serv'er** n.

ob·sess' v. haunt in mind; preoccupy greatly

ob·ses'sion n. idea, etc. that obsesses one

ob·sid'i·an n. hard, dark volcanic glass

ob'so·les'cent a. becoming obsolete —**ob'so·les'cence** n.

ob'so·lete' a. no longer used

ob·sta·cle n. obstruction

ob·stet'rics n. branch of medicine dealing with childbirth —**ob·stet'ric, ob·stet'ri·cal** a. —**ob'ste·tri'cian** n.

ob'sti·nate (-nət) a. 1 stubborn 2 hard to treat or cure —**ob'sti·na·cy** n.

ob·strep'er·ous a. unruly

ob·struct' v. 1 block 2 hinder —**ob·struc'tion** n. —**ob·struc'tive** a.

ob·tain' v. 1 get by trying 2 prevail; be in effect

ob·trude' v. 1 push out 2 to force oneself upon others —**ob·tru'sive** a.

ob·tuse' a. 1 more than 90°: said of an angle 2 blunt 3 slow to understand

ob·verse' (n.: äb'vʉrs') a. facing the observer —n. front or main side of a coin, etc.

ob'vi·ate' v. prevent, as by proper measures

ob'vi·ous a. easy to understand —**ob'vi·ous·ly** adv.

oc'a·ri'na (-rē'-) n. small, oval musical toy

oc·ca'sion n. 1 happening 2 special event 3 opportunity 4 cause —v. to cause —**on occasion** sometimes

oc·ca'sion·al a. 1 for special times 2 infrequent —**oc·ca'sion·al·ly** adv.

Oc'ci·dent (äk'sə-) n. Europe and the Western Hemisphere —**Oc'ci·den'tal** a., n.

oc·clude' v. to close or shut

oc·clu'sion n. the way the upper and lower teeth come together

oc·cult' a. 1 secret 2 mysterious 3 magical

oc'cu·pan·cy n., pl. **–cies** an occupying —**oc'cu·pant** n.

oc'cu·pa'tion n. 1 an occupying 2 work; vocation —**oc'cu·pa'tion·al** a.

oc'cu·py' v. **–pied', –py'ing** 1 take possession of 2 dwell in 3 employ

oc·cur' v. **–curred', –cur'ring** 1 exist 2 come to mind 3 happen —**oc·cur'rence** n.

o·cean (ō'shən) n. 1 body of salt water covering much of the earth 2 one of its four main divisions —**o'ce·an'ic** (ō'shē-) a.

o'ce·an·og'ra·phy (ō'shə näg'-) n. study of the ocean environment

o'ce·lot' (äs'ə-) n. large, spotted wildcat

o·cher, o·chre (ō'kər) n. yellow or red clay pigment

o'clock' adv. by the clock

oc'ta·gon n. figure with eight sides and eight angles —**oc·tag'o·nal** n.

oc'tane' number n. number representing certain property of a gasoline

oc'tave (-tiv) n. eight full steps of a musical scale

oc·tet', oc·tette' n. group of eight, esp. of musical performers

Oc·to'ber n. tenth month

oc'to·ge·nar'i·an n., a. (person) between 80 and 90 years old

oc'to·pus n. mollusk with soft body and eight arms

oc'u·lar (-yōō-) a. of, for, or by the eye

oc'u·list n. [Ar.] ophthalmologist

OD n., v. [Sl.] overdose, esp. fatal(ly)

odd a. 1 having a remainder of one when divided by two; not even 2 left over, as from a pair 3 with a few more 4 occasional 5 peculiar; strange —**odd'ly** adv.

odd'ball' a., n. [Sl.] peculiar (person)

odd'i·ty n. 1 odd quality 2 pl. **–ties** odd person or thing

odds n.pl. 1 advantage 2 betting ratio based on chances —**at odds** quarreling

odds and ends n.pl. remnants

odds'-on' a. having a very good chance of winning

ode n. lofty poem in praise

o'di·ous a. disgusting

o'di·um n. 1 hatred 2 disgrace

o·dom'e·ter n. device that measures distance traveled

o'dor n. smell; aroma —**o'dor·ous** a.

o'dor·if'er·ous a. giving off a strong odor

o'dour n. Br. sp. of ODOR

od·ys·sey (äd'ə sē) n. long journey with adventures

o'er (ō'ər) prep., adv. [Poet.] over

oeu·vre (ʉ'vr') n., pl. **oeu'vres** [Fr.] all the works of a writer, composer, etc.

of prep. 1 being or coming from 2 belonging to 3 having or containing 4 concerning; about 5 during

off adv. 1 farther away in space or time 2 so as to be no longer on 3 so as to be less —prep. 1 not on 2 dependent on 3 away from 4 below the standard of —a. 1 not on 2 on the way 3 away from work; absent 4 below standard 5 provided for 6 in error; wrong —**off and on** now and then

of·fal (ôf'əl) n. refuse; garbage

off'beat' a. [Col.] unconventional

off'-col'or a. not quite proper; risqué

of·fend' v. 1 commit an offense 2 make angry; displease —**of·fend'er** n.

of·fense' (or ô'fens') n. 1 sin or crime 2 an offending 3 an attacking —**give offense** make angry; insult —**take offense** become offended

of·fen'sive a. 1 attacking 2 disgusting —n. position for attacking

of'fer v. 1 to present or give 2 suggest —n. thing offered —**of'fer·ing** n.

of'fer·to·ry n., pl. **-ries** [often O-] 1 offering of bread and wine at Mass 2 collection of money at church service

off'hand' adv. without preparation —a. 1 said offhand 2 rude; curt Also **off'hand·ed**

of'fice n. 1 a favor 2 post of authority 3 place for doing business 4 rite

of'fice·hold·er n. 1 government official

of'fi·cer n. 1 one having a position of authority in business, the armed forces, etc. 2 policeman

of·fi'cial (-fish'əl) a. 1 authorized 2 formal —n. one holding an office —**of·fi'cial·ly** adv.

of·fi'ci·ate' (-fish'ē-) v. perform official duties or functions

of·fi'cious (-fish'əs) a. meddlesome

off'ing n. used chiefly in **in the offing**, at some future time

off'-key' a. not harmonious

off'·lim'its a. not to be gone to

off'-line' a. not connected to a computer's CPU

off'-price' a. selling high-quality clothing, etc. at a price lower than the retail price

off'-put'ting a. [Chiefly Br.] distracting, annoying, etc.

off'-sea'son n. time when usual activity is reduced

off'set' v. **-set'**, **-set'ting** compensate for

off'shoot' n. anything that comes from a main source

off'shore' a., adv. (moving) away from shore

off'side' a. not in proper position for play

off'spring' n. child or children

off'-white' a. grayish-white or yellowish-white

off year n. year of little production

oft adv. [Poet.] often

of·ten (ôf'ən) adv. many times: also **of'ten·times'**

o·gle (ō'gəl) v. look at in a boldly desirous way —n. ogling look

o'gre (-gər) n. 1 Folklore man-eating giant 2 cruel man

oh (ō) int., n., pl. **oh's** or **ohs** exclamation of surprise, fear, wonder, pain, etc.

ohm (ōm) n. unit of electrical resistance

-oid suf. like; resembling

oil n. 1 any greasy liquid 2 petroleum —v. lubricate with oil —a. of, from, or like oil —**oil'y** a.

oil'cloth' n. cloth waterproofed with oil or paint

oil color n. paint made of pigment ground in oil

oil painting n. painting in oil colors

oil shale n. shale from which oil can be distilled

oil'skin' n. cloth made waterproof with oil

oink v., n. (make) the vocal sound of a pig

oint'ment n. oily cream for healing the skin

OK, O.K. a., adv., int. all right —n. approval —v. **OK'd, O.K.'d, OK'ing, O.K.'ing** to approve Also sp. **o'kay'**

o'kra n. plant with green pods used in soups

old a. 1 having lived or existed for a long time 2 of a specified age 3 not new 4 former —n. time long past —**old'ness** n.

Old English n. English language before A.D. 1100

old'-fash'ioned a. of the past; out-of-date

old hand n. experienced person

old hat a. [Sl.] 1 old-fashioned 2 trite

old'ie, old'y n., pl. **-ies** [Col.] old joke, song, etc.

old lady n. [Sl.] one's mother or wife

old'-line' a. long-established, conservative, etc.

old maid n. spinster

old man n. [Sl.] one's father or husband

old'ster n. [Col.] old or elderly person

Old Testament Bible of Judaism, or the first part of the Christian Bible

old'-tim'er n. [Col.] longtime member, worker, etc.

o·lé (ō lā') int., n. [Sp.] shout of approval, etc.

o'le·ag'i·nous (-aj'-) a. oily; unctuous

o'le·an'der n. flowering evergreen shrub

o'le·o·mar'ga·rine, o'le·o·mar'ga·rin (-rin) n. margarine: also **o'le·o'**

ol·fac'to·ry a. of the sense of smell

ol'i·gar'chy (-gär'kē) n., pl. **-ies** 1 state rule by a few people 2 these people

ol'ive (-iv) n. 1 evergreen tree 2 its small, oval fruit 3 yellowish green

om'buds·man n., pl. **-men** official who investigates complaints about an organization, etc.

o·me'ga n. last letter of the Greek alphabet

om·e·let, om·e·lette (äm'lət) n. eggs beaten up and cooked as a pancake

o'men n. sign of something to come

om'i·nous a. threatening

o·mis'sion n. an omitting or thing omitted

o·mit' v. **o·mit'ted, o·mit'ting 1** leave out **2** fail to do

omni- pref. all; everywhere

om'ni·bus a. providing for, or including, many things at once

om·nip'o·tent a. all-powerful —**om·nip'o·tence** n.

om'ni·pres'ent a. present in all places at the same time

om·nis'cient (-nish'ənt) a. knowing all things —**om·nis'cience** n.

om·niv'o·rous a. **1** eating both animal and vegetable foods **2** taking in everything —**om'ni·vore'** n.

on prep. **1** held up by, covering, or attached to **2** near to **3** at the time of **4** connected with **5** in a state of **6** by using **7** concerning **8** [Sl.] using; addicted to —adv. **1** in a situation of touching, covering, or being held up by **2** toward **3** forward **4** continuously **5** into operation —a. in action

once adv. **1** one time **2** at any time **3** formerly —n. one time —**at once 1** immediately **2** simultaneously

once'-o'ver n. [Col.] quick look, examination, etc.

on·col'o·gy n. branch of medicine dealing with tumors —**on·col'o·gist** n.

on'com'ing a. approaching

one a. **1** being a single thing **2** united **3** a certain **4** some —n. **1** lowest number **2** single person or thing —pron. a person or thing —**one by one** individually

one'ness n. unity; identity

on'er·ous a. oppressive

one·self' pron. one's own self; himself or herself —**be oneself** function normally —**by oneself** alone

one'-sid'ed a. **1** unequal **2** partial

one'-time' a. former

one'-track' a. [Col.] limited in scope

one'-way' a. in one direction only

on'go'ing a. progressing

on·ion (un'yən) n. bulblike, sharp-tasting vegetable

on'ion-skin' n. tough, thin, translucent, glossy paper

on'-line' a. connected to a computer's CPU

on'look'er n. spectator

on'ly a. **1** alone of its or their kind **2** best —adv. **1** and no other **2** merely —con. [Col.] except that —**only too** very

on'rush' n. strong onward rush

on'set' n. **1** attack **2** start

on'slaught' n. violent attack

on'to prep. to and upon

o'nus n. **1** burden **2** blame

on'ward adv. forward: also **on'wards** —a. advancing

on'yx (-iks) n. kind of agate

ooze v. flow out slowly —n. **1** something that oozes **2** soft mud or slime

o'pal n. iridescent gem

o·paque' (-pāk') a. not transparent —**o·pac'i·ty** (-pas'-) n.

o'pen a. **1** not closed, covered, etc. **2** not enclosed **3** unfolded **4** free to be entered, used, etc. **5** not restricted **6** available **7** frank —v. **1** to cause to be or become open **2** begin **3** start operating —**open to** glad to consider —**o'pen·er** n. —**o'pen·ly** adv.

o'pen-air' a. outdoor

o'pen-and-shut' a. easily decided

o'pen-end'ed a. unlimited

o'pen-eyed' a. with the eyes wide open, as in surprise

o'pen-faced' a. **1** having a frank, honest face **2** without a top slice of bread

o'pen-hand'ed a. generous

open house n. **1** informal home reception **2** time when an institution is open to visitors

o'pen·ing n. **1** open place **2** beginning **3** favorable chance **4** unfilled job

o'pen-mind'ed a. impartial

o'pen·work' n. ornamental work with openings in it

op'er·a n. play set to music and sung with an orchestra —**op'er·at'ic** a.

op'er·a·ble a. that can be treated by surgery

op'er·ate' v. **1** be or keep in action **2** have an effect **3** perform an operation **4** manage —**op'er·a'tor** n.

op'er·a'tion n. **1** act or way of operating **2** a being in action **3** one process in a series **4** surgical treatment for an illness —**op'er·a'tion·al** a.

op'er·a·tive a. **1** operating **2** efficient

op'er·et'ta n. light opera

oph'thal·mol'o·gy (äf'-) n. branch of medicine dealing with diseases of the eye —**oph'thal·mol'o·gist** n.

o'pi·ate (-pē ət) n. narcotic drug containing opium

o·pine' v. think; suppose: usually humorous

o·pin'ion (-yən) n. **1** what one thinks true **2** estimation **3** expert judgment

o·pin'ion·at'ed a. obstinate in holding an opinion

o'pi·um n. narcotic drug made from a certain poppy

o·pos'sum n. small, tree-dwelling mammal

op·po'nent n. person against one in a fight, etc.

op'por·tune' adv. timely

op'por·tun'ist n. one willing to get ahead unethically —**op'por·tun'ism'** n. —**op'por·tun·is'tic** a.

op'por·tu'ni·ty n., pl. **–ties** fit time to do something

op·pose v. 1 to place opposite 2 fight or resist —**op'po·si'tion** (-zish'ən) n.

op'po·site (-zit) a. 1 entirely different 2 opposed to —n. anything opposed —prep. across from

op·press' v. 1 weigh down 2 rule in a cruel way —**op·pres'sion** n. —**op·pres'sor** n.

op·pres'sive a. 1 burdensome 2 cruel and unjust

op·pro'bri·ous a. 1 abusive 2 disgraceful

op·pro'bri·um n. disgrace

opt v. make a choice (for) —**opt out (of)** choose not to be or continue (in)

op'tic a. of the eye

op'ti·cal a. 1 of vision 2 aiding sight 3 of optics

op·ti'cian (-tish'ən) n. maker or seller of eyeglasses

op'tics n. science dealing with light and vision

op'ti·mism' n. tendency to be cheerful about life —**op'ti·mist** n. —**op'ti·mis'tic** a.

op'ti·mize' v. make the greatest use of

op'ti·mum n., a. (the) best: also **op'ti·mal** a.

op'tion n. choice or right to choose —**op'tion·al** a.

op·tom'e·trist n. one who tests eyes and fits eyeglasses —**op·tom'e·try** n.

op'u·lent a. 1 wealthy 2 abundant —**op'u·lence** n.

o'pus n., pl. **o'pe·ra** or **o'pus·es** a work, esp. of music

or con. word introducing an alternative, synonym, etc.

-or suf. person or thing that

or'a·cle n. ancient Greek or Roman priestess or priest who acted as prophet —**o·rac'u·lar** a.

o·ral (ôr'əl) a. 1 spoken 2 of the mouth —**o'ral·ly** adv.

or'ange n. 1 sweet, round, reddish-yellow citrus fruit 2 reddish yellow

or'ange·ade' n. drink of orange juice, water, and sugar

o·rang'u·tan' n. large ape

o·rate' v. speak pompously

o·ra'tion n. formal public speech —**or'a·tor** n.

or'a·to'ri·o' n., pl. **-os'** vocal and orchestral composition on a religious theme

or'a·to·ry n. skill in public speaking —**or'a·tor'i·cal** a.

orb n. (celestial) sphere

or'bit n. path of one heavenly body around another —v. put or go in an orbit

or'chard n. grove of fruit trees

or'ches·tra (-kis-) n. 1 group of musicians playing together 2 main floor of a theater —**or·ches'tral** (-kes'-) a.

or'ches·trate' v. arrange music for an orchestra —**or'ches·tra'tion** n.

or'chid (-kid) n. 1 plant having flowers with three petals, one of which is enlarged 2 light bluish red

or·dain' v. 1 to decree 2 admit to the ministry

or·deal' n. difficult or painful experience

or'der n. 1 peaceful, orderly, or proper state 2 monastic or fraternal brotherhood 3 general condition 4 a command 5 (a request for) items to be supplied 6 class; kind —v. 1 arrange 2 command 3 request (supplies) —**in order** so that —**in short order** quickly —**on the order of** 1 similar to 2 approximately

or'der·ly a. 1 neatly arranged 2 well-behaved —n., pl. **-lies** 1 soldier acting as an officer's servant 2 male hospital attendant —**or'der·li·ness** n.

or'di·nal number n. number used to show order in a series, as first, second, etc.

or'di·nance n. statute, esp. of a city government

or'di·nar'y a. 1 customary; usual; regular 2 common; average —**or'di·nar'i·ly** adv.

or·di·na'tion n. an ordaining or being ordained

ord'nance n. Mil. heavy guns, ammunition, etc.

ore n. rock or mineral containing metal

o·reg'a·no n. plant with fragrant leaves used as seasoning

or'gan n. 1 keyboard musical instrument using pipes, reeds, or electronic tubes 2 animal or plant part with a special function 3 agency or medium —**or'gan·ist** n.

or'gan·dy, or'gan·die n. sheer, stiff cotton cloth

or·gan'ic a. 1 of a body organ 2 systematically arranged 3 of or from living matter 4 of chemical compounds containing carbon

or'gan·ism' n. living thing

or'gan·i·za'tion n. 1 act of organizing 2 group organized for some purpose

or'gan·ize' v. 1 arrange according to a system 2 form into a group, union, etc. —**or'gan·iz'er** n.

or'gan·za n. stiff fabric of rayon, silk, etc.

or'gasm' n. climax of a sexual act

or'gy (-jē) n., pl. **-gies** 1 wild merrymaking, esp. with sexual activity 2 unrestrained indulgence

o'ri·ent v. adjust (oneself) to a specific situation —[O-] E Asia —**O'ri·en'tal** a., n. —**o'ri·en·ta'tion** n.

or'i·fice (-fis) n. mouth; opening

o·ri·ga·mi (ôr'ə gä'mē) n. Japanese art of folding paper to form flowers, etc.

or'i·gin *n.* 1 beginning 2 parentage 3 source

o·rig'i·nal *a.* 1 first 2 new; novel 3 inventive —*n.* an original work, form, etc. —**o·rig'i·nal'i·ty** *n.* —**o·rig'i·nal·ly** *adv.*

o·rig'i·nate' *v.* 1 create; invent 2 begin; start —**o·rig'i·na'tion** *n.* —**o·rig'i·na'tor** *n.*

o'ri·ole' *n.* bird with bright orange and black plumage

Or'lon' *trademark* synthetic fiber —*n.* [o—] this fiber

or'na·ment (-mənt; *v.*:-ment') *n.* decoration —*v.* decorate —**or'na·men'tal** *a.* —**or'na·men·ta'tion** *n.*

or·nate' *a.* showy —**or·nate'ly** *adv.*

or'ner·y *a.* -i·er, -i·est [Col.] mean; obstinate

or'ni·thol'o·gy *n.* study of birds —**or'ni·thol'o·gist** *n.*

o'ro·tund' *a.* 1 full and deep in sound 2 bombastic

or'phan *n.* child whose parents are dead —*v.* cause to be an orphan —**or'phan·age** *n.*

or'ris *n.* iris having a root (**or'ris·root'**) pulverized for perfume, etc.

or'tho·don'tics *n.* dentistry of teeth straightening: also **or'tho·don'ti·a** (-shə) —**or'tho·don'tist** *n.*

or'tho·dox' *a.* 1 holding to the usual or fixed beliefs; conventional 2 [O—] of a large eastern Christian church —**or'tho·dox'y** *n.*

or·thog'ra·phy *n.*, *pl.* **-phies** 1 correct spelling 2 spelling as a subject for study

or'tho·pe'dics *n.* surgery dealing with bones —**or'tho·pe'dic** *a.* —**or'tho·pe'dist** *n.*

-ory *suf.* 1 of or like 2 place or thing for

os'cil·late' (äs'ə-) *v.* 1 swing to and fro 2 fluctuate —**os'cil·la'tion** *n.*

os'cil'lo·scope' (ə sil'ə-) *n.* instrument showing an electrical wave on a fluorescent screen

os'cu·late' (-kyōō-) *v.* kiss —**os'cu·la'tion** *n.*

-ose *suf.* full of; like

o·sier (ō'zhər) *n.* willow with branches used for baskets and furniture

-osis *suf.* 1 condition or action 2 diseased condition

os·mo'sis *n.* diffusion of fluids through a porous membrane

os'prey (-prē) *n.*, *pl.* **-preys** large, fish-eating hawk

os'si·fy' *v.* **-fied'**, **-fy'ing** change into bone

os·ten'si·ble *a.* seeming; apparent —**os·ten'si·bly** *adv.*

os'ten·ta'tion *n.* showiness —**os'ten·ta'tious** *a.*

os'te·op'a·thy *n.* a school of medicine and surgery emphasizing interrelationship of muscles and bones —**os'te·o·path'** *n.*

os'te·o·po·ro'sis *n.* a disorder marked by porous, brittle bones

os'tra·cize' *v.* banish; shut out —**os'tra·cism'** *n.*

os'trich *n.* large, nonflying bird

oth'er *a.* 1 being the one(s) remaining 2 different 3 additional —*pron.* 1 the other one 2 some other one —*adv.* otherwise —**every other** every alternate

oth'er·wise' *adv.* 1 differently 2 in all other ways 3 if not; else —*a.* different

oth'er·world'ly *a.* apart from earthly interests

o·ti·ose (ō'shē ōs') *a.* 1 futile 2 useless

ot'ter *n.* weasellike animal

ot'to·man *n.* low, cushioned seat or footstool

ouch *int.* cry of pain

ought *v.* auxiliary verb showing: 1 duty 2 desirability 3 probability

oui (wē) *adv.* [Fr.] yes

ounce *n.* 1 unit of weight, $\frac{1}{16}$ pound 2 fluid ounce, $\frac{1}{16}$ pint

our *a.* of us

ours *pron.* that or those belonging to us

our·selves' *pron.* intensive or reflexive form of WE

-ous *suf.* having; full of; characterized by

oust *v.* force out; expel

oust'er *n.* dispossession

out *adv.* 1 away from a place, etc. 2 outdoors 3 into being or action 4 thoroughly 5 from a group —*a.* 1 not used, working, etc. 2 having lost —*n.* 1 [Sl.] excuse 2 *Baseball* retirement of a batter or runner from play —*v.* become known —*prep.* out of —**on the outs** [Col.] quarreling —**out for** trying to get or do —**out of** 1 from inside of 2 beyond 3 from (material) 4 because of 5 no longer having 6 so as to deprive

out- *pref.* 1 outside 2 outward 3 better or more than

out'age (-ij) *n.* accidental suspension of operation

out'-and-out' *a.* thorough

out'back' *a.* remote, sparsely settled region

out·bal'ance *v.* be greater than in weight, value, etc.

out'bid' *v.* **-bid'**, **-bid'ding** bid or offer more than (someone else)

out'board' *a.* located on the outer surface of a boat

out'bound' *a.* going outward

out'break' *n.* a breaking out, as of disease or rioting

out'build'ing *n.* building apart from the main one

out′burst′ n. sudden show of feeling, energy, etc.

out′cast′ a., n. shunned (person)

out′class′ v. surpass

out′come′ n. result

out′crop′ n. exposed rock layer

out′cry′ n., pl. **–cries′** 1 a crying out 2 strong protest

out′dat′ed a. out-of-date

out′dis′tance v. leave behind, as in a race

out′do′ v. do better than

out′door′ a. in the open

out′doors′ adv. in or into the open; outside —n. the outdoor world

out′er a. on or closer to the outside

out′er·most′ a. farthest out

outer space n. space beyond the earth's atmosphere

out′er·wear′ n. garments worn over the usual clothing

out′field′ n. Baseball the area beyond the infield —**out′field′er** n.

out′fit′ n. 1 equipment for some activity 2 group; esp., military unit —v. **–fit′ted, –fit′ting** equip

out′flank′ v. go around and beyond the flank of (troops)

out′fox′ v. outwit

out′go′ n. expenditure

out′go′ing a. 1 leaving or retiring 2 sociable

out′grow′ v. grow too large for

out′growth′ n. 1 result 2 an offshoot

out′guess′ v. outwit

out′house′ n. outdoor latrine

out′ing n. picnic, trip, etc.

out′land′ish a. 1 strange 2 fantastic

out′last′ v. endure longer than

out′law′ n. notorious criminal —v. declare illegal

out′lay′ n. money spent

out′let′ n. 1 passage or way out 2 market for goods

out′line′ n. 1 bounding line 2 sketch showing only outer lines 3 general plan

out′live′ v. live longer than

out′look′ n. 1 viewpoint 2 prospect

out′ly′ing a. remote

out′mod′ed (-mōd′-) a. obsolete; old-fashioned

out′num′ber v. be greater in number than

out′-of-date′ a. obsolete

out′-of-doors′ a. outdoor —n., adv. outdoors

out′-of-the-way′ a. secluded

out′pa′tient n. hospital patient treated without lodging or meals

out′post′ n. remote settlement or military post

out′put′ n. 1 total quantity produced in a given period 2 information from a computer 3 current or power delivered

out′rage′ n. 1 shocking act or crime 2 deep insult —v. commit an outrage on —**out·ra′geous** a.

out′right′ a. complete

out′set′ n. beginning

out′side′ n. 1 the exterior 2 area beyond —a. 1 outer 2 from some other 3 slight —adv. on or to the outside —prep. on or to the outside of

out′sid′er n. one not of a certain group

out′skirts′ n.pl. outlying districts of a city, etc.

out′smart′ v. outwit

out′spo′ken a. frank; bold

out′stand′ing a. 1 prominent 2 unpaid

out′stretched′ a. extended

out′strip′ v. **–stripped′, –strip′ping** excel

out′take′ n. faulty recording, film scene, etc. not used in the final version

out′ward a. 1 outer 2 visible —adv. toward the outside Also **out′wards** —**out′ward·ly** adv.

out′wear′ v. **–wore′, –worn′, –wear′ing** outlast

out′wit′ v. **–wit′ted, –wit′ting** to overcome by cleverness

o′va n. pl. of OVUM

o′val a., n. egg-shaped (thing)

o′va·ry n., pl. **–ries** 1 female gland where ova are formed 2 part of a flower where the seeds form —**o·var′i·an** (-ver′-) a.

o·va′tion n. loud and long applause or cheering

ov′en (uv′-) n. compartment for baking, drying, etc.

o′ver prep. 1 above 2 on; upon 3 across 4 during 5 more than 6 about —adv. 1 above or across 2 more 3 down 4 other side up 5 again —a. 1 finished 2 on the other side

over– pref. excessive or excessively: see list below

o′ver·a·bun′dance

o′ver·ac′tive

o′ver·anx′ious

o′ver·bur′den

o′ver·cau′tious

o′ver·con′fi·dent

o′ver·cook′

o′ver·crowd′

o′ver·eat′

o′ver·em′pha·size′

o′ver·es′ti·mate′

o′ver·ex·ert′

o′ver·ex·pose′

o′ver·heat′

o′ver·in·dulge′

o′ver·load′

o′ver·pop′u·late′

o′ver·pro·duc′tion

o′ver·ripe′

o′ver·stim′u·late′

o′ver·stock′

o′ver·sup·ply′

o′ver·a·chieve′ v. 1 do better in school than expected 2 drive oneself beyond reasonable goals

o′ver·all′ a. 1 end to end 2 total —n. pl. work trousers with attached bib

o′ver·awe′ v. subdue by inspiring awe

o′ver·bear′ing a. bossy

o′ver·blown′ a. 1 excessive 2 pompous

o′ver·board′ adv. from a ship into the water

o′ver·cast′ a. cloudy; dark

o′ver·coat′ n. coat worn over the usual clothing

o′ver·come′ v. get the better of; master

o′ver·do′ v. 1 do too much 2 cook too long

o′ver·dose′ (n.: ō′vər dōs′) v., n. (take) too large a dose

o′ver·draw′ v. draw on in excess of the amount credited to one —o′ver·draft′ n.

o′ver·drawn′ a. drawn on in excess of the amount credited to one

o′ver·dress′ v. dress too warmly, showily, or formally

o′ver·drive′ n. gear that reduces an engine's power without reducing its speed

o′ver·due′ a. past the time for payment, arrival, etc.

o′ver·flight′ n. flight of an aircraft over foreign territory

o′ver·flow′ (n.: o′vər flō′) v. 1 flood; run over 2 fill beyond capacity —n. 1 an overflowing 2 vent for overflowing liquids

o′ver·grow′ v. grow over all of 2 grow too much

o′ver·hand′ a., adv. with the hand held higher than the elbow

o′ver·haul′ v. check thoroughly and make needed repairs

o′ver·head′ a., adv. above the head —n. continuing business costs, as of rent

o′ver·hear′ v. hear a speaker without his knowledge

o′ver·joyed′ a. delighted

o′ver·kill′ n. much more than is needed, suitable, etc.

o′ver·land′ a., adv. by or across land

o′ver·lap′ v. lap over

o′ver·lay′ v. -laid′, -lay′ing 1 spread over 2 cover with decorative layer

o′ver·look′ v. 1 look down on 2 fail to notice 3 neglect 4 excuse

o′ver·ly adv. too much

o′ver·night′ (a.: ō′vər nīt′) adv. during the night —a. of or for a night

o′ver·pass′ n. bridge over a river, road, etc.

o′ver·pow′er v. subdue

o′ver·rate′ v. estimate too highly

o′ver·re·act′ v. react in an overly emotional way

o′ver·ride′ v. overrule

o′ver·rule′ v. 1 set aside 2 prevail over

o′ver·run′ v. 1 spread out over 2 swarm over

o′ver·seas′ a., adv. 1 across or beyond the sea 2 foreign

o′ver·see′ v. supervise —o′ver·se′er n.

o′ver·shad′ow v. be more important than

o′ver·shoe′ n. boot worn over the regular shoe to ward off dampness, etc.

o′ver·sight′ n. 1 failure to see 2 careless omission

o′ver·sim′pli·fy′ v. simplify to the point of distortion —o′ver·sim′pli·fi·ca′tion n.

o′ver·size′ a. 1 too large 2 larger than usual Also o′ver·sized′

o′ver·sleep′ v. sleep longer than intended

o′ver·stuffed′ a. upholstered with deep stuffing

o·vert′ (or ō′vʉrt′) a. 1 open; public 2 done openly

o′ver·take′ v. 1 catch up with 2 come upon suddenly

o′ver·tax′ v. 1 tax too much 2 put a strain on

o′ver·the-count′er a. sold without prescription, as some drugs

o′ver·throw′ (n.: ō′vər thrō′) v., n. defeat

o′ver·time′ n. 1 time beyond a set limit 2 pay for overtime work —a., adv. of or for overtime

o′ver·tone′ n. Mus. higher tone heard faintly when a main tone is played

o′ver·ture n. 1 Mus. introduction 2 proposal

o′ver·turn′ v. 1 turn over 2 conquer

o′ver·ween′ing a. haughty

o′ver·weight′ a. above the normal or allowed weight

o′ver·whelm′ v. 1 cover over completely 2 crush

o′ver·work′ v. work too hard —n. too much work

o′ver·wrought′ (-rôt′) a. too nervous or excited

o′vi·duct′ (or äv′i-) n. tube for passage of ova from ovary to uterus

o′void′ a. egg-shaped

ov·u·late′ (äv′yōō-) v. make and release ova —ov′u·la′tion n.

ov·ule n. 1 immature ovum 2 part of a plant that develops into a seed

o′vum n., pl. -va mature female germ cell

owe v. 1 be in debt (to) for a certain sum 2

feel obligated to give

ow'ing (ō'-) a. due; unpaid —**owing to** resulting from

owl n. night bird of prey with large eyes —**owl'ish** a.

owl'et n. small or young owl

own a. belonging to oneself or itself —n. what one owns —v. 1 possess 2 confess —**own'er** n. —**own'er·ship** n.

ox n., pl. **ox'en** 1 a cud-chewing animal, as a cow, bull, etc. 2 castrated bull

ox'blood n. deep-red color

ox'bow (-bō') n. U-shaped part of yoke for ox

ox'ford (-fərd) n. low shoe laced over the instep

ox'ide n. oxygen compound

ox'i·dize v. unite with oxygen —**ox'i·da'tion** n.

ox'y·gen n. colorless gas, commonest chemical element

ox'y·gen·ate v. treat or combine with oxygen

oys'ter n. edible mollusk with hinged shell

o'zone n. form of oxygen with a strong odor

P

pa n. [Col.] father

pab'lum n. simplistic or tasteless writing, ideas, etc.

pace n. 1 a step or stride 2 rate of speed 3 gait —v. 1 to walk back and forth across 2 measure by paces 3 set the pace for

pace'mak'er n. one leading the way: also **pace'set'ter** 2 electronic device placed in the body to regulate heart beat

pach'y·derm' (pak'ə-) n. large, thick-skinned animal

pach'y·san'dra n. low evergreen plant grown as ground cover

pa·cif'ic a. peaceful; calm

pac'i·fism' (pas'-) n. opposition to all war —**pac'i·fist** n.

pac'i·fy' v. —**fied'**, —**fy'ing** make calm —**pac'i·fi·ca'tion** n. —**pac'i·fi'er** n.

pack n. 1 bundle of things 2 package of a set number 3 a group of animals, etc. —v. 1 put (things) in a box, bundle, etc. 2 crowd; cram 3 fill tightly 4 send (off)

pack'age n. packed thing —v. make a package of

pack'et n. small package

packing house n. plant where meats, etc. are packed for sale

pack rat n. rat that hides small articles in its nest

pack'sad'dle n. saddle with fasteners to secure a load

pact n. compact; agreement

pad n. 1 soft stuffing or cushion 2 sole of an animal's foot 3 water lily leaf 4 paper sheets fastened at one edge —v. 1 stuff with material 2 walk softly

pad'ded, pad'ding 1 stuff with material 2 walk softly

pad'dle n. 1 oar for a canoe 2 similar thing for games, etc. —v. 1 propel with a paddle 2 spank

paddle wheel n. wheel with boards around it for propelling a steamboat

pad'dock n. small enclosure for horses

pad'dy n., pl. —**dies** rice field

pad'lock' n. a lock with a U-shaped arm —v. fasten with a padlock

pa·dre (pä'drā') n. father: title for a priest

pae·an (pē'ən) n. song of joy

pa'gan n., a. heathen —**pa'gan·ism'** n.

page n. 1 one side of a leaf of a book, etc. 2 the leaf 3 boy attendant —v. 1 number the pages of 2 try to find (a person) by calling his or her name

pag·eant (paj'ənt) n. elaborate show, parade, play, etc. —**pag'eant·ry** n.

pag'i·na'tion (paj'-) n. numbering of pages

pa·go'da n. towerlike temple of the Orient

paid v. pt. & pp. of PAY

pail n. bucket —**pail'ful'** n.

pain n. 1 hurt felt in body or mind 2 pl. great care —v. cause pain to —**pain'ful** a. —**pain'less** a.

pains'tak'ing a. careful

paint n. pigment mixed with oil, water, etc. —v. 1 make pictures (of) with paint 2 cover with paint —**paint'er** n. —**paint'ing** n.

pair n. two things, persons, etc. that match or make a unit —v. form pairs (of)

pais'ley (pāz'-) a. [also P—] having a complex pattern of swirls, etc.

pa·ja'mas (-jä'məz, -jam'əz) n.pl. matching trousers and top for sleeping

pal n. [Col.] close friend

pal'ace (-əs) n. 1 monarch's residence 2 magnificent building —**pa·la'tial** (-shəl) a.

pal'at·a·ble a. pleasing to the taste

pal'ate (-ət) n. 1 roof of the mouth 2 taste

pa·lav'er n., v. talk

pale a. 1 white; colorless 2 not bright or intense —v. 1 pointed fence stake 2 boundary —v. turn pale

pa'le·on·tol'o·gy n. study of fossils —**pa'le·on·tol'o·gist** n.

pal'ette (-ət) n. thin board on which artists mix paint

pal'frey (pôl'-) n., pl. —**freys** [Ar.] saddle horse

pal'in·drome' n. word, phrase, or sentence

pal′ing (pāl′-) n. fence made of pales

pal·i·sade (pal′ə sād′) n. **1** fence of large pointed stakes for fortification **2** pl. steep cliffs

pall (pôl) v. **palled, pall′ing** become boring —n. dark covering as for a coffin

pall′bear′er n. bearer of a coffin at a funeral

pal′let n. straw bed

pal′li·ate′ v. **1** relieve; ease **2** make seem less serious —**pal′li·a′tion** n. —**pal′li·a′tive** a., n.

pal′lid a. pale —**pal′lor** n.

palm (päm) n. **1** tall tropical tree topped with a bunch of huge leaves **2** its leaf: symbol of victory **3** inside of the hand —**palm off** [Col.] get rid of, sell, etc. by fraud

pal·met′to n., pl. **-tos** or **-toes** small palm tree

palm′is·try n. fortunetelling from the lines, etc. on a person's palm —**palm′ist** n.

palm′y a. **-i·er, -i·est** prosperous

pal′o·mi′no (-mē′-) n., pl. **-nos** pale-yellow horse with white mane and tail

pal′pa·ble a. **1** that can be touched, felt, etc. **2** obvious —**pal′pa·bly** adv.

pal′pi·tate′ v. to throb —**pal′pi·ta′tion** n.

pal·sy (pôl′zē) n. paralysis in part of the body, often with tremors —**pal′sied** a.

pal·try (pôl′trē) a. **-tri·er, -tri·est** trifling; petty

pam·pas (päm′pəz) n.pl. treeless plains of Argentina

pam′per v. to be overindulgent with

pam′phlet (-flət) n. a thin, unbound booklet

pan n. broad, shallow container used in cooking, etc. —v. **panned, pan′ning 1** move camera to view a panorama **2** [Col.] criticize adversely —**pan out** [Col.] turn out (well)

pan- pref. all; of all

pan′a·ce′a (-sē′-) n. supposed remedy for all diseases or problems

pa·nache′ (-nash′) n. dashing, elegant manner or style

pan′cake′ n. thin cake of batter fried in a pan

pan′chro·mat′ic (-krō-) a. describing film sensitive to all colors

pan′cre·as (-krē əs) n. gland that secretes a digestive juice —**pan′cre·at′ic** a.

pan′da n. white-and-black, bearlike animal of Asia

pan·dem′ic n., a. (disease) that is epidemic in a large area

pan′de·mo′ni·um n. wild disorder or noise

pan′der v. **1** act as a pimp **2** help other satisfy their desires —n. pimp

pane n. sheet of glass

pan′e·gyr′ic (-jir′-) n. speech or writing of praise

pan′el n. **1** flat section set off on a wall, door, etc. **2** group chosen for judging, discussing, etc. —v. provide with panels —**pan′el·ing** n. —**pan′el·ist** n.

pang n. sudden, sharp pain

pan′han′dle v. [Col.] beg on the streets

pan′ic n. sudden, wild fear —v. **-icked, -ick·ing** fill with panic —**pan′ick·y** a.

pan′ic-strick′en a. badly frightened

pan′nier, pan′ier (-yər) n. basket for carrying loads on the back

pan′o·ply (-plē) n., pl. **-plies 1** suit of armor **2** splendid display

pan′o·ram′a n. **1** unlimited view **2** constantly changing scene —**pan′o·ram′ic** a.

pan′sy (-zē) n., pl. **-sies** small plant with velvety petals

pant v. **1** breathe in pants **2** long (for) **3** gasp out —n. rapid, heavy breath

pan′ta·loons′ n.pl. trousers

pan′the·ism′ n. doctrine that all forces of the universe are God —**pan′the·ist** n.

pan′the·on′ n. temple for all the gods

pan′ther n. **1** cougar **2** jaguar **3** leopard

pant′ies n.pl. women's or children's short underpants

pan′to·mime′ v., n. (make) use of gestures without words to present a play

pan′try n., pl. **-tries** a room for food, pots, etc.

pants n.pl. trousers

pant′suit′ n. matched jacket and pants for women

pant′y·hose′ n. women's hose joined and extending to the waist: also **pant′y hose**

pap n. soft food

pa′pa n. father: child's word

pa′pa·cy (pā′-) n. position, authority, etc. of the Pope

pa′pal a. of the Pope or the papacy

pa·paw′ (pô′pô′) n. tree with yellow fruit

pa·pa·ya (pə pī′ə) n. tropical palmlike tree with large, orange fruit

pa′per n. **1** thin material in sheets, used to write or print on, wrap, etc. **2** sheet of this **3** essay **4** newspaper **5** wallpaper **6** pl. credentials —a. of or like paper —v. cover with wallpaper —**pa′per·y** a.

pa′per·back′ n. book bound in paper

pa′per·boy′ n. boy who sells or delivers newspapers —**pa′per·girl′** n.fem.

pa′per·weight′ n. object set on papers to hold them down

pa′pier-mâ·ché′ (-pər mə shā′) n. wet paper pulp, molded into various objects

pa·pil′la n., pl. **-lae** (-ē) small projection of tissue, as on the tongue

pa·poose′ n. North American Indian baby

pa·pri·ka (-prē´-) n. ground, mild, red seasoning

Pap test n. test for uterine cancer

pa·py·rus n. 1 paper made by ancient Egyptians from a water plant 2 this plant

par n. 1 equal rank 2 average 3 face value of stocks, etc. 4 expert score in golf

para– pref. 1 beside; beyond 2 helping; secondary

par·a·ble n. short, simple story with a moral

pa·rab·o·la n. curve formed when a cone is sliced parallel to its side

par·a·chute n. umbrellalike device used to slow down a person or thing dropping from an aircraft —v. drop by parachute —**par´a·chut´ist** n.

pa·rade n. 1 showy display 2 march or procession —v. 1 march in a parade 2 show off

par·a·digm (-dīm´) n. example

par·a·dise n. place or state of great happiness —[P–] heaven

par·a·dox n. contradictory statement that is or seems false —**par´a·dox´i·cal** a.

par·af·fin n. white, waxy substance used for making candles, sealing jars, etc.

par·a·gon n. model of perfection or excellence

par·a·graph n. distinct section of a piece of writing, begun on a new line and often indented

par·a·keet n. small parrot

par·a·le·gal a., n. (of) a lawyer's assistant

par·al·lax n. apparent change in object's position resulting from change in viewer's position

par·al·lel a. 1 in the same direction and at a fixed distance apart 2 similar —n. 1 parallel line, surface, etc. 2 one like another 3 imaginary line parallel to the equator, representing degrees of latitude —v. be parallel with

par·al·lel·o·gram´ n. four-sided figure with opposite sides parallel and equal

pa·ral´y·sis n. 1 loss of power to move any part of the body 2 a crippling —**par´a·lyt´ic** (-lit´-) a., n.

par·a·lyze (-līz´) v. 1 to cause paralysis in 2 to make ineffective

par·a·me´ci·um (-sē əm) n., pl. **–ci·a** a freshwater protozoan

par·a·med´i·cal a. of medical auxiliaries, as nurses' aides, midwives, etc.

pa·ram´e·ter n. boundary or limit

par·a·mil´i·tar´y a. of a private, often secret, military group

par·a·mount´ a. supreme

par·a·mour (-moor´) n. illicit lover or mistress

par·a·noi´a n. mental illness of feeling persecuted —**par·a·noid´** a., n.

par·a·pet n. wall for protection from enemy fire

par·a·pher·na´li·a n.pl. [sing. or pl. v.] belongings or equipment

par·a·phrase n. rewording —v. reword

par·a·ple·gi·a (-plē´jē ə, -jə) n. paralysis of the lower body —**par·a·ple´gic** a., n.

par·a·pro·fes´sion·al n. worker trained to assist a professional

par·a·site n. plant or animal that lives on or in another —**par´a·sit´ic** a.

par·a·sol´ (-sôl´) n. light umbrella used as a sunshade

par·a·thi´on (-thī´än´) n. a poisonous insecticide

par·a·thy´roid (-thī´-) a. of certain small glands near the thyroid

par·a·troops n.pl. unit of soldiers trained to parachute from airplanes behind enemy lines —**par´a·troop´er** n.

par·boil´ v. boil until partly cooked

par´cel (-səl) n. 1 package 2 piece (of land) —v. apportion: with out

parcel post n. postal branch which delivers parcels

parch v. 1 make hot and dry 2 make thirsty

parch´ment n. 1 skin of a sheep, etc. prepared as a surface for writing 2 paper resembling this

par·don v. 1 to release from punishment 2 excuse; forgive —n. act of pardoning —**par´don·a·ble** a.

pare v. 1 peel 2 reduce gradually

par·e·gor´ic n. medicine with opium, for diarrhea, pain, etc.

par·ent n. 1 father or mother 2 source —**pa·ren´tal** a. —**par´ent·hood´** n. —**par´ent·ing** n.

par´ent·age n. descent from parents or ancestors

pa·ren´the·sis n., pl. **–ses´** (-sēz´) 1 word of explanation put into a sentence 2 either of the marks ( ) used to set this off —**par´en·thet´i·cal, par´en·thet´ic·a** a.

pa·re´sis n. brain disease caused by syphilis

par·fait´ (-fā´) n. ice cream dessert in a tall glass

pa·ri´ah (-rī´ə) n. outcast

par´ing (per´-) n. strip peeled off

par·ish n. 1 part of a diocese under a priest, etc. 2 church congregation

pa·rish´ion·er n. member of a parish

par´i·ty n., pl. **–ties** equality of value at a given ratio between moneys, commodities, etc.

park n. public land for recreation or rest —v. leave (a vehicle) temporarily

par´ka n. hooded coat

Par´kin·son's disease *n.* disease causing tremors

park´way´ *n.* broad road lined with trees

par´lance *n.* mode of speech

par´lay *v.* 1 bet (wager plus winnings from one race, etc.) on another 2 exploit (an asset) successfully —*n.* bet or bets made by parlaying

par´ley (-lē) *v., n.* talk to settle differences, etc.

par´lia·ment (-lə-) *n.* legislative body, spec. [P–] of Great Britain, Canada, etc. —**par´lia·men´ta·ry** *a.*

par´lor *n.* 1 living room 2 business establishment, as a shop where hair is styled

Par´me·san´ cheese (-zän´) *n.* a dry Italian cheese

pa·ro´chi·al (-kē əl) *a.* 1 of a parish 2 limited; narrow

par´o·dy *v.* **–died, –dy·ing;** *n., pl.* **–dies** (write) a farcical imitation of a work

pa·role´ *v., n.* release from prison on condition of future good behavior

pa·rol´ee´ *n.* one on parole

par´ox·ysm´ (-əks iz´əm) *n.* spasm or outburst

par´quet´ (-kā´) *n.* flooring of parquetry

par´quet·ry (-kə trē) *n.* inlaid flooring of geometric forms

par´ri·cide´ *n.* 1 act of murdering one's parent 2 one who does this

par´rot *n.* brightly colored bird that can imitate speech —*v.* repeat or copy without full understanding

par´ry *v.* **–ried, –ry·ing** 1 ward off 2 evade

parse *v.* analyze (a sentence) grammatically

par´si·mo´ny *n.* stinginess —**par´si·mo´ni·ous** *a.*

pars´ley *n.* plant with leaves used to flavor some foods

pars´nip´ *n.* sweet white root used as a vegetable

par´son *n.* minister or clergyman

par´son·age *n.* parson's dwelling, provided by the church

part *n.* 1 portion, piece, element, etc. 2 duty 3 role 4 music for a certain voice or instrument in a composition 5 *usually pl.* region 6 dividing line formed in combing the hair —*v.* 1 divide; separate 2 go away from each other —*a.* less than whole —**part with** give up —**take part** participate

par·take´ *v.* **–took´, –tak´en, –tak´ing** 1 participate (*in*) 2 eat or drink (*of*)

par´tial (-shəl) *a.* 1 favoring one over another 2 not complete —**partial to** fond of —**par´ti·al´i·ty** (-shē al´-) *n.* —**par´tial·ly** *adv.*

par·tic´i·pate´ (-tis´-) *v.* have or take a share with others (*in*) —**par·tic´i·pant** *n.* —**par·tic´i·pa´tion** *n.*

par´ti·ci´ple *n.* verb form having the qualities of both a verb and adjective

par´ti·cle *n.* 1 tiny fragment 2 preposition, article, or conjunction

par´ti·col´ored *a.* having different colors in different parts

par·tic´u·lar *a.* 1 of one; individual 2 specific 3 hard to please —*n.* a detail —**par·tic´u·lar·ly** *adv.*

par·tic´u·late (-lit) *a.* of or formed of tiny, separate particles

part´ing *a., n.* 1 dividing 2 departing

par´ti·san *n.* 1 strong supporter; adherent 2 guerrilla —*a.* of a partisan

par·ti´tion (-tish´ən) *n.* 1 division into parts 2 thing that divides —*v.* divide into parts

part´ly *adv.* not fully

part´ner *n.* one who undertakes something with another; associate; mate —**part´ner·ship´** *n.*

part of speech *n.* class of word, as noun, verb, etc.

par´tridge *n.* game bird, as the pheasant, quail, etc.

part song *n.* song for several voices, without accompaniment

part time *n.* part of the usual time —**part´-time´** *a.*

par´tu·ri´tion (-rish´ən) *n.* childbirth

par´ty *n., pl.* **–ties** 1 group working together for a political cause, etc. 2 social gathering 3 one involved in a lawsuit, crime, etc. 4 [Col.] person —*v.* **–tied, –ty·ing** take part in social activity, esp. boisterously

party line *n.* 1 single circuit for two or more telephone users 2 a political party's policies

pas´chal (-kəl) *a.* of the Passover or Easter

pass *v.* 1 go by, beyond, etc. 2 go or change from one form, place, etc. to another 3 cease; end 4 approve or be approved 5 take a test, etc. successfully 6 cause or allow to go, move, qualify, etc. 7 throw 8 spend time 9 happen 10 give as an opinion, judgment, etc. —*n.* 1 a passing 2 free ticket 3 brief military leave 4 PASSAGE (*n.* 4) —**pass´a·ble** *a.*

pas´sage *n.* 1 a passing 2 right to pass 3 voyage 4 road, opening, etc. 5 part of something written

pas´sage·way´ *n.* narrow way, as a hall, alley, etc.

pass´book´ *n.* booklet recording depositor's bank account

pas·sé´ (pa sā´) *a.* out-of-date

pas´sen·ger *n.* one traveling in a train, car, etc.

pass′er-by′ n., pl. **pass′ers-by′** one who passes by

pass′ing a. 1 that passes 2 casual —in **passing** incidentally

pas′sion n. 1 strong emotion, as hate, love, etc. 2 an object of strong desire —**pas′sion-ate** a.

pas′sive a. 1 inactive, but acted upon 2 yielding; submissive —**pas-siv′i-ty** n.

passive resistance n. opposition to a law by refusal to comply or by nonviolent acts

pass′key′ n. key that fits a number of locks

Pass′o′ver n. Jewish holiday in the spring

pass′port′ n. government document identifying a citizen traveling abroad

pass′word′ n. secret word given to pass a guard

past a. 1 gone by 2 of a former time —n. 1 history 2 time gone by —prep. beyond in time, space, etc. —adv. to and beyond

pas′ta (päs′-) n. spaghetti, macaroni, etc.

paste n. 1 moist, smooth mixture 2 adhesive mixture with flour, water, etc. —v. make adhere, as with paste

paste′board′ n. stiff material of pasted layers of paper

pas-tel′ a., n. soft and pale (shade)

pas′teur-ize′ (-chər-, -tər-) v. kill bacteria (in milk, etc.) by heating —**pas′teur-i-za′tion** n.

pas-tiche′ (-tēsh′) n. artistic composition made up of bits from several sources

pas′time′ n. way to spend spare time

pas′tor n. clergyman in charge of a congregation

pas′to-ral a. 1 of a pastor 2 simple and rustic

past participle n. participle used to indicate a past time

pas-tra′mi (pə strä′-) n. spiced, smoked beef

pas′try (pās′-) n., pl. **-tries** fancy baked goods

pas′ture n. ground for grazing: also **pas′tur-age** (-ij) —v. let (cattle) graze

past′y a. **-i-er, -i-est** of or like paste

pat n. 1 gentle tap with something flat 2 small lump, as of butter —v. **pat′ted, pat′ting** give a gentle pat to —a. suitable

patch n. 1 piece of material used to mend a hole, etc. 2 spot —v. 1 put a patch on 2 to make crudely

patch′work′ n. quilt made of odd patches of cloth

pate (pāt) n. top of the head

pâ-té (pä tā′) n. meat paste or spread

pa-tel′la n., pl. **-las** or **-lae** (-lē) kneecap

pat′ent (pat′-; a. 2: pāt′-) n. document granting exclusive rights over an invention —a. 1 protected by patent 2

obvious —v. get a patent for

pat′ent leather (pat′-) n. leather with a hard, glossy finish

pa-ter′nal a. 1 fatherly 2 on the father's side —**pa-ter′nal-ism′** n. —**pa-ter′nal-is′tic** a.

pa-ter′ni-ty n. fatherhood

path n. 1 way worn by footsteps 2 line of movement 3 course of conduct

pa-thet′ic a. arousing pity —**pa-thet′i-cal-ly** adv.

path′o-gen′ic (-jen′-) a. producing disease

pa-thol′o-gy n. study of the nature and effect of disease —**path′o-log′i-cal** a. —**pa-thol′o-gist** n.

pa-thos (pā′thäs′) n. the quality in a thing which arouses pity

path′way′ n. path

pa′tient (-shənt) a. 1 enduring pain, delay, etc. without complaint 2 persevering —n. one receiving medical care —**pa′tience** n. —**pa′tient-ly** adv.

pat′i-na n. green oxidized coating on bronze or copper

pa′ti-o′ n., pl. **-os′** 1 courtyard 2 paved lounging area next to house

pa-tois′ (-wä′) n., pl. **-ois′** (-wäz′) dialect of a region

pa′tri-arch′ (-ärk′) n. 1 father and head of a family or tribe 2 dignified old man —**pa′tri-ar′chal** a.

pa-tri′cian (-trish′ən) a., n. aristocratic (person)

pat′ri-mo′ny n. inheritance from one's father

pa′tri-ot n. one who shows love and loyalty for his or her country —**pa′tri-ot′ic** a. —**pa′tri-ot-ism′** n.

pa-trol′ v. **-trolled′, -trol′ling** make trips around in guarding —n. a patrolling, or a group that patrols

pa-trol′man n., pl. **-men** policeman who patrols a certain area

pa′tron n. 1 a sponsor 2 regular customer

pa′tron-age n. 1 help given by a patron 2 customers, or their trade 3 political favors

pa′tron-ize′ v. 1 sponsor 2 be condescending to 3 be a regular customer of

pat′ro-nym′ic (-nim′-) n. name showing descent from a given person

pat′sy n., pl. **-sies** [Sl.] person easily imposed on

pat′ter n. 1 series of rapid taps 2 glib talk —v. make or utter (a) patter

pat′tern n. 1 one worthy of imitation 2 plan used in making things 3 design or decoration 4 usual behavior, procedure, etc. —v. copy as from a pattern

pat′ty n., pl. **-ties** flat cake of ground meat, etc.

pau'ci·ty (pô'-) n. 1 fewness 2 scarcity

paunch n. fat belly

pau'per n. very poor person

pause v., n. (make) temporary stop

pave v. surface (a road, etc.), as with asphalt

pave'ment n. paved road, sidewalk, etc.

pa·vil'ion (-yən) n. 1 large tent 2 building for exhibits, etc., as at a fair

paw n. foot of an animal with claws —v. 1 to touch, etc. with paws or feet 2 handle roughly

pawl n. a catch for the teeth of a ratchet wheel

pawn v. give as security for a loan —n. 1 chessman of lowest value 2 person who is subject to another's will

pawn'bro·ker n. one licensed to lend money on things pawned —**pawn'shop'** n.

pay v. **paid, pay'ing** 1 give (money) to (one) for goods or services 2 settle, as a debt 3 give, as a compliment 4 make, as a visit 5 be profitable (to) —n. wages —a. operated by coins, etc. —**pay out** pt. **payed out** let out, as a rope —**pay'ee'** n. —**pay'er** n. —**pay'ment** n.

pay'a·ble a. 1 that can be paid 2 due to be paid

pay'check' n. check in payment of wages or salary

pay'load' n. load carried by an aircraft, missile, etc.

pay'mas'ter n. official in charge of paying employees

pay'off' n. 1 reckoning or payment 2 [Col.] bribe

pay'roll' n. 1 list of employees to be paid 2 amount due them

PC n. personal computer, or microcomputer

pea n. plant with pods having round, edible seeds

peace n. 1 freedom from war or strife 2 agreement to end war 3 law and order 4 calm —**peace'a·ble** a.

peace'ful a. 1 not fighting 2 calm 3 of a time of peace —**peace'ful·ly** adv.

peace'mak'er n. one who settles quarrels, etc.

peach n. round, juicy, orange-yellow fruit

pea'cock' n. male of a large bird (**pea'fowl'**), with a long showy tail —**pea'hen'** n.fem.

peak n. 1 pointed end or top 2 mountain with pointed summit 3 highest point —v. come or bring to a peak

peak'ed a. thin and drawn

peal n. 1 loud ringing of bell(s) 2 loud, prolonged sound —v. to ring; resound

pea'nut' n. 1 vine with underground pods and edible seeds 2 the pod or a seed

peanut butter n. food paste made by grinding peanuts

pear n. soft, juicy fruit

pearl (purl) n. 1 smooth, roundish stone formed in oysters, used as a gem 2 mother-of-pearl 3 bluish gray —**pearl'y** a., **-i·er, -i·est**

peas'ant (pez'-) n. farm worker of Europe, etc. —**peas'ant·ry** n.

peat n. decayed plant matter in bogs, dried for fuel

peat moss n. peat made up of moss residues, used for mulch

peb'ble n. small, smooth stone —**peb'bly** a., **-bli·er, -bli·est**

pe·can' n. edible nut with a thin, smooth shell

pec·ca·dil'lo n., pl. **-loes** or **-los** minor or petty sin

pec'ca·ry n., pl. **-ries** wild piglike animal with tusks

peck v. strike as with a beak —n. 1 stroke made as with a beak 2 dry measure equal to 8 quarts

pec'tin n. substance in some fruits causing jelly to form

pec'to·ral a. of the chest

pec'u·late' v. embezzle

pe·cu'liar (-kyōol'yər) a. 1 of only one; exclusive 2 special 3 odd —**pe·cu'li·ar'i·ty** (-er'-) n., pl. **-ties**

pe·cu'ni·ar'y (-kyōo'nē-) a. of money

ped'a·gogue', ped'a·gog' (-gäg') n. teacher —**ped'a·gog'y** (-gä'jē) n. —**ped'a·gog'ic·al** a. —**ped'a·gog'i·cal** a.

ped'al n. lever worked by the foot —v. work by pedals —a. of the foot

ped'ant n. one who stresses trivial points of learning —**pe·dan'tic** a. —**ped'ant·ry** n.

ped'dle v. go from place to place selling —**ped'dler** n.

ped'es·tal n. base, as of a column, statue, etc.

pe·des'tri·an a. 1 going on foot 2 dull and ordinary —n. one who goes on foot; walker

pe'di·at'rics n. medical care and treatment of babies and children —**pe'di·a·tri'cian** (-trish'ən) n.

ped'i·cab' n. a three-wheeled carriage pedaled by the driver

ped'i·cure' n. a trimming, polishing, etc. of the toenails

ped'i·gree' n. ancestry; descent —**ped'i·greed'** a.

ped'i·ment n. ornamental triangular piece over a doorway

pe·dom'e·ter n. device measuring a distance walked

peek v. glance quickly and furtively —n. glance

peel v. 1 cut away (the rind, etc.) of 2 shed

skin, bark, etc. 3 come off in layers or flakes —n. rind or skin of fruit

peel'ing n. rind peeled off

peen n. end of hammer head opposite the striking surface

peep v. 1 make the chirping cry of a young bird 2 look through a small opening 3 peek 4 appear partially —n. 1 peeping sound 2 furtive glimpse —**peep'hole**' n.

peer n. 1 an equal 2 British noble —v. look closely —**peer'age** n.

peer'less a. without equal

peeve [Col.] v. make peevish —n. annoyance

pee'vish a. irritable

pee'wee' n. [Col.] something very small

peg n. 1 short pin or bolt 2 step or degree —v. **pegged, peg'ging** fix or mark as with pegs

peign·oir (pān wär') n. a woman's loose dressing gown

pe·jo'ra·tive a. derogatory

Pe'king·ese' (-kə nēz') n., pl. **-ese**' small dog with pug nose: also **Pe'kin·ese**'

pe'koe n. a black tea

pelf n. mere wealth

pel'i·can n. water bird with a pouch in its lower bill

pel·la'gra (-lā'-) n. a disease caused by vitamin deficiency

pel'let n. little ball

pell'-mell', pell'mell' adv. in reckless haste

pel·lu'cid (-loo'-) a. clear

pelt v. 1 throw things at 2 beat steadily —n. skin of a fur-bearing animal

pel'vis n. cavity formed by bones of the hip and part of the backbone —**pel'vic** a.

pem'mi·can n. dried food concentrate

pen n. 1 enclosure for animals 2 device for writing with ink 3 [Sl.] penitentiary —v. **penned, pent, pen'ning** 1 enclose as in a pen 2 write with a pen

pe'nal a. of or as punishment

pe'nal·ize (or pen'əl-) v. punish

pen'al·ty n., pl. **-ties** 1 punishment 2 handicap

pen'ance n. voluntary suffering to show repentance

pence n. [Br.] pl. of PENNY (n. 2)

pen'chant n. strong liking

pen'cil n. device with a core of graphite, etc. for writing, etc. —v. write with a pencil

pend v. await decision

pend'ant n. hanging object used as an ornament

pend'ent a. suspended

pend'ing a. not decided —prep. 1 during 2 until

pen'du·lous (-jə ləs, -dyə-) a. hanging freely

pen'du·lum n. weight hung so as to swing freely

pen'e·trate' v. 1 enter by piercing 2 to affect throughout 3 understand —**pen'e·tra·ble** a. —**pen'e·tra'tion** n.

pen'guin (-gwin) n. flightless bird of the antarctic

pen·i·cil'lin n. antibiotic drug obtained from a mold

pen·in'su·la n. land area almost surrounded by water —**pen·in'su·lar** a.

pe'nis n. male sex organ

pen'i·tent a. willing to atone —n. a penitent person —**pen'i·tence** n.

pen'i·ten'tia·ry (-sha rē) n., pl. **-ries** prison

pen'knife' n. small pocketknife

pen'man·ship' n. quality of handwriting

pen name n. pseudonym

pen'nant n. 1 long, narrow flag 2 championship

pen'ni·less a. very poor

pen'non n. flag or pennant

pen'ny n. 1 pl. **-nies** cent 2 pl. **pence** Br. coin, 1/100 pound (formerly, 1/12 shilling)

penny arcade n. public amusement hall with coin-operated games

pe·nol'o·gy n. study of prison management and reform

pen'sion n. regular payment to a retired or disabled person —v. pay a pension to

pen'sive (-siv) a. thoughtful; reflective

pent a. shut in; kept in: often with up

pen'ta·gon' n. figure with five angles and five sides

pen·tam'e·ter n. line of verse of five metrical feet

pen·tath'lon' n. athletic contest with five different events

pent'house' n. apartment on the roof of a building

pent'-up' a. confined; checked

pe·nu·che, pe·nu·chi (pə nōō'chē) n. fudgelike candy

pe·nul'ti·mate a. next to last

pe·nu'ri·ous (pe nyoor'ē-) a. stingy

pen'u·ry n. extreme poverty

pe'on' n. Latin American worker —**pe'on·age** n.

pe'o·ny n., pl. **-nies** plant with large showy flowers

peo'ple (pē'-) n.pl. 1 human beings 2 a populace 3 one's family —n., pl. **-ples** a nation, race, etc. —v. populate

pep [Col.] n. energy; vigor —v. **pepped, pep'ping** fill with pep: with up —**pep'py** a., **-pi·er, -pi·est**

pep'per n. 1 plant with a red or green, hot or sweet pod 2 the pod 3 spicy seasoning made from berries (**pep'per·corns**') of a tropical plant —v. 1 season with pepper

2 pelt with small objects

pepper mill *n.* hand mill used to grind peppercorns

pep'per·mint' *n.* mint plant yielding an oily flavoring

pep'per·o'ni *n.* highly spiced Italian sausage

pep'per·y *a.* 1 fiery 2 hot-tempered

pep'sin *n.* stomach enzyme that helps digest proteins

pep'tic *a.* of digestion

per *prep.* 1 by means of 2 for each

per·am'bu·late' *v.* walk through or over

per·am'bu·la'tor *n.* [Br.] a baby carriage

per an'num *a., adv.* by the year

per·cale' (-kāl') *n.* cotton cloth used for sheets

per cap'i·ta *a., adv.* for each person

per·ceive' (-sēv') *v.* 1 grasp mentally 2 become aware (of) through the senses

per·cent' *adv., a.* out of every hundred: also **per cent** —*n.* [Col.] percentage

per·cent'age *n.* 1 rate per hundred 2 portion

per·cen'tile' *n.* any of 100 equal parts

per·cep'ti·ble *a.* that can be perceived

per·cep'tion *n.* 1 ability to perceive 2 knowledge got by perceiving —**per·cep'tu·al** (-chōō-) *a.*

per·cep'tive *a.* able to perceive readily

perch *n.* 1 small food fish 2 a pole or branch that birds roost on —*v.* rest on a perch

per·chance' *adv.* [Ar.] 1 by chance 2 perhaps

per'co·late' *v.* 1 filter 2 make in a percolator

per'co·la'tor *n.* pot in which boiling water filters through ground coffee

per·cus'sion (-kush'ən) *n.* 1 hitting of one thing against another 2 musical instruments played by striking, as drums —**per·cus'sion·ist** *n.*

per di·em (dē'əm) *n.* daily

per·di'tion (-dish'ən) *n.* 1 hell 2 loss of one's soul

per'e·gri·na'tion *n.* a walking about

per·emp'to·ry *a.* 1 overbearing 2 not to be refused

per·en'ni·al *a.* 1 lasting a year 2 living more than two years —*n.* plant living more than two years

per'fect (*v.*: -ər fekt') *a.* 1 complete 2 excellent 3 completely accurate —*v.* make perfect —**per·fect'i·ble** *a.* —**per·fec'tion** *n.* —**per'fect·ly** *adv.*

per·fec'tion·ist *n.* one who strives for perfection

per'fi·dy *n., pl.* –**dies** treachery —**per·fid'i·ous** *a.*

per'fo·rate' *v.* pierce with a hole or holes

—**per'fo·ra'tion** *n.*

per·force' *adv.* necessarily

per·form' *v.* 1 do; carry out 2 act a role, play music, etc.

per·form'ance *n.* 1 a doing or thing done 2 display of one's skill or talent

per·form'ing arts *n.pl.* arts, as drama and dance, performed before an audience

per·fume' (*or* pur'fyōōm') *v.* scent with perfume —*n.* 1 fragrance 2 liquid with a pleasing odor

per·func'to·ry *a.* done without care or interest

per·go'la *n.* arbor with latticework roof

per·haps' *adv.* probably

per'i·gee' (-jē') *n.* point nearest earth in a satellite's orbit

per'il *v., n.* (put in) danger or risk —**per'il·ous** *a.*

pe·rim'e·ter *n.* outer boundary of a figure or area

pe'ri·od *n.* 1 portion of time 2 mark of punctuation (.)

pe'ri·od'ic *a.* recurring at regular intervals

pe'ri·od'i·cal *n.* magazine published every week, month, etc. —*a.* periodic —**pe'ri·od'i·cal·ly** *adv.*

per'i·o·don'tal *a.* around a tooth and affecting the gums

per'i·pa·tet'ic *a.* moving or walking about; itinerant

pe·riph'er·y (-rif') *n., pl.* –**ies** outer boundary or part —**pe·riph'er·al** *a.*

per'i·scope' *n.* tube with mirrors, etc., for seeing over or around an obstacle

per'ish *v.* be destroyed; die

per'ish·a·ble *n., a.* (food) liable to spoil

per'i·stal'sis (-stôl'-) *n.* action of intestines that moves food onward

per'i·to·ni'tis (-nīt'is) *n.* inflammation of the membrane (**per'i·to·ne'um**) lining the abdominal cavity

per'i·win'kle *n.* MYRTLE (n. 2)

per'jure *v.* tell a lie while under oath —**per'jur·er** *n.* —**per'ju·ry** *n., pl.* –**ries**

perk *v.* 1 raise or liven (*up*) 2 make stylish or smart 3 [Col.] percolate —*n.* [Col.] perquisite —**perk'y** *a.*, –**i·er**, –**i·est**

perm [Col.] *n.* a permanent —*v.* give a permanent to

per'ma·frost' *n.* permanently frozen subsoil

per'ma·nent *a.* lasting indefinitely —*n.* long-lasting hair wave —**per'ma·nence** *n.* —**per'ma·nent·ly** *adv.*

per'me·ate' *v.* diffuse; penetrate (*through* or *among*) —**per'me·a·ble** *a.*

per·mis'si·ble *a.* allowable

per·mis'sion *n.* consent

per·mis'sive *a.* not restricting

per·mit' (n.: pur'mit') v. –mit'ted, –mit'ting allow —n. document giving permission

per·mu·ta'tion (-myoo-) n. a change, as in order

per·ni'cious (-nish'əs) a. very harmful or damaging

per·o·ra'tion n. last part or summation of a speech

per·ox'ide' n. hydrogen peroxide

per·pen·dic'u·lar a. 1 at right angles to a given line or plane 2 vertical —n. perpendicular line

per'pe·trate' v. do (something evil, wrong, etc.) —**per'pe·tra'tion** n. —**per'pe·tra'tor** n.

per·pet'u·al (-pech'-) a. 1 lasting forever 2 constant

per·pet'u·ate' (-pech'-) v. cause to continue or be remembered —**per·pet'u·a'tion** n.

per'pe·tu'i·ty (-pə tōō'-) n. existence forever

per·plex' v. confuse or puzzle —**per·plex'i·ty** n., pl. –ties

per'qui·site (-kwi zit) n. privilege or profit incidental to one's employment

per' se' (-sā') by (or in) itself

per'se·cute' v. torment continuously for one's beliefs, etc. —**per'se·cu'tion** n. —**per'se·cu'tor** n.

per'se·vere' (-vir') v. to continue in spite of difficulty —**per'se·ver'ance** n.

Per'sian (-zhən) n. domestic cat with long, thick coat

Persian lamb n. karakul

per'si·flage' (-fläzh') n. playful or joking talk

per·sim'mon n. an orange-red, plumlike fruit

per·sist' v. continue insistently or steadily —**per·sist'ent** a. —**per·sist'ence** n.

per·snick'e·ty a. [Col.] fussy

per'son n. 1 human being 2 the body or self 3 Gram. any of the three classes of pronouns indicating the identity of the subject, as I, you, he, etc.

–person suf. person (without regard to sex)

per'son·a·ble a. pleasing in looks and manner

per'son·age n. (important) person

per'son·al a. 1 private; individual 2 of the body 3 of the character, conduct, etc. of a person 4 indicating person in grammar 5 other than real estate: said of property —**per'son·al·ize'** v. —**per'son·al·ly** adv.

personal computer n. microcomputer

personal effects n.pl. personal belongings worn or carried

per'son·al'i·ty n., pl. –ties 1 distinctive or attractive character of a person 2 notable person

per·so'na non gra'ta (-grät'ə) n. [L.] unwelcome person

per·son'i·fy' v. –fied', –fy'ing 1 represent as a person 2 typify —**per·son'i·fi·ca'tion** n.

per'son·nel' n. persons employed in any work, etc.

per·spec'tive n. 1 appearance of objects from their relative distance and positions 2 sense of proportion

per'spi·ca'cious a. having keen insight

per·spire' v. to sweat —**per'spi·ra'tion** n.

per·suade' v. to cause to do or believe by urging, etc. —**per·sua'sive** a.

per·sua'sion n. a persuading 2 belief

per·tain' v. 1 belong 2 have reference

per'ti·na'cious (-nā'shəs) a. persistent —**per'ti·nac'i·ty** (-nas'-) n.

per'ti·nent a. relevant; to the point —**per'ti·nence** n.

per·turb' v. alarm; upset

pe·ruse' (-rōōz') v. read —**pe·rus'al** n.

per·vade' v. spread or be prevalent throughout —**per·va'sive** a.

per·verse' a. 1 stubbornly contrary 2 erring 3 wicked —**per·ver'si·ty** n., pl. –ties

per·vert' (n.: pur'vurt') v. lead astray; corrupt —n. one who engages in abnormal sexual acts —**per·ver'sion** n.

pes'ky a. –ki·er, –ki·est [Col.] annoying

pe'so (pā'-) n., pl. –sos monetary unit of Mexico, Cuba, etc.

pes'si·mism' n. tendency to expect the worst —**pes'si·mist** n. —**pes'si·mis'tic** a.

pest n. person or thing that causes trouble, etc.

pes'ter v. annoy; vex

pes'ti·cide' n. chemical for killing insects, weeds, etc.

pes·tif'er·ous a. 1 noxious 2 [Col.] annoying

pes'ti·lence n. virulent or contagious disease —**pes'ti·lent** a.

pes'tle (-əl, -təl) n. tool used to pound or grind substances

pet n. 1 domesticated animal treated fondly 2 favorite 3 bad humor —v. pet'ted, pet'ting stroke gently

pet'al n. leaflike part of a blossom

pet'cock' n. small valve for draining pipes, etc.

pe·tite' (-tēt') a. small and trim in figure

pe·tit four (pet'ē) n. tiny frosted cake

pe·ti'tion n. solemn, earnest request, esp. in writing —v. address a petition to

pet'rel n. small sea bird

pet'ri·fy' v. –fied', –fy'ing 1 change into stony substance 2 stun, as with fear

pet'ro·chem'i·cal n. chemical derived from petroleum

pet′rol n. [Br.] gasoline

pe·tro·la′tum n. greasy, jellylike substance used for ointments: also **petroleum jelly**

pe·tro′le·um n. oily liquid found in rock strata: it yields kerosene, gasoline, etc.

pet′ti·coat n. skirt worn under an outer skirt

pet′ti·fog′ger n. unethical lawyer handling petty cases

pet′ty a. **-ti·er, -ti·est 1** of little importance **2** narrow-minded **3** low in rank

petty cash n. fund for incidentals

petty officer n. naval enlisted person of same rank as noncommissioned army officer

pet′u·lant (pech′ə-) a. impatient or irritable —**pet′u·lance** n.

pe·tu′ni·a (-tōōn′yə) n. plant with funnel-shaped flowers

pew (pyōō) n. row of fixed benches in a church

pew′ter n. alloy of tin with lead, brass, or copper

pe·yo·te (pā ō′tē) n. mescal cactus plant

PG trademark film rating indicting film content unsuitable for childern under 17

PG-13 trademark film rating indicting some content especially unsuitable for children under 13

pha·e·ton (fā′-) n. light, four-wheeled carriage

pha′lanx n. massed group of individuals

phal′lus n. image of the penis —**phal′lic** a.

phan′tasm (-taz′əm) n. figment of the mind

phan·tas·ma·go′ri·a (-taz′-) n. rapidly changing series of things seen, as in a dream

phan′ta·sy n., pl. **-sies** fantasy

phan′tom n. **1** ghost; specter **2** illusion —a. unreal

Phar·aoh (far′ō) n. title of ancient Egyptian rulers

phar′i·see′ (far′-) n. self-righteous person

phar′ma·ceu′ti·cal (fär′mə sōō′-) a. **1** of pharmacy **2** of or by drugs —n. a drug or medicine

phar′ma·cist n. one whose profession is pharmacy

phar′ma·col′o·gy n. study of drugs —**phar′ma·col′o·gist** n.

phar′ma·co·pe′ia (-pē′ə) n. official book listing drugs and medicines

phar′ma·cy n., pl. **-cies 1** science of preparing drugs and medicines **2** drugstore

phar·yn·gi·tis (far′in jīt′is) n. inflammation of the pharynx; sore throat

phar·ynx (-iŋks) n. cavity between mouth and larynx

phase n. **1** aspect; side **2** one of a series of changes

phase′out′ n. gradual withdrawal

pheas′ant (fez′-) n. game bird with a long tail

phe′no·bar′bi·tal′ n. white compound used as a sedative

phe·nom′e·non n., pl. **-na 1** observable fact or event **2** anything very unusual —**phe·nom′e·nal** a.

phi′al (fī′-) n. vial

phi·lan′der (fi-) v. make love insincerely —**phi·lan′der·er** n.

phi·lan′thro·py n. **1** desire to help mankind **2** pl. **-pies** thing done to help mankind —**phil′an·throp′ic** a. —**phi·lan′thro·pist** n.

phi·lat′e·ly n. collection and study of postage stamps —**phi·lat′e·list** n.

phil′har·mon′ic n. [Col.] orchestra

phi·lip′pic n. bitter verbal attack

phi·lis·tine (fil′i stēn′) n. one who is smugly conventional

phil′o·den′dron n. tropical American climbing plant

phi·los′o·pher n. one learned in philosophy

phi·los′o·phize′ v. to reason like a philosopher

phi·los′o·phy n. **1** study of ultimate reality, ethics, etc. **2** pl. **-phies** system of principles **3** mental calmness —**phil′o·soph′ic**, **phil′o·soph′i·cal** a.

phil′ter, phil′tre n. magic potion to arouse love

phle·bi·tis (fli bīt′is) n. inflammation of a vein

phlegm (flem) n. mucus in the throat, as during a cold

phleg·mat′ic (fleg-) a. sluggish, unexcitable, etc.

phlox (fläks) n. plant with clusters of flowers

pho′bi·a n. irrational, persistent fear of something

phoe·be (fē′bē) n. small bird

phoe′nix Egyptian myth. immortal bird

phone n., v. [Col.] telephone

pho′neme′ n. a set of speech sounds heard as one sound

pho·net′ics n. science of speech sounds and the written representation of them —**pho·net′ic** a.

phon′ics n. phonetic method of teaching reading

pho′no·graph′ n. instrument that reproduces sound from grooved records

pho·nol′o·gy n. (study of) speech sounds in a language —**pho′no·log′i·cal** a. —**pho·nol′o·gist** n.

pho′ny a., n. **-ni·er, -ni·est** [Col.] fake

phos′phate′ n. **1** salt of phosphoric acid **2**

fertilizer containing phosphates

phos′pho·res′cent *a.* giving off light without heat —**phos′pho·res′cence** *n.*

phos′pho·rus *n.* phosphorescent, waxy chemical element —**phos·phor′ic, phos′pho·rous** *a.*

pho′to *n., pl.* **–tos** photograph

pho′to·cop′y *n., pl.* **–ies** copy made by photographic device (**pho′to·cop′i·er**)

pho′to·e·lec′tric *a.* of the electric effects produced by light on some substances

pho′to·en·grav′ing *n.* reproduction of photographs in relief on printing plates —**pho′to·en·grav′er** *n.*

photo finish *n.* finish of a race so close the winner is known only by a photograph of the finish

pho′to·flash′ *a.* using a flashbulb synchronized with camera shutter

pho′to·gen′ic (-jen′-) *a.* attractive to photograph

pho′to·graph′ *n.* picture made by photography —*v.* take a photograph of —**pho·tog′ra·pher** *n.*

pho·tog′ra·phy *n.* process of producing images on a surface sensitive to light —**pho′to·graph′ic** *a.*

pho′ton′ *n.* unit of light or energy

pho′to·off′set′ *n.* offset printing in which photographic copies are transferred to metal plates, then to a press roller

pho′to·stat′ *n.* device for making photographic copies of printed matter, etc. 2 copy so made —*v.* make a photostat of —**pho′to·stat′ic** *a.*

pho′to·syn′the·sis (-sin′-) *n.* formation of carbohydrates in plants by the action of sunlight

phrase *n.* 1 a short, colorful expression 2 group of words, not a sentence or clause, conveying a single idea —*v.* express in words

phra′se·ol′o·gy *n.* wording

phy·lac′ter·y (fi-) *n., pl.* **–ies** small leather case holding Jewish Scripture text

phy′lum (fī′-) *n., pl.* **–la** basic division of plants or animals

phys′ic (fiz′-) *n.* cathartic

phys′i·cal *adv.* **1** of matter **2** of physics **3** of the body —*n.* physical examination —**phys′i·cal·ly** *adv.*

physical education *n.* instruction in the exercise and care of the body

physical science *n.* any science of inanimate matter, as physics or chemistry

physical therapy *n.* treatment of disease by massage, exercise, etc.

phy·si′cian (-zish′ən) *n.* doctor of medicine

phys′ics *n.* science that deals with matter and energy —**phys′i·cist** *n.*

phys′i·og′no·my *n., pl.* **–mies** the face

phys′i·ol′o·gy *n.* science of the functions of living organisms —**phys′i·o·log′i·cal** *a.* —**phys′i·ol′o·gist** *n.*

phys′i·o·ther′a·py (-zēk′) *n.* physical therapy

phy·sique′ (-zēk′) *n.* form or build of the body

pi (pī) *n.* symbol () for the ratio of circumference to diameter, about 3.1416

pi·a·nis′si·mo′ (pē′-) *a., adv. Mus.* very soft

pi·an′ist (*or* pē·an′ist) *n.* piano player

pi·a′no (*a., adv.:* -än′-) *n., pl.* **–nos** keyboard instrument with hammers that strike steel wires: also **pi·an′o·forte′** —*a., adv. Mus.* soft

pi·az′za (pē ät′sə, *n.* 2: -az′ə) *n.* **1** in Italy, a public square **2** veranda

pi′ca (pī′-) *n.* size of printing type

pic′a·resque′ (-resk′) *a.* of adventurous vagabonds

pic′a·yune′ *a.* trivial

pic′ca·lil′li *n.* relish of vegetables, mustard, etc.

pic′co·lo′ *n., pl.* **–los** small flute

pick *v.* **1** scratch or dig at with something pointed **2** gather, pluck, etc. **3** choose; select **4** provoke (a fight) —*n.* **1** choice **2** the best **3** pointed tool for breaking up soil, etc. **4** plectrum —**pick at** eat sparingly —**pick on** [Col.] criticize; tease —**pick out** choose —**pick up 1** lift **2** get, find, etc. **3** gain (speed) **4** improve —**pick′er** *n.*

pick′a·back′ *adv., a.* on the shoulders or back

pick′ax′, pick′axe′ *n.* pick with one end of the head pointed, the other axlike

pick′er·el *n.* fish with a narrow, pointed snout

pick′et *n.* **1** pointed stake **2** soldier(s) on guard duty **3** striking union member, etc. stationed outside a factory, etc. —*v.* place or be a picket at

picket line *n.* line of people serving as pickets

pick′ings *n.pl.* scraps

pick′le *n.* preserve in vinegar, brine, etc. —*n.* cucumber, etc. so preserved

pick′pock′et *n.* one who steals from pockets

pick′up′ *n.* **1** power of speeding up **2** small truck

pick′y *a.* **-i·er, -iest** [Col.] very fussy

pic′nic *n.* outing with an outdoor meal —*v.* **-nicked, -nick·ing** to hold a picnic —**pic′nick·er** *n.*

pi·cot′ (pē′kō) *n.* loop that is part of fancy edge on lace

pic′to·graph′ *n.* picturelike symbol used in a system of writing

pic·to′ri·al *a.* of or expressed in pictures

pic′ture *n.* **1** likeness made by painting,

photography, etc. **2** description **3** a FILM (n. 3) —v. **1** make a picture of **2** describe **3** imagine

pic'tur·esque' (-esk') a. **1** having natural beauty **2** quaint **3** vivid

pid'dle v. dawdle; trifle

pid'dling a. insignificant

pid·dly a. piddling

pidg'in English (pij'-) n. mixture of English and Chinese

pie n. fruit, meat, etc. baked on or in a crust

pie'bald' a. covered with patches of two colors

piece n. **1** part broken off or separated **2** part complete in itself **3** single thing —v. join (together) the pieces of

piece'meal' a., adv. (made or done) piece by piece

piece'work' n. work which one is paid for by the piece

pied (pīd) a. spotted with various colors

pier (pir) n. **1** landing place built out over water **2** heavy, supporting column

pierce v. **1** pass through as a needle does **2** make a hole in **3** sound sharply —**pierc'ing** a.

pi'e·ty (pī'-) n. devotion to religious duties, etc.

pif'fle n. [Col.] insignificant or nonsensical talk, etc.

pig n. **1** fat farm animal; swine **2** greedy or filthy person —**pig'gish** a.

pi·geon (pij'ən) n. plump bird with a small head

pi'geon·hole' v., n. (put in) a compartment, as in a desk, for filing papers

pi'geon-toed' a. having the toes or feet turned inward

pig'gy·back' adv. on the back

pig'head'ed a. stubborn

pig iron n. molten iron

pig'ment n. coloring matter

pig·men·ta'tion n. coloration in plants or animals

pig'my a., n., pl. —**mies** pygmy

pig'pen' n. a pen for pigs: also **pig'sty'**, pl. —**sties'**

pig'skin' n. **1** leather made from the skin of a pig **2** [Col.] a football

pig'tail' n. braid of hair hanging down the back

pike n. **1** slender, freshwater fish **2** turnpike **3** metal-tipped spear

pik'er n. [Sl.] petty or stingy person

pi·laf, pi·laff (pē'läf') n. boiled, seasoned rice with meat, etc.

pi·las'ter n. column projecting from a wall

pil'chard n. sardine

pile n. **1** mass of things heaped together **2** thick nap, as on a rug **3** heavy, vertical beam —v. **1** heap up **2** accumulate **3** to crowd

piles n.pl. hemorrhoids

pile'up' n. **1** accumulation **2** [Col.] collision of several cars

pil'fer v. steal; filch

pil'grim n. traveler to a holy place —**pil'grim·age** n.

pill n. pellet of medicine to be swallowed whole

pil'lage v., n. plunder

pil'lar n. upright support

pil'lion (-yən) n. extra seat on a horse or motorcycle

pil'lo·ry n., pl. —**ries** device with holes for head and hands, in which offenders were locked —v. —**ried**, —**ry·ing** expose to public scorn

pil'low n. bag of soft material, to support the head, as in sleeping —v. rest as on a pillow

pil'low·case' n. removable covering for a pillow: also **pil'low·slip'**

pi'lot n. **1** one whose job is steering ships in harbors, etc. **2** one who flies an airplane **3** guide —v. be pilot of, in, etc.

pi'lot·house' n. enclosure for helmsman on a ship

pilot light n. small gas jet kept burning to light burners

pi·men'to n., pl. —**tos** sweet, bell-shaped red pepper: also **pi·mien'to** (-myen'-)

pimp v., n. (act as) a prostitute's agent

pim'ple n. small, sore swelling of the skin —**pim'ply** a., —**pli·er**, —**pli·est**

PIN (pin) n. personal identification number, as for use at an ATM

pin n. **1** pointed piece of wire to fasten things together **2** thin rod to hold things with **3** thing like a pin **4** ornament with a pin to fasten it **5** thing at which a ball is bowled —v. **pinned**, **pin'ning** fasten as with a pin

pin'a·fore' n. apronlike garment for girls

pin'ball' machine n. game machine with pins and holes for scoring points made by rolling ball

pince-nez (pans'nā') n., pl. —**nez'** (-nāz') eyeglasses held in place only by a spring gripping bridge of nose

pin'cers n.pl. **1** tool for gripping things **2** claw of a crab, etc. Also **pinch'ers**

pinch v. **1** squeeze between two surfaces **2** to make look thin, gaunt, etc. **3** be stingy —n. **1** a squeeze **2** small amount **3** an emergency

pinch'-hit' v. —**hit'**, —**hit'ting** substitute (for someone)

pin'cush'ion n. small cushion to stick pins in

pine n. 1 evergreen tree with cones and needle-shaped leaves 2 its wood —v. 1 waste (away) through grief, etc. 2 yearn

pine′ap′ple n. large, juicy tropical fruit

pin′feath′er n. an undeveloped feather

ping n. sound of a bullet striking something sharply

Ping′-Pong′ trademark table tennis equipment —n. [p- p-] table tennis

pin′ion (-yən) n. 1 small cogwheel 2 wing or wing feather —v. bind the wings or arms of

pink n. 1 plant with pale-red flowers 2 pale red 3 finest condition —v. cut a sawtoothed edge on (cloth)

pink′eye n. acute, contagious conjunctivitis

pink′ie, pink′y n., pl. **-ies** smallest finger

pin′na·cle n. 1 slender spire 2 mountain peak 3 highest point

pi′noch′le (-nuk′-, -näk′-) n. card game using a double deck above the eight

pin′point′ v. show the precise location of

pin′prick′ n. 1 tiny hole made by a pin 2 minor annoyance

pin′set′ter n. person or machine that sets bowling pins: also **pin′spot′ter**

pin stripe n. fabric pattern of very narrow stripes

pint n. ½ quart

pin′to a., n. piebald (horse)

pinto bean n. mottled, kidney-shaped bean

pin′up′ n. [Col.] picture of a sexually attractive person

pin′wheel′ n. 1 small plastic wheel that turns in the wind 2 kind of firework wheel

pi′o·neer′ n. early settler, first investigator, etc. —v. be a pioneer

pi′ous a. having, showing, or pretending religious devotion —**pi′ous·ly** adv.

pip n. 1 seed of an apple, etc. 2 [Old Sl.] one much admired

pipe n. 1 long tube for conveying water, gas, etc. 2 tube with a bowl at one end, for smoking tobacco 3 tube for making musical sounds —v. 1 utter in a shrill voice 2 convey (water, etc.) by pipes 3 play (a tune) on a pipe —**pip′er** n.

pipe′line′ n. 1 line of pipes for water, gas, etc. 2 any means of conveying something

pip′ing n. 1 music made by pipes 2 shrill sound 3 pipelike cloth trimming

pip′it n. small songbird

pip′pin n. kind of apple

pip′squeak′ n. [Col.] insignificant person or thing

pi·quant (pē′kənt) a. 1 agreeably pungent 2 stimulating —**pi′quan·cy** n.

pi·qué or **pi·que** (pē kā′) n. cotton fabric with vertical cords

pique (pēk) n. resentment at being slighted

—v. 1 offend 2 excite

pi·ra·nha (pə rän′ə) n., pl. **-nhas** or **-nha** small fish that hunts in schools

pi′rate (-rət) n. 1 one who robs ships at sea 2 one who uses a copyrighted or patented work without authorization —v. take, use, etc. by piracy —**pi′ra·cy** n.

pi·ro·gi (pi rō′gē) n.pl. small pastry filled with meat, etc.

pir′ou·ette′ (-ōō et′) n. a whirling on the toes —**-et′ted, -et′ting** do a pirouette

pis′ca·to′ri·al a. of fishing

Pis·ces (pī′sēz′) 12th sign of the zodiac; Fish

pis′mire (or piz′-) n. [Ar.] ant

pis·tach·i·o (pi stash′ē ō′) n., pl. **-os′** greenish nut

pis′til n. seed-bearing organ of a flower

pis′tol n. small firearm held with one hand

pis′ton n. part that moves back and forth in a hollow cylinder from pressure caused by combustion, etc.

pit n. 1 stone of a plum, peach, etc. 2 hole in the ground 3 small hollow in a surface 4 section for the orchestra in front of the stage —v. **pit′ted, pit′ting** 1 remove the pit from (a fruit) 2 mark with pits 3 set in competition (against)

pi′ta (pē′-) n. round, flat bread of Middle East: also **pita bread**

pit′a-pat′ adv. with rapid, strong beating

pitch v. 1 set up (tents) 2 throw 3 plunge forward 4 set at some level, key, etc. 5 rise and fall, as a ship —n. 1 throw 2 point or degree 3 degree of slope 4 highness or lowness of a musical sound 5 black, sticky substance from coal tar, etc. —**pitch** in [Col.] begin working hard

pitch′blende′ n. dark, uranium-bearing mineral

pitch′er n. 1 container for holding and pouring liquids 2 baseball player who pitches to the batters

pitch′fork′ n. large fork for lifting and tossing hay

pitch pipe n. small musical pipe making a fixed tone as a standard of pitch for singers, etc.

pit′e·ous a. deserving pity —**pit′e·ous·ly** adv.

pit′fall′ n. 1 covered pit as a trap 2 hidden danger

pith n. 1 soft, spongy tissue in the center of plant stems 2 essential part

pith′y a. **-i·er, -i·est** full of meaning or force

pit′i·a·ble a. 1 deserving pity 2 deserving contempt —**pit′i·a·bly** adv.

pit′i·ful a. 1 arousing or deserving pity 2 contemptible —**pit′i·ful·ly** adv.

pit′i·less a. without pity

pit′tance *n.* small amount, esp. of money

pit′ter-pat′ter *n.* rapid series of tapping sounds

pi·tu′i·tar′y *a.* of a small endocrine gland (**pituitary gland**) attached to the brain

pit′y *n.* 1 sorrow for another's misfortune 2 cause for sorrow or regret —*v.* **-ied, -y·ing** feel pity (for)

piv′ot *n.* 1 person or thing on which something turns or depends 2 pivoting motion —*v.* provide with or turn on a pivot —**piv′ot·al** *a.*

pix′el *n.* any of the dots making up a TV image

pix′ie, pix′y *n., pl.* **-ies** fairy; sprite

pi·zazz′, piz·zazz′ *n.* [Col.] 1 vitality 2 stylishness

piz′za (pēt′sa) *n.* baked dish of thin dough topped with cheese, tomato sauce, etc.

piz′ze·ri′a *n.* a place where pizzas are made and sold

piz·zi·ca·to (pit′si kät′ō) *adv., a. Mus.* with the strings plucked

pj's *n.pl.* [Col.] pajamas

plac′ard *v., n.* (put up) a sign in a public place

pla′cate′ *v.* appease

place *n.* 1 space 2 region 3 city or town 4 residence 5 particular building, site, part, position, etc. 6 job or its duties —*v.* 1 put in a certain place 2 identify by some relationship —**in place of** rather than —**take place** occur

pla·ce′bo *n., pl.* **-bos** or **-boes** harmless preparation without medicine given to humor a patient

place′ment *n.* a placing, esp. in a job

pla·cen′ta *n., pl.* **-tas** or **-tae** (-tē) organ in the uterus to nourish the fetus

plac′er (plas′-) *n.* gravel with gold, etc. in it

plac′id (plas′-) *a.* calm

plack′et *n.* slit at the waist of a skirt or dress

pla′gia·rize′ (-jə rīz′) *v.* present another's writings as one's own —**pla′gia·rism′** *n.* —**pla′gia·rist** *n.*

plague (plāg) *n.* 1 affliction 2 deadly epidemic disease —*v.* vex; trouble

plaice *n.* kind of flatfish

plaid (plad) *n., a.* (cloth) with crisscross pattern

plain *a.* 1 clear 2 outspoken 3 obvious 4 simple 5 homely 6 not fancy 7 common —*n.* an extent of flat land —*adv.* clearly —**plain′ly** *adv.* —**plain′ness.**

plain′clothes′ man *n.* policeman who does not wear a uniform

plain′song′ *n.* very old church music chanted in unison

plaint *n.* complaint

plain′tiff *n.* one who brings a suit into a court of law

plain′tive (-tiv) *a.* sad; mournful

plait *v., n.* 1 braid 2 pleat

plan *n.* 1 outline; map 2 way of doing; scheme —*v.* **planned, plan′ning** 1 make a plan of or for 2 intend —**plan′ner** *n.*

plane *a.* flat —*n.* 1 flat surface 2 level or stage 3 airplane 4 carpenter's tool for leveling or smoothing —*v.* smooth or level with a plane

plan′et *n.* any of nine heavenly bodies revolving around the sun —**plan′e·tar′y** *a.*

plan′e·tar′i·um (-ter′-) *n.* large domed room for projecting images of the heavens

plane tree *n.* American sycamore

plank *n.* 1 long, broad, thick board 2 a principle in a political platform —*v.* cover with planks

plank′ton *n.* tiny animals and plants floating in bodies of water

plant *n.* 1 living thing that cannot move, as a tree, flower, etc. 2 factory —*v.* 1 to put in the ground to grow 2 set firmly in place

plan′tain (-tin) *n.* 1 weed with broad leaves 2 banana plant with coarse fruit

plan′tar (-tər) *a.* of the sole of the foot

plan·ta′tion *n.* estate with its workers living on it

plant′er *n.* container for plants

plaque (plak) *n.* 1 flat, decorative piece of wood or metal 2 thin film of bacteria on teeth

plas′ma (plaz′-) *n.* fluid part of blood or lymph

plas′ter *n.* lime, sand, and water, mixed as a coating that hardens on walls —*v.* cover as with plaster

plaster of Paris *n.* paste of gypsum and water that hardens quickly

plas′tic *a.* 1 that shapes or can be shaped 2 of plastic —*n.* substance that can be molded and hardened —**plas·tic′i·ty** (-tis′-) *n.*

plas′ti·cize′ *v.* make plastic

plastic surgery *n.* surgical grafting of skin or bone

plat *n.* 1 map 2 PLOT (*n.* 1)

plate *n.* 1 shallow dish 2 plated dinnerware 3 cast of molded type 4 engraved illustration 5 denture 6 home plate —*v.* coat with metal

pla·teau′ (pla tō′) *n.* 1 tract of high, level land 2 period of no progress

plat′en *n.* 1 plate that presses paper against printing type 2 typewriter roller on which keys strike

plat′form′ *n.* 1 raised horizontal surface 2 political party's stated aims

plat′i·num *n.* silvery, precious metal, a chemical element

plat'i·tude' n. trite remark

pla·ton'ic a. spiritual or intellectual, not sexual

pla·toon' n. small group, as of soldiers

plat'ter n. large serving dish

plat'y·pus n., pl. **-pus·es** or **-pi** (-pī') duck-bill

plau'dits (plô'-) n.pl. applause

plau'si·ble (-zə-) a. credible —**plau'si·bil'i·ty** n.

play v. 1 have fun 2 do in fun 3 take part in a game or sport 4 perform on a musical instrument 5 make a tape or disc machine give out sounds or images 6 trifle 7 cause 8 act in a certain way 9 act the part of —n. 1 recreation 2 fun 3 motion or freedom for motion 4 move in a game 5 drama —**play up** [Col.] emphasize —**play'er** n.

play'act' v. 1 pretend 2 act in dramatic way

play'back' n. playing of tape or disc that has been recorded

play'bill' n. program, poster, etc. for a play

play'boy' n. rich man given to pleasure-seeking

play'ful a. full of fun; frisky —**play'ful·ly** adv. —**play'ful·ness** n.

play'go'er n. one who attends plays frequently

play'ground' n. outdoor place for games and play

play'house' n. 1 theater 2 small house for children to play in

playing cards n.pl. cards in four suits for playing games

play'mate' n. companion in recreation

play'off' n. final match played to break a tie

play on words n. pun

play'pen' n. enclosure for infant to play in

play'thing' n. toy

play'wright' (-rīt') n. one who writes plays

pla·za (plä'zə, plaz'ə) n. public square

plea n. 1 appeal; request 2 statement in defense

plead v. 1 beg; entreat 2 argue (a law case) 3 offer as an excuse

pleas'ant a. pleasing; agreeable —**pleas'ant·ly** adv.

pleas'ant·ry n., pl. **-ries** 1 jocular remark 2 a polite social remark

please v. 1 satisfy 2 be the wish of 3 be obliging enough to: used in polite requests —**pleased** a.

pleas'ing a. giving pleasure —**pleas'ing·ly** adv.

pleas'ure (plezh'-) n. 1 delight or satisfaction 2 one's choice —**pleas'ur·a·ble** a.

pleat n. fold made by doubling cloth —v. make pleats in

ple·be'ian (-bē'ən) a., n. common (person)

pleb'i·scite' (-sīt') n. direct popular vote on an issue

plec'trum n., pl. **-trums** or **-tra** small device for plucking a guitar, etc.

pledge n. 1 thing given as security for a contract, etc. 2 promise —v. 1 give as security 2 promise

ple'na·ry a. full or fully attended

plen'i·po·ten'ti·ar'y (-shē-) a. having full authority —n., pl. **-ies** ambassador

plen'i·tude' n. 1 fullness 2 abundance

plen'ti·ful a. abundant: also **plen'te·ous**

plen'ty n. 1 prosperity 2 ample amount

pleth'o·ra n. overabundance

pleu'ri·sy (ploor'ə sē) n. inflammation of membrane lining the chest cavity

Plex'i·glas' trademark transparent plastic

plex'i·glass' n. material like Plexiglas

plex'us n. network of blood vessels, nerves, etc.

pli'a·ble a. easily bent; flexible —**pli'a·bil'i·ty** n.

pli'ant a. 1 flexible 2 compliant —**pli'an·cy** n.

pli'ers n.pl. small pincers

plight n. condition, esp. a bad or dangerous one —v. 1 pledge 2 betroth

plinth n. block at base of column, pedestal, etc.

plod v. **plod'ded, plod'ding** 1 trudge 2 work steadily —**plod'der** n.

plop n. sound of object falling into water —v. **plopped, plop'ping** fall with a plop

plot n. 1 piece of ground 2 diagram, plan, etc. 3 plan of action of a play, etc. 4 secret, esp. evil, scheme —v. **plot'ted, plot'ting** 1 make a map, plan, etc. of 2 scheme —**plot'ter** n.

plov'er (pluv'-) n. shorebird with long, pointed wings

plow (plou) n. 1 implement for cutting and turning up soil 2 machine for removing snow —v. 1 use a plow (on) 2 make one's way Also [Br.] **plough** —**plow'man** n., pl. **-men**

plow'share' n. blade of a plow

ploy n. ruse; trick

pluck v. 1 pull off or out 2 pull at and release quickly —n. 1 a pull 2 courage

pluck'y a. **-i·er, -i·est** brave; spirited

plug n. 1 stopper 2 device for making electrical contact 3 [Col.] insinuated advertisement 4 [Sl.] worn-out horse —v. **plugged, plug'ging** 1 stop up with a plug 2 [Col.] advertise with a plug 3 [Col.] work doggedly 4 [Sl.] hit with a bullet

plum n. 1 smooth-skinned, juicy fruit 2 choice thing

plum'age (ploom'-) n. a bird's feathers

plumb (plum) *n.* weight on a line for checking a vertical wall or sounding a depth —*a.* perpendicular —*adv.* **1** straight down **2** [Col.] entirely —*v.* **1** test with a plumb **2** solve

plumb′er *n.* one who fits and repairs water pipes, etc. —**plumb′ing** *n.*

plume *n.* feather or tuft of feathers —*v.* **1** adorn with plumes **2** preen

plum′met *v.* fall straight downward —*n.* plumb

plump *a.* full and rounded —*v.* drop heavily —*adv.* suddenly; heavily

plun′der *v.* rob by force —*n.* goods plundered

plunge *v.* **1** thrust suddenly (*into*) **2** dive or rush —*n.* dive or fall

plung′er *n.* **1** rubber suction cup to open drains **2** part that moves with a plunging motion

plunk *v.* **1** strum (a banjo, etc.) **2** put down heavily —*n.* sound of plunking

plu′ral (ploor′əl) *a.* more than one —*n.* *Gram.* word form designating more than one —**plu′ral·ize′** *v.*

plu·ral′i·ty *n.* **1** majority **2** excess of winner's votes over his nearest rival's

plus *prep.* added to —*a.* **1** designating a sign (+) showing addition **2** positive **3** more than —*n.* something added

plush *n.* fabric with a long pile —*a.* [Col.] luxurious

plu′to·crat′ *n.* wealthy person with great influence —**plu·toc′ra·cy** *n.*

plu·to′ni·um *n.* radioactive chemical element

ply *n.*, *pl.* **plies** one layer in plywood, folded cloth, etc. —*v.* **plied**, **ply′ing 1** work at (a trade) or with (a tool) **2** keep supplying (*with*) **3** travel back and forth (*between*)

ply′wood′ *n.* board made of glued layers of wood

p.m., P.M. after noon

pneu·mat′ic (nōō-) *a.* **1** of or containing air or gases **2** worked by compressed air

pneu·mo′ni·a *n.* acute disease of the lungs

poach *v.* **1** cook (an egg without its shell) in water **2** hunt or fish illegally —**poach′er** *n.*

pock′et *n.* **1** little bag or pouch, esp. when sewn into clothing **2** pouchlike cavity or hollow —*a.* that can be carried in a pocket —*v.* **1** put into a pocket **2** hide; suppress —**pock′et·ful′** *n.*

pock′et·book′ *n.* purse

pock′et·knife′ *n.*, *pl.* **-knives** small knife with folding blades

pock′mark′ *n.* scar left by a pustule: also **pock**

pod *n.* shell of peas, beans, etc. containing

the seeds

po·di′a·try (-dī′-) *n.* treatment of foot ailments —**po·di′a·trist** *n.*

po′di·um *n.*, *pl.* **-di·a** platform for an orchestra conductor

po′em *n.* piece of imaginative writing in rhythm, rhyme, etc.

po′et *n.* writer of poems —**po′et·ess** *n.fem.*

po′et·ry *n.* **1** writing of poems **2** poems **3** rhythms, deep feelings, etc. of poems —**po·et′ic, po·et′i·cal** *a.*

poi *n.* Hawaiian dish of taro paste

poign·ant (poin′yənt) *a.* **1** painful to the feelings **2** keen —**poign′an·cy** *n.*

poin·set′ti·a (-set′ə, -set′ē ə) *n.* plant with petallike red leaves

point *n.* **1** a dot **2** specific place or time **3** a stage or degree reached **4** item; detail **5** special feature **6** unit, as of a game score **7** sharp end **8** cape (land) **9** purpose; object **10** essential idea **11** mark showing direction on a compass —*v.* **1** sharpen to a point **2** call attention (*to*) **3** show **4** aim —**at the point** of very close to —**beside the point** irrelevant —**to the point** pertinent

point′-blank′ *a., adv.* **1** (aimed) straight at a mark **2** direct(ly)

point′ed *a.* **1** sharp **2** aimed at someone, as a remark

point′er *n.* **1** long, tapered rod for pointing **2** indicator **3** large hunting dog **4** [Col.] hint; suggestion

point′less *a.* without meaning —**point′less·ly** *adv.*

point of view *n.* way something is viewed or thought of

poise (poiz) *n.* **1** balance **2** ease and dignity of manner —*v.* balance

poi′son *n.* substance which can cause illness or death —*v.* **1** harm or kill with poison **2** put poison into **3** corrupt —**poi′son·ous** *a.*

poison ivy *n.* plant that can cause severe skin rash

poke *v.* **1** prod, as with a stick **2** search (*about* or *around*) **3** move slowly (*along*) —*n.* jab; thrust —**poke fun (at)** ridicule

pok′er *n.* **1** gambling game with cards **2** iron bar for stirring a fire

pok′y *a.* **-i·er, -i·est** [Col.] slow; dull: also **pok′ey**

po′lar *a.* **1** having opposite magnetic poles **2** opposite in character, nature, etc. —**po·lar′i·ty** *n.* —**po′lar·i·za′tion** *n.* —**po′lar·ize′** *v.*

polar bear *n.* large white bear of arctic regions

Po′lar·oid′ *trademark* a camera that produces a print within seconds

Pole *n.* Polish person

pole n. 1 long, slender piece of wood, metal, etc. 2 end of an axis, as of the earth 3 either of two opposed forces, as the ends of a magnet —v. propel (a boat) with a pole

pole'cat' n. 1 weasellike animal of Europe 2 skunk

po·lem'ics n. art or practice of disputation —**po·lem'ic** a., n.

pole vault n. a leap for height by vaulting with aid of a pole —**pole'-vault'** v.

po·lice' n. 1 department of a city, etc. for keeping law and order 2 [with pl. v.] members of such a department —v. control, etc. with police

po·lice'man n., pl. –**men** member of a police force —**po·lice'wom'an** n.fem., pl. –**wom'en**

police officer n. member of a police force

pol'i·cy n., pl. –**cies** 1 governing principle, plan, etc. 2 insurance contract

po'li·o·my'e·li'tis (-līt'is) n. virus disease often resulting in paralysis: also **po'li·o'**

Pol'ish (pōl'-) n., a. (language) of Poland

pol'ish (päl'-) v. 1 smooth and brighten, as by rubbing 2 refine (manners, etc.) —n. 1 surface gloss 2 elegance 3 substance used to polish

po·lite' a. 1 showing good manners; courteous 2 refined —**po·lite'ly** adv.

pol'i·tic adv. wise or shrewd

po·lit'i·cal a. of government, politics, etc. —**po·lit'i·cize'** v.

pol'i·ti'cian (-tish'ən) n. one active in politics

pol'i·tics n.pl. [sing. or pl. v.] 1 science of government 2 political affairs, methods, opinions, scheming, etc.

pol'i·ty n., pl. –**ties** 1 system of government 2 a state

pol'ka (pōl'-) n. fast dance for couples

pol'ka dot (pō'-) n. any of a pattern of dots on cloth

poll (pōl) n. 1 a counting or listing as of voters 2 number of votes recorded 3 pl. voting place 4 survey of opinion —v. 1 take the votes or opinions of 2 receive, as votes

pol'len n. powderlike sex cells on flower stamens

pol'li·nate' v. put pollen on the pistil of —**pol'li·na'tion** n.

pol'li·wog' n. tadpole

poll'ster n. taker of opinion polls

pol·lute' v. make unclean or impure —**pol·lu'tant** n. —**pol·lu'tion** n.

po'lo n. team game played on horseback

pol·troon' n. coward

poly- pref. much; many

pol'y·clin'ic n. clinic for treatment of various kinds of diseases

pol'y·es'ter n. synthetic substance used in plastics, fibers, etc.

po·lyg'a·my (-lig'-) n. a being married to more than one person at one time —**po·lyg'a·mist** n. —**po·lyg'a·mous** a.

pol'y·gon' n. figure with more than four angles and sides

pol'y·graph' n. device measuring bodily changes, used on one suspected of lying

pol'y·mer n. substance of giant molecules formed from smaller molecules of same kind

pol'yp (-ip) n. 1 slender water animal with tentacles 2 growth on a mucous membrane

pol'y·syl'la·ble n. word of more than three syllables —**pol'y·syl·lab'ic** a.

pol'y·tech'nic (-tek'-) a. giving instruction in many scientific and technical subjects

pol'y·the·ism' (-thē-) n. belief in more than one god —**pol'y·the·is'tic** a.

pol'y·un·sat'u·rat'ed a. of fats with low cholesterol

pol'y·vi'nyl a. of any of a group of polymer vinyl compounds

po·made' n. perfumed ointment for the hair

pome'gran'ate (päm'-, päm'ə-) n. round, red fruit with a hard rind and many seeds

pom'mel (pum'-) n. rounded, upward-projecting front part of a saddle —v. pummel

pomp n. stately or ostentatious display

pom'pa·dour' (-dôr') n. hair style with the hair brushed up high from the forehead

pom'pa·no' n., pl. –**no'** or –**nos'** food fish of the West Indies

pom'pom' n. tuft of fabric decorating hats, waved by cheerleaders, etc.: also **pom'pon'**

pom'pous a. pretentious —**pom·pos'i·ty** n.

pon'cho n., pl. –**chos** cloak like a blanket

pond n. small lake

pon'der v. think deeply (about)

pon'der·o'sa (pine) n. yellow pine of western North America

pon'der·ous a. heavy; clumsy

pone n. corn meal bread

pon·gee' n. soft, silk cloth

pon'iard (-yard) n. dagger

pon'tiff n. 1 bishop 2 [P-] the Pope —**pon·tif'i·cal** a.

pon·tif'i·cate' v. be dogmatic or pompous

pon·toon' n. one of the floats supporting a bridge or airplane on water

po'ny n., pl. –**nies** small horse

po'ny·tail' n. hairstyle in which hair is tied to hang in back

poo'dle n. curly-haired dog

pooh int. exclamation of contempt, disbelief, etc.

pool *n.* 1 small pond 2 puddle 3 tank for swimming 4 billiards on a table with pockets 5 common fund of money, etc. —*v.* put into a common fund

poop *n.* raised deck at the stern of a sailing ship

poor *a.* 1 having little money 2 below average; inferior 3 worthy of pity —**poor′ly** *adv.*

poor′-mouth′ *v.* [Col.] complain about one's lack of money

pop *n.* 1 light, explosive sound 2 flavored soda water —*v.* **popped, pop′ping** 1 make, or burst with, a pop 2 cause to pop 3 move, go, etc. suddenly 4 bulge —*adv.* like a pop —*a.* 1 of music popular with many people 2 intended for popular taste

pop (art) *n.* realistic art style

pop′corn′ *n.* corn with kernels that pop when heated

Pope *n.* head of the Roman Catholic Church

pop′gun′ *n.* toy gun that shoots pellets by compressed air

pop′lar *n.* tall tree

pop′lin *n.* ribbed cloth

pop′o′ver *n.* hollow muffin

pop′py *n., pl.* **–pies** plant with showy flowers

pop′py·cock′ *n.* nonsense

pop′u·lace (-ləs) *n.* the common people

pop′u·lar *a.* 1 of, by, or for people generally 2 very well liked —**pop′u·lar′i·ty** *n.* —**pop′u·lar·ize′** *v.*

pop′u·late *v.* inhabit

pop′u·la′tion *n.* total number of inhabitants

pop′u·lism *n.* movement to advance interests of common people —**pop′u·list** *a., n.*

pop′u·lous *a.* full of people

por′ce·lain (-lin) *n.* hard, fine, glazed earthenware

porch *n.* open or screen-enclosed room on the outside of a building

por′cine (-sīn′) *a.* of or like pigs

por′cu·pine *n.* gnawing animal with long, sharp spines in its coat

pore *v.* study or ponder (*over*) —*n.* tiny opening, as in the skin, for absorbing or discharging fluids

pork *n.* flesh of a pig used as food

pork barrel *n.* [Col.] government grants for political favors

por′nog·ra·phy *n.* writings, pictures, etc. intended to arouse sexual desire: also [Sl.] **por′no** or **porn** —**por′no·graph′ic** *a.* —**por·nog′ra·pher** *n.*

po′rous *a.* full of pores or tiny holes —**po·ros′i·ty** *n.*

por′poise (-pəs) *n.* 1 sea mammal with a blunt snout 2 dolphin

por′ridge *n.* cereal or meal boiled in water or milk

por′rin·ger (-jər) *n.* bowl for porridge, etc.

port *n.* 1 harbor 2 city with a harbor 3 sweet, dark-red wine 4 left side of a ship as one faces the bow 5 porthole 6 opening, as in a valve face

port′a·ble *a.* that can be carried —**port′a·bil′i·ty** *n.*

port′age *n.* 1 carrying of boats and supplies overland between waterways 2 route so used

por′tal *n.* doorway; gate

por·tend′ *v.* be an omen or warning of —**por′tent′** *n.* —**por·ten′tous** *a.*

por′ter *n.* 1 doorman 2 attendant who carries luggage, sweeps up, etc.

por′ter·house′ (steak) *n.* beef steak

port·fo′li·o′ *n., pl.* **–os′** briefcase

port′hole′ *n.* window in a ship's side

por′ti·co′ *n., pl.* **–coes′** or **–cos′** porch consisting of a roof supported by columns

por·tiere′, por·tière′ (-tyer′) *n.* curtain hung in a doorway

por′tion *n.* part; share —*v.* divide or give out in portions

port′ly *a.* stout and stately

port·man′teau (-tō) *n., pl.* **–teaus** or **–teaux** (-tōz) kind of suitcase

por′trait (-trit) *n.* a painting, photograph, etc. of a person

por·tray′ *v.* 1 make a portrait of 2 describe 3 represent on the stage —**por·tray′al** *n.*

Por′tu·guese′ (-chə gēz′) *n., pl.* **–guese′;** *a.* (native or language) of Portugal

por′tu·lac′a (-chə lak′ə)*n.* plant with small flowers

pose *v.* 1 present, as a question 2 assume a bodily posture, a false role, etc. —*n.* assumed posture, etc. —**pos′er, po·seur′** (-zur′) *n.*

posh *a.* [Col.] luxurious and fashionable

pos′it *v.* postulate

po·si′tion *n.* 1 way of being placed 2 opinion 3 place; location 4 status 5 job —*v.* to place

pos′i·tive *a.* 1 explicit; definite 2 sure or too sure 3 affirmative 4 real; absolute 5 of the electricity made by friction on glass 6 *Gram.* of an adjective, etc. in its uncompared degree 7 *Math.* greater than zero —*n.* 1 anything positive 2 battery plate of higher potential —**pos′i·tive·ly** *adv.*

pos′i·tron′ *n.* positive antimatter particle of an electron

pos′se (-ē) *n.* body of men called to help a sheriff

pos·sess′ *v.* 1 own 2 have as a quality, etc. 3 control —**pos·ses′sor** *n.*

pos·ses′sion n. 1 a possessing 2 thing possessed

pos·ses′sive a. 1 showing or desiring possession 2 Gram. of a form, etc. indicating possession —**pos′si·bil′i·ty** n., pl. **-ties** —**pos′si·bly** adv.

pos′sum n. opossum —**play possum** feign sleep, ignorance, etc.

post n. 1 piece of wood, etc. set upright as a support 2 place where a soldier or soldiers are stationed 3 job; position 4 mail —v. 1 put up (a notice, etc.) 2 assign to a post 3 to mail 4 inform

post- pref. after; following

post′age n. amount charged for mailing a letter, etc.

post′al a. of (the) mail

post·card n. card, often a picture card, sent by mail

post′date′ v. 1 mark with a later date 2 be later than

post′er n. large sign or notice posted publicly

pos·te′ri·or (-tir′ē-) a. 1 at the back 2 later —n. buttocks

pos·ter′i·ty n. all future generations

post exchange n. general store at an army camp

post′grad′u·ate a. of study after graduation

post′haste′ adv. speedily

post′hu·mous (päs′tyōō-, päs′chōō-) a. after one's death

post′lude′ n. concluding musical piece

post′man n., pl. **-men** mailman

post′mark′ v., n. mark to show the date and place of mailing at the post office

post′mas′ter n. person in charge of a post office

postmaster general n. head of a government's postal system

post′-mor′tem a. after death —n. autopsy

post′na′tal a. after birth

post office n. place where mail is sorted, etc.

post′op′er·a·tive a. after surgery

post′paid′ a. with the sender paying the postage

post′par′tum a. of the time after childbirth

post·pone′ v. put off; delay —**post·pone′ment** n.

post′script′ n. note added at the end of a letter, etc.

pos·tu·late (päs′chə lāt′; n.: -lət) v. assume to be true, real, etc. —n. something postulated

pos′ture n. way one holds the body —v. pose

post′war′ a. after the war

po′sy (-zē) n., pl. **-sies** flower or bouquet

pot n. round container for cooking, etc. —v.

pot′ted, pot′ting to put into a pot —**go to pot** go to ruin

po′ta·ble a. drinkable

pot′ash′ (pät′-) n. white substance obtained from wood ashes

po·tas′si·um n. soft, white, metallic chemical element

po·ta′to n., pl. **-toes** starchy tuber of a common plant, used as a vegetable

potato chip n. thin slice of potato fried crisp

pot′bel′ly n., pl. **-lies** belly that sticks out

po′tent a. 1 powerful 2 effective —**po′ten·cy** n.

po′ten·tate′ n. person having great power; ruler, etc.

po·ten′tial (-shəl) a. that can be; possible; latent —n. 1 something potential 2 voltage at a given point in a circuit —**po·ten′ti·al′i·ty** (-shē al′-) n., pl. **-ties** —**po·ten′tial·ly** adv.

poth′er (päth′-) n. fuss

pot′hold′er n. small pad for handling hot pots, etc.

po′tion n. a drink, esp. of medicine or poison

pot′luck′ n. whatever is available

potluck dinner (or **supper**) n. dinner in which everyone brings a dish of food to share

pot′pie′ n. meat pie

pot·pour·ri (pō′pər ē′) n. mixture

pot′sherd′ n. piece of broken pottery

pot′shot′ n. random shot, attack, etc.

pot′ter n. one who makes pots, dishes, etc. of clay

potter's field n. graveyard for paupers or unknown persons

potter's wheel n. rotating disk upon which bowls, etc. are made from clay

pot′ter·y n. earthenware

pouch n. 1 small sack or bag 2 baglike part

poul·tice (pōl′tis) n. hot, soft mass applied to a sore part of the body

poul′try n. domestic fowls

pounce v. leap or swoop down, as if to seize —n. a pouncing

pound n. 1 unit of weight, 16 ounces 2 British monetary unit 3 enclosure for stray animals —v. 1 hit hard 2 beat to pulp, powder, etc. 3 throb

pour (pôr) v. 1 flow or make flow steadily 2 rain heavily

pout v. 1 push out the lips, as in sullenness 2 sulk —n. a pouting

pov′er·ty n. 1 a being poor; need 2 inadequacy

pov′er·ty-strick′en a. very poor

pow′der n. dry substance of fine particles —v. 1 put powder on 2 make into powder —**pow′der·y** a.

pow'er *n.* **1** ability to do or act **2** strength or energy **3** authority **4** powerful person, nation, etc. **5** result of multiplying a number by itself —*a.* operated by electricity, fuel engine, etc. —**pow'er·less** *a.*

pow'er·ful *a.* strong; mighty --**pow'er·ful·ly** *adv.*

power of attorney *n.* written authority to act for another

pow'wow' *n.* conference of or with North American Indians

pox *n.* **1** smallpox or chicken pox **2** syphilis

prac'ti·ca·ble (-kə-) *a.* that can be done —**prac·ti·ca·bil'i·ty** *n.*

prac'ti·cal *a.* **1** of or obtained through practice **2** useful **3** sensible **4** virtual —**prac'ti·cal'i·ty** *n.* —**prac'ti·cal·ly** *adv.*

prac'tice (-tis) *v.* **1** do repeatedly so as to gain skill **2** make a habit of **3** work at as a profession —*n.* **1** a practicing **2** acquired skill **3** the work or business of a professional Also, chiefly Br. sp., **practise**

prac'ticed *a.* skilled

prac·ti'tion·er (-tish'ən-) *n.* one who practices a profession, etc.

prag·mat'ic *a.* **1** practical **2** tested by results

prag'ma·tism *n.* pragmatic behavior —**prag'ma·tist** *n.*

prai·rie (prer'ē) *n.* large area of grassy land

prairie dog *n.* small squirrellike animal

prairie schooner *n.* large covered wagon

praise *v.* **1** to say good things about **2** worship —*n.* a praising —**praise'wor'thy** *a.*

prance *v.* **1** move along on the hind legs, as a horse **2** strut —**pranc'er** *n.*

prank *v.* mischievous trick —**prank'ster** *n.*

prate *v.* talk foolishly

prat'tle *v.*, *n.* chatter or babble

prawn *n.* shellfish like a shrimp but larger

pray *v.* **1** implore **2** ask for by prayer **3** say prayers

pray'er *n.* **1** a praying **2** words of worship or entreaty to God **3** thing prayed for —**prayer'ful** *a.*

pray'ing mantis *n.* mantis

pre- *pref.* before

preach *v.* **1** give (a sermon) **2** urge or advise as by preaching —**preach'er** *n.*

pre·am·ble *n.* introduction

pre'ar·range' *v.* arrange beforehand

pre·car'i·ous *a.* not safe or sure; risky

pre·cau'tion *n.* care taken beforehand, as against danger —**pre·cau'tion·ar'y** *a.*

pre·cede' *v.* go or come before —**prec'e·dence** (pres'-) *n.*

prec'e·dent *n.* earlier case that sets an example

pre·cept' *n.* rule of ethics

pre·cep'tor *n.* teacher

pre'cinct' (-siŋkt') *n.* **1** subdivision of a city, ward, etc. **2** *pl.* grounds or environs

pre·cious (presh'əs) *a.* **1** of great value **2** beloved **3** too refined —**pre'cious·ly** *adv.*

prec'i·pice (-pis) *n.* steep cliff

pre·cip'i·tate' *v.* **1** bring on; hasten **2** hurl down **3** to separate out as a solid from solution —*a.* hasty; rash —*n.* precipitated substance

pre·cip'i·ta'tion *n.* **1** a precipitating **2** (amount of) rain, snow, etc.

pre·cip'i·tous *a.* **1** steep; sheer **2** hasty; rash

pré·cis (prā sē') *n.* summary

pre·cise' *a.* **1** exact; definite; accurate **2** strict; scrupulous —**pre·cise'ly** *adv.* —**pre·ci'sion** (-sizh' ən) *n.*

pre·clude' *v.* make impossible, esp. in advance

pre·co'cious (-shəs) *a.* advanced beyond one's age —**pre·coc'i·ty** (-käs'-) *n.*

pre'-Co·lum'bi·an *a.* of any period in the Americas before 1492

pre'con·ceive' *v.* form an opinion of beforehand —**pre'con·cep'tion** *n.*

pre'con·di'tion *v.* to prepare to react in a certain way under certain conditions

pre·cur'sor *n.* forerunner

pred'a·to'ry *a.* **1** plundering **2** preying on other animals

pre'de·cease' *v.* die before someone else

pred'e·ces'sor *n.* one preceding another, as in office

pre·des'tine (-tin) *v.* destine or determine beforehand —**pre·des'ti·na'tion** *n.*

pre'de·ter'mine *v.* set or decide beforehand

pred'i·ca·ment *n.* difficult situation

pred'i·cate' (-kāt'; *a.*, *n.*: -kət) *v.* base upon facts, conditions, etc. —*a.*, *n. Gram.* (of) the word or words that make a statement about the subject

pre·dict' *v.* tell about in advance —**pre·dict'a·ble** *a.* —**pre·dic'tion** *n.*

pre'di·gest' *v.* treat (food) with enzymes so it will digest easily when eaten

pred'i·lec'tion *n.* special liking; partiality

pre'dis·pose' *v.* make likely to get, etc.; incline —**pre'dis·po·si'tion** *n.*

pre·dom'i·nate' *v.* be greater in amount, power, etc.; prevail —**pre·dom'i·nance** *n.* —**pre·dom'i·nant** *a.*

pre·em'i·nent, **pre·em'i·nent** *a.* most outstanding —**pre·em'i·nence**, **pre·em'i·nence** *n.*

pre·empt', **pre·empt'** *v.* **1** to seize before anyone else can **2** to replace a scheduled radio or TV program —**pre·emp'tive**, **pre·emp'tive** *a.*

preen *v.* **1** groom (its feathers): said of a

bird 2 groom (oneself)

pre·fab′ n. [Col.] prefabricated building

pre·fab′ri·cat′ed a. made in sections ready for quick assembly, as a house

pref′ace (-əs) n. introduction to a book, speech, etc. —v. give or be a preface to —**pref′a·to′ry** a.

pre·fect′ n. administrator

pre·fer′ v. **-ferred′, -fer′ring** 1 like better 2 bring (charges) before a court —**pref′er·a·ble** a.

pref′er·ence n. 1 a preferring 2 thing preferred 3 advantage given to one over others —**pref′er·en′tial** a.

pre·fer′ment n. promotion

pre′fix′ n. syllable(s) added to the beginning of a word to alter its meaning

preg′nant a. 1 bearing a fetus in the uterus 2 filled (with) —**preg′nan·cy** n., pl. **-cies**

pre·hen′sile (-səl) a. adapted for grasping, as the hand

pre′his·tor′ic a. of times before recorded history

pre·judge′ v. judge beforehand

prej′u·dice (-dis) n. 1 preconceived idea 2 hatred or intolerance of other races, etc. 3 disadvantage —v. 1 harm 2 fill with prejudice —**prej′u·di′cial** a.

prel′ate (-ət) n. high-ranking clergyman

pre·lim′i·nar′y a. leading up to the main action —n., pl. **-ies** preliminary step

pre·lit′er·ate (-it) a. of a society lacking a written language

prel·ude (prel′yōōd′, prā′lōōd′) n. preliminary part, as of a musical piece

pre·mar′i·tal a. before marriage

pre′ma·ture′ a. before the proper or usual time

pre·med′i·tate′ v. think out or plan beforehand —**pre′med′i·ta′tion** n.

pre′men′stru·al a. before a menstrual period

pre·mier′ (-mir′) a. foremost —n. prime minister

pre·mière′, pre·miere′ (-mir′) n. first performance of a play, opera, etc.

prem′ise (-is) n. 1 a basic assumption 2 pl. piece of real estate

pre′mi·um n. 1 prize 2 extra charge 3 a payment 4 high value

prem′o·ni′tion n. feeling of imminent evil

pre·na′tal a. before birth

pre·oc′cu·py′ v. **-pied′, -py′ing** engross; absorb —**pre·oc′cu·pa′tion** n.

prep a. preparatory —v. **prepped, prep′ping** prepare (a patient) for surgery

preparatory school n. private school preparing students for college

pre·pare′ v. 1 make or get ready 2 equip 3 to put together —**prep′a·ra′tion** n. —**pre-**

par′a·to′ry a. —**pre·par′ed·ness** n.

pre′pay′ v. pay in advance —**pre′pay′ment** n.

pre·pon′der·ate′ v. predominate —**pre·pon′der·ance** n. —**pre·pon′der·ant** a.

prep′o·si′tion (-zish′ən) n. word that connects a noun or pronoun to another word —**prep′o·si′tion·al** a.

pre′pos·sess′ing a. making a good impression

pre·pos′ter·ous a. absurd

prep′py, prep′pie n., pl. **-pies** (former) student at a preparatory school

pre′re·cord′ v. record (a TV or radio program) for later broadcasting

pre·re·cord′ed a. of a magnetic tape on which sound, etc. has been recorded before its sale

pre·req′ui·site (-rek′wə zit) n., a. (something) required beforehand

pre·rog′a·tive n. exclusive privilege

pres′age (v.: prē sāj′) n. 1 warning 2 foreboding —v. 1 warn about 2 predict

pre′school′ a. younger than school age

pres·ci·ence (presh′əns) n. foresight —**pres′ci·ent** a.

pre·scribe′ v. 1 to order 2 order to take a certain medicine or treatment

pre′script′ n. prescribed rule —**pre·scrip′tive** a.

pre·scrip′tion n. 1 a prescribing, esp. by a doctor 2 medicine prescribed

pres′ence n. 1 a being present 2 one's appearance

presence of mind n. ability to think and act quickly in an emergency

pres′ent (v.: prē zent′) a. 1 being at a certain place 2 of or at this time —n. 1 present time 2 gift —v. 1 introduce 2 show 3 offer for consideration 4 give (to)

pre·sent′a·ble a. 1 fit to present 2 properly dressed

pres′en·ta′tion n. 1 a presenting 2 thing presented

pre·sen′ti·ment n. premonition

pres′ent·ly adv. 1 soon 2 now

pre·sent′ment n. presentation

present participle n. participle expressing present or continuing action

pre·serve′ v. 1 keep from harm, spoiling, etc. 2 maintain —n. pl. fruit cooked with sugar —**pre·serv′a·tive** a., n. —**pres′er·va′tion** n.

pre·set′ v. set (controls) beforehand

pre′shrunk′ a. shrunk to minimize shrinkage in laundering

pre·side′ (-zīd′) v. 1 act as chairman 2 have control

pres′i·dent n. chief executive of a republic, company, etc. —**pres′i·den·cy** n., pl. **-cies**

—**pres′i·den′tial** (-shal) a.

press v. 1 push against; squeeze 2 iron, as clothes 3 force 4 entreat 5 urge on 6 keep moving 7 crowd —n. 1 pressure 2 crowd 3 machine for crushing, printing, etc. 4 newspapers 5 journalists

press conference n. group interview of a celebrity by journalists

press′ing a. urgent

pres·sure (presh′ər) n. 1 a pressing 2 distress 3 strong influence 4 urgency 5 force of weight —v. try to influence

pres′sur·ize′ v. keep nearly normal air pressure inside (aircraft, etc.) at high altitude

pres·ti·dig′i·ta′tion (-dij′-) n. sleight of hand

pres·tige′ (-tēzh′) n. earned fame and respect

pres·ti′gious (-tij′əs) a. having prestige or distinction

pres′to adv., a. fast

pre·sume′ v. 1 dare 2 suppose 3 take liberties —**pre·sump′tion** n. —**pre·sump′tive** a.

pre·sump′tu·ous (-chō̄ əs) a. too bold or daring

pre′sup·pose′ v. assume beforehand

pre′teen′ n. child nearing a teenager

pre·tend′ v. 1 claim falsely 2 make believe 3 lay claim: with to

pre·tense′ (or prē′tens′) n. 1 claim 2 false claim or show 3 a making believe

pre·ten′sion n. 1 claim 2 pretext 3 show; display

pre·ten′tious a. showy; flashy

pre′ter·nat′u·ral a. supernatural

pre′text′ n. false reason used to hide the real one

pret′ty a. -ti·er, -ti·est attractive and dainty —adv. somewhat —**pret′ti·ly** adv. —**pret′ti·ness** n.

pret′zel n. hard, salted biscuit, twisted in a knot

pre·vail′ v. 1 win out or be successful 2 become more common

pre·vail′ing a. 1 superior 2 prevalent

prev′a·lent a. common; general —**prev′a·lence** n.

pre·var′i·cate′ v. evade the truth; lie —**pre·var′i·ca′tion** n. —**pre·var′i·ca′tor** n.

pre·vent′ v. stop or keep from doing or happening —**pre·vent′a·ble**, **pre·vent′i·ble** a. —**pre·ven′tion** n.

pre·ven′tive n., a. (something) that prevents: also **pre·vent′a·tive**

pre′view′ n. advance showing of (scenes from) a movie

pre′vi·ous a. coming before; prior —**pre′vi·ous·ly** adv.

pre′war′ a. before the war

prey (prā) n. 1 animal seized by another for food 2 victim —v. 1 hunt as prey 2 plunder; rob 3 harass

price n. 1 sum asked or paid for a thing 2 value —v. get or put a price on

price′less a. beyond price

prick v. 1 pierce with a sharp point 2 pain sharply 3 raise (the ears) —n. 1 a pricking 2 sharp pain —**prick up one's ears** listen closely

prick′le n. thorn or spiny point —v. tingle —**prick′ly** a., -li·er, -li·est

pride n. 1 too high opinion of oneself 2 self-respect 3 satisfaction in one's achievements 4 person or thing one is proud of —**pride oneself on** be proud of

priest n. one who conducts religious rites —**priest′ess** n.fem. —**priest′hood′** n. —**priest′ly** a.

prig n. smug, moralistic person —**prig′gish** a.

prim a. prim′mer, prim′mest stiffly proper —**prim′ly** adv.

pri′ma·cy n. supremacy

pri′ma don′na (prē′-) n. 1 chief woman singer in an opera 2 [Col.] one temperamental, vain, etc.

pri′mal a. 1 first in time; original 2 chief

pri′mar·y a. 1 most important 2 basic 3 first in order —n., pl. -ies preliminary election —**pri·mar′i·ly** adv.

pri′mate′ n. 1 archbishop 2 member of the order of mammals having hands and feet with five digits; man, ape, etc.

prime a. first in rank, importance, or quality —n. best period or part —v. make ready

prime minister n. chief official in some countries

prim′er (prim-) n. 1 explosive used to set off a larger explosive 2 preliminary coat of paint, etc.

prim′er (prim′-) n. elementary textbook, esp. for reading

prime time n. hours when radio or TV have largest audience

pri·me′val a. of the first age or ages

prim′i·tive a. 1 of earliest times 2 crude; simple —n. primitive person or thing

pri′mo·gen′i·ture (-jen′-) n. right of inheritance of eldest son

pri·mor′di·al (-dē-) a. primitive

primp v. groom oneself fussily

prim′rose′ n. plant with tubelike flowers in clusters

prince n. 1 monarch's son 2 ruler of a principality —**prince′ly** a. —**prin′cess** n.fem.

prin′ci·pal a. chief; main —n. 1 principal

person or thing **2** head of a school **3** sum owed, etc. aside from interest —**prin′ci·pal·ly** *adv.*

prin′ci·pal′i·ty *n., pl.* **–ties** land ruled by a prince

prin′ci·ple *n.* **1** basic truth, rule, action, etc. **2** rule of conduct **3** integrity

print *n.* **1** cloth stamped with a design **2** impression made by inked type, plates, etc. **3** photograph —*v.* **1** to impress inked type, etc. on paper **2** publish in print **3** write in letters like printed ones —**print′er** *n.* —**print′ing** *n., a.*

print′ed circuit *n.* electrical circuit in fine lines on an insulating sheet

print′out′ *n.* printed or typed computer output

pri′or *a.* preceding in time, order, or importance —*n.* head of a monastery or order —**pri′or·ess** *n.fem.* —**pri′or·y** *n., pl.* **–ries**

pri·or′i·ty *n., pl.* **–ties 1** precedence **2** prior right

prism *n.* clear glass, etc. of angular form, for dispersing light into its spectrum —**pris·mat′ic** *a.*

pris′on *n.* place of confinement —**pris′on·er** *n.*

pris′sy *a.* **–i·er, –i·est** [Col.] very prim or prudish

pris′tine′ (-tēn′) *n.* fresh and untouched

pri′vate′ *a.* **1** of or for a particular person or group; not public **2** secret —*n. Mil.* lowest rank of enlisted man —**pri′va·cy** *n.* —**pri′-vate·ly** *adv.*

pri′va·teer′ *n.* private ship commissioned to attack enemy ships

pri·va′tion *n.* lack of necessities

pri′va·tize′ *v.* turn over (public property, etc.) to private interests

priv′et *n.* evergreen shrub

priv′i·lege (-lij) *n.* special right, favor, etc. —*v.* grant a privilege to

priv′y *a.* private —*n., pl.* **–ies** outhouse —**privy to** privately informed about

prize *v.* value highly —*n.* **1** thing given to the winner of a contest, etc. **2** valued possession

prize′fight′ *n.* professional boxing match —**prize′fight′er** *n.*

pro *adv.* on the affirmative side —*n., pl.* **1** *pl.* pros reason or vote for **2** professional

pro– *pref.* in favor of

prob′a·ble *a.* likely to occur or to be so —**prob′a·bil′i·ty** *n., pl.* **–ties** —**prob′a·bly** *adv.*

pro′bate′ *v.* establish the validity of (a will) —*a.* of such action —*n.* a probating

pro·ba′tion *n.* **1** trial of ability, etc. **2** conditional suspension of a jail sentence —**pro·ba′tion·ar′y** *a.*

probation officer *n.* official who watches over persons on probation

probe *n.* **1** a slender surgical instrument for exploring a wound **2** investigation **3** spacecraft, etc. used to get information about an environment —*v.* **1** explore with a probe **2** investigate —**prob′er** *n.*

pro′bi·ty (prō′bə-) *n.* honesty

prob′lem *n.* **1** question to be solved **2** difficult matter, etc.

prob′lem·at′ic *a.* **1** hard to solve or deal with **2** uncertain Also **prob′lem·at′i·cal**

pro·bos′cis *n.* elephant's trunk, or similar snout

pro′caine′ *n.* drug used as a local anesthetic

pro·ce′dure (-jər) *n.* act or way of doing something

pro·ceed′ *v.* **1** go on after stopping **2** carry on an action **3** come forth

pro·ceed′ing *n.* **1** course of action **2** *pl.* transactions **3** *pl.* legal action

pro′ceeds′ *n.pl.* money from a business deal

proc′ess′ *n.* **1** series of changes in developing **2** act or way of doing something **3** court summons **4** projecting part —*v.* prepare by a special process

pro·ces′sion *n.* group moving forward, as in a parade

pro·ces′sion·al *n.* hymn or music for a procession

pro·claim′ *v.* announce officially —**proc′la·ma′tion** *n.*

pro·cliv′i·ty *n., pl.* **–ties** inclination; tendency

pro·cras′ti·nate′ *v.* put off; delay —**pro·cras′ti·na′tion** *n.* —**pro·cras′ti·na′tor** *n.*

pro′cre·ate′ *v.* produce (young) —**pro′cre·a′tion** *n.*

proc′tor *n.* one supervising students, as during a test

pro·cure′ *v.* get; obtain —**pro·cur′a·ble** *a.* —**pro·cure′ment** *n.* —**pro·cur′er** *n.*

prod *n., v.* **prod′ded, prod′ding** goad or jab

prod′i·gal *a.* very wasteful or generous —*n.* spendthrift —**prod′i·gal′i·ty** *n.*

pro·di′gious (-dij′əs) *a.* **1** amazing **2** enormous —**pro·di′gious·ly** *adv.*

prod′i·gy *n., pl.* **–gies** remarkable person or thing

pro·duce′ (*n.:* prō′dōōs′) *v.* **1** show **2** bring forth **3** manufacture **4** cause **5** get (a play, etc.) ready for the public —*n.* farm products —**pro·duc′er** *n.* —**pro·duc′tion** *n.*

prod′uct′ *n.* **1** thing produced **2** result **3** result of multiplying numbers

pro·duc′tive *a.* **1** producing much **2** causing —**pro′duc·tiv′i·ty** *n.*

pro·fane′ *a.* **1** not religious **2** scornful of sacred things —v. treat irreverently —**pro-fane′ly** adv.

pro-fan′i-ty n., pl. **–ties** swearing

pro-fess′ v. 1 declare openly 2 claim to have or be 3 declare one's belief in

pro-fes′sion n. 1 occupation requiring special study 2 its members 3 avowal

pro-fes′sion-al n., a. (one) of a profession, or (one) paid to play in games, etc. —**pro-fes′sion-al-ly** adv.

pro-fes′sor n. college teacher —**pro-fes-so′ri-al** a.

prof′fer v., n. offer

pro-fi′cient (-fish′ənt) a. skilled —**pro-fi′cien-cy** n.

pro′file′ n. 1 side view of the face 2 outline

prof′it n. 1 gain; benefit 2 net income from business —v. benefit —**prof′it-a-ble** a. —**prof′it-a-bly** adv. —**prof′it-less** a.

prof′it-eer′ n. one who makes excessive profits

prof′li-gate (-gət) a. 1 dissolute 2 wasteful —**prof′li-ga-cy** n.

pro-found′ a. 1 very deep 2 complete —**pro-fun′di-ty** n., pl. **–ties**

pro-fuse′ (-fyoos′) a. abundant —**pro-fuse′ly** adv. —**pro-fu′sion** n.

pro-gen′i-tor n. ancestor

prog′e-ny (präj′-) n. offspring

pro-ges′ter-one′ n. hormone secreted in the ovary

prog-no′sis n., pl. **–ses′** (-sēz′) prediction

prog-nos′ti-cate′ v. predict —**prog-nos′ti-ca′tion** n. —**prog-nos′ti-ca′tor** n.

pro′gram n. 1 list of things to be performed 2 plan of procedure 3 scheduled radio or TV broadcast 4 logical sequence of operations for electronic computer —v. 1 schedule in a program 2 plan a computer program for 3 furnish with a program Br. sp. **pro′gramme** —**pro′gram′ma-ble** a.

prog′ress (prō gres′; n.: präg′res) v. advance, develop, or improve —n. a progressing —**pro-gres′sion** n.

pro-gres′sive a. 1 progressing 2 favoring progress, reform, etc. —n. progressive person —**pro-gres′sive-ly** adv.

pro-hib′it v. 1 forbid, as by law 2 prevent —**pro-hib′i-tive, pro-hib′i-to′ry** a.

pro′hi-bi′tion (-bish′ən) n. a forbidding, esp. of the making or selling of liquor —**pro′hi-bi′tion-ist** n.

proj-ect′ (v.: prə jekt′) n. 1 scheme 2 undertaking —v. 1 propose 2 stick out 3 cause (a light, etc.) to fall upon a surface —**pro-jec′tion** n. —**pro-jec′tor** n.

pro-jec′tile (-təl) n. object to be shot forth, as a bullet

pro-jec′tion-ist n. operator of a film or slide projector

pro-lapse′ (n.: prō′laps′) v. fall or slip out of place —n. prolapsed condition

pro′le-tar′i-at n. working class —**pro′le-tar′i-an** a.

pro-lif′er-ate′ v. increase rapidly —**pro-lif′er-a′tion** n.

pro-lif′ic a. producing much

pro-lix′ a. wordy —**pro-lix′i-ty** n.

pro′logue (-lôg′) n. introduction to a poem, play, etc.

pro-long′ v. lengthen —**pro′lon-ga′tion** n.

prom n. formal dance at a college, etc.

prom′e-nade′ (-nād′, -näd′) n. 1 walk for pleasure 2 public place for walking —v. take a promenade

prom′i-nent a. 1 projecting 2 conspicuous; very noticeable 3 famous —**prom′i-nence** n.

pro-mis′cu-ous (-kyoo-) a. not discriminating —**prom′is-cu′i-ty** n.

prom′ise n. 1 agreement to do or not do something 2 sign as of future success —v. 1 to make a promise of or to 2 to cause to expect

prom′is-ing a. showing signs of future success

prom′is-so′ry a. containing or being a promise

prom′on-to′ry n., pl. **–ries** peak of high land jutting out into the sea

pro-mote′ v. 1 raise in rank 2 further the growth or sale of —**pro-mo′tion** n. —**pro-mot′er** n.

prompt a. ready; quick —v. 1 help with a cue 2 inspire or urge —**prompt′er** n. —**prompt′ly** adv.

promp′ti-tude′ n. quality of being prompt

prom′ul-gate′ v. proclaim; publish —**prom′ul-ga′tion** n.

prone a. 1 lying face downward 2 apt or likely

prong n. projecting point, as of a fork —**pronged** a.

prong′horn′ n. deer having curved horns

pro′noun′ n. word used in place of a noun —**pro-nom′i-nal** a.

pro-nounce′ v. 1 declare officially 2 utter the sounds of —**pro-nounce′a-ble** a. —**pro-nounce′ment** n.

pro-nounced′ a. definite; unmistakable

pron′to adv. [Sl.] at once; quickly

pro-nun′ci-a′tion n. act or way of pronouncing words

proof n. 1 convincing evidence 2 a test 3 strength of a liquor —a. strong enough to resist

–proof suf. impervious to

proof′read′ v. to read in order to correct errors

prop n. 1 a support or aid 2 propeller

—*v.* **propped, prop′ping** to support or lean against

prop′a·gan′da *n.* **1** systematic spreading of ideas **2** ideas so spread —**prop′a·gan′dist** *a., n.* —**prop′a·gan′dize** *v.*

prop′a·gate′ *v.* **1** produce offspring **2** raise; breed **3** spread (ideas) —**prop′a·ga′tion** *n.*

pro′pane′ *n.* a gas used as a fuel

pro·pel′ *v.* **-pelled′, -pel′ling** drive forward

pro·pel′lant, pro·pel′lent *n.* fuel for a rocket

pro·pel′ler *n.* blades on end of a revolving shaft for propelling a ship or aircraft

pro·pen′si·ty *n., pl.* **-ties** natural tendency

prop′er *a.* **1** suitable; fit **2** correct **3** genteel; respectable **4** belonging (*to*) **5** actual —**prop′er·ly** *adv.*

prop′er·ty *n., pl.* **-ties 1** thing owned **2** characteristic

proph′e·cy (-sē) *n., pl.* **-cies** prediction

proph′e·sy′ (-sī′) *v.* **-sied′, -sy′ing** to predict; foretell —**proph′et·ic** *a.*

proph′et *n.* **1** leader regarded as divinely inspired **2** one who predicts

pro′phy·lac′tic (-fə-) *n., a.* (medicine, device, etc.) that prevents disease, etc.

pro′phy·lax′is *n., pl.* **-lax′es** (-ēz) cleaning of the teeth

pro·pin′qui·ty *n.* nearness

pro·pi′ti·ate′ (-pish′ē-) *v.* to appease

pro·pi′tious *a.* favorable

prop′jet′ *n.* turboprop

pro·po′nent *n.* supporter

pro·por′tion *n.* **1** part in relation to the whole **2** ratio **3** symmetry **4** *pl.* dimensions —*v.* **1** make symmetrical **2** make fit —**pro·por′tion·al, pro·por′tion·ate** *a.*

pro·pose′ *v.* **1** suggest for considering **2** plan **3** offer marriage —**pro·pos′al** *n.*

prop′o·si′tion *n.* **1** a plan **2** subject for debate

pro·pound′ *v.* suggest for consideration

pro·pri′e·tar′y *a.* held under a patent, etc.

pro·pri′e·tor *n.* owner

pro·pri′e·ty *n.* fitness; correctness

pro·pul′sion *n.* a propelling or a force that propels —**pro·pul′sive** *a.*

pro·rate′ *v.* divide or assess proportionally

pro·sa′ic (-zā′-) *a.* commonplace

pro·sce′ni·um (-sē′-) *n., pl.* **-ni·ums** or **-ni·a** arch framing a conventional stage

pro·scribe′ *v.* forbid

prose *n.* nonpoetic language

pros′e·cute′ *v.* **1** engage in **2** take legal action against —**pros′e·cu′tion** *n.* —**pros′e·cu′tor** *n.*

pros′e·lyte′ (-līt′) *n., v.* convert —**pros′e·lyt·ize′** *v.*

pros′pect′ *n.* **1** outlook **2** likely customer, etc. **3** *pl.* apparent chance for success —*v.*

search (*for*) —**pros′pec′tor** *n.*

pro·spec′tive *a.* expected

pro·spec′tus *n.* report outlining a new work, etc.

pros′per *v.* thrive

pros·per′i·ty *n.* wealth —**pros′per·ous** *a.* —**pros′per·ous·ly** *adv.*

pros′tate′ *a.* of a gland at the base of the bladder in males

pros·the′sis *n., pl.* **-ses** (-sēz′) (use of) artificial body part(s) —**pros·thet′ic** *a.*

pros′ti·tute′ *n.* one who engages in sexual intercourse for pay —*v.* sell (one's talents, etc.) for base purposes —**pros′ti·tu′tion** *n.*

pros′trate′ *a.* **1** lying flat, esp. face downward **2** overcome —*v.* **1** lay flat **2** overcome —**pros·tra′tion** *n.*

pro·tag′o·nist *n.* main character or leading figure

pro′te·an *a.* readily taking on many forms

pro·tect′ *v.* shield from harm —**pro·tec′tion** *n.* —**pro·tec′tive** *a.* —**pro·tec′tor** *n.*

pro·tec′tor·ate (-ət) *n.* territory controlled and protected by a strong state

pro·té·gé (prōt′ə zhā′) *n.* one under another's patronage

pro·tein′ (-tēn′) *n.* nitrogenous substance essential to diet

pro·test′ (*n.:* prō′test′) *v.* **1** to object **2** assert —*n.* objection —**prot′es·ta′tion** *n.* —**pro·test′er, pro·tes′tor** *n.*

Prot′es·tant *n.* Christian not of the Roman Catholic or Eastern Orthodox Church —**Prot′es·tant·ism′** *n.*

proto- *pref.* original

pro′to·col′ (-kôl′) *n.* code of etiquette among diplomats, etc.

pro′ton′ *n.* positive particle in the nucleus of an atom

pro′to·plasm′ *n.* essential matter in all living cells —**pro′to·plas′mic** *a.*

pro′to·type′ *n.* first thing of its kind

pro′to·zo′an *n., pl.* **-zo′a** one-celled animal

pro·tract′ *v.* draw out; prolong —**pro·trac′tion** *n.*

pro·trac′tor *n.* device for drawing and measuring angles

pro·trude′ *v.* jut out —**pro·tru′sion** *n.*

pro·tu′ber·ance *n.* bulge —**pro·tu′ber·ant** *a.*

proud *a.* **1** haughty **2** feeling or causing pride **3** splendid —**proud of** highly pleased with —**proud′ly** *adv.*

proud flesh *n.* excessive growth of flesh around a healing wound

prove (prōōv) *v.* **proved, proved** or **prov′en, prov′ing 1** test by experiment **2** establish as true

prov′e·nance *n.* origin; source

prov′en·der *n.* fodder

prov′erb′ *n.* wise saying —**pro·ver′bi·al** *a.*

pro·vide′ *v.* 1 supply; furnish (with) 2 prepare (*for* or *against*) 3 stipulate —**pro·vid′er** *n.*

pro·vid′ed *con.* on condition (*that*): also **pro·vid′ing**

prov′i·dence *n.* 1 prudent foresight 2 guidance of God or Nature —[P–] God —**prov′i·dent** *a.* —**prov′i·den′tial** (-shal) *a.*

prov′ince *n.* 1 division of a country 2 *pl.* parts of a country outside major cities 3 sphere

pro·vin′cial (-shal) *a.* 1 of a province 2 narrow-minded —**pro·vin′cial·ism′** *n.*

proving ground *n.* place for testing new equipment, etc.

pro·vi′sion (-vizh′ən) *n.* 1 a providing 2 *pl.* stock of food 3 stipulation —*v.* supply with provisions

pro·vi′sion·al *a.* temporary

pro·vi′so′ *n., pl.* **-sos**′ or **-soes**′ stipulation

prov′o·ca′tion *n.* 1 a provoking 2 thing that provokes —**pro·voc′a·tive** *a.*

pro·voke′ *v.* 1 anger 2 stir up or evoke

prow′est′ (-vōst′) *n.* high executive official, as in some colleges

prow (prou) *n.* forward part of a ship

prow′ess *n.* 1 bravery; valor 2 superior skill, etc.

prowl *v.* roam or stalk furtively

prox·im′i·ty *n.* nearness

prox′y *n., pl.* **-ies** (one with) authority to act for another

prude *n.* one overly modest or proper —**prud′er·y** *n.* —**prud′ish** *a.*

pru′dent *a.* wisely careful —**pru′dence** *n.* —**pru·den′tial** (-shal) *a.*

prune *n.* dried plum —*v.* trim twigs, etc. from

pru′ri·ent (proor′ē-) *a.* lustful —**pru′ri·ence** *n.*

pry *n., pl.* **pries** lever —*v.* **pried**, **pry′ing** 1 raise with a lever 2 look closely or inquisitively

psalm (säm) *n.* sacred song or poem —**psalm′ist** *n.*

pseu′do (sōō′dō) *a.* false

pseudo– *pref.* sham; counterfeit

pseu′do·nym′ (-nim′) *n.* fictitious name assumed by an author, etc.

pshaw (shô) *int., n.* exclamation of disgust, etc.

pso·ri′a·sis (sə rī′ə-) *n.* skin disease with scaly, reddish patches

psych (sīk) *v.* [Sl.] 1 probe behavior psychologically so as to outwit or control: often with *out* 2 prepare (oneself) psychologically: with *up*

psy′che (sī′kē) *n.* 1 soul 2 mind

psy′che·del′ic *a.* of or causing extreme

changes in the conscious mind

psy·chi′a·try (-kī′-) *n.* branch of medicine dealing with mental illness —**psy′chi·at′ric** (-kē-) *a.* —**psy·chi′a·trist** *n.*

psy′chic (-kik) *a.* 1 of the mind 2 supernatural Also **psy′chi·cal** —*n.* one sensitive to psychic phenomena

psy′cho (-kō) [Col.] *n., pl.* **-chos** psychopath —*a.* psychopathic

psycho– *pref.* mind; mental processes: also **psych–**

psy′cho·a·nal′y·sis *n.* method of treating neuroses —**psy′cho·an′a·lyst** *n.* —**psy′cho·an′a·lyze**′ *v.*

psy·chol′o·gy *n.* science dealing with the mind and behavior —**psy′cho·log′i·cal** *a.* —**psy′cho·log′i·cal·ly** *adv.* —**psy·chol′o·gist** *n.*

psy′cho·path′ic *a.* of mental disorder —**psy′cho·path**′ *n.*

psy·cho′sis *n., pl.* **-ses**′ (-sēz′) severe mental illness —**psy·chot′ic** *a., n.*

psy′cho·so·mat′ic *a.* of a physical disorder caused by emotional disturbance

psy′cho·ther′a·py *n.* treatment of mental illness —**psy′cho·ther′a·pist** *n.*

ptar′mi·gan (tär′-) *n.* northern grouse

pter·o·dac′tyl (ter′ə dak′təl) *n.* extinct flying reptile

pto·maine′ (tō′-) *n.* a substance in decaying matter

pub *n.* [Br. Col.] bar; tavern: in full **public house**

pu′ber·ty (pyōō′-) *n.* time of maturing sexually

pu′bic *a.* of or in the region of the groin

pub′lic *a.* 1 of people as a whole 2 for everyone 3 known by all —*n.* the people —**in public** in open view —**pub′lic·ly** *adv.*

pub′li·ca′tion *n.* 1 printing and selling of books, etc. 2 thing published

public domain *n.* condition of being free from copyright or patent

pub′li·cist *n.* publicity agent

pub·lic′i·ty (-lis′-) *n.* 1 public attention 2 information meant to bring one this —**pub′li·cize**′ *v.*

public servant *n.* government official or employee

pub′lish *v.* 1 issue (a printed work) for sale 2 announce —**pub′lish·er** *n.*

puce *n.* brownish purple

puck *n.* hard rubber disk used in ice hockey

puck′er *n., v.* wrinkle

puck′ish *a.* mischievous

pud′ding (pood′-) *n.* soft food of flour, milk, eggs, etc.

pud′dle *n.* small pool of water

pudg′y *a.* **-i·er**, **-i·est** short and fat

pueb′lo (pweb′-) *n., pl.* **-los** American

Indian village of SW U.S.

pu·er·ile (pyoor′il) *a.* childish —**pu′er·il′i·ty** *n.*

puff *n.* 1 brief burst of wind, etc. 2 draw at a cigarette 3 light pastry shell 4 soft pad —*v.* 1 blow in puffs 2 breathe rapidly 3 smoke 4 swell —**puff′i·ness** *n.* —**puff′y** *a.*, **-i·er, -i·est**

puff′ball′ *n.* round, white fungus

puf′fin *n.* northern seabird

pug *n.* small dog

pu·gil·ism (pyoo′jə liz′əm) *n.* sport of boxing —**pu′gil·ist** *n.* —**pu′gil·is′tic** *a.*

pug·na′cious *a.* quarrelsome —**pug·na′cious·ly** *adv.* —**pug·nac′i·ty** (-nas′-) *n.*

pug nose *n.* a short, thick nose that is turned up at the end —**pug′-nosed′** *a.*

puke *v.*, *n.* [Col.] vomit

puk′ka *a.* 1 first-rate 2 genuine; real

pul′chri·tude′ (-krə-) *n.* beauty

pull *v.* 1 to make (something) move toward one 2 pluck out 3 rip 4 strain 5 [Col.] do; perform 6 move (*away, ahead, etc.*) —*n.* 1 act or effort of pulling 2 handle, etc. 3 [Col.] influence —**pull for** [Col.] cheer on —**pull off** accomplish —**pull in** 1 depart 2 quit or withdraw —**pull over** drive toward, and stop at, the curb —**pull through** [Col.] get over (an illness, etc.)

pul′let (pool′-) *n.* young hen

pul′ley *n.*, *pl.* **-leys** wheel with a grooved rim in which a rope runs, for raising weights

Pull′man (car) *n.* railroad car with berths for sleeping

pull′out′ *n.* removal, withdrawal, etc.

pull′o′ver *n.* sweater, etc. to be pulled over the head

pul′mo·nar′y *a.* of the lungs

pulp *n.* 1 soft, inside part, as of fruit 2 moist wood fiber, ground to make paper —**pulp′y** *a.*, **-i·er, -i·est**

pul′pit *n.* clergyman's platform for preaching

pul′sar′ *n.* celestial object emitting pulses of radiation

pul·sate′ *v.* throb —**pul·sa′tion** *n.*

pulse *n.* regular beat, as of blood in the arteries

pul′ver·ize′ *v.* grind or crush into powder

pu′ma (pyoo′-, poo′-) *n.* cougar

pum′ice *n.* light, spongy rock, used for cleaning, etc.

pum′mel *v.* hit with repeated blows, esp. with the fist

pump *n.* machine that forces fluids in or out 2 low-cut, strapless shoe —*v.* 1 move or empty (fluids) with a pump 2 move like a pump 3 question persistently

pum′per·nick′el *n.* coarse, dark rye bread

pump′kin *n.* large, round, orange-yellow gourd

pun *n.* humorous use of different words that sound alike —*v.* **punned, pun′ning** make puns

punch *n.* 1 tool for piercing, etc. 2 fruit drink 3 blow with the fist —*v.* 1 pierce, etc. with a punch 2 hit with the fist

punch′-drunk′ *a.* [Col.] dazed

punch′y *a.* **-i·er, -i·est** [Col.] 1 forceful 2 dazed

punc·til′i·ous *a.* 1 careful in behavior 2 precise

punc′tu·al (-choo əl) *a.* on time —**punc′tu·al′i·ty** *n.*

punc′tu·ate′ *v.* use periods, commas, etc. in (writing) —**punc′tu·a′tion** *n.*

punc′ture *n.* hole made by a sharp point —*v.* pierce as with a point

pun′dit *n.* very learned person

pun′gent *a.* 1 sharp in taste or smell 2 keen and direct —**pun′gen·cy** *n.*

pun′ish *v.* make suffer pain, loss, etc. as for a crime or offense —**pun′ish·a·ble** *a.* —**pun′ish·ment** *n.*

pu′ni·tive *a.* of or inflicting punishment

punk *n.* 1 substance that smolders, used to light fireworks 2 [Sl.] insignificant young person

pun′ster *n.* one who makes puns: also **pun′ner**

punt *v.* 1 kick a dropped football before it touches the ground 2 move (a boat) using a long pole —*n.* 1 a punting 2 square, flat-bottomed boat

pu′ny *a.* **-ni·er, -ni·est** small or weak

pup *n.* young dog, wolf, etc.

pu·pa (pyoo′-) *n.*, *pl.* **-pae** (-pē) or **-pas** insect just before the adult stage

pu′pil *n.* 1 person being taught 2 contracting opening in iris of the eye

pup′pet *n.* 1 doll moved manually by strings, etc. 2 person controlled by another —**pup′pet·eer′** *n.*

pup′py *n.*, *pl.* **-pies** young dog

pup tent *n.* small, portable tent

pur′chase (-chəs) *v.* buy —*n.* 1 thing bought 2 act of buying —**pur′chas·er** *n.*

pure *a.* 1 unmixed 2 clean 3 mere 4 faultless 5 chaste 6 abstract —**pure′ly** *adv.* —**pu′ri·fy′** *v.* —**pu′ri·fi·ca′tion** *n.* —**pu′ri·ty** *n.*

pure′bred′ *a.* belonging to a breed of unmixed descent

pu·rée, pu·ree (pyoo rā′) *n.* 1 mashed, strained food 2 thick soup

pur′ga·tive (-gə-) *a.* purging —*n.* a laxative

pur′ga·to′ry *R.C.Ch.* state or place for expiating sins after death

purge *v.* 1 cleanse; make pure 2 move (the

bowels) **3** get rid of —*n.* **1** a purging **2** a laxative

pur′ist *n.* person who strictly observes rules in art, etc.

pu′ri·tan (pyoor′ə-) *n.* one very strict in morals and religion —**pu′ri·tan′i·cal**, **pu′ri·tan′ic·a** *a.*

purl *v.* invert (stitches) in knitting to form ribbing

pur·lieu (purl′yoō′) *n.* outlying part; suburb

pur·loin′ *v.* steal

pur′ple *n., a.* bluish red

pur·port′ (*n.:* pur′pôrt′) *v.* seem or claim to mean or be —*n.* meaning

pur′pose (-pəs) *n.* **1** intention; aim **2** determination —**on purpose** intentionally —**pur′pose·ful** *a.* —**pur′pose·less** *a.* —**pur′pose·ly** *adv.*

purr *v., n.* (make) the sound of a cat at ease

purse *n.* **1** small bag for money **2** woman's handbag **3** prize money —*v.* to pucker (the lips)

purs′er *n.* ship's officer in charge of accounts, etc.

pur·su′ant *a.* following —**pursuant to** according to

pur·sue′ *v.* **1** try to overtake; chase **2** go on with **3** seek —**pur·su′ance** *n.*

pur·suit′ *n.* **1** a pursuing **2** occupation

pu′ru·lent (pyoō′roō-) *a.* of or discharging pus —**pu′ru·lence** *n.*

pur·vey′ (-vā′) *v.* supply, as food —**pur·vey′or** *n.*

pur′view′ *n.* scope or extent of control, activity, etc.

pus *n.* yellowish matter forming in infections

push *v.* **1** to move by pressing against **2** urge on —*n.* **1** a pushing **2** an advance

push′er *n.* [Sl.] one who sells drugs illegally

push′o′ver *n.* [Sl.] **1** anything easy to do **2** one easily persuaded, defeated, etc.

push′-up′, **push′up′** *n.* exercise of raising one's prone body by pushing down on the palms

push′y *a.* **-i·er**, **-i·est** [Col.] annoyingly aggressive

pu′sil·lan′i·mous *a.* cowardly; timid

puss (poos) *n.* [Col.] cat: also **puss′y**, **puss′y·cat′**

puss′y·foot′ *v.* [Col.] **1** move cautiously **2** avoid taking a stand

pussy willow *n.* willow with soft, silvery catkins

pus′tule (-tyoōl′, -choōl′) *n.* inflamed, pus-filled pimple

put *v.* put, put′ting **1** make be in some place, state, relation, etc. **2** impose or assign **3** express **4** go (*in, out,* etc.) —**put down 1** repress **2** [Sl.] belittle or humiliate —**put in for** apply for —**put off 1** postpone **2** perturb —**put on 1** pretend **2** [Sl.] to hoax —**put out 1** extinguish **2** inconvenience —**put up 1** preserve (fruits, etc.) **2** give lodgings to **3** provide (money) —**put upon** impose on —**put up with** tolerate —**stay put** [Col.] remain; stay

pu′ta·tive *a.* supposed

put′-down′ *n.* [Sl.] belittling remark

put′-on′ *n.* [Sl.] hoax

pu′tre·fy′ *v.* **-fied′**, **-fy′ing** rot —**pu′tre·fac′tion** *n.*

pu′trid *a.* rotten; stinking

putt *v., n.* *Golf* (make) a stroke to roll the ball into the hole

put′ter *v.* busy oneself aimlessly —*n.* *Golf* club for putting

put′ty *n.* pliable substance to fill cracks, etc. —*v.* **-tied**, **-ty·ing** fill with putty

puz′zle *v.* perplex —*n.* **1** thing that puzzles **2** problem to test cleverness

pyg′my (pig′-) *n., pl.* **-mies** dwarf

py·ja·mas *n.pl.* Br. sp. of PAJAMAS

py′lon′ (pī-) *n.* towerlike shaft

py·lo′rus *n., pl.* **-ri′** (-rī′) opening from the stomach into intestines —**py·lor′ic** *a.*

py·or·rhe·a, **py·or·rhoe·a** (pī′ə rē′ə) *n.* infection of the gums and tooth sockets

pyr′a·mid (pir′-) *n.* solid figure or structure with triangular sides meeting at a point —*v.* build up —**py·ram′i·dal** *a.*

pyre (pīr) *n.* pile of wood for burning a dead body

py′ro·ma′ni·a *n.* compulsion to start fires —**py′ro·ma′ni·ac′** *n.*

py′ro·tech′nics *n.pl.* **1** display of fireworks **2** dazzling display

py′thon′ *n.* large snake that crushes its prey to death

Q

quack *v.* utter the cry of a duck —*n.* **1** this cry **2** one who practices medicine fraudulently —**quack′er·y** *n.*

quad′ran′gle *n.* **1** plane figure with four angles and four sides **2** four-sided area surrounded by buildings: also **quad**

quad′rant *n.* quarter section of a circle

quad′ra·phon′ic *a.* using four channels to record and reproduce sound

quad·ren′ni·al *a.* lasting or occurring every four years

quad′ri·lat′er·al *a., n.* four-sided (figure)

qua·drille′ *n.* dance in which four couples form a square, etc.

quad′ri·ple′gi·a (-plē′jē ə) *n.* paralysis of

the body from the neck down —**quad′ri-ple′gic** a., n.

quad′ru-ped′ n. four-footed animal

quad·ru·ple a., adv. four times as much —v. make or become quadruple

quad·ru·plet n. any of four children born at one birth

quad·ru·pli·cate (-kāt′; a., n.: -kət)v. make four copies of —a. made in four identical copies —n. one of these copies

quaff (kwäf) v. drink deeply —n. a quaffing

quag′mire′ n. a bog

qua′hog′, qua′haug′ (kwô′-) n. edible, hard-shelled clam

quail v. draw back in fear —n. game bird

quaint a. pleasingly odd or old-fashioned —**quaint′ly** adv. —**quaint′ness** n.

quake v. shake —n. **1** a quaking **2** earthquake

qual′i·fied′ a. **1** skilled; able **2** limited

qual′i·fy′ v. **-fied′, -fy′ing 1** make or be fit for a job, etc. **2** modify; restrict **3** moderate —**qual′i·fi·ca′tion** n. —**qual′i·fi′er** n.

qual′i·ty n., pl. **-ties 1** characteristic **2** kind **3** degree of (excellence) —**qual′i·ta′tive** a.

qualm (kwäm) n. scruple; misgiving

quan′da·ry n., pl. **-ries** state of perplexity; dilemma

quan′ti·ty n., pl. **-ties 1** amount **2** large amount **3** number or symbol expressing measure —**quan′ti·ta′tive** a.

quan′tum n., pl. **-ta** Physics basic unit of energy, etc.

quar′an·tine′ (-tēn′) n. isolation to keep contagious disease from spreading —v. place under quarantine

quark n. assumed basic unit of matter

quar′rel v., n. (have) an argument or disagreement —**quar′rel·some** a.

quar′ry n., pl. **-ries 1** animal, etc. being hunted down **2** place where stone is excavated —v. **-ried, -ry·ing** excavate from a quarry

quart n. ¼ gallon

quar′ter n. **1** any of four equal parts; ¼ **2** 25-cent coin **3** district **4** pl. lodgings **5** mercy —v. **1** divide into quarters **2** provide lodgings for —**at close quarters** at close range

quar′ter·back′ n. Football back who calls signals and passes the ball

quar′ter·deck′ n. after part of a ship's top deck

quar′ter·ly a. occurring regularly four times a year —adv. once every quarter of the year —n., pl. **-lies** publication issued quarterly

quar′ter·mas′ter n. army officer in charge of supplies

quar·tet′, quar·tette′ n. musical composition for four performers

quar′to n. book-page size about 9 X 12 in.

quartz n. bright mineral

quartz crystal n. Electronics piece of quartz that vibrates at a particular frequency

qua′sar′ n. a distant celestial object that emits immense quantities of light and radio waves

quash (kwäsh) v. **1** annul **2** suppress

qua·si (kwā′zī′, kwä′zē′) a., adv. seeming(ly)

quat′rain′ n. stanza of four lines

qua′ver v. **1** tremble **2** be tremulous: said of the voice —n. tremulous tone

quay (kē) n. wharf

quea′sy (kwē′-) a. **-si·er, -si·est** feeling nausea

queen n. **1** wife of a king **2** woman monarch **3** female in an insect colony **4** playing card with a queen's picture **5** most powerful chess piece

queer a. **1** odd **2** [Col.] eccentric —**queer′ly** adv.

quell v. subdue or quiet

quench v. **1** extinguish **2** satisfy —**quench′less** a.

quer′u·lous (kwer′-) a. **1** fretful **2** complaining

que′ry (kwir′-) n., pl. **-ries**; v. **-ried, -ry·ing** question

quest n. a seeking —v. seek

ques′tion n. **1** inquiry **2** thing asked **3** doubt **4** problem **5** point being debated —v. **1** inquire **2** doubt **3** challenge —**out of the question** impossible —**ques′tion·er** n.

ques′tion·a·ble a. **1** doubtful **2** not well thought of

question mark n. mark of punctuation (?)

ques′tion·naire′ n. list of questions for gathering information

queue (kyōō) n. **1** pigtail **2** line of persons

quib′ble v. evade a point by carping

quiche (kēsh) n. hot custard pie made with cheese, spinach, etc.

quiche Lor·raine′ (lô rān′) n. custard pie made with cheese and bacon

quick a. **1** swift **2** prompt —adv. rapidly —n. **1** the living **2** one's deepest feelings —**quick′ly** adv.

quick′en v. **1** enliven **2** hasten

quick′-freeze′ v., **-froze′, -froz′en, -freez′ing** freeze (food) suddenly for storage

quick′ie n. [Sl.] anything done or made quickly

quick′lime′ n. unslaked lime

quick′sand′ n. wet, deep sand that engulfs heavy things

quick'sil'ver n. mercury

quick'-tem'pered a. easily angered

quick'-wit'ted a. alert

quid n. 1 piece of tobacco to be chewed 2 [Br. Col.] one pound sterling

qui·es'cent (kwī-) a. quiet; inactive

qui'et a. 1 still 2 silent 3 gentle —n. 1 stillness 2 silence —v. make or become quiet —**qui'et·ly** adv. —**qui'et·ness** n.

qui'e·tude' n. calmness

quill n. 1 large feather 2 pen made from this 3 spine of a porcupine

quilt v., n. (make) a bedcover stitched in layers

quince n. yellowish fruit

qui'nine' n. alkaloid used in treating malaria

quin'sy (-zē) n. sore throat

quin·tes'sence n. 1 pure essence 2 perfect example

quin·tet', quin·tette' n. musical composition for five performers

quin·tu'plet (-tup'lət) n. any of five children born at one birth

quip v., n. **quipped, quip'ping** (make) a witty remark

quire n. set of 24 or 25 sheets of the same paper

quirk n. peculiarity

quirt n. riding whip with braided leather lash

quis'ling (kwiz'-) n. traitor

quit v. **quit, quit'ted, quit'ting** 1 give up 2 leave 3 stop —a. free

quit'claim' n. deed resigning a claim, as to property

quite adv. 1 completely 2 really 3 very or fairly —**quite a few** [Col.] many

quits a. on even terms —**call it quits** [Col.] stop working, being friendly, etc.

quit'tance n. 1 discharge of a debt 2 recompense

quit'ter n. [Col.] one who gives up easily

quiv'er v. tremble —n. 1 tremor 2 case for arrows

quix·ot'ic a. idealistic but impractical

quiz n., pl. **quiz'zes** test of knowledge —v. **quizzed, quiz'zing** give a quiz to

quiz'zi·cal a. 1 comical 2 perplexed —**quiz'zi·cal·ly** adv.

quoit n. 1 ring thrown to encircle an upright peg 2 pl. game so played

quon'dam a. former

Quon'set hut n. metal shelter with a curved roof

quo'rum n. minimum number needed to transact business at an assembly

quo'ta n., pl. **-tas** share assigned to each one

quo·ta'tion n. 1 a quoting 2 words quoted 3 current price of a stock or bond

quotation marks n. marks ("...") around quoted words

quote v. 1 repeat (the words of) 2 state (the price of) —n. [Col.] 1 quotation 2 quotation mark —**quot'a·ble** a.

quoth (kwōth) v. [Ar.] said

quo'tient (-shənt) n. number got by dividing one number into another

R

R trademark film rating indicating anyone under 17 admitted only with a parent or guardian

rab'bi (-ī) n., pl. **-bis** ordained teacher of the Jewish law —**rab·bin'i·cal** a.

rab'bit n. burrowing rodent with soft fur and long ears

rab'ble n. a mob

rab'ble-rous'er n. one who tries to incite others to anger or violence

rab'id a. 1 fanatical 2 of or having rabies

ra'bies n. disease of dogs, etc., transmitted by biting

rac·coon' n. small, furry mammal with black-ringed tail

race n. 1 a competition, esp. of speed 2 swift current 3 division of mankind, esp. based on skin color 4 any group or class —v. 1 be in a race 2 move swiftly —**rac'er** n. —**ra'cial** (-shəl) a.

race'horse' n. horse bred and trained for racing

ra·ceme' n. flower cluster

race track n. course for racing

race'way' n. race track for harness races or one for drag races, etc.

rac'ism' n. racial discrimination or persecution —**rac'ist** a., n.

rack n. 1 framework for holding things 2 ancient torture device 3 great torment 4 toothed bar meshing with a gearwheel —v. to torture —**rack one's brain** think hard

rack'et n. 1 noisy confusion 2 dishonest scheme 3 netted frame used as a bat in tennis: also sp. **rac'quet**

rack'et·eer' n. one who gets money by fraud, extortion, etc. —**rack'et·eer'ing** n.

rac'on·teur' (-tur') n. one clever at telling stories

rac'quet·ball' n. game like handball played with rackets

rac·y (rā'sē) a. **-i·er, -i·est** 1 lively 2 risqué

ra'dar' n. device for locating objects by their reflection of radio waves

ra'di·al a. of or like a ray or rays

radial (ply) tire n. tire with ply cords at right angles to the center line of tread

ra′di·ant a. 1 beaming 2 shining bright 3 issuing in rays —**ra′di·ance** n.

ra′di·ate′ v. 1 send out rays, as of heat or light 2 branch out as from a center

ra′di·a′tion n. 1 a radiating 2 rays sent out 3 nuclear particles

ra′di·a′tor n. device for radiating heat

rad′i·cal a. 1 basic 2 favoring extreme change —n. 1 one with radical views 2 Chem. group of atoms acting as one —**rad′i·cal·ism′** n. —**rad′i·cal·ly** adv.

ra′di·o′ n., pl. -**os′** 1 way of sending sounds through space by electromagnetic waves 2 set for receiving radio waves 3 broadcasting by radio —a. of radio —v. -**oed′**, -**o′ing** send by radio

ra′di·o·ac′tive a. emitting radiant energy by the disintegration of atomic nuclei —**ra′di·o·ac·tiv′i·ty** n.

ra′di·o·gram′ n. message sent by radio

ra′di·ol′o·gy n. medical use of radiant energy —**ra′di·ol′o·gist** n.

ra′di·o·ther′a·py n. treatment of disease by X-rays or rays from radioactive substance

rad′ish n. edible pungent root of certain plant

ra′di·um n. radioactive metallic chemical element

ra′di·us n., pl. -**di·i′** (-dē ī′) or -**di·us·es** straight line from the center to the outside of a circle or sphere

ra′don n. radioactive gas, a chemical element

raf′fi·a n. fiber from leaves of a palm, used in weaving

raff′ish a. 1 disreputable 2 tawdry

raf′fle n. lottery —v. offer as a prize in a raffle

raft n. floating platform of logs fastened together

raf′ter n. beam in a roof

rag n. 1 piece of torn or waste cloth 2 pl. tattered clothes —**rag′ged** a.

rag′a·muf′fin n. dirty, ragged child

rage n. 1 furious anger 2 craze; fad —v. 1 show violent anger 2 be unchecked

rag′lan n. designating a sleeve that continues in one piece to the collar

ra·gout (ra gōō′) n. stew

rag′time′ n. early jazz

rag′weed′ n. common weed whose pollen causes hay fever

raid n. sudden attack or invasion —v. make a raid on

rail n. 1 bar put between posts as a guard or support 2 either of the bars of a railroad track 3 railroad 4 small wading bird —v. speak bitterly

rail′ing n. fence made of rails and posts

rail′ler·y n. playful teasing

rail′road′ n. 1 road with steel rails for trains 2 system of such roads —v. [Col.] rush through unfairly

rail′way′ n. 1 [Br.] railroad 2 track with rails for cars

rai′ment (rā′-) n. [Ar.] attire

rain n. water falling in drops from the clouds —v. fall as or like rain —**rain′drop′** n. —**rain′fall′** n. —**rain′storm′** n. —**rain′y** a., -**i·er**, -**i·est**

rain′bow′ n. arc of colors formed by sunshine on rain

rain′coat′ n. waterproof coat

rain′drop′ n. single drop of rain

rain′fall′ n. 1 fall of rain 2 amount of rain over an area during a given time

rain′storm′ n. storm with heavy rain

raise v. 1 lift up 2 increase in amount, degree, etc. 3 build or put up 4 bring up 5 collect 6 make grow —n. a pay increase

rai′sin n. sweet, dried grape

ra·jah, ra·ja (rä′jə) n. prince in India

rake n. 1 long-handled tool with teeth at one end 2 debauched man —v. 1 gather (leaves, etc.) with a rake 2 search carefully 3 sweep with gunfire

rake′-off′ n. [Sl.] illegal commission or share

rak′ish (rāk′-) a. jaunty

ral′ly v. -**lied**, -**ly·ing** 1 regroup to set in order 2 gather for a common aim 3 revive —n., pl. -**lies** 1 a rallying 2 mass meeting

ram n. 1 male sheep 2 battering ram —v. -**rammed**, **ram′ming** 1 strike against with force 2 force into place

RAM (ram) n. computer memory allowing direct access of data: also **ran′dom·ac′cess memory**

ram′ble v. 1 stroll; roam 2 talk or write aimlessly 3 spread, as vines —n. a stroll —**ram′bler** n.

ram·bunc′tious (-shəs) a. disorderly; unruly

ram′e·kin n. small baking dish

ram′i·fy′ v. -**fied′**, -**fy′ing** spread out into branches —**ram′i·fi·ca′tion** n.

ramp n. sloping passage joining different levels

ram·page′ (n.: ram′pāj)v. rush wildly about —n. wild, angry action: usually in **on** the (or **a**) **rampage**

ramp′ant a. 1 raging; wild 2 rearing up

ram′part′ n. fortified embankment

ram′rod′ n. rod for ramming down a charge in a gun

ram′shack′le a. rickety

ran v. pt. of RUN

ranch n. large farm for raising livestock —**ranch′er, ranch′man** n., pl. -**men**

ran′cid a. stale, as oil or fat; spoiled

ran'cor n. bitter hate or ill will —**ran'cor·ous** a.

ran'dom a. haphazard —**at random** haphazardly

ran'dy a. **–di·er, –di·est** lustful

rang v. pt. of RING

range v. 1 set in rows 2 roam about 3 extend —n. 1 row or line, esp. of mountains 2 effective distance 3 extent 4 open land 5 place for shooting practice 6 cooking stove

rang'er n. 1 trooper who patrols a region 2 warden who patrols forests

rang·y (rān'jē) a. **–i·er, –i·est** long-limbed and thin

rank n. 1 row; line 2 class or grade 3 pl. enlisted soldiers —v. 1 to place in, or hold, a certain rank 2 outrank —a. 1 growing wildly 2 bad in taste or smell 3 utter —**rank and file** 1 enlisted men and women 2 common people

rank'ing a. 1 of highest rank 2 prominent

ran'kle v. cause mental pain, resentment, etc.

ran'sack' v. 1 search thoroughly 2 plunder; loot

ran'som n. 1 the freeing of a captive by paying money 2 price asked —v. buy a captive's freedom

rant v. talk wildly; rave

rap v. **rapped, rap'ping** 1 strike or knock sharply 2 [Sl.] to chat; talk —n. quick, sharp knock

ra·pa'cious (-shəs) a. greedy voracious —**ra·pac'i·ty** n.

rape n. 1 crime of attacking sexually 2 plant whose leaves are used for fodder —v. commit rape (on) —**rap'ist** n.

rap'id a. swift —**ra·pid'i·ty** n. —**rap'id·ly** adv.

rap'ids n.pl. part of a river with very swift current

ra'pi·er n. light, sharp sword

rap·ine (rap'in) n. plunder

rap·port' (-pôr') n. sympathetic relationship; harmony

rap·proche·ment (ra'prōsh män') n. an establishing of friendly relations

rap·scal'lion (-yən) n. rascal

rapt a. engrossed (in)

rap'ture n. ecstasy

rare a. 1 scarce; uncommon 2 very good 3 not dense 4 partly raw —**rare'ness** n. —**rar'i·ty** n., pl. **–ties**

rare'bit n. Welsh rabbit

rar·e·fy' v. **–fied', –fy'ing** make or become less dense

rare'ly adv. seldom

ras'cal n. 1 rogue 2 mischievous child —**ras·cal'i·ty** n.

rash a. too hasty; reckless —n. red spots on the skin —**rash'ly** adv.

rash'er n. slice of bacon

rasp v. 1 scrape harshly 2 irritate —n. 1 rough file 2 grating sound

rasp'ber'ry n., pl. **–ries** 1 shrub with red or black berries 2 the berry

rat n. long-tailed rodent, larger than a mouse —v. **rat'ted, rat'ting** [Sl.] inform on others

ratch'et n. wheel or bar with slanted teeth that catch on a pawl

rate n. 1 relative amount or degree 2 price per unit 3 rank —v. 1 appraise 2 rank 3 [Col.] deserve

rath'er adv. 1 preferably 2 with more reason 3 more truly 4 on the contrary 5 somewhat

raths'kel'ler n. restaurant below street level

rat·i·fy' v. **–fied', –fy'ing** approve formally —**rat'i·fi·ca'tion** n.

rat'ing n. 1 rank 2 appraisal

ra'tio (-shō, -shē ō') n., pl. **–tios** relation of one thing to another in size, etc.

ra·ti·o·ci·na'tion (rash'ē ō'sə-) n. reasoning by logic

ra·tion (rash'ən, rā'shən) n. fixed share, as of food —v. to give in rations —**ra'tion·ing** n.

ra'tion·al (rash'-) a. 1 able to reason 2 reasonable —**ra'tion·al'i·ty** n. —**ra'tion·al·ly** adv.

ra'tion·ale' (rash'ə nal') n. reasons or explanation

ra'tion·al·ism' n. belief in reason as the only authority

ra'tion·al·ize' v. give plausible explanations for —**ra'tion·al·i·za'tion** n.

rat·tan' n. palm stems used in wickerwork, etc.

rat'tle v. 1 make or cause to make a series of sharp, short sounds 2 chatter 3 [Col.] upset —n. 1 a rattling sound 2 baby's toy that rattles

rat'tle·snake' n. snake with a tail that rattles: also **rat'tler**

rau·cous (rô'kəs) a. loud or rowdy

raun'chy a. **–chi·er, –chi·est** [Sl.] risqué, lustful, etc.

rav'age v., n. ruin

rave v. 1 talk wildly 2 praise greatly —n. [Sl.] enthusiastic praise

rav'el v. untwist; fray

ra'ven n. large black crow —a. black and shiny

rav'e·nous a. greedily hungry —**rav'e·nous·ly** adv.

ra·vine' (-vēn') n. long, deep hollow in the earth

rav′ing a. 1 frenzied 2 [Col.] remarkable

ra·vi·o′li (rav′ē-) n. dough casings holding meat, cheese, etc.

rav′ish v. 1 fill with great joy 2 rape

rav′ish·ing a. delightful

raw a. 1 uncooked 2 unprocessed 3 inexperienced 4 sore and inflamed 5 cold and damp 6 [Sl.] unfair —**raw′ness** n.

raw′boned′ a. lean; gaunt

raw′hide′ n. untanned cattle hide

ray n. 1 thin beam of light 2 stream of radiant energy 3 tiny amount 4 broad, flat fish

ray′on n. fabric made from cellulose

raze v. demolish

ra′zor n. sharp-edged instrument for shaving

razz v. [Sl.] make fun of

raz′zle-daz′zle n. [Sl.] flashy display

re (rē) prep. regarding

re— pref. 1 back 2 again: add again to meaning of base word in list below

  re′ad·just′
  re′af·firm′
  re′ap·pear′
  re′ap·point′
  re·arm′
  re′as·sem′ble
  re′as·sign′
  re′a·wak′en
  re·born′
  re·build′
  re·cap′ture
  re′con·sid′er
  re′con·struct′
  re′dis·cov′er
  re·do′
  re·dou′ble
  re·ed′u·cate′
  re′e·lect′
  re′en·act′
  re′en·list′
  re′en·ter
  re′ex·am′ine
  re·fill′
  re·fu′el
  re·heat′
  re′in·vest′
  re·load′
  re·lo′cate′
  re·make′
  re·mar′ry
  re·o′pen
  re·or′der
  re·phrase′
  re·play′
  re·print′
  re·read′
  re·tell′
  re′u·nite′

reach v. 1 extend the hand, etc. 2 touch 3 get to 4 influence 5 get in touch with 6 try to get —n. act or extent of reaching

re·act′ v. 1 respond to stimulus 2 return to an earlier state 3 act with another substance in a chemical change —**re·ac′tion** n.

re·act′ant n. any substance involved in a chemical reaction

re·ac′tion·ar′y a.; n., pl. —**ies** ultraconservative

re·ac′ti·vate′ v. make or become active again

re·ac′tor n. device for producing atomic energy

read (rēd) v. **read** (red), **read′ing** 1 understand or utter (written or printed matter) 2 to study 3 to register, as a gauge 4 access computer data —**read′er** n.

read′er·ship′ n. all the readers of a magazine, etc.

read′ing n. 1 act of one that reads 2 thing to be read 3 interpretation

read′out′ n. displayed information

read′y a. **-i·er, -i·est** 1 prepared to act 2 willing 3 available —v. **-ied, -y·ing** prepare —**read′i·ly** adv. —**read′i·ness** n.

read′y-made′ a. ready for use or sale at once

re·a′gent n. chemical used to detect or convert another

re′al a. 1 actual; true 2 genuine —adv. [Col.] very —**re′al·ly** adv.

real estate n. land, including buildings, etc., on it

re′al·ism′ n. awareness of things as they really are —**re′al·ist** n. —**re′al·is′tic** a. —**re′al·is′ti·cal·ly** adv.

re·al′i·ty n., pl. —**ties** 1 state of being real 2 real thing; fact

re′al·ize′ v. 1 achieve 2 understand fully 3 make real 4 gain —**re′al·i·za′tion** n.

real′-life′ a. actual

realm (relm) n. 1 kingdom 2 region; sphere

Re′al·tor trademark certified real estate broker —n. [r—] real estate agent

re′al·ty n. real estate

ream n. quantity of 480 to 516 sheets of paper —v. enlarge (a hole) —**ream′er** n.

re·an′i·mate′ v. give new life or vigor to —**re·an′i·ma′tion** n.

reap v. cut and gather (grain, etc.) —**reap′er** n.

re′ap·por′tion v. adjust the representation pattern of (a legislature) —**re′ap·por′tion·ment** n.

rear n. back part or place —a. of or at the rear —v. 1 bring up; raise 2 rise on the hind legs

rear admiral n. naval officer above a captain

re′ar·range′ v. arrange in a different way —**re′ar·range′ment** n.

rea'son n. 1 explanation 2 cause 3 power to think 4 good sense —v. think or argue with logic —**rea'son·ing** n.

rea'son·a·ble a. 1 fair 2 sensible 3 not expensive —**rea'son·a·bly** adv.

re·as·sure' v. restore to confidence —**re'as·sur'ance** n.

re'bate' v., n. return (of) part of a payment

reb·el' (v.: rē bel') n. one who openly resists authority —a. rebellious —v. **re·bel'**, **-belled'**, **-bel'ling** resist authority —**re·bel'lion** n. —**re·bel'lious** a.

re·bound' v., n. recoil

re·buff' v., n. snub

re·buke' (-byōōk') v. to scold sharply —n. sharp scolding

re'bus n. puzzle in which pictures stand for words

re·but' v. **-but'ted**, **-but'ting** contradict formally —**re·but'tal** n.

re·cal'ci·trant a. refusing to obey —**re·cal'ci·trance** n.

re·call' (n.: rē'kôl) v. 1 call back 2 remember 3 revoke —n. a recalling

re·cant' v. to renounce (one's beliefs)

re'cap' (v. 1: also rē kap') v. **-capped'**, **-cap'ping** 1 put new tread on (worn tire) 2 recapitulate —n. a recapped tire 2 recapitulation

re'ca·pit'u·late' (-pich'ə-) v. summarize —**re'ca·pit'u·la'tion** n.

re·cede' v. move or slope backward

re·ceipt' (-sēt') n. 1 a receiving 2 written acknowledgment of sum received 3 pl. amount received

re·ceiv'a·ble a. due

re·ceive' v. 1 get; be given 2 greet (guests) 3 react to

re·ceiv'er n. 1 one who receives 2 one holding in trust property in bankruptcy, etc. 3 apparatus that converts electrical signals into sound or light, as in radio and TV

re'cent a. of a short time ago —**re'cent·ly** adv.

re·cep'ta·cle n. container

re·cep'tion n. 1 a receiving or being received 2 social function 3 the receiving of signals on radio or TV

re·cep'tion·ist n. employee who receives callers, etc.

re·cep'tive a. ready to receive suggestions

re·cep'tor n. nerve ending that feels heat, pressure, pain, etc.

re'cess (or rē ses') n. 1 hollow in a wall 2 break from work —v. 1 take a recess 2 set back

re·ces'sion n. temporary falling off of business

re·ces'sion·al n. hymn at end of church service when clergy and choir march out

re·ces'sive a. tending to recede

re·cher·ché (rə sher'shā) a. 1 rare 2 too refined

rec·i·pe (res'ə pē') n. directions for preparing dish or drink

re·cip'i·ent n. one that receives

re·cip'ro·cal a. 1 done, etc. in return 2 mutual —**re·cip'ro·cal·ly** adv. —**re·cip'ro·cate'** v. —**rec'i·proc'i·ty** (-präs'-) n.

re·cit'al (-sīt'-) n. 1 account told 2 musical program

re·cite' v. 1 repeat something memorized 2 narrate —**rec'i·ta'tion** n.

reck'less a. heedless; rash —**reck'less·ly** adv. —**reck'less·ness** n.

reck'on v. 1 count 2 estimate 3 [Col.] suppose —**reckon with** deal with

reck'on·ing n. 1 a figuring out 2 settlement of accounts

re·claim' v. restore for use —**rec'la·ma'tion** n.

re·cline' v. lie down or lean back

rec'luse n. one who lives a secluded, solitary life

rec'og·nize' v. 1 to identify as known before 2 to perceive 3 acknowledge; notice formally —**rec'og·ni'tion** n. —**rec'og·niz'a·ble** a.

re·coil' (n.: rē'koil) v. pull back —n. a recoiling

rec'ol·lect' v. remember —**rec'ol·lec'tion** n.

rec'om·mend' v. 1 suggest as fit or worthy 2 advise —**rec'om·men·da'tion** n.

rec'om·pense' v. pay or pay back —n. compensation

rec'on·cile' (-sīl') v. 1 make friendly again 2 settle (a quarrel) 3 to make agree or fit 4 to make acquiescent (to) —**rec'on·cil'a·ble** a. —**rec'on·cil'i·a'tion** (-sil'ē-) n.

rec'on·dite' a. abstruse

re'con·di'tion v. put back in good condition

re·con'nais·sance (-kän'ə səns) n. a spying on an area

rec'on·noi'ter v. examine or spy on an area

re·cord' (n., a.: rek'ərd) v. 1 keep a written account of 2 show on a dial, etc. 3 put (sound, images, etc.) on a disc, tape, etc. —n. 1 official account 2 known facts 3 a disc with recorded sound 4 the best yet done —a. best

re·cord'er n. 1 a person or machine that records 2 early form of flute

re·cord'ing n. 1 what is recorded on a disc, tape, etc. 2 the record itself

re·count' v. narrate

re'count' (n.: rē'kount) v. count again —n. second count

re·coup' (-kōōp') v. make up for, as a loss

re′course n. 1 a turning for aid 2 source of aid

re·cov′er (-kuv′-) v. 1 get back; regain 2 become normal 3 keep from a fall 4 reclaim —**re·cov′er·y** n., pl. –**ies**

recovery room n. hospital room where patients are first cared for after surgery

rec′re·ant a. 1 cowardly 2 disloyal —n. 1 coward 2 traitor

rec′re·a′tion n. refreshing play —**rec′re·a′tion·al** a.

re·crim′i·nate′ v. accuse one's accuser —**re·crim′i·na′tion** n.

re′cru·des′cence n. a breaking out again, esp. of something bad —**re′cru·des′cent** a.

re·cruit′ n. new member, soldier, etc. —v. enlist (recruits) —**re·cruit′ment** n.

rec′tal a. of, for, or near the rectum

rec′tan′gle n. four-sided figure with four right angles —**rec·tan′gu·lar** a.

rec′ti·fy′ v. –**fied′**, –**fy′ing** 1 to correct 2 convert (alternating current) to direct current —**rec′ti·fi·ca′tion** n. —**rec′ti·fi′er** n.

rec′ti·lin′e·ar a. bounded or formed by straight lines

rec′ti·tude′ n. honesty

rec′tor n. head of some schools or parishes

rec′to·ry n., pl. –**ries** rector's residence

rec′tum n. lowest part of the intestine —**rec′tal** a.

re·cum′bent a. lying down

re·cu′per·ate′ v. recover health, losses, etc. —**re·cu′per·a′tion** n.

re·cur′ v. –**curred′**, –**cur′ring** 1 occur again 2 return in talk, etc. —**re·cur′rence** n. —**re·cur′rent** a.

re·cy′cle v. 1 pass through a cycle again 2 use (metal, paper, etc.) again (and again)

red n. 1 color of blood 2 [R–] communist —a. **red′der**, **red′dest** of the color red —**in the red** losing money —**red′dish** a. —**red′ness** n.

red′cap′ n. porter in a railroad or bus station

red carpet n. very grand or impressive welcome: used with the —**red′-car′pet** a.

red′coat′ n. British soldier in a uniform with a red coat

red′den v. make or become red

re·deem′ v. 1 buy back 2 pay off 3 turn in for a prize 4 free, as from sin 5 atone for —**re·deem′a·ble** a. —**re·deem′er** n. —**re·demp′tion** n.

red′-hand′ed a. while committing a crime

red′head′ n. person with red hair —**red′head′ed** a.

red herring n. something used to divert attention from the basic issue

red′-hot′ a. 1 glowing hot 2 very excited 3 very new

red′-let′ter a. memorable

re·do′ v. –**did′**, –**done′**, –**do′ing** 1 do again 2 redecorate

red′o·lent a. 1 fragrant 2 smelling (of) 3 suggesting —**red′o·lence** n.

re·doubt′ (-dout′) n. stronghold

re·doubt′a·ble a. 1 formidable 2 deserving respect

re·dound′ v. have a result

re·dress′ (n.: rē′dres′) v. correct and make up for —n. a redressing

red snapper n. ocean food fish

red tape n. rules and details that waste time and effort

re·duce′ v. 1 lessen; decrease 2 change the form of 3 lower 4 lose weight —**re·duc′tion** n.

re·dun′dant a. 1 excess; superfluous 2 wordy —**re·dun′dan·cy** n., pl. –**cies**

red′wood′ n. 1 giant evergreen 2 its reddish wood

reed n. 1 a hollow-stemmed grass 2 musical pipe made of this 3 vibrating strip in some musical instruments —**reed′y** a., –**i·er**, –**i·est**

reef n. ridge of land near the surface of water —v. take in part of a sail

reek v., n. (emit) a strong, offensive smell

reel n. 1 spool or frame on which thread, film, etc. is wound 2 amount wound on it 3 lively dance —v. 1 to wind (in or out) on a reel 2 tell fluently: with off 3 stagger

re-en′try, re-en′try n., pl. –**tries** a coming back, as of a spacecraft into the earth's atmosphere

ref n., v. referee

re·fec′tion n. light meal

re·fec′to·ry n., pl. –**ries** dining hall, as in a college

re·fer′ v. –**ferred′**, –**fer′ring** 1 go to, or direct someone to, for aid, information, etc. 2 allude (to)

ref′er·ee′ n. 1 one chosen to decide something 2 a judge in sports —v. act as referee in

ref′er·ence n. 1 a referring 2 relation or connection 3 mention of a source of information 4 recommendation, or person giving it —**make reference to** mention

ref′er·en′dum n. submission of a law to direct popular vote

re·fer′ral n. 1 a referring or being referred 2 person referred to another person

re·fine′ v. free from impurities, coarseness, etc. —**re·fine′ment** n.

re·fined′ a. 1 purified 2 cultivated or elegant

re·fin'er·y n., pl. **-ies** plant for purifying materials

re·flect' v. 1 throw back, as an image or sound 2 result in (credit, etc.) —**reflect on** (or **upon**) 1 ponder 2 cast blame —**re·flec'tion** n. —**re·flec'tive** a. —**re·flec'tor** n.

re·flex' a., n. (designating of or) an involuntary reaction to a stimulus

re·flex'ive a. 1 designating a verb whose subject and object are the same 2 designating a pronoun used as object of such a verb

re·form' v. 1 improve 2 behave or make behave better —n. improvement —**re·form'er** n.

ref'or·ma'tion n. a reforming —**the Reformation** 16th-c. movement establishing the Protestant churches

re·form'a·to·ry n., pl. **-ries** institution for reforming young lawbreakers

re·fract' v. bend (a light ray, etc.) —**re·frac'tion** n.

re·frac'to·ry a. obstinate

re·frain' v. hold back (from) —n. repeated verse of a song

re·fresh' v. make fresh or stronger; renew or revive

re·fresh'ing a. 1 that refreshes 2 pleasingly new or different

re·fresh'ment n. a refreshing 2 pl. food or drink

re·frig'er·ate' (-frij'-) v. make cold, as to preserve —**re·frig'er·a'tion** n. —**re·frig'er·ant** a., n.

re·frig'er·a'tor n. box or room for refrigerating

ref'uge (-yōōj) n. protection from danger or pursuit

ref'u·gee' n. one who flees to seek refuge

re·ful'gent (-ful'jənt) a. shining; radiant

re·fund' (n.: rē'fund') v. give back (money, etc.) —n. amount refunded

re·fur'bish v. renovate

re·fuse' (rē fyōōz'; n.: ref'yōōs) v. 1 reject 2 decline (to do, etc.) —n. rubbish —**re·fus'al** n.

re·fute' v. prove wrong —**ref'u·ta'tion** n.

re·gain' v. get back; recover

re'gal a. royal

re·gale' v. entertain, as with a feast

re·ga'li·a n.pl. insignia or decorations, as of a rank

re·gard' n. 1 concern 2 affection and respect 3 reference 4 pl. good wishes —v. 1 to gaze upon 2 think of; consider 3 concern —**as regards** concerning —**re·gard'ful** a. —**re·gard'less** a., adv.

re·gard'ing prep. about

re·gat'ta (-gät'-) n. boat race

re·gen'er·ate' v. 1 give new life to; renew

2 improve —**re·gen'er·a'tion** n.

re'gent n. interim ruler in place of a monarch —**re'gen·cy** n., pl. **-cies**

reg·gae (reg'ā) n. type of popular Jamaican music

reg'i·cide' n. killer or killing of a king

re·gime' (rā zhēm') n. political or ruling system

reg'i·men n. system of diet, exercise, etc.

reg'i·ment n. section of an army division —v. to control and discipline strictly —**reg'i·men'tal** a. —**reg'i·men·ta'tion** n.

re'gion n. area, division, or part —**re'gion·al** a.

re'gion·al·ism' n. 1 regional quality or character 2 word, etc. peculiar to some region

reg'is·ter n. 1 list of names, etc. 2 recording device, as for cash transactions 3 a device for adjusting passage of air 4 musical range —v. 1 enter in a list 2 show 3 make an impression —**reg'is·trant** (-trənt) n. —**reg'is·tra'tion** n.

reg'is·tered nurse n. trained nurse who has passed a State examination

reg'is·trar' (-trär') n. keeper of records, as in a college

re·gress' v. go backward —**re·gres'sion** n. —**re·gres'sive** a.

re·gret' v. **-gret'ted, -gret'ting** be sorry for (a mistake, etc.) —n. a being sorry —**re·gret'ful** a. —**re·gret'ta·ble** a.

reg'u·lar a. 1 according to rule; orderly 2 usual 3 unchanging —**reg'u·lar'i·ty** n. —**reg'u·lar·ize'** v. —**reg'u·lar·ly** adv.

reg'u·late' v. 1 control 2 adjust to a standard, etc. —**reg'u·la'tor** n. —**reg'u·la·to'ry** a.

reg'u·la'tion n. 1 a regulating 2 a rule —a. usual

re·gur'gi·tate' (-jə-) v. bring up from the stomach —**re·gur'gi·ta'tion** n.

re'ha·bil'i·tate' v. restore to earlier state —**re'ha·bil'i·ta'tion** n.

re'hash' v. repeat; go over again —n. a rehashing

re·hearse' (-hurs') v. 1 recite 2 practice for a performance —**re·hears'al** n.

reign (rān) n. (period of) a sovereign's rule —v. rule as sovereign

re'im·burse' v. pay back —**re'im·burse'ment** n.

rein (rān) n. 1 strap hooked to a bit for controlling a horse 2 pl. means of controlling —**give (free) rein** to free from restraint

re'in·car·na'tion n. rebirth (of the soul) —**re'in·car'nate** v.

rein'deer' n., pl. **-deer'** large northern deer

re'in·force' v. strengthen —**re'in·force'ment** n.

re·in·state' v. restore —**re·in·state'ment** n.

re·it'er·ate' v. repeat —**re·it'er·a'tion** n.

re·ject' (n.: rē'jekt) v. **1** refuse to accept **2** discard —n. thing rejected —**re·jec'tion** n.

re·joice' v. be or make happy —**re·joic'ing** n.

re·join' v. **1** join again **2** answer —**re·join'der** n.

re·ju've·nate' v. make young again —**re·ju've·na'tion** n.

re·lapse' (n.: also rē'laps) v., n. fall back into a past state

re·late' v. **1** narrate **2** connect, as in meaning **3** have reference (to)

re·lat'ed a. of the same family or kind

re·la'tion n. **1** a relating or being related **2** kinship **3** a relative **4** pl. dealings, as between people —**re·la'tion·ship'** n.

rel'a·tive a. **1** related **2** relevant **3** comparative —n. related person

rel'a·tiv'i·ty n. **1** a being relative **2** modern theory of the universe

re·lax' v. **1** loosen up **2** rest, as from work —**re'lax·a'tion** n.

re'lay n. fresh group of workers, runners, etc. —v. get and pass on

relay race n. a race between teams, each member of which goes part of the distance

re·lease' v. **1** set free **2** allow to be issued —n. **1** a releasing **2** device to release a catch

rel'e·gate' v. **1** exile **2** put into a lower position **3** assign —**rel'e·ga'tion** n.

re·lent' v. become less stern

re·lent'less a. **1** pitiless **2** persistent

rel'e·vant a. pertinent —**rel'e·vance, rel'e·van·cy** n.

re·li'a·ble a. that can be relied on —**re·li'a·bil'i·ty** n. —**re·li'a·bly** adv.

re·li'ance n. trust or confidence —**re·li'ant** a.

rel'ic n. **1** something from the past **2** sacred object

re·lief' n. **1** a relieving **2** thing that relieves **3** public aid, as to the poor **4** sculpted figures projecting from a flat surface

re·lieve' v. **1** to ease; comfort **2** give aid to **3** to free by replacing **4** bring a pleasant change to

re·li'gion n. **1** belief in God or gods **2** system of worship —**re·li'gious** a.

re·lin'quish v. let go

rel'ish n. **1** pleasing flavor **2** enjoyment **3** pickles, etc. served with a meal —v. enjoy

re·live' v. experience again

re·luc'tant a. unwilling —**re·luc'tance** n. —**re·luc'tant·ly** adv.

re·ly' v. **-lied', -ly'ing** to trust; depend on or upon

rem n., pl. **rem** a standard unit of absorbed radiation

re·main' v. **1** be left when part is gone **2** stay **3** continue —**re·main'der** n.

re·mains' n.pl. **1** part left **2** dead body

re·mand' v. send back

re·mark' v., n. (make) a brief comment or observation

re·mark'a·ble a. unusual —**re·mark'a·bly** adv.

re·me'di·al a. corrective

rem'e·dy n., pl. **-dies** thing that corrects, etc.

re·mem'ber v. **1** think of again **2** to bear in mind —**re·mem'brance** n.

re·mind' v. cause to remember —**re·mind'er** n.

rem'i·nis'cence n. **1** memory **2** pl. an account of remembered events —**rem'i·nisce'** (-nis') v. —**rem'i·nis'cent** a.

re·miss' a. careless; negligent

re·mit' v. **-mit'ted, -mit'ting 1** forgive **2** refrain from exacting **3** slacken **4** send money —**re·mis'sion** n. —**re·mit'tance** n.

rem'nant n. part left over

re·mod'el v. rebuild

re·mon'strate' v. say in protest —**re·mon'strance** n.

re·morse' n. deep sense of guilt —**re·morse'ful** a.

re·mote' a. **1** distant **2** slight —**re·mote'ly** adv.

remote control n. **1** control from a distance **2** hand-held device for controlling TV, etc.

re·move' v. **1** take away **2** dismiss **3** get rid of —**re·mov'a·ble** a. —**re·mov'al** n.

re·mu'ner·ate' (-myōō'-) v. pay for; reward —**re·mu'ner·a'tion** n. —**re·mu'ner·a'tive** a.

ren'ais·sance' (-ə säns') n. rebirth; revival: also **re·nas'cence** —the **Renaissance** period in Europe, 14th-16th c.

re'nal a. of the kidneys

rend v. rent, rend'ing tear; split apart

ren'der v. **1** submit **2** give in return **3** cause to be **4** perform **5** translate **6** melt (fat) —**ren·di'tion** n.

ren·dez·vous (rän'dā vōō') n. appointed meeting (place) —v. meet as agreed

ren'e·gade' n. traitor

re·nege' (-nig') v. go back on a promise

re·new' v. **1** make new again **2** begin again **3** replenish (a supply) —**re·new'al** n.

re·nounce' v. **1** give up (a claim, etc.) **2** disown —**re·nounce'ment** n.

ren'o·vate' v. make like new; restore —**ren'o·va'tion** n. —**ren'o·va'tor** n.

re·nown' n. fame —**re·nowned'** a.

rent n. **1** payment for the use of property **2** a rip —v. get or give rent (for)

rent´al n. 1 rate of rent 2 thing for rent —a. of or for rent

re-nun´ci-a´tion n. a renouncing, as of a right

rep n. [Col.] a representative

re-pair´ v. 1 fix; mend 2 make amends for 3 go (to) —n. a repairing or being repaired

rep´a-ra´tion n. 1 a making of amends 2 often pl. compensation, as for war damage

rep-ar-tee´ (-tē´, -tä´) n. quick, witty reply or conversation

re-past´ n. a meal

re-pa´tri-ate´ v. return to country of birth, etc. —re-pa´tri-a´tion n.

re-pay´ v. –paid´, –pay´ing pay back —re-pay´ment n.

re-peal´ v. revoke; annul (a law) —n. revocation

re-peat´ v. say or do again —n. 1 a repeating 2 thing repeated —re-peat´ed-ly adv. —re-peat´er n.

re-pel´ v. –pelled´, –pel´ling 1 force back 2 disgust —re-pel´lent a., n.

re-pent´ v. feel sorry for (a sin, etc.) —re-pent´ance n. —re-pent´ant a.

re´per-cus´sion (-kush´ən) n. 1 echo 2 reaction, often an indirect one

rep´er-toire´ (-twär´) n. stock of plays, songs, etc. one is prepared to perform: also **rep´er-to´ry**, pl. –ries

rep´e-ti´tion (-tish´ən) n. 1 a repeating 2 thing repeated —rep´e-ti´tious a. —rep-et´i-tive a.

re-pine´ v. feel or express discontent (at)

re-place´ v. 1 put back 2 take the place of 3 put another in place of —re-place´ment n.

re-plen´ish v. fill again —re-plen´ish-ment n.

re-plete´ a. filled —re-ple´tion n.

rep´li-ca n. exact copy

re-ply´ v. –plied´, –ply´ing; n., pl. –plies´ answer

re-port´ v. 1 give an account of 2 tell as news; announce 3 denounce (an offender, etc.) to someone in authority 4 present oneself —n. 1 statement or account 2 rumor 3 explosive noise —re-port´ed-ly adv.

report card n. periodic written report on a student's progress

re-port´er n. one who gathers and reports news

re-pose´ v., n. rest

re-pos´i-to´ry n., pl. –ries a place where things may be put for safekeeping

re´pos-sess´ v. take back from a defaulting buyer

rep´re-hen´si-ble a. deserving scolding or blame

rep´re-sent´ v. 1 to portray or describe 2 symbolize 3 act in place of 4 be an example of —rep´re-sen-ta´tion n.

rep´re-sent´a-tive a. 1 representing 2 typical —n. 1 typical example 2 one chosen to act for others 3 [R–] Congressional or State legislator

re-press´ v. 1 hold back 2 subdue 3 force (painful ideas, etc.) into the unconscious —re-pres´sion n. —re-pres´sive a.

re-prieve´ n., v. delay (in) the execution of (one sentenced to die)

rep´ri-mand´ n., v. rebuke

re-pris´al (-prī´zəl) n. injury done for injury received

re-proach´ v. blame; rebuke —n. 1 disgrace 2 a scolding or blaming —re-proach´ful a.

rep´ro-bate´ a., n. depraved (person)

re´pro-duce´ v. produce copies, offspring, etc. —re´pro-duc´tion n. —re´pro-duc´tive a.

re-proof´ n. a reproving; rebuke: also **re-prov´al**

re-prove´ v. find fault with

rep´tile n. coldblooded, creeping vertebrate, as a snake, lizard, etc. —rep-til´i-an a.

re-pub´lic n. government by elected representatives —re-pub´li-can a., n.

re-pu´di-ate´ v. disown; cast off —re-pu´di-a´tion n.

re-pug´nant a. 1 opposed 2 distasteful; offensive —re-pug´nance n.

re-pulse´ v. 1 repel 2 rebuff —re-pul´sion n.

re-pul´sive a. disgusting

rep´u-ta-ble a. having a good reputation

rep´u-ta´tion n. 1 others' opinion of one 2 good character 3 fame

re-pute´ v. consider to be —n. reputation —re-put´ed a. —re-put´ed-ly adv.

re-quest´ n. 1 an asking for 2 thing asked for —v. ask for

Re´qui-em´ (rek´wē-, rā´kwē-) n. R.C.Ch. [also r–] Mass for the dead

re-quire´ v. 1 demand 2 need —re-quire´ment n.

req´ui-site (rek´wə zit) n., a. (something) necessary

req´ui-si´tion n. written order —v. to demand or take

re-quite´ v. repay for —re-quit´al n.

re-route´ v. send by a different route

re´run´ n. showing of a movie, etc. after the first showing

re-scind´ (-sind´) v. cancel; repeal —re-scis´sion n.

res´cue v. free or save —n. a rescuing —res´cu-er n.

re´search´ (or rē surch´) v., n. (do) careful study in a subject

re-sec´tion n. surgical removal of part of an organ, etc.

re-sem´ble v. be like —re-sem´blance n.

re·sent′ v. feel anger at —**re·sent′ful** a. —**re·sent′ment** n.

res′er·va′tion n. 1 a reserving, as of a hotel room 2 public land set aside, as for North American Indians

re·serve′ v. keep back; set aside —n. 1 thing reserved 2 limitation 3 reticence 4 pl. troops subject to call —**re·served′** a.

res′er·voir′ (-vwär′, -vôr′) n. 1 place for storing water 2 large supply

re·side′ v. 1 live (in or at) 2 be present (in)

res′i·dence n. 1 a residing 2 home —**res′i·dent** a., n. —**res′i·den′tial** (-shəl) a.

res′i·den·cy n., pl. —**cies** period of advanced medical training

res′i·due′ n. part that is left —**re·sid′u·al** (-zij′-) a.

re·sign′ v. 1 give up, as a claim, position, etc. 2 be submissive —**res′ig·na′tion** n. —**re·signed′** a.

re·sil′ient a. bouncing back; elastic —**re·sil′ience** or **re·sil′ien·cy** n.

res′in n. 1 substance from trees used in varnish, etc. 2 rosin —**res′in·ous** a.

re·sist′ v. withstand; fight against

re·sist′ance n. 1 power to resist 2 opposition to another force —**re·sist′ant** a.

re·sis′tor n. device in electrical circuit providing resistance

re·sole′ v. put a new sole on (a shoe, etc.)

res′o·lute′ n. firm; determined —**res′o·lute′ly** adv.

res′o·lu′tion n. 1 a resolving 2 formal statement 3 determination

re·solve′ v. 1 decide 2 solve 3 change —n. fixed purpose —**re·solved′** a.

res′o·nant a. 1 resounding 2 intensifying sound —**res′o·nance** n.

res′o·na′tor n. device that produces resonance

re·sort′ v. 1 go often 2 turn for help (to) —n. 1 place for a vacation, etc. 2 source of help

re·sound′ (-zound′) v. make an echoing sound

re·sound′ing a. 1 reverberating 2 complete

re·source′ (or ri sôrs′) n. 1 emergency supply 2 pl. wealth 3 resourcefulness

re·source′ful a. able to handle problems, etc. effectively

re·spect′ v. 1 think highly of 2 show concern for —n. 1 honor 2 concern 3 pl. regards 4 reference —**re·spect′ful** a. —**re·spect′ful·ly** adv.

re·spect′a·ble a. 1 of good reputation 2 good enough —**re·spect′a·bil′i·ty** n.

re·spect′ing prep. concerning; about

re·spec′tive a. of or for each separately —**re·spec′tive·ly** adv.

res′pi·ra′tion n. act or process of breathing —**res′pi·ra·to′ry** a.

res′pi·ra′tor n. device to aid breathing artificially

res·pite (-pit) n. 1 a delay 2 period of relief or rest

re·splend′ent a. dazzling

re·spond′ v. 1 to answer 2 react —**re·spond′ent** n.

re·sponse′ n. 1 a reply 2 reaction —**re·spon′sive** a.

re·spon′si·ble a. 1 obliged to do or answer for 2 involving duties 3 dependable —**re·spon′si·bil′i·ty** n., pl. —**ties**

rest n. 1 ease or inactivity 2 peace 3 a support 4 a pause 5 remainder —v. 1 get, or be at, ease 2 become still 3 lie or lay 4 depend —**rest′ful** a.

res′tau·rant′ (-tə ränt′, -tränt′) n. place for buying and eating meals

res′ti·tu′tion n. 1 a giving back 2 reimbursement

res′tive a. restless

rest′less a. 1 uneasy 2 disturbed 3 active

re·store′ v. 1 give back 2 return to a former position, condition, etc. —**res′to·ra′tion** n. —**re·stor′a·tive** a., n.

re·strain′ v. to hold back from action; suppress

re·straint′ n. 1 a restraining 2 thing that restrains 3 self-control

re·strict′ v. limit; confine —**re·stric′tion** n. —**re·stric′tive** a.

rest′room′ n. public room with toilets and washbowls: also **rest room**

re·struc′ture v. plan or provide a new structure, etc. for

re·sult′ v. 1 happen as an effect 2 to end (in) —n. 1 what is caused; outcome 2 mathematical answer —**re·sult′ant** a.

re·sume′ v. 1 take again 2 continue after interrupting —**re·sump′tion** n.

ré·su·mé (rez′ə mā′) n. summary, esp. of one's employment history

re·sur′face v. 1 put a new surface on 2 come to the surface again

re·sur′gent a. rising again —**re·sur′gence** n.

res′ur·rect′ v. bring back to life, use, etc. —**res′ur·rec′tion** n.

re·sus′ci·tate′ (-sus′ə-) v. revive, as one almost dead —**re·sus′ci·ta′tion** n.

re·tail′ n. sale of goods in small amounts to consumers —a. of such a sale —v. sell at retail —**re′tail′er** n.

re·tain′ v. 1 keep in possession, use, etc. 2 keep in mind 3 hire (a lawyer)

re·tain′er n. 1 servant to a rich person or family 2 fee paid to hire a lawyer

re·take′ (n.: rē′tāk′) v. —**took′**, —**tak′en**, —**tak′ing** take again —n. scene photographed again

re·tal'i·ate v. return injury for injury —re·tal'i·a'tion n. —re·tal'i·a·to'ry a.

re·tard' v. slow down; delay —re'tar·da'tion n.

re·tard'ant n. substance delaying chemical reaction

re·tard'ed a. slowed in development, esp. mentally

retch v. strain to vomit

re·ten'tion n. 1 a retaining 2 ability to retain —re·ten'tive a.

ret'i·cent a. disinclined to speak —ret'i·cence n.

ret'i·na n. cells lining the interior of the eyeball, on which images are formed

ret'i·nue n. attendants on a person of rank

re·tire' v. 1 withdraw or retreat 2 withdraw from one's career, etc. 3 go to bed —re·tire'ment n.

re·tired' a. no longer working because of age, etc.

re·tir·ee' n. one who has retired from work, business, etc.

re·tir'ing a. shy; modest

re'tool' v. adapt (factory machinery) for different use

re·tort' v. reply sharply or cleverly —n. 1 sharp or clever reply 2 container for distilling, etc.

re'touch' v. touch up

re·trace' v. go back over

re·tract' v. 1 draw back or in 2 withdraw, as a charge —re·trac'tion n.

re'tread' (n.: rē'tred') v., n. recap

re·treat' n. 1 withdrawal, esp. under attack 2 quiet place 3 period of contemplation —v. withdraw

re·trench' v. economize —re·trench'ment n.

ret'ri·bu'tion n. deserved punishment

re·trieve' v. 1 get back or bring back 2 make good (a loss or error)

re·triev'er n. dog trained to retrieve game

ret'ro·ac'tive a. effective as of a prior date

ret'ro·fire' v. fire a retrorocket

ret'ro·grade' a. 1 moving backward 2 getting worse

ret'ro·gress' v. move backward, esp. into a worse state —ret'ro·gres'sion n.

ret'ro·rock'et n. small rocket on spacecraft fired opposite to flight direction to reduce landing speed

ret'ro·spect' n. contemplation of the past —ret'ro·spec'tive a.

ret·si'na n. Greek wine flavored with pine resin

re·turn' v. 1 go or come back 2 bring or send back 3 repay (a visit, etc.) 4 yield (profit) —n. 1 a going or coming back 2 something returned 3 recurrence 4 requital 5 often pl. yield or profit 6 official report —a. of or for a return —in return as a return

re·u'ni·fy' v. —fied', -fy'ing unify again —re·u'ni·fi·ca'tion n.

re·un'ion n. a coming together again

rev v. **revved, rev'ving** [Col.] increase engine speed: with up

re·vamp' v. renovate; redo

re·veal' v. 1 make known, as a secret 2 show

rev·eil·le (rev'ə lē) n. Mil. morning signal to wake up

rev'el v. 1 make merry 2 take pleasure (in) —n. merrymaking —rev'el·ry n., pl. -ries

rev'e·la'tion n. 1 a revealing 2 striking disclosure

re·venge' v., n. harm in retaliation —re·venge'ful a.

rev'e·nue' n. a government's income from taxes, etc.

re·ver'ber·ate' v. 1 to echo again; resound 2 have repercussions —re·ver'ber·a'tion n.

re·vere' v. show deep respect or love for —rev'er·ence n. —rev'er·ent a.

rev'er·end a. respected: [R-] used with the for a member of the clergy

rev'er·ie (-ē) n. daydream(ing)

re·vers' (-vir') n., pl. -vers' (-virz') lapel

re·verse' a. opposite —n. 1 the opposite 2 the back of a coin, etc. 3 change for the worse 4 gear for reversing —v. 1 turn about or inside out 2 revoke 3 go or make go in the opposite direction —re·ver'sal n. —re·vers'i·ble a.

re·vert' v. go back to a former state, owner, etc. —re·ver'sion n.

rev'er·y n., pl. -ies reverie

re·view' n. 1 general survey 2 reexamination 3 a criticism of a book, play, etc. 4 formal inspection —v. to survey 2 study again 3 to inspect formally 4 write a review of (a book, etc.) —re·view'er n.

re·vile' v. use abusive language (to or about)

re·vise' v. change, esp. after reading —re·vi'sion n.

re·viv'al n. 1 a reviving 2 meeting to stir up religious feeling —re·viv'al·ist n.

re·vive' v. return to life, health, use, etc.

re·voke' v. put an end to; cancel —rev'o·ca·ble a. —rev'o·ca'tion n.

re·volt' v. 1 to rebel 2 disgust or be disgusted —n. a rebellion —re·volt'ing a.

rev'o·lu'tion n. 1 movement in an orbit 2 complete cycle 3 complete change 4 overthrow of a government, etc. —rev'o·lu'tion·ar'y a.; n., pl. -ies —rev'o·lu'tion·ist n.

rev'o·lu'tion·ize' v. make a drastic change in

re·volve' v. 1 rotate 2 move in an orbit 3 think about

re·volv'er n. pistol with a revolving cylinder for bullets

re·vue' n. musical show

re·vul'sion n. disgust

re·ward' n. thing given in return for something done —v. give a reward to or for

re·wind' v. **-wound', -wind'ing** wind (film or tape) back on reel

re·word' v. put into other words

re·write' v. **-wrote', -writ'ten, -writ'ing** revise

rhap'so·dize' (rap'-) v. speak or write ecstatically

rhap'so·dy n., pl. **-dies** 1 ecstatic speech or writing 2 a musical piece of free form —**rhap·sod'i·cal, rhap·sod'ic** a.

rhe·a (rē'ə) n. large, ostrichlike bird

rhe'o·stat' n. device for regulating electric current

rhe'sus (monkey) n. small, brownish monkey of India

rhet'o·ric n. effective or showy use of words —**rhe·tor'i·cal** a. —**rhet'o·ri'cian** (-rish'ən) n.

rhetorical question n. question with an obvious answer

rheum (room) n. watery discharge from nose, eyes, etc.

rheumatic fever n. disease with fever, aching joints, etc.

rheu'ma·tism' (roo'-) n. painful condition of the joints, etc. —**rheu·mat'ic** a., n. —**rheu'ma·toid'** a.

rheumatoid arthritis n. chronic disease with swollen joints

Rh factor n. antigen group in some human blood

rhine'stone' (rīn'-) n. artificial gem of glass, etc.

rhi·ni'tis (rī-) n. inflammation in the nose

rhi'no n., pl. **-nos** rhinoceros

rhi·noc'er·os n. large mammal with one or two horns on the snout

rhi'zome' n. creeping stem with leaves near its tips and roots growing underneath

rho'do·den'dron (rō'-) n. shrub with showy flowers

rhom'boid' (räm'-) n. a parallelogram with oblique angles and only opposite sides equal

rhom'bus n., pl. **-bus·es** or **-bi'** (-bī') equilateral parallelogram with oblique angles

rhu'barb' (roo'-) n. 1 plant with edible leafstalks 2 [Sl.] heated argument

rhyme (rīm) n. 1 likeness of end sounds in words 2 verse using this —v. make (a) rhyme

rhythm (rith'əm) n. pattern of regular beat, accent, etc. —**rhyth'mi·cal, rhyth'mic** a. —**rhyth'mi·cal·ly** adv.

rib n. 1 any of the curved bones around the chest 2 anything riblike —v. **ribbed, rib'bing** form with ribs 2 [Sl.] tease

rib'ald a. coarsely joking —**rib'ald·ry** n.

rib'bon n. 1 narrow strip, as of silk, etc. 2 pl. shreds

ri'bo·fla'vin n. a vitamin in milk, eggs, etc.

rice n. food grain grown in warm climates

rich a. 1 wealthy 2 well supplied 3 costly 4 full of fats or sugar 5 full and deep 6 producing much —**the rich** wealthy people —**rich'ly** adv. —**rich'ness** n.

rich'es n.pl. wealth

rick n. stack of hay, etc.

rick'ets n. disease causing a softening of the bones

rick'et·y a. weak; shaky

rick'rack' n. flat, zigzag braid for trimming dresses, etc.

rick'shaw', rick'sha' n. jinrikisha

ric'o·chet' (-shā') n., v. **-cheted'** (-shād'), **-chet'ing** (-shā'iŋ) rebound at an angle

ri·cot'ta (ri-) n. soft Italian cheese

rid v. **rid** or **rid'ded, rid'ding** to free or relieve of —**get rid of** dispose of —**rid'dance** n.

rid'dle n. puzzling question, thing, etc. —v. perforate

ride v. **rode, rid'den, rid'ing** 1 sit on and make go 2 move along, as in a car 3 be carried along on or by 4 dominate 5 [Col.] tease —n. 1 a riding 2 thing to ride in at an amusement park

rid'er n. 1 one who rides 2 addition to a contract or legislative bill

rid'er·ship' n. passengers of a transportation system

ridge n. 1 crest 2 narrow, raised strip —v. form into ridges

ridge'pole' n. beam at the ridge of a roof, to which rafters are attached

rid'i·cule' n. remarks meant to make fun of another —v. make fun of

ri·dic'u·lous a. foolish; absurd —**ri·dic'u·lous·ly** adv.

rife a. 1 widespread 2 abounding

riff n. constantly repeated musical phrase in jazz

rif'fle n. 1 ripple in a stream 2 way of shuffling cards

riff'raff' n. people thought of as low, common, etc.

ri'fle n. gun with spiral grooves in the barrel —v. rob —**ri'fle·man** n., pl. **-men**

rift n., v. crack; split

rig v. **rigged, rig'ging** 1 equip 2 arrange dishonestly —n. 1 equipment 2 arrangement of sails

rig′ging n. ropes, etc. to work the sails of a ship

right a. 1 straight 2 just and good 3 correct 4 suitable 5 normal 6 of that side toward the east when one faces north —n. 1 what is right 2 right side 3 power or privilege 4 conservative party, etc. —adv. 1 directly 2 properly 3 completely 4 toward the right —v. set right —**right away** at once —**right′ful** a.

right angle n. 90-degree angle

right·eous (rī′chəs) a. 1 virtuous 2 morally right —**right′eous·ly** adv. —**right′eous·ness** n.

right′-hand′ed a. 1 using the right hand more easily 2 for the right hand

right′ist n., a. conservative or reactionary

right′-mind′ed a. having sound principles

right of way n. legal right to proceed, pass over, etc.

rig′id (rij′-) a. 1 stiff and firm 2 severe; strict —**ri·gid′i·ty** n.

rig′ma·role′ n. nonsense

rig′or n. strictness; hardship —**rig′or·ous** a.

rig′or mor′tis n. stiffening of muscles after death

rile v. [Col.] to anger

rill n. little brook

rim n. edge, esp. of something round —v. **rimmed, rim′ming** form a rim around

rime n., v. rhyme

rime n. white frost

rind n. firm outer layer

ring v. **rang, rung** 1 make, or cause to make, the sound of a bell 2 seem 3 resound 4 encircle —n. 1 sound of a bell 2 band for the finger 3 hollow circle 4 group with selfish aims 5 enclosed area —**ring′er** n.

ring′lead′er n. leader of a group, as of lawbreakers

ring′let n. long curl

ring′mas′ter n. director of circus performances

ring′side′ n. space just outside the ring at boxing match, etc.

ring′worm′ n. skin disease

rink n. smooth area for skating

rinse v. 1 wash lightly 2 wash soap from —n. rinsing or liquid for this

ri′ot v., n. (take part in) mob violence —**ri′ot·er** n. —**ri′ot·ous** a.

rip v. **ripped, rip′ping** 1 tear apart roughly 2 become torn —n. torn place

rip cord n. cord pulled to open parachute during descent

ripe a. 1 ready to be harvested, eaten, etc. 2 ready —**rip′en** v. —**ripe′ness** n.

rip′-off′ n. [Sl.] a stealing, cheating, etc.

ri·poste′, ri·post′ (ri-) n. sharp retort

rip′ple v. to form small surface waves —n. small wave

rip′saw′ n. saw for cutting wood along the grain

rise v. **rose, ris′en, ris′ing** 1 stand up 2 come or go up 3 increase 4 begin 5 revolt —n. 1 ascent 2 upward slope 3 an increase 4 origin

ris·er (rī′zər) n. vertical piece between steps

ris′i·bil′i·ty (riz′-) n. laughter

risk n. chance of harm, loss, etc. —v. 1 put in danger 2 take the chance of —**risk′y** a., -i·er, -i·est

ris·qué′ (-kā′) a. almost indecent

rite n. ceremonial act

rit′u·al (rich′-) a. of a rite —n. system of rites

ri′val n. competitor —a. competing —v. compete with —**ri′val·ry** n., pl. -ries

riv′en a. split

riv′er n. large stream —**riv′er·side′** n., a.

river basin n. area drained by a river and its tributaries

riv′et n. metal bolt used to fasten by hammering the ends into heads —v. fasten firmly —**riv′et·er** n.

riv′u·let (-yōō-) n. little stream

roach n. cockroach

road n. 1 way made for traveling 2 way; path —**road′side′** n., a.

road′bed′ n. foundation for railroad tracks or highway

road′block′ n., v. blockade

road′run′ner n. desert bird of southwestern U.S.

road′show′ n. touring theatrical show

roam v. wander about; rove

roan a. reddish-brown, etc. thickly sprinkled with white —n. roan horse

roar v., n. 1 (make) a loud, deep, rumbling sound 2 (burst out in) loud laughter

roast v. cook (meat, etc.) in an oven or over an open fire —n. roasted meat —a. roasted —**roast′er** n.

rob v. **robbed, rob′bing** take property from unlawfully by force —**rob′ber** n. —**rob′ber·y** n., pl. -ies

robe n. 1 long, loose, outer garment 2 covering —v. dress as in a robe

rob′in n. red-breasted North American thrush

ro′bot′ n. automatic manlike device

ro·bust′ a. strong and healthy —**ro·bust′ness** n.

rock n. 1 mass or pieces of stone 2 popular music based on jazz, folk music, etc. —v. move back and forth —**on the rocks** [Col.] 1 in serious trouble 2 served with ice cubes —**rock′i·ness** n. —**rock′y** a., -i·er, -i·est

rock'-and-roll' *n.* popular music with a strong rhythm

rock bottom *n.* lowest level

rock'-bound' *a.* covered with rocks

rock'er *n.* chair mounted on curved pieces for rocking: also **rock'ing chair**

rocker panel *n.* panel below automobile door

rock'et *n.* projectile propelled by the thrust of escaping gases

rock'et·ry *n.* building and launching of rockets

rock salt *n.* common salt in masses

rock wool *n.* fibrous insulation made from molten rock

ro·co'co *a.* full of elaborate decoration

rod *n.* **1** straight stick or bar **2** linear measure, 5½ yd.

rode *v.* pt. of RIDE

ro'dent *n.* gnawing mammal, as a rat, rabbit, etc.

ro·de·o' *n., pl.* **-os'** public exhibition of the skills of cowboys

roe *n.* **1** fish eggs **2** pl. roe or roes small deer

roent·gen (rent'gən) *n.* unit for measuring radiation

rogue (rōg) *n.* **1** scoundrel **2** mischievous person —**ro'guish** (-gish) *a.*

rogues' gallery *n.* police collection of pictures of criminals

roil *v.* make muddy or cloudy

roist'er *v.* revel; carouse —**roist'er·er** *n.*

role, rôle *n.* **1** part played by an actor **2** function taken on by someone

roll *v.* **1** move by turning **2** move on wheels **3** wind into a ball or cylinder **4** flatten with a roller **5** rock **6** trill —*n.* **1** a rolling **2** scroll **3** list of names **4** small cake of bread **5** a swaying motion **6** loud, echoing sound —**roll'er** *n.*

roller coaster *n.* ride with cars on tracks that dip and curve sharply

roller skate *n.* frame or shoe with four small wheels, for gliding on floor, etc. —**roll'er-skate'** *v.*

rol'lick·ing (räl'-) *a.* lively and carefree

roll'ing pin *n.* cylinder used to roll out dough

roll'-top' *a.* of a desk having a flexible, sliding top

ro·ly-po'ly *a.* pudgy

ROM *n.* computer memory that can be read but not altered

ro·maine' *n.* type of lettuce having long leaves and head

Ro'man *a.* of Rome —*n.* **1** a native of Rome **2** [r-] type with non-slanting letters

Roman Catholic *a.* of the Christian church headed by the Pope —*n.* member of this church

ro·mance' *a.* [R-] of any language derived

from Latin. **1** tale of love; —adventure, etc. **2** exciting quality **3** love affair —*v.* [Col.] make love to

Roman numerals *n.pl.* Roman letters used as numerals: I=1, V=5, X=10, L=50, C=100, D=500, M=1,000

ro·man'tic *a.* **1** of romance **2** visionary **3** full of feelings of romance —*n.* a romantic person —**ro·man'ti·cal·ly** *adv.* —**ro·man' ti·cism'** *n.*

ro·man'ti·cize' *v.* act in a romantic way

romp *v.* play boisterously —*n.* a romping

romp'ers *n.pl.* loose, one-piece outer garment for a small child

rood (rōōd) *n.* crucifix

roof *n., pl.* **roofs** outside top covering of a building —*v.* cover as with a roof

roof'ing *n.* material for roofs

roof'top' *n.* roof of building

rook *n.* **1** European crow **2** chess piece moving horizontally or vertically

rook'ie *n.* [Sl.] beginner

room *n.* **1** enough space **2** space set off by walls **3** pl. living quarters; apartment —*v.* to lodge —**room'er** *n.* —**room'ful'** *n.* —**room'mate'** *n.* —**room'y** *a.*, **-i·er, -i·est**

roost *n.* perch for birds —*v.* perch on a roost

roost'er *n.* male chicken

root (rōōt, root) *n.* **1** underground part of a plant **2** embedded part, as of a tooth **3** cause **4** quantity multiplied by itself —*v.* **1** take root **2** place firmly **3** dig (*up* or *out*) with snout **4** rummage about **5** [Col.] support a team, etc.: with *for* —**take root 1** grow by putting out roots **2** become fixed

root beer *n.* carbonated drink made of root extracts

rope *n.* strong cord of twisted strands —*v.* **1** mark off with a rope **2** catch with a lasso

Roque'fort (cheese) (rōk'-) *trademark* strong cheese with bluish mold

ro'sa·ry *n., pl.* **-ries** string of beads used when praying

rose *n.* **1** sweet-smelling flower that has a prickly stem **2** pinkish red —**rose'bud'** *n.* —**rose'bush'** *n.* —**rose'-col'ored** *a.*

ro·sé' (-zā') *n.* a pink wine

ro'se·ate (-zē-) *a.* rose-colored

rose'mar'y *n.* fragrant herb used in cooking

ro·sette' *n.* roselike ornament

rose'wood' *n.* reddish wood

ros'in (räz'-) *n.* hard resin

ros'ter *n.* list; roll

ros'trum *n.* speakers' platform

ros'y *a.* **-i·er, -i·est 1** rose red or pink **2** bright or promising —**ros'i·ly** *adv.* —**ros' i·ness** *n.*

rot v. **rot′ted, rot′ting** decay; spoil —n. **1** a rotting **2** plant disease

ro′ta·ry a. **1** rotating **2** having rotating parts

ro′tate v. **1** turn around, as a wheel **2** alternate —**ro·ta′tion** n.

rote n. fixed routine —**by rote** by memory alone

ro·tis′ser·ie (-ē-) n. electric grill with a turning spit

ro′tor n. rotating blades on a helicopter, etc.

rot′ten a. **1** decayed **2** corrupt —**rot′ten·ness** n.

ro·tund′ a. round; plump —**ro·tun′di·ty** n.

ro·tun′da n. round building with a dome

rouge (rōōzh) n. **1** cosmetic to redden cheeks and lips **2** red polish for jewelry —v. put rouge on

rough a. **1** not smooth; uneven **2** disorderly **3** harsh **4** not perfected **5** [Col.] difficult —adv. in a rough way —n. rough part —v. **1** treat roughly: with up **2** shape roughly —**rough it** live without comforts —**rough′en** v.

rough′age n. coarse food

rough′house′ v. [Sl.] play or fight boisterously

rough′neck′ n. [Sl.] a rowdy

rou·lette (rōō let′) n. gambling game played with a ball in a whirling bowl

round a. **1** that forms a circle or curve **2** complete **3** that is a whole number **4** vigorous —n. **1** thigh of beef **2** a course or series **3** often pl. regular circuit **4** single gun shot **5** outburst **6** period of action or time **7** simple song for three or four voices —v. **1** make round **2** finish **3** turn **4** pass around —adv. **1** in a circle **2** through a cycle **3** from one to another **4** in the opposite direction —prep. **1** so as to encircle **2** near **3** in a circuit through —**round up** collect in a herd, etc.

round′a·bout′ a. indirect

round′house′ n. round building for repairing and storing locomotives

round′-shoul′dered a. having the shoulders stooped

round steak n. a cut from a round of beef

round table n. group discussion

round′-the-clock′ a., adv. without interruption

round trip n. trip to a place and back

round′up′ n. a bringing together, esp. of cattle

round′worm′ n. unsegmented worm

rouse (rouz) v. **1** excite **2** wake

roust′a·bout′ n. unskilled, transient worker

rout n. **1** confused flight **2** crushing defeat —v. **1** make flee **2** defeat **3** force out **4** gouge out

route (rōōt, rout) n. course traveled, as to make deliveries —v. send by a certain route

rou·tine (rōō tēn′) n. regular procedure —a. regular; customary —**rou·tine′ly** adv.

rove v. roam —**rov′er** n.

row (rō) n. **1** line of people, seats, etc. **2** a trip by rowboat —v. move (in) a boat with oars

row (rou) n., v. quarrel; brawl

row′boat′ n. boat to row

row′dy a. **-di·er, -di·est** rough, disorderly, etc. —n., pl. **-dies** rowdy person —**row′di·ness** n.

row′el (rou′-) n. small wheel with points, as on a spur

roy′al a. of a monarch, kingdom, etc. —**roy′al·ist** a., n. —**roy′al·ly** adv.

roy′al·ty n., pl. **-ties 1** royal rank, person, or persons **2** set payment for use of copyright or patent

R.S.V.P. please reply

rub v. **rubbed, rub′bing 1** move over a surface with pressure and friction **2** spread on, erase, injure, etc. by rubbing —n. **1** a rubbing **2** difficulty; trouble —**rub down** to massage

ru·ba′to (-bät′ō) a., adv. not in strict musical tempo

rub′ber n. **1** elastic substance **2** an overshoe —**rub′ber·ize′** v. —**rub′ber·y** a.

rubber stamp n. **1** rubbery printing stamp **2** [Col.] automatic or routine approval —**rub′ber-stamp′** v.

rub′bish n. **1** trash; worthless material **2** nonsense

rub′ble n. broken stones, bricks, etc.

rub′down′ n. a massage

ru·bel′la n. contagious disease with red skin spots

ru′bi·cund′ a. reddish

ru′ble n. monetary unit of U.S.S.R. and Russia

ru′bric n. title of a chapter, section, etc.

ru′by n., pl. **-bies** deep-red precious stone

ruck′sack′ n. knapsack

ruck′us n. [Col.] noisy confusion; disturbance

rud′der n. steering piece at ship's stern or aircraft's tail

rud′dy a. **-di·er, -di·est 1** healthily red **2** reddish —**rud′di·ness** n.

rude a. **1** coarse; crude **2** impolite —**rude′ly** adv. —**rude′ness** n.

ru′di·ment n. **1** first principle of a subject **2** trace —**ru′di·men′ta·ry** a.

rue v. regret —**rue′ful** a.

ruff n. **1** high, frilled collar **2** raised ring

of feathers or fur about a bird's or beast's neck

ruf′fi·an n. brutal, lawless person

ruf′fle v. 1 to ripple 2 make ruffles in or on 3 make (feathers, etc.) stand up 4 disturb —n. narrow, pleated cloth trimming

rug n. floor covering of thick fabric in one piece

rug′by n. English game like football

rug′ged a. 1 uneven; rough 2 harsh; severe 3 strong

ru′in n. 1 anything destroyed, etc. 2 pl. remains of this 3 downfall; destruction —v. bring or come to ruin —**ru′in·a′tion** n. —**ru′in·ous** a.

rule n. 1 a set guide for conduct, etc. 2 custom; usage 3 government 4 RULER (n. 2) 5 straight line —v. 1 to guide 2 govern 3 decide officially 4 mark lines on —**as a rule** usually —**rule out** exclude —**rul′ing** a., n.

rule of thumb n. crude but practical method

rul′er n. 1 one who governs 2 straight-edged strip for drawing lines, measuring, etc.

rum n. alcoholic liquor made from molasses, etc.

rum′ba n. Cuban dance

rum′ble v., n. (make) a deep rolling sound

ru′mi·nant a. cud-chewing —n. cud-chewing mammal

ru′mi·nate′ v. 1 chew the cud 2 meditate —**ru′mi·na′tion** n.

rum′mage v. search thoroughly

rummage sale n. sale of miscellaneous articles

rum′my n. card game

ru′mor n. unconfirmed report or story —v. spread as a rumor

rump n. 1 animal's hind part 2 buttocks

rum′ple n., v. wrinkle

rum′pus n. [Col.] uproar

run v. **ran, run, run′ning** 1 go by moving the legs fast 2 make a quick trip 3 compete (in) 4 unravel 5 spread (over) 6 continue 7 operate 8 follow (a course) 9 undergo 10 cause to run —n. 1 act or period of running 2 journey; trip 3 brook 4 a kind 5 enclosed area 6 freedom 7 unraveled part in a fabric 8 Baseball point scored by a circuit of the bases —**run across** happen on —**run down** 1 cease operating 2 knock down, capture, or kill 3 disparage —**run out** expire —**run out of** use up —**run over** 1 ride over 2 overflow

run′a·round′ n. [Col.] series of evasions

run′a·way′ n. person or animal that has run away or fled —a. 1 running away 2 out of control

run′down′ n. quick summary

run′-down′ a. 1 not wound, as a watch 2 in poor condition

rung v. pp. of RING —n. rodlike step of a ladder, etc.

run′-in′ n. [Col.] a quarrel

run′ner n. 1 one that runs 2 long, narrow rug 3 unraveled part 4 either of the pieces on which a sled slides

run′ner-up′ n. the second to finish in a contest

run′ning a. 1 that runs 2 measured straight 3 continuous —adv. in succession —n. act of one that runs —**in** (or **out of**) **the running** in (or out of) the competition

running mate n. lesser candidate, as for Vice President

run′ny a. —**ni·er, –ni·est** 1 flowing too freely 2 discharging mucus

run′off′ n. a deciding contest

run′-of-the-mill′ a. ordinary

runt n. stunted animal or plant

run′-through′ n. a complete rehearsal

run′way′ n. a landing strip

ru′pee n. monetary unit of India, Pakistan, etc.

rup′ture n. 1 a breaking apart 2 hernia —v. 1 burst 2 induce a hernia

ru′ral a. of or living in the country

ruse (rooz) n. artful trick

rush v. 1 move, push, attack, etc. swiftly 2 hurry —n. 1 a rushing 2 busyness 3 grassy marsh plant

rush hour n. time when traffic is heavy

rusk n. (piece of) sweet bread toasted brown

rus′set n., a. yellowish (or reddish) brown

Rus′sian n., a. (native or language) of Russia

rust n. 1 reddish-brown coating formed on iron, etc. 2 plant disease —v. 1 form rust on 2 deteriorate, as through disuse —**rust′y** a., **–i·er, –i·est**

rus′tic a. 1 rural 2 plain or rough —n. country person

rus′tle (-əl) v. make soft sounds of slight motion, as stirring leaves —n. these sounds —**rus′tler** n.

rut n. 1 groove as made by wheels 2 fixed routine 3 sexual excitement in animals —v. **rut′ted, rut′ting** make ruts in

ru′ta·ba′ga n. yellow turnip

ruth′less a. without pity

RV n., pl. **RVs** recreational vehicle for camping trips, etc.

-ry suf. —ERY

rye (rī) n. 1 cereal grass 2 its grain, used for flour

S

Sab′bath (-əth) *n.* day of rest and worship; Saturday for Jews, Sunday for many Christians

sab·bat′i·cal *n.* period of absence with pay for study, travel, etc., as for teachers

sa′ber, sa′bre *n.* cavalry sword

sa′ble *n.* animal like the weasel, with dark fur

sab′o·tage′ (-täzh′) *n.* destruction of factories, etc. by enemy agents, strikers, etc. —*v.* destroy by sabotage

sab′o·teur′ (-tur′) *n.* one who commits sabotage

sac *n.* pouchlike part

sac·cha·rin (sak′ə rin) *n.* sugar substitute

sac′cha·rine′ (-rin′) *a.* very sweet —*n.* saccharin

sac′er·do′tal (sas′-) *a.* of priests

sa·chet (sa shā′) *n.* small bag of perfumed powder

sack *n.* 1 bag 2 large, coarse bag 3 plunder 4 [Sl.] bed —*v.* 1 put in sacks 2 plunder 3 [Sl.] dismiss from a job —**hit the sack** [Sl.] go to sleep

sack′cloth′ *n.* coarse cloth worn to show sorrow

sack′ing *n.* coarse cloth for making sacks

sac′ra·ment *n.* sacred Christian rite, as Communion —**sac′ra·men′tal** *a.*

sa′cred *a.* 1 consecrated to a god or God 2 venerated 3 inviolate —**sa′cred·ly** *adv.* —**sa′cred·ness** *n.*

sac′ri·fice′ *v.* 1 offer (something) to a deity 2 give up something for another 3 take a loss in selling —*n.* a sacrificing —**sac′ri·fi′cial** (-fish′əl) *a.*

sac′ri·lege (-lij) *n.* desecration of sacred things —**sac′ri·le′gious** (-lij′əs) *a.*

sac′ris·ty *n., pl.* **–ties** room in a church for sacred vessels, etc.

sac′ro·il′i·ac′ *n.* joint at lower end of the spine

sac′ro·sanct′ *a.* very holy

sad *a.* **sad′der, sad′dest** showing or causing sorrow; unhappy —**sad′den** *v.* —**sad′ly** *adv.* —**sad′ness** *n.*

sad′dle *n.* seat for a rider on a horse, etc. —*v.* 1 put a saddle on 2 burden

sad′dle·bag′ *n.* 1 bag hung behind a horse's saddle 2 similar bag on a bicycle, etc.

saddle shoes *n.* white oxfords with dark band over the instep

sa′dist *n.* one who gets pleasure from hurting others —**sa′dism** *n.* —**sa·dis′tic** *a.*

sad′o·mas′o·chist (-kist) *n.* one who gets pleasure from causing or being hurt

—**sad′o·mas′o·chism′** *n.* —**sad′o·mas′o·chis′tic** *a.*

sa·fa′ri *n.* hunting trip, esp. in Africa

safe *a.* 1 free from danger 2 unharmed 3 trustworthy 4 cautious —*n.* metal box with a lock —**safe′ly** *adv.* —**safe′ty** *n.*

safe′-con′duct *n.* permission to travel safely

safe′-de·pos′it *a.* of a bank box, etc. for storing valuables: also **safe′ty-de·pos′it**

safe′guard′ *n.* protection; precaution —*v.* protect

safe′keep′ing *n.* protection

safety glass *n.* glass that resists shattering

safety match *n.* match that strikes only on a prepared surface

safety pin *n.* bent pin with the point held in a guard

safety razor *n.* razor with a detachable blade held between guards

saf′flow′er *n.* plant whose seeds yield an edible oil

saf′fron *n.* orange-yellow dye and seasoning

sag *v.* **sagged, sag′ging** 1 sink in the middle 2 hang unevenly 3 lose strength —*n.* place that sags

sa′ga (sä′-) *n.* long story of heroic deeds

sa·ga′cious (-gā′shəs) *a.* very wise or shrewd —**sa·gac′i·ty** (-gas′-) *n.*

sage *a.* very wise —*n.* 1 very wise old man 2 green leaves used as seasoning 3 sagebrush

sage′brush′ *n.* shrub of the western plains of the U.S.

Sag′it·tar′i·us (saj′-) *n.* ninth sign of the zodiac; Archer

sa·hib (sä′ib′, -ēb′) *n.* title for a European, once used in India

said *v.* pt. & pp. of SAY —*a.* aforesaid

sail *n.* 1 canvas sheet to catch the wind and move a vessel 2 boat trip —*v.* 1 move by means of sails 2 travel on water 3 glide —**set sail** begin a trip by water —**sail′boat′** *n.*

sail′fish′ *n.* ocean fish with a tall dorsal fin

sail′or *n.* 1 enlisted man in the navy 2 one who sails

saint *n.* holy person —**saint′ly** *a.*, **–li·er, –li·est** —**saint′li·ness** *n.*

saith (seth) *v.* [Ar.] says

sake *n.* 1 motive; cause 2 behalf

sa·ke (sä′kē) *n.* Japanese alcoholic beverage

sa·laam (sə läm′) *n.* Oriental greeting of bowing low

sal′a·ble, sale′a·ble *a.* that can be sold

sa·la′cious (-lā′shəs) *a.* obscene

sal′ad *n.* mixture of vegetables, fruit, etc., with salad dressing

salad dressing n. oil, vinegar, spices, etc. put on a salad

sal'a·man'der n. amphibian resembling a lizard

sa·la'mi n. spiced, salted sausage

sal'a·ry n., pl. **–ries** fixed payment at regular intervals for work —**sal'a·ried** a.

sale n. 1 a selling 2 special selling of goods at reduced prices —**for sale** to be sold —**on sale** for sale at a reduced price

sales'clerk' n. one employed to sell goods in a store

sales'man n., pl. **–men** man employed to sell goods or services —**sales'wom'an** n.fem., pl. **–wom'en** —**sales'man·ship'** n.

sales'per'son n. one employed to sell goods or services

sales slip n. bill of sale

sal'i·cyl'ic acid (-sil'-) n. pain-relieving compound, as in aspirin

sa·lient (sāl'yənt) a. 1 prominent; conspicuous 2 jutting —**sa'lience** n.

sa·line (-līn, -lēn) a. salty

sa·li'va n. watery fluid secreted by glands in the mouth —**sal'i·var'y** a.

sal'low a. sickly yellow

sal'ly n., pl. **–lies** 1 sudden rush forward 2 quip 3 short trip —v. **–lied**, **–ly·ing** start out briskly

salm'on (sam'-) n. large, edible ocean fish

sal'mo·nel'la (sal'mə-) n. bacillus causing food poisoning and typhoid

sa·lon' n. 1 parlor 2 gathering of notables

sa·loon' n. 1 public place where liquor is sold and drunk 2 large public room

sal'sa (säl'-) n. sauce made with chilies, tomatoes, etc.

salt n. 1 white substance found in the earth, sea water, etc., used to flavor food 2 a compound formed from an acid 3 [Col.] sailor —a. containing salt —v. add salt to —**salt'i·ness** n. —**salt'y** a., **-i·er**, **-i·est**

salt'cel'lar n. 1 small dish for salt 2 salt-shaker

salt·ine' (-ēn') n. flat, salted cracker

salt lick n. rock salt for animals to lick

salt'pe'ter n. niter

salt'shak'er n. salt container with holes on top

salt'wa'ter a. of salt water, or of the sea

sa·lu'bri·ous a. healthful

sal'u·tar'y (-yōō-) a. 1 healthful 2 beneficial

sal'u·ta'tion n. act or form of greeting

sa·lute' n. formal gesture, act, etc. expressing respect —v. to greet with a salute

sal'vage (-vij) n. 1 rescue of a ship, etc. from shipwreck 2 reclaimed property or goods —v. 1 save from shipwreck, etc. 2 utilize (damaged goods, etc.) —**sal'vage·a·ble** a.

sal·va'tion n. 1 a saving or being saved 2 one that saves 3 saving of the soul

salve (sav) n. soothing ointment —v. soothe

sal'ver n. tray

sal'vo' n., pl. **–vos'** or **–voes'** discharge of a number of guns together

sam'ba n. Brazilian dance, or music for it

same a. 1 being the very one 2 alike 3 unchanged 4 before-mentioned —pron. the same person or thing —adv. in like manner —**all** (or just) **the same** nevertheless —**same'ness** n.

sam'o·var' n. metal urn to heat water for tea

sam'pan' n. small Oriental boat, rowed with a scull

sam'ple n. 1 part typical of a whole 2 example —v. take a sample of

sam'pler n. cloth embroidered with designs, mottoes, etc.

sam'u·rai' (-ə rī') n., pl. **–rai'** member of a military class in feudal Japan

san'a·to'ri·um n. [Chiefly Br.] sanitarium

sanc'ti·fy' v. to make holy or free from sin —**sanc'ti·fi·ca'tion** n.

sanc'ti·mo'ni·ous a. pretending to be pious —**sanc'ti·mo'ny** n.

sanc'tion n. 1 authorization 2 approval 3 punitive measure against a nation: often used in pl. —v. 1 authorize 2 approve

sanc'ti·ty n. 1 holiness 2 sacredness

sanc'tu·ar'y (-chōō-) n., pl. **–ies** holy place, as a church 2 place of refuge

sanc'tum n. 1 sacred place 2 one's own private room

sand n. 1 loose grains of disintegrated rock 2 pl. area of sand —v. to sandpaper —**sand'er** n.

san'dal n. open shoe with sole tied to the foot by straps

san'dal·wood' n. tree with sweet-smelling wood

sand'bag' n. sand-filled bag for ballast, etc. —v. **–bagged'**, **–bag'ging** 1 put sandbags around 2 [Col.] force into doing something

sand'bar' n. ridge of sand along a shore: also **sand'bank'**

sand'blast' v. clean with a blast of air and sand

sand'box' n. box with sand, as for children to play in

sand'hog' n. laborer in underground or underwater construction

sand'lot' a. of baseball played by amateurs

sand'man' n. mythical bringer of sleep to children

sand'pa'per n. paper coated with sand —v. to smooth or polish with sandpaper

sand'pip'er n. shorebird with a long bill

sand'stone' n. kind of rock much used in building

sand'storm' n. windstorm with clouds of blown sand

sand'wich n. slices of bread with meat, etc. between them —v. squeeze in or between

sand'y a. **-i·er, -i·est 1** of or like sand **2** dull yellow

sane a. **1** mentally healthy **2** sensible —**sane'ly** adv.

sang v. pt. of SING

san'gui·nar'y (-gwi-) a. **1** of or with bloodshed **2** bloodthirsty

san'guine (-gwin) a. **1** blood-red **2** cheerful or optimistic

san'i·tar'i·um n. institution for invalids, etc.

san'i·tar'y a. **1** of health **2** clean and healthful —**san'i·tize'** v.

sanitary napkin n. absorbent pad worn during menstruation

san'i·ta'tion n. **1** hygienic conditions **2** sewage disposal

san'i·ty n. soundness of mind or judgment

sank v. pt. of SINK

sans prep. without

sap n. **1** juice of a plant **2** vigor **3** [Sl.] a fool —v. **1** undermine **2** weaken —**sap'py** a., **-pi·er, -pi·est**

sa'pi·ent a. wise —**sa'pi·ence** n.

sap'ling n. young tree

sap·phire (saf'īr) n. deep-blue precious stone

sap'suck'er n. small woodpecker

sa·ran' n. plastic for wrapping material, fabric, etc.

sar'casm' n. taunting, ironic remark(s) —**sar·cas'tic** a.

sar·co'ma n., pl. **-mas** or **-ma·ta** malignant tumor

sar·coph'a·gus (-käf'-) n., pl. **-gi** (-jī') or **-gus·es** stone coffin

sar·dine' (-dēn') n. small herring preserved in oil

sar·don'ic a. bitterly sarcastic

sa·ri (sä'rē) n. long, draped outer garment of Hindu women

sa·rong' n. skirtlike garment of East Indies

sar'sa·pa·ril'la (sas'pə-) n. sweetened, root-flavored drink

sar·to'ri·al a. **1** of tailors **2** of (men's) clothing

sash n. **1** band worn over the shoulder or around the waist **2** sliding frame for glass in a window

sass v., n. [Col.] (use) impudent talk

sas'sa·fras' n. tree whose root bark is used for flavoring

sass'y a. **-i·er, -i·est** [Col.] impudent

sat v. pt. & pp. of SIT

Sa'tan the Devil —**sa·tan'ic** a.

Sa'tan·ism' n. worship of Satan —**Sa'tan·ist** n.

satch'el n. small traveling bag

sate v. **1** satisfy fully **2** satiate

sa·teen' n. satinlike cotton cloth

sat'el·lite' n. **1** small planet revolving around a larger one **2** man-made object orbiting in space **3** small state dependent on a larger one

sa'ti·ate' (-shē-) v. give too much to, causing disgust —**sa·ti'e·ty** (-tī'-) n.

sat'in n. smooth and glossy silk, nylon, or rayon cloth

sat'in·wood' n. a tree yielding smooth wood used in fine furniture

sat'ire' n. **1** use of ridicule, irony, etc. to attack vice or folly **2** literary work in which this is done —**sa·tir'i·cal** (-tir'-), **sa·tir'ic** a. —**sat'i·rist** n.

sat'i·rize' v. attack with satire

sat·is·fy' v. **-fied', -fy'ing 1** fulfill the needs and desires of **2** fulfill the requirements of **3** convince **4** pay in full —**sat'is·fac'tion** n. —**sat'is·fac'to·ry** a.

sa·to·ri (sä tôr'ē) n. Buddhism spiritual enlightenment

sa'trap' (sā'-, sa'-) n. petty tyrant

sat'u·rate' (sach'-) v. **1** soak thoroughly **2** fill completely —**sat'u·rat'ed** a. —**sat'u·ra'tion** n.

Sat'ur·day n. seventh day of the week

sat'ur·nine' a. gloomy

sa'tyr (sāt'ər) n. Gr. myth. woodland god with goat's legs

sauce n. **1** tasty, liquid or soft dressing for food **2** mashed, stewed fruit **3** flavored syrup

sauce'pan' n. metal cooking pot with a long handle

sau'cer n. shallow dish, esp. one for holding a cup

sau'cy a. **-ci·er, -ci·est 1** impudent **2** lively and bold —**sau'ci·ly** adv. —**sau'ci·ness** n.

sau·er·bra·ten (sour'brät''n) n. beef marinated before cooking

sau'er·kraut' (-krout') n. chopped, fermented cabbage

sau'na n. bath with exposure to hot, dry air

saun'ter v., n. stroll

sau'sage n. chopped, seasoned pork, etc., often stuffed into a casing

sau·té (sō tā') v. **1** fry quickly in a little fat

sau·ternes (sō turn') n. a white table wine: also **sau·terne'**

sav'age a. **1** fierce; untamed **2** primitive; barbarous —n. an uncivilized or brutal person —**sav'age·ly** adv. —**sav'age·ry** n.

sa·van·na, sa·van'nah n. treeless, grassy plain

sa·vant (sə vänt′) n. scholar

save v. 1 rescue; keep safe 2 keep or store (up) for future use 3 avoid waste (of) —prep., con. except; but

sav′ing a. that saves —n. 1 reduction in time, cost, etc. 2 pl. money saved

sav′ior, sav′iour (-yər) n. one who saves or rescues —[S—] Jesus Christ

sa·voir-faire (sav′wär fer′) n. social poise; tact

sa′vor v., n. (have) a special taste, smell, or quality

sa′vor·y a. -i·er, -i·est tasting or smelling good

sav′vy [Sl.] n. shrewdness —a. shrewd

saw n. 1 thin, metal blade with sharp teeth, for cutting 2 proverb —v. 1 pt. of SEE 2 cut with a saw —**saw′yer** n.

saw′dust n. fine bits of wood formed in sawing wood

sawed′-off a. short or shortened

saw′horse n. rack to hold wood while sawing it: also **saw′buck**

sax′o·phone n. single-reed, metal wind instrument

say v. **said, say′ing** 1 speak 2 to state 3 suppose —n. 1 chance to speak 2 power to decide —**that is to say** in other words

say′ing n. proverb

say′-so n. [Col.] 1 (one's) word, assurance, etc. 2 power to decide

scab n. 1 crust over a healing sore 2 worker who rejects union or breaks a strike —v. **scabbed, scab′bing** form a scab

scab′bard (-ərd) n. sheath for a sword, dagger, etc.

sca·bies (skā′-) n. itch caused by mites

scab′rous a. 1 scaly 2 indecent, shocking, etc.

scads n.pl. [Col.] very large number or amount

scaf′fold n. 1 framework to hold workmen, painters, etc. 2 platform on which criminals are executed

scald (skôld) v. 1 burn with hot liquid or steam 2 heat almost to a boil —n. burn caused by scalding

scale n. 1 series of gradations or degrees 2 ratio of a map, etc. to the thing represented 3 any of the thin, hard plates on a fish, snake, etc. 4 flake 5 either pan of a balance 6 often pl. balance or weighing machine 7 Mus. series of consecutive tones —v. 1 climb up 2 set according to a scale 3 scrape scales from 4 flake off in scales —**scal′y** a., -i·er, -i·est —**scal′i·ness** n.

scal′lion (-yən) n. green onion

scal′lop n. 1 edible mollusk 2 any of the curves forming a fancy edge —v. 1 to edge

in scallops 2 to bake with a milk sauce, etc.

scalp n. skin on top of the head —v. 1 cut the scalp from 2 [Col.] sell (tickets, etc.) above current prices —**scalp′er** n.

scal′pel n. sharp knife used in surgery, etc.

scam n. [Sl.] a trick or swindle

scamp n. rascal

scam′per v. run quickly —n. quick dash

scam′pi n., pl. **-pi** or **-pies** large, edible prawns

scan v. **scanned, scan′ning** 1 look at quickly 2 examine 3 analyze the meter in verse

scan′dal n. 1 disgrace or thing that disgraces 2 gossip —**scan′dal·ous** a.

scan′dal·ize v. outrage one's feeling of decency

scan′dal·mon′ger (-muŋ′-, -mäŋ′-) n. one who spreads gossip

scant a. not enough —**scant′y** a., -i·er, -i·est —**scant′i·ly** adv. —**scant′i·ness** n.

scape′goat n. one who is blamed for others' mistakes

scape′grace n. rogue

scap′u·la n. shoulder bone

scar n. mark left after a wound has healed —v. **scarred, scar′ring** to mark with or form a scar

scar′ab (skar′-) n. beetle

scarce a. 1 not common 2 hard to get —adv. scarcely —**scarce′ness** n. —**scar′ci·ty** n., pl. **-ties**

scarce′ly adv. hardly

scare v. frighten —n. sudden fear —[Col.] **scar′y** a., -i·er, -i·est

scare′crow n. human figure set up to scare away birds from crops

scarf n., pl. **scarfs** or **scarves** long or broad cloth piece for the neck, etc.

scar′let n. bright red

scarlet fever n. contagious disease with fever and a rash

scat int. [Col.] go away!

scath′ing (skāth′-) a. harsh; bitter —**scath′ing·ly** adv.

scat′o·log′i·cal a. of obscenity

scat′ter v. 1 throw about 2 move in several directions

scat′ter·brain′ n. one incapable of clear thinking —**scat′ter-brained′** a.

scatter rug n. small rug

scav′eng·er n. 1 one who collects refuse 2 animal that eats decaying matter —**scav′enge** v.

sce·nar′i·o′ (sə ner′-, -när′-) n., pl. **-os′** 1 movie script 2 outline for proposed action

scene (sēn) n. 1 place; setting 2 view 3 division of a play, film, etc. 4 show of emotion

sce′ner·y n., pl. **-ies** 1 painted backdrops for a stage play 2 outdoor views

sce′nic a. 1 of scenery 2 picturesque

scent (sent) v. **1** to suspect **2** to perfume —n. **1** odor **2** perfume **3** sense of smell

scep´ter (sep´-) n. a staff as symbol of a ruler's power: also [Chiefly Br.] **scep´tre**

scep´tic (skep´-) n. chiefly Br. sp. of SKEPTIC

sched·ule (ske´jool) n. **1** timetable **2** timed plan **3** list of details —v. to place in a schedule

scheme (skēm) n. **1** plan; system **2** plot; intrigue **3** diagram —v. plot —**sche·mat´ic** a. —**schem´er** n.

scher·zo (sker´tsō) n., pl. **-zos** or **-zi** (-tsē) lively musical movement in ¾ time

schism (siz´əm) n. split, esp. in a church, over doctrine —**schis·mat´ic** a.

schist (shist) n. rock in layers

schiz·o·phre´ni·a (skits´ə frē´-) n. severe mental illness —**schiz´o·phren´ic** (-fren´-) a., n.

schlock a., n. [Sl.] cheap or inferior (thing)

schmaltz n. [Sl.] very sentimental music, writing, etc.

schnapps (shnäps) n., pl. **schnapps** flavored gin

schnau´zer (shnou´-) n. small terrier

schol·ar (skä´lər) n. **1** learned person **2** student —**schol´ar·ly** a.

schol´ar·ship´ n. **1** academic knowledge; learning **2** money given to help a student

scho·las´tic a. of schools, students, teachers, etc.

school n. **1** place for teaching and learning **2** its students and teachers **3** education **4** group with the same beliefs **5** group of fish —v. train; teach —a. of, in, or for school —**school´mate´** n. —**school´teach´er** n.

school board n. group in charge of local public schools

school´ing n. training or education

schoon´er n. ship with two or more masts

schwa (shwä) n. vowel sound in an unaccented syllable: symbol (ə)

sci·at´ic (sī-) a. of or in the hip or its nerves

sci·at´i·ca n. neuritis in the hip and thigh

sci´ence n. systematized knowledge or a branch of it —**sci´en·tif´ic** a. —**sci´en·tif´i·cal·ly** adv.

science fiction n. imaginative fiction involving scientific phenomena

sci´en·tist n. expert in science

scim´i·tar (sim´-) n. curved sword

scin·til´la (sin-) n. tiny bit

scin´til·late´ v. **1** sparkle **2** be clever and witty —**scin´til·la´tion** n.

sci´on (sī´-) n. **1** a bud or shoot **2** descendant

scis´sors (siz´-) n.pl. cutting tool with two opposing blades that move on a pivot

scle·ro´sis (skli-) n. a hardening of body tissues

scoff n. scornful remark —v. mock or jeer (at)

scoff´law´ n. [Col.] habitual violator of traffic laws, etc.

scold v. find fault with angrily —n. one who scolds

sconce n. wall bracket for candles

scone n. small tea cake

scoop n. **1** small, shovellike utensil **2** bucket of a dredge, etc. **3** a scooping —v. **1** take up with a scoop **2** hollow out

scoot v. [Col.] scurry off

scoot´er n. **1** child's two-wheeled vehicle **2** small motorcycle

scope n. **1** range of understanding, action, etc. **2** chance

-scope suf. instrument, etc. for seeing

scorch v. **1** burn slightly **2** parch —n. surface burn

score n. **1** points made in a game, etc. **2** grade on a test **3** piece of music showing all parts **4** scratch or mark **5** twenty **6** pl. very many **7** debt —v. **1** make a score or scores **2** evaluate **3** achieve **4** keep score **5** upbraid —**scor´er** n.

score´board´ n. large board or screen posting scores, etc., as in a stadium

score´less a. having scored no points

scorn n. contempt; disdain —v. **1** treat with scorn **2** refuse —**scorn´ful** a. —**scorn´ful·ly** adv.

Scor´pi·o´ eighth sign of the zodiac; Scorpion

scor´pi·on n. arachnid with a poisonous sting

Scot n. native or inhabitant of Scotland

Scotch n. whiskey made in Scotland —a. Scottish —v. [**s-**] put an end to

Scotch tape trademark a thin, transparent adhesive tape

scot´-free´ a. unpunished

Scot´tie, Scot´ty n., pl. **-ties** [Col.] Scottish terrier

Scot´tish a., n. (of) the people or language of Scotland

Scottish terrier n. short-legged terrier with wiry hair

scoun´drel n. villain

scour v. **1** to clean by rubbing with abrasives **2** go through thoroughly, as in search

scourge (skurj) n., v. **1** whip **2** torment; plague

scout n., v. (one sent ahead) to spy, search, etc.

scout´mas´ter n. adult leader of a troop of Boy Scouts

scow n. flat-bottomed boat

scowl v., n. (to have) an angry frown

scrag´gly a. **-gli·er, -gli·est** rough; jagged

scram v. scrammed, scram′ming [Sl.] get out

scram′ble v. 1 climb, crawl, etc. hurriedly 2 struggle for something 3 to mix; jumble 4 stir and cook (eggs) 5 make (signals) unclear —n. a scrambling

scrap n. 1 fragment 2 discarded material 3 pl. bits of food —a. discarded —v. scrapped, scrap′ping 1 discard 2 [Col.] fight —scrap′py a., -pi·er, -pi·est

scrap′book′ n. book in which to paste pictures, etc.

scrape v. 1 rub smooth or rub away 2 scratch 3 gather bit by bit —n. 1 scraped place 2 harsh sound 3 predicament —scrap′er n.

scrap′heap′ n. pile of discarded material or things

scratch v. 1 cut the surface 2 scrape or dig with one's nails 3 scrape noisily 4 cross out —n. mark from scratching —a. for hasty notes, etc. —from scratch from nothing —scratch′y a., -i·er, -i·est

scrawl v. write carelessly —n. poor handwriting

scraw′ny a. -ni·er, -ni·est lean; thin

scream v., n. (make) a loud, shrill cry or noise

screech v., n. (give) a harsh, shrill shriek

screen n. 1 thing used to shield, conceal, etc. 2 wire mesh in a frame 3 surface for showing video images, films, etc. —v. 1 conceal or shelter 2 sift or sift out

screen′play′ n. script for a motion picture

screw n. 1 naillike fastener with a spiral groove 2 propeller —v. 1 to turn; twist 2 fasten, as with a screw

screw′ball′ a., n. [Sl.] erratic or unconventional (person)

screw′driv′er n. tool for turning screws

screw′y a. -i·er, -i·est [Sl.] 1 crazy 2 peculiar or eccentric

scrib′ble v. 1 write carelessly 2 draw marks —n. scribbled writing

scribe n. writer; author

scrim′mage (-ij) n. Football 1 play that follows the pass from center 2 practice game —v. take part in a scrimmage

scrimp v. spend or use as little as possible

scrip n. certificate redeemable for stocks, money, etc.

script n. 1 handwriting 2 working copy of a play

Scrip′ture n. 1 often pl. the Bible 2 [s—] any sacred writing —Scrip′tur·al a.

scrod n. young cod or haddock

scrof′u·la n. tuberculosis of the lymphatic glands

scroll n. 1 roll of paper, etc. with writing on it 2 coiled or spiral design

scro′tum n. skin pouch containing the testicles

scrounge v. [Col.] hunt around for and take; pilfer

scrub v. scrubbed, scrub′bing rub hard, as in washing —n. 1 a scrubbing 2 a growth of stunted trees or bushes —a. 1 inferior 2 undersized —scrub′by a., -bi·er, -bi·est

scruff n. back of the neck; nape

scruff′y a. -i·er, -i·est shabby or unkempt

scrump′tious a. [Col.] delicious

scrunch v. 1 crumple or crunch 2 huddle, squeeze, etc.

scru′ple n. a doubt as to what is right, proper, etc. —v. hesitate from doubt

scru′pu·lous a. 1 showing or having scruples 2 precise

scru′ti·nize′ v. examine closely —scru′ti·ny n.

scu′ba n. equipment, as an air tank, for breathing underwater

scud v. scud′ded, scud′ding move swiftly

scuff v. 1 scrape with the feet 2 wear a rough place on —n. worn spot

scuf′fle v. rough, confused fight —v. be in a scuffle

scull n. 1 large oar at the stern of a boat 2 light rowboat for racing —v. propel with a scull

scul′ler·y n., pl. -ies room for rough kitchen work

sculp′ture v. carve wood, stone, etc. into statues, etc. —n. art of sculpturing or work sculptured —sculp′tor n. —sculp′tur·al a.

scum n. 1 surface impurities on a liquid 2 [Col.] vile person or people —scum′my a., -mi·er, -mi·est

scup′per n. side opening for water to run off a deck

scurf n. scales shed by skin

scur′ri·lous a. vulgarly abusive —scur·ril′i·ty n., pl. -ties

scur′ry v., n. -ried, -ry·ing scamper

scur′vy a. -vi·er, -vi·est low; mean —n. disease due to vitamin C deficiency

scut′tle n. bucket for coal —v. -tled, -tling 1 scamper 2 cut holes in (a ship) to sink it

scut′tle·butt′ n. [Col.] rumor

scythe (sīth) n. long-bladed tool to cut grass, etc.

sea n. 1 the ocean 2 a smaller body of salt water 3 large body of fresh water 4 heavy wave

sea anemone n. sea polyp with gelatinous body

sea′bird′ n. bird that lives near the sea, as a gull

sea′board′ n. land along the sea: also sea′coast′

sea′far′ing (-fer′-) a., n. (of) sea travel or a

sailor's work —sea'far'er n.

sea'food' n. ocean fish or shellfish used as food

sea'go'ing a. 1 made for use on the open sea 2 seafaring

sea gull n. a gull (bird)

sea horse n. small fish with a head like that of a horse

seal n. 1 sea mammal with flippers 2 official design stamped on a letter, etc. 3 thing that seals —v. 1 certify as with a seal 2 close tight 3 settle finally

seal'ant n. substance, as wax, plastic, etc. used for sealing

sea level n. mean level of the sea's surface

sea lion n. seal of N Pacific

seam n. 1 line where two pieces are sewn or welded together 2 layer of ore or coal —v. join with a seam

sea'man n., pl. —men 1 sailor 2 navy enlisted man

seam'stress n. woman whose work is sewing

seam'y a. -i-er, -i-est unpleasant or sordid

sé·ance (sā'äns) n. spiritualists' meeting

sea'plane' n. airplane which can land on water

sea'port' n. port for ocean ships

sear a. withered —v. 1 wither 2 burn the surface of

search v. look through or examine to find something —n. a searching

search'light' n. 1 strong light 2 device to project it

search warrant n. writ authorizing a police search

sea'shell' n. mollusk shell

sea'shore' n. land along the sea

sea'sick'ness n. nausea caused by a ship's rolling —sea'sick' a.

sea'son n. 1 any of the four divisions of the year 2 special time —v. 1 to flavor 2 age 3 accustom —sea'son·al a.

sea'son·a·ble a. timely

sea'son·ing n. flavoring for food

seat n. 1 place to sit 2 thing or part one sits on 3 right to sit as a member 4 chief location —v. 1 set on a seat 2 have seats for

seat belt n. strap across the hips to protect a seated passenger

sea urchin n. small sea animal with a spiny shell

sea'way' n. inland waterway for ocean-going ships

sea'weed' n. any sea plant(s)

sea'wor'thy a. fit for travel on the sea: said of a ship

se·ba'ceous (-shəs) a. of or secreting fat, etc.

seb'or·rhe'a, seb'or·rhoe'a (-rē'ə) n. oily skin condition

se·cede' (-sēd') v. withdraw formally from a group, etc. —se·ces'sion (-sesh'ən) n.

se·clude' v. isolate —se·clu'sion n.

sec'ond a. 1 next after the first 2 another, like the first —n. 1 one that is second 2 thing not of the first quality 3 assistant 4 ¹⁄₆₀ of a minute —v. support (a suggestion, motion, etc.) —adv. in the second place, etc. —sec'ond·ly adv.

sec'ond·ar'y a. 1 second in order 2 less important 3 derivative

secondary school n. high school

sec'ond-class' a. 1 of the class, rank, etc. next below the highest 2 inferior

sec'ond-guess' v. [Col.] use hindsight in judging

sec'ond·hand' a. 1 not from the original source 2 used before

second lieutenant n. Mil. commissioned officer of the lowest rank

second nature n. deeply fixed, acquired habit

sec'ond-rate' a. inferior

sec'ond-string' a. [Col.] playing as a substitute at a specified position, as in sports

second thought n. change in thought after reconsidering

se'cret a. 1 kept from being known by others 2 hidden —n. secret fact, etc. —se'cre·cy n. —se'cret·ly adv.

sec're·tar'i·at (-ter'-) n. staff headed by a secretary

sec're·tar'y n., pl. —ies 1 one who keeps records, writes letters, etc. for a person or group 2 head of a department of government 3 tall desk —sec're·tar'i·al a.

se·crete' v. 1 to hide 2 make (a body substance), as a gland —se·cre'tion n.

se'cre·tive a. not frank or open —se'cre·tive·ly adv.

sect n. group having the same beliefs, esp. in religion

sec·tar'i·an (-ter'-) a. 1 of or like a sect 2 narrow-minded

sec'tion n. distinct part —v. divide into sections —sec'tion·al a.

sec'tor n. 1 part of a circle like a pie slice 2 district for military operations

sec'u·lar a. not connected with church or religion

sec'u·lar·ize' v. to change from religious to civil control

se·cure' a. 1 free from danger, care, etc. 2 firm; stable 3 sure —v. 1 make secure 2 get —se·cure'ly adv.

se·cu'ri·ty n., pl. —ties 1 secure state or feeling 2 protection 3 thing given as a pledge of repayment, etc. 4 pl. stocks, bonds, etc.

se·dan' n. closed automobile with front and rear seats

se·date' a. quiet and dignified —**se·date'ly** adv.

sed'a·tive (-tiv) a. making one calmer —n. sedative medicine —**se·da'tion** n.

sed'en·tar·y a. characterized by much sitting

Se·der (sā'dər) n. feast on the eve of Passover

sedge n. coarse, grasslike plant of marshes

sed'i·ment n. matter that settles from a liquid —**sed'i·men'ta·ry** a.

se·di'tion (-dish'ən) n. stirring up a rebellion —**se·di'tious** a.

se·duce' v. 1 to lead astray 2 entice into sexual intercourse, esp. for the first time —**se·duc'er** n. —**se·duc'tion** n. —**se·duc'tive** a.

sed'u·lous (sej'-) a. diligent

see v. saw, seen, see'ing 1 look at 2 understand 3 find out 4 make sure 5 escort 6 meet; visit with 7 consult 8 have the power of sight —n. office or district of a bishop —**see to** attend to

seed n., pl. **seeds** or **seed** 1 the part of a plant from which a new one will grow 2 source 3 sperm —v. 1 plant with seed 2 take the seeds from —**seed'less** a.

seed'ling n. young plant grown from a seed

seed money n. money to begin a project or attract more funds for it

seed'y a. -i·er, -i·est 1 full of seeds 2 shabby; untidy

see'ing con. considering

seek v. sought, seek'ing 1 search for 2 try to get

seem v. look, feel, etc. (to be)

seem'ing a. not actual —**seem'ing·ly** adv.

seem'ly a. -li·er, -li·est suitable, proper, etc.

seep v. leak through; ooze —**seep'age** n.

seer n. prophet

seer'suck·er n. crinkled fabric

see'saw n. balanced plank ridden at the ends for swinging up and down —v. to move up and down or back and forth

seethe (sēth) v. boil

seg'ment (-mənt; v.: -ment) n. section —v. divide into segments

seg're·gate' v. set apart —**seg're·ga'tion** n.

seine (sān) n. fishing net

seis'mic (sīz'-) a. of an earthquake

seis'mo·graph' n. instrument to record earthquakes

seize (sēz) v. 1 take suddenly or by force 2 attack 3 capture —**sei'zure** n.

sel'dom adv. rarely

se·lect' a. 1 chosen with care 2 exclusive —v. choose; pick out —**se·lec'tion** n. —**se·lec'tive** a.

selective service n. compulsory military training

se·lect'man n., pl. -men New England town official

self n., pl. **selves** one's own person, welfare, etc.

self- pref. of, by, in, to, or with oneself or itself: see list below

self'-ad·dressed'
self'-ap·point'ed
self'-de·ni'al
self'-dis'ci·pline
self'-ed'u·cat'ed
self'-es·teem'
self'-ex·plan'a·to'ry
self'-ex·pres'sion
self'-in·dul'gence
self'-pit'y
self'-pres·er·va'tion
self'-re·li'ance
self'-re·spect'
self'-sat'is·fied'
self'-sup·port'ing
self'-taught'

self'-as·sur'ance n. self-confidence

self'-cen'tered a. selfish

self'-con'fi·dent a. sure of oneself —**self'-con'fi·dence** n.

self'-con'scious a. ill at ease

self'-con·tained' a. 1 self-controlled 2 reserved 3 self-sufficient

self'-con·tra·dic'to·ry a. having elements that contradict each other

self'-con·trol' n. control of one's emotions, actions, etc. —**self'-con·trolled'** a.

self'-de·fense' n. defense of oneself or of one's rights, etc.

self'-de·struct' v. destruct

self'-de·ter'mi·na'tion n. 1 free will 2 right to choose one's government

self'-ev'i·dent a. evident without proof

self'-gov'ern·ment n. government of a group by its own members —**self'-gov'ern·ing** a.

self'-im'age n. one's idea of oneself, one's worth, etc.

self'-im·por'tance n. pompous conceit —**self'-im·por'tant** a.

self'-in'ter·est n. (selfish) interest in one's own welfare

self'ish a. caring too much about oneself —**self'ish·ly** adv. —**self'ish·ness** n.

self'less a. unselfish

self'-love' n. excessive regard for oneself, one's interests, etc.

self'-made' a. successful, rich, etc. through one's own efforts

self'-pos·ses'sion n. full control over one's actions, etc. —**self'-pos·sessed'** a.

self'-re·straint' n. self-control —**self'-re·strained'** a.

self'-right'eous a. feeling more righteous than others

self'same' a. identical

self'-serv'ice n. practice of serving oneself in a store, cafeteria, etc.

self'-serv'ing a. serving one's selfish interests

self'-styled' a. so called by oneself

self'-suf-fi'cient a. independent —**self'-suf-fi'cien-cy** n.

self'-sus-tain'ing a. 1 supporting oneself 2 able to continue once begun

self'-willed' a. stubborn

self'-wind'ing a. wound automatically, as some watches

sell v. **sold, sell'ing** 1 exchange for money 2 offer for sale 3 be sold (for) —**sell out** 1 sell completely 2 [Col.] betray

sell'out' n. [Col.] show, game, etc. for which all seats have been sold

sel'vage, sel'vedge (-vij) n. edge woven to prevent raveling

se-man'tics n. study of words —**se-man'tic** a.

sem'a-phore' n. flags or lights for signaling

sem'blance n. outward show

se'men n. reproductive fluid of the male

se-mes'ter n. either of the terms in a school year

sem'i' (-ī') n. semitrailer: also used of semitrailer and its attached TRACTOR (n. 2)

semi- pref. 1 half 2 partly 3 twice in some period —**sem'i-an'nu-al, sem'i-month'ly, sem'i-week'ly**

sem'i-cir'cle n. half circle

sem'i-co'lon n. mark of punctuation (;)

sem'i-con-duc'tor n. substance, as silicon, used in transistors, etc. to control current flow

sem'i-fi'nal n., a. (contest) just before the finals

sem'i-nal a. primary

sem'i-nar' (-när') n. supervised course of research

sem'i-nar'y (-ner'-) n., pl. **-ies** 1 school for women 2 school, esp. for training ministers, etc.

sem'i-pre'cious a. less valuable than precious gems

sem'i-pri'vate a. of a hospital room with two, three, or sometimes four beds

sem'i-skilled' a. of manual work requiring little training

sem'i-tone' n. Mus. half of a whole tone

sem'i-trail'er n. detachable trailer attached to a TRACTOR (n. 2)

sem'i-week'ly a., adv. twice a week

sem'o-li'na (-lē'-) n. coarsely ground durum

sen'ate n. 1 lawmaking assembly 2 [S—] upper branch of Congress or a State legislature —**sen'a-tor** n. —**sen'a-to'ri-al** a.

send v. **sent, send'ing** 1 cause to go or be carried 2 impel; drive —**send for** summon —**send'er** n.

send'-off' n. [Col.] farewell demonstration for someone leaving

se'nile a. 1 of old age 2 weak in mind and body —**se-nil'i-ty** n.

sen'ior (-yər) a. 1 the older: written *Sr.* 2 of higher rank, etc. —n. high school or college student in the last year

senior citizen n. elderly person, esp. one retired

sen-ior'i-ty (-yôr'-) n. status gained by length of service

sen'na n. laxative derived from a cassia plant

se-ñor (se nyôr') n. [Sp.] Mr.

se-ño'ra n. [Sp.] Mrs.

se'ño-ri'ta n. [Sp.] Miss

sen-sa'tion n. 1 sense impression or the power to receive it 2 exciting thing

sen-sa'tion-al a. shocking —**sen-sa'tion-al-ism'** n.

sense n. 1 power to see, hear, taste, feel, etc. 2 sound judgment 3 meaning —v. perceive —**in a sense** to some extent —**make sense** be intelligible

sense'less a. 1 unconscious 2 foolish or stupid

sen'si-bil'i-ty n., pl. **-ties** 1 power of feeling 2 pl. delicate feelings

sen'si-ble a. 1 reasonable; wise 2 aware 3 noticeable —**sen'si-bly** adv.

sen'si-tive (-tiv') a. 1 quick to feel, notice, etc. 2 susceptible to stimuli 3 tender or sore 4 touchy —**sen'si-tiv'i-ty** n.

sen'si-tize' v. make sensitive

sen'sor n. device for detecting heat, light, etc.

sen'so-ry a. of the senses

sen'su-al (-shōō-) a. of or enjoying the pleasures of the body —**sen'su-al-ly** adv. —**sen'su-al'i-ty** n.

sen'su-ous a. having to do with the senses

sent v. pt. & pp. of SEND

sen'tence n. 1 group of words stating something 2 court decision 3 punishment —v. pronounce punishment on

sen-ten'tious a. 1 pithy 2 pompously boring

sen'tient (-shənt) a. conscious

sen'ti-ment n. 1 a feeling 2 opinion 3 tender feelings 4 maudlin emotion —**sen'ti-men'tal** a. —**sen'ti-men'tal-ist** n. —**sen'ti-men-tal'i-ty** n. —**sen'ti-men'tal-ly** adv.

sen'ti-men'tal-ize' v. treat or think of in a sentimental way

sen'ti-nel n. guard; sentry

sen'try n., pl. **-tries** guard posted to protect a group

se'pal n. leaf at the base of a flower

sep'a-rate' (-rāt'; a.: -rət) v. 1 divide; set

apart **2** keep apart **3** go apart —*a.* set apart; distinct —**sep′a·ra·ble** *a.* —**sep′a·rate·ly** *adv.* —**sep′a·ra′tion** *n.* —**sep′a·ra′tor** *n.*

sep′a·ra·tism′ *n.* advocacy of separation, racially, politically, etc.

se′pi·a *n.*, *a.* reddish brown

sep′sis *n.* blood infection —**sep′tic** *a.*

Sep·tem′ber *n.* ninth month

septic tank *n.* tank into which house waste drains

sep′tum *n.*, *pl.* **-tums** or **-ta** *Biol.* partition, as in the nose

sep′ul·cher (-kər) *n.* tomb: also, Br. sp., **sep′ul·chre** —**se·pul′chral** *a.*

se′quel *n.* **1** result **2** book, etc. that continues an earlier one

se′quence *n.* **1** succession or the order of this **2** series **3** scene; episode

se·ques′ter *v.* confiscate; isolate —**se′ques·tra′tion** *n.*

se′quin *n.* small, shiny disk for decorating cloth

se·quoi′a (-kwoi′-) *n.* giant evergreen tree

se·rag′lio (-ral′yō) *n.*, *pl.* **-lios** HAREM (sense 1)

se·ra·pe (sə rä′pē) *n.* blanket worn over the shoulders

ser′aph (-əf) *n.*, *pl.* **-aphs** or **-a·phim′** angel of the highest rank —**se·raph′ic** *a.*

sere (sir) *a.* [Poet.] withered

ser′e·nade′ *v.*, *n.* (perform) music sung or played at night, esp. by a lover

ser′en·dip′i·ty *n.* the making of lucky discoveries by chance

se·rene′ (-rēn′) *a.* undisturbed; calm —**se·rene′ly** *adv.* —**se·ren′i·ty** (-ren′-) *n.*

serf *n.* feudal farmer, almost a slave —**serf′dom** *n.*

serge *n.* twilled, worsted fabric

ser·geant (sär′jənt) *n.* **1** low-ranking police officer **2** noncommissioned officer above a corporal

ser′geant-at-arms′ *n.*, *pl.* **ser′geants-at-arms′** one who keeps order, as in a court

se′ri·al (sir′ē-) *a.* of, in, or published in a series —*n.* serial story —**se′ri·al·i·za′tion** *n.* —**se′ri·al·ize′** *v.*

serial number *n.* one of a series of numbers given for identification

se′ries *n.*, *pl.* **se′ries** number of similar things coming one after another

se′ri·ous *a.* **1** earnest **2** important **3** dangerous

ser′mon *n.* **1** religious speech by a clergyman **2** serious talk on duty, etc.

ser′pent *n.* snake

ser′pen·tine (-tēn′, -tīn′) *a.* winding

ser′rate′ *a.* edged like a saw: also **ser′rat′ed**

ser′ried (-ēd) *a.* placed close together

se·rum (sir′əm) *n.* **1** yellowish fluid in blood **2** antitoxin from the blood of an immune animal —**se′rous** *a.*

serv′ant *n.* one hired to work in another's home

serve *v.* **1** be a servant to **2** aid **3** do official service **4** spend a prison term **5** offer (food, etc.) to **6** be used by **7** deliver **8** hit a ball to start play —*n.* a hitting of a ball in tennis, etc. —**serv′er** *n.*

serv′ice *n.* **1** a serving **2** governmental work **3** armed forces **4** religious ceremony **5** set of silverware, etc. **6** aid —*v.* **1** supply **2** repair —**of service** helpful —**serv′ice·a·ble** *a.*

serv′ice·man′ *n.*, *pl.* **-men′** member of the armed forces

service mark *n.* mark used like a trademark by supplier of services

service station *n.* place selling gasoline, oil, etc.

ser′vile (-vəl, -vīl) *a.* humbly submissive —**ser·vil′i·ty** *n.*

ser′vi·tude′ *n.* slavery

ser′vo·mech′a·nism′ *n.* automatic remote control system

ses′a·me′ *n.* edible seeds

ses′qui·cen·ten′ni·al (ses′kwi-) *n.* 150th anniversary

ses′sion *n.* meeting of a court, legislature, class, etc.

set *v.* **set**, **set′ting 1** put; place **2** put in the proper condition, position, etc. **3** make or become firm or fixed **4** establish; fix **5** sit on eggs, as a hen **6** start **7** mount (gems) **8** furnish (an example) **9** sink below the horizon **10** fit (words) to music —*a.* **1** fixed **2** obstinate **3** ready —*n.* **1** way in which a thing is set **2** scenery for a play **3** group of like persons or things **4** assembled parts, as of a radio —**set about** (or **in** or **to**) begin —**set forth** state —**set off 1** show by contrast **2** explode —**set on** (or **upon**) attack —**set up 1** erect **2** establish

set′back′ *n.* relapse

set·tee′ *n.* small sofa

set′ter *n.* long-haired hunting dog

set′ting *n.* **1** that in which a thing is set **2** time, place, etc., as of a story **3** surroundings

set′tle *v.* **1** put in order **2** set in place firmly or comfortably **3** go to live in **4** deposit sediment, etc. **5** calm **6** decide **7** pay, as a debt **8** come to rest **9** sink —**set′tler** *n.*

set′tle·ment *n.* **1** a settling **2** a colonizing of new land **3** colony **4** village **5** an agreement **6** payment

set′-to′ *n.*, *pl.* **-tos′** [Col.] fight or argument

set′up′ *n.* details or makeup of organization, equipment, plan, etc.

sev′en a., n. one more than six —**sev′enth** a., n.

sev′en·teen′ a., n. seven more than ten —**sev′en·teenth′** a., n.

sev′en·ty a.; n., pl. **-ties** seven times ten —**sev′en·ti·eth** a., n.

sev′er v. cut off; separate —**sev′er·ance** n.

sev′er·al a. 1 more than two but not many 2 separate —n. several persons or things —**sev′er·al·ly** adv.

se·vere′ a. 1 harsh; strict 2 grave 3 very plain 4 intense —**se·vere′ly** adv. —**sever′i·ty** n.

sew (sō) v. **sewed**, **sewn** or **sewed**, **sew′ing** fasten, make, etc. by means of needle and thread —**sew′er** n. —**sew′ing** n.

sew′age (sōō′-) n. waste matter carried off by sewers

sew′er n. underground drain for water and waste matter

sex n. 1 either of the two divisions of organisms, male or female 2 character of being male or female 3 attraction between the sexes 4 sexual intercourse —**sex′u·al** a. —**sex′u·al·ly** adv.

sex′ism′ n. unfair treatment of one sex by the other, esp. of women by men —**sex′ist** a.

sex′tant n. ship's instrument for navigation

sex′ton n. official who maintains church property

sex′y a. **-i·er**, **-i·est** [Col.] exciting sexual desire

shab′by a. **-bi·er**, **-bi·est** 1 worn out 2 clothed poorly 3 mean —**shab′bi·ly** adv. —**shab′bi·ness** n.

shack n. shanty

shack′le n. metal fastening for a prisoner's wrist or ankle —v. 1 put shackles on 2 restrain

shad n. saltwater fish

shade n. 1 partial darkness caused by cutting off light rays 2 device to cut off light 3 degree of darkness of a color 4 small difference —v. 1 to screen from light 2 change slightly 3 represent shade in (a painting, etc.) —**shad′y** a., **-i·er**, **-i·est**

shad′ing n. 1 a shielding against light 2 slight variation

shad′ow n. 1 shade cast by a body blocking light rays 2 sadness 3 small amount —v. follow in secret —**shad′ow·y** a.

shad′ow·box′ v. spar with imaginary boxing opponent

shaft n. 1 arrow or spear, or its stem 2 long, slender part or thing 3 vertical opening 4 bar that transmits motion to a mechanical part

shag n. long nap on cloth

shag′gy a. **-gi·er**, **-gi·est** 1 having long, coarse hair 2 unkempt

shah (shä) n. title of former rulers of Iran

shake v. **shook**, **shak′en**, **shak′ing** 1 move quickly up and down, back and forth, etc. 2 tremble 3 weaken, disturb, upset, etc. 4 clasp (another's hand), as in greeting —n. a shaking —**shake off** get rid of —**shake up** 1 mix by shaking 2 jar 3 reorganize —**shak′y** a., **-i·er**, **-i·est**

shake′down′ n. [Sl.] extortion of money

shak′er n. 1 device used in shaking 2 [S-] member of celibate religious sect

shake′-up′ n. extensive reorganization

shak′o (shak′-) n., pl. **-os** high, stiff military dress hat

shale n. rock of hard clay

shall v. pt. **should** auxiliary verb showing: 1 future time 2 determination or obligation

shal·lot′ n. onionlike plant

shal′low a. not deep —n. shoal

shalt v. [Ar.] shall: used with *thou*

sham n., a. (something) false or fake —v. **shammed**, **sham′ming** pretend

sham′ble v. walk clumsily —n. pl. scene of great destruction

shame n. 1 guilt, embarrassment, etc. felt for a wrong act 2 dishonor 3 a misfortune —v. 1 make ashamed 2 dishonor 3 force by a sense of shame —**shame′ful** a.

shame′faced′ a. 1 bashful 2 ashamed

shame′less a. showing no shame or modesty

sham·poo′ v. wash (the hair, etc.) —n. a shampooing, or soap, etc. used for this

sham′rock′ n. cloverlike plant with three leaflets

shang·hai′ (-hī′) v. **-haied′**, **-hai′ing** to kidnap for service aboard ship

shank n. the leg, esp. between the knee and ankle

shan't shall not

shan′tung′ n. silk fabric

shan′ty n., pl. **-ties** small, shabby dwelling

shape n. 1 outer form 2 definite form 3 [Col.] condition —v. form or adapt —**shape up** [Col.] 1 come to definite form 2 behave as one should —**take shape** become definite —**shape′less** a.

shape′ly a. **-li·er**, **-li·est** well-shaped

shard n. broken piece

share n. 1 part each gets or has 2 equal part of stock in a corporation —v. 1 give in shares 2 have a share (*in*) 3 use in common with

share′crop′ v. **-cropped′**, **-crop′ping** work (land) for a share of the crop —**share′crop′per** n.

share′hold′er n. an owner of share(s) of corporation stock

shark n. a large, fierce fish

shark′skin′ n. smooth, silky cloth

sharp a. 1 having a fine point or cutting edge 2 abrupt 3 distinct 4 clever or shrewd 5 vigilant 6 harsh or intense 7 Mus. above the true pitch —n. Mus. a note one half step above another: symbol (♯) —adv. 1 in a sharp way 2 precisely —**sharp'en** v. —**sharp'en·er** n. —**sharp'ly** adv. —**sharp'ness** n.

sharp'er n. swindler; cheat

sharp'-eyed a. having keen sight or perception

sharp'shoot·er n. good marksman

sharp'-tongued a. sarcastic; highly critical

sharp'-wit·ted a. thinking quickly

shat'ter v. 1 break into pieces 2 damage badly —**shat'ter·proof** a.

shave v. shaved, shaved or shav'en, shav'ing 1 cut thin slices from 2 cut the hair or beard (of) to the skin —n. act of shaving —**close shave** [Col.] narrow escape —**shav'er** n.

shav'ing n. 1 act of one who shaves 2 thin piece shaved off

shawl n. cloth covering for the head and shoulders

shay n. [Dial.] light carriage

she pron. the female mentioned

sheaf n., pl. **sheaves** bundle of stalks, papers, etc.

shear v. sheared, sheared or shorn, shear'ing 1 cut or cut off as with shears 2 clip hair from —n.pl. large scissors

sheath (shēth) n. 1 case for a knife blade, etc. 2 any covering like this

sheathe (shēth) v. put into or cover with a sheath

she-bang' n. [Col.] affair, thing, contrivance, etc.

shed n. small shelter or storage place —v. shed, shed'ding 1 make flow 2 radiate 3 throw or cast off

she'd 1 she had 2 she would

sheen n. luster; gloss

sheep n., pl. **sheep** cud-chewing animal with heavy wool —**sheep'skin'** n.

sheep'ish a. bashful or embarrassed

sheer v. to swerve —a. 1 very thin 2 absolute 3 very steep —adv. completely

sheet n. 1 large cloth of cotton, etc. used on beds 2 piece of paper 3 broad, thin piece of glass, etc. 4 rope to control a sail

sheet'ing n. cloth material for sheets

sheik, sheikh (shēk, shāk) n. Arab chief

shek'el n. ancient Hebrew coin

shelf n., pl. **shelves** 1 thin, flat board for holding things 2 ledge or reef

shell n. 1 hard outer covering, as of an egg 2 narrow rowboat for racing 3 missile from a large gun 4 cartridge —v. 1 remove the shell from 2 bombard

she'll 1 she will 2 she shall

shel·lac', **shel·lack'** n. thin varnish of resin and alcohol —v. -lacked', -lack'ing 1 put shellac on 2 [Sl.] to beat

shell'fish' n. aquatic animal with a shell

shel'ter n. something that covers or protects —v. give shelter to

shelve v. 1 put on a shelf 2 lay aside

shelv'ing n. 1 material for shelves 2 shelves

she·nan'i·gans n.pl. [Col.] mischief; trickery

shep'herd (-ərd) n. 1 one who herds sheep 2 religious leader —v. be a shepherd —**shep'herd·ess** n.fem.

sher'bet n. frozen dessert of fruit juice, milk, etc.

sher'iff n. chief law officer of a county

sher'ry n., pl. **-ries** a strong wine

she's 1 she is 2 she has

shib'bo·leth' n. password

shield n. 1 armor carried on the arm 2 thing that protects —v. protect

shift v. 1 move or change from one person, place, direction, etc. to another 2 get along —n. 1 a shifting 2 time at work 3 trick

shift'less a. lazy

shift'y a. -i·er, -i·est tricky; evasive

shill n. [Sl.] one who pretends to buy, bet, etc. to lure others

shil·le·lagh (shi lā'lē) n. Irish cudgel

shil'ling n. former British coin, 1/20 of a pound

shil'ly-shal'ly v. -lied, -ly·ing hesitate

shim n. wedge for filling space

shim'mer v., n. (shine with) a wavering light

shim'my n., v. -mied, -my·ing shake or wobble

shin n. front of the leg between knee and ankle —v. shinned, shin'ning climb, as a rope, with hands and legs: also **shin'ny**, -nied, -ny·ing

shin'bone' n. tibia

shin'dig n. [Col.] informal party, dance, etc.

shine v. shone or (esp. for v. 3) shined, shin'ing 1 be or make be bright 2 excel 3 make shiny by polishing —n. 1 brightness 2 polish

shin'gle n. 1 piece of wood, slate, etc. for roofing 2 [Col.] small signboard —v. put shingles on (a roof)

shin'gles n. virus skin disease along a nerve

shin'guard' n. padded guard for the shin, worn in sports

shin'splints' n. muscle strain of lower leg

shin'y a. -i·er, -i·est bright; shining

ship n. 1 large water craft 2 aircraft —v. shipped, ship'ping 1 put or go in a ship 2 transport —**on shipboard** on a ship —**ship'**

load′ n. —**ship**′**ment** n. —**ship**′**per** n.

-ship suf. **1** state of **2** rank of **3** skill as

ship′**mate**′ n. fellow sailor

ship′**shape**′ a. neat; trim

ship′**wreck**′ v., n. (cause) loss or ruin of a ship

ship′**yard**′ n. place where ships are built and repaired

shire n. county in England

shirk v. to neglect (a duty) —**shirk**′**er** n.

shirr v. **1** pull stitches tight in rows **2** bake (eggs) with crumbs

shirt n. **1** upper garment for men **2** undershirt

shirt′**waist**′ n. woman's blouse tailored like a shirt

shish kebab n. dish of small chunks of meat and vegetables broiled on a skewer

shiv′**er** v. **1** shake or tremble **2** shatter —n. **1** a trembling **2** sliver

shoal n. **1** school of fish **2** shallow place in water

shock n. **1** sudden blow or jar **2** sudden emotional upset **3** effect of electric current on the body **4** bundle of grain **5** thick mass of hair —v. **1** astonish; horrify **2** give an electric shock to

shock′**proof**′ a. able to stand shock without damage

shod′**dy** a. —**di-er, –di-est** inferior —**shod**′**di-ness** n.

shoe n. **1** outer covering for the foot **2** horseshoe **3** part of a brake that presses on the wheel —v. **shod, shoe**′**ing** put shoes on

shoe′**horn**′ n. device to help slip a shoe on the foot

shoe′**lace**′ n. LACE (n. 1)

shoe′**string**′ n. **1** shoelace **2** small amount of capital

shoe tree n. form put in a shoe to hold its shape

sho′**gun**′ n. hereditary governor of Japan: absolute rulers until 1867

shone v. pt. & pp. of SHINE

shoo int. go away! —v. drive away abruptly

shoo′**-in**′ n. [Col.] one expected to win easily

shook v. pt. of SHAKE

shoot v. **shot, shoot**′**ing 1** send out, or move, with force, speed, etc. **2** send a bullet, etc. from **3** wound or kill with a bullet, etc. **4** to photograph **5** to score (a point, etc.) in sports **6** grow rapidly **7** to mark in spots, etc. (with color) —n. new growth; sprout —**shoot**′**er** n.

shop n. **1** place where things are sold **2** manufacturing place —v. **shopped, shop**′**ping** look at or buy goods in shops —**shop**′**per** n.

shop′**lift**′**er** n. one who steals from a store

during shopping hours —**shop**′**lift** v.

shopping center n. complex of stores with common parking area

shop′**talk**′ n. **1** specialized words for certain work **2** talk about work after hours

shore n. **1** land next to water **2** prop; support —v. prop (up)

short a. **1** not measuring much **2** not tall **3** brief **4** brusque **5** less than enough —n. **1** short movie **2** pl. short pants **3** short circuit —adv. abruptly or briefly —v. short-circuit —**in short** briefly —**short**′**en** v. —**short**′**ness** n.

short′**age** n. **1** lack; deficiency **2** deficit

short′**cake**′ n. light biscuit or sweet cake

short′**change**′ v. [Col.] give less change than is due

short circuit n. side circuit of low resistance that deflects electric current —**short**′**-cir**′**cuit** v.

short′**com**′**ing** n. defect

short′**cut**′ n. **1** shorter route **2** way of saving time, etc.

short′**en-ing** n. fat used to make baked goods flaky

short′**hand**′ n. system of symbols for writing fast

short′**-hand**′**ed** a. short of workers or helpers

short′**horn**′ n. kind of cattle with short, curved horns

short′**-lived**′ (-līvd′, -livd′) a. lasting only a short time

short′**ly** adv. **1** briefly **2** soon **3** curtly

short shrift n. little attention

short′**sight**′**ed** a. lacking in foresight

short′**stop**′ n. Baseball infielder between second and third basemen

short subject n. short movie

short′**-tem**′**pered** a. easily angered

short′**-term**′ a. for a short time

short′**wave**′ n. radio wave 60 meters or less in length

short′**-wind**′**ed** (-win′dəd) a. easily put out of breath

shot v. pt. & pp. of SHOOT —n. **1** act of shooting **2** range; scope **3** attempt **4** throw, etc., as of a ball **5** projectile(s) for a gun **6** marksman **7** photograph **8** dose or drink —a. worn out —**shot**′**gun**′ n.

shot put n. track event in which a heavy metal ball is thrown

should v. pt. of SHALL: should is used to express obligation, probability, etc.

shoul′**der** n. **1** part of the body to which an arm or foreleg is connected **2** edge of a road —v. **1** push with the shoulder **2** assume the burden of

shout v., n. (utter) a loud, sudden cry or call

shove v. **1** push along a surface **2** push

roughly —n. a push

shov'el n. tool with a broad scoop and a handle —v. move or dig with a shovel —**shov'el·ful'** n., pl. **-fuls**

show v. **showed, shown** or **showed, show'ing** 1 bring into sight; reveal 2 appear 3 be noticeable 4 guide 5 point out 6 prove; explain —n. 1 a display, performance, etc. 2 pompous display 3 pretense —**show off** make a display of —**show up** 1 expose 2 arrive —**show'case'** n. —**show'room'** n.

show'boat' n. boat with theater and actors who play river towns

show'down' n. [Col.] disclosure of facts to force a settlement

show'er n. 1 brief fall of rain 2 any sudden fall or flow 3 party with gifts for a bride, etc. 4 bath of fine water spray —v. 1 to spray with water 2 give, or fall, abundantly 3 bathe under a shower —**show'er·y** a.

show'man n., pl. **-men** one who produces shows skillfully —**show'man·ship** n.

show'piece' n. a fine example

show'y a. **-i·er, -i·est** 1 of striking appearance 2 gaudy; flashy —**show'i·ly** adv. —**show'i·ness** n.

shrap'nel n. fragments of an exploded artillery shell

shred n. 1 torn strip 2 fragment —v. **shred'ded** or **shred, shred'ding** cut or tear into shreds

shrew n. 1 small, mouselike mammal 2 nagging woman —**shrew'ish** a.

shrewd a. clever or sharp in practical affairs —**shrewd'ly** adv. —**shrewd'ness** n.

shriek (shrēk) v., n. (utter) a loud, piercing cry

shrike n. shrill-voiced bird of prey

shrill a. high-pitched and piercing in sound —**shrill'ness** n. —**shril'ly** adv.

shrimp n. 1 small, long-tailed, edible shellfish 2 [Col.] small person

shrine n. saint's tomb or other sacred place

shrink v. **shrank** or **shrunk, shrunk** or **shrunk'en, shrink'ing** 1 lessen in size; contract 2 draw back —**shrink'age** n.

shriv'el v. dry up; wither

shroud n. 1 cloth used to wrap a corpse 2 cover; veil 3 pl. ropes supporting ship's masts —v. 1 hide; cover

shrub n. bush —**shrub'ber·y** n.

shrug v., n. **shrugged, shrug'ging** (draw up the shoulders in) a gesture of doubt, indifference, etc.

shtick n. [Sl.] 1 comic act 2 attention-getting device

shuck v., n. husk; shell

shud'der v. shake, as in horror —n. a shuddering

shuf'fle v. 1 walk with feet dragging 2 mix or jumble together —n. a shuffling

shuf'fle·board' n. game in which disks are pushed toward numbered squares

shun v. **shunned, shun'ning** keep away from

shunt v. 1 move to one side 2 switch or shift

shush int. be quiet! —v. say "shush" to

shut v. **shut, shut'ting** 1 close (a door, etc.) 2 prevent entrance to —a. closed —**shut down** cease operating —**shut off** prevent passage of or on —**shut out** prevent scoring —**shut up** 1 enclose 2 [Col.] stop talking

shut'-eye' n. [Sl.] sleep

shut'-in' a. confined indoors by illness —n. invalid

shut'out' n. game in which a team is kept from scoring

shut'ter n. 1 movable window cover 2 light-controlling device on a camera lens

shut'tle n. device to carry thread back and forth in weaving —v. move rapidly to and fro

shut'tle·cock' n. feathered cork ball in badminton

shy a. **shy'er** or **shi'er, shy'est** or **shi'est** 1 timid 2 bashful 3 distrustful 4 [Sl.] lacking —v. **shied, shy'ing** 1 be startled 2 hesitate 3 fling sideways —**shy'ly** adv. —**shy'ness** n.

shy'ster (shī'-) n. [Sl.] dishonest lawyer

Si'a·mese' twins n. pair of twins born joined

sib'i·lant a., n. hissing (sound) —**sib'i·lance** n.

sib'ling n. a brother or sister

sib'yl (-al) n. prophetess of ancient Greece or Rome

sic v. **sicked, sick'ing** to urge to attack

sick a. 1 having disease; ill 2 nauseated 3 of or for sick people 4 disgusted 5 [Col.] morbid —v. **sic** —**the sick** sick people —**sick'ness** n.

sick bay n. ship's hospital

sick'bed' n. sick person's bed

sick'en v. make or become sick —**sick'en·ing** a.

sick'le n. curved blade with a short handle, for cutting tall grass

sick'ly a. **-li·er, -li·est** 1 in poor health 2 faint or weak

side n. 1 right or left half 2 a bounding line 3 a surface 4 aspect 5 relative position 6 party; faction —a. 1 of, at, or to a side 2 secondary —**side with** support —**take sides** support one faction

side'arm' a., adv. with the arm from the side, below the shoulder

side arms n.pl. weapons worn at the side

side'board' n. dining-room cabinet for linen, etc.

side′burns *n.pl.* hair on the cheeks, beside the ears

side dish *n.* separate dish along with the main course of food

side′kick′ *n.* [Sl.] 1 close friend 2 partner

side′light′ *n.* bit of incidental information

side′line′ *n.* secondary line of merchandise, work, etc. —*v.* remove from active participation —**on the sidelines** not actively participating

side′long′ *adv., a.* toward or to the side

si·de′re·al (-dir′ē-) *a.* of or measured by the stars

side′show′ *n.* small show connected to main show

side′split′ting *a.* very hearty or very funny

side′step′ *v.* avoid as by stepping aside

side′swipe′ *v.* hit along the side in passing —*n.* such a hit

side′track′ *v.* turn aside from a course, subject, etc.

side′walk′ *n.* path for pedestrians alongside a street

side′wall′ *n.* side of a tire

side′ways′ *a., adv.* 1 to or from one side 2 side first Also **side′wise′**

sid′ing (sīd′-) *n.* 1 outside boards, etc. on a building 2 short railroad track off the main track

si′dle *v.* move sideways cautiously

siege (sēj) *n.* 1 encircling of a place to effect its capture 2 persistent attack

si·es′ta (sē-) *n.* brief rest or nap, esp. in the afternoon

sieve (siv) *n.* strainer with many small holes

sift *v.* 1 pass through a sieve, as to separate 2 examine with care, as evidence

sigh (sī) *v.* 1 let out a deep breath, as in sorrow 2 long (*for*) —*n.* a sighing

sight *n.* 1 something seen 2 act or power of seeing 3 range of vision 4 aiming device —*v.* 1 to see 2 aim (a gun, etc.) —**at** (or **on**) **sight** as soon as seen —**sight′less** *a.*

sight′ed *a.* not blind

sight′ly *a.* **–li·er, –li·est** pleasing to look at

sight′see′ing *n.* visiting of places of interest

sign (sīn) *n.* 1 mark or symbol 2 meaningful gesture 3 signboard, road marker, etc. 4 trace; vestige —*v.* write one's name (on) —**sign off** stop broadcasting —**sign′er** *n.*

sig′nal *n.* 1 gesture, device, etc. to warn, order, etc. 2 radio wave —*a.* notable —*v.* make signals (to)

sig′nal·ize′ *v.* 1 make noteworthy 2 point out

sig′nal·ly *adv.* notably

sig′na·to′ry *n., pl.* **–ries** nation signing a pact, etc.

sig′na·ture *n.* one's name written by oneself

sign′board′ *n.* board bearing advertising

sig′net *n.* small official seal

sig·nif′i·cance *n.* 1 meaning 2 importance —**sig·nif′i·cant** *a.*

sig·ni·fy′ *v.* **–fied′, –fy′ing** 1 to mean 2 make known, as by a sign —**sig′ni·fi·ca′tion** *n.*

si′lage *n.* green fodder preserved in a silo

si′lence *n.* absence of sound —*v.* 1 make silent 2 repress —*int.* be silent!

si′lent *a.* 1 not speaking 2 still; quiet 3 inactive —**si′lent·ly** *adv.*

sil′hou·ette′ (-ōō-) *v., n.* (make) a dark shape against a light background

sil′i·ca *n.* glassy mineral found as sand, etc.

sil′i·con′ *n.* chemical element forming silica, etc.

sil′i·cone′ *n.* silicon compound resistant to water, etc.

sil′i·co′sis *n.* chronic lung disease from inhaling silica dust

silk *n.* thread or fabric of soft fiber made by silkworms —**silk′en** *a.* —**silk′y,** -i-er, -i-est

silk′worm′ *n.* moth caterpillar that spins silk fiber

sill *n.* bottom of a door frame or window frame

sil′ly *a.* **–li·er, –li·est** foolish; absurd —**sil′li·ness** *n.*

si′lo *n., pl.* **–los** tower for storing green fodder

silt *n.* fine particles of soil floating or left by water —*v.* fill with silt

sil′ver *n.* 1 white, precious metal, a chemical element 2 silver coins 3 silverware 4 grayish white —*a.* of silver —*v.* cover as with silver —**sil′ver·y** *a.*

sil′ver·fish′ *n.* wingless insect found in damp places

silver lining *n.* hope or comfort in the midst of despair

sil′ver·smith′ *n.* one who makes things of silver

sil′ver-tongued′ *a.* eloquent

sil′ver·ware′ *n.* tableware of or plated with silver

sim′i·an *n.* ape or monkey

sim′i·lar *a.* nearly alike —**sim′i·lar′i·ty** *n., pl.* **–ties** —**sim′i·lar·ly** *adv.*

sim′i·le′ (-lē′) *n.* a likening of dissimilar things

si·mil′i·tude′ *n.* likeness

sim′mer *v., n.* (keep at or near) a gentle boiling

si′mon-pure′ *a.* genuine

si′mo·ny (or sim′ə-) *n.* buying or selling of sacred things

sim·pa′ti·co (-pä′-) *a.* compatible or congenial

sim′per *v.* smile in a silly way —*n.* silly smile

sim′ple a. 1 having only one or a few parts 2 easy to do or understand 3 plain 4 natural 5 common 6 foolish —**sim·plic′i·ty** n., pl. —**ties**

simple interest n. interest computed on principal alone

sim′ple-mind′ed a. 1 naive 2 foolish 3 mentally retarded

sim′ple·ton n. fool

sim′pli·fy′ v. -**fied′**, -**fy′ing** make easier —**sim′pli·fi·ca′tion** n.

sim·plis′tic a. oversimplifying or oversimplified

sim′ply adv. 1 in a simple way 2 merely 3 completely

sim′u·late′ v. pretend —**sim′u·la′tion** n.

si′mul·ta′ne·ous a. done, etc. at the same time —**si′mul·ta′ne·ous·ly** adv.

sin n. breaking of religious or moral law —v. **sinned**, **sin′ning** commit a sin —**sin′ful** a. —**sin′ner** n.

since adv., prep. 1 from then until now 2 at some time between then and now —con. 1 after the time that 2 because

sin·cere′ a. 1 without deceit 2 genuine —**sin·cere′ly** adv. —**sin·cer′i·ty** n.

si′ne·cure′ n. well-paid job with little work

sin′ew (-yo̅o̅) n. 1 tendon 2 strength —**sin′ew·y** a.

sing v. **sang**, **sung**, **sing′ing** 1 make musical sounds with the voice, etc. 2 perform by singing 3 hum, buzz, etc. 4 tell in song —n. [Col.] group singing —**sing′er** n.

singe v. **singed**, **singe′ing** burn superficially —n. a singeing

sin′gle a. 1 one only 2 of or for one person or family 3 unmarried —v. select from others: with out —n. 1 single person or thing 2 pl. tennis game with only two players 3 Baseball hit on which the batter reaches first base —**sin′gle·ness** n.

single file n. column of persons one behind the other

sin′gle-hand′ed a. without help

sin′gle-mind′ed a. with only one purpose

sin′gly adv. 1 alone 2 one by one

sing′song′ a., n. (having) a monotonous cadence

sin′gu·lar a. 1 unique 2 separate 3 exceptional 4 unusual —n. Gram. word form designating only one —**sin′gu·lar′i·ty** n. —**sin′gu·lar·ly** adv.

sin′is·ter a. 1 threatening 2 wicked or evil

sink v. **sank** or **sunk**, **sunk**, **sink′ing** 1 go or put beneath the surface of water, etc. 2 go down slowly 3 become lower 4 pass gradually (into sleep, etc.) 5 invest 6 defeat —n. basin with a drain pipe —**sink in** [Col.] be understood fully

sink′er n. lead weight used on a fishing line

sinking fund n. fund built up to pay off a debt

sin′u·ous a. 1 bending or winding in and out 2 crooked

si′nus n., pl. -**nus·es** any air cavity in the skull opening into the nasal cavities

si′nus·i′tis n. inflammation of the sinuses

sip v. **sipped**, **sip′ping** drink a little at a time —n. a small amount sipped

si′phon n. tube for carrying liquid from one container to another below it —v. drain through a siphon

sir n. 1 polite title for a man 2 [S—] title for a knight or baronet

sire n. male parent —v. be the male parent of

si′ren n. 1 warning device with a wailing sound 2 a seductive woman

sir′loin′ n. choice cut of beef from the loin

si·roc′co n., pl. -**cos** hot wind blowing from N Africa into S Europe

sir′up n. syrup —**sir′up·y** a.

sis n. [Col.] sister

si′sal n. strong rope fiber

sis′sy n., pl. -**sies** [Col.] unmanly boy or man —**sis′si·fied′** a.

sis′ter n. 1 female related to one by having the same parents 2 female fellow member 3 nun —**sis′ter·hood′** n. —**sis′ter·ly** a.

sis′ter-in-law′ n., pl. **sis′ters-in-law′** 1 sister of one's spouse 2 brother's wife

sit v. **sat**, **sit′ting** 1 rest on one's buttocks or haunches 2 perch 3 be in session 4 pose, as for a portrait 5 be located 6 baby-sit —**sit down** take a seat —**sit in** take part —**sit out** take no part in —**sit′ter** n.

si·tar′ n. lutelike instrument of India

sit′-down′ n. strike, demonstration, etc. in which participants refuse to leave

site n. location; scene

sit′-in′ n. strike or demonstration in which participants refuse to work or leave

sit′ting n. 1 session, as of court 2 time of being seated

sitting duck [Col.] easy target; one easily attacked

sit′u·ate′ (sich′o̅o̅-) v. put or place; locate

sit′u·a′tion n. 1 location 2 condition 3 job

six a., n. one more than five —**sixth** a., n.

six′teen′ a., n. six more than ten —**six′teenth′** a., n.

sixth sense n. intuitive power

six′ty a., n., pl. -**ties** six times ten —**six′ti·eth** a., n.

siz′a·ble, **size′a·ble** a. fairly large

size n. 1 dimensions 2 any of a series of measures, often numbered 3 pasty glaze: also **siz′ing** —v. 1 arrange by SIZE (n. 2) 2 apply SIZE (n. 3) —**size up** [Col.] 1 to estimate 2 meet requirements

siz′zle v. to hiss when hot —n. such a sound

skate n. 1 ice skate 2 roller skate —v. glide or roll on skates

skeet n. trapshooting from different angles

skein (skān) n. coil of yarn or thread

skel′e·ton n. framework, as of the bones of a body —**skel′e·tal** a.

skep′tic n. one who questions matters generally accepted —**skep′ti·cal** a. —**skep′ti·cism′** n.

sketch n. 1 rough drawing or design 2 outline —v. make a sketch (of) —**sketch′y** a., -i·er, -i·est

skew (skyō) v., n. slant

skew′er n. long pin to hold meat together as it cooks

ski (skē) n., pl. **skis** long, flat runner fastened to the shoe for snow travel —v. travel on skis —**ski′er** n.

skid n. 1 plank, log, etc. on which to support or slide something heavy 2 act of skidding —v. **skid′ded, skid′ding** slide sideways

skid′dy a. -di·er, -di·est having a slippery surface

skid row n. city area where vagrants gather

skiff n. small sailboat

skill n. 1 great ability 2 art or craft involving use of the hands or body —**skilled** a. —**skill′ful, skil′ful** a.

skil′let n. frying pan

skim v. **skimmed, skim′ming** 1 take floating matter from a liquid 2 read quickly 3 glide lightly

skim milk n. milk with the cream removed

skimp v. [Col.] scrimp

skimp′y a. -i·er, -i·est [Col.] barely enough; scanty

skin n. 1 tissue covering the body 2 pelt 3 covering like skin, as fruit rind —v. **skinned, skin′ning** remove the skin from

skin diving n. underwater swimming with special equipment —**skin′-dive′** v.

skin′flint′ n. miser

skin′ny a. -ni·er, -ni·est very thin —**skin′ni·ness** n.

skin′ny-dip′ v. **-dipped′, -dip′ping** [Col.] swim in the nude

skip v. **skipped, skip′ping** 1 move by hopping on alternate feet 2 leap lightly (over) 3 bounce 4 omit —n. act of skipping

skip′per n. ship's captain

skir′mish v., n. (take part in) a small, brief battle

skirt n. 1 part of a dress, coat, etc. below the waist 2 woman's garment that hangs from the waist —v. go along the edge of

skit n. short, funny play

skit′tish a. 1 lively; playful 2 very nervous

skiv′vies n.pl. [Sl.] men's underwear

skul·dug′ger·y n. [Col.] mean trickery

skulk v. to move or lurk in a stealthy way

skull n. bony framework of the head

skunk n. small mammal that ejects a smelly liquid

sky n., pl. **skies** often pl. upper atmosphere or space around the earth

sky′cap′ n. porter at an air terminal

sky diving n. parachute jumping

sky′lark′ n. lark of Europe and Asia, famous for its song

sky′light′ n. window in a roof or ceiling

sky′line′ n. outline of a city, etc. seen against the sky

sky′rock′et n. fireworks rocket —v. rise fast

sky′scrap′er n. very tall building

sky′ward a., adv. toward the sky: also **sky′wards** adv.

slab n. flat, thick piece

slack a. 1 loose 2 not busy 3 slow; sluggish —n. slack part or time —**slack off** (or **up**) slacken

slack′en v. 1 slow down 2 loosen

slack′er n. one who shirks

slacks n.pl. trousers

slag n. smelting refuse

slain v. pp. of SLAY

slake v. 1 satisfy (thirst) 2 mix (lime) with water

sla′lom n. downhill ski race over a zig-zag course

slam v. **slammed, slam′ming** shut, hit, etc. with force —n. heavy impact

slan′der n. spoken falsehood harmful to another —v. speak slander against —**slan′der·ous** a.

slang n. vigorous, short-lived, informal language

slant v., n. 1 incline; slope 2 (show) a special attitude

slap n. a blow with something flat —v. **slapped, slap′ping** strike with a slap

slap′dash′ a., adv. hurried(ly) or careless(ly)

slap′-hap′py a. [Sl.] 1 dazed 2 silly or giddy

slap′stick′ n. crude comedy

slash v. 1 cut at with a knife 2 cut slits in 3 reduce —n. a slashing; cut

slat n. narrow strip

slate n. 1 bluish-gray rock in thin layers 2 tile, etc. of slate 3 list of candidates —v. designate

slat′tern n. untidy woman —**slat′tern·ly** a., adv.

slaugh′ter v. 1 kill (animals) for food 2 kill (people) brutally —n. a slaughtering

slaugh′ter·house′ n. place for butchering animals

slave n. human being owned by another —v. to toil —**slav′ish** a.

slave driver n. merciless taskmaster

slav′er (slav′-) v. drool

slav′er·y n. 1 condition of slaves 2 ownership of slaves 3 drudgery

Slav′ic (släv′-) a. of the Russians, Poles, Slovaks, etc.

slaw n. coleslaw

slay v. **slew, slain, slay′ing** kill by violent means —**slay′er** n.

sleaze n. [Sl.] 1 sleaziness 2 something or someone sleazy

slea′zy a. **-zi·er, -zi·est** 1 flimsy; thin 2 morally low, shabby, shoddy, etc. —**slea′zi·ness** n.

sled n. vehicle with runners, for snow —v. **sled′ded, sled′ding** ride a sled

sledge n. 1 long, heavy hammer 2 heavy sled

sleek a. 1 glossy 2 well-groomed —v. make sleek

sleep n. natural regular rest, as at night —v. **slept, sleep′ing** to be in a state of sleep —**sleep′less** a.

sleep′er n. 1 one who sleeps 2 railway car with berths

sleeping bag n. warmly lined bag for sleeping in outdoors

sleep′y a. **-i·er, -i·est** 1 drowsy 2 dull; quiet

sleet n. partly frozen rain —v. to shower as sleet

sleeve n. 1 part of a garment covering the arm 2 protective cover —**sleeve′less** a.

sleigh (slā) n. vehicle on runners for travel on snow

sleight of hand (slīt) n. 1 skill in doing tricks with the hands 2 such tricks

slen′der a. 1 long and thin 2 small in size or force

slen′der·ize′ v. make or become slender

slept v. pt. & pp. of SLEEP

sleuth (slooth) n. [Col.] detective

slew v. pt. of SLAY —n. [Col.] large number or amount

slice n. 1 thin, broad piece cut off 2 share —v. cut into slices or as a slice —**slic′er** n.

slick v. make smooth —a. 1 smooth 2 slippery 3 clever —n. smooth area, as of oil on water

slick′er n. loose, waterproof coat

slide v. **slid, slid′ing** 1 move along a smooth surface 2 glide 3 slip —n. 1 a sliding 2 inclined surface to slide on 3 picture for projection on a screen —**let slide** fail to take proper action

slide fastener n. fastener with interlocking tabs worked by a sliding part

slid′er n. Baseball fast pitch that curves sharply

slide rule n. device for calculating that looks like a ruler

sliding scale n. schedule of costs, etc. that varies with given conditions

slight a. 1 slender 2 unimportant 3 small or weak —v., n. neglect or snub —**slight′ly** adv.

slim a. **slim′mer, slim′mest** 1 long and thin 2 small —v. **slimmed, slim′ming** make or become slim

slime n. soft, wet, sticky matter —**slim′y** a., **-i·er, -i·est**

sling n. 1 device for hurling stones 2 band or looped cloth for raising or supporting —v. **slung, sling′ing** hurl as with a sling

sling′shot′ n. Y-shaped piece with elastic band for shooting stones, etc.

slink v. **slunk, slink′ing** move in a sneaking way

slink′y a. **-i·er, -i·est** [Sl.] sinuous and graceful in movement, line, etc.

slip v. **slipped, slip′ping** 1 go quietly 2 put or pass smoothly or quickly 3 slide accidentally 4 escape from 5 become worse —n. 1 dock for ships 2 woman's undergarment 3 a falling down 4 error: also [Col.] —**slip′-up′** 5 plant stem or root, for planting, etc. 6 small piece of paper

slip′knot′ n. knot that can slip along a rope

slip′page (-ij) n. a slipping

slipped disk n. ruptured disk between vertebrae

slip′per n. light, low shoe

slip′per·y a. **-i·er, -i·est** 1 that can cause slipping 2 tending to slip 3 tricky

slip′shod′ a. careless

slit v. **slit, slit′ting** cut or split open —n. a straight, narrow opening

slith′er (slith′-) v. slide or glide along

sliv′er n. thin, pointed piece cut or split off

slob n. [Col.] sloppy or coarse person

slob′ber v., n. drool

sloe n. dark-blue fruit

slog v. **slogged, slog′ging** plod

slo′gan n. motto or phrase, as for advertising purposes

sloop n. boat with one mast

slop n. 1 spilled liquid 2 slush 3 watery food 4 often pl. liquid waste —v. **slopped, slop′ping** splash

slope n. 1 rising or falling surface, line, etc. 2 amount of this —v. have a slope

slop′py a. **-pi·er, -pi·est** 1 slushy 2 careless

slosh v. to splash

slot n. narrow opening

sloth (slôth, slōth) n. 1 laziness 2 South American mammal living in trees —**sloth′ful** a.

slouch n. 1 a lazy person 2 drooping posture —v. have a drooping posture

slough (sluf; n.: sloo) v. to shed; discard —n. swamp

slov′en (sluv′-) n. slovenly person

slov′en·ly a. careless or untidy

slow *a.* 1 taking longer than usual 2 low in speed 3 behind the right time 4 stupid 5 sluggish —*v.* make or become slow —*adv.* in a slow way —**slow′ly** *adv.* —**slow′ness** *n.*

slow′-mo·tion *a.* of film or video showing action slowed down

slow′poke′ *n.* [Sl.] one who acts slowly

slow′-wit′ted *a.* mentally slow; dull

sludge *n.* 1 mud or mire 2 slimy waste

slue *n., v.* turn or swerve

slug *n.* 1 small mollusk 2 bullet 3 false coin —*v.* **slugged, slug′ging** [Col.] hit hard —**slug′ger** *n.*

slug′gard *n.* lazy person

slug′gish *a.* slow-moving

sluice (slōōs) *n.* water channel or gate to control it

slum *n.* populous area with very poor living conditions

slum′ber *v., n.* sleep

slump *v.* 1 fall suddenly 2 to slouch —*n.* sudden fall

slur *v.* **slurred, slur′ring** 1 pass over quickly 2 pronounce indistinctly 3 insult —*n.* 1 a slurring 2 insult

slurp [Sl.] *v.* drink or eat noisily —*n.* loud sipping or sucking sound

slush *n.* partly melted snow —**slush′y** *a.*

slut *n.* immoral woman

sly *a.* **sli′er** or **sly′er, sli′est** or **sly′est** 1 cunning; crafty 2 playfully mischievous —**on the sly** secretly —**sly′ly** *adv.*

smack *n.* 1 slight taste 2 sharp noise made by parting the lips suddenly 3 sharp slap 4 loud kiss 5 fishing boat —*v.* 1 have a trace 2 make a smack with one's lips 3 slap loudly —*adv.* directly

small *a.* 1 little in size, extent, etc. 2 trivial 3 mean; petty —*n.* small part —**small′ish** *a.*

small arms *n.* firearms of small caliber, as pistols or rifles

small′pox′ *n.* contagious disease with fever and sores

smart *v.* 1 cause or feel stinging pain 2 suffer —*a.* 1 that smarts 2 brisk; lively 3 bright; clever 4 neat 5 stylish —**smart′ly** *adv.*

smart al′eck, smart al′ec *n.* [Col.] conceited, insolent person

smart bomb *n.* [Sl.] bomb guided to a target electronically

smart′en *v.* make or become smarter

smash *v.* 1 break violently 2 crash 3 to destroy —*n.* 1 a smashing 2 wreck; collision

smash′up′ *n.* very damaging collision

smat′ter·ing *n.* a little knowledge

smear *v.* 1 make greasy, dirty, etc. 2 spread 3 slander —*n.* a smearing

smear′case′ *n.* cottage cheese

smell *v.* **smelled** or [Br.] **smelt, smell′ing** 1 catch the odor of 2 sniff 3 have an odor —*n.* 1 power to smell 2 thing smelled; odor

smell′y *a.* **-i·er, -i·est** having a bad smell

smelt *n.* small, silvery food fish —*v.* melt (ore or metal) so as to remove the impurities —**smelt′er** *n.*

smidg·en (smij′ən) *n.* [Col.] tiny amount

smile *v.* 1 to show pleasure, amusement, etc. by curving the mouth upward 2 show with a smile —*n.* act of smiling

smirch *v., n.* smear

smirk *v.* to smile in a conceited or annoyingly complacent way —*n.* such a smile

smite *v.* **smote, smit′ten, smit′ing** 1 hit or strike hard 2 affect strongly

smith *n.* one who makes or repairs metal objects

smith′er·eens′ *n.pl.* [Col.] bits; fragments

smith′y *n., pl.* **-ies** blacksmith's shop

smock *n.* loose, protective outer garment

smog *n.* fog and smoke —**smog′gy** *a.,* **-gi-er, -gi-est**

smoke *n.* vapor, as from something burning —*v.* 1 give off smoke 2 use cigarettes, a pipe, etc. 3 cure (meats, etc.) with smoke —**smoke′less** *a.* —**smok′er** *n.* —**smok′y** *a.,* **-i-er, -i-est**

smoke′stack′ *n.* tall chimney

smol′der *v.* 1 burn without flame 2 exist suppressed Br. sp. **smoul′der**

smooch *n., v.* [Sl.] kiss

smooth *a.* 1 having no roughness or bumps; even 2 with no trouble 3 ingratiating —*v.* to make smooth —*adv.* in a smooth way —**smooth′ness** *n.*

smor′gas·bord′ (-gas-) *n.* variety of tasty foods served buffet style

smoth′er (smu*th*′-) *v.* 1 suffocate 2 cover thickly

smudge *n.* 1 dirty spot 2 fire with dense smoke —*v.* to smear —**smudg′y** *a.*

smug *a.* **smug′ger, smug′gest** too self-satisfied —**smug′ly** *adv.*

smug′gle *v.* bring in or take out secretly or illegally —**smug′gler** *n.*

smut *n.* 1 dirt 2 obscene matter 3 plant disease —**smut′ty** *a.,* **-ti-er, -ti-est**

snack *n.* light meal

snaf′fle *n.* horse's bit with a joint in the middle

snag *n.* 1 sharp projection 2 tear made by this 3 hidden difficulty —*v.* **snagged, snag′ging** 1 tear on a snag 2 hinder

snail *n.* mollusk with a spiral shell

snake *n.* long, legless reptile —*v.* twist like a snake —**snak′y** *a.,* **-i-er, -i-est**

snap *v.* **snapped, snap′ping** 1 bite or grasp

suddenly 2 shout (at) 3 break suddenly 4 make a cracking sound 5 move quickly 6 take a snapshot of —*n.* 1 sharp sound 2 fastening that clicks shut 3 [Sl.] easy job —*a.* quick —**snap′per** *n.* —**snap′pish** *a.*

snap′drag′on *n.* plant with red or yellow flowers

snap′py *a.* **-pi·er, -pi·est** [Col.] 1 lively; brisk 2 stylish; smart

snap′shot′ *n.* picture taken with a hand camera

snare *n.* 1 trap for small animals 2 dangerous lure 3 string across the bottom of a drum —*v.* to trap

snarl *v.* 1 growl, baring the teeth 2 speak sharply 3 tangle —*n.* 1 a snarling 2 tangle; disorder

snatch *v.* seize; grab —*n.* 1 brief time 2 fragment

sneak *v.* move, do, etc. secretly —*n.* one who sneaks —**sneak′y** *a.*, **-i·er, -i·est**

sneak′er *n.* canvas shoe with a rubber sole

sneer *v.* show scorn —*n.* sneering look or remark

sneeze *v.* expel breath from the nose and mouth in a sudden, uncontrolled way —*n.* act of sneezing

snick′er *v., n.* (give) a silly, partly stifled laugh

snide *a.* slyly malicious

sniff *v.* inhale forcibly through the nose, as in smelling —*n.* act of sniffing

snif′fle *v., n.* sniff to check mucus flow —**the sniffles** [Col.] a head cold

snif′ter *n.* goblet with a small opening, as for brandy

snig′ger *v., n.* snicker

snip *v.* **snipped, snip′ping** cut in a quick stroke —*n.* small piece cut off

snipe *n.* wading bird —*v.* shoot at from a hidden place —**snip′er** *n.*

snip′pet *n.* small piece; bit

snip′py *a.* **-pi·er, -pi·est** [Col.] insolently curt

snitch [Sl.] *v.* inform; tattle (on) —*n.* informer; tattler

sniv′el *v.* 1 cry and sniffle 2 whine

snob *n.* one who disdains his supposed inferiors —**snob′bish** *a.* —**snob′ber·y** *n.*

snood *n.* kind of hair net

snoop [Col.] *v.* pry in a sneaky way —*n.* one who snoops: also **snoop′er**

snoot′y *a.*, **-i·er, -i·est** [Col.] snobbish

snooze *v., n.* (take) a nap

snore *v.* breathe noisily while asleep —*n.* a snoring

snor′kel *n.* **-keled, -kel·ing;** *n.* (use a) breathing tube for swimming underwater

snort *v.* force breath audibly from the nose

—*n.* a snorting

snot *n.* [Sl.] 1 nasal mucus 2 insolent young person —**snot′ty** *a.*, **-ti·er, -ti·est**

snout *n.* projecting nose and jaws of an animal

snow *n.* flakes of frozen water vapor from the sky —*v.* 1 fall as snow 2 cover with snow 3 [Sl.] deceive —**snow under** overwhelm or defeat —**snow′drift′** *n.* —**snow′fall′** *n.* —**snow′flake′** *n.* —**snow′storm′** *n.* —**snow′y** *a.*, **-i·er, -i·est**

snow′ball′ *n.* ball of packed snow —*v.* increase rapidly

snow′bound′ *a.* confined by snow

snow′drift′ *n.* pile of snow heaped up by the wind

snow′fall′ *n.* fall of snow or the amount of this

snow′flake′ *n.* single snow crystal

snow′man′ *n., pl.* **-men′** crude human figure made of packed snow

snow′mo·bile′ *n.* motor vehicle for snow travel, with runners and tractor treads

snow′plow′ *n.* machine for removing snow

snow′shoe′ *n.* racketlike footgear for walking on snow

snow′storm′ *n.* storm with a heavy snowfall

snow′suit′ *n.* child's lined garment, often with a hood

snow tire *n.* tire with a deep tread for added traction

snub *v.* **snubbed, snub′bing** 1 treat with scorn 2 stop abruptly —*n.* a slight —*a.* short and turned up, as a nose

snuff *v.* put out (a candle, etc.) —*n.* powdered tobacco —**up to snuff** [Col.] up to the usual standard

snug *a.* **snug′ger, snug′gest** 1 cozy 2 compact 3 tight in fit

snug′gle *v.* cuddle; nestle

so *adv.* 1 in such a way 2 to such a degree 3 very 4 therefore 5 more or less 6 also 7 then 8 [Col.] very much —*con.* 1 in order (that) 2 [Col.] with the result (that) —*int.* word showing surprise —**and so on** (or **forth**) and the rest

soak *v.* 1 make wet 2 stay in liquid —**soak up** absorb

soap *n.* substance that makes suds in water for washing —*v.* rub with soap —**soap′y** *a.*, **-i·er, -i·est**

soap′box′ *n.* improvised platform for public speaking

soap opera *n.* [Col.] melodramatic daytime TV serial drama

soar *v.* fly high in the air

sob *v.* **sobbed, sob′bing** weep aloud with short gasps —*n.* act of sobbing

so′ber *a.* 1 not drunk 2 serious; sedate

3 plain —v. make or become sober —**so'-bri'e·ty** n.

so'-called' a. called thus, but usually in-accurately

soc'cer n. kind of football

so'cia·ble (-sha-) a. 1 friendly; agreeable —**so'cia·bil'i·ty** n. —**so'cia·bly** adv.

so'cial a. 1 of society 2 living in groups 3 sociable 4 of social work —n. a party —**so'cial·ly** adv.

so'cial·ism' n. public ownership of the means of production —**so'cial·ist** n., a. —**so'cial·is'tic** a.

so'cial·ite n. person prominent in fashion-able society

so'cial·ize' v. 1 put under public ownership 2 take part in social affairs

social science n. field of study dealing with society

social security n. federal insurance for old age, unemployment, etc.

social work n. work of clinics, agencies, etc. to improve living conditions

so·ci'e·ty n., pl. **-ties** 1 community of people 2 all people 3 companionship 4 organized group 5 the fashionable class

so'ci·ol'o·gy (-sē-) n. study of the organi-zation, problems, etc. of society —**so'ci·o·log'i·cal** a. —**so'ci·ol'o·gist** n.

sock n. 1 short stocking 2 [Sl.] a blow —v. [Sl.] hit with force

sock'et n. hollow part into which some-thing fits

sock'eye' n. red salmon

sod n. earth surface with grass —v. **sod'ded**, **sod'ding** cover with sod

so'da n. 1 substance containing sodium 2 soda water 3 beverage of soda water and ice cream

soda cracker n. crisp cracker

soda pop n. flavored, carbonated soft drink

soda water n. carbonated water

sod'den a. soaked or dough

so'di·um n. silver-white metallic chemical element

sodium bi·car'bon·ate (-ət) n. baking soda

sodium chloride n. common salt

sodium hydroxide n. lye

sodium nitrate n. a clear salt used in explo-sives, etc.

sod'om·y n. sexual intercourse held to be abnormal

so'fa n. couch with back and arms

sofa bed n. sofa that can be opened into a bed

soft a. 1 not hard; easy to crush, cut etc. 2 not harsh; mild, gentle, etc. 3 without minerals that hinder lathering 4 weak 5 nonalcoholic —adv. gently —**soft'ly** adv. —**soft'ness** n.

soft'ball' n. game like baseball played with

a larger and softer ball

soft'-boiled' a. boiled briefly to keep the egg's yolk soft

soft drink n. nonalcoholic drink, esp. one carbonated

soft'en (sôf'-) v. make or become soft —**soft'en·er** n.

soft'heart'ed a. 1 compassionate 2 lenient

soft landing n. safe landing, as of a space-craft on the moon

soft'-ped'al v. [Col.] make less emphatic; tone down

soft sell n. subtle selling

soft soap n. [Col.] smooth talk or flattery —**soft'-soap'** v.

soft'ware' n. programs, etc. for a computer or other electronic equipment

soft'y n., pl. **-ies** [Col.] overly sentimental or trusting person

sog'gy a. **-gi·er**, **-gi·est** very wet and heavy; soaked

soil n. earth or ground, esp. the surface layer —v. make or become dirty

soi·ree, soi·rée (swä rā') n. an evening social

so'journ (-jurn) n., v. visit, as in a for-eign land

sol'ace n. relief or comfort —v. comfort

so'lar a. of or having to do with the sun

so·lar'i·um n. glassed-in room for sunning

solar system n. the sun and all its planets

sold v. pt. & pp. of SELL

sol'der (säd'ər) n. metal alloy for joining metal parts —v. join with solder

sol·dier (sōl'jər) n. member of an army, esp. one who is not an officer —v. be a soldier

sole n. 1 bottom of the foot, or of a shoe 2 sea flatfish —v. put a sole on (a shoe) —a. one and only

sole'ly adv. 1 alone 2 only

sol'emn (-əm) a. 1 formal 2 serious —**sol'emn·ly** adv.

so·lem'ni·ty n., pl. **-ties** 1 solemn ritual 2 seriousness

sol'em·nize' v. celebrate or perform for-mally

so'le·noid' n. coil of wire acting like a mag-net

so·lic'it (-lis'-) v. ask for —**so·lic'i·ta'tion** n.

so·lic'i·tor n. 1 one who solicits trade, etc. 2 in England, lawyer not a barrister 3 in U.S., lawyer for a city, etc.

so·lic'i·tous a. 1 showing concern 2 anxious —**so·lic'i·tude'** n.

sol'id a. 1 firm or hard 2 not hollow 3 three-dimensional 4 of one piece, color, etc. —n. 1 firm or hard substance 2 three-dimensional object —**so·lid'i·fy'** v., **-fied'**, **-fy'ing** —**so·lid'i·ty** n.

sol'i·dar'i·ty n. firm unity

so·lil'o·quy (-kwē) n., pl. **-quies** a talking to

oneself —**sol·lil′o·quize′** v.

sol′i·taire′ (-ter′) n. **1** gem set by itself **2** card game for one person

sol′i·tar′y a. **1** alone; lonely **2** single

sol′i·tude′ n. loneliness

so′lo n., a. (piece of music) for one performer —**so′lo·ist** n.

sol′stice (-stis) n. longest day (June 21 or 22) or shortest day (Dec. 21 or 22)

sol′u·ble a. **1** that can be dissolved **2** solvable —**sol′u·bil′i·ty** n.

sol′ute′ (-yōōt′) n. substance dissolved

so·lu′tion n. **1** solving of a problem **2** explanation or answer **3** liquid with something dissolved in it

solve v. find the answer to —**solv′a·ble** a.

sol′vent a. **1** able to pay one's debts **2** able to dissolve a substance —n. substance used to dissolve another —**sol′ven·cy** n.

som′ber a. **1** dark and gloomy **2** sad Br. sp. **som′bre**

som·bre′ro (-brer′ō) n., pl. **-ros** broad-brimmed hat

some a. **1** certain but unspecified **2** of indefinite quantity **3** about —pron. indefinite quantity —adv. **1** approximately **2** [Col.] somewhat **3** [Col.] to a great extent —**some** suf. tending to (be)

some′bod′y n., pl. **-ies** important person —pron. person not named or known

some′day′ adv. sometime

some′how′ adv. in some way

some′one′ pron. somebody

som·er·sault (sum′ər sôlt′) v., n. (perform) a turning of the body, heels over head

some′thing n. thing not named or known

some′time′ adv. at some unspecified time —a. former

some′times adv. at times

some′what′ n. some part, amount, etc. —adv. a little

some′where′ adv. in, to, or at some unnamed place

som·nam′bu·lism′ n. act of walking while asleep

som′no·lent a. sleepy —**som′no·lence** n.

son n. male in relation to his parents

so·na′ta n. piece of music for one or two instruments

song n. **1** music, or poem, to be sung **2** singing sound

song′bird′ n. bird that makes vocal sounds like music

song′ster n. singer —**song′stress** n.fem.

son′ic a. of or having to do with sound

sonic barrier n. large increase of air resistance as an aircraft nears the speed of sound

sonic boom n. explosive sound of supersonic jets overhead

son′-in-law′ n., pl. **sons′-** husband of one's daughter

son′net n. 14-line poem

soon adv. **1** in a short time **2** early **3** readily

soot n. black particles in smoke —**soot′y** a., **-i·er, -i·est**

soothe (sōōth) v. **1** make calm, as by kindness **2** ease, as pain —**sooth′ing·ly** adv.

sooth′say′er (sōōth′-) n. one who pretends to prophesy

sop n. bribe —v. **sopped, sop′ping** soak (up)

so·phis′ti·cat′ed a. **1** knowledgeable, subtle, etc. **2** highly complex; advanced —**so·phis′ti·cate** (-kət) n. —**so·phis′ti·ca′tion** n.

soph′ist·ry, soph′ism′ n. clever but misleading reasoning —**soph′ist** n.

soph′o·more′ n. second-year student in high school or college

soph′o·mor′ic a. immature

sop′o·rif′ic n., a. (drug) causing sleep

sop′ping a. very wet: also **sop′py, -i·er, -i·est**

so·pra′no (-pran′ō, -prä′nō) n., pl. **-nos** highest female voice

sor′bet′ (-bā′) n. tart ice, as of fruit juice

sor′cer·y n. witchcraft —**sor′cer·er** n. —**sor′cer·ess** n.fem.

sor′did a. **1** dirty; filthy **2** mean; selfish

sore a. **1** painful **2** sad **3** [Col.] angry —n. injured body tissue —**sore′ness** n.

sore′ly adv. greatly

sor′ghum (-gəm) n. grass grown for grain, syrup, etc.

so·ror′i·ty n., pl. **-ties** social club for women

sor′rel n. **1** reddish brown **2** horse of this color

sor′row n. (feel) sadness —**sor′row·ful** a.

sor′ry a. **-ri·er, -ri·est 1** full of sorrow, regret, etc. **2** pitiful; wretched

sort n. kind; class —v. arrange according to kind —**of sorts** or **of a sort** of an inferior kind —**out of sorts** [Col.] slightly ill —**sort of** [Col.] somewhat

sor′tie (-tē) n. **1** raid by besieged troops **2** one mission by a single military plane

SOS n. signal of distress

so′-so′ a., adv. fair or fairly well: also **so so**

sot n. habitual drunkard

souf·flé (sōō flā′) n. food made puffy by being baked with beaten egg whites

sought v. pt. & pp. of SEEK

soul n. **1** spiritual part of a person **2** vital part **3** person —**soul′ful** a.

sound n. **1** that which is heard **2** strait or inlet of the sea —v. **1** (cause) to make a sound **2** seem **3** measure the depth of water **4** seek the opinion of: often with **out** —a. **1** free from defect; healthy, secure, wise, etc. **2** deep or thorough —adv. in a sound way —**sound′ly** adv. —**sound′ness** n.

sound barrier n. sonic barrier

sound′ing board′ n. person used to test ideas on

sound′proof′ v., a. (make) impervious to sound

sound′track′ n. sound record along one side of a film

soup n. liquid food with meat, vegetables, etc. in it

soup′y a. **-i·er, -i·est** like soup 2 [Col.] foggy

sour a. 1 having an acid taste 2 fermented 3 unpleasant —v. make or become sour —**sour′ness** n.

source n. 1 starting point 2 place of origin

sour grapes n. scorning of something impossible to get or do

souse n. 1 pickled food 2 brine 3 [Sl.] drunkard —v. 1 to pickle 2 soak in liquid

south n. direction or region to the left of one facing the sunset —a., adv. in, toward, or from the south —**south′er·ly** a., adv. —**south′ern** a. —**south′ern·er** n. —**south′ward** a., adv. —**south′wards** adv.

south′east′ n. direction or region between south and east —a., adv. in, toward, or from the southeast —**south′east′er·ly** a., adv. —**south′east′ern** a. —**south′east′ward** a., adv. —**south′east′wards** adv.

south′paw′ n. [Sl.] left-handed person, esp. a baseball pitcher

South Pole southern end of the earth's axis

south′west′ n. direction or region between south and west —a., adv. in, toward, or from the southwest —**south′west′er·ly** a., adv. —**south′west′ern** a. —**south′west′ward** a., adv. —**south′west′wards** adv.

sou·ve·nir (sōō′və nir′) n. thing kept as a reminder

sov·er·eign (säv′rən) a. 1 chief; supreme 2 independent —n. 1 monarch 2 former Br. gold coin —**sov′er·eign·ty** n., pl. **-ties**

so′vi·et′ n. elected governing council, as in the U.S.S.R.

sow (sou) n. adult female pig

sow (sō) v. **sowed, sown** or **sowed, sow′ing** scatter, or plant with, seed for growing

soy n. sauce from soybeans

soy′bean′ n. seed of a plant of the pea family

spa n. (resort having) a mineral spring

space n. 1 limitless expanse containing all things 2 distance or area 3 interval of time —v. divide by spaces

space′craft′ n., pl. **-craft′** vehicle or satellite for outer-space travel, exploration, etc.

spaced′-out′ a. [Sl.] under the influence of

a drug, etc.: also **spaced**

space heater n. small heating unit for a room

space′man′ n., pl. **-men′** astronaut

space′port′ n. center for launching spacecraft

space′ship′ n. spacecraft, esp. if manned

space′suit′ n. garment pressurized for use by spacemen

space′y, spac′y a. **-i·er, -i·est** [Sl.] eccentric —**spac′i·ness** n.

spa′cious (-shəs) a. having much space; vast

Spack′le trademark paste that dries hard, used to fill holes in wood, etc. —n. [**s**-] this substance

spade n. 1 flat-bladed digging tool 2 playing card marked with a ♠ —v. dig with a spade

spade′work′ n. preparatory work, esp. when tiresome

spa·ghet′ti (-get′-) n. (cooked) strings of dried flour paste

span n. 1 nine inches 2 extent 3 period of time —v. extend over

span′gle n. shiny decoration, as a sequin —v. to decorate with spangles

span′iel (-yəl) n. dog with large drooping ears

Span′ish a., n. (of) the people or language of Spain

spank v., n. slap on the buttocks

spank′ing adv. [Col.] wholly or completely

spar n. pole supporting a ship's sail —v. **sparred, spar′ring** box cautiously

spare v. 1 save or free from something 2 avoid using 3 give up, as time or money —a. 1 extra 2 lean; meager —n. extra thing

spare′ribs n.pl. thin end of pork ribs

spar′ing a. frugal

spark n. 1 small glowing piece from a fire 2 particle 3 flash from an electrical discharge across a gap —v. 1 make sparks 2 excite

spar′kle v. 1 give off sparks 2 glitter 3 effervesce —n. glitter —**spar′kler** n.

spark plug n. piece in an engine cylinder, that ignites the fuel mixture

spar′row n. small songbird

sparse a. thinly spread —**sparse′ly** adv. —**spar′si·ty, sparse′ness** n.

Spar′tan a. brave; hardy

spasm (spaz′əm) n. 1 involuntary muscular contraction 2 short, sudden burst of activity —**spas·mod′ic** a.

spas′tic n., a. (one) having muscular spasms

spat v. pt. & pp. of SPIT —n. 1 [Col.] a brief quarrel 2 cloth ankle covering

spate n. unusually large outpouring, as of words

spa'tial (-shəl) *a.* of, or existing in, space

spat'ter *v.* 1 spurt out in drops 2 splash —*n.* mark made by spattering

spat'u·la (spach'ə-) *n.* tool with a broad, flexible blade

spawn *n.* 1 eggs of fishes, etc. 2 offspring —*v.* produce (spawn)

spay *v.* sterilize (a female animal)

speak *v.* **spoke, spo'ken, speak'ing** 1 utter words 2 tell; express 3 make a speech 4 use (a language) in speaking —**speak for** ask for

speak'er *n.* 1 one who speaks 2 loud-speaker

spear *n.* long, slender sharp-pointed weapon —*v.* pierce or stab as with a spear

spear'head' *n.* leading person or group, as in an attack

spear'mint' *n.* fragrant mint

spe·cial (spesh'əl) *a.* 1 distinctive 2 unusual 3 main; chief 4 for a certain use —*n.* special thing —**spe'cial·ly** *adv.*

spe'cial·ize' *v.* concentrate on a certain type of study, work, etc. —**spe'cial·ist** *n.* —**spe'cial·i·za'tion** *n.*

spe'cial·ty *n., pl.* **–ties** 1 special feature, interest, etc 2 special article

spe·cie (-shē, -sē) *n.* metal money

spe'cies *n., pl.* **–cies** distinct kind of plant or animal

spe·cif'ic *a.* definite; explicit —**spe·cif'i·cal·ly** *adv.*

spec'i·fi·ca'tion *n.* 1 a specifying 2 *pl.* detailed description

spec'i·fy' *v.* **–fied', –fy'ing** state explicitly

spec'i·men *n.* sample

spe'cious (-shəs) *a.* plausible but not genuine

speck *n.* small spot or bit —*v.* mark with specks

speck'le *n., v.* speck

specs *n.pl.* [Col.] specifications

spec'ta·cle *n.* 1 unusual sight 2 public show 3 *pl.* eyeglasses

spec·tac'u·lar *a.* showy; striking

spec'ta·tor *n.* one who watches

spec'ter *n.* ghost: Br. sp. **spec'tre** —**spec'tral** *a.*

spec'tro·scope' *n.* instrument that forms spectra from a ray

spec'trum *n., pl.* **–tra** or **–trums** row of colors formed by diffraction

spec'u·late' *v.* 1 ponder 2 take risky chances in business —**spec'u·la'tion** *n.* —**spec'u·la'tor** *n.*

speech *n.* 1 act or way of speaking 2 power to speak 3 something said 4 public talk —**speech'less** *a.*

speed *n.* 1 rapid motion 2 rate of movement —*v.* **sped, speed'ing** 1 move fast 2 aid

—**speed'y** *a.,* **–i·er, –i·est**

speed'boat' *n.* fast motorboat

speed·om'e·ter *n.* device to indicate speed

speed'ster *n.* very fast driver, runner, etc.

speed'way' *n.* track for racing automobiles or motorcycles

spe'le·ol'o·gy *n.* scientific study of caves

spell *n.* 1 supposedly magic words 2 fascination; charm 3 period of work, duty, etc. —*v.* 1 give in order the letters of (a word) 2 mean 3 [Col.] relieve (another)

spell'bind' *v.* **–bound', –bind'ing** cause to be spellbound —**spell'bind'er** *n.*

spell'bound' *a.* fascinated

spell'er *n.* 1 one who spells words 2 spelling textbook

spell'ing *n.* 1 a forming words from letters 2 way a word is spelled

spelling bee *n.* spelling contest: also **spell'down'**

spe·lunk'er *n.* cave explorer

spend *v.* **spent, spend'ing** 1 use up 2 pay out (money) 3 pass (time)

spend'thrift' *n.* one who wastes money —*a.* wasteful

sperm *n.* 1 semen 2 any of the germ cells in it

sperm whale *n.* large, toothed whale of warm seas

spew *v.* throw up; vomit

sphere (sfir) *n.* 1 globe; ball 2 place or range of action —**spher'i·cal** (sfer'-, sfir'-) *a.*

sphe·roid (sfir'oid) *n.* almost spherical body

sphinx (sfinks) *n.* 1 [S-] statue in Egypt with a lion's body and man's head 2 one difficult to know or understand

spice *n.* 1 any aromatic seasoning 2 stimulating quality —*v.* add spice to —**spic'y** *a.,* **–i·er, –i·est**

spick'-and-span' *a.* fresh or tidy

spi'der *n.* arachnid that spins webs

spiff'y *a.* **–i·er, –i·est** [Sl.] spruce or dapper

spig'ot *n.* faucet or tap

spike *n.* 1 sharp-pointed projection 2 long, heavy nail 3 ear of grain 4 long flower cluster —*v.* 1 fasten or pierce as with a spike 2 thwart

spill *v.* **spilled** or **spilt, spill'ing** 1 let run over 2 overflow 3 shed (blood) 4 [Col.] make fall —*n.* a fall

spill'way' *n.* channel for excess water

spin *v.* **spun, spin'ning** 1 twist fibers into thread 2 make a web, cocoon, etc. 3 tell (a story) 4 to whirl 5 move fast —*n.* 1 whirling movement 2 fast ride

spin'ach *n.* plant with dark-green, edible leaves

spi'nal *a.* of the spine

spinal column *n.* long row of connected bones in the back

spinal cord n. cord of nerve tissue in the spinal column

spin'dle n. 1 rod used in spinning thread 2 rod that acts as an axis

spin'dly a. **-dli-er, -dli-est** long and thin: also **spin'dling**

spine n. 1 thorn, quill, etc. 2 spinal column **—spin'y** a., **-i-er, -i-est**

spine'less a. 1 having no spine 2 weak or cowardly

spin'et n. small upright piano

spinning wheel n. simple spinning machine driven by a large wheel

spin'off' n. secondary benefit, product, etc.

spin'ster n. unmarried, older woman

spi'ral a. circling around a center —n. spiral curve or coil —v. move in a spiral

spire n. tapering, pointed part, as of a steeple

spir'it n. 1 soul 2 ghost, angel, etc. 3 pl. mood 4 courage 5 loyalty 6 essential quality 7 pl. alcoholic liquor —v. carry away secretly

spir'it-ed a. lively

spir'it-u-al a. 1 of the soul 2 religious; sacred —n. Negro religious song —**spir'it-u-al'i-ty** n.

spir'it-u-al-ism' n. seeming communication with the dead —**spir'it-u-al-ist** n.

spit n. 1 thin rod to roast meat on 2 shoreline narrowed to a point 3 saliva —v. **spit'ted** or (v. 2) **spit** or [Br.] **spat, spit'ting** 1 fix as on a spit 2 eject (saliva, etc.) from the mouth

spite n. malice —v. annoy; hurt —**in spite of** regardless of —**spite'ful** a.

spit'tle n. spit; saliva

spit-toon' n. container to spit into

splash v. dash liquid, etc. (on) —n. 1 a splashing 2 a spot made by splashing —**make a splash** [Col.] attract great attention

splash'down' n. landing of a spacecraft on water

splash'y a. **-i-er, -i-est** [Col.] spectacular

splat'ter n., v. splash

splay v., a. spread out

spleen n. 1 large abdominal organ 2 malice; spite —**sple-net'ic** a.

splen'did a. magnificent; grand —**splen'dor** n.

splice v., n. (make) a joint with ends overlapped

splint n. stiff strip to hold a broken bone in place

splin'ter n. thin, sharp piece —v. split in splinters

split v. **split, split'ting** separate into parts —n. break; crack —a. divided

split-lev'el a. having adjacent floor levels staggered about a half story apart

split'ting a. severe

splotch n., v. spot; stain —**splotch'y** a., **-i-er, -i-est**

splurge v., n. [Col.] (make) a showy display, etc.

splut'ter v. 1 make spitting sounds 2 speak confusedly —n. a spluttering

spoil v. spoiled or spoilt, spoil'ing to damage, ruin, decay, etc. —n.pl. plunder —**spoil'age** n.

spoil'sport' n. one who ruins the fun of others

spoke v. pt. of SPEAK —n. rod from hub to rim

spo'ken v. pp. of SPEAK —a. oral; voiced

spokes'man n., pl. **-men** one who speaks for another —**spokes'per'son** n.

sponge n. 1 absorbent substance made from a sea animal, plastic, etc. 2 the sea animal —v. 1 clean, etc. with a sponge 2 [Col.] live off others —**spon'gy** a., **-gi-er, -gi-est**

sponge bath n. bath taken by using a wet sponge or cloth without getting into water

sponge'cake' n. light, spongy cake without shortening

spon'sor n. 1 promoter; supporter 2 advertiser who pays for a radio or TV program —v. be sponsor for

spon-ta'ne-ous a. 1 without effort 2 within or by itself —**spon'ta-ne'i-ty** (-nē'-, -nā'-) n.

spoof n. light satire —v. satirize playfully

spook n. [Col.] ghost —**spook'y** a., **-i-er, -i-est**

spool n. cylinder upon which thread, etc. is wound

spoon n. small bowl with a handle, used in eating —**spoon'ful** n., pl. **-fuls**

spoon'-feed' v. pamper

spoor n. wild animal's trail or track

spo-rad'ic a. not regular —**spo-rad'i-cal-ly** adv.

spore n. tiny reproductive cell of mosses, fern, etc.

sport n. 1 athletic game 2 fun 3 abnormal plant or animal —v. 1 [Col.] display 2 play —a. for play

sport'ing a. 1 of sports 2 fair 3 risky

sports a. sport

sports (or sport) car n. small, expensive car with powerful engine

sports'man n., pl. **-men** 1 participant in sports 2 one who plays fair —**sports'man-like'** a.

sport utility vehicle n. station wagon on a small truck chassis

sport'y a. **-i-er, -i-est** [Col.] flashy or showy

spot n. 1 stain; mark 2 place —v. **spot'ted, spot'ting** 1 mark with spots 2 see —a. made at random —**spot'less** a.

spot'-check v. check at random —n. such a checking

spot'light' n. 1 strong beam of light, or lamp that throws it 2 public notice

spot'ty a. **-ti·er, -ti·est** 1 spotted 2 not uniform

spouse n. husband or wife —**spous·al** (spou'zəl) a.

spout n. 1 pipe, etc. by which a liquid pours 2 stream of liquid —v. 1 shoot out with force 2 talk loudly and on and on

sprain v. twist a muscle or ligament in a joint —n. injury caused by this

sprang v. pt. of SPRING

sprat n. small herring

sprawl v. sit or spread out in a relaxed or awkward way —n. sprawling position

spray n. 1 mist or stream of tiny liquid drops 2 branch with leaves, flowers, etc. 3 spray gun —v. apply, or emit in, a spray

spray can n. can in which gas under pressure sprays out the contents

spray gun n. device that sprays a liquid, as paint

spread v. **spread, spread'ing** 1 open out 2 extend in time or space 3 make known 4 cover 5 go or make go —n. 1 act or extent of spreading 2 a cloth cover 3 butter, jam, etc.

spread'sheet' n. computer program organizing data into rows and columns on a video screen

spree n. 1 lively time 2 drinking bout

sprig n. little twig

spright'ly a. **-li·er, -li·est** brisk; lively —adv. briskly

spring v. **sprang** or **sprung, sprung, spring'ing** 1 leap 2 grow; develop 3 snap back or shut 4 make or become bent, split, etc. 5 make known —n. 1 a leap 2 resilience 3 resilient coil of wire, etc. 4 flow of water from the ground 5 source 6 season after winter —a. of, for, or in the season of spring —**spring'y** a., **-i·er, -i·est**

spring'board' n. springy board, as to dive from

sprin'kle v. 1 scatter drops of or on 2 rain lightly —n. a sprinkling

sprint v., n. race at full speed for a short distance

sprite n. elf, fairy, etc.

sprock'et n. any tooth in a series on a wheel made to fit the links of a chain

sprout v. begin to grow —n. new growth; shoot

spruce n. evergreen tree —v., a. (make) neat or trim

sprung v. pp. & alt. pt. of SPRING

spry a. **spri'er** or **spry'er, spri'est** or **spry'est** lively

spud n. [Col.] potato

spume n. foam; froth

spu·mo'ni n. Italian ice cream

spun v. pt. and pp. of SPIN

spunk [Col.] n. courage —**spunk'y** a., **-i·er, -i·est**

spur n. 1 pointed device on a shoe to prick a horse 2 stimulus 3 projecting part —v. **spurred, spur'ring** 1 to prick with spurs 2 urge on

spu'ri·ous (spyoor'-) a. false; not genuine

spurn v. reject in scorn

spurt v. 1 shoot forth; squirt 2 make a sudden effort —n. a spurting

sput'nik n. Russian man-made satellite

sput'ter v. 1 speak in a fast, confused way 2 spit out bits 3 make hissing sounds —n. a sputtering

spu'tum n. saliva

spy v. **spied, spy'ing** 1 watch closely and secretly 2 see —n., pl. **spies** one who spies, esp. to get another country's secrets

spy'glass' n. small telescope

squab (skwäb) n. young pigeon

squab'ble v., n. quarrel over a small matter

squad n. small group

squad'ron n. unit of warships, aircraft, etc.

squal'id a. 1 foul; unclean 2 wretched —**squal'or** n.

squall n. 1 brief, violent windstorm 2 harsh, loud cry —v. cry loudly

squan'der v. spend or use wastefully

square n. 1 rectangle with all sides equal 2 area with streets on four sides 3 tool for making right angles 4 product of a number multiplied by itself 5 [Sl.] person who is SQUARE (a. 6) —v. 1 make square 2 make straight, even, etc. 3 settle; adjust 4 multiply by itself —a. 1 shaped like a square 2 forming a right angle 3 straight, level, or even 4 just; fair 5 [Col.] filling, as a meal 6 [Sl.] old-fashioned, unsophisticated, etc. —adv. in a square way —**square'ly** adv. —**square'ness** n.

square dance n. lively dance with couples grouped in a square

square root n. quantity that when squared produces another, given quantity

squash v. 1 press into a soft, flat mass 2 to suppress —n. 1 a squashing 2 game played with rackets in a walled court 3 fleshy vegetable growing on a vine

squat v. **squat'ted, squat'ting** 1 crouch 2 settle on land without title to it —a. short and heavy —n. position of squatting —**squat'ter** n.

squaw n. a North American Indian woman or wife: now considered offensive

squawk v. 1 utter a loud, harsh cry 2 [Col.]

complain —n. a squawking —**squawk′er** n.

squeak v. make a sharp, high-pitched sound —n. such a sound —**squeak′y** a., **-i-er, -i-est**

squeal v., n. (utter) a long, shrill cry

squeam′ish a. 1 easily nauseated 2 easily shocked

squee′gee (-jē) n. rubber-edged tool used in washing windows

squeeze v. 1 press hard 2 extract by pressure 3 force by pressing 4 hug —n. a squeezing —**squeez′er** n.

squelch v. suppress or silence completely

squib n. short, witty verbal attack

squid n. long, slender sea mollusk with ten arms

squig′gle n. short, wavy line —**squig′gly** a.

squint v. 1 peer with eyes partly closed 2 be cross-eyed —n. a squinting

squire n. English country gentleman —v. escort

squirm v. twist and turn

squir′rel n. tree-dwelling rodent with a bushy tail

squirt v., n. (shoot out in) a jet or spurt

squish [Col.]v., n. 1 (make) a soft, splashing sound when squeezed 2 SQUASH (v. 1, n. 1) —**squish′y** a., **-i-er, -i-est**

stab v. **stabbed, stab′bing** pierce or wound as with a knife —n. 1 a thrust, as with a knife 2 [Col.] a try

sta′bi-lize′ v. 1 make stable, or firm 2 keep from changing —**sta′bi-li-za′tion** n. —**sta′bi-liz′er** n.

sta′ble a. not apt to change; firm —n. building for horses or cattle —v. keep in a stable —**sta-bil′i-ty** n.

stac-ca-to (stə kät′ō) a., adv. Mus. with abrupt tones

stack n. 1 orderly pile 2 smokestack 3 set of bookshelves —v. to pile in a stack

sta′di-um n. place for outdoor games, surrounded by tiers of seats

staff n., pl. (n. 1, 2, 3) **staffs** or (n. 1 & 3) **staves** 1 stick or rod used for support, etc. 2 group of people assisting a leader 3 the five lines on and between which music is written —v. provide with workers

stag n. full-grown male deer —a. for men only

stage n. 1 platform, esp. one on which plays are presented 2 the theater 3 part of a journey 4 period in growth or development —v. 1 to present as on a stage 2 carry out

stage′coach′ n. horse-drawn public coach for long trips

stage fright n. fear of speaking before an audience

stage′hand′ n. one who sets up scenery, etc. for a play

stage′-struck′ a. eager to become an actor or actress

stag′ger v. 1 (cause to) totter, reel, etc. 2 shock 3 arrange alternately —n. a staggering

stag′ger-ing a. astonishing

stag′nant a. 1 not flowing, therefore foul 2 sluggish

stag′nate′ v. become stagnant —**stag-na′tion** n.

staid a. sober; sedate

stain v. 1 discolor; spot 2 dishonor 3 color (wood, etc.) with a dye —n. 1 a spot; mark 2 dishonor 3 dye for wood, etc. —**stain′less** a.

stainless steel n. alloyed steel almost immune to rust and corrosion

stair n. 1 one of a series of steps between levels 2 usually pl. flight of stairs: also **stair′case′** or **stair′way′**

stair′well′ n. shaft containing a staircase

stake n. 1 pointed stick to be driven into the ground 2 often pl. money risked as a wager —v. 1 mark the boundaries of 2 wager —**at stake** being risked

sta-lac′tite n. stick of lime hanging from a cave roof

sta-lag′mite n. stick of lime built up on a cave floor

stale a. 1 no longer fresh 2 trite

stale′mate′ n. deadlock

stalk v. 1 stride haughtily 2 track secretly —n. 1 a stalking 2 plant stem —**stalk′er** n.

stall n. 1 section for one animal in a stable 2 market booth —v. 1 put in a stall 2 stop 3 delay by evading

stal′lion (-yən) n. uncastrated male horse

stal′wart a. strong or brave —n. stalwart person

sta′men n. pollen-bearing part of a flower

stam′i-na n. endurance

stam′mer v., n. pause or halt in speaking

stamp v. 1 put the foot down hard 2 pound with the foot 3 cut out with a die 4 impress a design on 5 put a stamp on —n. 1 a stamping 2 gummed piece of paper, as for postage 3 a stamped mark 4 stamping device —**stamp out** 1 crush or put out by treading on 2 suppress or put down

stam-pede′ n. sudden, headlong rush, as of a herd —v. move in a stampede

stamp′ing ground n. [Col.] favorite gathering place

stance n. way one stands

stanch (stônch, stanch) v. check the flow of blood from a wound —a. staunch

stan′chion (-chən) n. upright support

stand v. **stood, stand′ing** 1 be or get in an

upright position **2** place or be placed **3** hold a certain opinion **4** halt **5** endure or resist —*n*. **1** a halt **2** a position **3** platform, rack, counter, etc. **4** a growth (of trees) —**stand by** be ready to help —**stand for 1** represent **2** [Col.] tolerate —**stand in for** be a substitute for —**stand out** to project, be prominent, etc. —**stand up 1** prove valid, durable, etc. **2** [Sl.] fail to keep a date with

stand'ard *n.* **1** flag, banner, etc. **2** thing set up as a rule or model **3** upright support —*a.* **1** that is a standard or rule **2** proper

stand'ard·ize' *v.* make standard or uniform

standard time *n.* official civil time for a region: the 24 time zones are one hour apart

stand·by' *n., pl.* **-bys'** person or thing that is dependable, a possible substitute, etc.

stand'-in' *n.* a substitute

stand'ing *n.* **1** status or rank **2** duration —*a.* **1** upright **2** continuing

stand'off' *n.* tie in a contest

stand'off'ish *a.* aloof

stand'point' *n.* viewpoint

stand'still' *n.* a stop or halt

stank *v.* alt. pt. of STINK

stan'za *n.* group of lines making a section of a poem

staph'y·lo·coc'cus *n., pl.* **-ci'** (-sī') kind of spherical bacteria

sta'ple *n.* **1** main product, part, etc. **2** basic trade item, as flour **3** U-shaped metal fastener —*v.* fasten with a staple —*a.* regular or principal —**sta'pler** *n.*

star *n.* **1** celestial body seen as a point of light at night **2** flat figure with five or more points **3** asterisk **4** one who excels or plays a leading role as in acting —*v.* **starred, star'ring 1** mark with stars **2** present in, or play, a leading role —**star'ry** *a.,* **-ri·er, -ri·est**

star'board (-bərd) *n.* right side of a ship, etc. as one faces the bow

starch *n.* **1** white food substance in potatoes, etc. **2** powdered form of this —*v.* stiffen (laundry) with starch —**starch'y** *a.,* **-i·er, -i·est**

star'dom *n.* status of a STAR (*n.* 4)

stare *v.* gaze steadily —*n.* long, steady look

star'fish' *n.* small, star-shaped sea animal

star'gaze' *v.* **1** gaze at the stars **2** to daydream —**star'gaz'er** *n.*

stark *a.* **1** bleak **2** complete; utter —*adv.* entirely —**stark'ly** *adv.*

stark'-nak'ed *a.* entirely naked

star'ling *n.* bird with shiny, black feathers

star'ry-eyed' *a.* with sparkling eyes

star'-span'gled *a.* studded with stars

start *v.* **1** begin to go, do, etc. **2** set in motion **3** jump or jerk —*n.* **1** a starting **2** a jump or jerk **3** place or time of beginning **4** a lead; advantage —**start in** begin to do —**start out** (or **off**) begin a trip, etc. —**start'er** *n.*

star'tle *v.* **1** frighten suddenly **2** surprise —**star'tling** *a.*

starve *v.* **1** suffer or die from lack of food **2** cause to starve —**star·va'tion** *n.*

stash [Col.] *v.* hide away —*n.* something hidden

stat *n.* [Col.] statistic

state *n.* **1** the way a person or thing is **2** formal style **3** nation **4** [often **S-**] a unit of a federal government —*v.* to express in words

stat'ed *a.* fixed; set

state'ly *a.,* **-li·er, -li·est** grand or dignified

state'ment *n.* **1** a stating **2** something stated **3** report, as of money owed

state'room' *n.* private room in a ship or railroad car

states'man *n., pl.* **-men** person skillful in government

stat'ic *a.* **1** at rest **2** of electricity caused by friction —*n.* electrical disturbances in radio reception

sta'tion *n.* **1** assigned place **2** stopping place **3** place for radio or TV transmission **4** social rank —*v.* assign to a station

sta'tion·ar'y *a.* not moving or changing

sta'tion·er'y *n.* writing materials

station wagon *n.* automobile with a back end that opens

sta·tis'tics *n.* analysis of numerical data —*n.pl.* the data —**sta·tis'ti·cal** *a.* —**stat'is·ti'cian** (-tish'ən) *n.*

stat'u·ar'y *n.* statues

stat·ue (stach'ōō) *n.* likeness done in stone, metal, etc.

stat'u·esque' (-esk') *a.* tall and stately

stat'u·ette' *n.* small statue

stat·ure (stach'ər) *n.* **1** person's height **2** level of attainment or esteem

sta'tus *n.* **1** rank **2** condition

status quo *n.* existing state of affairs

status symbol *n.* a possession regarded as a sign of social status

stat'ute (stach'-) *n.* a law

stat'u·to'ry *a.* authorized, or punishable, by statute

staunch (stônch) *a.* firm, loyal, etc. —*v.* stanch

stave *n.* **1** any of the wooden side strips of a barrel **2** staff **3** stanza —*v.* **staved** or **stove, stav'ing smash** (in) —**stave off** hold off

staves *n.* **1** alt. pl. of STAFF (*n.* **1** & **3**) **2** pl. of STAVE

stay *v.* **1** remain **2** dwell **3** stop or delay **4** to support —*n.* **1** a staying **2** prop **3** guy rope **4** stiffening strip

stay′ing power n. endurance

stead (sted) n. place for a substitute

stead′fast a. constant; firm

stead′y a. **-i·er, -i·est 1** firm **2** regular **3** calm **4** reliable —v. **-ied, -y·ing** make or become steady

steak n. slice of meat or fish

steal v. **stole, stol′en, steal′ing 1** take dishonestly and secretly **2** move stealthily

stealth (stelth) n. secret action —**stealth′i·ly** adv. —**stealth′y** a., **-i·er, -i·est**

steam n. wa′ter changed to a vapor by boiling: source of heat and power —a. using steam —v. **1** expose to steam **2** cook with steam **3** give off steam —**steam′boat′, steam′ship′** n. —**steam′y** a., **-i·er, -i·est**

steam′er n. thing run by steam

steam′roll′er n. heavy steam-driven roller —v. move, crush, override, etc. as (with) a steamroller

steed n. [Poet.] riding horse

steel n. hard alloy of iron with carbon —a. of steel —v. make strong —**steel′y** a.

steel wool n. steel shavings used for cleaning, etc.

steel′yard′ n. weighing scale

steep a. having a sharp rise or slope —v. soak or saturate

stee′ple n. high tower

stee′ple·chase′ n. horse race over a course with obstacles

steer v. guide; direct —n. male of beef cattle; ox

steer′age n. part of a ship for passengers paying least

stein (stīn) n. beer mug

stel′lar a. **1** of or like a star **2** most important

stem n. **1** stalk of a plant, flower, etc. **2** stemlike part **3** prow of a ship **4** root of a word —v. **stemmed, stem′ming 1** remove the stem of **2** advance against **3** stop **4** derive

stench n. offensive smell

sten′cil n. sheet cut with letters, etc. to print when inked over —v. mark with a stencil

ste·nog′ra·phy n. transcription of dictation in shorthand —**ste·nog′ra·pher** n.

sten·to′ri·an (-tôr′ē-) adj. very loud

step n. **1** one foot movement, as in walking **2** footstep **3** way of stepping **4** stair tread **5** degree; rank **6** act in a series —v. **1** move with a step **2** press the foot down —**in** (or **out of**) **step** (not) in rhythm with others —**step up 1** advance **2** increase in rate

step′broth′er n. stepparent's son

step′child′ n. spouse's child (**step′daugh′-** **ter** or **step′son′**) by a former marriage

step′-down′ n. decrease, as in amount, intensity, etc.

step′lad′der n. four-legged ladder with flat steps

step′par′ent n. the spouse (**step′fa′ther** or **step′moth′er**) of one's remarried parent

steppe (step) n. great plain

step′ping-stone′ n. **1** stone to step on, as in crossing a stream **2** means of bettering oneself

step′sis′ter n. a stepparent's daughter

step′-up′ n. increase, as in amount, intensity, etc.

ster′e·o′ n., pl. **-os′** stereophonic system, etc. —a. stereophonic

ster′e·o·phon′ic a. of a blend of sounds reproduced through separate speakers

ster′e·o·scope′ n. device for giving three-dimensional effect to pictures

ster′e·o·type′ v., n. (express or conceive in) a set, trite form —**ster′e·o·typ′i·cal, ster′e·o·typ′ic** a.

ster′ile (-al) a. **1** not able to reproduce itself or oneself **2** free of germs —**ste·ril′i·ty** n.

ster′i·lize′ v. to make sterile —**ster′i·li·za′tion** n.

ster′ling a. **1** (made) of silver at least 92.5% pure **2** of British money **3** excellent

stern a. severe; unyielding —n. rear end of a ship, etc.

ster′num n. front chest bone to which ribs are joined

ster′oid′ n. any of a group of compounds including cholesterol, sex hormones, etc.

steth′o·scope′ n. instrument for hearing chest sounds

ste′ve·dore′ n. one hired to load and unload ships

stew v. cook by boiling slowly —n. meat with vegetables, cooked in this way

stew′ard n. **1** one put in charge of funds, supplies, etc. **2** servant on a ship, airplane, etc. —**stew′ard·ess** n.fem.

stick n. **1** small branch broken or cut off **2** long, thin piece, as of wood —v. **stuck, stick′ing 1** pierce **2** attach or be attached as by pinning or gluing **3** extend **4** become fixed, jammed, etc. **5** persevere **6** hesitate **7** be puzzled

stick′er n. gummed label

stick′-in-the-mud′ n. [Col.] one who resists change, etc.

stick′le·back′ n. small fish with sharp spines on its back

stick′ler n. one who is stubbornly fussy

stick′pin′ n. ornamental pin worn in a necktie, etc.

stick shift n. car gearshift, operated manually by a lever

stick′up′ n. [Sl.] robbery

stick′y a. **-i·er, -i·est** adhesive **—stick′i·ness** n.

stiff a. **1** hard to bend or move **2** thick; dense **3** strong, as a wind **4** difficult **5** tense **—stiff′en** v. **—stiff′ly** adv.

stiff′-necked′ a. stubborn

sti′fle v. **1** suffocate **2** suppress; restrain

stig′ma n., pl. **-mas** or **-ma·ta 1** sign of disgrace **2** upper tip of a pistil

stig′ma·tize′ v. mark as disgraceful

stile n. step(s) for climbing over a fence or wall

sti·let′to n., pl. **-tos** or **-toes** small, thin dagger

still a. **1** quiet **2** motionless **3** calm **—**n. device to distill liquor **—**adv. **1** until then or now **2** even; yet **3** nevertheless **—**con. nevertheless **—**v. to make or become still **—still′ness** n.

still′born′ a. dead at birth **—still′birth′** n.

still life n. painting of inanimate objects, as fruit

stilt n. supporting pole, esp. one of a pair for walking high off the ground

stilt′ed a. pompous

stim′u·lant n. thing that stimulates, as a drug

stim′u·late′ v. make (more) active **—stim′u·la′tion** n.

stim′u·lus n., pl. **-li′** (-lī′) anything causing activity

sting v. **stung, sting′ing 1** hurt with a sting **2** cause or feel sharp pain **—**n. **1** a stinging, or pain from it **2** sharp part in some plants, bees, etc. that pricks: also **sting′er**

stin′gy (-jē) a. **-gi·er, -gi·est** miserly; grudging

stink v. **stank** or **stunk, stunk, stink′ing**; n. (have) a strong, unpleasant smell

stint v. restrict to a small amount **—**n. **1** limit **2** assigned task

sti′pend n. regular payment

stip′ple v. paint or draw in small dots

stip′u·late′ v. specify as an essential condition

stir v. **stirred, stir′ring 1** move, esp. slightly **2** move around as with a spoon **3** excite **—**n. **1** a stirring **2** commotion

stir′-cra′zy a. [Sl.] mentally affected by long confinement

stir′-fry′ v. fry (vegetables, meat, etc.) quickly while stirring

stir′rup n. ring hung from a saddle as a footrest

stitch n. **1** single movement or loop made by a needle in sewing, knitting, etc. **2** sudden pain **—**v. sew

stock n. **1** tree trunk **2** ancestry **3** biological breed **4** rifle part holding the barrel **5** pl.

frame with holes for feet and hands, once used for punishment **6** broth from meat or fish **7** livestock **8** goods on hand **9** shares in a business **—**v. supply or keep in stock **—**a. **1** kept in stock **2** common **—in** (or **out of**) **stock** (not) available

stock·ade′ n. defensive wall of tall stakes

stock′bro′ker n. a broker for stocks and bonds

stock car n. standard automobile, modified for racing

stock exchange, stock market n. place of sale for stocks and bonds

stock′hold′er n. one owning stock in a company

stock′ing n. knitted covering for the leg and foot

stocking cap n. long, tapered, knitted cap

stock′pile′ v., n. (accumulate) a reserve supply

stock′-still′ a. motionless

stock′y a. **-i·er, -i·est** short and heavy

stock′yard′ n. place to pen livestock till slaughtered

stodg·y (stä′jē) a. **-i·er, -i·est 1** dull; uninteresting **2** stubbornly conventional

sto′gie, sto′gy n., pl. **-gies** long cigar

sto′ic a., n. stoical (person)

sto′i·cal a. indifferent to grief, pain, etc. **—sto′i·cism′** n.

stoke v. stir up and feed fuel to (a fire) **—stok′er** n.

stole v. pt. of STEAL **—**n. long fur piece worn by women around the shoulders

stol′en v. pp. of STEAL

stol′id (stäl′-) a. unexcitable

stom·ach (stum′ək) n. **1** digestive organ into which food passes **2** abdomen **3** appetite **—**v. tolerate

stom′ach·ache′ n. pain in the stomach or abdomen

stomp v. STAMP (v. **1 & 2**)

stone n. **1** solid nonmetallic mineral matter **2** piece of this **3** seed of certain fruits **4** abnormal stony mass in the kidney, etc. **5** pl. **stone** [Br.] **14** pounds **—**v. throw stones at

stoned a. [Sl.] under the influence of liquor, a drug, etc.

stone's throw n. short distance

stone′wall′ v. [Col.] impede by refusing to help, cooperate, etc.

ston′y a. **-i·er, -i·est 1** full of stones **2** unfeeling

stood v. pt. & pp. of STAND

stooge (stōōj) n. [Col.] lackey

stool n. **1** single seat with no back or arms **2** feces

stoop v. **1** bend the body forward **2** lower one's dignity **—**n. **1** position of stooping **2**

small porch

stop v. **stopped, stop′ping 1** close by filling, shutting off, etc. **2** cease; end; halt **3** to block; obstruct **4** stay —n. **1** a stopping **2** a place stopped at **3** obstruction, plug, etc. —**stop off** stop for a while —**stop′page** n.

stop′cock′ n. valve to regulate the flow of a liquid

stop′gap′ n. temporary substitute

stop′light′ n. **1** traffic light, esp. when red **2** rear light on a vehicle that lights up when the brakes are applied

stop′o′ver n. brief stop at a place during a journey

stop′per n. something inserted to close an opening

stop′watch′ n. watch that can be started and stopped instantly, as to time races

stor′age n. **1** a storing **2** place for, or cost of, storing goods

storage battery n. battery capable of being recharged

store n. **1** supply; stock **2** establishment where goods are sold —v. put aside for future use —**in store** set aside for the future

store′front′ n. front room or ground floor, for use as retail store

store′house′ n. warehouse

store′keep′er n. a person in charge of a store

store′room′ n. a room where things are stored

stork n. large, long-legged wading bird

storm n. **1** strong wind with rain, snow, etc. **2** any strong disturbance **3** strong attack —v. blow violently, rain, etc. **2** rage **3** rush or attack violently —**storm′y** a., **-i·er, -i·est**

storm door (or **window**) n. door (or window) put outside the regular one as added protection

sto′ry n., pl. **-ries 1** a telling of an event **2** fictitious narrative **3** one level of a building **4** [Col.] a falsehood —**sto′ried** a.

sto′ry·book′ n. book of stories, esp. one for children

sto′ry·tell′er n. one who narrates stories

stout n. **1** brave **2** firm; strong **3** fat —n. strong, dark beer —**stout′ly** adv.

stove n. apparatus for heating, cooking, etc. —v. alt. pt. & pp. of STAVE

stove′pipe′ n. metal pipe to carry off stove smoke

stow (stō) v. pack or store away —**stow away** hide aboard a ship, etc. for a free ride —**stow′a·way′** n.

strad′dle v. **1** sit or stand astride **2** take both sides of (an issue)

strafe v. attack with machine guns from aircraft

strag′gle v. **1** wander from the group **2** spread out unevenly —**strag′gler** n.

straight a. **1** not crooked, bent, etc. **2** direct **3** in order **4** honest or frank **5** undiluted **6** [Sl.] conventional **7** [Sl.] heterosexual —adv. **1** in a straight line **2** directly **3** without delay —**straight a·way** (or off) without delay —**straight′en** v.

straight′a·way′ n. straight part of a track, road, etc. —adv. at once

straight face n. facial expression showing no emotion —**straight′-faced′** a.

straight′for′ward a. **1** direct **2** honest

straight′way′ adv. at once

strain v. **1** stretch tight or to the utmost **2** strive hard **3** sprain **4** filter —n. **1** a straining or being strained **2** excessive demand on one's emotions, etc. **3** ancestry **4** inherited tendency **5** trace; streak **6** often pl. tune —**strain′er** n.

strait n. often pl. **1** narrow waterway **2** distress

strait′en v. impoverish

strait′ened a. impoverished

strait′jack′et n. coatlike device for restraining a person

strait′-laced′ a. strict

strand n. **1** any of the threads, wires, etc. that form a string, cable, etc. **2** string, as of pearls **3** shore —v. put into a helpless position

strange a. **1** unfamiliar **2** unusual **3** peculiar; odd —**strange′ly** adv.

stran′ger n. **1** newcomer **2** person not known to one

stran′gle v. **1** choke to death **2** stifle —**stran′gler** n.

strap n. narrow strip of leather, etc., as for binding things —v. **strapped, strap′ping** fasten with a strap —**strap′less** a.

strapped a. [Col.] without money

strap′ping a. [Col.] robust

strat′a·gem (-jəm) n. tricky ruse or move to gain an end

strat′e·gy n., pl. **-gies 1** science of military operations **2** artful maneuvering; plan —**stra·te′gic** a. —**stra·te′gi·cal·ly** adv. —**strat′e·gist** n.

strat′i·fy′ v. form in layers —**strat′i·fi·ca′tion** n.

strat′o·sphere′ n. upper atmosphere from 12 to 31 miles

stra′tum n., pl. **-ta** or **-tums** any of a series of layers

stra·tus (strat′əs) n., pl. **-ti** long, low, gray cloud layer

straw n. **1** grain stalk or stalks after threshing **2** tube for sucking a drink

straw′ber′ry n., pl. **–ries** small, red, juicy fruit of a vinelike plant

straw boss n. [Col.] person having subordinate authority

straw vote n. unofficial poll of public opinion

stray v. 1 wander; roam 2 deviate —a. 1 lost 2 isolated —n. lost domestic animal

streak n. 1 long, thin mark 2 layer 3 tendency in behavior 4 spell, as of luck —v. 1 mark with streaks 2 go fast

stream n. 1 small river 2 steady flow, as of air —v. 1 flow in a stream 2 move swiftly

stream′er n. long, narrow flag or strip

stream′line′ v., a. (to make) streamlined

stream′lined′ a. 1 shaped to move easily in air, etc. 2 made more efficient

street n. road in a city

street′car′ n. passenger car on rails along streets

street′walk′er n. prostitute

street′wise′ a. [Col.] knowing how to deal with conditions in crowded, dangerous, etc. urban areas

strength n. 1 force; power; vigor 2 durability 3 intensity 4 potency —**on the strength of** based upon or relying on —**strength′en** v.

stren′u·ous a. needing or showing much energy

strep′to·coc′cus (-käk′əs) n., pl. **-coc′ci** (-käk′sī′) kind of spherical bacteria

strep′to·my′cin (-mī′sin) n. antibiotic drug

stress n. 1 strain; pressure 2 importance; emphasis 3 special force on a syllable, etc. —v. 1 to strain 2 accent 3 emphasize

stretch v. 1 reach out 2 draw out to full extent 3 strain 4 exaggerate —n. 1 a stretching 2 ability to be stretched 3 extent

stretch′er n. 1 canvas-covered frame to carry the sick 2 one that stretches

strew v. **strewed**, **strewed** or **strewn**, **strew′ing** 1 scatter 2 cover as by scattering

stri′at′ed a. striped

strick′en a. struck, wounded, afflicted, etc.

strict a. 1 exact or absolute 2 rigidly enforced or enforcing —**strict′ly** adv. —**strict′ness** n.

stric′ture n. strong criticism

stride v. **strode**, **strid′den**, **strid′ing** walk with long steps —n. 1 long step 2 pl. progress

stri′dent a. shrill; grating

strife n. a quarrel(ing)

strike v. **struck**, **struck** or **strick′en**, **strik′ing** 1 hit 2 sound by hitting some part 3 ignite (a match) 4 make by stamping 5 attack 6 reach or find 7 occur to 8 assume (a pose) 9 take down or apart 10 stop working until demands are met —n. 1 a striking 2 Baseball a pitched ball struck at but missed, etc. 3 Bowling a knocking down of all the pins at once —**strike out** 1 erase 2 go out on three strikes —**strike up** begin —**strik′er** n.

strik′ing a. very attractive, impressive, etc.

string n. 1 thick thread, etc. used as for tying 2 numbers of things on a string or in a row 3 thin cord bowed, etc. to make music, as on a violin 4 pl. condition attached to a plan, offer, etc. —v. strung, **string′ing** 1 provide with strings 2 put on a string 3 extend —**pull strings** use influence to gain advantage —**string′y** a., **-i·er, -i·est**

string bean n. thick bean pod, eaten as a vegetable

strin′gent (-jənt) a. strict

strip v. **stripped**, **strip′ping** 1 take off clothing, covering, etc. (of) 2 make bare 3 break the teeth of (a gear, etc.) —n. long, narrow piece

stripe n. 1 narrow band of different color or material 2 kind; sort —v. mark with stripes

strip′ling n. a youth

strive v. **strove** or **strived**, **striv′en** or **strived**, **striv′ing** 1 try very hard 2 struggle

strobe (light) n. electronic tube emitting rapid, bright flashes of light

strode v. pt. of STRIDE

stroke n. 1 sudden blow, attack, action, etc. 2 a single movement of the arm, a tool, etc. 3 striking sound —v. draw one's hand, etc. gently over

stroll n. leisurely walk —v. 1 take a stroll 2 wander

stroll′er n. chairlike cart for a baby

strong a. 1 powerful 2 healthy 3 durable 4 intense —**strong′ly** adv.

strong′-arm′ a. [Col.] using physical force —v. [Col.] use force upon

strong′box′ n. heavily made box or safe for valuables

strong′hold′ n. fortress

stron′ti·um (-shəm) n. chemical element with radioactive isotope

strove v. pt. of STRIVE

struck v. pt. & pp. of STRIKE

struc′ture n. 1 thing built 2 plan, design, etc. —**struc′tur·al** a.

stru′del n. pastry of thin dough and filling, rolled up and baked

strug′gle v. 1 fight 2 strive —n. a struggling

strum v. **strummed, strum′ming** play (a guitar, etc.) with long strokes, often casually

strum′pet n. prostitute

strung v. pt. & pp. of STRING

strut v. **strut′ted, strut′ting** walk arrogantly —n. 1 strutting walk 2 rod used as a support

strych′nine (strik′-) n. poisonous drug used as a stimulant

stub n. short, leftover, or blunt part —v. **stubbed, stub′bing** bump (one's toe)

stub′ble n. 1 short grain stumps 2 short growth

stub′born a. obstinate —**stub′born·ness** n.

stub′by a. **-bi·er, -bi·est** short and thick

stuc′co v., **-coed, -co·ing**; n. (cover with) rough plaster

stuck v. pt. & pp. of STICK

stuck′-up a. [Col.] snobbish

stud n. 1 decorative nail 2 removable button 3 upright support in a wall 4 breeding stallion —v. **stud′ded, stud′ding** be set thickly in

stu′dent n. one who studies

stud′ied a. done on purpose

stu′di·o n., pl. **-os′** 1 artist's work area 2 place for producing movies, radio or TV programs, etc.

studio couch n. couch that opens into a full-sized bed

stu′di·ous a. 1 fond of study 2 attentive

stud′y v. **-ied, -y·ing** 1 learn by reading, thinking, etc. 2 investigate —n., pl. **-ies** 1 act of studying 2 pl. education 3 deep thought 4 place to study

stuff n. 1 material; substance 2 (worthless) objects —v. 1 fill 2 cram —**stuff′ing** n.

stuffed shirt n. [Sl.] pompous, pretentious person

stuff′y a. **-i·er, -i·est** 1 poorly ventilated 2 stopped up 3 [Col.] dull

stul′ti·fy v. **-fied′, -fy′ing** make seem foolish, etc.

stum′ble v. 1 walk unsteadily; trip 2 speak confusedly 3 come by chance —n. a stumbling

stum′bling block n. difficulty

stump n. part left after cutting off the rest —v. 1 make a speaking tour 2 walk heavily 3 [Col.] baffle

stun v. **stunned, stun′ning** 1 make unconscious, as by a blow 2 shock deeply

stung v. pt. & pp. of STING

stunk v. pp. & alt. pt. of STINK

stun′ning a. [Col.] very attractive

stunt v. keep from growing —n. daring show of skill

stu′pe·fy v. **-fied′, -fy′ing** stun —**stu′pe·fac′tion** n.

stu·pen′dous a. overwhelming

stu′pid a. 1 not intelligent 2 foolish 3 dull —**stu·pid′i·ty** n., pl. **-ties**

stu′por n. dazed condition

stur′dy a. **-di·er, -di·est** 1 firm 2 strong

stur′geon (-jən) n. food fish

stut′ter n., v. stammer

sty n., pl. **sties** pigpen

sty, stye n., pl. **sties** swelling on the rim of the eyelid

style n. 1 way of making, writing, etc. 2 fine style 3 fashion —v. 1 name 2 design the style of

styl′ish a. fashionable

styl′ize v. design or depict in a style rather than naturally

sty′lus n. 1 pointed writing tool 2 phonograph needle

sty′mie v. **-mied, -mie·ing** to obstruct; block

styp′tic (stip′-) a. that halts bleeding; astringent

styptic pencil n. piece of a styptic substance to stop minor bleeding

Sty′ro·foam′ trademark rigid, light, porous plastic —n. [s—] this substance

suave (swäv) a. smoothly polite —**suav′i·ty** n.

sub- pref. 1 under; below 2 somewhat 3 being a division

sub′a·tom′ic a. smaller than an atom

sub·con′scious a., n. (of) one's feelings, wishes, etc. of which one is unaware

sub·cu·ta′ne·ous (-kyōō-) a. beneath the skin

sub′di·vide′ v. 1 divide again 2 divide (land) into small sections for sale —**sub′di·vi′sion** n.

sub·due′ v. 1 get control over 2 make less intense

sub′ject (v.: səb jekt′) a. 1 that is a subject 2 liable 3 contingent upon —n. 1 one controlled by another 2 topic of discussion or study 3 Gram. word or words about which something is said —v. 1 bring under the control of 2 make undergo —**sub·jec′tion** n.

sub·jec′tive a. of one's feelings rather than from facts —**sub′jec·tiv′i·ty** n.

sub′ju·gate′ v. conquer

sub′lease′ (v.: sub lēs′) n. lease granted by a lessee —v. grant or hold a sublease of

sub·let′ v. 1 sublease 2 let out work one has contracted to do

sub′li·mate′ v. 1 to sublime 2 express (unacceptable impulses) in acceptable forms —**sub′li·ma′tion** n.

sub·lime′ a. noble; lofty —v. purify (a solid) by heating and then condensing —**sub·lim′i·ty** n.

sub·lim′i·nal a. below the threshold of awareness

sub·ma·chine′ gun *n.* portable, automatic firearm

sub·mar′gin·al *a.* below minimum standards

sub·ma·rine′ *n.* warship operating under water

submarine sandwich *n.* hero sandwich

sub·merge′ *v.* put or go under water —**sub·mer′gence** *n.*

sub·merse′ *v.* submerge —**sub·mer′sion** *n.*

sub·mis′sion *n.* 1 a submitting 2 obedience —**sub·mis′sive** *a.*

sub·mit′ *v.* -**mit′ted**, -**mit′ting** 1 to present for consideration, etc. 2 surrender

sub·nor′mal *a.* below normal, as in intelligence

sub·or′di·nate (-nət; *v.:* -nāt′) *a.* lower in rank; secondary —*n.* subordinate person —*v.* to make subordinate

sub·orn′ *v.* induce (another) to commit perjury

sub·poe·na, sub·pe·na (sə pē′nə) *n.* legal paper ordering one to appear in court —*v.* to order with a subpoena

sub·scribe′ *v.* 1 give support or consent (to) 2 promise to contribute (money) 3 agree to take and pay for a periodical, etc.: with *to* —**sub·scrip′tion** *n.*

sub′se·quent *a.* following

sub·ser′vi·ent *a.* servile

sub·side′ *v.* 1 to sink lower 2 become quieter

sub·sid′i·ar′y *a.* helping in a lesser way —*n.*, *pl.* -**ies** company controlled by another

sub·si·dize′ *v.* support with a subsidy

sub′si·dy *n.*, *pl.* -**dies** (government) grant of money

sub·sist′ *v.* continue to live or exist

sub·sist′ence *n.* 1 a subsisting 2 livelihood

sub′soil′ *n.* layer of soil beneath the surface soil

sub·son′ic *a.* moving at a speed less than sound

sub′stance *n.* 1 essence 2 physical matter 3 central meaning 4 wealth

sub·stand′ard *a.* below standard

sub·stan′tial (-shəl) *a.* 1 material 2 strong 3 large 4 wealthy 5 in essentials

sub·stan′ti·ate′ (-shē-) *v.* prove to be true or real

sub′sti·tute′ *n.* one that takes the place of another —*v.* use as or be a substitute —**sub′sti·tu′tion** *n.*

sub′ter·fuge′ *n.* scheme used to evade something

sub′ter·ra′ne·an *a.* 1 underground 2 secret

sub′text′ *n.* underlying meaning, theme, etc.

sub′ti·tle *n.* 1 secondary title 2 line translating dialogue, etc. as at the bottom of a film image

sub·tle (sut′'l) *a.* 1 keen; acute 2 crafty 3 delicate 4 not obvious —**sub′tle·ty** *n.*, *pl.* -**ties** —**sub′tly** *adv.*

sub·tract′ *v.* take away, as one number from another —**sub·trac′tion** *n.*

sub′tra·hend′ *n.* quantity to be subtracted from another

sub′urb′ *n.* district, town, etc. on the outskirts of a city —**sub·ur′ban** *a.* —**sub·ur′ban·ite′** *n.*

sub·ur′bi·a *n.* suburbs or suburbanites collectively

sub·vert′ *v.* overthrow (something established) —**sub·ver′sion** *n.* —**sub·ver′sive** *a.*, *n.*

sub′way′ *n.* underground electric railroad in a city

suc·ceed′ *v.* 1 come next after 2 have success

suc·cess′ *n.* 1 favorable result 2 the gaining of wealth, fame, etc. 3 successful one —**suc·cess′ful** *a.* —**suc·cess′ful·ly** *adv.*

suc·ces′sion *n.* 1 a coming after another 2 series —**suc·ces′sive** *a.*

suc·ces′sor *n.* one who succeeds another, as in office

suc·cinct′ (-siŋkt′) *a.* terse

suc′cor (-ər) *v.*, *n.* help

suc′co·tash′ *n.* beans and corn kernels cooked together

suc′cu·lent *a.* juicy

suc·cumb′ (-kum′) *v.* 1 give in; yield 2 die

such *a.* 1 of this or that kind 2 whatever 3 so much —*pron.* such a one —**such as** for example

suck *v.* 1 draw into the mouth 2 suck liquid from 3 dissolve in the mouth —*n.* act of sucking

suck′er *n.* 1 one that sucks or clings 2 sprout 3 lollipop 4 [Sl.] dupe

suck′le *v.* give or get milk from the breast or udder

suck′ling *n.* unweaned child or young animal

su′crose′ *n.* sugar found in sugar cane, sugar beets, etc.

suc′tion *n.* creation of a vacuum that sucks in fluid, etc. —*a.* worked by suction

sud′den *a.* 1 unexpected 2 hasty —**sud′den·ly** *adv.*

suds *n.pl.* foam on soapy water —**suds′y** *a.*, -**i·er**, -**i·est**

sue *v.* 1 begin a lawsuit against 2 petition

suede (swād) *n.* 1 leather with one side buffed into a nap 2 cloth like this

su′et *n.* hard animal fat

suf'fer v. 1 undergo or endure (pain, loss, etc.) 2 tolerate —**suf'fer·ance** n.

suf·fice' v. be enough

suf·fi'cient (-fish'ənt) a. enough —**suf·fi'cien·cy** n. —**suf·fi'cient·ly** adv.

suf'fix n. syllable(s) added at the end of a word to alter its meaning, etc.

suf'fo·cate' v. 1 kill by cutting off air 2 die from lack of air 3 stifle —**suf'fo·ca'tion** n.

suf'frage n. right to vote

suf·fuse' (-fyōōz') v. overspread, as with color

sug'ar n. sweet carbohydrate found in sugar cane, etc.

sugar beet n. beet with a white root of high sugar content

sugar cane n. tall tropical grass grown for its sugar

sug'ar-coat' v. make seem more pleasant

sug·gest' v. 1 bring to mind 2 propose as a possibility 3 imply —**sug·ges'tion** n.

sug·gest'i·ble a. readily influenced by suggestion

sug·ges'tive a. suggesting ideas, esp. indecent ideas

su'i·cide' n. 1 act of killing oneself intentionally 2 one who commits suicide —**su'i·ci'dal** a.

suit n. 1 coat and trousers (or skirt) 2 any of the four sets of playing cards 3 lawsuit 4 a suing, pleading, etc. —v. 1 be suitable for 2 make suitable 3 please —**follow suit** follow the example set

suit'a·ble a. appropriate; fitting —**suit'a·bly** adv.

suit'case' n. traveling bag

suite (swēt) n. 1 group of connected rooms 2 set of matched furniture

suit'or n. man who courts a woman

su·ki·ya·ki (-kē yä'kē) n. Japanese dish of thinly sliced meat and vegetables

sul'fa a. of a family of drugs used in combating certain bacterial infections

sul'fate' n. salt of sulfuric acid

sul'fide' n. compound of sulfur

sul'fur n. yellow solid substance, a chemical element —**sul·fu'ric** (-fyoor'ik), **sul'fu·rous** a.

sulfuric acid n. acid formed of hydrogen, sulfur, and oxygen

sulk v. be sulky —n. sulky mood: also **the sulks**

sulk'y a. -i·er, -i·est sullen; glum —n., pl. -ies light, two-wheeled carriage —**sulk'i·ly** adv.

sul'len a. 1 showing ill-humor by morose withdrawal 2 gloomy —**sul'len·ly** adv.

sul'ly v. -lied, -ly·ing soil, stain, defile, etc.

sul'phur n. Br. sp. of SULFUR

sul'tan n. Muslim ruler

sul'try a. -tri·er, -tri·est 1 hot and humid 2 inflamed, as with passion

sum n. 1 amount of money 2 summary 3 total —v. **summed, sum'ming** summarize

su·mac, su·mach (shōō' mak, sōō'-) n. plant with lance-shaped leaves and red fruit

sum'ma·rize' v. make or be a summary of

sum'ma·ry n., pl. -ries brief report; digest —a. 1 concise 2 prompt —**sum·mar'i·ly** adv.

sum·ma'tion n. summarizing of arguments, as in a trial

sum'mer n. warmest season of the year —a. of or for summer —v. pass the summer —**sum'mer·y** a.

sum'mer-house' n. small, open structure in a garden, etc.

summer sausage n. hard, dried sausage, not spoiling easily

sum'mit n. highest point

sum'mon v. 1 call together 2 send for 3 rouse

sum'mons n. official order to appear in court

su'mo (wrestling) n. Japanese wrestling by large, extremely heavy men

sump'tu·ous (-choo əs) a. costly; lavish

sun n. 1 incandescent body about which (the) planets revolve 2 heat or light of the sun —v. **sunned, sun'ning** expose to sunlight

sun'bathe' v. expose the body to sunlight or a sunlamp —**sun bath** n. —**sun'bath'er** n.

sun'beam' n. beam of sunlight

sun'block' n. sunscreen

sun'bon'net n. bonnet for shading the face, neck, etc. from the sun

sun'burn' n. inflammation of the skin from exposure to the sun —v. give or get sunburn

sun'burst' n. 1 sudden sunlight 2 decoration representing the sun's rays

sun'dae n. ice cream covered with syrup, nuts, etc.

Sun'day first day of the week

sun'der v. break apart

sun'di'al n. instrument that shows time by the shadow cast by the sun

sun'down' n. sunset

sun'dries n.pl. sundry items

sun'dry a. various

sun'fish' n. 1 small freshwater fish 2 large sea fish

sun'flow'er n. tall plant with big, daisylike flowers

sung v. pp. of SING

sun'glass'es n.pl. eyeglasses with tinted lenses

sunk v. pp. & alt. pt. of SINK

sunk′en *a.* 1 sunk in liquid 2 depressed; hollow

sun′lamp′ *n.* an ultraviolet-ray lamp, used for tanning the body, etc.

sun′light′ *n.* light of the sun

sun′lit′ *a.* lighted by the sun

sun′ny *a.* **–ni·er, –ni·est** 1 full of sunshine 2 cheerful

sun′rise′ *n.* daily rising of the sun in the east

sun′roof′ *n.* car roof with a panel to let in air and light

sun′screen′ *n.* chemical used in creams, etc. to block ultraviolet rays and reduce sunburn

sun′set′ *n.* daily setting of the sun in the west

sun′shine′ *n.* 1 shining of the sun 2 light from the sun —**sun′shin′y** *a.*

sun′spot′ *n.* temporary dark spot on sun

sun′stroke′ *n.* illness from overexposure to the sun

sun′suit′ *n.* short pants with a bib and shoulder straps, worn by young children

sun′tan′ *n.* skin darkened by exposure to the sun

sup *v.* **supped, sup′ping** have supper

su′per *a.* [Col.] outstanding

super– *pref.* 1 over; above 2 very; very much 3 greater than others 4 extra

su′per·an′nu·at′ed *a.* 1 retired on a pension 2 too old to work or use

su·perb′ *a.* excellent

su′per·charge′ *v.* increase an engine's power

su′per·cil′i·ous (-sil′-) *a.* disdainful; haughty

su′per·con·duc·tiv′i·ty *n.* lack of electrical resistance in some metals at low temperatures

su′per·fi′cial (-fish′əl) *a.* 1 of or on the surface 2 shallow; hasty —**su′per·fi′cial·ly** *adv.*

su·per′flu·ous *a.* unnecessary —**su′per·flu′i·ty** *n.*

su′per·high′way′ *n.* expressway

su′per·hu′man *a.* 1 divine 2 greater than normal

su′per·im·pose′ *v.* put on top of something else

su′per·in·tend′ *v.* direct or manage —**su′per·in·tend′ent** *n.*

su·pe′ri·or *a.* 1 higher in rank, etc. 2 above average 3 haughty —*n.* one that is superior —**superior to** unaffected by —**su·pe′ri·or′i·ty** *n.*

su·per′la·tive *a.* of the highest degree; supreme —*n.* 1 highest degree 2 third degree in the comparison of adjectives and adverbs

su′per·man′ *n., pl.* **–men** seemingly superhuman man

su′per·mar′ket *n.* large, self-service food store

su′per·nat′u·ral *a.* beyond known laws of nature —**the supernatural** supernatural things

su′per·nu′mer·ar′y *a.; n., pl.* **–ies** extra (person or thing)

su′per·scribe′ *v.* write on the top or outside of

su′per·script′ *n.* figure, letter, etc. written above and to the side of another

su′per·sede′ *v.* replace, succeed, or supplant

su′per·son′ic *a.* 1 traveling faster than sound 2 ultrasonic

su′per·star′ *n.* famous athlete, entertainer, etc.

su′per·sti′tion *n.* belief or practice based on fear or ignorance —**su′per·sti′tious** *a.*

su′per·struc′ture *n.* 1 part above a ship's deck 2 upper part of a building

su′per·tank′er *n.* extremely large oil tanker

su′per·vene′ *v.* come unexpectedly

su′per·vise′ *v.* oversee or direct —**su′per·vi′sion** *n.* —**su′per·vi′sor** *n.* —**su′per·vi′so·ry** *a.*

su′pine′ *a.* 1 lying on the back 2 lazy

sup′per *n.* evening meal

sup·plant′ *v.* take the place of, esp. by force

sup′ple *a.* flexible

sup′ple·ment *n.* something added —*v.* add to —**sup′ple·men′tal, sup′ple·men′ta·ry** *a.*

sup′pli·cate′ *v.* implore —**sup′pli·ant, sup′pli·cant** *n., a.* —**sup′pli·ca′tion** *n.*

sup·ply′ *v.* **–plied′, –ply′ing** 1 furnish; provide 2 make up for —*n., pl.* **–plies′** 1 amount available 2 *pl.* materials —**sup·pli′er** *n.*

sup·port′ *v.* 1 hold up 2 help 3 provide for 4 help prove —*n.* 1 a supporting 2 that which supports

sup·port′ive *a.* giving support, help, or approval

sup·pose′ *v.* 1 take as true; assume 2 guess; think 3 expect —**sup·posed′** *a.* —**sup′po·si′tion** *n.*

sup·pos′i·to′ry *n., pl.* **–ries** medicated substance put in the rectum or vagina

sup·press′ *v.* 1 put down by force 2 keep back; conceal —**sup·pres′sion** *n.*

sup′pu·rate′ (-yōō-) *v.* become filled with pus

su′pra·na′tion·al *a.* of, for, or above all or a number of nations

su·prem′a·cy *n.* supreme power or authority

su·preme′ *a.* highest in rank, power, or degree

sur·cease′ n. end or cessation

sur·charge′ n. 1 extra charge 2 overload —v. put a surcharge in or on

sure a. 1 reliable; certain 2 without doubt 3 bound to happen or do —adv. [Col.] surely —**for sure** certainly —**sure enough** [Col.] without doubt

sure′-fire′ a. [Col.] sure to be successful

sure′-foot′ed a. not likely to stumble, err, etc.

sure′ly adv. 1 with confidence 2 without doubt

sur′e·ty n., pl. —**ties** 1 security 2 guarantor of another's debts

surf n. ocean waves breaking on a shore or reef

sur·face n. 1 outside of a thing 2 any face of a solid 3 outward look —a. superficial —v. 1 give a surface to 2 rise to the surface

surf′board′ n. long board used in riding the surf

sur·feit (-fit) n. 1 excess, as of food 2 sickness caused by this —v. overindulge

surf′ing n. sport of riding the surf on a surfboard

surge v., n. (move in) a large wave or sudden rush

sur′geon n. doctor who practices surgery

sur′ger·y n. 1 treatment of disease or injury by operations 2 a room for this —**sur′gi·cal** a.

sur′ly a. —**li·er**, —**li·est** bad-tempered; uncivil

sur·mise′ (-mīz′) n., v. guess

sur·mount′ v. 1 to overcome 2 climb over 3 top —**sur·mount′a·ble** a.

sur·name′ n. family name

sur·pass′ v. 1 excel 2 go beyond the limit of

sur′plice (-plis) n. clergyman's loose, white tunic

sur′plus′ n., a. (quantity) over what is needed or used

sur·prise′ v. 1 come upon unexpectedly 2 astonish —n. 1 a surprising or being surprised 2 thing that surprises —**sur·pris′ing** a.

sur·re′al a. fantastic or bizarre

sur·re′al·ism′ n. art depicting the unconscious mind —**sur·re′al·ist** a., n.

sur·ren′der v. 1 give oneself up 2 give up; abandon —n. act of surrendering

sur′rep·ti′tious (-tish′əs) a. secret; stealthy

sur′rey n., pl. —**reys** light, four-wheeled carriage

sur′ro·gate (-gət) n., a. (a) substitute

sur·round′ v. encircle on all sides

sur·round′ings n.pl. things, conditions, etc. around a person or thing

sur′tax′ n. extra tax on top of the regular tax

sur·veil′lance (-vā′-) n. watch kept over a person

sur·vey′ (n.: sur′vā′) v. 1 examine in detail 2 determine the form, boundaries, etc. of a piece of land —n. 1 general or comprehensive study 2 act of surveying an area —**sur·vey′or** n.

sur·vey′ing n. science or work of making land surveys

sur·vive′ v. 1 outlive 2 continue to live —**sur·viv′al** n. —**sur·viv′or** n.

sus·cep′ti·ble (sə sep′-) a. easily affected; sensitive

su′shi n. Japanese dish of rice cakes, raw fish, etc.

sus·pect′ (n.: sus′pekt′) v. 1 believe to be guilty on little evidence 2 distrust 3 surmise —n. one suspected

sus·pend′ v. 1 exclude, stop, etc. for a time 2 hold back (judgment, etc.) 3 hang —**sus·pen′sion** n.

sus·pend′ers n.pl. shoulder straps to hold up trousers

sus·pense′ n. tense uncertainty

suspension bridge n. bridge suspended by anchored cables from supporting towers

sus·pi·cion (sə spish′ən) n. 1 a suspecting or being suspected 2 feeling of one who suspects 3 trace —**sus·pi′cious** a.

sus·tain′ v. 1 maintain; prolong 2 provide for 3 support 4 suffer 5 uphold as valid 6 confirm

sus′te·nance n. 1 means of livelihood 2 food

su′ture (-chər) n. 1 stitching up of a wound, or stitch so used

su′ze·rain′ (-rin′, -rān′) n. state having some control over another state

svelte a. 1 slender and graceful 2 suave

swab n. 1 a mop 2 piece of cotton, etc. used to medicate or clean the throat, etc. —v. **swabbed**, **swab′bing** clean with a swab

swad′dle v. wrap (a baby) in narrow bands of cloth

swage (swāj) n. tool for shaping or bending metal

swag′ger v. 1 walk with a bold stride 2 brag loudly —n. swaggering walk

swain n. [Poet.] lover

swal′low v. 1 pass (food, etc.) from the mouth into the stomach 2 take in; absorb 3 tolerate 4 suppress —n. 1 act of swallowing 2 amount swallowed 3 small, swift-flying bird

swam v. pt. of SWIM

swa′mi n. Hindu religious teacher

swamp n. piece of wet, spongy ground —v. 1 flood with water 2 overwhelm —**swamp′y** a., —**i·er**, —**i·est**

swamp buggy n. vehicle for traveling over swampy ground

swan n. large water bird with a long graceful neck

swank a. [Col.] ostentatiously stylish: also **swank′y**, **-i-er**, **-i-est**

swan song n. last act, final work, etc. of a person

swap n., v. **swapped**, **swap′ping** [Col.] trade

sward n. grass-covered soil

swarm n. 1 colony of bees 2 large, moving mass of insects, etc. —v. move in a swarm

swarth·y (swôr′thē) a. **-i-er**, **-i-est** dark-skinned

swash′buck′ler n. swaggering fighting man

swas′ti·ka n. cross with bent arms: Nazi emblem

swat v., n. **swat′ted**, **swat′ting** (hit with) a quick, sharp blow —**swat′ter** n.

swatch n. sample bit of cloth

swath n. a strip cut by a scythe, mower, etc.

swathe (swāth, swä*th*) v. 1 wrap up in a bandage 2 envelop

sway v. 1 swing from side to side or to and fro 2 incline 3 influence —n. 1 a swaying 2 influence

swear v. **swore**, **sworn**, **swear′ing** 1 make a solemn declaration or promise 2 curse 3 make take an oath

swear′word′ n. profane or obscene word or phrase

sweat n. 1 salty liquid given off through the skin 2 moisture collected on a surface —v. **sweat** or **sweat′ed**, **sweat′ing** 1 give forth sweat 2 work so hard as to cause sweating —**sweat′y** a., **-i-er**, **-i-est**

sweat′er n. knitted garment for the upper body

sweat shirt n. heavy jersey worn to absorb sweat

sweat′shop′ n. shop having many hours of work at low wages

Swed′ish a., n. (of) the people or language of Sweden

sweep v. **swept**, **sweep′ing** 1 clean, or clear away, with a broom 2 carry away or pass over swiftly 3 extend in a long line —n. 1 a sweeping 2 range or extent —**sweep′ing** a.

sweep′ings n.pl. things swept up

sweep′stakes′ n., pl. **-stakes′** lottery on a horse race

sweet a. 1 tasting of sugar 2 pleasant 3 fresh —n. a candy —**sweet′en** v. —**sweet′ly** adv.

sweet′bread′ n. calf's pancreas or thymus, used as food

sweet′bri′er, **sweet′bri′ar** n. kind of rose

sweet corn n. kind of corn cooked and eaten before it is ripe

sweet′en·er n. sugar substitute

sweet′heart′ n. loved one

sweet′meat′ n. a candy

sweet pea n. climbing plant with fragrant flowers

sweet pepper n. 1 red pepper producing a large, mild fruit 2 the fruit

sweet potato n. thick, yellow root of a tropical vine

sweet′-talk′ v. [Col.] to flatter

sweet tooth n. [Col.] fondness for sweet foods

swell v. **swelled**, **swelled** or **swol′len**, **swell′ing** 1 bulge 2 increase in size, force, etc. 3 fill, as with pride —n. 1 a swelling 2 large wave —a. [Sl.] excellent

swell′head′ n. [Col.] conceited person

swell′ing n. 1 swollen part 2 increase

swel·ter v. feel oppressed with great heat

swel·ter·ing a. very hot

swept v. pt. & pp. of SWEEP.

swerve v., n. (make) a quick turn aside

swift a. 1 moving fast 2 prompt —n. swallowlike bird —**swift′ly** adv.

swig [Col.] v. **swigged**, **swig′ging** drink in large gulps —n. large gulp

swill v. drink greedily —n. garbage fed to pigs

swim v. **swam**, **swum**, **swim′ming** 1 move in water by moving the limbs, fins, etc. 2 float on a liquid 3 overflow 4 be dizzy —n. a swimming —**swim′mer** n.

swimming hole n. deep place in a creek, etc. used for swimming

swim′suit′ n. garment worn for swimming

swin′dle v. defraud; cheat —n. a swindling

swine n., pl. **swine** pig or hog —**swin′ish** a.

swing v. **swung**, **swing′ing** 1 sway back and forth 2 turn, as on a hinge 3 manage to get, win, etc. 4 to strike (at) —n. 1 a swinging 2 a sweeping blow 3 musical rhythm 4 seat hanging from ropes

swipe n. [Col.] hard, sweeping blow —v. 1 [Col.] hit with a swipe 2 [Sl.] steal

swirl v., n. whirl; twist

swish v., n. (move with) a hissing or rustling sound

Swiss a., n. (of) the people of Switzerland

Swiss chard n. chard

Swiss (cheese) n. pale-yellow cheese with large holes

Swiss steak n. round steak pounded with flour and braised

switch n. 1 thin stick used for whipping 2 control device for an electric circuit 3 movable section of railroad track 4 shift; change —v. 1 to whip 2 jerk 3 turn a light, etc. on or off 4 move a train to another track 5 shift

switch′blade′ (knife) n. jackknife opened by a spring release

switch′board′ n. control panel for electric switches

switch′-hit′ter n. baseball player who bats left-handed and right-handed

swiv′el n. fastening with free-turning parts —v. turn as on a swivel

swiz′zle stick′ n. small rod for stirring mixed drinks

swol·len (swō′lən) v. alt. pp. of SWELL —a. bulging

swoon v., n. faint

swoop v. sweep down or pounce upon —n. a swooping

sword (sôrd) n. weapon with a handle and a long blade

sword′fish′ n. large ocean fish with a sword-like jaw

sword′play′ n. the act or skill of using a sword

swore v. pt. of SWEAR

sworn v. pp. of SWEAR —a. bound by an oath

swum v. pp. of SWIM

syc′a·more′ (sik′-) n. shade tree with shedding bark

syc·o·phant (sik′ə fənt) n. flatterer

syl·lab′i·fy′ v. -fied′, -fy′ing divide into syllables: also **syl·lab′i·cate′** —**syl·lab′i·fi·ca′tion** n.

syl′la·ble n. 1 single vocal sound 2 written form of this —**syl·lab′ic** a.

syl′la·bus n., pl. -**bus·es** or -**bi′** (-bī′) summary or outline

syl′lo·gism′ (-jiz′əm) n. two premises and a conclusion

sylph (silf) n. slender, graceful woman

syl′van a. of, living in or covered with trees

sym·bi·ot′ic (-bī-, -bē-) a. mutually dependent

sym′bol n. object, mark, etc. that represents another object, an idea, etc. —**sym·bol′ic, sym·bol′i·cal** a. —**sym′bol·ize′** v.

sym′bol·ism′ n. 1 use of symbols 2 set of symbols

sym′me·try n. balance of opposite parts in position or size —**sym·met′ri·cal** a.

sym′pa·thet′ic a. of, in, or feeling sympathy —**sym′pa·thet′i·cal·ly** adv.

sym′pa·thize′ v. feel or show sympathy

sym′pa·thy n., pl. -**thies** 1 sameness of feeling 2 agreement 3 compassion

sym′pho·ny n., pl. -**nies** full orchestra or composition for it —**sym·phon′ic** a.

sym·po′si·um n., pl. -**ums** or -**a** meeting for discussion

symp′tom n. indication or sign, as of disease —**symp′to·mat′ic** a.

syn′a·gogue (-gäg′) n. building where Jews worship

sync, synch (siŋk) v. **synced** or **synched, sync′ing** or **synch′ing** synchronize —n. synchronization

syn′chro·nize′ v. 1 move or occur at the same time or rate 2 make agree in time or rate —**syn′chro·ni·za′tion** n.

syn′co·pate′ v. Mus. shift the beat to unaccented notes —**syn′co·pa′tion** n.

syn′di·cate (-kət; v.: -kāt′) n. 1 business association of bankers, corporations, etc. 2 organization selling news stories, etc. —v. publish through a syndicate

syn′drome n. set of symptoms characterizing a disease or condition

syn′od n. council of churches or church officials

syn′o·nym (-nim) n. word meaning the same as another —**syn·on′y·mous** a.

syn·op′sis n., pl. -**ses** (-sēz′) summary

syn′tax′ n. the way words are arranged in a sentence —**syn·tac′ti·cal** a.

syn′the·sis n., pl. -**ses** (-sēz′) combining of parts into a whole —**syn′the·size′** v.

syn′the·siz′er n. an electronic device for producing musical sounds without instruments

syn·thet′ic a. 1 of or using synthesis 2 artificial; not natural —n. synthetic thing —**syn·thet′i·cal·ly** adv.

syph′i·lis (sif′-) n. infectious venereal disease —**syph′i·lit′ic** a., n.

sy·ringe (sə rinj′) n. ball with a tube, for ejecting fluids

syr′up n. sweet, thick liquid, as of sugar boiled in water —**syr′up·y** a.

sys′tem n. 1 whole formed of related things 2 set of organized facts, rules, etc. 3 orderly way of doing things —**sys′tem·a·tize′** v.

sys·tem·at′ic a. orderly; methodical —**sys′tem·at′i·cal·ly** adv.

sys·tem′ic a. of or affecting the body as a whole

sys′to·le′ (-tə le′) n. usual rhythmic contraction of the heart, esp. of the ventricles —**sys·tol′ic** a.

T

tab n. small flap or tag —**keep tab on** —**keep tabs on** [Col.] keep informed about

tab′by n., pl. -**bies** pet cat

tab·er·nac′le (-nak′əl) n. large place of worship

ta′ble n. 1 flat surface set on legs 2 table set with food 3 orderly list or arrangement —v. postpone

tab′leau′ (-lō′) n., pl. -**leaux** (-lōz′) or -**leaus** scene by persons posing in costume

ta′ble-cloth′ n. cloth for covering a table at meals

ta′ble-hop′ v. -**hopped′**, -**hop′ping** leave

one's table and visit about at other tables

ta'ble·land' n. plateau

ta'ble·spoon' n. spoon holding ½ fluid ounce —**ta'ble·spoon'ful** n., pl. —**fuls**

tab'let n. 1 flat, inscribed piece of stone, metal, etc. 2 writing pad 3 flat, hard cake of medicine

table tennis n. game like tennis, played on a table

ta'ble·ware' n. dishes, forks, etc. used for eating

tab'loid' n. small newspaper with sensational news stories

ta·boo', ta·bu' n. sacred or social prohibition —v. prohibit

tab'u·lar a. of or arranged in a table or list

tab'u·late' v. put in tabular form —**tab'u·la'tion** n.

ta·chom'e·ter (ta käm'-) n. a device showing rate of rotation of a shaft

tac'it (tas'-) a. not expressed openly, but implied

tac'i·turn' (tas'-) a. usually silent —**tac'i·tur'ni·ty** n.

tack n. 1 short, flat-headed nail 2 a course of action 3 ship's direction relative to position of sails —v. 1 fasten with tacks 2 add 3 change course

tack'le n. 1 equipment 2 set of ropes and pulleys 3 a tackling —v. 1 undertake 2 Football bring down (the ball carrier)

tack'y a. **-i·er, -i·est** 1 slightly sticky 2 [Col.] in poor taste —**tack'i·ness** n.

ta'co (tä'-) n., pl. **-cos** folded, fried tortilla, filled with meat, etc.

tact n. skill in dealing with people —**tact'ful** a. —**tact'less** a.

tac'tic n. skillful method

tac'tics n. science of battle maneuvers —**tac'ti·cal** a. —**tac·ti'cian** (-tish'ən) n.

tad n. small amount

tad'pole' n. frog or toad in an early stage

taf'fe·ta n. stiff silk cloth

taff'rail' n. rail around a ship's stern

taf'fy n. a chewy candy

tag n. 1 hanging end 2 card, etc. attached as a label 3 children's chasing game —v. 1 provide with a tag 2 touch as in game of tag 3 [Col.] follow closely: with along, after, etc.

tail n. 1 appendage at rear end of an animal's body 2 hind or end part —v. [Col.] follow closely —a. at or from the rear —**tail'less** a.

tail'bone' n. coccyx

tail'gate' n. hinged door or gate at the back of a truck, etc. —v. to drive too closely behind (another vehicle)

tail'light' n. red light at the back of a vehicle

tai'lor n. one who makes or alters clothes

—v. 1 make by a tailor's work 2 form, alter, etc. to suit

tail'pipe' n. exhaust pipe at the rear of a car or truck

tail'spin' n. sharp downward plunge of a plane with tail spinning in circles

taint v. 1 spoil; rot 2 make corrupt or depraved —n. trace of contamination

take v. **took, tak'en, tak'ing** 1 grasp 2 capture, seize, win, etc. 3 obtain, select, assume, etc. 4 use, consume, etc. 5 buy; rent 6 travel by 7 deal with 8 occupy 9 derive from 10 write down 11 make (a photograph) 12 require 13 engage in 14 understand 15 have or feel 16 carry, lead, etc. 17 remove 18 subtract —n. amount taken —**take after** act or look like —**take in** 1 admit; receive 2 make smaller 3 understand 4 trick —**take over** begin managing —**take up** 1 make tighter or shorter 2 absorb 3 engage in

take'off' n. 1 a leaving the ground, as for flight 2 [Col.] mocking imitation; caricature Also **take'-off**

tak'ing a. attractive; charming —n. pl. profits

tal'cum (powder) n. powder for the body and face made from a soft mineral (**talc**)

tale n. 1 story 2 lie 3 gossip

tale'bear'er n. one who spreads scandal, etc.; gossip

tal'ent n. special, natural ability —**tal'ent·ed** a.

tal'is·man n., pl. **-mans** anything supposed to have magic power

talk v. 1 says words; speak 2 gossip 3 confer 4 discuss —n. 1 a talking 2 conversation 3 speech 4 conference 5 gossip —**talk back** answer impertinently —**talk'er** n.

talk'a·tive a. talking a great deal: also **talk'y**

talk'ing-to' n. [Col.] a scolding

tall a. high, as in stature

tal'low n. hard animal fat used in candles and soap

tal'ly n., pl. **-lies** record, account, etc. —v. 1 record; score 2 add 3 agree

tal'ly·ho' int. fox hunter's cry —n., pl. **-hos'** coach drawn by four horses

Tal·mud' (täl'mood) body of early Jewish law

tal'on n. claw of a bird of prey

tam n. tam-o'-shanter

ta·ma'le (-mä'lē) n. peppery chopped meat rolled in corn meal

tam'a·rack' n. swamp larch

tam'bou·rine' (-ba rēn') n. small, shallow drum with metal disks around it

tame a. 1 trained from a wild state 2 gentle 3 not lively; dull —v. make tame —**tame'ly** adv. —**tam'er** n.

tam'-o'-shan'ter n. flat, round Scottish cap

tamp v. pack down by tapping —**tamp'er** n.

tam'per v. interfere (with)

tam'pon' n. plug of cotton for absorbing blood, etc.

tan n. yellowish brown —a. **tan'ner, tan'nest** yellowish-brown —v. **tanned, tan'ning** 1 make (hide) into leather by soaking in tannic acid 2 brown by sun's rays

tan'a·ger n. American songbird

tan'bark' n. tree bark containing tannic acid

tan'dem adv. one behind another

tang n. strong taste or odor —**tang'y** a., **-i·er, -i·est**

tan'ge·lo' (-jə-) n., pl. **-los'** fruit that is a hybrid of the tangerine and grapefruit

tan'gent a. touching a curve at one point —n. a tangent curve, line, etc. —**go off at** (or **on**) **a tangent** change suddenly to another line of action —**tan·gen'tial** (-jen'shəl) a.

tan'ge·rine' (-jə·rēn') n. small, loose-skinned orange

tan'gi·ble a. 1 real or solid 2 definite

tan'gle v. 1 make or become knotted, confused, etc. 2 catch, as in a snare —n. tangled mass or condition

tan'go n., pl. **-gos** South American dance —v. dance the tango

tank n. 1 large container for liquid or gas 2 armored vehicle carrying guns

tank'ard n. large drinking cup with a hinged lid

tank'er n. ship for transporting liquids, esp. oil

tank truck n. motor truck for transporting gasoline, etc.

tan'ner·y n., pl. **-ies** place where leather is made by tanning hides —**tan'ner** n.

tan'nic acid n. acid used in tanning, dyeing, etc.: also **tan'nin**

tan'sy (-zē) n., pl. **-sies** plant with small, yellow flowers

tan'ta·lize' v. show but withhold something; tease

tan'ta·mount' a. equal (to)

tan'trum n. fit of rage

tap v. **tapped, tap'ping** 1 hit lightly 2 make a hole in 3 draw off, as liquid 4 connect into —n. 1 light blow 2 faucet or spigot 3 plug or cork 4 place for connection

tap dance n. dance done with sharp taps of the foot, toe, or heel —**tap'-dance'** v.

tape n. narrow strip of cloth, paper, etc. —v. 1 to bind with a tape 2 record on tape

tape measure n. tape with marks for measuring

ta'per v. decrease or lessen gradually in thickness, loudness, etc. —n. 1 a tapering

2 slender candle

tape recorder n. recording device using magnetic tape

tap'es·try n., pl. **-tries** cloth with woven designs

tape'worm' n. tapelike worm found in the intestines

tap'i·o'ca n. starchy substance from cassava roots

ta'pir (-pər) n. hoglike animal

tap'room' n. barroom

tap'root' n. main root

taps n. bugle call for funerals and the end of the day

tar n. 1 black liquid distilled from wood or coal 2 [Col.] sailor —v. **tarred, tar'ring** cover with tar —**tar'ry** a.

ta·ran'tu·la (-chə lə) n. large, hairy spider

tar'dy a. **-di·er, -di·est** 1 slow 2 late

tare n. 1 a weed 2 container's weight

tar'get n. thing aimed at, shot at, or attacked

tar'iff n. 1 tax on exports or imports 2 list of prices, charges, etc.

tar'nish v. stain; discolor —n. dullness; stain

ta·ro (ter'ō) n. tropical plant with edible root

tar·ot (tar'ō) n. [often **T**–] any of a set of fortunetelling cards

tar·pau'lin (-pô'-) n. waterproofed canvas

tar'pon n. large ocean fish

tar'ra·gon' (tar'ə-) n. seasoning of fragrant leaves of wormwood

tar'ry (tar'ē) v. **-ried, -ry·ing** 1 linger 2 delay

tart a. 1 sour; acid 2 sharp in meaning —n. pastry filled with jam, etc. —**tart'ly** adv. —**tart'ness** n.

tar'tan n. plaid cloth

tar'tar n. hard deposit forming on the teeth

tartar sauce n. sauce of mayonnaise with chopped pickles, olives, etc.

task n. work that must be done —v. burden; strain —**take to task** scold

task force n. group, esp. a military unit, assigned a task

task'mas'ter n. one who assigns severe tasks

tas'sel n. 1 bunch of threads hanging from a knob 2 tuft of corn silk

taste v. 1 notice or test the flavor of in one's mouth 2 eat or drink sparingly 3 have a certain flavor —n. 1 sense for telling flavor 2 flavor 3 small amount 4 sense of the beautiful, proper, etc. 5 liking —**taste'ful** a. —**taste'less** a.

taste bud n. taste organ in the tongue

tast'y a. **-i·er, -i·est** that tastes good

tat v. **tat'ted, tat'ting** make lace with a

hand shuttle

tat′ter n. 1 rag; shred 2 pl. ragged clothes —**tat′tered** a.

tat′ting n. fine lace made by looping and knotting thread

tat′tle v. 1 tell secrets 2 gossip —n. gossip —**tat′tler** n.

tat′tle-tale′ n. informer

tat-too′ v. -**tooed′**, -**too′ing** make designs on the skin —n., pl. -**toos′** 1 tattooed design 2 steady beating, as on a drum

taught v. pt. & pp. of TEACH

taunt v. mock; tease —n. scornful remark

taupe (tōp) n. dark, brownish gray

Tau′rus second sign of the zodiac; Bull

taut a. 1 tightly stretched 2 tense

tau-tol′o-gy (tô-) n. statement that is true by definition —**tau′to-log′i-cal** a.

tav′ern n. saloon or inn

taw′dry a. -**dri-er**, -**dri-est** gaudy and cheap

taw′ny a. -**ni-er**, -**ni-est** dark yellow or tan

tax n. 1 compulsory payment to a government 2 burden; strain —v. 1 levy, or make pay, a tax 2 burden 3 accuse; charge —**tax′a-ble** a. —**tax-a′tion** n. —**tax′pay′er** n.

tax′i n., pl. -**is** taxicab —v. -**ied**, -**i-ing** or -**y-ing** 1 go in a taxicab 2 move along the ground or water, as an airplane

tax′i-cab′ n. automobile for passengers who pay

tax′i-der′my n. art of stuffing animal skins —**tax′i-der′mist** n.

tax-on′o-my n. classification of animals and plants

TB tuberculosis

T′-bone′ steak n. beefsteak with a T-shaped bone

tea n. 1 leaves of an Asian shrub 2 drink made from these 3 similar drink made from other plants, etc. 4 afternoon party with tea —**tea′cup′** n.

tea′ber′ry n., pl. -**ries** wintergreen

teach v. **taught**, **teach′ing** give lessons (in) —**teach′er** n.

teak n. East Indian tree

tea′ket′tle n. kettle with a spout, used to heat water

teal n. 1 wild duck 2 grayish or greenish blue

team n. 1 two or more animals harnessed together 2 group working or playing together —v. join in a team —**team′mate′** n. —**team′work′** n.

team′ster n. truck driver

tea′pot′ n. pot with spout and handle for brewing tea

tear (ter) v. **tore**, **torn**, **tear′ing** 1 pull apart, up, etc. by force 2 make by tearing 3 move fast —n. 1 a tearing 2 torn place —**tear down** wreck

tear (tir) n. drop of liquid from the eye: also **tear′drop′** —**in tears** weeping —**tear′ful**, **tear′y** a.

tear gas n. gas that blinds the eyes with tears: used in warfare

tea′room′ n. restaurant that serves tea, light lunches, etc.

tease v. 1 annoy by poking fun at, etc. 2 fluff up, as hair —n. one who teases

tea′sel (-zal) n. bristly plant with prickly flowers

tea′spoon′ n. small spoon —**tea′spoon·ful′** n., pl. -**fuls′**

teat n. nipple on a breast or udder

tech′ni-cal (tek′-) a. 1 dealing with industrial arts or skills 2 of a specific art, science, etc. 3 of technique —**tech′ni-cal-ly** adv.

tech′ni-cal′i-ty n., pl. -**ties** 1 technical detail 2 minute, formal point

tech-ni′cian (-nish′ən) n. one skilled in a technique or in a technical area

tech-nique′ (-nēk′) n. method of procedure, as in art

tech′no-crat′ n. one who believes in government by scientists, etc. —**tech-noc′ra-cy** n.

tech-nol′o-gy n. study of applied arts and sciences —**tech′no-log′i-cal** a.

ted′dy bear n. child's stuffed toy that looks like a bear

te′di-ous a. tiring; boring

te′di-um n. a being tedious

tee Golf n. 1 small peg to rest the ball on 2 starting place for each hole —v. **teed**, **tee′ing** hit a ball from a tee: with off

teem v. abound; swarm

teen n. 1 pl. numbers or years from 13 through 19 2 teenager —a. teenage

teen′age′ a. 1 in one's teens 2 of or for those in their teens —**teen′ag′er** n.

tee′ny a. -**ni-er**, -**ni-est** [Col.] tiny: also **teen′sy** or **tee′ny-wee′ny**

tee′pee n. tepee

tee shirt n. T-shirt

tee′ter v., n. seesaw

tee′ter-tot′ter n., v. seesaw

teeth n. pl. of TOOTH

teethe (tēth) v. have teeth growing through the gum

tee′to′tal-er, **tee′to′tal-ler** n. one who never drinks liquor

Tef′lon′ trademark nonsticking coating for cookware, etc. —n. [t-] this finish

tel′e-cast′ v. -**cast′** or -**cast′ed**, -**cast′ing** broadcast over television —n. television broadcast

tel′e-com-mu′ni-ca′tion n. [also pl., with sing. or pl. v.] electronic communication using radio, computers, etc.

tel′e-gram′ n. message sent by telegraph

tel′e·graph′ n. device or system for sending messages by electric signals through a wire —v. send a message by telegraph —**te·leg′ra·pher** n. —**tel′e·graph′ic** a. —**te·leg′ra·phy** n.

tel·e·me′ter n. device for transmitting data about temperature, etc. from a remote point —**te·lem′e·try** n.

te·lep′a·thy n. supposed communication between minds without help of speech, sight, etc. —**tel′e·path′ic** a.

tel′e·phone′ n. device or system for talking over distances through wires —v. talk (to) by telephone

tel′e·pho′to a. of a camera lens producing a large image of a distant object

tel′e·scope′ n. device with lenses that magnify distant objects —v. slide one into another —**tel′e·scop′ic** a.

tel′e·thon′ n. televised campaign seeking donations

tel′e·vise′ v. transmit by television

tel·e·vi′sion n. 1 way of sending pictures through space by radio waves to a receiving set 2 such a set

tell v. **told, tell′ing** 1 report; narrate 2 put into words 3 show 4 inform 5 recognize 6 order —**tell off** [Col.] criticize sharply

tell′er n. 1 one who tells 2 cashier at a bank

tell′ing a. forceful

tell′tale′ a. revealing what is meant to be secret

tem′blor (-blôr′, blər) n. earthquake

te·mer′i·ty n. rashness; boldness

tem′per v. 1 make less intense 2 make hard, as steel —n. 1 state of mind 2 self-control 3 rage 4 tendency to become angry

tem′per·a n. painting with pigments mixed with egg, etc.

tem′per·a·ment (-prə mənt, -pər-) n. (moody or excitable) disposition —**tem′per·a·men′tal** a.

tem′per·ance n. 1 self-restraint; moderation 2 abstinence from liquor

tem′per·ate (-ət) a. 1 moderate; self-restrained 2 neither very hot nor very cold

tem′per·a·ture (-prə chər) n. 1 degree of hotness or coldness 2 fever

tem′pered a. having a certain kind of temper

tem′pest n. wild storm —**tem·pes′tu·ous** (-chōō-) a.

tem′plate (-plit) n. pattern for making an exact copy

tem′ple n. 1 a building for worship service or for some special purpose 2 area between the eye and ear

tem′po n., pl. **-pos** or **-pi** (-pē) rate of speed, esp. for playing music

tem′po·ral a. 1 worldly 2 of time

tem′po·rar′y a. lasting only a while —**tem′po·rar′i·ly** adv.

tempt v. 1 entice, esp. to an immoral act 2 provoke 3 to incline strongly —**temp·ta′tion** n.

tem·pu′ra (-poor′ə) n. Japanese dish of deep-fried fish, vegetables, etc.

ten a., n. one more than nine —**tenth** a., n.

ten′a·ble a. that can be defended or believed

te·na′cious (-shəs) a. 1 holding firmly 2 retentive 3 stubborn —**te·nac′i·ty** (-nas′-) n.

ten′ant n. occupant (who pays rent) —**ten′an·cy** n.

tend v. 1 take care of 2 be apt; incline 3 lead

tend′en·cy n., pl. **-cies** a being likely to move or act in a certain way

ten′der a. 1 soft or delicate 2 sensitive 3 loving 4 young —n. 1 thing offered, as in payment 2 car with locomotive's coal 3 one who tends —v. give to one to take —**ten′der·ly** adv.

ten′der·foot′ n., pl. **-foots′** or **-feet′** newcomer, esp. one not used to hardships

ten′der-heart′ed a. quick to feel compassion

ten′der·ize′ v. make tender

ten′der·loin′ n. tenderest part of a loin of meat

ten′don n. cord of tissue binding a muscle to a bone

ten′dril n. threadlike, clinging part of a climbing plant

ten′e·ment n. apartment house, esp. an old one

ten′et n. opinion or belief

ten′nis n. game played by hitting a ball over a net with a racket

tennis shoe n. sneaker

ten′on n. projecting part to fit in a mortise

ten′or n. 1 highest male voice 2 general course 3 meaning

ten′pins′ n. bowling

tense a. 1 taut 2 anxious —v. make or become tense —n. verb form showing time

ten′sile (-səl) a. of or under tension

ten′sion n. 1 a stretching 2 stress from this 3 nervous strain 4 voltage

tent n. shelter of canvas, nylon, etc. supported by poles and stakes

ten′ta·cle n. slender growth on an animal's head, for feeling, grasping, etc.

ten′ta·tive a. not final

ten′ter·hook′ n. hooked nail —**on tenterhooks** in anxious suspense

ten′u·ous (-yōō-) a. 1 thin; fine 2 not dense 3 flimsy

ten′ure (-yər) n. right or duration of holding a position, etc.

te′pee n. cone-shaped tent

tep′id a. lukewarm

te·qui′la (-kē′-) n. strong alcoholic liquor

of Mexico

term n. 1 fixed time period 2 pl. conditions of a contract, etc. 3 pl. personal relationship 4 word or phrase 5 either part of a fraction, etc. —v. name —**come to terms** arrive at an agreement —**in terms of** regarding; concerning

ter'ma·gant n. nagging woman

ter'mi·nal a. 1 of or at the end 2 final —n. 1 end (part) 2 main station, as for buses 3 keyboard and video screen connected to a computer

ter'mi·nate' v. 1 stop; end 2 form the end of —**ter'mi·na'tion** n.

ter'mi·nol'o·gy n., pl. **-gies** special words or phrases

term insurance n. life insurance that expires after a specified period

ter'mi·nus n., pl. **-nus·es** or **-ni'** (-nī') an end, limit, etc.

ter'mite' n. antlike insect that eats wood

tern n. gull-like seabird

ter'race (-as) n. 1 patio 2 flat mound with sloping side 3 row of houses on this —v. make a terrace of

ter'ra cot'ta n. brownish-red earthenware or its color

ter'ra fir'ma n. solid ground

ter·rain' n. area of land with regard to its fitness for use

ter'ra·pin n. freshwater turtle

ter·rar'i·um (-rer'-) n., pl. **-ums** or **-i·a** glass enclosure for small plants, etc.

ter·raz'zo (-rät'sō, -raz'ō) n. polished flooring of small marble chips in cement

ter·res'tri·al a. 1 worldly 2 of the earth 3 of, or living on, land

ter'ri·ble a. 1 causing terror 2 extreme 3 [Col.] very bad —**ter'ri·bly** adv.

ter'ri·er n. breed of small, lively dog

ter·rif'ic a. 1 terrifying 2 [Col.] very great, etc.

ter'ri·fy' v. **-fied'**, **-fy'ing** fill with terror

ter'ri·to'ry n., pl. **-ries** 1 land ruled by a nation 2 national region not yet a State 3 region —**ter'ri·to'ri·al** a.

ter'ror n. great fear, or cause of this

ter'ror·ism' n. use of force and threats to intimidate —**ter'ror·ist** n., a.

ter'ror·ize' v. 1 terrify 2 coerce by terrorism

ter'ry (cloth) n. cloth having a pile of uncut loops

terse a. concise; to the point —**terse'ly** adv.

ter'ti·ar'y (-shē-) a. third

test n. examination or trial to determine a thing's value, a person's knowledge, etc. —v. subject to a test

tes'ta·ment n. 1 [T—] either part of the Bible 2 legal will

tes'ta·tor n. one who has made a will

tes'ti·cle n. either of the two male sex glands

tes'ti·fy' v. **-fied'**, **-fy'ing** 1 give evidence in court 2 indicate

tes'ti·mo'ni·al n. 1 statement of recommendation 2 thing given as a tribute

tes'ti·mo'ny n., pl. **-nies** 1 statement of one who testifies in court 2 indication

tes'tis n., pl. **-tes** (-tēz') testicle

tes·tos'ter·one' (-ōn') n. male sex hormone

test tube n. tubelike glass container

tes'ty a. **-ti·er**, **-ti·est** irritable; touchy

tet'a·nus n. acute infectious disease

tête-à-tête (tāt'ə tāt') a., n. (of) a private talk between two people

teth'er (teth'-) n. rope or chain tied to an animal to confine it —v. tie as with this

tet'ra n. tropical fish

tet'ra·eth'yl lead n. lead compound added to gasoline to prevent engine knock

text n. 1 author's words 2 main part of a printed page 3 textbook 4 Biblical passage 5 topic —**tex'tu·al** (-chōō-) a.

text'book' n. book used in teaching a subject

tex'tile (-til', -tǝl) n. woven fabric —a. 1 of weaving 2 woven

tex'ture n. 1 look and feel of a fabric 2 structure —**tex'tur·al** a.

thal'a·mus n., pl. **-mi'** (-mī') gray matter at the base of the brain

than con. compared to

thank v. give thanks to —**thank you** I thank you

thank'ful a. showing thanks —**thank'ful·ly** adv.

thank'less a. ungrateful or unappreciated

thanks n.pl. expression of gratitude —int. I thank you —**thanks to** 1 thanks be given to 2 because of

thanks'giv'ing n. 1 thanks to God 2 [T—] U.S. holiday: fourth Thursday in November

that pron., pl. **those** 1 the one mentioned 2 the farther one or other one 3 who, whom, or which 4 when —a., pl. **those** being that one —con. That is used to introduce certain dependent clauses —adv. to that extent —**all that** [Col.] so very —**that is** 1 to be specific 2 in other words

thatch v., n. (cover with) a roof of straw, etc.

thaw v. melt or become so warm that ice melts —n. period of thawing weather

the a., definite article that or this one in particular or of a certain kind —adv. that much or by that much

the'a·ter, the'a·tre n. 1 place where plays, movies, etc. are shown 2 scene of events 3 dramatic art —**the·at'ri·cal** a.

thee *pron.* objective case of THOU

theft *n.* act of stealing

their *a.* of them

theirs *pron.* that or those belonging to them

the'ism' *n.* belief in god(s) —**the'ist** *n., a.*

them *pron.* objective case of THEY

theme *n.* 1 topic 2 short essay 3 main melody

them·selves' *pron.* intensive or reflexive form of THEY

then *adv.* 1 at that time 2 next 3 in that case 4 besides —*n.* that time

thence *adv.* from that place

thence'forth' *adv.* from that time on: also **thence'for'ward**

the·oc'ra·cy *n., pl.* **-cies** (a) government by a church

the·ol'o·gy *n.* study of God and of religious beliefs —**the'o·lo'gi·an** (-lō'jən) *n.* —**the'o·log'i·cal** *a.*

the'o·rem *n. Math.* statement (to be) proved

the'o·ret'i·cal *a.* based on theory, not on practice

the'o·ry *n., pl.* **-ries** 1 explanation based on scientific study and reasoning 2 principles of an art or science 3 guess, conjecture, etc. —**the'o·rize'** *v.*

ther'a·peu'tic (-pyōō'-) *a.* serving to cure or heal

ther'a·peu'tics *n.* therapy

ther'a·py *n., pl.* **-pies** method of treating disease or disorders —**ther'a·pist** *n.*

there *adv.* 1 at, in, or to that place 2 at that point 3 in that respect —*n.* that place

there'a·bouts' *adv.* near that place, time, amount, etc.: also **there'a·bout'**

there·af'ter *adv.* after that

there·by' *adv.* by that

there'fore' *adv.*, *con.* for this or that reason

there·in' *adv.* in that place, matter, writing, etc.

there·of' *adv.* 1 of that 2 from that as a cause

there·on' *adv.* 1 on that 2 thereupon

there·to' *adv.* to that place, thing, etc.

there'to·fore' *adv.* up to that time

there'up·on' *adv.* 1 just after that 2 because of that

there·with' *adv.* 1 with that or this 2 just after that

ther'mal *a.* of heat

thermal pollution *n.* harmful discharge of heated liquids into lakes, rivers, etc.

ther'mo·dy·nam'ics *n.* science of changing heat into other forms of energy

ther·mom'e·ter *n.* device for measuring temperature

ther'mo·nu'cle·ar *a.* of or using the heat energy released in nuclear fission

ther'mo·plas'tic *a.* soft and moldable when heated —*n.* thermoplastic substance

ther'mos (bottle) *n.* container for keeping liquids at the same temperature

ther'mo·stat' *n.* device for regulating temperature

the·sau'rus (-sôr'əs) *n.* book containing lists of synonyms or related words

these *pron.*, *a.* pl. of THIS

the'sis *n., pl.* **-ses'** (-sēz') 1 statement to be defended 2 essay written to obtain an academic degree

Thes'pi·an *n.* [often t–] actor

thews *n.pl.* muscles or sinews

they *pron.* 1 the ones mentioned 2 people

they'd 1 they had 2 they would

they'll 1 they will 2 they shall

they're they are

they've they have

thi·a·mine (thī'ə min) *n.* vitamin B$_1$, found in liver, etc.

thick *a.* 1 great in extent from side to side 2 as measured from side to side 3 dense 4 not clear —*n.* the most active part —**thick'en** *v.* —**thick'ly** *adv.* —**thick'ness** *n.*

thick'et *a.* thick growth of shrubs or small trees

thick'set' *a.* thick in body

thick'-skinned' *a.* unfeeling

thief *n., pl.* **thieves** one who steals

thieve *v.* steal —**thiev'er·y** *n., pl.* **-ies** —**thiev'ish** *a.*

thigh *n.* the leg between the knee and the hip

thim'ble *n.* protective cap worn on the finger in sewing

thin *a.* **thin'ner, thin'nest** 1 small in extent from side to side 2 lean; slender 3 sparse 4 watery 5 weak 6 transparent; flimsy —*v.* **thinned, thin'ning** make or become thin —**thin'ness** *n.*

thine [Ar.] *pron.* yours —*a.* [Ar.] your

thing *n.* 1 real object or substance 2 a happening, act, event, etc. 3 matter or affair 4 *pl.* belongings

think *v.* **thought, think'ing** 1 form in or use the mind 2 consider 3 believe 4 remember: with *of* or *about* 5 have an opinion of: with *of* or *about* 6 consider: with *about* 7 conceive (*of*) —**think better of** reconsider —**think up** invent, plan, etc.

think tank *n.* [Sl.] group organized for intensive research

thin'ner *n.* substance added to paint, etc. for thinning

thin'-skinned' *a.* sensitive

Thin'su·late' *trademark* synthetic material for heat insulation, esp. in clothing

third *a.* preceded by two others —*n.* 1 third one 2 one of three equal parts

third'-class' *a.* of the class, etc. next below

the second

third degree n. [Col.] cruel treatment to force confession

third dimension n. 1 depth 2 quality of seeming real

third'-rate' a. very inferior

third world n. [often T- W-] underdeveloped countries

thirst n. 1 need or craving for water 2 strong desire —v. feel thirst —**thirst'y** a.

thir'teen' a., n. three more than ten —**thir'teenth'** a., n.

thir'ty a., n., pl. –ties three times ten —**thir'ti·eth** a., n.

this a., pron., pl. **these** (being) the one mentioned or nearer —adv. to this extent

this'tle (-əl) n. prickly plant

thith'er (thith'-) adv. there

tho, tho' con., adv. though

thong n. strip of leather used as a lace, strap, etc.

tho'rax' n. 1 CHEST (n. 3) 2 middle segment of an insect

thorn n. short, sharp point on a plant stem —**thorn'y** a.

thor·ough (thur'ō) a. 1 complete 2 very exact

thor'ough·bred' n., a. (an animal) of pure breed

thor'ough·fare' n. main highway

thor'ough·go'ing a. very thorough

those a., pron. pl. of THAT

thou pron. [Ar.] you (sing. subject of v.)

though (thō) con. 1 although 2 yet 3 even if —adv. however

thought v. pt. & pp. of THINK —n. 1 act or way of thinking 2 idea, plan, etc.

thought'ful a. 1 full of thought 2 considerate

thought'less a. 1 careless 2 inconsiderate

thou'sand a., n. ten hundred —**thou'sandth** a., n.

thrash v. 1 thresh 2 beat 3 toss about violently

thrash'er n. thrushlike songbird

thread n. 1 fine cord of spun cotton, silk, etc. 2 spiral ridge of a screw, etc. —v. 1 put a thread through a needle 2 make one's way

thread'bare' a. shabby

threat n. 1 warning of plan to harm 2 sign of danger

threat'en v. make or be a threat

three a., n. one more than two

three'-di·men'sion·al a. having depth or thickness

three'fold' a. 1 having three parts 2 having three times as much or as many —adv. three times as much or as many

three'score' a. sixty

thresh v. beat out (grain) from its husk

—**thresh'er** n.

thresh'old' n. 1 sill of a door 2 beginning point

threw v. pt. of THROW

thrice adv. three times

thrift n. careful managing of money, etc. —**thrift'i·ly** adv. —**thrift'less** a. —**thrift'y** a., -i·er, -i·est

thrill v., n. (feel or make feel) great excitement

thrill'er n. suspenseful novel, film, etc.

thrive v. throve or thrived, thrived or thriv'en, thriv'ing 1 be successful 2 grow luxuriantly

throat n. 1 front of the neck 2 upper passage from mouth to stomach or lungs

throb v. throbbed, throb'bing beat or vibrate strongly —n. a throbbing

throe (thrō) n. pang of pain: used in pl.

throm·bo'sis n. a clotting in the circulatory system

throne n. 1 official chair, as of a king 2 his power

throng n., v. crowd

throt'tle n. valve to control fuel mixture —v. choke

through (thrō̄) prep. 1 from end to end of 2 by way of 3 to places in 4 throughout 5 by means of 6 because of —adv. 1 in and out of 2 all the way 3 entirely —a. 1 open; free 2 to the end without stops 3 finished

through·out' adv., prep. in every part (of)

through'way' n. expressway

throw v. threw, thrown, throw'ing 1 send through the air from the hand 2 make fall 3 put suddenly 4 move, as a switch 5 direct, cast, etc. —n. 1 a throwing 2 distance thrown —**throw off** get rid of, expel, etc. —**throw together** to assemble hastily —**throw up** 1 give up 2 vomit

throw'a·way' a. designed to be discarded after use

throw'back' n. (a) return to an earlier type

throw rug n. small rug

thru prep., adv., a. [Col.] through

thrush n. any of a large group of songbirds

thrust v. thrust, thrust'ing push with sudden force —n. 1 sudden push 2 stab 3 forward force

thru'way n. expressway

thud v., n. thud'ded, thud'ding (hit with) a dull sound

thug n. rough criminal

thumb n. short, thick finger nearest the wrist

thumb'nail' n. nail of the thumb —a. brief

thumb'tack' n. tack with wide, flat head

thump n. 1 a blow with a heavy, blunt thing 2 its dull sound —v. hit or pound with a thump

thun′der n. loud noise after lightning —v. 1 cause thunder 2 shout loudly —**thun′der·ous** a.

thun′der·bolt′ n. flash of lightning and its thunder

thun′der·cloud′ n. storm cloud producing thunder

thun′der·show′er n. shower with thunder and lightning

thun′der·storm′ n. storm with thunder and lightning

thun′der·struck′ a. amazed

Thurs′day n. fifth day of the week

thus adv. 1 in this way 2 to this or that degree 3 therefore

thwack v., n. whack

thwart v. block; hinder

thy (thī) a. [Ar.] your

thyme (tīm) n. plant of the mint family

thy′mus (thī′-) n. small gland in the throat

thy′roid′ a., n. (of) a gland secreting a growth hormone

thy·self′ pron. [Ar.] yourself

ti·a·ra (tē er′ə, -är′-) n. woman's crownlike headdress

tib′i·a n. thicker bone of the lower leg

tic n. muscle spasm

tick n. 1 light clicking sound 2 blood-sucking insect —v. make a ticking sound

tick′er n. 1 one that ticks 2 telegraphic device recording stock prices on paper tape

tick′et n. 1 printed card entitling one to a theater seat, etc. 2 tag, label, etc. 3 list of a party's candidates —v. put a ticket on

tick′ing n. cloth holding a pillow's contents

tick′le v. 1 stroke lightly and make twitch or laugh 2 feel tickled 3 amuse; delight —n. a tickling

tick′ler n. file for noting items to be remembered

tick′lish a. 1 sensitive to tickling 2 touchy

tid′al a. of, having, or caused by a tide

tidal wave n. very large, destructive wave caused by an earthquake or strong wind

tid′bit′ n. choice morsel

tide n. 1 rise and fall of the ocean twice a day 2 trend —v. chiefly in **tide over** help through a difficulty

tide′land′ n. land covered by tide

tide′wa′ter n. 1 water affected by tide 2 seaboard

ti′dings n.pl. news

ti′dy a. -di·er, -di·est 1 neat; orderly 2 [Col.] quite large —v. -died, -dy·ing make tidy

tie v. tied, ty′ing 1 fasten with string, rope, etc. 2 make (a knot) 3 bind in any way 4 to equal, as in a score —n. 1 thing that ties or joins 2 necktie 3 contest with equal scores

tie′-dye′ n. dyeing method affecting only exposed areas —v. dye in this way

tie′-in′ n. connection

tier (tir) n. any of a series of rows, one above another

tie′-up′ n. 1 temporary stoppage, as of traffic 2 connection

tiff n. slight quarrel

ti′ger n. large, striped jungle cat —**ti′gress** n.fem.

tight a. 1 made to keep water, air, etc. out or in 2 fitting closely or too closely 3 taut 4 difficult 5 [Col.] stingy —adv. closely —**tight′en** v. —**tight′ly** adv.

tight′fist′ed a. stingy

tight′-lipped′ a. secretive

tight′rope′ n. taut rope on which acrobats perform

tights n.pl. tight garment from the waist to the feet

tight′wad′ n. [Sl.] miser

til′de (-də) n. diacritical mark (~)

tile n. thin piece of baked clay, stone, plastic, etc. for roofing, flooring, etc. —v. cover with tiles

till prep., con. until —v. cultivate land for crops —n. drawer for money

till′er n. bar or handle to turn a boat's rudder

tilt v., n. 1 slope; tip 2 joust —**at full tilt** at full speed

tim′ber n. 1 wood for building houses, etc. 2 wooden beam 3 trees

tim·bre (tam′bər) n. the distinctive sound of a voice or musical instrument

time n. 1 period; duration 2 the right instant, hour, etc. 3 the passing hours, day, etc.; or, system of measuring them 4 an occasion 5 set period of work, or pay for this 6 tempo or rhythm —v. 1 choose a right time for 2 measure the speed of —a. 1 of time 2 set to work at a give time —**at times** sometimes —**in time** 1 eventually 2 before it is too late —**on time** 1 not late 2 by installment payments —**tim′er** n.

time′-hon′ored a. honored because of long existence

time′keep′er n. one who records time played, as in games, or hours worked

time′less a. eternal

time′ly a. -li·er, -li·est at the right time

time′out′ n. temporary suspension of play in sports

time′piece′ n. clock; watch

times prep. multiplied by

time′ta′ble n. schedule of arrivals and departures

time′worn′ a. 1 worn out 2 trite

tim′id a. shy; easily frightened —**ti·mid′i·ty** n.

tim′ing n. regulation of speed, etc. to improve performance

tim'or·ous *a.* timid

tim'o·thy *n.* a tall grass used for fodder

tim'pa·ni *n.pl.* kettledrums

tin *n.* soft, silvery metal, a chemical element —**tin'ny** *a.,* **-ni·er, -ni·est**

tinc'ture *n.* solution of medicine in alcohol —*v.* tinge

tin'der *n.* any dry, easily ignited material

tin'der·box' *n.* 1 flammable object, etc. 2 place, etc. likely to have trouble or war

tine *n.* prong, as of a fork

tin'foil' *n.* 1 thin sheet of tin 2 [Col.] tin sheet of aluminum

tinge *n.* 1 tint 2 slight trace —*v.* give a tinge to

tin'gle *v.* sting slightly; prickle —*n.* a tingling

tin'ker *n.* mender of pots and pans —*v.* 1 mend clumsily 2 to putter

tin'kle *v.* ring of a small bell —*n.* make a tinkle

tin plate *n.* thin sheets of iron or steel plated with tin

tin'sel *n.* 1 thin strips of metal foil, for decorating 2 showy, cheap thing

tin'smith' *n.* one who works with tin: also **tin'ner**

tint *n.* 1 light color 2 a shading of a color —*v.* give a tint to

ti'ny *a.,* **-ni·er, -ni·est** very small

-tion *suf.* 1 act of 2 condition of being 3 thing that is

tip *n.* 1 a point or end 2 thing fitted to an end 3 light blow; tap 4 secret information 5 a warning 6 gratuity 7 slant —*v.* **tipped, tip'ping** 1 make or put a tip on 2 give a tip 3 overturn 4 slant —**tip one's hand** [Sl.] reveal a secret, etc.

tip'-off' *n.* a TIP (*n.* 4 & 5)

tip'ple *v.* drink liquor

tip'ster *n.* [Col.] one who sells tips, as on horse races

tip'sy *a.* **-si·er, -si·est** 1 unsteady 2 drunk

tip'toe' *n.* tip of the toes —*v.* **-toed', -toe'-ing** walk stealthily on one's toes

tip'top' *a., adv., n.* (at) the highest point

ti'rade *n.* long, angry speech

tire *v.* make or become weary, bored, etc. —*n.* hoop or rubber tube around a wheel —**tire'less** *a.*

tired *a.* weary; exhausted

tire'some *a.* tiring

tis·sue (tish'ōō) *n.* 1 tissue paper 2 cellular material of organisms 3 thin cloth

tissue paper *n.* thin, soft paper

ti'tan *n.* giant —**ti·tan'ic** *a.*

tit for tat this for that

tithe (tīth) *v., n.* (pay) a tenth part of one's income

ti·tian (tish'ən) *n., a.* reddish yellow

tit'il·late' *v.* excite pleasurably —**tit'il·la'tion** *n.*

ti'tle *n.* 1 name of a book, picture, etc. 2 word showing rank or occupation 3 legal right 4 championship —*v.* name

ti'tlist *n.* champion in some sport or competition

tit'mouse' *n., pl.* **-mice'** small, dull-colored bird

tit'ter *v., n.* giggle

tit'u·lar (tich'-) *a.* 1 in name only 2 of or having a title

tiz'zy *n., pl.* **-zies** [Col.] frenzied excitement

TNT *n.* an explosive

to *prep.* 1 toward 2 as far as 3 on, onto, or against 4 until 5 causing 6 with 7 in each *To* may indicate an infinitive or a receiver of action —*adv.* 1 forward 2 shut

toad *n.* froglike land animal

toad'stool' *n.* poisonous mushroom

toad'y *n., pl.* **-ies** servile flatterer —*v.* **-ied, -y·ing** be a toady (to)

toast *v.* 1 brown by heating, as bread 2 warm 3 drink in honor of —*n.* 1 toasted bread 2 a toasting

toast'mas'ter *n.* one who presides at a banquet

to·bac'co *n., pl.* **-cos** plant with leaves dried for smoking, chewing, etc.

to·bog'gan *v., n.* (coast on) a flat, runnerless sled

toc'sin *n.* alarm bell

to·day' *adv.* 1 during this day 2 nowadays —*n.* this day or time

tod'dle *v.* walk unsteadily, as a child —**tod'dler** *n.*

tod'dy *n., pl.* **-dies** whiskey, etc. mixed with hot water, sugar, etc.

to-do' *n.* [Col.] a fuss

toe *n.* any of five end parts of the foot —*v.* **toed, toe'ing** touch with the toes —**on one's toes** alert —**toe the line** (or **mark**) follow orders, etc. strictly —**toe'nail'** *n.*

toe dance *n.* dance performed on the tips of the toes

toe'hold' *n.* slight footing or advantage

tof'fee, tof'fy *n.* taffy

to'fu *n.* Japanese cheeselike food made from soybeans

to'ga *n.* loose garment worn in ancient Rome

to·geth'er *adv.* 1 in one group or place 2 at the same time 3 so as to meet, agree, etc. —**to·geth'er·ness** *n.*

tog'gle switch *n.* switch with a lever to open or close an electric circuit

togs *n.pl.* [Col.] clothes

toil *v.* 1 work hard 2 go with effort —*n.* hard work

toi'let *n.* 1 fixture to receive body waste 2

bathroom **3** one's grooming: also **toi·lette′** (twä-, toi-)

toilet paper *n.* soft paper used after evacuation

toi′let·ry *n., pl.* **–ries** soap, cosmetics, etc.

toilet water *n.* cologne

toils *n.pl.* snare or net

toil′some *a.* laborious

to′ken *n.* **1** sign or symbol **2** keepsake **3** metal disk, as for fare —*a.* pretended

told *v.* pt. & pp. of TELL

tole *n.* lacquered or enameled metalware, as for lamps

tol′er·a·ble *a.* **1** endurable **2** fairly good —**tol′er·a·bly** *adv.*

tol′er·ance *n.* **1** a tolerating, as of another's ways **2** power to resist a drug's effect **3** deviation allowed —**tol′er·ant** *a.*

tol′er·ate′ *v.* **1** to put up with; endure **2** permit

toll *n.* **1** charge on a turnpike, for a long-distance phone call, etc. **2** the number lost, etc. —*v.* ring with slow, regular strokes, as a bell

toll′gate′ *n.* gate where tolls are paid

toll road *n.* road on which tolls must be paid

tom′a·hawk′ *n.* light ax used by North American Indians

to·ma′to *n., pl.* **–toes** red, round, juicy vegetable

tomb (tōōm) *n.* vault or grave for the dead

tom′boy′ *n.* girl who behaves like an active boy

tomb′stone′ *n.* stone marking a tomb or grave

tom′cat′ *n.* male cat

tome *n.* large book

tom′fool′er·y *n., pl.* **–ies** foolish behavior; silliness

to·mor′row *adv., n.* (on) the day after today

tom′-tom′ *n.* primitive drum

ton *n.* 2,000 pounds

to·nal′i·ty *n.* **1** KEY (*n.* 7) **2** tonal character

tone *n.* **1** vocal or musical sound; spec., a full interval of a diatonic scale **2** style, character, feeling, etc. **3** shade or tint **4** healthy condition, as of muscles —**tone down** give a less intense tone to —**ton′al** *a.*

tone arm *n.* arm containing the pickup of a phonograph

tongs *n.pl.* device for seizing, lifting, etc., made of two long, hinged arms

tongue (tuŋ) *n.* **1** movable muscle in the mouth, used in eating and speaking **2** act or manner of speaking **3** language **4** tonguelike part

tongue′-lash′ing *n.* [Col.] harsh scolding

tongue′-tied′ *a.* speechless

tongue twister *n.* phrase or sentence hard to say fast

ton′ic *n.* medicine, etc. that invigorates

to·night′ *adv., n.* (on) this night

ton′nage (-ij) *n.* **1** amount in tons of shipping, etc. **2** carrying capacity of a ship

ton′sil *n.* either of two masses of tissue at the back of the mouth

ton′sil·lec′to·my *n., pl.* **–mies** surgical removal of the tonsils

ton′sil·li′tis (-līt′is) *n.* inflammation of the tonsils

ton·so′ri·al (-sôr′ē-) *a.* of a barber or barbering

ton′sure *n.* shaven crown of a priest's or monk's head

too *adv.* **1** also **2** more than enough **3** very

took *v.* pt. of TAKE

tool *n.* **1** instrument, implement, etc. used for some work **2** stooge —*v.* shape or work with a tool

toot *v., n.* (make) a short blast on a horn, etc.

tooth *n., pl.* **teeth 1** any of a set of bony structures in the jaws, used for biting and chewing **2** toothlike part, as of a saw, gear, etc. —**tooth and nail** with all one's strength —**tooth′ache′** *n.* —**tooth′brush′** *n.*

toothed (tōōtht, tōō*th*d) *a.* having teeth

tooth′paste′ *n.* paste for brushing the teeth

tooth′pick′ *n.* pointed stick for picking food from between the teeth

tooth′some *a.* tasty

tooth′y *a.* **-i·er, -i·est** having prominent teeth

top *n.* **1** highest point or surface **2** uppermost part or covering **3** highest degree or rank **4** toy that spins round —*a.* of, at, or being the top —*v.* **topped, top′ping 1** provide with a top **2** be at the top of **3** surpass; exceed —**on top of 1** resting upon **2** besides —**top off** complete

to′paz′ *n.* yellow gem

top′coat′ *n.* light overcoat

top′-draw′er *a.* of first importance

top′-flight′ *a.* first-rate

top hat *n.* man's tall, black hat

top′-heav′y *a.* too heavy at the top and, thus, unstable

top′ic *n.* subject of an essay, speech, etc.

top′i·cal *a.* of current or local interest

top′knot′ *n.* tuft of hair or feathers on top of the head

top′less *a.* without a top covering, as a dancer with breasts exposed

top′-lev′el *a.* of or by persons of the highest rank

top′mast′ *n.* second mast above the deck of a ship

top′most *a.* uppermost

top′-notch′ *a.* [Col.] first-rate

to·pog′ra·phy *n.* **1** surface features of a region **2** science of showing these, as on maps —**top´o·graph´i·cal, top´o·graph´ic** a.

top´ple v. (make) fall over

top´sail´ n. sail next above the lowest sail on a mast

top´-se´cret a. designating or of the most secret information

top´side´ adv. on or to an upper deck or the main deck of a ship

top´soil´ n. upper layer of soil, usually richer

top´sy-tur´vy adv., a. 1 upside down 2 in disorder

to´rah (-rə) n. Jewish scriptures; spec. [T-] first five books of the Bible

torch n. 1 portable flaming light 2 device that makes a very hot flame, as in welding —**torch´light´** n.

tore v. pt. of TEAR (pull apart)

tor´e·a·dor´ (-ē ə-) n. bullfighter

tor´ment´ (v.: tôr ment´) n. great pain —v. make suffer —**tor·men´tor** n.

torn v. pp. of TEAR (pull apart)

tor·na´do n., pl. **–does** violent wind with a whirling, funnel-shaped cloud

tor·pe´do n., pl. **–does** large, cigar-shaped, underwater projectile —v. **-doed, -do·ing** to destroy or ruin

tor´pid a. dull; sluggish —**tor´por** n.

torque (tôrk) n. force that gives a twisting motion

tor´rent n. swift, violent stream —**tor·ren´tial** (-shəl) a.

tor´rid a. very hot

tor´sion n. a twisting or being twisted

torsion bar n. metal bar having resilience under torsion

tor´so n., pl. **–sos** human body minus head and limbs

tort n. Law wrongful act, injury, etc.

torte n. rich cake

tor´tel·li´ni n. tiny, ring-shaped pasta

tor·til´la (-tē´ə) n. flat, unleavened corn cake

tor´toise (-təs) n. turtle, esp. one living on land

tor´toise-shell´ a. made of a mottled, yellow-and-brown substance

tor´tu·ous (-chōō-) a. full of twists and turns

tor´ture n. 1 inflicting of great pain 2 great pain —v. 1 subject to torture 2 twist

To·ry (tôr´ē) n., pl. **–ries** 1 Br. loyalist in American Revolution 2 [often **t-**] a conservative

toss v. 1 throw lightly 2 throw lightly from the hand 2 fling or be flung about 3 jerk upward —n. a tossing

toss´up´ n. 1 flipping of a coin to decide 2 even chance

tot n. young child

to´tal n. the whole amount; sum —a. 1 entire; whole 2 complete —v. add (up to) —**to·tal´i·ty** n. —**to´tal·ly** adv.

to·tal´i·tar´i·an a. of a dictatorship

tote v. [Col.] carry; haul

to´tem pole n. pole with animal symbol(s), made by Indians of NW North America

tot´ter v. 1 rock as if about to fall 2 stagger

tou·can´ (tōō´-) n. tropical bird with a large beak

touch v. 1 put the hand, etc. on so as to feel 2 bring or come into contact 3 tap lightly 4 handle; use 5 concern 6 arouse pity, etc. in 7 treat in passing: with on or upon —n. 1 a touching 2 way things feel 3 sense of this 4 small bit 5 contact —**in touch** in contact —**touch on** mention —**touch up** improve by additions

touch´-and-go´ a. uncertain, risky, etc.

touch´down´ n. 1 goal scored in football, for six points 2 moment when an aircraft lands

touched´ a. 1 emotionally affected 2 slightly demented

touch´ing a. arousing tender emotions; moving

touch´stone´ n. criterion

touch´y a. **-i-er, -i-est** 1 irritable 2 difficult

tough a. 1 hard to chew, cut, break, etc. 2 strong or rough 3 very difficult —n. ruffian —**tough´en** v.

tou·pee´ (tōō pā´) n. small wig for a bald spot

tour n. long trip, as to see sights, put on plays, etc. —v. go on a tour (through) —**tour´ist** n., a.

tour´ism´ n. tourist travel

tour´na·ment n. 1 series of contests for a championship 2 knights' jousting contest

tour´ney n., pl. **–neys** tournament

tour´ni·quet (-kət) n. device for compressing a blood vessel to stop bleeding

tou·sle (tou´zəl) v. muss

tout (tout) [Col.] v. 1 praise highly 2 sell tips on (race horses) —n. one who touts

tow v. pull by a rope or chain —n. a towing

toward (tôrd, twôrd) prep. 1 in the direction of 2 concerning 3 near 4 for Also **towards**

tow´el n. piece of cloth or paper to wipe things dry

tow´el·ing, tow´el·ling n. material for making towels

tow´er n. high structure, often part of another building —v. rise high

tow´head´ (tō´-) n. person with light yellow hair

tow´hee´ (tō´-) n. small North American sparrow

tow´line´ n. rope, etc. for towing

town n. 1 small city 2 business center —**towns´peo´ple, towns´folk´** n.pl.

town crier *n.* one who formerly cried public announcements through the streets

town hall *n.* town building housing offices of officials, etc.

town house *n.* two-story dwelling in a complex of such houses

town meeting *n.* meeting of the voters of a town

town'ship *n.* **1** part of a county **2** U.S. land unit 6 miles square

towns'man *n., pl.* **-men** one who lives in a town

tow'path' *n.* path by a canal

tow'rope' *n.* rope for towing

tox·e'mi·a *a.* condition of toxins or poisons spread throughout the blood

tox'ic·a **1** of or caused by a toxin **2** poisonous

tox'i·col'o·gy *n.* science of poisons and their effects —**tox'i·col'o·gist** *n.*

tox'in *n.* poison, esp. from bacteria, viruses, etc.

toy *n.* thing to play with —*a.* small —*v.* play (*with*)

trace *n.* **1** mark or track left **2** small bit **3** harness strap connecting to vehicle —*v.* **1** follow (the trial or course of) **2** draw, outline, etc. —**trac'er** *n.*

trac'er·y *n., pl.* **-ies** design of interlacing lines

tra'che·a (-kē-) *n.* air passage from the larynx to the bronchial tubes

tra'che·ot'o·my *n., pl.* **-mies** emergency incision of the trachea, as to allow breathing

trac'ing *n.* something traced

track *n.* **1** footprint, wheel rut, etc. **2** path, trail, or course **3** running sports, etc. **4** pair of rails a train runs on —*v.* **1** follow the track of **2** leave footprints on —**keep** (or **lose**) **track of** keep (or fail to keep) informed about

tract *n.* **1** large stretch of land **2** system of bodily organs **3** booklet

trac'ta·ble *a.* manageable

trac'tion *n.* **1** power to grip a surface **2** a pulling

trac'tor *n.* **1** motor vehicle to pull farm machines, etc. **2** truck to haul a trailer

trac'tor-trail'er *n.* coupled TRACTOR (*n.* 2) and trailer or semitrailer

trade *n.* **1** skilled work **2** buying and selling **3** an exchange —*v.* **1** buy and sell **2** exchange

trade'-in' *n.* thing used as part payment

trade'mark' *n.* special mark or name (**trade name**) put on a product

trade'-off' *n.* exchange of a benefit for one more desirable

trades'man *n., pl.* **-men** [Chiefly Br.] storekeeper

trade union *n.* labor union

trade wind *n.* wind that blows toward the equator

trad'ing post *n.* store in an outpost, where trading is done

tra·di'tion *n.* **1** custom, etc. handed down from the past **2** such handing down —**tra·di'tion·al** *a.*

tra·duce' *v.* to slander

traf'fic *n.* **1** vehicles moving along streets, etc. **2** amount of business done **3** TRADE (*n.* 2) —*v.* **-ficked, -fick·ing** do business, esp. illegally

traffic circle *n.* circular road at the intersection of several streets

traffic light (or **signal**) *n.* set of signal lights to regulate traffic

tra·ge'di·an (trə jē'-) *n.* actor of tragedy —**tra·ge'di·enne'** *n.fem.*

trag'e·dy *n., pl.* **-dies 1** serious play with a sad ending **2** tragic event

trag'ic·a 1 of or like tragedy **2** very sad —**trag'i·cal·ly** *adv.*

trail *v.* **1** drag or lag behind **2** follow or drift behind **3** dwindle —*n.* **1** thing trailing behind **2** beaten path

trail'blaz'er *n.* **1** one who blazes a trail **2** pioneer in any field

trail'er *n.* wagon or van pulled by a car or truck, sometimes used as a home

trailer park *n.* area designed for trailers, esp. mobile homes

train *n.* **1** a thing that drags behind **2** procession **3** connected series **4** locomotive with cars —*v.* **1** guide the development of **2** instruct or prepare **3** aim —**train·ee'** *n.*

traipse *v.* [Col. or Dial.] to walk, tramp, etc.

trait *n.* characteristic

trai'tor *n.* disloyal person —**trai'tor·ous** *a.*

tra·jec'to·ry *n., pl.* **-ries** curved path of a missile

tram'mel *n., v.* (thing) to hinder or restrain

tramp *v.* **1** walk, or step, heavily **2** roam about —*n.* **1** vagrant **2** a tramping

tram'ple *v.* step hard on or crush underfoot

tram'po·line' (-lēn') *n.* apparatus with springs and taut canvas, used for acrobatic tumbling

trance *n.* state of shock, hypnosis, or deep thought

tran'quil *a.* calm; quiet —**tran·quil'li·ty, tran·quil'i·ty** *n.*

tran'quil·ize', tran'quil·lize' *v.* make tranquil —**tran'quil·iz'er, tran'quil·liz'er** *n.*

trans- *pref.* over, across, beyond

trans·act' *v.* do; complete —**trans·ac'tion** *n.*

tran·scend' (-send') *v.* exceed —**tran·scend'ent** *a.*

tran·scen·den'tal *a.* 1 transcendent 2 supernatural

tran·scribe' *v.* 1 write or type out 2 record for rebroadcast —**tran·scrip'tion** *n.*

tran'script' *n.* written or typewritten copy

tran'sept' *n.* shorter part of a cross-shaped church

trans·fer' *v.* **-ferred', -fer·ring** move or change from one person, place, etc. to another —*n.* 1 a transferring 2 ticket letting one change to another bus, etc. —**trans·fer'a·ble** *a.* —**trans'fer·ence** *n.*

trans·fig'ure *v.* 1 transform 2 make seem glorious —**trans·fig'u·ra'tion** *n.*

trans·fix' *v.* pierce through

trans·form' *v.* change the form or condition of —**trans'for·ma'tion** *n.*

trans·form'er *n.* device that changes voltage

trans·fuse' *v.* 1 imbue; fill 2 transfer blood to another —**trans·fu'sion** *n.*

trans·gress' *v.* 1 break a law; do wrong 2 go beyond —**trans·gres'sion** *n.* —**trans·gres'sor** *n.*

tran'si·ent (-shənt, -sē ənt) *a.* temporary —*n.* one who stays only a short time

tran·sis'tor *n.* small electronic device that controls current flow

trans'it *n.* 1 passage across 2 a conveying

tran·si'tion *n.* a passing from one condition, place, etc. to another

tran'si·tive *a.* taking a direct object, as some verbs

tran'si·to'ry *a.* temporary

trans·late' *v.* put into another language, form, etc. —**trans·la'tion** *n.* —**trans·la'tor** *n.*

trans·lu'cent *a.* letting light pass through but not transparent

trans·mis'si·ble *a.* capable of being transmitted

trans·mis'sion *n.* 1 a transmitting 2 car part sending power to wheels

trans·mit' *v.* **-mit'ted, -mit'ting** 1 transfer 2 pass or convey 3 send out radio or TV signals —**trans·mit'ter** *n.*

trans·mute' *v.* change from one form, nature, etc. into another

tran'som *n.* small window above a door or window

trans·par'ent *a.* that can be seen through; clear —**trans·par'en·cy** *n., pl.* **-cies**

tran·spire' *v.* 1 become known 2 happen

trans·plant' (*n.:* trans'plant') *v.* 1 dig up and plant in another place 2 to transfer (tissue or organ) from one to another; graft —*n.* something transplanted

trans·pon'der *n.* radio transmitter and receiver that automatically transmits signals

trans·port' (*n.:* trans'pôrt') *v.* 1 carry from one place to another 2 carry away with emotion —*n.* thing for transporting —**trans'por·ta'tion** *n.*

trans·pose' *v.* 1 to interchange 2 *Mus.* change the key of

trans·sex'u·al *n.* one who identifies with the opposite sex, sometimes so strongly as to undergo sex-change surgery

trans·verse' *a.* situated, placed, etc. across

trans·ves'tite *n.* one who gets sexual pleasure from wearing clothes of the opposite sex

trap *n.* 1 device for catching animals 2 tricky ruse 3 bend in a drainpipe —*v.* **trapped, trap'ping** 1 catch in a trap 2 set traps for animals —**trap'per** *n.*

trap'door' *n.* hinged or sliding door in a roof or floor

tra·peze' *n.* swinglike bar for acrobats

trap'e·zoid' *n.* figure with two of four sides parallel

trap'pings *n.pl.* adornments

trap'shoot'ing *n.* sport of shooting clay disks sprung into the air from throwing devices (**traps**)

trash *n.* rubbish —**trash'y** *a.,* **-i·er, -i·est**

trau'ma *n.* emotional shock with lasting psychic effects —**trau·mat'ic** *a.*

tra·vail (trə vāl') *n.* 1 labor 2 agony

trav'el *v.* 1 make a journey (through) 2 move or pass —*n.* 1 a traveling 2 *pl.* journeys —**trav'el·er** *n.*

trav'e·logue', trav'e·log' *n.* illustrated lecture or movie of travels

tra·verse' (*a.:* trav'ərs) *v.* to cross —*a.* of drapes drawn by pulling cords

trav'es·ty *n., pl.* **-ties** farcical imitation —*v.* **-tied, -ty·ing** to make a travesty of

trawl *v., n.* (fish with) a large dragnet —**trawl'er** *n.*

tray *n.* flat, low-sided server to carry things

treach'er·ous (trech'-) *a.* 1 disloyal 2 not safe or reliable —**treach'er·y** *n.*

trea'cle (trē'-) *n.* [Br.] molasses

tread (tred) *v.* **trod, trod'den** or **trod, tread'ing** 1 walk on, along, over, etc. 2 trample —*n.* 1 way or sound of treading 2 part for treading or moving on

trea·dle (tred'l) *n.* foot pedal to operate a wheel, etc.

tread'mill' *n.* device worked by treading an endless belt

trea·son (trē'zən) *n.* betrayal of one's country —**trea'son·a·ble, trea'son·ous** *a.*

treas'ure *n.* 1 accumulated money, jewels, etc. 2 valued person or thing —*v.* 1 save up 2 cherish

treas'ure-trove' *n.* 1 treasure found hidden 2 valuable discovery

treas'ur·y *n., pl.* **-ies** 1 place where money

is kept 2 funds of a state, corporation, etc.
—**treas′ur·er** n.

treat v. 1 deal with or act toward 2 pay for the food, etc. of 3 subject to a process, medical care, etc. —n. 1 food, etc. paid for by another 2 thing giving pleasure —**treat′ment** n.

trea·tise (trēt′is) n. a formal writing on a subject

trea′ty n., pl. —**ties** agreement between nations

tre·ble (treb′əl) a. 1 triple 2 of or for the treble —n. 1 Mus. highest part 2 high-pitched voice or sound —v. to triple

tree n. large, woody plant with one main trunk and many branches —v. **treed, tree′ing** to chase up a tree

tre′foil n. 1 plant with three-part leaves 2 design like such a leaf

trek v., n. **trekked, trek′king** (make) a slow, hard journey

trel′lis n. lattice on which vines, etc. are grown

trem·ble v. 1 shake from cold, fear, etc. 2 quiver or vibrate —n. act or fit of trembling

tre·men′dous a. 1 very large 2 [Col.] wonderful

trem·o·lo′ n., pl. —**los′** tremulous effect of repeating the same tone

trem′or n. a trembling, shaking, etc.

trem′u·lous (-yoo-) a. trembling

trench n. ditch, esp. one dug for cover in battle

trench′ant a. incisive

trench coat n. belted raincoat in a military style

trench foot n. foot disorder from exposure to wet and cold

trench mouth n. infectious disease of the mouth

trend v., n. (have) a general direction or tendency

trend′y a. **-i·er, -i·est** [Col.] of or in the latest style

trep′i·da′tion n. fearful uncertainty

tres′pass v. 1 enter another's property unlawfully 2 sin —n. a trespassing —**tres′pass·er** n.

tress n. lock of hair

tres·tle (-əl) n. 1 framework support, as for a bridge 2 sawhorse

trey (trā) n. playing card with three spots

tri- pref. three

tri′ad′ n. group of three

tri′al n. 1 hearing and deciding of a case in a law court 2 attempt 3 test 4 pain, trouble, etc.

trial and error n. the making of repeated tests or trials, as to find a solution

trial balloon n. something done to test public opinion

tri′an′gle n. three-sided figure with three angles —**tri·an′gu·lar** a.

tribe n. 1 group of people living together under a chief 2 group or class —**trib′al** a. —**tribes′man** n., pl. —**men**

trib′u·la′tion (-yoo-) n. great misery or distress

tri·bu′nal n. law court

trib′une′ n. public defender

trib′u·tar′y (-ter′-) n., pl. —**ies** river that flows into a larger one

trib′ute n. 1 forced payment, as by a weak nation to a stronger 2 gift, speech, etc. showing respect

tri·cen·ten′ni·al n. 300th anniversary

trich′i·no′sis (trik′i-) n. disease caused by worms in the intestines and muscles

trick n. 1 something done to fool, cheat, etc. 2 prank 3 clever act or skillful way 4 turn at work 5 personal habit 6 cards played in one round —v. fool or cheat —**trick′er·y** n.

trick′le v. 1 flow in drops or a thin stream 2 move slowly —n. slow flow

trick′y a. **-i·er, -i·est** 1 deceitful 2 difficult

tri′col·or n. flag having three colors

tri′cy·cle (-si-) n. three-wheeled vehicle

tri′dent n. three-pronged spear

tried v. pt. & pp. of TRY —a. tested or trustworthy

tri′fle n. 1 thing of little value 2 small amount —v. 1 act jokingly 2 play

tri′fling a. unimportant

trig′ger n. lever pressed in firing a gun

trig·o·nom′e·try n. mathematics dealing with relations between sides and angles of triangles —**trig′o·no·met′ric** a.

trill v., n. (sing or play with) a rapid alternation of two close notes

tril′lion n. thousand billions —**tril′lionth** a., n.

tril′o·gy n., pl. —**gies** set of three novels, plays, etc.

trim v. **trimmed, trim′ming** 1 clip, lop, etc. 2 decorate 3 put (sails) in order —n. 1 good condition 2 decoration —a. **trim′mer, trim′mest** 1 orderly; neat 2 in good condition —**trim′mer** n.

trim′ming n. 1 decoration 2 pl. parts trimmed off

Trin′i·ty Father, Son, and Holy Ghost as one God

trin′ket n. small ornament

tri·o (trē′ō) n., pl. —**os** musical composition for three performers

trip v. **tripped, trip′ping** 1 move with light, rapid steps 2 stumble or make stumble 3 err or cause to err —n. a journey

tri·par'tite' a. 1 having three parts 2 between three parties, as a treaty

tripe n. stomach of a cow, etc. used as food

trip'ham'mer n. heavy power-driven hammer, alternately raised and dropped

tri·ple (trip'əl) a. 1 of or for three 2 three times as much or as many —n. Baseball hit putting the batter on third —v. to make or become triple —**tri'ply** adv.

tri'plet n. any of three children born at one birth

trip'li·cate (-kət) a. triple —n. one of three exact copies

tri'pod' n. three-legged stool, support, etc.

trite a. worn-out; stale

tri'umph n. victory; success —v. gain victory or success —**tri·um'phal, tri·um'phant** a.

tri·um'vi·rate (-rət) n. government by three persons

triv'et n. three-legged stand for holding pots

triv'i·a n.pl. trifles

triv'i·al a. unimportant —**triv'i·al'i·ty** n.,pl. **-ties**

tro'che (-kē) n. small medicinal lozenge

trod v. pt. & alt. pp. of TREAD

trod'den v. alt. pp. of TREAD

trog'lo·dyte' (-dīt') n. 1 cave dweller 2 hermit

troll (trōl) v. 1 fish with a moving line 2 sing loudly —n. Folklore cave-dwelling giant

trol'ley n.,pl. **-leys** 1 overhead device that sends electric current to a streetcar 2 electric streetcar: also **trolley car**

trol'lop n. prostitute

trom'bone' n. brass-wind instrument with a sliding tube

troop n. 1 group of persons 2 pl. soldiers 3 cavalry unit —v. move in a group

troop'er n. 1 cavalryman 2 mounted policeman

tro'phy n.,pl. **-phies** souvenir of victory, etc.

trop'ic n. 1 either of two parallels of latitude (**Tropic of Cancer** and **Tropic of Capricorn**) N and S of the equator 2 [also T–] pl. hot region between these latitudes —**trop'i·cal** a.

tro'pism' n. tendency to grow or turn in response to a stimulus, as light

trop'o·sphere' (trō'pə-) n. atmosphere from the earth's surface to about 6 to 12 miles above

trot v. **trot'ted, trot'ting** go at a trot —n. 1 running gait of a horse 2 slow, jogging ruin —**trot'ter** n.

troth (trôth, trōth) n. [Ar.] 1 promise, esp. to marry 2 truth

trou·ba·dour (trōō'bə dôr') n. medieval lyric poet

trou'ble n. 1 worry, distress, bother, etc. 2 disturbance 3 difficulty —v. be or give trouble to —**trou'ble·some** a.

trou'ble·mak'er n. one who makes trouble for others

trou'ble·shoot'er n. one who finds and fixes what is out of order

trounce v. beat; flog

troupe (trōōp) n. troop of actors, etc. —**troup'er** n.

trou'sers n.pl. man's two-legged outer garment

trous·seau (trōō sō') n., pl. **-seaus'** or **-seaux'** (-sōz') bride's outfit of clothes, linen, etc.

trout n. freshwater food fish related to the salmon

trow'el (trou'-) n. 1 flat tool for smoothing 2 scooplike tool for digging

troy (weight) n. system of weights for gold, silver, etc. in which 12 oz. = 1 lb.

tru'ant n. 1 pupil who stays away from school without leave 2 one who shirks his or her duties —**tru'an·cy** n.

truce n. cessation of fighting by mutual agreement

truck n. 1 large motor vehicle for carrying loads 2 wheeled frame 3 vegetables raised for market 4 [Col.] dealings —v. carry on a truck —**truck'er** n.

truck farm n. farm where vegetables are grown for market

truck'le v. be servile

trudge v. walk wearily

true a. 1 loyal 2 not false 3 accurate 4 lawful 5 real; genuine —adv. exactly —n. that which is true —**tru'ly** adv.

true'-blue' a. very loyal

truf'fle n. fleshy, edible underground fungus

tru'ism' n. an obvious truth

trump n. (playing card of) a suit ranked highest —v. take with a trump —**trump up** devise deceitfully

trump'er·y n., pl. **-ies** showy but worthless thing

trum'pet n. brass instrument with a flared end —v. proclaim loudly

trun'cate' v. cut off a part —**trun·ca'tion** n.

trun'cheon (-chən) n. short, thick club

trun'dle v. roll along

trundle bed n. low bed on small wheels

trunk n. 1 main stem of a tree 2 body, not including the head and limbs 3 long snout of an elephant 4 large box for clothes, etc. 5 main line 6 pl. very short pants worn for sports

trunk line n. main line of a railroad, telephone system, etc.

truss v. tie, fasten, or tighten —n. supporting framework or device

trust n. 1 belief in the honesty, reliability, etc. of another 2 one trusted 3 responsibility 4 custody CREDIT (n. 4) 6 property managed for another 7 a monopolistic group of corporations —v. 1 have trust in 2 put in the care of 3 believe 4 hope 5 let buy on credit —**trust′ful** a. —**trust′wor′thy** a.

trust·ee′ n. 1 one put in charge of another's property 2 member of a controlling board —**trust·ee′ship** n.

trust fund n. money, stock, etc. held in trust

trust′y a. **-i·er, -i·est** dependable —n., pl. **-ies** a convict with privileges

truth n. 1 a being true, honest, etc. 2 that which is true 3 established fact —**truth′ful** a.

try v. **tried, try′ing** 1 conduct the trial of 2 test 3 afflict 4 attempt —n., pl. **tries** attempt; effort

try′ing a. hard to bear

try′out′ n. test of fitness

tryst (trist) n. appointment to meet made by lovers

T′-shirt′ n. short-sleeved, pull-over undershirt

T square n. T-shaped ruler

tsu·na·mi (tsōō nä′mē) n., pl. **-mis** huge sea wave

tub n. 1 large, open container 2 bathtub

tu′ba n. large, deep-toned brass instrument

tub′by (-ē) a. **-bi·er, -bi·est** fat and short

tube n. 1 slender pipe for fluids 2 tubelike, sealed container 3 electron tube —**tu′bu·lar** a.

tu′ber n. thickened part of an underground stem —**tu′ber·ous** a.

tu′ber·cle n. 1 small, round projection 2 hard growth

tu·ber·cu·lo′sis n. wasting disease, esp. of the lungs —**tu·ber′cu·lous, tu·ber′cu·lar** a.

tube′rose′ n. flower with a bulblike root

tuck v. 1 gather up in folds 2 push the edges of something under 3 cover snugly 4 press into a small space —n. sewn fold

tuck′er v. [Col.] tire (out)

-tude suf. quality; state

Tues′day n. third day of the week

tuft n. bunch of hairs, grass, etc. growing or tied together —v. form in tufts

tug v. **tugged, tug′ging** pull; drag —n. 1 hard pull 2 tugboat

tug′boat′ n. small boat for towing or pushing ships

tug of war n. contest with two teams pulling at a rope

tu·i′tion (-ish′ən) n. charge for instruction

tu′lip n. bulb plant with cup-shaped flower

tulle (tōōl) n. fine netting for veils, etc., made of silk, etc.

tum′ble v. 1 fall or move suddenly or clumsily 2 toss about 3 do acrobatics —n. 1 a fall 2 disorder

tum′ble-down′ a. dilapidated

tum′bler n. 1 drinking glass 2 acrobat 3 part of a lock moved by a key

tum′ble·weed′ n. plant that breaks off and is blown about

tu′mid a. 1 swollen; bulging 2 inflated; pompous

tum′my n., pl. **-mies** stomach: child's word

tu′mor n. abnormal growth in or on the body

tu′mult′ n. 1 uproar 2 confusion —**tu·mul′tu·ous** (-chōō əs) a.

tun n. large cask

tu′na (fish) n. large ocean fish with oily flesh

tun′dra n. large arctic plain without trees

tune n. 1 melody 2 Mus. right pitch 3 agreement —v. 1 put in TUNE (n. 2) 2 adjust to proper performance —**tune in** adjust radio or TV set to receive (a station, program, etc.) —**tun′er** n.

tune′ful a. full of melody

tune′-up′, tune′-up′ n. an adjusting, as of an engine, to proper condition

tung′sten n. hard metal in alloys, a chemical element

tu′nic n. 1 loose gown worn in ancient Greece and Rome 2 long, belted blouse

tun′ing fork n. two-pronged steel device struck to sound a tone in perfect pitch

tun′nel n. underground passageway —v. make a tunnel

tun′ny n., pl. **-nies** tuna

tur′ban n. scarf wound round the head, as in the Middle East

tur′bid a. 1 muddy or cloudy 2 confused

tur′bine (-bin, -bīn′) n. engine driven by the pressure of air, steam, or water on the vanes of a wheel

tur′bo·jet′ n. airplane engine with a jet-driven turbine to work the air compressor

tur′bo·prop′ n. airplane engine with a jet-driven turbine to drive the propeller

tur′bot (-bət) n. large, edible European flatfish

tur′bu·lent a. 1 disorderly 2 agitated —**tur′bu·lence** n.

tu·reen′ n. large, deep dish with a lid, for soup, etc.

turf n. top layer of earth with grass —**the turf** (track for) horse racing

tur'gid (-jid) *a.* 1 swollen 2 pompous —**tur·gid'i·ty** *n.*

Turk *n.* native of Turkey

tur'key *n.* 1 large bird with a spreading tail 2 its flesh, used as food

turkey buzzard *n.* dark-colored American vulture

Turk'ish *n., a.* (language) of Turkey

tur'mer·ic *n.* plant whose powdered root is used for seasoning, etc.

tur'moil' *n.* noisy, excited condition

turn *v.* 1 revolve or rotate 2 change in position or direction 3 make or perform 4 reverse 5 change in feelings, etc. 6 change in form, etc. 7 drive, set, etc. 8 to wrench or twist 9 divert; deflect 10 upset 11 depend 12 reach or pass 13 become 14 become sour —*n.* 1 a turning around 2 change in position or direction 3 short walk, ride, etc. 4 bend; twist 5 chance; try 6 deed 7 turning point 8 style; form 9 sudden shock —**in** (or **out of**) **turn** (in or not in) proper order —**turn down** to reject —**turn in** 1 hand in 2 [Col.] go to bed —**turn off** 1 shut off 2 [Sl.] cause to be bored, etc. —**turn on** 1 make go on 2 [Sl.] make or become elated, etc. —**turn out** 1 shut off 2 come 3 make 4 result —**turn over** to rely on —**turn up** happen, appear, etc.

turn'a·bout' *n.* reversal

turn'a·round' *n.* 1 wide area for turning a vehicle around 2 time taken by a business to complete a job

turn'buck'le *n.* metal loop used as a coupling

turn'coat' *n.* traitor

turn'ing point *n.* point in time for a decisive change

tur'nip *n.* plant with an edible, round root

turn'key' *n., pl.* **-keys'** jailer

turn'off' *n.* place to turn off a highway, etc.

turn'out' *n.* gathering of people

turn'o'ver *n.* 1 small pie with crust folded over 2 rate of replacement of workers, goods, etc.

turn'pike' *n.* highway, esp. one on which a toll is paid

turn'stile' *n.* gate admitting only one at a time

turn'ta'ble *n.* round, revolving platform

tur'pen·tine' *n.* oil from trees, used in paints, etc.

tur'pi·tude' *n.* vileness

tur'quoise' (-kwoiz', -koiz') *n.* greenish-blue gem

tur'ret *n.* 1 small tower on a building 2 armored dome, as on a tank 3 lathe part holding cutting tools

tur'tle *n.* hard-shelled land and water reptile

tur'tle-dove' *n.* wild dove

tur'tle-neck' *n.* a high, snug, turned-down collar

tusk *n.* long, projecting tooth, as of an elephant

tus'sle *n., v.* struggle

tus'sock (-ək) *n.* thick tuft or clump of grass, etc.

tu·te·lage (tōōt''l ij) *n.* 1 instruction 2 protection

tu'tor *n.* private teacher —*v.* teach —**tu·to'ri·al** (-tôr'ē-) *a.*

tut·ti-frut·ti (tōōt'ē frōōt'ē) *n., a.* (ice cream, etc.) made with mixed fruits

tux·e'do *n., pl.* **-dos** man's semiformal suit

TV *n.* 1 television 2 *pl.* **TVs** or **TV's** television set

TV dinner *n.* precooked dinner frozen in a tray, heated, and served

twad·dle (twäd'l) *n.* nonsense

twain *n., a.* [Poet.] two

twang *n.* 1 sharp, vibrating sounds 2 nasal sound —*v.* to make, or utter with, a twang

'twas it was

tweak *v., n.* (give) a sudden, twisting pinch

tweed *n.* 1 rough wool fabric 2 *pl.* clothes of tweed

tweet *v., n.* chirp

tweet'er *n.* small speaker for high-frequency sounds

tweez'ers *n.pl.* small pincers for plucking hairs

twelve *a., n.* two more than ten —**twelfth** *a., n.*

twen'ty *a., n., pl.* **-ties** two times ten —**twen'ti·eth** *a., n.*

twerp *n.* [Sl.] insignificant or contemptible person

twice *adv.* 1 two times 2 two times as much

twid'dle *v.* twirl idly

twig *n.* small branch

twi'light' *n.* 1 dim light after sunset 2 gradual decline

twill *n.* cloth woven with parallel diagonal lines

twin *n.* 1 either of two born at the same birth 2 either of two very much alike —*a.* being a twin or twins

twine *n.* strong cord made of twisted strands —*v.* 1 interweave 2 wind around

twinge *v., n.* (have) a sudden pain or a qualm

twin'kle *v.* 1 sparkle 2 light up —*n.* a twinkling

twirl *v., n.* spin; twist

twist *v.* 1 to wind together or around something 2 force out of shape 3 pervert meaning of 4 sprain 5 rotate 6 curve —*n.* 1

something twisted 2 a twisting

twist'er n. [Col.] tornado or cyclone

twitch v. pull or move with a sudden jerk —n. sudden, spasmodic motion

twit'ter v. 1 chirp rapidly 2 tremble excitedly —n. a twittering

two a., n. one more than one —in two in two parts

two'-bit' a. [Sl.] cheap, inferior, etc.

two'-faced' a. deceitful

two'-fist'ed a. [Col.] virile

two'fold' a. 1 having two parts 2 having twice as much or as many —adv. twice as much or as many

two'-ply' a. having two layers, strands, etc.

two'some n. couple

two'-time' v. [Sl.] be unfaithful to

two'-way' a. allowing passage in two directions

-ty suf. quality or condition of

ty·coon' (-ti-) n. powerful industrialist

ty'ing v. prp. of TIE

tyke (tīk) n. [Col.] small child

tym·pan'ic membrane (tim-) n. eardrum

tym'pa·num (-) n. 1 cavity beyond eardrum 2 eardrum

type (tīp) n. 1 kind or sort 2 model; example 3 metal piece or pieces for printing 4 printed letters, etc. —v. 1 classify 2 typewrite

type'cast' v. to cast (an actor) repeatedly in similar role

type'script' n. typewritten matter

type'set' v. —set', —set'ting set in type —type'set'ter n.

type'write' v. write with a typewriter

type'writ·er n. a keyboard machine for making printed letters on paper

ty'phoid' n. infectious disease with fever, intestinal disorders, etc.: also typhoid fever

ty·phoon' n. cyclonic storm, esp. in the W Pacific

ty'phus n. infectious disease with fever, skin rash, etc.: also typhus fever

typ'i·cal (tip'-) a. 1 being a true example of its kind 2 characteristic —typ'i·cal·ly adv.

typ'i·fy' (tip'-) v. —fied', —fy'ing be typical of; exemplify

typ'ist (tīp'-) n. one who operates a typewriter

ty'po n., pl. —pos [Col.] typographical error; mistake in typing

ty·pog'ra·phy n. 1 setting of, and printing with, type 2 style, design, etc. of matter printed from type —ty·pog'ra·pher n. —ty'po·graph'i·cal a.

ty·ran'no·saur' (-sôr') n. huge, two-footed dinosaur

tyr·an'ny (tir'-) n. 1 government of a tyrant

2 cruel and unjust use of power —ty·ran'ni·cal a. —tyr'an·nize' v.

ty'rant (tī'-) n. 1 absolute ruler 2 cruel, unjust ruler

ty'ro n., pl. —ros novice

tzar (tsär, zär) n. czar

U

u·biq·ui·tous (yoo bik'wə təs) a. everywhere at the same time —u·biq'ui·ty n.

U'-boat' n. German submarine

ud'der n. large, milk-secreting gland of cows, etc.

UFO n., pl. **UFOs** or **UFO's** unidentified flying object

ugh int. exclamation of disgust, horror, etc.

ug'ly a. —li·er, —li·est 1 unpleasant to see 2 bad 3 dangerous —ug'li·ness n.

u'kase' (yoo'-) n. official decree

u·ku·le·le (yoo'kə lā'lē) n. small, four-stringed guitar

ul'cer n. open sore, as on the skin —ul'cer·ate' v. —ul'cer·ous a.

ul'na n., pl. —nae (-nē) or —nas larger bone of the forearm

ul·te'ri·or (-tir'ē-) a. beyond what is expressed

ul'ti·mate (-mət) a. 1 farthest 2 final 3 basic —n. final point or result —ul'ti·mate·ly adv.

ul'ti·ma'tum n. final offer or demand

ultra- pref. 1 beyond 2 extremely

ul'tra·ma·rine' a. deep-blue

ul·tra·son'ic a. above the range of humanly audible sound

ul'tra·sound' n. ultrasonic waves used in medical diagnosis, therapy, etc.

ul'tra·vi'o·let a. of the invisible rays just beyond the violet end of the spectrum

um'bel n. cluster of flowers with stalks of equal length

um'ber n. reddish brown

um·bil'i·cal cord n. cord connecting a fetus with the placenta

um'brage (-brij) n. resentment and displeasure

um·brel'la n. cloth screen on a folding frame, carried for protection against rain

um'pire n. 1 one who judges a dispute 2 an official in certain sports —v. act as umpire

un- pref. 1 not, lack of 2 back: reversal of action See list below

un·a'ble

un·a·fraid'

un·aid'ed

un·a·shamed'

un·au·thor·ized'

un·a·void·a·ble

un·bear′a·ble
un′be·liev′a·ble
un·bi′ased
un·bro′ken
un·but′ton
un·changed′
un·com′fort·a·ble
un′con·trol′la·ble
un′con·ven′tion·al
un′de·served′
un′de·sir′a·ble
un′de·vel′oped
un′dis·cov′ered
un·earned′
un′em·ployed′
un′em·ploy′ment
un·e′ven
un′ex·plained′
un′ex·plored′
un·fair′
un·fas′ten
un·fa′vor·a·ble
un·fit′
un′fore·seen′
un·for′tu·nate
un·gra′cious
un·harmed′
un·heed′ed
un·hurt′
un′i·den′ti·fied′
un′im·por′tant
un′in·hab′it·ed
un·in′jured
un·in′ter·est·ing
un′in·vit′ed
un·just′
un·kind′
un·lace′
un·man′ly
un·mar′ried
un·named′
un·nec′es·sar′y
un·no′ticed
un′of·fi′cial
un·o′pened
un·or′gan·ized′
un·paid′
un·pop′u·lar
un′pre·pared′
un′pro·fes′sion·al
un′pro·tect′ed
un·qual′i·fied′
un′re·li′a·ble
un·ripe′
un′sat′is·fac′to·ry
un·scram′ble
un·self′ish
un·sight′ly
un·skilled′
un·skill′ful

un·sound′
un·spoiled′
un·suit′a·ble
un·ti′dy
un·tir′ing
un·tried′
un·trou′bled
un·true′
un·want′ed
un·war′rant·ed
un·war′y
un·whole′some
un·will′ing
un·wise′
un·wor′thy
un·wrap′
un·yield′ing

un′a·bridged′ *a.* not abridged; complete
un′ac·count′a·ble *a.* **1** inexplicable **2** not responsible
un′ac·cus′tomed *a.* **1** not accustomed (*to*) **2** unusual
u·nan′i·mous (yōō-) *a.* without dissent —u′na·nim′i·ty *n.* —u·nan′i·mous·ly *adv.*
un′ap·proach′a·ble *a.* **1** aloof **2** without equal
un·armed′ *a.* having no weapon
un′as·sum′ing *a.* modest
un′at·tached′ *a.* **1** not attached **2** not engaged or married
un′a·vail′ing *a.* useless
un′a·ware′ *a.* not aware —*adv.* unawares
un′a·wares′ *adv.* **1** unintentionally **2** by surprise
un·bal′anced *a.* **1** not in balance **2** mentally ill
un·bar′ *v.* –barred′, –bar′ring unbolt; open
un′be·com′ing *a.* **1** not suited **2** not proper
un′be·lief′ *n.* lack of belief, esp. in religion —un′be·liev′er *n.*
un·bend′ *v.* –bent′ or –bend′ed, –bend′ing **1** relax **2** straighten
un·bend′ing *a.* **1** rigid; stiff **2** firm; unyielding
un·blush′ing *a.* shameless
un·bolt′ *v.* withdraw the bolt of (a door, etc.); open
un·born′ *a.* **1** not born **2** not yet born; future
un·bos′om (-booz′-) *v.* to tell (secrets)
un·bound′ed *a.* not restrained
un·bri′dled *a.* **1** with no bridle on **2** uncontrolled
un·bur′den *v.* relieve by disclosing (guilt, etc.)
un·called′-for′ *a.* unnecessary and out of place
un·can′ny *a.* **1** weird **2** unusually good, acute, etc.
un′cer·e·mo′ni·ous *a.* rudely abrupt
un·cer′tain *a.* **1** not sure or certain **2** vague

3 not steady or constant —**un·cer'tain·ty** n., pl. **-ties**

un·char'i·ta·ble a. severe or harsh

un'cle n. 1 brother of one's father or mother 2 husband of one's aunt

un·coil' v. unwind

un·com·mit'ted a. not pledged or taking a stand

un·com'mon a. 1 not usual 2 extraordinary

un·com'pro·mis'ing a. unyielding; firm

un'con·cern' n. lack of interest or worry; indifference —**un'con·cerned'** a.

un'con·di'tion·al a. without conditions or limits

un'con·scion·a·ble (-shən-) a. 1 unscrupulous 2 unreasonable

un·con'scious (-shəs) a. 1 not conscious 2 not aware (of) 3 unintentional —**the unconscious** part of the mind storing feelings, desires, etc. of which one is unaware

un·count'ed a. 1 not counted 2 innumerable

un·couth' (-kooth') a. rude; crude

un·cov'er v. 1 to disclose 2 remove the cover from

unc'tion n. 1 an anointing 2 anything soothing

unc'tu·ous (-choo-) a. 1 oily 2 insincerely earnest

un·cut' a. 1 not shaped: said of a gem 2 not abridged

un·daunt'ed a. not hesitating because of fear

un·de·cid'ed a. not (having) decided

un'de·ni'a·ble a. that cannot be denied

un'der prep. 1 lower than; below; beneath 2 covered by 3 less than 4 below and across 5 subject to 6 undergoing —adv. 1 in or to a lower position 2 so as to be covered —a. lower

under- pref. 1 below 2 less than usual or proper

un'der·a·chieve' v. fail to do as well as expected

un'der·age' a. below the legal age

un'der·arm' a. 1 for the armpit 2 UNDERHAND (a. 1)

un'der·brush' n. small trees, bushes, etc. in a forest

un'der·car'riage n. supporting frame

un'der·clothes' n.pl. underwear: also **un'der·cloth'ing**

un'der·cov'er a. secret

un'der·cur'rent n. underlying tendency, opinion, etc.

un'der·de·vel'oped a. inadequately developed, esp. economically

un'der·dog' n. one that is expected to lose

un'der·es'ti·mate' v. make too low an estimate

un'der·foot' adv., a. 1 under the feet 2 in the way

un'der·gar'ment n. piece of underwear

un'der·go' v. **-went', -gone', -go'ing** experience; endure

un'der·grad'u·ate (-ət) n. college student who does not yet have a degree

un'der·ground' a., adv. 1 beneath the earth's surface 2 secret 3 unconventional, radical, etc. —n. secret revolutionary movement

un'der·growth' n. underbrush

un'der·hand' a. 1 with the hand held below the elbow 2 underhanded; sly —adv. 1 with an underhand motion 2 in an underhanded way

un'der·hand'ed a. sly, deceitful, etc.

un'der·lie' v. 1 lie beneath 2 to support

un'der·line' v. 1 to draw a line under 2 to stress

un'der·ling n. subordinate

un'der·ly'ing a. basic

un'der·mine' v. 1 dig beneath 2 weaken gradually

un'der·neath' adv., prep. under; below

un'der·pants' n.pl. undergarment of short pants

un'der·pass' n. road under a railway or highway

un'der·pin'ning n. prop or foundation

un'der·priv'i·leged a. needy; poor

un'der·rate' v. rate too low

un'der·score' v. underline

un'der·sec're·tar'y n., pl. **-ies** assistant secretary

un'der·sell' v. sell for less than

un'der·shirt' n. undergarment worn under a shirt

un'der·shorts' n.pl. men's or boys' short underpants

un'der·shot' a. with the lower part extending past the upper

un'der·stand' v. **-stood', -stand'ing** 1 get the meaning (of) 2 take as a fact 3 know or perceive the nature, etc. of 4 sympathize with —**un'der·stand'a·ble** a.

un'der·stand'ing n. 1 comprehension 2 intelligence 3 mutual agreement

un'der·state' v. say with little or no emphasis

un'der·stud'y v. **-ied, -y·ing**; n., pl. **-ies** (be ready to) substitute for an actor

un'der·take' v. **-took', -tak'en, -tak'ing** 1 begin (a task, etc.) 2 promise —**un'der·tak'ing** n.

un'der·tak'er n. funeral director

un'der·things' n.pl. women's or girls' underwear

un'der·tone' n. subdued tone

un'der·tow' (-tō') n. strong flow of water

back under breaking waves

un'der·wa'ter a., adv. beneath the surface of the water

un'der·wear' n. clothes worn next to the skin

un'der·weight' a. weighing too little

un'der·world' n. 1 the world of criminals 2 Hades

un'der·write' v. –wrote', –writ'ten, –writ'ing 1 agree to finance 2 write insurance for —**un'der·writ'er** n.

un·do' v. –did', –done', –do'ing 1 open, untie, etc. 2 cancel or destroy

un·do'ing n. 1 a bringing to ruin 2 cause of ruin

un·done' a. 1 not done 2 ruined

un·doubt'ed a. certain

un·dress' v. take the clothes off

un·due' a. more than is proper —**un·du'ly** adv.

un'du·late (-jōō-, -dyōō-) v. 1 move in waves 2 have or give a wavy form —**un'du·la'tion** n.

un·dy'ing a. eternal

un·earth' v. 1 dig up from the earth 2 find

un·earth'ly a. 1 supernatural 2 weird

un·eas'y a. –i·er, –i·est uncomfortable —**un·eas'i·ness** n.

un·e'qual a. 1 not equal in size, value, etc. 2 not adequate (to)

un·e'qualed a. without equal

un'e·quiv'o·cal a. straightforward; clear

un'ex·pect'ed a. not expected; sudden —**un'ex·pect'ed·ly** adv.

un·fail'ing a. always dependable

un·faith'ful a. 1 not faithful 2 adulterous

un'fa·mil'iar a. 1 not well-known 2 not acquainted (with)

un·feel'ing a. 1 insensible 2 hardhearted; cruel

un·feigned' (-fānd') a. real; genuine

un·fin'ished a. 1 incomplete 2 not painted, etc.

un·flap'pa·ble a. [Col.] not easily excited

un·flinch'ing a. steadfast

un·fold' v. 1 spread out 2 make or become known

un·found'ed a. not based on fact or reason

un·friend'ly a. not friendly, kind, or favorable

un·furl' v. unfold

un·gain'ly a. awkward

un·gov'ern·a·ble a. unruly

un·guard'ed a. 1 unprotected 2 frank; candid 3 careless

un'guent (-gw**ə**nt) n. salve

un'gu·late (-gyōō l**ə**t, -lāt') a. having hoofs —n. ungulate mammal

un·hand' v. let go of

un·hap'py a. –pi·er, –pi·est 1 unlucky 2

sad; wretched

un·health'y a. –i·er, –i·est 1 not well 2 harmful to health

un·heard' a. not heard or listened to

un·heard'-of' a. never known or done before

un·hinge' v. 1 remove from the hinges 2 unbalance (the mind)

un·ho'ly a. –li·er, –li·est 1 not sacred 2 wicked; sinful

un·horse' v. make fall from a horse

uni- pref. having only one

u'ni·corn' (yōōn'**ə**-) n. mythical horse with a horn in its forehead

u'ni·form' a. 1 never changing 2 all alike —n. special clothes for some group —v. dress in a uniform —**u'ni·form'i·ty** n.

u'ni·fy' v. –fied', –fy'ing make into one —**u'ni·fi·ca'tion** n.

u'ni·lat'er·al a. 1 of one side only 2 involving only one of several parties

un'im·peach'a·ble a. without fault

un'in·ter·est·ed a. not interested; indifferent

un·ion (yōōn'y**ə**n) n. 1 a uniting 2 group of nations or states united 3 marriage 4 a labor union

un'ion·ize' v. organize into a labor union

u·nique (yōō nēk') a. 1 one and only 2 without equal 3 unusual

u'ni·sex' a. not differentiated for the sexes

u'ni·son n. 1 Mus. sameness of pitch 2 agreement

u'nit n. 1 single part of a whole 2 a special part 3 a standard measure 4 one

u·nite' v. 1 put together as one; combine 2 join together (in)

u'ni·ty n., pl. –ties 1 a being united 2 harmony; agreement

u'ni·ver'sal a. 1 of or for all 2 present everywhere —**u'ni·ver'sal·i·ty** n.

u'ni·ver'sal·ly adv. 1 in every case 2 everywhere

u'ni·verse' n. 1 space and all things in it 2 the world

u'ni·ver'si·ty n., pl. –ties school made up of college and, often, graduate schools

un·kempt' a. untidy; messy

un·known' a., n. unfamiliar or unidentified (person or thing)

un·law'ful a. against the law —**un·law'ful·ly** adv.

un·lead'ed a. not containing lead compounds, as gasoline

un·learn'ed a. not educated

un·leash' v. release as from a leash

un·less' con. except if

un·let'tered a. 1 ignorant 2 illiterate

un·like' a. not alike —prep. not like

un·like'ly a. not likely to happen, be true,

succeed, etc.

un·lim′it·ed *a.* without limits or bounds

un·load′ *v.* 1 remove (a load) 2 take a load from 3 get rid of

un·lock′ *v.* open by undoing a lock

un·luck′y *a.* –i·er, –i·est having or bringing bad luck

un·make′ *v.* –made′, –mak′ing 1 undo 2 ruin 3 depose

un·man′ *v.* –manned′, –man′ning deprive of manly courage —**un·man′ly** *a.*

un·manned′ *a.* without people aboard and operated remotely

un·mask′ *v.* 1 remove a mask (from) 2 expose

un′mis·tak′a·ble *a.* that cannot be mistaken; clear —**un′mis·tak′a·bly** *adv.*

un·mit′i·gat′ed *a.* 1 not lessened 2 absolute

un·nat′u·ral *a.* 1 abnormal 2 artificial

un·nerve′ *v.* to make (someone) lose nerve, courage, etc.

un·num′bered *a.* 1 countless 2 not numbered

un·pack′ *v.* take things out of a trunk, box, etc.

un·par′al·leled′ *a.* that has no equal or counterpart

un·pleas′ant *a.* offensive; disagreeable

un·prec′e·dent′ed *a.* having no precedent; unique

un·prin′ci·pled *a.* without good principles

un·print′a·ble *a.* not fit to be printed

un·ques′tion·a·ble *a.* certain —**un·ques′tion·a·bly** *adv.*

un′quote′ *int.* that ends the quotation

un·rav′el *v.* 1 undo the threads of 2 make clear

un·read′ (-red′) *a.* 1 not having been read 2 having read little

un·re′al *a.* fantastic

un·re′al·ized′ *a.* not having been achieved

un·rea′son·a·ble *a.* 1 not reasonable 2 excessive

un′re·gen′er·ate (-it) *a.* stubbornly defiant

un′re·lent′ing *a.* 1 refusing to relent 2 cruel

un·rest′ *n.* 1 restlessness 2 angry discontent

un·ri′valed, un·ri′valled *a.* having no rival or equal

un·roll′ *v.* to open (something rolled up)

un·ruf′fled *a.* calm; smooth

un·rul′y (-rōōl′ē) *a.* –i·er, –i·est not obedient or orderly

un·sa′vor·y *a.* 1 tasting or smelling bad 2 disgusting

un·scathed′ (-skā*th*d′) *a.* uninjured

un·screw′ *v.* detach or loosen by removing screws

un·scru′pu·lous *a.* without scruples; dishonest

un·seal′ *v.* to open

un·sea′son·a·ble *a.* not usual for the season

un·seat′ *v.* 1 throw from a seat 2 remove from office

un·seem′ly *a.* improper

un·set′tle *v.* disturb, displace, or disorder

un′so·phis′ti·cat′ed *a.* simple, naive, etc.

un·speak′a·ble *a.* so bad, evil, etc. that description is impossible

un·sta′ble *a.* 1 not fixed, firm, etc. 2 changeable 3 emotionally unsettled

un·stead′y *a.* unstable

un·struc′tured *a.* not strictly organized; loose, free, open, etc.

un·strung′ *a.* nervous; upset

un·stuck′ *a.* loosened or freed from being stuck

un·stud′ied *a.* spontaneous; natural

un′sub·stan′tial *a.* not solid, firm, real, etc.

un·sung′ *a.* not honored

un·tan′gle *v.* free from tangles; straighten out

un·taught′ *a.* 1 uneducated 2 got without teaching

un·think′a·ble *a.* that cannot be considered

un·think′ing *a.* thoughtless

un·tie′ *v.* unfasten (something tied or knotted)

un·til′ *prep.* 1 up to the time of 2 before —*con.* 1 to the point, degree, etc. that 2 before

un·time′ly *a.* 1 premature 2 at the wrong time —*adv.* too soon —**un·time′li·ness** *n.*

un·to′ *prep.* [Poet.] to

un·told′ *a.* 1 not told or revealed 2 very great

un·to′ward (-tō′ərd) *a.* 1 unfortunate 2 hard to control

un·truth′ *n.* lie; falsehood —**un·truth′ful** *a.*

un·tu′tored *a.* uneducated

un·used′ *a.* 1 not in use 2 unaccustomed (to) 3 never used before

un·u′su·al *a.* not usual; rare —**un·u′su·al·ly** *adv.*

un·ut′ter·a·ble *a.* that cannot be spoken or described —**un·ut′ter·a·bly** *adv.*

un·var′nished *a.* 1 plain; simple 2 not varnished

un·veil′ *v.* remove a veil from; disclose

un·well′ *a.* not well; sick

un·wield′y *a.* –i·er, –i·est 1 hard to handle because of size, etc. 2 clumsy —**un·wield′i·ness** *n.*

un·wind′ *v.* 1 make or become undone or uncoiled 2 relax

un·wit′ting *a.* 1 not knowing 2 not intentional —**un·wit′ting·ly** *adv.*

un·wont′ed *a.* unusual; rare

un·writ′ten *a.* 1 not in writing 2 observed

through custom, as some rules

up *adv.* 1 to, in, or on a higher place, level, etc. 2 to a later time 3 upright 4 into action, discussion, etc. 5 aside; away 6 so as to be even 7 completely 8 apiece —*prep.* up along, on, in, etc. —*a.* 1 put, brought, going, or gone up 2 at an end —*v.* upped, up′ping [Col.] increase —**ups and downs** changes in fortune —**up to** [Col.] 1 doing or scheming 2 capable of 3 as many as 4 as far as 5 dependent upon

up′-and-com′ing *a.* 1 promising 2 gaining prominence

up′beat′ *a.* [Col.] cheerful or optimistic

up·braid′ *v.* scold

up′bring′ing *n.* training received as a child

up′com′ing *a.* coming soon

up·date′ (*n.:* up′dāt′) *v.* make conform to most recent facts, etc. —*n.* updated information

up·end′ *v.* set on end

up·front′ *a.* [Col.] 1 forthright 2 in advance

up′grade′ *n.* upward slope —*v.* raise in grade or rank

up·heav′al *n.* 1 a heaving up 2 quick, violent change

up′hill′ *a., adv.* 1 upward 2 with difficulty

up·hold′ *v.* 1 support 2 confirm; sustain

up·hol′ster *v.* fit out (furniture) with coverings, etc. —**up·hol′ster·y** *n.*

up′keep′ *n.* 1 maintenance 2 cost of maintenance

up·lift′ (*n.:* up′lift′) *v.* 1 lift up 2 raise to a better level —*n.* a lifting up

up·on′ *prep., adv.* on, or up and on

up′per *a.* higher in place, rank, etc. —*n.* part of a shoe above the sole

up′per·case′ *a., n.* (of or in) capital letters

upper hand *n.* a position of advantage or control

up′per·most′ *a.* highest in place, power, etc. —*adv.* in the highest place; first

up·raise′ *v.* raise up; lift

up′right′ *a.* 1 standing up; erect 2 honest; just —*adv.* in an upright position —*n.* upright pole, beam, etc.

up′ris′ing *n.* a revolt

up′roar′ *n.* loud, confused noise or condition

up·roar′i·ous *a.* 1 making an uproar 2 boisterous

up·root′ *v.* 1 pull up by the roots 2 remove entirely

up′scale′ *a.* for affluent or stylish people

up·set′ (*n.:* up′set′) *v.* -set′, -set′ting 1 overturn 2 disturb or distress 3 defeat unexpectedly —*n.* an upsetting —*a.* 1 overturned 2 disturbed

up′shot′ *n.* result; outcome

up′side′ down *adv.* 1 with the top part underneath 2 in disorder —**up′side′-down′** *a.*

up′stage′ *v.* draw attention away from

up′stairs′ *adv., a.* to or on an upper floor —*n.* upper floor or floors

up′stand′ing *a.* honorable

up′start′ *n.* presumptuous newcomer

up′stream′ *adv., a.* against the current of a stream

up′swing′ *n.* upward trend

up′take′ *n.* a taking up —**quick (or slow) on the uptake** [Col.] quick (or slow) to understand

up′tight′ *a.* [Sl.] very tense, nervous, etc.: also **up′-tight′**

up′-to-date′ *a.* 1 having the latest facts, ideas, etc. 2 of the newest or latest kind

up′town′ *n.* part of city away from the business district

up′turn′ *n.* upward trend

up′ward *adv., a.* toward a higher place, position, etc.: also **up′wards** *adv.* —**upward(s) of** more than

u·ra′ni·um *n.* radioactive metallic chemical element

ur′ban *a.* of or in a city —**ur′ban·ize′** *v.*

ur·bane′ *a.* suave; refined —**ur·ban′i·ty** *n.*

ur′chin *n.* small mischievous child, esp. a boy

-ure *suf.* 1 act, result, or means of 2 state of being

u·re′a *n.* substance found in urine

u·re′mi·a *n.* toxic condition caused by kidney failure —**u·re′mic** *a.*

u·re′ter *n.* tube from a kidney to the bladder

u·re′thra *n.* duct for discharge of urine from bladder

urge *v.* 1 insist on 2 to force onward 3 plead with 4 incite —*n.* impulse

ur′gent *a.* 1 needing quick action 2 insistent —**ur′gen·cy** *n.*

u·ric (yoor′ik) *a.* of or from urine

u·ri′nal (yoor′ə-) *n.* fixture in which to urinate

u′ri·nar′y *a.* of the organs that secrete or discharge urine

u′ri·nate′ *v.* discharge urine from the body

u·rine (yoor′in) *n.* waste fluid from the kidneys, which passes through the bladder

urn *n.* 1 footed vase 2 container with a faucet

us *pron.* the objective case of WE

us′a·ble, use′a·ble *a.* that can be used

us′age *n.* 1 treatment 2 custom; habit

use (yooz; *n.:* yoos) *v.* 1 put into action 2 treat 3 consume —*n.* 1 a using or being used 2 power or right to use 3 need to use 4 utility or function —**used to** 1 did once 2 familiar with

used *a.* not new; secondhand

use′ful *a.* that can be used; helpful —**use′ful·ness** *n.*

use′less *a.* worthless

us′er *n.* one that uses something; spec., 1) drug addict 2) computer operator

us′er-friend′ly *a.* easy to use or understand, as a computer program

ush′er *v.* show the way to or bring in —*n.* one who ushers

u′su·al *a.* in common use; ordinary —**u′su·al·ly** *adv.*

u·surp′ *v.* take by force and without right —**u′sur·pa′tion** *n.* —**u·surp′er** *n.*

u·su·ry (yōō′zhər ē) *n.* lending of money at an excessive interest rate —**u′su·rer** *n.* —**u·su′ri·ous** *a.*

u·ten′sil *n.* container or tool for a special purpose

u′ter·ine (-in) *a.* of the uterus

u′ter·us *n.* hollow female organ in which a fetus grows

u·til′i·tar′i·an (-ter′-) *a.* useful or practical

u·til′i·ty *n., pl.* **-ties** 1 usefulness 2 water, gas, etc. for public use 3 company providing this

utility room *n.* room containing laundry appliances, etc.

u′ti·lize′ *v.* put to use —**u′ti·li·za′tion** *n.*

ut′most′ *a.* 1 most distant 2 greatest or highest —*n.* the most possible

U·to′pi·a, u·to′pi·a *n.* any imaginary place where all things are perfect —**U·to′pi·an, u·to′pi·an** *a., n.*

ut′ter *a.* complete; absolute —*v.* express with the voice —**ut′ter·ly** *adv.*

ut′ter·ance *n.* 1 an uttering 2 something said

ut′ter·most′ *a., n.* utmost

u′vu·la (yōō′vyōō-) *n., pl.* **-las** or **-lae** (-lē′) small part hanging down above the back of the tongue

V

va′cant *a.* 1 empty; unoccupied 2 free from work 3 stupid —**va′can·cy** *n., pl.* **-cies**

va′cate *v.* 1 make a place empty 2 annul

va·ca′tion *n.* rest from work, study, etc. —**va·ca′tion·er, va·ca′tion·ist** *n.*

vac·cine′ (-sēn′) *n.* preparation injected for immunity to a disease —**vac′ci·nate′** *v.* —**vac′ci·na′tion** *n.*

vac′il·late′ (vas′-) *v.* 1 waver 2 show indecision —**vac′il·la′tion** *n.*

vac′u·ous *a.* 1 empty 2 stupid; senseless —**va·cu′i·ty** *n., pl.* **-ties**

vac′u·um (-yōō əm, -yōōm′) *n.* 1 completely empty space 2 space with most of the air or gas taken out —*a.* of, having, or working by a vacuum —*v.* use a vacuum cleaner

vacuum cleaner *n.* machine that cleans by means of suction

vac′u·um-packed′ *a.* packed in airtight container to keep fresh

vacuum tube *n.* electron tube

vag′a·bond′ *a., n.* vagrant

va·gar′y (*or* vā′gər ē) *n., pl.* **-ies** odd action or idea

va·gi′na (-jī′-) *n.* canal leading to the uterus —**vag′i·nal** *a.*

va′grant *n.* homeless wanderer; tramp —*a.* 1 nomadic 2 wayward —**va′gran·cy** *n.*

vague (vāg) *a.* indefinite; unclear —**vague′ly** *adv.* —**vague′ness** *n.*

vain *a.* 1 conceited 2 futile 3 worthless —**in vain** 1 without success 2 profanely

vain′glo′ry *n.* boastful pride —**vain′glo′ri·ous** *a.*

val′ance (val′-) *n.* short drapery forming a border

vale *n.* [Poet.] valley

val′e·dic′to·ry *n.* farewell speech, as at graduation —**val′e·dic·to′ri·an** *n.*

va′lence (vā′-) *n. Chem.* combining capacity of an element

val′en·tine′ *n.* sweetheart or card for St. Valentine's Day

val′et (val′et, va lā′) *n.* male servant to another man

val′iant (-yənt) *a.* brave

val′id *a.* 1 true or sound 2 having legal force —**val′i·date′** *v.* —**va·lid′i·ty** *n.*

va·lise′ (-lēs′) *n.* suitcase

val′ley *n., pl.* **-leys** 1 low land between hills 2 land drained by a river system

val′or *n.* courage; bravery —**val′or·ous** *a.*

val′u·a·ble *a.* 1 having value 2 worth much money —*n.* valuable thing: *usually used in pl.*

val′u·a′tion *n.* 1 the fixing of a thing's value 2 value set on a thing

val′ue *n.* 1 importance, desirability, utility, etc. 2 worth in money 3 buying power 4 *pl.* standards —*v.* 1 set the value of 2 think highly of —**val′ue·less** *a.*

valve *n.* 1 device in a pipe, etc. to control the flow of a gas or liquid 2 body membrane like this

vamp *n.* part of a shoe over the instep

vam′pire *n.* 1 one who preys on others 2 bat that lives on other animals' blood: also **vampire bat**

van *n.* 1 vanguard 2 large closed truck

van′dal *n.* one who destroys another's property on purpose

van′dal·ize′ *v.* destroy maliciously —**van′dal·ism′** *n.*

Van·dyke′ (beard) (-dīk′) *n.* short, pointed beard

vane *n.* **1** device that swings to show wind direction **2** blade of a windmill, etc.

van′guard′ *n.* **1** front part of an army **2** leading group or position in a movement

va·nil′la *n.* flavoring made from the pods of an orchid

van′ish *v.* disappear

van′i·ty *n., pl.* **–ties 1** being vain, or conceited **2** futility **3** low table with mirror

van′quish *v.* conquer

van′tage *n.* **1** advantage **2** position allowing a clear view, etc.: also **vantage point**

vap′id *a.* tasteless; dull

va′por *n.* **1** thick mist, as fog or steam **2** gas formed by heating a liquid or solid **—va′por·ous** *a.*

va′por·ize′ *v.* change into vapor **—va′por·i·za′tion** *n.* **—va′por·iz′er** *n.*

var′i·a·ble *a.* that varies or can be varied **—n.** variable thing

var′i·ance *n.* a varying **—at variance** disagreeing

var′i·ant *a.* slightly different **—n.** variant form

var′i·a′tion *n.* **1** change in form, etc. **2** amount of change

var′i·col′ored *a.* of several or many colors

var′i·cose′ *a.* swollen, as veins

var′ied *a.* **1** of different kinds **2** changed

var′i·e·gat′ed *a.* **1** marked with different colors **2** varied

va·ri′e·ty *n., pl.* **–ties 1** change **2** kind; sort **3** number of different kinds

var′i·ous *a.* **1** of several kinds **2** several or many

var′mint, var′ment *n.* [Col. or Dial.] vermin; vile creature

var′nish *n.* resinous liquid forming a hard, glossy surface **—v.** cover with this

var′si·ty *n., pl.* **–ties** school's main team in contests, esp. in athletic events

var′y *v.* **-ied, -y·ing 1** make or become different; change **2** differ

vas′cu·lar *a.* of vessels carrying blood, etc.

vase *n.* open container for flowers, etc.

vas·ec′to·my *n., pl.* **-mies** removal or tying of sperm ducts

Vas′e·line (-lēn′) *trademark* petrolatum **—n.** [v–] petrolatum

vas′sal *n.* **1** feudal tenant **2** subject, servant, etc.

vast *a.* very great in size, degree, etc. **—vast′ly** *adv.* **—vast′ness** *n.*

vat *n.* large tank or cask

vaude·ville (vôd′vil) *n.* stage show with song and dance acts, skits, etc.

vault *n.* **1** arched roof or ceiling **2** arched room **3** burial chamber **4** room for keeping money, etc. as in a bank **5** a vaulting or leap **—v. 1** provide with a vault **2** leap over, balancing on a pole or the hands **—vault′er** *n.*

vaunt *n., v.* boast

VCR *n.* videocassette recorder

VDT *n.* video display terminal

veal *n.* meat from a calf

veer *v., n.* shift; turn

veg′e·ta·ble (vej′tə-) *n.* **1** plant eaten raw or cooked **2** any plant

veg′e·tar′i·an *n.* one who eats no meat **—a. 1** of vegetarians **2** of vegetables only

veg′e·tate′ *v.* live or grow like a plant

veg′e·ta′tion *n.* plant life

ve·he·ment (-ə-) *a.* **1** showing strong feeling **2** violent **—ve′he·mence** *n.*

ve′hi·cle (-ə-) *n.* **1** means of conveying, esp. a device on wheels **2** means **—ve·hic′u·lar** *a.*

veil (vāl) *n.* **1** piece of thin fabric worn by women over the face or head **2** thing that conceals **—v. 1** cover with a veil **2** conceal

veiled *a.* **1** wearing a veil **2** hidden **3** not openly expressed

vein (vān) *n.* **1** blood vessel going to the heart **2** line in a leaf or an insect's wing **3** body of minerals in a fissure or zone of rock **4** colored streak **5** trace or quality **—v.** mark as with veins

Vel′cro *trademark* nylon material for fastenings, with opposing strips of tiny hooks and clinging pile **—n.** [v–] this material

veld, veldt (velt) *n.* South African grassy land

vel′lum *n.* fine parchment

ve·loc′i·ty *n.* speed

ve·lour′, ve·lours′ (-loor′) *n., pl.* **–lours** (-loorz′, loor′) fabric with a velvety nap

ve·lure′ *n.* velvet or a fabric like velvet

vel′vet *n.* fabric of silk, rayon, etc. with a soft, thick pile **—vel′vet·y** *a.*

vel′vet·een′ *n.* cotton cloth with a nap like velvet

ve′nal *a.* open to bribery **—ve·nal′i·ty** *n.*

vend *v.* sell **—ven′dor, vend′er** *n.*

ven·det′ta *n.* feud, esp. vengeful one between families

vend′ing machine *n.* a coin-operated machine for selling small articles

ve·neer′ *n.* thin, covering layer, as of fine wood **—v.** cover with a veneer

ven′er·a·ble *a.* worthy of respect because of age, etc. **—ven′er·a·bil′i·ty** *n.*

ven′er·ate′ *v.* show deep respect for **—ven′er·a′tion** *n.*

ve·ne′re·al (-nir′ē-) *a.* of or passed on by sexual intercourse

Ve·ne′tian blind (-shən) *n.* [also v– b–] window blind of thin, adjustable slats

venge′ance n. revenge —**with a vengeance** 1 with great force 2 very much

venge′ful a. seeking revenge

ve′ni·al a. pardonable

ven′i·son n. flesh of deer

ven′om n. 1 poison of some snakes, spiders, etc. 2 malice —**ven′om·ous** a.

vent n. 1 outlet 2 opening to let gas, etc. out —v. let out

ven′ti·late′ v. circulate fresh air in —**ven′ti·la′tion** n. —**ven′ti·la′tor** n.

ven′tral a. of, near, or on the belly

ven′tri·cle n. either lower chamber of the heart

ven·tril′o·quism′ n. art of making one's voice seem to come from another point —**ven·tril′o·quist** n.

ven′ture n. risky undertaking —v. 1 place in danger 2 dare to do, say, etc.

ven′ture·some a. 1 daring; bold 2 risky

ven′tur·ous a. venturesome

ven′ue′ (-yōō′) n. 1 locality of a crime, trial, etc. 2 locale of a large gathering

ve·ra′cious (-shəs) a. truthful or true —**ve·rac′i·ty** (-ras′-) n.

ve·ran′da, ve·ran′dah n. open, roofed porch

verb n. word expressing action or being

ver′bal a. 1 of or in words 2 in speech 3 like or derived from a verb —n. verbal derivative, as a gerund —**ver′bal·ly** adv.

ver′bal·ize′ v. 1 use words for communication 2 express in words

verbal noun n. noun derived from a verb

ver·ba′tim adv., a. word for word

ver·be′na n. ornamental plant with showy flowers

ver′bi·age (-bē ij′) n. wordiness

ver·bose′ a. wordy —**ver·bos′i·ty** (-bäs′-) n.

ver′dant a. covered with green vegetation

ver′dict n. decision, as of a jury in a law case

ver′di·gris′ (-grēs′) n. greenish coating on brass, copper, or bronze

ver′dure (-jər) n. 1 green vegetation 2 color of this

verge v., n. (be on) the edge or border

ver′i·fy′ v. -**fied′**, -**fy′ing** 1 prove to be true 2 test the accuracy of —**ver′i·fi′a·ble** a. —**ver′i·fi·ca′tion** n.

ver′i·ly adv. [Ar.] really

ver′i·si·mil′i·tude′ n. appearance of being real

ver′i·ta·ble a. true; real

ver′i·ty n., pl. -**ties** (a) truth

ver·mi·cel′li (-sel′-, -chel′-) n. pasta that is like thin spaghetti

ver·mil′ion n. bright yellowish red

ver′min n., pl. -**min** small, destructive animal, as a fly or rat

ver·mouth′ (-mōōth′) n. a white wine

ver·nac′u·lar a., n. (of) the everyday speech of a country or place

ver′nal a. 1 of or in the spring 2 springlike

ver′sa·tile (-təl) a. able to do many things well —**ver′sa·til′i·ty** n.

verse n. 1 poetry 2 stanza 3 short division of a Bible chapter

versed a. skilled

ver′si·fy′ v. -**fied′**, -**fy′ing** 1 write poetry 2 tell in verse —**ver′si·fi·ca′tion** n. —**ver′si·fi′er** n.

ver′sion n. 1 translation 2 an account; report

ver′sus prep. against

ver′te·bra n., pl. -**brae** (-brē′, -brā′) or -**bras** any single bone of the spinal column

ver′te·brate (-brət) n., a. (animal) having a spinal column

ver′tex′ n., pl. -**tex′es** or -**ti·ces** (-tə sēz′) highest or farthest point

ver′ti·cal n., a. (line, plane, etc.) that is straight up and down

ver·ti′go′ n. dizzy feeling

verve n. vigor; enthusiasm

ver′y a. 1 complete; absolute 2 same; identical 3 actual —adv. 1 extremely 2 truly

ves′i·cle n. small, membranous cavity, sac, etc. —**ve·sic′u·lar** a.

ves′pers n. [also V-] evening prayer or service

ves′sel n. 1 container 2 ship or boat 3 tube of the body, as a vein

vest n. 1 man's sleeveless garment 2 undershirt —v. 1 to clothe 2 give power over or right to

ves′ti·bule′ (-byōōl′) n. 1 small entrance hall 2 enclosed passage

ves′tige (-tij) n. a trace or mark, esp. of something gone —**ves·tig′i·al** a.

vest′ing n. retention by an employee of pension rights, etc., when changing jobs, etc.

vest′ment n. garment, esp. one for a clergyman

vest′pock′et a. very small

ves′try n., pl. -**tries** 1 church meeting room 2 lay church group with certain powers

vet n. 1 veteran 2 veterinarian 3 veterinary

vetch n. plant grown for fodder

vet′er·an a. experienced —n. 1 former member of the armed forces 2 long-time employee, etc.

vet′er·i·nar′i·an n. doctor for animals

vet′er·i·nar′y a. of the medical care of animals —n. veterinarian

ve′to n., pl. -**toes** 1 power, or right, to prohibit or reject 2 use of this —v. -**toed**, -**to·ing** use a veto on

vex v. annoy; disturb —**vex·a′tion** n. —**vex·a′tious** a.

VHS *trademark* electronic system for recording videocassettes

vi·a (vī′ə, vē′ə) *prep.* by way of

vi′a·ble *a.* able to exist

vi′a·duct′ *n.* bridge held up by a series of towers

vi′al *n.* small bottle

vi′and *n.* 1 article of food 2 *pl.* fine food

vibes *n.* [Col.] vibraphone —*n.pl.* [Sl.] qualities producing emotional reaction

vi′brant *a.* 1 quivering 2 resonant 3 energetic

vi′bra·phone′ *n.* musical instrument like a xylophone, with electrically enhanced sound

vi′brate′ *v.* 1 move rapidly back and forth; quiver 2 thrill —**vi·bra′tion** *n.* —**vi′bra′tor** *n.*

vi·bra′to (-brä′-) *n., pl.* —**tos** pulsating effect made by slight wavering of a tone

vi·bur′num *n.* shrub or small tree with white flowers

vic′ar *n.* 1 Church of England priest 2 *R.C.Ch.* deputy of a bishop, etc.

vic′ar·age *n.* vicar's residence

vi·car′i·ous (-ker′-) *a.* 1 felt by imagined participation 2 taking another's place —**vi·car′i·ous·ly** *adv.*

vice *n.* 1 bad or evil conduct 2 bad or evil habit

vice– *pref.* substitute or subordinate

vice′-pres′i·dent *n.* officer next in rank to a president

vice′roy′ *n.* deputy ruler for a sovereign

vi′ce ver′sa (vī′sə-, vīs′-) *adv.* the other way around

vi·cin′i·ty *n., pl.* —**ties** 1 nearness 2 nearby area

vi·cious (vish′əs) *a.* 1 evil 2 unruly 3 malicious —**vi′cious·ly** *adv.* —**vi′cious·ness** *n.*

vi·cis′si·tude′ (-sis′ə-) *n.* any of one's ups and downs; change

vic′tim *n.* 1 one killed, hurt, etc. 2 one cheated, tricked, etc. —**vic′tim·ize′** *v.*

vic′tor *n.* winner

vic·to′ri·ous *a.* having won a victory; conquering

vic′to·ry *n., pl.* —**ries** success in war or any struggle

vict·uals (vit′'lz) *n.pl.* [Dial. or Col.] food

vi·cu′na (-kyōōn′ə) *n.* 1 small llama 2 its soft, shaggy wool

vid·e·o′ *a., n.* 1 (of) television 2 (of) performance on videotape —**vid′e·o·tape′** *n.*

vid′e·o′cas·sette′ *n.* cassette containing videotape, recorded on and played back esp. by using a **videocassette recorder**

vid′e·o·tape′ *n.* magnetic tape for recording and playing back images and sounds —*v.*

to record on a videotape

vie *v.* **vied**, **vy′ing** to compete as in a contest

view *n.* 1 a looking 2 range of vision 3 idea or thought 4 scene 5 opinion 6 aim; goal —*v.* 1 look at or see 2 consider —**in view of** because of

view′er *n.* 1 one who views 2 device for looking at slides

view′point′ *n.* 1 place of observation 2 attitude

vig′il *n.* 1 watchful staying awake 2 watch kept 3 eve of a religious festival

vig′i·lant *a.* watchful —**vig′i·lance** *n.*

vig′i·lan′te (-tē) *n.* one of a group illegally organized to punish crime

vi·gnette′ (vin yet′) *n.* 1 short literary sketch 2 picture that shades off at the edges

vig′or *n.* active force; strength and energy —**vig′or·ous** *a.* —**vig′or·ous·ly** *adv.*

vik′ing *n.* [also V–] Scandinavian pirate of the Middle Ages

vile *a.* 1 evil; wicked 2 disgusting 3 lowly and bad

vil′i·fy′ *v.* —**fied′**, —**fy′ing** defame or slander

vil′la *n.* showy country house

vil′lage *n.* small town

vil′lain (-ən) *n.* evil or wicked person —**vil′lain·ous** *a.* —**vil′lain·y** *n.*

vim *n.* energy; vigor

vin′ai·grette′ (-ə-) *n.* dressing of vinegar, oil, herbs, etc.

vin′di·cate′ *v.* 1 clear from criticism, blame, etc. 2 justify —**vin′di·ca′tion** *n.*

vin·dic′tive *a.* 1 revengeful in spirit 2 done in revenge

vine *n.* plant with a stem that grows along the ground or climbs up a support

vin′e·gar *n.* sour liquid made by fermenting cider, wine, etc. —**vin′e·gar·y** *a.*

vine′yard (vin′yərd) *n.* land where grapevines are grown

vin′tage (-tij) *n.* wine of a certain region and year

vint′ner *n.* 1 wine merchant 2 one who makes wine

vi′nyl (-nəl) *a.* of a group of chemical compounds used in making plastics

vi·o′la (vē-) *n.* instrument like, but larger than, the violin —**vi·ol′ist** *n.*

vi′o·late′ *v.* 1 break (a law, etc.) 2 rape 3 desecrate 4 disturb —**vi′o·la′tion** *n.* —**vi′o·la′tor** *n.*

vi′o·lent *a.* 1 showing or acting with wild force or feeling 2 intense —**vi′o·lence** *n.*

vi′o·let *n.* delicate spring flower, usually bluish-purple

vi′o·lin′ *n.* four-stringed instrument

played with a bow —vi′o·lin′ist n.

vi′o·lon·cel′lo (vē′-) n., pl. –los cello

VIP (vē′ī pē′) n. very important person

vi′per n. 1 venomous snake 2 treacherous person

vi·ra′go (vi rä′-) n., pl. –goes or –gos shrewish woman

vir′gin n. person, esp. a woman, who has not had sexual intercourse —a. chaste, untouched, pure, etc. —vir·gin′i·ty n.

vir′gi·nal a. virgin

Vir·gin′ia creeper n. woodbine

Virginia reel n. American reel danced by couples facing in two lines

Vir′go′ sixth sign of the zodiac; Virgin

vir′ile (-əl) a. 1 masculine 2 strong, vigorous, etc. —vi·ril′i·ty n.

vir′tu·al (-chōō-) a. being so in effect if not in fact —vir′tu·al·ly adv.

vir′tue n. 1 moral excellence 2 good quality, esp. a moral one 3 chastity —by (or in) virtue of because of —vir′tu·ous a.

vir′tu·o′so n., pl. –sos musician, etc. having great skill —vir′tu·os′i·ty n.

vir′u·lent (-yōō-) a. 1 deadly 2 full of hate —vir′u·lence n.

vi′rus n. 1 infective agent that causes disease 2 harmful influence 3 unauthorized computer program instructions added as a joke or to sabotage —vi′ral a.

vi·sa (vē′zə) n. endorsement on a passport, granting entry into a country

vis·age (viz′ij) n. the face

vis-à-vis (vēz′ə vē′) prep. in relation to

vis′cer·a (-ər ə) n.pl. internal organs of the body —vis′cer·al a.

vis′cid (-id) a. viscous

vis′count′ (vī′-) n. nobleman above a baron

vis′cous (-kəs) a. thick, syrupy, and sticky —vis·cos′i·ty n.

vise n. device with adjustable jaws for holding an object firmly

vis′i·bil′i·ty n. distance within which things can be seen

vis′i·ble a. that can be seen; evident —vis′i·bly adv.

vi′sion n. 1 power of seeing 2 something seen in a dream, trance, etc. 3 mental image 4 foresight

vi′sion·ar′y a., n., pl. –ies idealistic and impractical (person)

vis′it v. 1 go or come to see 2 stay with as a guest 3 afflict —n. a visiting —vis′i·tor n.

vis′it·a′tion n. 1 visit to inspect 2 punishment sent by God

vi′sor n. 1 movable part of a helmet, covering the face 2 brim on a cap for shading the eyes

vis′ta n. view; scene

vis′u·al (vizh′-) a. 1 of or used in seeing 2 visible

vis′u·al·ize′ v. form a mental image of

vi′tal a. 1 of life 2 essential to life 3 very important 4 full of life —vi′tal·ly adv.

vi·tal′i·ty n. 1 energy; vigor 2 power to survive

vi′tal·ize′ v. give life or vigor to

vital signs n.pl. pulse, respiration, and body temperature

vital statistics n.pl. data on births, deaths, etc.

vi′ta·min n. any of certain substances vital to good health: vitamins A and D are found in fish-liver oil, eggs, etc.; vitamin B (complex), in liver, yeast, etc.; vitamin C, in citrus fruits

vi′ti·ate′ (vish′ē-) v. make bad; spoil —vi′ti·a′tion n.

vit′re·ous a. of or like glass

vit′ri·fy′ v. –fied′, –fy′ing change into glass by heating

vit′ri·ol (-ôl) n. caustic remarks —vit′ri·ol′ic (-äl′-) a.

vi·tu′per·ate′ v. berate

vi·va′cious (-shəs) a. spirited; lively —vi·vac′i·ty n.

viv′id a. 1 full of life 2 bright; intense 3 strong; active —viv′id·ly adv.

viv′i·fy′ v. –fied′, –fy′ing give life to

vi·vip′a·rous a. bearing living young, as most mammals

viv′i·sec′tion n. surgery on living animals for medical research

vix′en n. 1 female fox 2 shrewish woman

vi·zier (vi zir′) n. in Muslim countries, a high government official

vo·cab′u·lar′y n., pl. –ies all the words used by a person, group, etc. or listed in a dictionary, etc.

vo′cal a. 1 of or by the voice 2 speaking freely —vo′cal·ly adv.

vocal cords n.pl. membranes in the larynx that vibrate to make voice sounds

vo·cal′ic a. of or like a vowel or vowels

vo′cal·ist n. singer

vo′cal·ize′ v. speak or sing

vo·ca′tion n. one's profession, trade, or career —vo·ca′tion·al a.

vo·cif′er·ous (-sif′-) a. loud; clamorous —vo·cif′er·ate′ v.

vod′ka n. Russian alcoholic liquor made from grain

vogue (vōg) n. 1 current fashion 2 popularity

voice n. 1 sound made through the mouth 2 ability to make such sound 3 sound like this 4 right to express one's opinion, etc. 5 expression —v. utter or express

voice box n. larynx

voice mail n. electronic storage and delivery of telephone messages

voice'-o'ver n. voice of an unseen speaker, as on TV

void a. 1 empty; vacant 2 lacking 3 of no legal force —n. empty space —v. 1 to empty 2 cancel

voile (voil) n. thin fabric

vol'a·tile (-tal) a. 1 quickly evaporating 2 changeable —**vol'a·til'i·ty** n.

vol·ca'no n., pl. **–noes** or **–nos** mountain formed by erupting molten rock —**vol·can'ic** a.

vo·li'tion n. WILL (n. 3)

vol'ley n., v., pl. **–leys** 1 discharge (of) a number of weapons together 2 return (of) a tennis ball before it hits the ground

vol'ley·ball' n. game between teams hitting a large, light ball back and forth over a net

volt n. unit of electromotive force

volt'age n. electromotive force, shown in volts

vol·ta'ic a. of or producing electricity by chemical action

volt'me'ter n. instrument for measuring voltage

vol'u·ble a. talkative

vol'ume n. 1 a book 2 cubic measure 3 amount 4 loudness of sound

vo·lu'mi·nous a. 1 filling or producing volumes 2 large; full

vol'un·tar'y a. 1 by choice; of one's own free will 2 controlled by the will —**vol'un·tar'i·ly** adv.

vol'un·teer' v. offer, give, etc. of one's own free will —n. one who volunteers

vo·lup'tu·ous (-chōō əs) a. sensual

vom'it v., n. (have) matter from the stomach ejected through the mouth

voo'doo' n. religion of the West Indies, based on magic, charms, etc.

vo·ra'cious (-shəs) a. 1 greedy or ravenous 2 very eager

vor'tex' n., pl. **-tex'es** or **-ti·ces'** (-tə sēz') 1 whirlpool 2 whirlwind

vo'ta·ry n., pl. **–ries** worshiper; devotee

vote n. 1 a decision or choice shown on a ballot, etc. 2 all the votes 3 the right to vote —v. 1 cast a vote 2 decide by vote —**vot'er** n.

vo'tive a. given or done to fulfill a vow or promise

vouch v. give or be a guarantee (for)

vouch'er n. a paper serving as proof of payment, etc.

vouch·safe' v. be kind enough to grant

vow n., v. (make) a solemn promise or statement —**take vows** enter a religious order

vow'el n. speech sound of the letters a, e, i, o, u

voy'age n., v. journey by ship

voy·eur' (vwä yur') n. one having very strong interest in viewing sexual activities, etc.

vul'can·ize' v. treat rubber to make it stronger and more elastic

vul'gar a. 1 popular 2 lacking culture; crude —**vul'gar·ly** adv.

vul'gar·ism' n. coarse word or phrase that is considered improper

vul·gar'i·ty (-ger'-) n. 1 vulgar state or quality 2 pl. **–ties** vulgar act, etc.

vul'ner·a·ble a. 1 that can be hurt, attacked, etc. 2 easily hurt; sensitive —**vul'ner·a·bil'i·ty** n.

vul'ture n. 1 large bird of prey 2 greedy, ruthless person

vul'va n. external female sex organs

W

wab'ble n., v. wobble

wack'y a. **-i·er, -i·est** [Sl.] erratic, eccentric, or irrational

wad n. 1 small, soft mass 2 small lump —v. **wad'ded, wad'ding** 1 roll into a wad 2 stuff as with padding

wad'ding n. any soft material used in padding, packing, etc.

wad'dle v., n. walk with short steps, swaying from side to side

wade v. 1 walk through water, mud, etc. 2 proceed with difficulty 3 cross by wading

wad'er n. 1 one who wades 2 pl. high, waterproof boots, often with trousers

wad'ing bird n. long-legged shore bird that wades in shallows

wa'fer n. 1 thin, crisp cracker 2 disklike thing

waf'fle n. crisp cake baked between two flat, studded plates (**waffle iron**)

waft v. carry or move lightly over water or through the air —n. 1 odor, sound, etc. carried through the air 2 wafting motion

wag v. **wagged, wag'ging** move rapidly back and forth or up and down —n. 1 a wagging 2 a wit; comic

wage v. take part in —n. pl. money paid for work done

wa'ger n., v. bet

wag'gish a. 1 roguishly merry 2 said, done, etc. in jest

wag'gle v. wag abruptly

wag'on n. four-wheeled vehicle, esp. for hauling

waif n. homeless child

wail v., n. **1** (make a) loud, sad cry **2** lament

wain'scot n. wall paneling of wood —v. panel with wood

waist n. **1** body part between the ribs and the hips **2** waistline

waist'band' n. band fitting around the waist on slacks, a skirt, etc.

waist'coat' (or wes'kət) n. [Br.] man's vest

waist'line' n. middle or narrow part of the waist

wait v. **1** remain until something occurs **2** remain undone **3** serve food at **4** await —n. act or time of waiting —**wait on** (or **upon**) **1** be a servant to **2** serve

wait'er n. man who serves food at table —**wait'ress** n.fem.

wait'ing a. **1** that waits **2** of or for a wait —n. **1** act of one that waits **2** period of waiting

waiting list n. list of applicants, as for a vacancy

waiting room n. room where people wait, as in a doctor's office

waive v. **1** give up, as a right **2** postpone

waiv'er n. Law waiving of a right, claim, etc.

wake v. **woke** or **waked**, **waked** or **wok'en**, **wak'ing 1** come or bring out of a sleep **2** become alert (to) **3** stir up —n. **1** all-night vigil over a corpse **2** track or trail left behind

wake'ful a. **1** watchful **2** unable to sleep

wak'en v. to wake

wale n. **1** welt **2** ridge, as on corduroy

walk v. **1** go on foot at moderate speed **2** walk along, over, with, etc. **3** Baseball advance to first base by a walk —n. **1** way of walking **2** stroll; hike **3** path for walking **4** Baseball advancement by batter to first base on four pitches not strikes —**walk of life** way of living

walk'ie-talk'ie n. portable radio for sending and receiving

walk'ing stick n. stick carried when walking; cane

walk'out' n. **1** labor strike **2** abrupt departure in protest

walk'-up' n. apartment house without an elevator

wall n. upright structure that encloses, divides, etc. —v. to divide, or close up with a wall

wal'la·by (wäl'-) n., pl. **-bies** or **-by** small kangaroo

wall'board' n. fibrous material in thin slabs for making or covering walls

wal'let n. flat case for carrying money, cards, etc.

wall'eye' n. North American freshwater food fish

wall'flow'er n. [Col.] shy or unpopular person

wal'lop [Col.] v. **1** hit hard **2** defeat completely —n. a hard blow

wal'low v. **1** roll around in mud or filth, as pigs do **2** live selfishly

wall'pa'per v., n. (apply) paper for covering walls or ceilings

wall'-to-wall' a. covering a floor completely

wal'nut' n. **1** tree bearing an edible nut in a hard shell **2** its nut **3** its wood

wal'rus n. large seallike animal with two tusks

waltz n. ballroom dance in 3/4 time —v. dance a waltz

wam'pum (wäm'-) n. beads used as money by North American Indians

wan (wän) a. sickly pale

wand n. slender rod, as one of supposed magic power

wan'der v. **1** roam idly about **2** go astray; stray —**wan'der·er** n.

wan'der·lust' n. strong urge to wander or travel

wane v. **1** get smaller, weaker, etc. **2** approach the end —n. a waning

wan'gle v. [Col.] get by sly or tricky means

want v. **1** wish for; desire **2** need **3** lack —n. **1** lack; need **2** poverty **3** desire

want ad n. [Col.] advertisement for something wanted

want'ing a. **1** lacking **2** inadequate —prep. minus

wan'ton a. **1** senseless and cruel **2** irresponsible **3** immoral —n. wanton person

wap·i·ti (wäp'ət ē) n. North American elk

war n. **1** armed conflict, as between nations **2** any fight —v. **warred**, **war'ring** carry on war —**war'like'** a.

war'ble v. sing with trills, runs, etc. —n. a warbling —**war'bler** n.

ward n. **1** one under the care of a guardian **2** division of a hospital **3** voting district of a city —**ward off** turn aside

-ward suf. in a (specified) direction: also **-wards**

war'den n. **1** one who takes care of something **2** head official of a prison

ward'er n. watchman; guard

ward'robe' n. **1** a closet for clothes **2** all one's clothes

ware n. **1** thing for sale: usually used in pl. **2** pottery

ware'house' n. building where goods are stored

war'fare' n. war or any conflict

war'head' n. front part of a bomb, etc., with the explosive

war'horse' n. [Col.] veteran of many struggles

war'lock' n. wizard: male witch

warm a. 1 moderately hot 2 enthusiastic 3 kind and loving —v. make or become warm —**warm'ly** adv.

warm'blood'ed a. 1 having a relatively constant body temperature 2 ardent

warmed'-o'ver a. 1 reheated 2 presented again, without significant change

warm'heart'ed a. kind; loving

war'mon'ger (-muŋ'-, -mäŋ'-) n. one who tries to cause war

warmth n. 1 a being warm 2 strong feeling

warn v. 1 tell of danger; advise to be careful 2 inform; let know —**warn'ing** n., a.

warp v. 1 bend or twist out of shape 2 distort —n. 1 a warping or twist 2 long threads in a loom

war'rant n. 1 justification 2 legal writ authorizing an arrest, search, etc. —v. 1 authorize 2 justify

warrant officer n. officer just above enlisted man

war'ran-ty n., pl. **-ties** GUARANTEE (n. 1)

war'ren n. (limited) area in which rabbits are raised

war'ri-or n. soldier

war'ship' n. ship for combat use

wart n. small, hard growth on the skin —**wart'y** a.

war-y (wer'ē) a. **-i-er, -i-est** on guard; cautious —**wary of** careful of —**war'i-ly** adv.

was v. pt. of BE: used with *he, she,* or *it*

wash v. 1 clean with water 2 wash clothes 3 flow over or against 4 remove by washing 5 coat thinly —n. 1 a washing 2 clothes (to be) washed 3 rush of water 4 eddy from propeller, oars, etc. —a. that can be washed —**wash'a-ble** a.

wash'-and-wear' a. needing little or no ironing after washing

wash'board' n. ridged board to scrub clothes on

wash'bowl' n. bowl for washing the hands and face: also **wash'ba'sin**

wash'cloth' n. small cloth to wash the face or body

washed'-out' a. [Col.] 1 tired 2 pale

washed'-up' a. 1 [Col.] tired 2 [Sl.] having failed

wash'er n. 1 machine for washing 2 flat ring used to make a bolt, nut, etc. fit tight 3 one who washes

wash'ing n. 1 act of one that washes 2 clothes, etc. to be washed

washing machine n. machine for washing clothes, etc.

wash'out' n. 1 washing away of soil, etc. 2 [Sl.] a failure

wash'room' n. restroom

wash'stand' n. plumbing fixture with a washbowl

wash'tub' n. tub, often with faucets and a drain, to wash clothes, etc.

was'n't was not

wasp n. flying insect: some have a sharp sting

wasp'ish a. bad-tempered

was-sail (wäs'əl) n. toast (drink)

waste v. 1 use up needlessly 2 fail to take advantage of 3 wear away 4 lose strength or weaken 5 destroy —a. 1 barren or wild, as land 2 left over —n. 1 a wasting 2 wasted matter; refuse; etc. 3 wasteland —**go to waste** be wasted —**lay waste (to)** devastate —**waste'ful** a.

waste'bas'ket n. container for discarded paper, etc.

waste'pa'per n. paper thrown away after use

wast-rel (wās'trəl) n. profligate person

watch n. 1 act of guarding or observing 2 guard(s), or period of guard duty 3 small clock for wrist or pocket 4 Naut. period of duty, or crew on duty —v. 1 keep vigil 2 observe 3 guard or tend 4 be alert (for) —**watch out** be alert or careful —**watch'ful** a.

watch'band' n. band for holding a watch on the wrist

watch'dog' n. 1 dog kept to guard property 2 one that watches to prevent waste, etc.

watch'man n., pl. **-men** person hired to guard

watch'tow'er n. high tower from which a sentinel watches for enemies, etc.

watch'word' n. slogan

wa'ter n. 1 colorless liquid of rivers, lakes, etc. 2 water solution 3 body secretion, as urine —v. 1 to supply with water 2 dilute with water 3 fill with tears 4 secrete saliva —a. of, for, in, or by water

water buffalo n. oxlike work animal of Asia and Africa

wa'ter-col'or n. 1 paint made by mixing pigment and water 2 picture painted with such paints

wa'ter-cooled' a. cooled by circulating water

wa'ter-course' n. river, brook, canal, etc.

wa'ter-craft' n., pl. **-craft'** boat, ship, or other water vehicle

wa'ter-cress' n. water plant with leaves used in salads

wa'ter-fall' n. steep fall of water, as from a cliff

wa'ter-fowl' n. swimming bird

wa'ter-front' n. land or docks at the edge of a river, harbor, etc.

wa'ter·lil'y n., pl. **-ies** water plant with large, showy flowers

wa'ter·logged' a. soaked or filled with water

wa'ter·mark' n. 1 mark showing how high water has risen 2 design pressed into paper —v. to mark (paper) with a watermark

wa'ter·mel'on n. large melon with juicy, red pulp

water moccasin n. large, poisonous snake of southern U.S.

wa'ter·proof' v., a. (to make) impervious to water

wa'ter·shed' n. 1 area a river systems drains 2 ridge between two such areas

wa'ter·ski' v. be towed over water on a kind of ski

wa'ter·spout' n. whirling water funnel rising from sea

water table n. level below which the ground is saturated with water

wa'ter·tight' a. so tight no water can get through

water tower n. elevated tank for water storage, etc.

wa'ter·way' n. navigable river, lake, canal, etc.

wa'ter·works' n.pl. system of reservoirs, pumps, etc. supplying water to a city

wa'ter·y a. 1 of, like, or full of water 2 diluted

watt n. unit of electric power —**watt'age** n.

wat'tle (wät''l) n. 1 sticks woven with twigs 2 flap of skin hanging at the throat of a chicken, etc.

wave v. 1 move to and fro 2 wave the hand, etc., or signal thus 3 arrange in curves —n. 1 curving swell moving along on the ocean, etc. 2 wavelike vibration 3 curve(s), as in the hair 4 a waving, as of the hand —**wav'y** a., **-i·er**, **-i·est**

wave'length' n. distance between any point in a wave, of light or sound, to the same point in the next wave

wa'ver v. 1 flutter, falter, flicker, etc. 2 show indecision —n. a wavering

wax n. 1 plastic substance secreted by bees 2 substance like this, as paraffin —v. 1 put polish or wax on 2 get larger, stronger, etc. 3 to become —**wax'y** a., **-i·er**, **-i·est** —**wax'en** a.

wax bean n. bean with long, edible yellow pods

wax museum n. exhibit of wax figures of famous people: also **wax'works'**

wax paper n. paper made moisture-proof by a wax coating: also **waxed paper**

wax'works' n. exhibition of human figures made of wax

way n. 1 road or route 2 movement forward 3 method, manner, etc. 4 distance 5 direction 6 particular 7 wish; will 8 pl. framework on which a ship is built —adv. [Col.] far —**by the way** incidentally —**by way of** 1 passing through 2 as a means of —**give way** 1 yield 2 break down —**under way** moving ahead

way'far'er (-fer'-) n. traveler, esp. on foot —**way'far'ing** a., n.

way·lay' v. **-laid'**, **-lay'ing** to ambush

way'-out' a. [Col.] very unusual or unconventional

ways and means n.pl. methods of raising money

way'side' a., n. (at or along) the edge of a road

way'ward a. 1 willful; disobedient 2 irregular —**way'ward·ness** n.

we pron. persons speaking or writing

weak a. lacking strength, power, etc.; not strong effective, etc. —**weak'en** v.

weak'-kneed' a. timid; cowardly

weak'ling n. weak person

weak'ly a. **-li·er**, **-li·est** sickly —adv. in a weak way

weak'ness n. 1 a being weak 2 fault 3 special liking

weal n. skin welt

wealth (welth) n. 1 riches 2 large amount —**wealth'y** a., **-i·er**, **-i·est**

wean v. 1 stop suckling 2 withdraw from a certain habit, etc.

weap'on (wep'-) n. 1 thing used for fighting 2 means of attack or defense

weap'on·ry n. weapons

wear v. **wore**, **worn**, **wear'ing** 1 have on the body as clothes 2 make or become damaged by use 3 endure in use 4 to tire or exhaust —n. 1 clothing 2 impairment

wear and tear (ter) n. loss and damage resulting from use

wea·ry (wir'ē) a. **-ri·er**, **-ri·est** 1 tired 2 bored —v. **-ried**, **-ry·ing** make or become weary —**wea'ri·ness** n. —**wea'ri·some** a.

wea·sel (wē'zəl) n. small, flesh-eating mammal —v. [Col.] avoid or evade a commitment: with out

weath'er (weth'-) n. condition outside as to temperature, humidity, etc. —v. 1 to pass through safely 2 wear, discolor, etc. by exposure to sun, rain, etc.

weath'er-beat'en a. roughened, etc. by the weather

weath'er·ize' v. insulate (a building) to conserve heat

weath'er·man' n., pl. **-men'** weather forecaster

weath'er·proof' v., a. (make) able to withstand exposure to the weather

weath′er·strip′ n. strip of metal, felt, etc. for covering joints to keep out drafts, etc.: also **weath′er·strip′ping** —v. provide with weatherstrips

weather vane n. VANE (n. 1).

weave v. **wove**, **wo′ven**, **weav′ing** 1 make cloth by interlacing threads, as on a loom 2 twist or move from side to side or in and out —n. pattern of weaving

web n. 1 network, esp. one spun by a spider 2 skin joining the toes of a duck, frog, etc.

web′bing n. strong fabric woven in strips

web′foot′ n., pl. **–feet′** foot with a WEB (n. 2) —**web′-foot′ed** a.

wed v. **wed′ded**, **wed′ded** or **wed**, **wed′ding** 1 marry 2 unite

we'd 1 we had 2 we should 3 we would

wed′ding n. ceremony of marrying

wedge n. piece of wood, etc. tapering to a thin edge —v. 1 fix in place with a wedge 2 pack tightly

wed′lock′ n. matrimony

Wednes′day (wenz′-) n. fourth day of the week

wee a. very small; tiny

weed n. unwanted plant, as in a lawn —v. 1 remove weeds 2 take (out) as useless; etc.

weeds n.pl. black clothes for mourning

weed′y a. **–i·er**, **–i·est** 1 full of weeds 2 like a weed

week n. 1 period of seven days, esp. Sunday through Saturday 2 the hours or days one works each week

week′day′ n. any day of the week except Sunday and, often, Saturday

week′end′, **week′-end′** n. Saturday and Sunday —v. spend the weekend

week′ly a. 1 lasting a week 2 done, etc. once a week —adv. once a week —n., pl. **–lies** periodical coming out weekly

weep v. **wept**, **weep′ing** 1 shed tears 2 mourn (for)

weep′ing n. act of one who weeps —a. 1 that weeps 2 having drooping branches

weep′y a. **–i·er**, **–i·est** weeping or inclined to weep

wee′vil n. beetle larva that destroys cotton, grain, etc.

weft n. threads woven across the warp in a loom

weigh (wā) v. 1 determine the heaviness of, as on a scale 2 have a certain weight 3 consider well 4 burden: with down 5 hoist (an anchor)

weight n. 1 (amount of) heaviness 2 unit of heaviness 3 solid mass 4 burden 5 importance or influence —v. to burden —**weight′y** a., **–i·er**, **–i·est**

weight′less a. having little or no apparent weight

weight lift′ing n. athletic exercise or sport of lifting barbells

weir (wir) n. 1 low dam in a river, etc. 2 fencelike barrier in a stream, etc. for catching fish

weird (wird) a. 1 mysterious 2 bizarre

weird′o n., pl. **–os** [Sl.] bizarre person or thing

wel′come a. 1 gladly received 2 freely permitted 3 under no obligation —n. a welcoming —v. greet with pleasure

weld v. unite by melting together —n. welded joint

wel′fare′ n. health, happiness, and comfort —**on welfare** receiving government aid because of poverty, etc.

well n. 1 natural spring 2 hole dug in the earth to get water, oil, etc. 3 hollow shaft 4 source —v. gush or flow —adv. **bet′ter**, **best** 1 in a pleasing, good, or right way 2 prosperously 3 much 4 thoroughly —a. in good health —int. exclamation of surprise —**as well (as)** in addition (to) 2 equally (with)

we'll 1 we shall 2 we will

well′-ap·point′ed a. excellently furnished

well′-be′ing n. welfare

well′-bred′ a. showing good manners; courteous

well′-dis·posed′ a. friendly or receptive

well′-done′ a. 1 done with skill 2 thoroughly cooked

well′-fixed′ a. [Col.] rich

well′-found′ed a. based on facts or good judgment

well′-ground′ed a. having good basic knowledge of a subject

well′-heeled′ a. [Sl.] rich; prosperous

well′-in·formed′ a. having extensive knowledge of a subject or many subjects

well′-known′ a. famous or familiar

well′-man′nered a. polite

well′-mean′ing a. with good intentions —**well′-meant′** a.

well′-nigh′ adv. almost

well′-off′ a. 1 fortunate 2 prosperous

well′-read′ (-red′) a. having read much

well′spring′ n. source of a stream, continual supply, etc.

well′-to-do′ a. wealthy

well′-worn′ a. much worn or used

Welsh a., n. (of) the people or language of Wales

Welsh rabbit (or **rarebit**) n. melted cheese on toast

welt n. 1 leather strip in the seam between shoe sole and upper 2 ridge raised on the skin by a blow

wel′ter v. wallow —n. confusion

wen n. skin cyst

wench *n.* young woman: derogatory or humorous

wend *v.* proceed or go on (one's way)

went *v.* pt. of GO

wept *v.* pt. & pp. of WEEP

were *v.* pt. of BE: used with *you, we,* or *they*

we're we are

weren't were not

were'wolf' (wir'-, wer'-) *n., pl.* **-wolves'** *Folklore* a person changed into a wolf

west *n.* 1 direction in which sunset occurs 2 region in this direction 3 [W-] Europe and North and South America —*a., adv.* in, toward, or from the west —**west'erly** *a., adv.* —**west'ern** *a.* —**west'erner** *n.* —**west'ward** *a., adv.* —**west'wards** *adv.*

wet *a.* **wet'ter, wet'test** 1 covered or soaked with water 2 rainy 3 not dry yet —*n.* water, rain, etc. —*v.* **wet** or **wet'ted, wet'ting** make or become wet

wet blanket *n.* one who lessens the gaiety of others

wet suit *n.* closefitting rubber suit worn by divers

we've we have

whack *v., n.* hit or slap with a sharp sound

whack'y *a.* **-i-er, -i-est** wacky

whale *n.* huge, fishlike sea mammal —*v.* 1 hunt for whales 2 [Col.] beat

whale'bone' *n.* horny substance from a whale's jaw

whal'er *n.* a person or ship engaged in hunting whales

wham *int.* sound imitating a heavy blow —*n.* heavy blow

wham'my *n., pl.* **-mies** [Sl.] a jinx

wharf (hwôrf) *n., pl.* **wharves** or **wharfs** platform at which ships dock to load, etc.

what *pron.* 1 which thing, event, etc.? 2 that which —*a.* 1 which or which kind of 2 as much or as many as 3 how great! —*adv.* 1 how 2 partly —*int.* exclamation of surprise, etc. —**what for?** why? —**what if** suppose

what·ev'er *pron.* 1 anything that 2 no matter what 3 what —*a.* 1 of any kind 2 no matter what

what'not' *n.* set of open shelves, as for bric-a-brac

what'so·ev'er *pron., a.* whatever

wheal *n.* weal

wheat *n.* cereal grass with seed ground for flour, etc.

whee'dle *v.* coax

wheel *n.* round disk turning on an axle —*v.* 1 move on wheels 2 turn, revolve, etc.

wheel'bar'row *n.* single-wheeled cart with handles

wheel'base' *n.* distance from front to rear axle

wheel'chair' *n.* chair mounted on wheels, as for an invalid

wheeze *v., n.* (make) a whistling, breathy sound

whelk *n.* large sea snail with a spiral shell

whelp *n.* puppy or cub —*v.* give birth to whelps

when *adv.* at what time? —*con.* 1 at what time 2 at which 3 at the time that 4 if —*pron.* what or which time

whence *adv.* from where

when·ev'er *adv.* [Col.] when —*con.* at whatever time

where *adv.* 1 in or to what place? 2 in what way? 3 from what source? —*con.* 1 in or at what place 2 in or at which place 3 to the place that —*pron.* 1 what place? 2 the place at which

where'a·bouts' *adv.* at what place? —*n.* location

where·as' *con.* 1 because 2 while on the contrary

where·by' *adv.* by which

where'fore' *adv.* why? —*con.* therefore —*n.* the reason

where·in' *con.* in which

where·of' *adv.* of what, which, or whom

where·on' *con.* on which

where·up·on' *con.* at or after which —*adv.* on what?

wher·ev'er *adv.* [Col.] where? —*con.* in or to whatever place

where·with' *con.* with which

where'with·al' *n.* necessary means, esp. money

whet *v.* **whet'ted, whet'ting** 1 sharpen, as by grinding 2 to stimulate

wheth'er *con.* 1 if it is true or likely that 2 in either case that

whet'stone' *n.* abrasive stone for sharpening knives

whew *int.* exclamation of relief, surprise, etc.

whey (hwā) *n.* watery part of curdled milk

which *pron.* 1 what one or ones of several 2 the one or ones that 3 that —*a.* 1 what one or ones 2 whatever

which·ev'er *pron., a.* any one that; no matter which

whiff *n.* 1 light puff of air 2 slight odor

while *n.* period of time —*con.* 1 during the time that 2 although —*v.* to spend (time) pleasantly: often with *away*

whi·lom (hwī'lom) *a.* former

whim *n.* sudden notion

whim'per *v., n.* (make) a low, broken cry

whim'sy (-zē) *n., pl.* **-sies** 1 whim 2 fanciful humor —**whim'si·cal** *a.*

whine *v., n.* (make) a long, high cry, as in complaining

whin'ny v., n. **-nied, -ny·ing** (make) a low, neighing sound

whip v. **whipped, whip'ping 1** move suddenly **2** strike, as with a strap **3** beat (cream, etc.) into a froth **4** [Col.] defeat —n. **1** rod with a lash at one end **2** dessert of whipped cream, fruit, etc. —**whip up 1** rouse (interest, etc.) **2** [Col.] to prepare quickly

whip'cord' n. strong worsted cloth with diagonal ribs

whip'lash' n. severe jolting of the neck back and forth

whip'per-snap'per n. impertinent youngster

whip'pet n. small, swift dog

whip'poor·will' n. North American bird active at night

whir v. **whirred, whir'ring** fly or revolve with a buzzing sound —n. this sound

whirl v. **1** move or spin rapidly **2** seem to spin —n. **1** a whirling **2** confused condition

whirl'i·gig' n. child's toy that whirls or spins

whirl'pool' n. water in violent, whirling motion

whirl'wind' n. air whirling violently and moving forward

whisk v. move, pull, etc. with a quick, sweeping motion —n. this motion

whisk broom n. small broom

whisk'er n. **1** pl. the hair on a man's face **2** a long hair, as on a cat's upper lip

whis'key n., pl. **-keys** or **-kies** strong liquor made from grain: also sp. **whis'ky**, pl. **-kies**

whis'per v. **1** say very softly **2** tell as a secret —n. a whispering

whist n. card game like bridge

whis'tle (-əl) v. **1** make, or move with, a high, shrill sound **2** blow a whistle —n. **1** device for making whistling sounds **2** a whistling

whis'tle-stop' n. small town

whit n. least bit; jot

white a. **1** of the color of snow **2** pale **3** pure; innocent **4** having light skin —n. **1** color of pure snow **2** a white thing, as egg albumen —**white'ness** n.

white ant n. termite

white'cap' n. wave with its crest broken into foam

white'-col'lar a. of clerical or professional workers

white elephant n. useless thing expensive to maintain

white'fish' n. white, freshwater fish in cool Northern lakes

white flag n. white banner, a signal of truce or surrender

white goods n. household linens, as sheets, towels, etc.

white lead n. poisonous lead compound, used in paint

white lie n. lie about a trivial matter

whit'en v. make or become white

white'wall' n. tire with a white band on the side

white'wash' n. mixture of lime, water, etc. as for whitening walls —v. **1** cover with whitewash **2** conceal the faults of

whith'er (hwith'-) adv. where

whit'ing (hwīt'-) n. any of various edible sea fishes

whit'ish a. somewhat white

whit'tle v. **1** cut shavings from wood with a knife **2** reduce gradually

whiz, whizz v., n. **whizzed, whiz'zing** (make) the hissing sound of a thing rushing through air

who pron. **1** what person? **2** which person **3** that

whoa int. stop!: command to a horse

who·ev'er pron. **1** any person that **2** no matter who

whole a. **1** not broken, damaged, etc. **2** complete **3** not divided up **4** healthy —n. **1** entire amount **2** thing complete in itself —**on the whole** in general —**whole'ness** n.

whole'heart'ed a. sincere

whole milk n. milk from which no butterfat has been removed

whole'sale' n. sale of goods in large amounts, as to retailers —a. **1** of such sale **2** extensive —v. to sell at wholesale —**whole'sal'er** n.

whole'some a. **1** healthful **2** improving one's morals **3** healthy —**whole'some·ness** n.

whol'ly adv. completely

whom pron. objective case of WHO

whoop v., n. (to utter) a loud shout, cry, etc.

whoop'ing cough n. infectious disease, esp. of children

whop'per n. [Col.] **1** any large thing **2** big lie

whop'ping a. [Col.] very large or great

whore (hôr) n. prostitute

whorl (hwôrl, hwurl) n. design of circular ridges

who's **1** who is **2** who has

whose pron. that or those belonging to whom —a. of whom or of which

who'so·ev'er pron. whoever

why adv. **1** for what reason **2** because of which **3** reason for which —n., pl. **whys** the reason —int. exclamation of surprise, etc.

wick n. piece of cord, etc. for burning, as in a candle

wick'ed a. **1** evil **2** unpleasant **3** naughty

wick′er n. 1 long, thin twigs or strips 2 wickerwork —a. made of wicker

wick′er·work′ n. baskets, etc. made of wicker

wick′et n. 1 small door, gate, or window 2 wire arch used in croquet

wide a. 1 great in width, amount, degree, etc. 2 of a specified width 3 far from the goal —adv. 1 over or to a large extent 2 so as to be wide —**wide′ly** adv. —**wid′en** v.

wide′-a·wake′ a. 1 completely awake 2 alert

wide′-eyed′ a. surprised, fearful, or naive

wide′spread′ a. occurring over a wide area

wid′ow n. woman whose husband has died —v. make a widow of —**wid′ow·hood′** n.

wid′ow·er n. man whose wife has died

width n. 1 distance side to side 2 a piece so wide

wield (wēld) v. 1 handle with skill 2 use (power, etc.)

wie′ner n. frankfurter

wife n., pl. **wives** married woman —**wife′ly** a.

wig n. false covering of hair for the head

wig′gle v., n. twist and turn from side to side —**wig′gly** a., **-gli·er**, **-gli·est**

wig′wag′ v. **-wagged′**, **-wag′ging** 1 wag 2 send messages by visible code

wig′wam′ n. cone-shaped tent of North American Indians

wild a. 1 in its natural state 2 not civilized 3 unruly 4 stormy 5 enthusiastic 6 reckless 7 missing the target —adv. in a wild way —n. pl. wilderness

wild′cat′ n. fierce cat of medium size, as the bobcat —a. 1 risky 2 unauthorized

wil′der·ness n. wild region

wild′-eyed′ a. 1 staring wildly 2 very foolish

wild′fire′ n. rapidly spreading fire, hard to put out

wild′fowl′ n. wild bird, esp. a game bird: also **wild fowl**

wild′-goose′ chase n. futile pursuit, search, or endeavor

wild′life′ n. wild animals

wild rice n. 1 aquatic grass 2 its edible grain

wile v., n. trick; lure

will n. 1 wish; desire 2 strong purpose 3 power of choice 4 attitude 5 legal document disposing of one's property after death —v. 1 decide 2 control by the will 3 bequeath —**at will** when one wishes

will v. pt. **would** auxiliary verb showing: 1 future time 2 determination or obligation 3 ability or capacity

will′ful a. 1 done deliberately 2 stubborn

Also sp. **wil′ful** —**will′ful·ly** adv. —**will′ful·ness** n.

will′ing a. 1 consenting 2 doing or done gladly —**will′ing·ly** adv. —**will′ing·ness** n.

will′-o′-the-wisp′ n. anything elusive

wil′low n. a tree with narrow leaves

wil′low·y a. slender

will′pow′er n. self-control

wil′ly-nil′ly a., adv. (happening) whether one wishes it or not

wilt v. 1 make or become limp 2 make or become weak

wil′y a. **-li·er**, **-li·est** crafty; sly —**wil′i·ness** n.

wimp n. [Sl.] weak, dull person —**wimp′y**, **wimp′ish** a.

win v. **won**, **win′ning** 1 gain a victory 2 get by work, effort, etc. 3 persuade —n. [Col.] victory

wince v. draw back; flinch

winch n. machine for hoisting by a cable, etc. wound on a drum

wind (wīnd) v. **wound**, **wind′ing** 1 turn, coil, or twine around 2 cover, or tighten, by winding 3 move or go indirectly —n. a turn —**wind up** finish

wind (wind) n. 1 air in motion 2 gales 3 breath 4 smell —v. put out of breath

wind′break′ n. fence, trees, etc. protecting a place from the wind

wind′ed a. out of breath

wind′fall′ n. unexpected gain, as of money

wind instrument n. Mus. instrument played by blowing air, esp. breath, through it

wind′lass (-ləs) n. winch

wind′mill′ n. machine operated by the wind's rotation of a wheel of vanes

win′dow n. 1 opening for light and air in a building, car, etc. 2 glass in a frame set in this

win′dow·pane′ n. pane of glass in a window

win′dow-shop′ v. **-shopped′**, **-shop′ping** look at goods in store windows without buying

win′dow·sill′ n. sill of a window

wind′pipe′ n. trachea

wind′shield′ n. in cars, etc. glass shield in the front

wind′up (wīnd′-) n. end

wind′ward a., adv., n. (in or toward) the direction from which the wind blows

wind′y a. **-i·er**, **-i·est** 1 with much wind; breezy 2 long-winded, pompous, etc.

wine n. fermented juice of grapes or of other fruits —v. entertain with wine

wing n. 1 organ used by a bird, insect, etc. in flying 2 thing like a wing in use or position 3 political faction —v. 1 to fly 2 send swiftly 3 wound in the wing or arm 4 extension of a building —**on the wing** in flight —**take wing** fly away —**under one's wing** under one's protection, etc. —**winged** *a.* —**wing'less** *a.*

wing'span' *n.* distance between tips of an airplane's wings

wing'spread' *n.* 1 distance between tips of fully spread wings 2 wingspan

wink *v.* 1 close and open the eyelids quickly 2 do this with one eye, as a signal 3 twinkle —*n.* 1 a winking 2 an instant

win'ner *n.* one that wins

win'ning *a.* 1 victorious 2 charming —*n.* 1 a victory 2 *pl.* something won

win'now (-ō) *v.* 1 blow the chaff from grain 2 sort out

win'o *n., pl.* —**os** [Sl.] alcoholic who drinks cheap wine

win'some (-sam) *a.* charming

win'ter *n.* coldest season of the year —*a.* of or for winter —*v.* spend the winter

win'ter·green' *n.* oil from the leaves of an evergreen plant, used for flavoring

win'ter·ize' *v.* put into condition for winter

win'try *a.* —**tri·er**, —**tri·est** of or like winter

wipe *v.* 1 clean or dry by rubbing 2 rub (a cloth, etc.) over something —*n.* a wiping —**wipe out** 1 remove 2 kill —**wip'er** *n.*

wire *n.* 1 metal drawn into a long thread 2 telegraph 3 telegram —*a.* made of wire —*v.* 1 furnish or fasten with wire(s) 2 telegraph

wire'hair' *n.* fox terrier with a wiry coat: also **wire-haired terrier**

wire'less *a.* operating by electric waves, not with conducting wire —*n.* 1 wireless telegraph or telephone 2 [Chiefly Br.] radio

wire service *n.* agency sending news stories electronically or by telegraph to newspapers, etc.

wire'tap' *v.* tap (telephone wire) to get information secretly —*n.* 1 act of wiretapping 2 device for wiretapping

wir'ing *n.* system of wires, as for carrying electricity

wir'y *a.* —**i·er**, —**i·est** 1 like wire; stiff 2 lean and strong —**wir'i·ness** *n.*

wis'dom *n.* 1 a being wise; good judgment 2 knowledge

wisdom tooth *n.* back tooth on each side of each jaw

wise *a.* 1 having good judgment 2 informed or learned —*n.* manner —**wise'ly** *adv.*

—**wise** *suf.* 1 in a certain direction, position, or manner 2 with regard to

wise'a'cre *n.* one annoyingly conceited in claiming knowledge

wise'crack' *v., n.* [Sl.] (make) a flippant remark

wish *v.* 1 to want; desire 2 express a desire concerning 3 request —*n.* 1 a wishing 2

something wished for 3 request

wish'bone' *n.* forked bone in front of a bird's breastbone

wish'ful *a.* showing a wish

wish'y-wash'y *a.* weak

wisp *n.* slight thing or bit —**wisp'y** *a.*, —**i·er**, —**i·est**

wis·te'ri·a (-tir'ē-) *n.* twining shrub with clusters of flowers

wist'ful *a.* yearning —**wist'ful·ly** *adv.*

wit *n.* 1 (one with) the ability to make clever remarks 2 *pl.* powers of thinking —**to wit** namely

witch *n.* woman supposed to have evil, magic power

witch'craft' *n.* power or practices of witches

witch doctor *n.* one thought to have magical power in curing disease, etc.

witch'er·y *n.* 1 witchcraft 2 bewitching charm

witch hazel *n.* lotion made from a plant extract

with *prep.* 1 against 2 near to; in the care or company of 3 into 4 as a member of 5 concerning 6 compared to 7 as well as 8 in the opinion of 9 as a result of 10 by means of 11 having or showing 12 to; onto 13 from 14 after

with·draw' *v.* —**drew'**, —**drawn'**, —**draw'ing** 1 take back 2 move back 3 leave —**with·draw'al** *n.*

with·drawn' *a.* shy, reserved, etc.

with'er (*with'*-) *v.* wilt

with'ers (*with'*-) *n.pl.* highest part of a horse's back

with·hold' *v.* —**held'**, —**hold'ing** 1 keep back; restrain 2 refrain from granting

with·in' *adv.* in or to the inside —*prep.* 1 inside 2 not beyond

with·out' *adv.* on the outside —*prep.* 1 outside 2 lacking 3 avoiding

with·stand' *v.* —**stood'**, —**stand'ing** resist; endure

wit'less *a.* stupid

wit'ness *n.* 1 one who saw and can testify to a thing 2 testimony; evidence 3 an attesting signer —*v.* 1 see 2 act as a witness of 3 be proof of —**bear witness** testify

wit'ti·cism' *v.* witty remark

wit'ty *a.* —**ti·er**, —**ti·est** cleverly amusing

wives *n., pl.* of WIFE

wiz'ard *n.* magician

wiz'ard·ry *n.* magic

wiz'ened (-ənd) *a.* dried up and wrinkled

wob'ble *v.* move unsteadily from side to side —*n.* a wobbling —**wob'bly** *a.*

woe *n.* grief or trouble —**woe'ful** *a.* —**woe'ful·ly** *adv.*

woe'be·gone' *a.* showing woe

wok *n.* bowl-shaped frying pan

woke v. pt. of WAKE

wolf n., pl. **wolves** 1 wild, doglike animal 2 cruel or greedy person —v. eat greedily —**cry wolf** give a false alarm —**wolf'ish** a.

wolf'hound' n. breed of large dog

wol'ver·ine' (-ēn') n. strong animal like a small bear

wom'an n., pl. **wom'en** adult female person —**wom'an·hood'** n. —**wom'an·ly** a.

wom'an·ish a. like a woman

wom'an·kind' n. women in general

womb (wōōm) n. uterus

wom'bat' (wäm'-) n. burrowing marsupial like a small bear

wom'en·folk' n.pl. [Col.] women

won v. pt. of WIN

won'der n. 1 amazing thing; marvel 2 feeling caused by this —v. 1 feel wonder 2 be curious about

won'der·ful a. 1 causing wonder 2 [Col.] excellent

won'der·land' n. place of wonders, great beauty, etc.

won'der·ment n. amazement

won'drous a., adv. [Poet.] amazing(ly)

wont (wônt, wänt) a. accustomed —n. habit —**wont'ed** a.

won't will not

woo v. seek to win, esp. as one's spouse

wood n. 1 hard substance under a tree's bark 2 lumber 3 pl. forest —a. 1 of wood 2 of the woods —**wood'ed** a.

wood alcohol n. poisonous alcohol used as fuel, etc.

wood'bine' n. climbing plant

wood'chuck' n. North American burrowing animal

wood'cut' n. print made from a wood engraving

wood'en a. 1 made of wood 2 lifeless, dull, etc.

wood'land' n., a. forest

wood'peck'er n. bird that pecks holes in bark

wood'wind' a., n. (of) any of the wind instruments, esp. of wood, as the clarinet, oboe, flute, etc.

wood'work' n. wooden doors, frames, moldings, etc.

wood'work'ing n. art or work of making wooden items

wood'y a. **-i-er, -i-est** 1 tree-covered 2 of or like wood

woof n. weft

woof'er n. large loudspeaker for low sounds

wool n. 1 soft curly hair of sheep, goats, etc. 2 yarn or cloth made of this

wool'en a. of wool —n. pl. woolen goods

wool'gath'er·ing n. daydreaming

wool'ly a. **-li-er, -li-est** of, like, or covered with wool: also sp. **wool'y**

wooz'y a. **-i-er, -i-est** [Col.] dizzy or dazed, as from drink

word n. 1 a sound or sounds as a speech unit 2 letter or letters standing for this 3 brief remark 4 news 5 promise 6 pl. quarrel —v. put into words

word'ing n. choice and arrangement of words

word'y a. **-i-er, -i-est** using too many words —**word'i·ness** n.

wore v. pt. of WEAR

work n. 1 effort of doing or making; labor 2 occupation, trade, etc. 3 task; duty 4 thing made, done, etc. 5 pl. factory 6 pl. engineering structures, as bridges 7 workmanship —v. **worked** or **wrought**, **work'ing** 1 do work; toil 2 to function 3 cause to work 4 be employed 5 bring about 6 come or bring to some condition 7 solve (a problem) —**at work** working —**the works** 1 working parts (of) 2 everything: also **the whole works** —**work off** get rid of —**work on** 1 influence 2 try to persuade —**work out** 1 develop or result 2 to exercise —**work up** 1 advance 2 develop 3 excite; arouse —**work'a·ble** a. —**work'er** n. —**work'man** n., pl. **-men**

work'a·day' a. ordinary

work'a·hol'ic n. person having an uncontrollable need to work

work'book' n. book of exercises, etc. for students

work'day' n. day or part of a day during which work is done

work'horse' n. reliable worker

work'house' n. jail where prisoners are put to work

work'ing a. 1 that works 2 of or used in work 3 enough to get work done

work'ing·man' n., pl. **-men** worker, esp. in industry

work'man·like' a. done well

work'man·ship' n. worker's skill or product

work'out' n. strenuous exercise, practice, etc.

work'shop' n. room or building where work is done

work'sta'tion n. person's work area, esp. including a computer terminal

world n. 1 the earth 2 the universe 3 all people 4 any sphere or domain 5 secular life 6 often pl. great deal

world'ly a. **-li-er, -li-est** 1 of the world; secular 2 sophisticated

world'ly-wise' a. wise in the ways of the world

World Wide Web n. group of Internet sources giving access to text, images, sound, etc.

worm n. 1 long, slender creeping animal 2 thing like a worm 3 pl. disease caused by worms —v. 1 move like a worm 2 get in a sneaky way —**worm'y** a.

worm'wood' n. bitter herb

worn v. pp. of WEAR

worn'-out' a. 1 no longer usable 2 very tired

wor'ry v. **-ried, -ry-ing** 1 make, or be, troubled or uneasy 2 annoy 3 shake with the teeth —n., pl. **-ries** 1 troubled feeling 2 cause of this —**wor'ri-er** n. —**wor'ri-some** a.

wor'ry-wart' n. [Col.] one who worries too much

worse a. 1 more evil, bad, etc. 2 more ill —adv. in a worse way —n. that which is worse

wor'sen v. make or become worse

wor'ship n. 1 prayer, service, etc. in reverence to a deity 2 intense love or admiration —v. 1 show reverence for 2 take part in worship service

worst a. most evil, bad, etc. —adv. in the worst way —n. that which is worst

wor-sted (woos'tid, wur'stid) n. smooth wool fabric

worth n. 1 value or merit 2 equivalent in money —a. 1 deserving 2 equal in value to —**worth'less** a.

worth'while' a. worth the time or effort spent

wor'thy a. **-thi-er, -thi-est** 1 having worth or value 2 deserving —n. worthy person —**wor'thi-ness** n.

would v. pt. of WILL: would is used to express a condition, a wish, a request, etc.

would'-be' a. wishing, pretending, or meant to be

wound (woond) n. 1 injury to the body tissue 2 scar 3 injury to the feelings, etc. —v. injure; hurt

wound (wound) v. pt. & pp. of WIND (turn)

wove v. pt. of WEAVE

wo'ven v. pp. of WEAVE

wow int. expression of surprise, pleasure, etc.

wrack n. destruction

wraith n. ghost

wran'gle v., n. quarrel; dispute

wrap v. **wrapped** or **wrapt**, **wrap'ping** 1 wind or fold (a covering) around 2 enclose in paper, etc. —n. outer garment —**wrap'per** n.

wrap'ping n. often pl. material for wrapping something

wrap'-up' n. [Col.] concluding, summarizing report

wrath n. great anger; rage —**wrath'ful** a.

wreak (rēk) v. 1 inflict (vengeance, etc.) 2 give vent to (anger, etc.)

wreath (rēth) n., pl. **wreaths** twisted ring of leaves, etc.

wreathe (rēth) v. 1 encircle 2 decorate with wreaths

wreck n. 1 remains of a thing destroyed 2 rundown person 3 a wrecking —v. 1 destroy or ruin 2 tear down —**wreck'age** (-ij) n. —**wreck'er** n.

wren n. small songbird

wrench n. 1 sudden, sharp twist 2 injury caused by a twist 3 tool for turning nuts, bolts, etc. —v. 1 twist or jerk sharply 2 injure with a twist

wrest v. take by force

wres'tle (-əl) v. 1 struggle with (an opponent) trying to throw him 2 contend (with) —n. a struggle —**wres'tler** n. —**wres'tling** n.

wretch n. 1 very unhappy person 2 person despised

wretch'ed a. 1 very unhappy 2 distressing 3 unsatisfactory —**wretch'ed-ness** n.

wrig'gle v. twist and turn, or move along thus —n. a wriggling —**wrig'gler** n.

wring v. **wrung, wring'ing** 1 squeeze and twist 2 force out by this means 3 get by force —**wring'er** n.

wrin'kle n. 1 small crease or fold 2 [Col.] clever idea, etc. —v. form wrinkles (in)

wrist n. joint between the hand and forearm

writ n. formal court order

write v. **wrote, writ'ten, writ'ing** 1 form (words, letters, etc.) 2 produce (writing or music) 3 write a letter —**write off** cancel, as a debt —**writ'er** n.

writhe (rīth) v. twist and turn, as in pain

wrong a. 1 not right or just 2 not true or correct 3 not suitable 4 mistaken 5 out of order 6 not meant to be seen —adv. incorrectly —n. something wrong —v. treat unjustly

wrong'do'ing n. unlawful or bad behavior —**wrong'do'er** n.

wrong'ful a. unjust, unlawful, etc. —**wrong'ful-ly** adv.

wrong'head'ed a. stubbornly holding to false ideas, etc.

wrought (rôt) a. 1 made 2 shaped by hammering

wrought iron n. tough, malleable iron used for fences, etc. —**wrought'-i'ron** a.

wrought'-up' a. very disturbed or excited

wrung v. pt. & pp. of WRING

wry (rī) a. **wri'er, wri'est** twisted or distorted —**wry'ly** adv. —**wry'ness** n.

wy'vern n. Heraldry two-legged dragon with wings

X

Xe-rox (zir'äks') *trademark* device for copying printed material electrically —v. [x-] to copy using this device —n. [x-] a copy made with this device

X'mas n. [Col.] Christmas

X'ray' n. 1 ray that can penetrate solid matter 2 photograph made with X-rays —a. of or by X-rays —v. photograph, treat, or examine with X-rays Also sp. **X ray, x-ray,** or **x ray**

xy'lem (zī'-) n. woody plant tissue

xy'lo-phone' (zī'-) n. musical instrument of a row of wooden bars struck with hammers

Y

-y *suf.* 1 full of or like 2 rather 3 apt to 4 state of being 5 act of

yacht (yät) n. small ship —v. sail in a yacht —**yachts'man** n., pl. **-men**

yak [Sl.] v. **yakked, yak'king** talk much or idly —n. a yakking

yak n. wild ox of Asia

yam n. starchy, edible root of a tropical plant 2 [Dial.] sweet potato

yam'mer v. [Col.] whine or complain

yank v., n. [Col.] jerk

Yan'kee n. 1 U.S. citizen 2 native of a northern State

yap v., n. **yapped, yap'ping** (make) a sharp, shrill bark

yard n. 1 measure of length, three feet 2 ground around a building 3 enclosed place 4 slender spar

yard'age (-ij) n. distance or length in yards

yard'stick' n. 1 measuring stick one yard long 2 standard for judging

yarn n. 1 spun strand of wool, cotton, etc. 2 [Col.] tale or story

yaw v., n. turn from the course, as of a ship

yawl n. kind of sailboat

yawn v. open the mouth widely, as when one is sleepy —n. a yawning

yaws n. tropical, infectious skin disease

ye (yē; a.: *thə*) [Ar.] *pron.* you —a. the

yea (yā) adv. 1 yes 2 truly —n. vote of "yes"

yeah (ya) adv. [Col.] yes

year n. 1 period of 365 days (366 in leap year) or 12 months 2 pl. age 3 pl. a long time

year'book' n. book with data of the preceding year

year'ling n. animal in its second year

year'ly a. 1 every year 2 of a year —adv. every year

yearn (yurn) v. feel longing —**yearn'ing** n., a.

year'-round' a. open, in use, etc. throughout the year

yeast n. 1 frothy substance causing fermentation 2 yeast mixed with flour or meal

yell v., n. scream; shout

yel'low a. 1 of the color of ripe lemons 2 [Col.] cowardly —n. yellow color —v. to make or become yellow —**yel'low-ish** a.

yellow fever n. tropical disease carried by a mosquito

yellow jacket n. bright-yellow wasp or hornet

yelp v., n. (utter) a short, sharp cry or bark

yen n. [Col.] deep longing

yeo'man (yō'-) n., pl. **-men** U.S. Navy clerk

yes adv. 1 it is so 2 not only that, but more —n., pl. **yes'es** 1 consent 2 affirmative vote

yes man n. [Sl.] one who always approves what his superior says

yes'ter-day' n. 1 day before today 2 recent time —adv. on the day before today

yet adv. 1 up to now 2 now 3 still; even now 4 nevertheless —con. nevertheless

yew n. evergreen tree

Yid'dish n. German dialect using the Hebrew alphabet

yield v. 1 produce; give 2 surrender 3 concede; grant 4 give way to force —n. amount produced

yield'ing a. flexible; submissive

yip v. **yipped, yip'ping**; n. [Col.] yelp or bark

yo'del v. sing with abrupt, alternating changes to the falsetto —n. a yodeling

yo'ga n. Hindu discipline for uniting self with supreme spirit through various exercises

yo'gi (-gē) n., pl. **-gis** one who practices yoga

yo'gurt, yo'ghurt n. thick, semisolid food made from fermented milk

yoke n. 1 frame for harnessing together a pair of oxen, etc. 2 thing that binds or unites 3 servitude 4 part of a garment at the shoulders —v. 1 harness to 2 join together

yo'kel n. person living in rural area: contemptuous term

yolk (yōk) n. yellow part of an egg

Yom Kip-pur (kip'ər) n. Jewish holiday and day of fasting

yon a., adv. [Dial.] yonder

yon'der a., adv. over there

yore adv. [Obs.] long ago

you *pron.* [*sing. or pl. v.*] **1** the person(s) spoken to **2** person(s) generally

you'd 1 you had **2** you would

you'll 1 you will **2** you shall

young *a.* **1** in an early stage of life or growth **2** fresh —*n.* young offspring —**with young** pregnant —**young'ish** *a.*

young'ster *n.* child

your *a.* of you

you're you are

yours *pron.* that or those belonging to you

your·self' *pron.*, *pl.* **-selves'** intensive or reflexive form of YOU

yours truly *pron.* [Col.] I or me

youth *n.* **1** state or quality of being young **2** adolescence **3** young people **4** young man —**youth'ful** *a.*

you've you have

yowl *v., n.* howl; wail

yo'-yo' *n., pl.* **-yos'** spool-like toy on a string on which it is made to spin up and down

yuc'ca *n.* lilylike plant

yuck [Sl.] *n.* something disgusting, etc. —*int.* an expression of disgust —**yuck'y** *a.*, *-i·er*, *-i·est*

yule *n.* [*often* Y–] Christmas

yule'tide' *n.* [*often* Y–] Christmas time

yum'my *a.* **-mi·er**, **-mi·est** [Col.] very tasty; delicious

yup'pie *n.* [Col.] affluent, ambitious, young professional

Z

za'ny *a.* **-ni·er**, **-ni·est** of or like a foolish or comical person —*n.*, *pl.* **-nies** such a person —**za'ni·ness** *n.*

zap *v.* **zapped**, **zap'ping** [Sl.] move, kill, etc. suddenly and with great speed —*int.* exclamation used to express such action

zeal *n.* eager endeavor or devotion

zeal'ot (zel'-) *n.* one showing zeal, esp. fanatic kind

zeal'ous (zel'-) *a.* full of zeal —**zeal'ous·ly** *adv.*

ze'bra *n.* striped African animal similar to the horse

ze'bu' *n.* oxlike animal with a hump

Zen *n.* form of Buddhism seeking intuitive knowledge through meditation

ze'nith *n.* **1** point in the sky directly overhead **2** the highest point

zeph·yr (zef'ar) *n.* breeze

zep'pe·lin *n.* dirigible

ze'ro *n., pl.* **-ros** or **-roes 1** the symbol 0 **2** point marked 0 in a scale **3** nothing —*a.* of or at zero

zero hour *n.* **1** the time an attack is to begin **2** crucial point

zero population growth *n.* condition in which the birth rate equals the death rate

ze'ro·sum' *a.* of a situation in which a gain for one means a loss for another

zest *n.* **1** stimulating quality **2** keen enjoyment —**zest'ful** *a.*

zig'zag' *n.* line with sharp turns back and forth —*a., adv.* in a zigzag —*v.* **-zagged'**, **-zag'ging** to move or form in a zigzag

zilch *n.* [Sl.] nothing; zero

zil'lion *n.* [Col.] very large, indefinite number

zinc *n.* bluish-white metal, a chemical element

zing *n.* [Sl.] shrill, whizzing sound

zin'ni·a *n.* daisylike flower thick with petals

zip *v.* **zipped**, **zip'ping 1** make a short, sharp hissing sound **2** [Col.] move fast **3** fasten with a zipper —*n.* **1** a zipping sound **2** [Col.] energy; vigor —**zip'py** *a.*, *-pi·er*, *-pi·est*

ZIP code *n.* mail delivery system using code numbers for zones

zip'per *n.* fastener with interlocking tabs worked by a sliding panel

zir'con' *n.* transparent gem

zit *n.* [Sl.] pimple, esp. on face

zith'er *n.* stringed instrument, played by plucking

zo'di·ac' *n.* imaginary belt along the sun's apparent path divided into 12 parts named for constellations

zom'bie *n.* **1** animated corpse in folklore **2** [Sl.] one listless, machine-like, etc.

zone *n.* **1** any of the five areas into which the earth is divided according to climate **2** area set apart in some way —*v.* mark off into zones —**zoned** *a.*

zonked *a.* [Sl.] **1** drunk or under drug influence **2** exhausted

zoo *n.* place with wild animals on exhibition

zo'o·log'i·cal garden (zō'-) *n.* zoo

zo·ol'o·gy (zō-) *n.* science of animal life —**zo'o·log'i·cal** *a.* —**zo·ol'o·gist** *n.*

zoom *v.* **1** make a loud, buzzing sound **2** speed upward or forward —*n.* a zooming

zoom lens *n.* system of lenses adjustable for close or distant shots always in focus

zuc·chi·ni (zōō kē'nē) *n.* cucumberlike squash

zwie·back (swē'bäk', swī'-) *n.* dried, toasted slices of a kind of bread

zy'gote' *n.* fertilized egg cell before it divides

PUNCTUATION

The **Period** (.) is used: 1) at the end of a sentence; 2) after many abbreviations; 3) in a decimal fraction; 4) as one of a series (usually three spaced periods) to indicate an omission, an interruption, or a break in continuity.

The **Comma** (,) is used: 1) between short independent clauses in parallel construction and between clauses joined by conjunctions such as *and, but, or, nor, yet,* and *for;* 2) after a fairly long dependent clause that precedes an independent one; 3) before and after a dependent clause that comes in the middle of a sentence; 4) to set off a nonrestrictive word, phrase, or clause; 5) to set off transitional words and phrases; 6) to separate words, phrases, or clauses in series; 7) to set off the word indicating the one spoken to in direct address; 8) to set off a direct quotation; 9) to set off a title, an address, a place name, a date, etc.; 10) after the salutation of an informal letter; 11) after the complimentary close of any letter.

The **Semicolon** (;) is used: 1) in a compound sentence between independent clauses that are not joined by connectives, or between such clauses joined by a conjunctive adverb (such as *thus*); 2) between phrases or clauses that contain internal punctuation.

The **Colon** (:) is used: 1) before a long series; 2) before a lengthy quotation; 3) between chapter and verse, volume and page, hour and minute, etc.; 4) after the salutation of a business letter.

The **Question Mark** (?) is used: 1) after a direct question; 2) as an indication of uncertainty or doubt.

The **Exclamation Point** (!) is used after a word, phrase, or sentence to indicate strong emotion, surprise, etc.

The **Hyphen** (-) is used: 1) to separate the parts of a compound word or numeral; 2) to indicate syllabification.

The **Dash** (—) is used: 1) between sentence parts, to show a break in continuity; 2) between numbers, dates, times, places, etc. that mark limits.

Quotation Marks: *Double* (" ") are used: 1) to enclose a direct quotation; 2) to enclose the titles of articles, short stories, short poems, etc., or the divisions or chapters of books, periodicals, long poems, etc. *Single* (' ') are used to enclose a quotation within a quotation.

Italic Type is used: 1) to set off the titles of books, periodicals, newspapers, etc.; 2) to indicate foreign words or phrases; 3) to emphasize a word within a sentence.

The **Apostrophe** (') is used: 1) in place of an omitted letter or letters in a word or contraction; 2) with an added *s* to form the possessive case of all nouns that do not end in an *s* or *z* sound; 3) with an added *s* to form the possessive of monosyllabic singular nouns that end in an *s* or *z* sound; 4) without an added *s* to form the possessive of all nouns that end in an *s* or *z* sound except monosyllabic singular nouns and nouns ending in -*ce*; 5) with a letter, a number, etc., to form its plural.

Parentheses, ( ), are used: 1) to enclose nonessential material in a sentence; 2) to enclose letters or numbers of reference, as in an outline.

Brackets, [ ], are used to indicate an insertion, a comment, a correction, etc. made by a person other than the original author of the material.

A **Capital Letter** is used: 1) to begin a sentence, or a quotation or direct question within a sentence; 2) to begin every word, except conjunctions, articles, and short prepositions that are not the first word, in the name of a book, magazine, work of music or art, business, agency, religion, holiday, etc.; 3) to begin every main word in a proper noun; 4) to begin every main word in the name of a day, month, era, etc.; 5) to begin many abbreviations; 6) to begin a noun or a pronoun referring to the Deity; 7) to begin the salutation and the complimentary close of a letter.

ABBREVIATIONS

Many abbreviations can be written in various ways (p.m., P.M., pm, PM). The most commonly used forms are listed here.

a. adjective
A *Sports* assist(s)
AA, A.A. Associate in Arts
AB, A.B. Bachelor of Arts
abbr., abbrev. abbreviated; abbreviation
AC air conditioning; alternating current
acct. account
A.D. in the year of our Lord
adj. adjective
Adm. Admiral
admn. administration
adv. adverb
AFDC Aid to Families with Dependent Children
agcy. agency
Ala. Alabama
Alas. Alaska
alt. alternate; altitude
a.m., A.M. before noon
AM, A.M. Master of Arts
Am. America(n)
anon. anonymous
Apr. April
apt. apartment
Ariz. Arizona
Ark. Arkansas
assn. association
assoc. associate
asst. assistant
Attn. attention
atty. attorney
Aug. August
av. average (also **avg.**); avoirdupois
Av(e). Avenue
b. born
BA, B.A. Bachelor of Arts
bbl. barrel(s)
B.C. before Christ
biol. biology
bldg. building
Blvd. Boulevard
Br., Brit. Britain, British
Bros. Brothers
BS, B.S. Bachelor of Science
Btu British thermal unit(s)
bu. bushel(s)
bur. bureau
c centimeter; copyright
c. century
C Celsius (or centigrade)
C. cup(s)
c(a). circa (about)
Cal., Calif. California

cal. calorie(s)
Can. Canada; Canadian (also **Cdn.**)
cap. capacity; capital(ize)
Capt. Captain
cc carbon copy; cubic centimeter(s)
cent. century; centuries
cert. certificate; certified
cf. compare
cg centigram(s)
Ch. Church
ch., chap. chapter(s)
chem. chemistry
chg(d). charge(d)
CIA Central Intelligence Agency
cm centimeter(s)
Cmdr. Commander
CO Commanding Officer
C/O, c/o care of
Co. Company; County
COD collect on delivery
Col. Colonel
Colo. Colorado
Cong. Congress
Conn. Connecticut
cont. continued
Corp. Corporal; Corporation
CPA Certified Public Accountant
CST Central Standard Time
cu. cubic
d. degree(s); diameter; died
DA, D.A. District Attorney
dba doing business as
D.C. District of Columbia
DC direct current
DD, D.D. Doctor of Divinity
DDS, D.D.S. Doctor of Dental Surgery
dec. deceased
Dec. December
Del. Delaware
Dem. Democrat(ic)
dept. department; deputy
dir. director
dist. district
div. division
d(o)z. dozen(s)
Dr. Doctor; Drive
DST Daylight Savings Time
DWI driving while intoxicated
E *Baseball* error(s)
E, E. east(ern)
ea. each
EC European Community
econ. economics
ed. edited (by); edition; editor; education

ABBREVIATIONS

e.g. for example
EKG electrocardiogram
elem. elementary
enc(l). enclosure
Eng. England; English
EPA Environmental Protection Agency
ERA earned run average; Equal Rights Amendment
ESP extrasensory perception
esp. especially
Esq. Esquire
EST Eastern Standard Time
est. established (also **estab.**); estimate(d)
ETA estimated time of arrival
et al. and (the) others
et seq. and the following
ex. example; exchange
exec. executive; executor
ext. extension
f. folio
F Fahrenheit; female
FBI Federal Bureau of Investigation
FCC Federal Communications Commission
FDA Food and Drug Administration
Feb. February
Fed. Federal; Federation
fem. feminine
ff. folios; following (pages, etc.)
FG *Sports* field goal(s)
FICA Federal Insurance Contributions Act
fig. figuratively; figure(s)
fl. flourished; fluid
Fla. Florida
Fr. Father; French
Fri. Friday
FT *Basketball* free throw(s)
ft. foot; feet
Ft. Fort
FTC Federal Trade Commission
g *Sports* goal(s); gram(s)
Ga. Georgia
gal. gallon(s)
Gen. General
gen., genl. general
Ger. German(y)
GM General Manager
GOP Grand Old (Republican) Party
Gov. Governor
gov., govt. government
GP, G.P. general practitioner
Gr. Greece; Greek
grad. graduate(d)
gram. grammar
Gr. Brit. Great Britain
guar. guaranteed
H *Baseball* hit(s)
hdqrs. headquarters

hist. history
H.J. here lies
HMO health maintenance organization
HP horsepower
HQ headquarters
HR *Baseball* home run(s)
HR, H.R. House of Representatives
hr. hour
HS, H.S. high school
ht. height
hwy. highway
Hz, hz hertz
Ia. Iowa
ib., ibid. in the same place
ICC Interstate Commerce Commission
id. the same
Ida. Idaho
i.e. that is (to say)
Ill. Illinois
illus. illustrated; illustration; illustrator
in. inch(es)
Inc., inc. incorporated
incl. including; inclusive
Ind. Indiana
ins. insurance
Inst. Institute; Institution
int. interest; interjection; international (also **intl.**)
IRA Independent Retirement Account
IRS Internal Revenue Service
It., Ital. Italian; Italy
ital. italic type
IV intravenous
Jan. January
JD, J.D. Doctor of Laws
JP, J.P. Justice of the Peace
Jpn. Japan(ese)
Jr. Junior
Jul. July
Jun. June
k karat(s); kilogram(s); kilometer(s)
K karat(s); kilobyte(s); kilometer(s); *Baseball* strikeout(s)
Kans. Kansas
KB kilobyte(s)
kc kilocycle(s)
kg kilogram(s)
kHz, khz kilohertz
km kilometer(s)
KO *Boxing* knockout
Ky. Kentucky
l. line
L *Sports* loss(es)
L, l liter(s)
L. Lake; Latin
LA, L.A. Los Angeles
La. Louisiana
Lat. Latin
lat. latitude

ABBREVIATIONS

lb. pound(s)

l.c. in the place cited; lowercase

Lieut. Lieutenant

lit. literal(ly); literature

ll. lines

LLB, LL.B. Bachelor of Laws

LLD, LL.D. Doctor of Laws

loc. cit. in the place cited

long. longitude

LPN, L.P.N. Licensed Practical Nurse

Lt. Lieutenant

Ltd., ltd. limited

m meter(s); mile(s) (also **m.**)

M male

M. Monsieur

MA, M.A. Master of Arts

Maj. Major

Mar. March

masc. masculine

Mass. Massachusetts

math. mathematics

max. maximum

MB megabyte(s)

MC Master of Ceremonies

MD, M.D. Doctor of Medicine

Md. Maryland

mdse. merchandise

Me. Maine

med. medical; medicine; medium

met. metropolitan

Mex. Mexican; Mexico

mfg. manufacturing

mfr. manufacture(r)

mg milligram(s)

mgr. manager

MHz, Mhz megahertz

mi. mile(s)

Mich. Michigan

mil. military

min. minimum; minute(s)

Minn. Minnesota

misc. miscellaneous

Miss. Mississippi

mkt. market

ml milliliter(s)

Mlle. Mademoiselle

mm millimeter(s)

Mme. Madame

MO mode of operation; money order

Mo. Missouri

mo. month

Mon. Monday

Mont. Montana

MP Member of Parliament (also **M.P.**); Military Police

mpg miles per gallon

mph miles per hour

MS, M.S. Master of Science

MS manuscript; multiple sclerosis

MST Mountain Standard Time

Mt., mt. mount; mountain

mtg. meeting; mortgage

mun. municipal

mus. museum; music

myth. mythology

n. noun

N, N. north(ern)

N.A. North America

NASA National Aeronautics and Space Administration

NATO North Atlantic Treaty Organization

naut. nautical

n.b. note well

N.C. North Carolina

NCO noncommissioned officer

N.D., N.Dak. North Dakota

NE, N.E. northeast(ern)

Neb., Nebr. Nebraska

neg. negative

Nev. Nevada

N.H. New Hampshire

N.J. New Jersey

N.M., N.Mex. New Mexico

no. number

non seq. it does not follow

Nov. November

nt. wt. net weight

NW, N.W. northwest(ern)

N.Y. New York

NYC, N.Y.C. New York City

O *Baseball* out(s)

O. Ohio

Oct. October

off. office; officer; official

Okla. Oklahoma

op. cit. in the work cited

Oreg. Oregon

orig. origin(al)(ly)

OT overtime

oz. ounce(s)

p. page; participle; past

PA public address (system)

Pa. Pennsylvania

PAC political action committee

pat. patent(ed)

pc. piece

PC personal computer

pct. percent

pd. paid

Penn., Penna. Pennsylvania

pg. page

PhD, Ph.D. Doctor of Philosophy

phys. physical; physician; physics

pk. pack; park; peck

pkg. package(s)

pl. place; plate; plural

PM, P.M. Postmaster; Prime Minister

p.m., P.M. after noon

PO, P.O. Post Office (box)

ABBREVIATIONS

pop. popularly; population
pos. positive
POW prisoner of war
PP parcel post
pp. pages; past participle
ppd. postpaid
ppr. present participle
P.R. public relations (also **PR**);
Puerto Rico
pr. pair(s); price
prec. preceding
pref. preferred; prefix
prelim. preliminary
prep. preparatory; preposition
Pres. President
pres. present
prim. primary
prob. probably; problem
Prof. Professor
pron. pronoun; pronunciation
prop. proper(ly); property; proprietor
P.S. postscript
PST Pacific Standard Time
pt. part; past tense; pint; point
pub. public; published; publisher
Pvt. Private
Q question
qb *Football* quarterback
Q.E.D. which was to be demonstrated
qt. quart(s)
qty. quantity
quot. quotation
q.v. which see
R *Baseball* run(s)
RAM random-access memory
rbi, RBI *Baseball* runs batted in
R.C. Roman Catholic
Rd. Road
recd., rec'd. received
ref. referee; reference; reformed; refund
reg. registered; regular; regulation
rel. relative(ly); religion
Rep. Representative; Republic(an)
rep. report(ed)
rept. report
res. reserve; residence; resigned
ret. retired; return(ed)
Rev. Reverend
rev. revenue; revise(d); revolution
R.I. Rhode Island
R.I.P., RIP may he (she) rest in peace
RN, R.N. Registered Nurse
Rom. Roman
ROM read-only memory
ROTC Reserve Officers Training Corps
rpm revolutions per minute
RR railroad; rural route
R.S.V.P. please reply
Rte. Route
S, S. south(ern)

Sat. Saturday
S.C. South Carolina
ScD, Sc.D. Doctor of Science
S.D., S.Dak. South Dakota
SE, S.E. southeast(ern)
sec. second(s); secondary; secretary
(also **secy.**); section(s) (also **sect.**)
Sen. Senate; Senator
Sept. September
seq(q). the following (ones)
Sgt. Sergeant
shpt. shipment
sing. singular
soc. social; society
Sp. Spain; Spanish
sp. special; spelling
spec. special; specifically (also
specif.); specification
sq. square
Sr. Senior; Sister
SST supersonic transport
St. Saint; Strait; Street
STD sexually transmitted disease
suf. suffix
Sun. Sunday
Supt. Superintendent
SW, S.W. southwest(ern)
t. teaspoon(s); tense; ton(s)
T. tablespoon(s)
TB tuberculosis
tbs. tablespoon(s)
TD *Football* touchdown
tech. technical; technology
tel. telegram; telephone
temp. temperature; temporary
Tenn. Tennessee
Tex. Texas
theol. theology
Thur., Thurs. Thursday
TKO *Boxing* technical knockout
TM trademark
tr. translated (by); translation;
translator; transpose
trans. translated (by); translation;
translator; transportation
treas. treasurer; treasury
tsp. teaspoon(s)
Tue., Tues. Tuesday
U. Union; United; University
u.c. uppercase
UHF ultrahigh frequency
UK, U.K. United Kingdom
UN United Nations
Univ. University
U.S., US United States of America
USA United States of America (also
U.S.A.); United States Army
USAF United States Air Force
USDA United States Department
of Agriculture

ABBREVIATIONS

USMC United States Marine Corps
USN United States Navy
U.S.S.R., USSR Union of Soviet Socialist Republics
Ut. Utah
v. verb; verse; versus; very
V, v volt(s)
VA Veterans Administration
Va. Virginia
VD venereal disease
vet. veteran; veterinary
VHF very high frequency
viz. namely
vol. volume
VP, V.P. Vice President
vs. versus

Vt. Vermont
W watt(s) (also **w**); west(ern) (also **W.**); *Sports* win(s)
Wash. Washington
Wed. Wednesday
Wis., Wisc. Wisconsin
wk. week
wt. weight
W.Va. West Virginia
Wyo. Wyoming
yd. yard(s)
YMCA Young Men's Christian Association
yr. year
YWCA Young Women's Christian Association

WEIGHTS AND MEASURES

Linear

12 inches	=	1 foot
3 feet	=	1 yard
5 ½ yards	=	1 rod
40 rods	=	1 furlong
8 furlongs	=	1 mile

Liquid

4 gills	=	1 pint
2 pints	=	1 quart
4 quarts	=	1 gallon
31½ gals.	=	1 barrel
2 barrels	=	1 hogshead

Metric Equivalents

1 inch	=	2.5400 centimeters
1 foot	=	0.3048 meter
1 yard	=	0.9144 meter
1 mile	=	1.6093 kilometers
1 centimeter	=	0.3937 inch
1 decimeter	=	3.9370 inches
1 meter	=	39.3701 inches
1 kilometer	=	0.6214 mile
1 quart (dry)	=	1.1012 liters
1 quart (liquid)	=	0.9464 liter
1 gallon	=	3.7854 liters
1 liter	=	0.9081 dry quart
1 liter	=	1.0567 liquid quarts

Square

144 sq. inches	=	1 sq. ft.
9 sq. feet	=	1 sq. yard
30¼ sq. yds.	=	1 sq. rod
160 sq. rods	=	1 acre
640 acres	=	1 sq. mile

Circular

60 sec.	=	1 min.
60 min.	=	1 degree
90 degrees	=	1 quadrant
180 degrees	=	1 semicircle
360 degrees	=	1 circle

Metric Equivalents

1 sq. inch	=	6.452 sq. centimeters
1 sq. foot	=	929.030 sq. centimeters
1 sq. mile	=	2.590 sq. kilometers
1 sq. centimeter	=	0.155 sq. inch
1 sq. meter	=	1.196 sq. yards
1 sq. kilometer	=	0.386 sq. mile

Cubic

1,728 cu. inches	=	1 cu. foot
27 cu. feet	=	1 cu. yard
128 cu. feet	=	1 cord (wood)

Dry

2 pints	=	1 quart
8 quarts	=	1 peck
4 pecks	=	1 bushel

Metric Equivalents

1 cu. inch	=	16.3871 cu. centimeters
1 cu. inch	=	0.0164 liter
1 cu. foot	=	0.0283 cu. meter
1 cu. foot	=	28.3169 liters
1 cu. meter	=	35.3147 cu. feet
1 ounce (avdp.)	=	28.3495 grams
1 pound	=	0.4536 kilogram
1 gram	=	0.0353 ounce
1 kilogram	=	2.2046 lbs.
1 ton (2000 lbs.)	=	907.1848 kilograms

Longitude and Time

1 second of longitude	=	1/15 sec. of time
1 minute " "	=	4 sec. of time
1 degree " "	=	4 min. of time
15 degrees " "	=	1 hour
360 degrees " "	=	24 hours

NATIONS OF THE WORLD

Nation	Capital	Currency
Afghanistan	Kabul	afghani
Albania	Tirana	lek
Algeria	Algiers	dinar
Andorra	Andorra la Vella	*(Fr.)* franc; *(Sp.)* peseta
Angola	Luanda	kwanza
Antigua and Barbuda	St. John's	dollar
Argentina	Buenos Aires	peso
Armenia	Yerevan	dram
Australia	Canberra	dollar
Austria	Vienna	schilling
Azerbaijan	Baku	manat
Bahamas	Nassau	dollar
Bahrain	Manama	dinar
Bangladesh	Dhaka	taka
Barbados	Bridgetown	dollar
Belarus	Minsk	ruble
Belgium	Brussels	franc
Belize	Belmopan	dollar
Benin	Porto Novo	franc
Bhutan	Thimphu	ngultrum
Bolivia	La Paz; Sucre	boliviano
Bosnia and Herzegovina	Sarajevo	dinar
Botswana	Gaborone	pula
Brazil	Brasília	real
Brunei	Bandar Seri Begawan	dollar
Bulgaria	Sofia	lev
Burkina Faso	Ouagadougou	franc
Burundi	Bujumbura	franc
Cambodia	Phnom Penh	riel
Cameroon	Yaoundé	franc
Canada	Ottawa	dollar
Cape Verde	Praia	escudo
Central African Republic	Bangui	franc
Chad	N'Djamena	franc
Chile	Santiago	peso
China	Beijing	yuan
Colombia	Bogotá	peso
Comoros	Moroni	franc
Congo	Brazzaville	franc
Costa Rica	San José	colón
Croatia	Zagreb	kuna
Cuba	Havana	peso
Cyprus	Nicosia	pound
Czech Republic	Prague	koruna
Denmark	Copenhagen	krone
Djibouti	Djibouti	franc
Dominica	Roseau	dollar
Dominican Republic	Santo Domingo	peso
Ecuador	Quito	sucre
Egypt	Cairo	pound
El Salvador	San Salvador	colón
Equatorial Guinea	Malabo	franc
Eritrea	Asmara	birr
Estonia	Tallinn	kroon

NATIONS OF THE WORLD

Nation	Capital	Currency
Ethiopia	Addis Ababa	birr
Fiji	Suva	dollar
Finland	Helsinki	markka
France	Paris	franc
Gabon	Libreville	franc
Gambia	Banjul	dalasi
Georgia	Tbilisi	lari
Germany	Berlin	deutsche mark
Ghana	Accra	cedi
Greece	Athens	drachma
Grenada	St. George's	dollar
Guatemala	Guatemala City	quetzal
Guinea	Conakry	franc
Guinea-Bissau	Bissau	peso
Guyana	Georgetown	dollar
Haiti	Port-au-Prince	gourde
Honduras	Tegucigalpa	lempira
Hungary	Budapest	forint
Iceland	Reykjavik	króna
India	New Delhi	rupee
Indonesia	Jakarta	rupiah
Iran	Tehran	rial
Iraq	Baghdad	dinar
Ireland	Dublin	pound
Israel	Jerusalem	shekel
Italy	Rome	lira
Ivory Coast	Yamoussoukro	franc
Jamaica	Kingston	dollar
Japan	Tokyo	yen
Jordan	Amman	dinar
Kazakhstan	Almaty	tenge
Kenya	Nairobi	shilling
Kiribati	Tarawa	*(Austral.)* dollar
Korea, North	Pyongyang	won
Korea, South	Seoul	won
Kuwait	Kuwait	dinar
Kyrgyzstan	Bishkek	som
Laos	Vientiane	kip
Latvia	Riga	lats
Lebanon	Beirut	pound
Lesotho	Maseru	loti
Liberia	Monrovia	dollar
Libya	Tripoli	dinar
Liechtenstein	Vaduz	*(Swiss)* franc
Lithuania	Vilnius	litas
Luxembourg	Luxembourg	franc
Macedonia	Skopje	denar
Madagascar	Antananarivo	franc
Malawi	Lilongwe	kwacha
Malaysia	Kuala Lumpur	ringgit
Maldives	Malé	rufiyaa
Mali	Bamako	franc
Malta	Valletta	lira
Marshall Islands	Dalap-Uliga-Darrit	dollar
Mauritania	Nouakchott	ouguiya
Mauritius	Port Louis	rupee
Mexico	Mexico City	peso
Micronesia	Palikir	dollar

NATIONS OF THE WORLD

Nation	Capital	Currency
Moldova	Chisinau	leu
Monaco	Monaco	*(Fr.)* franc
Mongolia	Ulan Bator	tugrik
Morocco	Rabat	dirham
Mozambique	Maputo	metical
Myanmar	Yangon	kyat
Namibia	Windhoek	dollar
Nauru	—	*(Austral.)* dollar
Nepal	Katmandu	rupee
Netherlands	Amsterdam	guilder
New Zealand	Wellington	dollar
Nicaragua	Managua	córdoba
Niger	Niamey	franc
Nigeria	Abuja	naira
Norway	Oslo	krone
Oman	Muscat	rial
Pakistan	Islamabad	rupee
Palau	Koror	dollar
Panama	Panama City	balboa
Papua New Guinea	Port Moresby	kina
Paraguay	Asunción	guaraní
Peru	Lima	sol
Philippines	Manila	peso
Poland	Warsaw	złoty
Portugal	Lisbon	escudo
Qatar	Doha	riyal
Romania	Bucharest	leu
Russia	Moscow	ruble
Rwanda	Kigali	franc
San Marino	San Marino	*(It.)* lira
São Tomé and Príncipe	São Tomé	dobra
Saudi Arabia	Riyadh	riyal
Senegal	Dakar	franc
Seychelles	Victoria	rupee
Sierra Leone	Freetown	leone
Singapore	Singapore	dollar
Slovakia	Bratislava	koruna
Slovenia	Ljubljana	tolar
Solomon Islands	Honiara	dollar
Somalia	Mogadishu	shilling
South Africa	Pretoria	rand
Spain	Madrid	peseta
Sri Lanka	Colombo	rupee
St. Kitts and Nevis	Basseterre	dollar
St. Lucia	Castries	dollar
St. Vincent and the Grenadines	Kingstown	dollar
Sudan	Khartoum	pound
Suriname	Paramaribo	guilder
Swaziland	Mbabane	lilangeni
Sweden	Stockholm	krona
Switzerland	Bern	franc
Syria	Damascus	pound
Taiwan	Taipei	dollar
Tajikistan	Dushanbe	ruble
Tanzania	Dodoma	shilling
Thailand	Bangkok	baht
Togo	Lomé	franc

NATIONS OF THE WORLD

Nation	Capital	Currency
Tonga	Nukualofa	pa'anga
Trinidad and Tobago	Port-of-Spain	dollar
Tunisia	Tunis	dinar
Turkey	Ankara	lira
Turkmenistan	Ashgabat	manat
Tuvalu	Fongafale	*(Austral.)* dollar
Uganda	Kampala	shilling
Ukraine	Kiev	hryvnia
United Arab Emirates	Abu Dhabi	dirham
United Kingdom	London	pound
United States	Washington, D.C.	dollar
Uruguay	Montevideo	peso
Uzbekistan	Tashkent	som
Vanuatu	Vila	vatu
Vatican City	—	*(It.)* lira
Venezuela	Caracas	bolívar
Vietnam	Hanoi	dong
Western Samoa	Apia	tala
Yemen	Sana	rial
Yugoslavia	Belgrade	dinar
Zaire	Kinshasa	zaire
Zambia	Lusaka	kwacha
Zimbabwe	Harare	dollar

THE UNITED STATES

State	Capital	Postal Code
Alabama	Montgomery	AL
Alaska	Juneau	AK
Arizona	Phoenix	AZ
Arkansas	Little Rock	AR
California	Sacramento	CA
Colorado	Denver	CO
Connecticut	Hartford	CT
Delaware	Dover	DE
[Dist. of Columbia	—	DC]
Florida	Tallahassee	FL
Georgia	Atlanta	GA
Hawaii	Honolulu	HI
Idaho	Boise	ID
Illinois	Springfield	IL
Indiana	Indianapolis	IN
Iowa	Des Moines	IA
Kansas	Topeka	KS
Kentucky	Frankfort	KY
Louisiana	Baton Rouge	LA
Maine	Augusta	ME
Maryland	Annapolis	MD
Massachusetts	Boston	MA
Michigan	Lansing	MI
Minnesota	St. Paul	MN
Mississippi	Jackson	MS
Missouri	Jefferson City	MO
Montana	Helena	MT
Nebraska	Lincoln	NE
Nevada	Carson City	NV
New Hampshire	Concord	NH
New Jersey	Trenton	NJ
New Mexico	Santa Fe	NM
New York	Albany	NY
North Carolina	Raleigh	NC
North Dakota	Bismarck	ND
Ohio	Columbus	OH
Oklahoma	Oklahoma City	OK
Oregon	Salem	OR
Pennsylvania	Harrisburg	PA
Rhode Island	Providence	RI
South Carolina	Columbia	SC
South Dakota	Pierre	SD
Tennessee	Nashville	TN
Texas	Austin	TX
Utah	Salt Lake City	UT
Vermont	Montpelier	VT
Virginia	Richmond	VA
Washington	Olympia	WA
West Virginia	Charleston	WV
Wisconsin	Madison	WI
Wyoming	Cheyenne	WY

U.S. TERRITORIES

Territory	Capital	Postal Code
American Samoa	Pago Pago	AS
Guam	Agana	GU
Northern Marianas	Saipan	MP
Puerto Rico	San Juan	PR
Virgin Islands	Charlotte Amalie	VI

PROVINCES AND TERRITORIES OF CANADA

Province or Territory	Capital	Postal Code
Alberta	Edmonton	AB
British Columbia	Victoria	BC
Manitoba	Winnipeg	MB
New Brunswick	Fredericton	NB
Newfoundland	St. John's	NF
Northwest Territories	Yellowknife	NT
Nova Scotia	Halifax	NS
Ontario	Toronto	ON
Prince Edward Island	Charlottetown	PE
Quebec	Quebec	QC
Saskatchewan	Regina	SK
Yukon Territory	Whitehorse	YT

U.S. CITIES BY POPULATION

Rank	City, State	1990 Census Population
1.	New York, NY	7,322,564
2.	Los Angeles, CA	3,485,557
3.	Chicago, IL	2,783,726
4.	Houston, TX	1,629,902
5.	Philadelphia, PA	1,585,577
6.	San Diego, CA	1,110,623
7.	Detroit, MI	1,027,974
8.	Dallas, TX	1,007,618
9.	Phoenix, AZ	983,403
10.	San Antonio, TX	935,393
11.	San Jose, CA	782,224
12.	Indianapolis, IN	741,952
13.	Baltimore, MD	736,014
14.	San Francisco, CA	723,959
15.	Jacksonville, FL	672,971
16.	Columbus, OH	632,945
17.	Milwaukee, WI	628,088
18.	Memphis, TN	610,337
19.	Washington, DC	606,900
20.	Boston, MA	574,283
21.	Seattle, WA	516,259
22.	El Paso, TX	515,342
23.	Nashville, TN	510,784
24.	Cleveland, OH	505,616
25.	New Orleans, LA	496,938
26.	Denver, CO	467,610
27.	Austin, TX	465,648
28.	Fort Worth, TX	447,619
29.	Oklahoma City, OK	444,724
30.	Portland, OR	438,802
31.	Kansas City, MO	434,829
32.	Long Beach, CA	429,321
33.	Tucson, AZ	405,323
34.	St. Louis, MO	396,685
35.	Charlotte, NC	395,925
36.	Atlanta, GA	393,929
37.	Virginia Beach, VA	393,089
38.	Albuquerque, NM	384,619
39.	Oakland, CA	372,242
40.	Pittsburgh, PA	369,879
41.	Sacramento, CA	369,365
42.	Minneapolis, MN	368,383
43.	Tulsa, OK	367,302
44.	Honolulu, HI	365,272
45.	Cincinnati, OH	364,114
46.	Miami, FL	358,648
47.	Fresno, CA	354,091
48.	Omaha, NE	335,719
49.	Toledo, OH	332,943
50.	Buffalo, NY	328,175
51.	Wichita, KS	304,017
52.	Santa Ana, CA	293,827
53.	Mesa, AZ	288,104
54.	Colorado Springs, CO	280,430
55.	Tampa, FL	280,015

Rank	City, State	1990 Census Population
56.	Newark, NJ	275,221
57.	St. Paul, MN	272,235
58.	Louisville, KY	269,555
59.	Anaheim, CA	266,406
60.	Birmingham, AL	265,347
61.	Arlington, TX	261,721
62.	Norfolk, VA	261,229
63.	Las Vegas, NV	258,204
64.	Corpus Christi, TX	257,428
65.	St. Petersburg, FL	240,318
66.	Rochester, NY	230,356
67.	Jersey City, NJ	228,517
68.	Riverside, CA	226,546
69.	Anchorage, AK	226,338
70.	Lexington, KY	225,366
71.	Akron, OH	223,019
72.	Aurora, CO	222,103
73.	Baton Rouge, LA	219,531
74.	Raleigh, NC	212,050
75.	Stockton, CA	210,943
76.	Richmond, VA	202,798
77.	Shreveport, LA	198,518
78.	Jackson, MS	196,637
79.	Mobile, AL	196,263
80.	Des Moines, IA	193,189
81.	Lincoln, NE	191,972
82.	Madison, WI	190,766
83.	Grand Rapids, MI	189,126
84.	Yonkers, NY	188,082
85.	Hialeah, FL	188,008
86.	Montgomery, AL	187,543
87.	Lubbock, TX	186,206
88.	Greensboro, NC	183,894
89.	Dayton, OH	182,005
90.	Huntington Beach, CA	181,519
91.	Garland, TX	180,635
92.	Glendale, CA	180,038
93.	Columbus, GA	178,681
94.	Spokane, WA	177,165
95.	Tacoma, WA	176,664
96.	Little Rock, AR	175,727
97.	Bakersfield, CA	174,978
98.	Fremont, CA	173,339
99.	Fort Wayne, IN	172,971
100.	Newport News, VA	171,439

U.S. METROPOLITAN CORE AREAS
BY POPULATION

Rank	Metropolitan Core Area, State	1990 Census Population
1.	Los Angeles–Long Beach, CA	8,863,164
2.	New York, NY	8,546,846
3.	Chicago, IL	6,069,974
4.	Philadelphia, PA–NJ	4,856,881
5.	Detroit, MI	4,382,299
6.	Washington, DC–MD–VA	3,923,574
7.	Houston, TX	3,301,937
8.	Boston, MA	2,870,669
9.	Atlanta, GA	2,833,511
10.	Nassau–Suffolk, NY	2,609,212
11.	Riverside–San Bernardino, CA	2,588,793
12.	Dallas, TX	2,553,362
13.	San Diego, CA	2,498,016
14.	Minneapolis–St. Paul, MN–WI	2,464,124
15.	St. Louis, MO–IL	2,444,099
16.	Anaheim–Santa Ana, CA	2,410,556
17.	Baltimore, MD	2,382,172
18.	Phoenix, AZ	2,122,101
19.	Oakland, CA	2,082,914
20.	Tampa–St. Petersburg–Clearwater, FL	2,067,959
21.	Pittsburgh, PA	2,056,705
22.	Seattle, WA	1,972,961
23.	Miami–Hialeah, FL	1,937,094
24.	Cleveland, OH	1,831,122
25.	Newark, NJ	1,824,321
26.	Denver, CO	1,622,980
27.	San Francisco, CA	1,603,678
28.	Kansas City, MO–KS	1,566,280
29.	San Jose, CA	1,497,577
30.	Sacramento, CA	1,481,102
31.	Cincinnati, OH–KY–IN	1,452,645
32.	Milwaukee, WI	1,432,149
33.	Norfolk–Virginia Beach–Newport News, VA	1,396,107
34.	Columbus, OH	1,377,419
35.	Fort Worth–Arlington, TX	1,332,053
36.	San Antonio, TX	1,302,099
37.	Bergen–Passaic, NJ	1,278,440
38.	Fort Lauderdale–Hollywood–Pompano Beach, FL	1,255,488
39.	Indianapolis, IN	1,249,822
40.	Portland, OR	1,239,842
41.	New Orleans, LA	1,238,816
42.	Charlotte–Gastonia–Rock Hill, NC–SC	1,162,093
43.	Orlando, FL	1,072,748
44.	Salt Lake City–Ogden, UT	1,072,227
45.	Middlesex–Somerset–Hunterdon, NJ	1,019,835
46.	Rochester, NY	1,002,410
47.	Monmouth–Ocean, NJ	986,327
48.	Nashville, TN	985,026
49.	Memphis, TN–AR–MS	981,747
50.	Buffalo, NY	968,532

PRESIDENTS OF THE UNITED STATES

Name	Lived	Birthplace	Term	Political party
George Washington	1732–1799	Va.	1789–1797	Fed.
John Adams	1735–1826	Mass.	1797–1801	Fed.
Thomas Jefferson	1743–1826	Va.	1801–1809	Rep.
James Madison	1751–1836	Va.	1809–1817	Rep.
James Monroe	1758–1831	Va.	1817–1825	Rep.
John Quincy Adams	1767–1848	Mass.	1825–1829	Rep.
Andrew Jackson	1767–1845	S.C.	1829–1837	Dem.
Martin Van Buren	1782–1862	N.Y.	1837–1841	Dem.
William H. Harrison	1773–1841	Va.	1841	Whig
John Tyler	1790–1862	Va.	1841–1845	Whig
James K. Polk	1795–1849	N.C.	1845–1849	Dem.
Zachary Taylor	1784–1850	Va.	1849–1850	Whig
Millard Fillmore	1800–1874	N.Y.	1850–1853	Whig
Franklin Pierce	1804–1869	N.H.	1853–1857	Dem.
James Buchanan	1791–1868	Pa.	1857–1861	Dem.
Abraham Lincoln	1809–1865	Ky.	1861–1865	Rep.
Andrew Johnson	1808–1875	N.C.	1865–1869	Rep.
Ulysses S. Grant	1822–1885	Ohio	1869–1877	Rep.
Rutherford B. Hayes	1822–1893	Ohio	1877–1881	Rep.
James A. Garfield	1831–1881	Ohio	1881	Rep.
Chester A. Arthur	1829–1886	Vt.	1881–1885	Rep.
Grover Cleveland	1837–1908	N.J.	1885–1889	Dem.
			1893–1897	Dem.
Benjamin Harrison	1833–1901	Ohio	1889–1893	Rep.
William McKinley	1843–1901	Ohio	1897–1901	Rep.
Theodore Roosevelt	1858–1919	N.Y.	1901–1909	Rep.
William H. Taft	1857–1930	Ohio	1909–1913	Rep.
Woodrow Wilson	1856–1924	Va.	1913–1921	Dem.
Warren G. Harding	1865–1923	Ohio	1921–1923	Rep.
Calvin Coolidge	1872–1933	Vt.	1923–1929	Rep.
Herbert Hoover	1874–1964	Iowa	1929–1933	Rep.
Franklin D. Roosevelt	1882–1945	N.Y.	1933–1945	Dem.
Harry S Truman	1884–1972	Mo.	1945–1953	Dem.
Dwight D. Eisenhower	1890–1969	Tex.	1953–1961	Rep.
John F. Kennedy	1917–1963	Mass.	1961–1963	Dem.
Lyndon B. Johnson	1908–1973	Tex.	1963–1969	Dem.
Richard M. Nixon	1913–1994	Cal.	1969–1974	Rep.
Gerald R. Ford	1913–	Neb.	1974–1977	Rep.
Jimmy Carter	1924–	Ga.	1977–1981	Dem.
Ronald Reagan	1911–	Ill.	1981–1989	Rep.
George Bush	1924–	Mass.	1989–1993	Rep.
Bill Clinton	1946–	Ark.	1993–	Dem.

CONTINENTS OF THE WORLD

Continent	Area (sq. mi.)	Area (sq. km)	Population
Africa	11,700,000	30,303,000	705,000,000
Antarctica	5,400,000	13,985,000	0
Asia	17,400,000	45,066,000	3,451,000,000
Australia	2,966,150	7,682,000	16,849,000
Europe	3,800,000	9,842,000	710,000,000
North America	9,400,000	24,346,000	449,000,000
South America	6,900,000	17,871,000	318,000,000

OCEANS AND SEAS OF THE WORLD BY SIZE

Rank	Ocean or Sea	Area (sq. mi.)	Area (sq. km)
1.	Pacific Ocean	64,186,300	166,241,875
2.	Atlantic Ocean	33,420,000	86,557,466
3.	Indian Ocean	28,350,500	73,427,511
4.	Arctic Oceen	5,105,700	13,223,711
5.	South China Sea	1,148,500	2,974,604
6.	Caribbean Sea	971,400	2,515,916
7.	Mediterranean Sea	969,100	2,509,959
8.	Bering Sea	873,000	2,261,061
9.	Sea of Okhotsk	537,500	1,392,120
10.	Sea of Japan	391,100	1,012,945
11.	East China Sea	256,600	664,591
12.	Andaman Sea	218,100	564,877
13.	Black Sea	196,100	507,897
14.	Red Sea	174,900	452,989
15.	North Sea	164,900	427,089
16.	Baltic Sea	147,500	382,024
17.	Yellow Sea	113,500	293,964

HIGHEST MOUNTAINS OF THE WORLD

Rank	Mountain	Location	Altitude (ft.)	Altitude (m)
1.	Everest	Nepal/China	29,028	8,848
2.	K2	India	28,250	8,611
3.	Kanchenjunga	India/Nepal	28,168	8,586
4.	Lhotse I (Everest)	Nepal/China	27,923	8,511
5.	Makalu I	Nepal/China	27,824	8,481
6.	Lhotse II (Everest)	Nepal/China	27,560	8,400
7.	Dhaulagiri	Nepal	26,810	8,172
8.	Manaslu I	Nepal	26,760	8,156
9.	Cho Oyu	Nepal/China	26,750	8,153
10.	Nanga Parbat	India	26,660	8,126

LONGEST RIVERS OF THE WORLD

Rank	River	Empties into	Length (mi.)	Length (km)
1.	Nile	Mediterranean Sea	4,160	6,695
2.	Amazon	Atlantic Ocean	4,000	6,437
3.	Chang Jiang	East China Sea	3,964	6,379
4.	Huang	Yellow Sea	3,395	5,464
5.	Ob-Irtysh	Gulf of Ob	3,362	5,410
6.	Amur	Tatar Strait	2,744	4,416
7.	Lena	Laptev Sea	2,734	4,400
8.	Congo	Atlantic Ocean	2,718	4,374
9.	Mekong	South China Sea	2,600	4,184
10.	Niger	Gulf of Guinea	2,590	4,168

Discover the
WEB
in WEBster's New World™

Webster's New World™ College Dictionary is available in its entirety on the Web. The definitive guide to American English, renowned for clarity and ease of use, is also easy to access.

Visit our web site at
http://www.mgr.com/websters

- Browse or search Webster's New World™ College Dictionary and see why it is the preferred dictionary of the Associated Press and leading newspapers.

- Test your vocabulary with the WNW word-of-the-day game.

- Discover our complete line of dictionaries and other language reference books.

- Take advantage of special book offers.

- Check out the Macmillan SuperLibrary for other fine Macmillan products.

- Shop at home with our on-line bookstore.

It's a new world . . . speak the language!